THE DOMAIN TESTING WORKBOOK

CEM KANER · SOWMYA PADMANABHAN · DO

context driven press

Library of Congress Cataloging-in-Publication Data:

Kaner, Cem; Padmanabhan, Sowmya; & Hoffman, Douglas

The Domain Testing Workbook

Library of Congress Control Number: 2013947216

ISBN 978-0-9898119-0-3

The Context-Driven Press logo and The Domain Testing Workbook cover design are by Susan Handman, Handman Design, New York.

Editor: Rebecca L. Fiedler

Copy Editor: Karen Fioravanti

These materials are partially based on research that was supported by National Science Foundation research grants EIA-0113539 ITR/SY+PE: Improving the Education of Software Testers and CCLI-0717613 Adaptation & Implementation of an Activity-Based Online or Hybrid Course in Software Testing. Any opinions, findings and conclusions or recommendations expressed in this material are those of the author(s) and do not necessarily reflect the views of the National Science Foundation.

A SCHEMA FOR DOMAIN TESTING: AN OVERVIEW ON ONE PAGE

Here is a list of several tasks that people often do as part of a domain testing analysis. We organized the book's chapters around this list because it puts the tasks into a logical order.

Please note that for any particular product or variable, you might skip several of these tasks or do them in a different order than we list here.

1. CHARACTERIZE THE VARIABLE

- A. Identify the potentially interesting variables.
- B. Identify the variable(s) you can analyze now. This is the variable(s) of interest.
- C. Determine the primary dimension of the variable of interest.
- D. Determine the type and scale of the variable's primary dimension and what values it can take.
- E. Determine whether you can order the variable's values (from smallest to largest).
- F. Determine whether this is an input variable or a result.
- G. Determine how the program uses this variable.
- H. Determine whether other variables are related to this one.

2. ANALYZE THE VARIABLE AND CREATE TESTS

- I. Partition the variable (its primary dimension).
  - – If the dimension is ordered, determine its sub-ranges and transition points.
  - – If the dimension is not ordered, base partitioning on similarity.
- J. Lay out the analysis in a classical boundary/equivalence table. Identify best representatives.
- K. Create tests for the consequences of the data entered, not just the input filter.
- L. Identify secondary dimensions. Analyze them in the classical way.
- M. Summarize your analysis with a risk/equivalence table.

3. GENERALIZE TO MULTIDIMENSIONAL VARIABLES

- N. Analyze independent variables that should be tested together.
- O. Analyze variables that hold results.
- P. Analyze non-independent variables. Deal with relationships and constraints.

4. PREPARE FOR ADDITIONAL TESTING

- Q. Identify and list unanalyzed variables. Gather information for later analysis.
- R. Imagine and document risks that don't necessarily map to an obvious dimension.

DEDICATION

This book is dedicated to my step-mother, Rosemary Kaner, and the spirit of my father, Harry, who raised me in their businesses and taught me to cherish integrity, skepticism, the applicability of mathematics in all situations and the transcendant value of the Person in each of them, of the fundamental importance of data, and the delight in well-designed tables.

— Cem Kaner

To my children who are my inspiration and motivation in life: Ria, my wonderful daughter, and Simba, my awesome dog.

— Sowmya Padmanabhan

I'd like to dedicate my work to the ladies in my life, Connie and Jackie who have stoically endured my sometimes long absences, many of which were for collaboration on this book.

— Doug Hoffman

CONTENTS

PREFACE

People learn what they do. To develop skills, people need to practice. To practice, people need examples to practice on, time to work on them, and feedback.

This book is about a single software testing technique, ***domain testing***. You might know it as *equivalence class analysis* or ***boundary testing***. It is our field's most widely-taught technique.

TESTING TECHNIQUES

Testing is a cognitively complex activity. Developing competence with cognitively complex skills requires mastery of routine tasks and formation of schemas (cognitive maps) that can guide you as you do tasks that require more conscious effort (van Merrienboer, 1997).

The fundamental problem underlying testing's complexity is that every tester, of every nontrivial program, must choose from an impossibly large set of potential tests. Test techniques provide a cognitive toolkit for making these choices.

A test technique is both, a design tool and a selection tool:

- As a design tool, it tells you what to include in the test.
- As a selection tool, it provides a method for sampling a relatively small number of interesting tests from the vast set of possibilities.

Domain testing is primarily a sampling strategy:

- Divide the possible values of a variable into subsets of values that are similar in some way (we'll call them ***equivalent***).
- Design your tests to use only one or two values from each subset. Pick extreme values (we'll call them ***boundaries***) that maximize the likelihood of exposing a bug.

A critical problem with much industrial and academic training is that we teach test techniques as if there were obvious procedures to generate the correct set of tests. There are no such procedures. Instead, each technique involves its own way of thinking; one you get better at over time as you gain experience.

To learn a test technique is to learn a way of thinking about how to test well, not how to follow a procedure.

DOMAIN TESTING AS A TEST TECHNIQUE

According to the domain-testing way of thinking, we focus test designs on the values of variables. We select values for those tests by partitioning variables' values into equivalence classes. We pick values from within those classes that are the most extreme (such as the boundaries) because we're looking for the values most likely to drive the program to failure.

As a sampling strategy, domain testing helps testers:

- Improve their efficiency (testers don't run redundant tests).

- Improve their effectiveness (testers are more likely to find bugs because they design tests to be more powerful).

DOMAIN TESTING IS NOT THE ONLY TECHNIQUE

There are over 100 software testing techniques. Each points to different possible tests. Some are more popular than others, but no technique is "best." The challenge of skilled testing is not just to know how to apply techniques but to understand which technique is likely to yield the most useful information at *this* time, with *this* program, on *this* project.

Some test groups rely on a single technique to guide all of their testing. This is a mistake. We focus on only one technique in this book because our goal is to help you develop skill with that technique. But please don't confuse the narrow focus of this book with a suggestion that you can get by with only this technique.

A good technique, well-used, might expose a lot of problems, but relying on that *one* is like restricting your testing to a single corner of a large room. The better goal is to learn many techniques well, along with a deeper understanding of when to use them and how best to combine them in the context of a particular project. This approach requires skill and judgment at many levels. We explore the diversity of test techniques in the BBST® lectures on test design, available at http://www.testingeducation.org/BBST. For books that introduce the field's test techniques, we suggest Ainapure (2007); Black (2007); Craig & Jaskiel (2002); Kaner, Bach & Pettichord (2002); Jorgensen (2008); Myers, Sandler, Badgett & Thomas (2004); and Page, Johnston & Rollison (2009).

WHO THIS BOOK IS FOR

Testers

This book is primarily for software testing practitioners—people who make their living as software testers—and people studying to become testers or trying to understand what testers do in order to work with them or manage them.

- ***We expect that you already know a bit about testing.*** You have either studied some techniques already or applied them on the job. We're extending your knowledge, not introducing you to the field.

  We don't expect everyone to have the same knowledge, even the same basic knowledge. Therefore, we review many basics of testing as we go. But if you're new to testing, we recommend that you start with a general introduction to testing and return to this book when you have a more general background.

- ***We expect you to know some basic facts about programming, but we don't expect you to know how to program.*** In our experience, many people who work in this field have little or no experience as programmers. Several testers come from other technical fields (such as customer support) or from the application industry (for example, people who know insurance very well joining a group that tests insurance-related software). We're trying to deepen your skills as system testers.

  To do this, we have to introduce some technical concepts at a level that some readers will find difficult and other readers will have already mastered. Included in this category are discussions of the nature of data. Domain testing focuses on the values of variables, so you need to know about Integers, Fixed-Point, Floating-Point, Strings, multidimensional Records, and so forth.

- *We expect you to practice on the examples, not to just read them.* A person's preferences for how they're taught vary over time. To succeed with this book, you must approach it with an active mindset. Even though it appears to offer a memorizable structure, what it really offers is a collection of experiences.

You will learn more by trying things for yourself than by reading, listening or watching what someone else has done. You will learn more from explaining your solutions to others than from taking in others' explanations. The more active you are in your learning, the more you will learn and the more deeply you will learn.

INSTRUCTORS AND PROFESSORS

This book provides useful material for courses in black-box testing or test design. In a university course on software testing that is primarily focused on the underlying theory of testing, this book offers a practice-oriented supplement that complements texts like Ammann & Offutt (2008) and Tian (2005).

Please see the Appendix for more on how to use this book in your teaching.

PROGRAMMERS?

Several reviewers have suggested that we create examples that walk through code samples. Some have provided detailed suggestions for analyzing the same problem from an external (black-box) view and from the underlying code.

We like this idea. In a university course on software engineering, we would do this. However, after careful consideration, we decided not to include code samples in this book because we felt it would change the character of the book and chase away potential readers—many of whom are nonprogrammers—studying on their own.

That doesn't mean there's nothing in this book for programmers. Like any book on black-box testing, this book speaks to how people experience the code when they use it. It gives a different perspective on how code can break or be inadequate. And it suggests ways for you to test when you use someone else's code (e.g., library functions) but don't have their source code and aren't allowed to reverse engineer it.

HOW TO USE THIS BOOK

This book comes in three sections that differ in character:

SECTION 1 PROVIDES AN OVERVIEW OF DOMAIN TESTING AND KEY TECHNICAL CONCEPTS

If you're new to domain testing, *skim this. Don't get bogged down in it.* Don't worry about parts you don't understand. Work through the examples. They apply many points made here. Come back after a few examples and skim it again. At some point, you'll find Section 1 easier to read. You'll probably find it helps you organize what you learn from the examples into a more coherent structure. *There is no need to rush this.*

SECTION 2 WORKS THROUGH THE DOMAIN TESTING SCHEMA

The Schema is a list of 18 tasks that we suggest you use to organize your test designs and testing. Each chapter describes one task. Each chapter clarifies its description with worked examples and then asks you to work through some exercises.

- The examples are numbered. Each has its own chapter in Section 3.

- ***Don't read the solutions to the exercises before you try them yourself. Even if you know you can't do the exercise, complete as much as you can.*** The more you try for yourself, the more you will learn. If you let us tell you the answer, you will lose the learning experience that comes from figuring out the answer for yourself.

SECTION 3 PROVIDES A COLLECTION OF EXAMPLES

We work through each example, one per chapter, showing how to apply the Schema.

We don't apply every item on the list to every example. We do what we think is useful and skip the rest.

THE EXAMPLES ARE SIMPLE, INCREASING IN COMPLEXITY

Many examples are from other books or courses that presented material well. You might find it instructional to compare our solutions to theirs.

Many examples in this book are artificially simple. We designed examples to bring different Tasks of the Schema into focus. You'll see this as you work through Section 3 (the worked examples). The solution for an example emphasizes some Tasks and deals only briefly with the others. The more advanced tasks call for more complex examples.

Even the simple examples reflect real-world software. When you use domain testing, you focus on variables. Every application has many variables that you can test. It makes sense to test variables individually before testing them in combination. Domain testing suggests ways to do one-variable testing efficiently.

- What we call the classical approach requires almost no contextual information about the variable. If you can identify a variable, you can usually figure out its type and boundaries using a combination of experimentation (testing) and research (such as reading documents and asking people).

  Examples of the classical approach, illustrate a straightforward technique you can apply to many types of data. When you test a program, it should be easy to find many variables to test this way.

- The Schema generalizes this to an explicitly risk-based approach. This reflects what we've seen in the practices of skilled testers. The more you know about the application, the more basis you'll have for imagining risks and designing tests to trigger those risks.

  Our design goal for the more complex tasks in the Schema was to create the simplest examples that can help you imagine what questions to ask or where to look for risk-relevant information.

WE DELIBERATELY REPEAT INFORMATION

We hope you'll read the *Introduction to Domain Testing* and skim the *Summaries of Key Technical Concepts*. We expect that many readers will skip through the rest of the book in whatever order feels most useful at the time.

To make it easier for you to read chapters on their own, we deliberately repeat some text. You are particularly likely to notice text from Section 2, used to explain a Task, reappearing in Section 3 to explain an Example.

WE WRITE IN A SPIRAL

A spiral presentation covers the same concepts several times with new information about it or a new application of it, each time. The goal of a spiral presentation is to give you a lot of information about a concept without drowning you in details that you won't need until later.

In this type of writing:

- A concept appears first in a relatively short or simplified form. (In many cases, you'll see the concept first in the *Summaries of Key Technical Concepts*.)
- The concept appears again with details relevant to a particular Task or Example.
- The concept might appear several times with new details each time.
- We often present a concept in detail and refer back to that presentation as needed.
- If a technical topic is presented without enough detail early in the book, check the index. We probably cover it again later.
- If you see a technical topic later in the book and the discussion assumes you know more than you should, look for a cross-reference to a previous presentation of the topic. If you don't see one, check the index.

DON'T JUST READ THE EXAMPLES—WORK THROUGH THEM YOURSELF

The more actively engaged you're in solving these exercises yourself and teaching solutions to colleagues, the richer your learning will be and the more of that learning you will be able to transfer to real-world tasks.

We recommend that you work through the exercises and examples with a friend.

- *Attempt each exercise on your own.*
- *Explain how you solved it to your friend.*
- *Critique your friend's work.* Be friendly, but be specific. You will learn from this and your friend will learn from this.
- *Only then should you* compare your ideas with the solution.
- If your friend still doesn't get it, *try another example.*

Explaining things involves different cognitive processes than reading about them or doing them. To explain something to someone else, you have to organize your knowledge more effectively and fill in the gaps.

NOTICE THE REFERENCES

We cite the books, papers, and presentations:

- That we relied on in writing this book.

- Or that you might find useful for understanding or applying this material.

The reference format (name, date) can be a little distracting at first. You'll get used to it. It carries information that you won't get as easily in any other way. When you pay attention to who says what, who agrees or disagrees with them, who cites their work and who ignores it, you'll start to see patterns. These patterns can teach you about the social networks that structure communication in our field. Understanding these networks can give you a much deeper insight into the context and meaning of the papers you read and the talks and classes you attend (Moody, 2001; Price, 1965; Small, 1978, 2003; Upham, Rosenkopf & Ungar, 2010).

A field's social networks are the fabric on which the field's data are written.

OTHER TESTING BOOKS AND COURSES

Over the past 30 years, there has been tremendous growth in the number and quality of books and courses on software testing.

BOOKS FOR PRACTITIONERS

As I wrote this note, I skimmed through some of my favorite books that address black-box testing: Beizer (1995), Black (2002), Copeland (2004), Craig & Jaskiel (2002), Graham & Fewster (2012), Kaner, Bach & Pettichord (2002), Kaner, Falk & Nguyen (1993), Koskela (2008), Myers (1979), Nguyen, Johnson & Hackett (2003), Page, Johnston & Rollison (2009), Perry (2006), Perry & Rice (1997), Rainsberger (2004), Weinberg (2008), and Whittaker (2003).

- Each of these has been valuable to practitioners. They explain important testing concepts and controversies, suggest ways to think through testing problems, consider the goals and management of the testing effort.

- These books teach by describing and explaining. They offer excellent examples, but they don't set many exercises for the students or provide feedback to help the students develop their skills.

BOOKS FOR UNIVERSITY STUDENTS

The last decade has seen a new generation of university textbooks for testing, such as Ammann & Offutt (2008), Jorgensen (2008), and Tian (2005). I like all three of these books, have taught from them, and expect to teach from them again. As you would expect from university texts, these have more exercises than the books for practitioners. The exercises were designed to support the instructional objectives of the books.

These books assume knowledge of programming and discrete mathematics. They work well for students with those strengths. Many of these students would benefit from a supplementary collection of problems that emphasize practical applications.

WHY WRITE AN ENTIRE BOOK ON DOMAIN TESTING?

The main ideas of domain testing are easy to explain. In a lecture, I can teach the key concepts in 15 minutes. There are many good, easy-to-read explanations. Glen Myers (1979) did an excellent job of laying out the basics. Jorgensen (2008) and Kaner, Falk & Nguyen (1993) are two other popular examples of clear introductory presentations.

In my classes, most students can give me a description of domain testing and use it in simple situations after a short explanation with an example or two. *That doesn't mean they understand domain testing or that they can use it on the job.*

The most common problem in training is that students can go to a class, learn a technique, but can't apply it on the job. This problem presents itself in several ways:

- Testers recognize the opportunity to apply a new skill and should be able to use it, but it is harder than they expect. It takes them more time. They make errors. **This illustrates the problem of skill.**

- Testers recognize an opportunity to apply a new skill but it contains elements different from what they've studied. Maybe the type of data are a little different, the context is a little different or the risks are a little more complex. They have trouble extending what they've learned to this new case. **This illustrates the problem of transfer of learning.** We offer additional notes on this in the Appendix.

- Testers face a testing problem and don't recognize it as an opportunity to apply a skill or technique that they've learned. **This also illustrates the problem of transfer of learning.**

What good is training if you can't apply it with enough skill to do your job?

When you work as a tester, it doesn't matter whether you can define a test technique or apply it to a simple textbook example. It doesn't matter whether you can answer multiple-choice test questions about it. What matters is whether you can apply the technique to the software you're trying to test. If you can't do that, you didn't learn what you needed in your training. Too much teaching about testing doesn't give you the practice you need to apply new skills and techniques.

I saw these problems for many years, through the eyes of a test manager, a test-management consultant, and a commercial trainer.

As a trainer, I started developing collections of examples and exercises for several test techniques. I could use *some* of these materials in general survey courses on software testing, but these types of courses didn't allow enough time for enough examples or practice.

My models for this work were the *Schaum's Outlines* books and more advanced practice books like Sveshnikov (1968). These books present basic ideas and many worked examples, running from simple to complex, from straightforward applications of theory to more challenging word problems.

I gained experience with these types of books as a student, tutor, and teacher of mathematics. The books were effective when students created their own solutions for the examples and checked their own work against the book. For those students, the diversity of the collection was important.

My goal in creating *The Domain Testing Workbook* was to collect a set of examples:

- Broad enough for you to learn the scope of the technique.
- Detailed enough for you to develop skill, which I think requires trying something, getting feedback, and trying it again until you can do it well.

At first glance, *The Domain Testing Workbook* looks like a long book. However, I urge you to think of it instead as a collection of worked examples. Work through them at your own pace, getting feedback as you go.

Cem Kaner

August, 2013

ACKNOWLEDGMENTS

We got a lot of help from a lot of people:

Thanks to our many reviewers, who waded through drafts from 2010 through 2013: Scott Allman, Dani Almog, Ajay Balamurugadas, Richard Bender, Ajay Bhagwat, Lalitkumar Bhamare, Rex Black, Cole Boehmer, Michael Bolton, Pat Bond, Laurent Bossavit, Paul Carvalho, Ross Collard, Adriano Comai, Mike Dedolph, Tom Delmonte, Joe DeMeyer, Rikard Edgren, Jack Falk, Rebecca Fiedler, Keith Gallagher, Markus Gärtner, W. Morven Gentleman, Paul Gerrard, Dorothy Graham, Sam Guckenheimer, Michael Hackett, Jon Hagar, Dick Hamlet, Linda Hamm, Parimala Hariprasad, Jean-Anne Harrison, Dan Hoffman, Justin Hunter, Martin Jansson, Karen Johnson, Jesse Johnson, Paul Jorgensen, Adam Jubaer, Nawwar Kabbani, Geordie Keitt, Chris Kenst, Vipul Kocher, Jonathan Kohl, Darko Marinov, John McConda, Iain McCowatt, Pat McGee, Grigori Melnick, Zoltán Molnár, Hung Nguyen, Ray Oei, Brian Osman, Jane Owen, Louise Perold, Dale Perry, Erik Petersen, Curtis Pettit, Ron Pihlgren, Dee Ann Pizzica, Meeta Prakash, Maaret Pyhajarvi, BJ Rollison, Rob Sabourin, Huib Schoots, Parimala Shankaralah, Aleksander Simic, Ben Simo, Ajoy Kumar Singha, Michael Stahl, Keith Stobie, Andy Tinkham, Aleksis Tulonen, Peter Walen, and Christin Wiedemann.

Thanks also to students who worked in Florida Tech's Center for Software Testing Education & Research and helped us with projects directly related to the content of this book: Ayuba Audu, Pushparani Bhallamudi, Thomas Bedran, Karishma Bhatia, Nathan Christie, Tim Coulter, Sabrina Fay, Ajay Jha, Kishore Kattamuri, Jiahui Liu, Pat McGee, Tauhida Parveen, Amit Singh, Umesh Subramanyan, Andy Tinkham and Giridhar Vijayaraghavan.

This book's approach was informed by our instructional research and course development at Florida Institute of Technology. That work was supported by National Science Foundation research grants *EIA-0113539 ITR/SY+PE: Improving the Education of Software Testers* and *CCLI-0717613 Adaptation & Implementation of an Activity-Based Online or Hybrid Course in Software Testing.* (Any opinions, findings, conclusions or recommendations expressed in this book are ours and do not necessarily reflect the views of the National Science Foundation.)

Much appreciation to *Panera Bread* at 245 Palm Bay Road in West Melbourne, Florida, for providing warm hospitality, unlimited good coffee and a comfortable table where we wrote much of this book.

Special thanks to BJ Rollison for a Chapter 24 better than anything we could have written, to Pat Bond and Morven Gentleman for freely sharing their knowledge of mathematics and their wisdom about presenting technical ideas to readers who are more interested in the application of the concepts than the theoretical underpinnings, and to Bill Shoaff, Chair of Computer Sciences at Florida Tech, for his ongoing encouragement and support over so many years.

SECTION 1: WHAT IS DOMAIN TESTING?

This Section[1] has two Chapters:

1. Introduction to Domain Testing

2. Summaries of Key Technical Concepts

We suggest that you read the Introduction before the rest of the book. After this, you can proceed to:

- The next chapter, which provides short discussions of several key terms and concepts of the book.

- Section 2, which works through the book's Schema for Domain Testing in detail (one Chapter per Task).

- Section 3, which works through the book's collection of Examples.

The Chapters on Key Technical Concepts and on the Schema provide background information that will help you understand the Examples. If you go to the Examples first, you'll sometimes find it useful to skim earlier chapters.

---

1   If you haven't read *How to Use This Book* on page xvii (in the Preface), we recommend that you read it now.

SECTION 1. PART 1: INTRODUCTION TO DOMAIN TESTING

The essence of domain testing is that you partition a *domain* (a set of values) into subdomains (*equivalence classes*) and select *representatives* of each subdomain for your tests.

- *Equivalence class analysis is about similarity.* Two values belong in the same class if they are so similar the program will treat them the same way.

  Testing with only one or two representatives of each class allows you to substantially reduce the number of tests.

- *Picking representatives is about risk.* As used in this book, a *risk* is a way the program can fail. Look for a value that is a little more likely to cause the program to fail than the others. This value is often at the boundary of a class. Picking powerful representatives lets you keep the number of tests small without increasing the risk of missing bugs by much.

Simple examples make partitioning look misleadingly simple. Two partitions can be equivalent in some respects but different in others. Therefore, testers must create alternative groups of equivalence classes. The process of partitioning requires imagination, experience and exercise of judgment. (Product knowledge helps too.)

AN EXAMPLE TEST SERIES

Long ago, we started *Testing Computer Software* (Kaner, 1988) with a simple example that illustrated this technique. Let's work through that example again:

> You've been given the program and the following description of it:
>
> > The program is designed to add two numbers, which you enter. Each number should be one or two digits. The program will echo your entries, then print the sum. Press <Enter> after each number. To start the program, type ADDER.

The book's analysis of this example:

- Started with simple tests to discover how the program worked and the nature of the variables involved, such as:

2 + 3	*Does the program work at all?*
99 + 99	*Is 99 the actual upper boundary?*
-9 + -9	*Are negative numbers acceptable?*

- Progressed to consideration of simple risks that seemed obvious at the time:[2]

0 + 0	*What does it do with zeros?*
-99 + -99	*How does it handle numbers with 2 digits but 3 characters?*
100 + 100	*How does it handle values just beyond the boundary?*
-100 + -100	
<Enter> + <Enter>	*What if there is no input?*
123456 + 0	*How many digits will it accept?*

- Checked the input filter, the code that ensures the program accepts only legitimate numbers. For example:

---

2 Today, many of the Kaner (1988) tests seem quaint. They were products of a time when people still wrote complex applications in Assembler or in quirky application programming languages that were space-and-speed-optimized to produce programs that ran well on computers with 48K of RAM and a 1-MHz clock. Many bugs that just won't appear in code today roamed the Silicon Wilds freely back then. We will ignore some of those antique tests.

1.2 + 5	*Decimal points? If it rejects this, what about 1. or 1.0?*
A + b	*Letters?*
/ + 1 or 1 + :	*The ASCII codes for digits run from 48 (0) to 57 (9). ASCII 47 is / and ASCII 58 is :*
\<Space\> 1 + 1	*Try arbitrarily many leading and trailing spaces.*

- Considered the processing of the user's actions during entry of the numbers, such as:

  ◦ *Wait for some time between digits or entries. Is there a timeout?*

  ◦ *Edit the numbers repeatedly before entering them. You might be able to overflow the input string if the program processes all the keystrokes at one time when you press \<Enter\>. (Today we would call that input string an input buffer and think of this as a very simple test for a buffer overflow.)*

- And considered the possible values of the result variable (the sum of the two numbers):

  ◦ If the program holds the input values and the sum as 1-byte Integers, the range of values it can hold is -128 to 127.[3] Any test that drives the sum beyond 127, such as 64+64, might expose an overflow (a number too big to be stored in the space available for it).

The example made several points about testing and the environment of testing that you're probably familiar with:

- When testing part of a program that collects and processes data, you have to take into account:

  ◦ **User Interface**: The software that supports the entry and receipt of data and the display of results.

  ◦ **Storage**: How the data are stored.

  ◦ **Calculations and Result Variables:** The calculations that will be done using the data and the variables that will hold the results of those calculations.

  ◦ **Consequences**: How the data will be used and how those uses might be affected by the values of the data.

- Most (and maybe all) specifications (or requirements documents) (or user stories) are ambiguous and incomplete. For much information you need, you'll probably have to figure it out for yourself, by using ***active reading / active learning*** strategies:

  ◦ Asking questions.

  ◦ Reading other source material.

  ◦ Running tests that go beyond the information in the specification.

  The book called this supplemental information-gathering, ***exploratory testing,*** a term that has since gained some popularity.

- Even a very simple part of a program (as simple as collecting and adding two numbers) can be tested in many ways, with many different values:

  ◦ ***Don't try to design or run all the tests at once.*** Start with simpler tests and increase difficulty and complexity as the program gets more stable.

---

3   *Why would anyone try to optimize this way?* A **byte** holds 8 bits of memory. In computers like the Apple 2, the basic word size of the computer was 1 byte. When Kaner started training staff from this example (1984), many programmers had learned how to program (as he had) on Digital Equipment Corporation minicomputers that had 4K (4096 words) of 12-bit RAM. Today (2013) your computer probably has at least 4 billion words of RAM, with a word size of 32 or 64 bits. But back then, every byte was precious. Good programmers optimized their use of memory. Because of optimizations, overflows from simple arithmetic were much more common. You can still have overflow errors and you still have to test for them. But today's overflows will usually require much more extreme values.

- ◦ *Don't try to run every test.* Look for ways to organize tests into groups of tests that are so similar to each other that there is little reason to run more than one test from the group.
- ◦ *Look for boundary values* or other values that will probably be troublesome for the program.
- ◦ *Think in terms of risk.* Imagine ways the program can fail. For each way, choose tests that probably *will* make it fail that way if it *can* fail that way. (For example, 99+99 will cause an overflow IF the program stores sums in a byte. But if the program doesn't have that vulnerability, this test won't make the program fail that way.)

In 1988, we presented and explained these test ideas, but didn't place the collection into a coherent structure. Our impression is that this is a prevalent problem. Many authors have described the technique but no one has explored their full process. They stop after describing what they see as the most important parts.

Everyone describes a different part of the elephant,[4] yielding a collection of incomplete and often contradictory analyses. We created the Schema as our description of the whole elephant. Not the **One True Elephant of Domain Testing,** *just the one we ride when we hunt domain bugs. With this Schema, we can solve many types of problems using one coherent mental structure. This book is organized around this Schema.*

THE EXAMPLE TEST SERIES AGAIN, USING THE SCHEMA

Let's look at the example again, using the Schema. Each item in the Schema is a distinct Task.

You might not understand every Task in the Schema at this point. Don't worry about that. Section 2 works through the Schema in detail, with a chapter for each Task. What we hope you get from this presentation is an impression of the flow of the work involved in the analysis.

1. CHARACTERIZE THE VARIABLE

Start by trying to understand the variable(s) you're working with.

A. IDENTIFY THE POTENTIALLY INTERESTING VARIABLES

Variables? What variables?

- The Example doesn't name any variables. It says that you enter two numbers and the program computes the sum of them.
- You don't have access to the code, so you can't see any variables.

Black-box testers work with ***notional variables***. The tester analyzes the program *as if* these variables were part of the code, but they may or may not actually exist or be used in the way the tester assumes.

In this case, the *analysis* works on three variables:

- `FirstNumber`
- `SecondNumber`
- `Sum`

---

4   https://en.wikipedia.org/wiki/Blind_men_and_an_elephant

These are related by:

`Sum = FirstNumber + SecondNumber`

The program might not have these variables. But if you treat the program *as if* it had them, you can probably imagine many risks the program might be vulnerable to and define tests for them.

B. IDENTIFY THE VARIABLE(S) YOU CAN ANALYZE NOW. THIS IS THE VARIABLE(S) OF INTEREST

The analysis works with all three of them.

C. DETERMINE THE PRIMARY DIMENSION OF THE VARIABLE OF INTEREST

What *is* the dimension? Are you entering a length and a width of something? A pair of prices? You don't know, because the example is artificially simple.

- In the real world, if you didn't know, you would find out, probably by reading something or asking someone.
- In the textbook world, you make do with what the textbook tells you (`FirstNumber` and `SecondNumber` have one or two digits).

D. DETERMINE THE TYPE AND SCALE OF THE VARIABLE'S PRIMARY DIMENSION AND WHAT VALUES IT CAN TAKE

`FirstNumber` and `SecondNumber` are Integers. Integers have values like 1, 2, 3. All digits. No fractions, no numbers with decimal points. There are a few exceptions:

- Leading or trailing spaces aren't digits but they might be OK (a leading space is before the number. A trailing space is after the number).
- The numbers might be Hexadecimal. If so, A, B, C, D, E and F are digits with values (in Decimal) of 10 through 15.
- Minus signs and plus signs might be OK.

Probably, the range of values for `FirstNumber` and `SecondNumber` is 0 to 99, but it might be -99 to 99 or -FF to FF.

- In the real world, you'd probably check the range by running tests to find out what the program accepts and by asking people whether the results are correct.
- In the textbook world, you make do with what the textbook tells you and design the tests to find out how the program behaves.

Some testers behave as if they're paralyzed when they aren't given this type of information. In our experience, in most companies, you won't get this information from specifications and if you ask programmers about every little thing, they'll get tired of you. You will learn a lot by experimentation (testing), including follow-up tests that check whether the program can cope with the values you've entered.

E. DETERMINE WHETHER YOU CAN ORDER THE VARIABLE'S VALUES (FROM SMALLEST TO LARGEST)

Yes, you can.

F. DETERMINE WHETHER THIS IS AN INPUT VARIABLE OR A RESULT

- `FirstNumber` and `SecondNumber` are input variables
- `Sum` is a result. You don't enter data directly into `Sum`. Instead, `Sum` gets its value from a calculation that uses the values of the input variables.

G. Determine how the program uses this variable

This textbook example doesn't tell you a thing about how the program uses the variables. In the real world, you'd either know this because you knew more about what the program does or you'd use this as a reason to investigate the program further.

H. Determine whether other variables are related to this one

All that you know is `Sum` = `FirstNumber` + `SecondNumber`.

2. ANALYZE THE VARIABLE AND CREATE TESTS

The goal of characterizing the variable is to discover what the variable is, what the program does with it and what else it's related to. Having learned as much as you can about the variable, it's time to design and run some tests.

I. Partition the variable (its primary dimension)

Start by assuming that the valid values for `FirstNumber` and `SecondNumber` are 0 through 99. Under that assumption:

- Any value less than 0 is too small.
- Any value greater than 99 is too big.
- Any value from 0 to 99 is OK.

Your three partitions are the sets of values that are too small, too large or OK.

The central idea underlying the partitioning is that the values in each set are pretty much equivalent to each other:

- The program should reject all numbers less than 0 because they're all too small. In this respect, it is treating all the negative numbers the same way.
- The program should accept all numbers from 0 to 99 and use them to compute the value of `Sum`. It is treating all valid values the same way.
- The program should reject all numbers larger than 99 because they're all too big. In this respect, it is treating all numbers > 99 the same way.

Because the program treats everything within each set the same way, we call the members of each set *equivalent* to each other and we call the sets of values *equivalence sets* or *equivalence classes*. (A class is the same thing as a set.)

Will the program *really* treat equivalent variables the same way?

In the black-box testing world, it's hard to make that claim. Heck, we don't even know if the variables we're talking about are the *real* variables.

---

*We know how the program is **supposed to** work (or how some aspects are supposed to work). We create **models**[5] of the program that we **don't expect** to be complete or perfectly accurate but that we **do expect** to be useful. A model, for testers, is useful if it is similar enough to the program under test to help us discover good tests of the real program.[6]*

---

5   "All models are wrong, but some are useful." George Box. https://en.wikiquote.org/wiki/George_E._P._Box

6   If the idea that testers design tests from a model of the program and not from the program itself is a new and interesting idea for you, you might be interested in some of the work of Paul Gerrard. *See* Gerrard (2009) and http://testaxioms.com. This article is a fairly gentle introduction that new testers will find readable.

J. LAY OUT THE ANALYSIS IN A CLASSICAL BOUNDARY/EQUIVALENCE TABLE. IDENTIFY BEST REPRESENTATIVES

You have three equivalence classes:

- The set of values that are too small (< 0) is infinitely large. You can't test them all. Test with the element of the set that is *almost* in the valid set. This is the upper boundary of this set. In this case, that's -1.

- The set of values the program is supposed to accept and use to calculate **Sum**. The tradition is to call this the set of *valid* values.

  There are 100 of these. *Unless you have a reason to suspect problems with other values*, you'll typically test with the set's boundary values, the smallest (0) and the largest (99).

- The set of values that are too big (> 99). The relevant boundary of this set is 100.

There is a widely-used table to show this analysis.

- It shows the equivalence classes:
  - It calls *invalid* any set of values that you could imagine trying to store in the variable, but the program is supposed to reject.
  - It calls *valid* any set of values that you could imagine trying to store in the variable and the program is supposed to accept and process further.
- It also shows the boundary values of the sets.

Not surprisingly, this is sometimes called the Equivalence Class table, the Boundary Value Analysis table or the Equivalence Class and Boundaries table. We call it ***Boundary-Equivalence Table.*** We also call it the ***classical table*** because it has been around so long and is widely taught and used.

Variable	Valid case equivalence class	Invalid case equivalence class	Boundaries and special cases	Notes
FirstNumber	0 - 99		0	Test with the smallest valid value
			99	Test with the largest valid value
		0 <	-1	Test with the largest value that is "too small"
		> 99	100	Test with the smallest value that is "too large"

Most of the table shows the analysis. Testers use the values in the "Boundaries and special cases" column as their test values.

- Some people prefer a version of this table with an Expected Results column that tells you what response you should get from the program when you run the test.

- We like to know what the expected results are too, but quite often we use domain analysis while we explore the program. We aren't necessarily sure how the program will behave when we run a certain test or even how the program *should* behave. We run the test without expected results when we think that studying what the program actually does can help us discover obvious errors or figure out what it is supposed to do. Because we do a lot of exploration, we don't insist on an Expected Results column in our tables.

K. CREATE TESTS FOR THE CONSEQUENCES OF THE DATA ENTERED, NOT JUST THE INPUT FILTER

If a program does something or cannot do something as a result of data that you entered, that's a consequence of the entry of the data.

This Example doesn't say much about consequences, nor do most descriptions of domain testing. However, we've come to think of this as important.

As we see it now, the difference between the experienced tester and the novice is that the skilled domain tester realizes that setting extreme values is just the first step in the test. It's like spreading banana peels all over the floor. The novice is happy to mess up the floor. The professional makes the program walk on it.

Students are often confused about the difference between a *consequence* and a *result variable*. Here is an example that might make it clearer.

Suppose that you were working with a presentation program, like *PowerPoint*. You decided to put a table on a slide. The dialog to create a table asked you to specify the number of rows in the table and the number of columns.

Here are some possible consequences of your entries into `NumberOfRows` and `NumberOf-Columns`:

- The program would create a table with `NumberOfRows` rows and `NumberOfColumns` columns.
- The height of the rows and the width of the columns in this table would be influenced by `NumberOfRows` and `NumberOfColumns`. To fit 100 columns on a 10-inch-wide slide, the columns will have to be pretty skinny.
- The program might note how many cells there are in the table. It might store that in a variable, `NumberOfCells` = `NumberOfRows` × `NumberOfColumns`.
- The program might set aside memory to hold the data in each cell of the table. If `NumberOfCells` is very large and if you stick memory-consuming things in each cell (such as graphics), the program might run out of memory.
- If `NumberOfCells` is large, the program might work very slowly when it does anything with the table.
- If you create a table with an odd number of columns, you won't be able to divide the table evenly into one half that has blue columns and one half that has red columns.
- Suppose you have data about 21 people and you want to show this in a table, with one row per person. If you create a table with 20 rows, you won't be able to copy in 21 rows of data. If you create a table with 30 rows, you'll have 9 extra (empty) rows.

One of the consequences in this list is that the program sets a value of a variable: `NumberOfCells` = `NumberOfRows` × `NumberOfColumns`.

- `NumberOfCells` is a result variable.
- *It is often useful to do a domain analysis on a result variable*. In this example, look for equivalence classes and boundary values of the variable `NumberOfCells`. Result variables call for a special type of domain analysis because you can't enter values into `NumberOfCells` directly. Instead, you have to figure out what values of `NumberOfRows` and `NumberOfColumns` will generate the values of `NumberOfCells` that you want to test.

L. IDENTIFY SECONDARY DIMENSIONS. ANALYZE THEM IN THE CLASSICAL WAY

The classical table showed only four tests: -1, 0, 99 and 100.

What about all those other tests?

- Tests with non-digits, such as A, b, / and :
- Tests with non-Integers, such as 1.5
- Tests with formulas, such as 6 / 3 (the *result* is an Integer, but will the program accept it?)
- Tests with Really Big numbers, such as 123456 or 12345678901234567890123456789
- Tests with characters that should be ignored, such as leading and trailing spaces or parentheses (((5))) or +1 and with lots of these characters, such as ++++++++++1
- There are lots of others. If you want a Very Long List, see *The Risk/Equivalence Table (Integers)* on page 155.

These variations have little or nothing to do with the goal of entering two numbers in order to add them up. The program should reject most of these variations and ignore the others.

However, programmers sometimes fail to anticipate what odd things a person (or their cat) might type into a data entry field or what might be (inappropriately) stored in a data file the program will read from. If the program runs into something the programmer never prepared for, **bad things can happen**.

Testers like to make programs do bad things, so they test with strange values. Because of that, strange tests have appeared in many of the books, courses and practitioner presentations on testing that introduced testers to domain testing (which they often called boundary value analysis or equivalence class analysis). However, we have never seen clear guidelines for deciding which, if any, of these types of variations belong in a domain analysis.

We decided to call these types of variation, **secondary dimensions**. We call each type of variation a dimension because you can feed the variable under test with inputs that vary quite a bit in one specific way but are the same in every other way. For example:

- Consider an input value of 10. Arithmetically, 10 is the same as +++++++++++++10. What varies is the number of plus signs.
- Consider an input that is too long. 100 and 1000000000 are both invalid for the same reason (too big) but they differ in length.
- It is harder to order non-Integer numbers. For example, 1.5 and 2.5 are both equally distant from the nearest Integer. You'll have to sample from them to test non-Integer numbers, because there are infinitely many potential values to test.

Traditional presentations of domain analysis showed these values in the classical table. The expanded table looks like this:

Variable	Valid case equivalence class	Invalid case equivalence class	Boundaries and special cases	Notes
First-Number	0 - 99		0	Test with the smallest valid value
			99	Test with the largest valid value
		0 <	-1	Largest value that is "too small"
		> 99	100	Smallest value that is "too large"
	ASCII digits: 48 to 57		0 (ASCII 48)	

Variable	Valid case equivalence class	Invalid case equivalence class	Boundaries and special cases	Notes
			9 (ASCII 57)	
		Letters	A	ASCII code 65. This letter's code is closest to the digits
			z	As far from the digits as letters get
			Σ, ώ, etc.	Greek letters: Unicode values even further from digits than z. (There are plenty of other alphabets in Unicode too.)
		Not alphanumeric	/ (ASCII 47)	In modern programs, these are no longer interesting tests. Very few programs will fail them.
			: (ASCII 58)	
	1 or 2 digits		0, 99	You've done these tests already
		lots of digits	123456	in the original example, the program rejected anything longer than 6 digits
			999999...99999	Lots and lots of digits because, why not?
		lots of characters but still 2 digits	\<space\>99	With the \<space\> in front, there are three characters but only two digits
			\<space\> ... \<space\>999	Lots and lots of leading spaces

The individual tests in the table are clear.

- The reasoning behind the choice of each test is probably clear to a reasonably experienced tester.
- You can give a table like this to a person who has only a modest level of training/experience in testing and they'll know how to use it.
- You can highlight the individual cells in the Boundaries and Special Cases column as you run the tests, making a record of which tests you ran. A few weeks or years later, that record might be useful.

The classical table documents the basic partitioning and boundary analysis very well. However, when you extend its use to a broader collection of risks, there are common problems:

- The table doesn't show why a test designer included some risks and ignored others.
- It is not obvious what risks are missing from the table. In our experience evaluating tables like these:
  - Testers and students often created inconsistent tables. When we asked why a secondary dimension was analyzed for one variable but not another, we discovered that a given risk had occurred to someone one time but had simply not come to mind the next.
  - The tables themselves did not make these inconsistencies obvious. We had to read tables with care to recognize inconsistencies.

To make the risk analysis more visible, we created a different type of table for domain analysis, which we call the Risk/Equivalence table.

- Given a risk, you can imagine:
  - Some values of the variable under test that expose the program to that risk (the program might fail the test if you use one of these values for the variable) and

- ○ Other values that will not expose the program to that risk.

  For example, if you imagine that the program might fail (overflow) if it tries to process inputs longer than 30 digits, the set of possible inputs with 31 or more digits expose the program to that risk and the set of possible inputs with 0 to 30 digits do not.

- You can partition each set into one or more equivalence classes and sample from each class.

M. SUMMARIZE YOUR ANALYSIS WITH A RISK/EQUIVALENCE TABLE

Here is an example of the risk/equivalence table.

Variable	Risk (potential failure)	Classes that should not trigger failure	Classes that might trigger failure	Test cases (best representatives)	
First-Number	misclassifies valid inputs	anything out of bounds	0 to 99	0	
				99	
	mishandles values that are too small	≥ 0	< 0	-1	At lower bound of range - 1
	mishandles values that are too large	≤ 99	> 99	100	At upper bound of range + 1
				999...999 (16384 nines)	Far above the upper bound of range
	too few characters	any input value	empty field	enter nothing	
				clear the field	Empty the field (clear the default value)
				space character	Whitespace only (tab, space)
	too many characters	1 - 2 characters	> 2 characters	+99	Leading +
				++++++++++99	lots of leading +
				<space>99	Leading space
				<space>--99	Leading space plus a sign (+ or --)
				<space><space><space> ... <space>99	Many leading spaces
				099	Leading zeros
				+099	Leading zero plus a sign (+ or --)
				000...000999	Many leading zeros

For an example of a much more complete table of this kind, see *The Risk/Equivalence Table (Integers)* on page 155.

3. GENERALIZE TO MULTIDIMENSIONAL VARIABLES

In this Example, you enter a value into each of two variables, **FirstNumber** and **SecondNumber**. Rather than treating these as two distinct variables, you might treat them as one variable that has two dimensions: (**FirstNumber, SecondNumber**).

The Example's description gives no reason to prefer to treat these as one two-dimensional variables or two individual variables.

To understand what we mean by a multidimensional variable, consider a different situation: American students often take entrance exams (the SAT or the ACT) when they apply to university. Each student's application includes the student's name and the student's scores on the two tests. These three values are stored together, retrieved together and examined together. In this case, rather than seeing these as three distinct variable, you should see them as related (*this* score goes with *that* student). The three-dimensional variable is (**StudentName, SATscore, ACTscore**).[7]

N. ANALYZE INDEPENDENT VARIABLES THAT SHOULD BE TESTED TOGETHER

An important factor driving test design is the independence (or non-independence) of the variables. We say that two variables are independent if the value of one variable has no effect on the range of valid values of the other variable.

There are other definitions of independence. For example, statistical independence requires the variables to be uncorrelated. We do not. Two variables might be highly correlated, so that if one has a large value, the other is very likely to have a high value and very unlikely to have a small value. However, when testing, our concern is with which tests are *possible*, not which are *probable*. If (high value, small value) is a valid pair, we see it as a valid test it even if it is improbable.

- Testing variables together that you know are independent is an expensive use of time. There's almost no limit on the number of combination tests you could run. What will you learn from testing lots of combinations that you wouldn't learn from testing the variables on their own? Where do you stop?

- It's useful to test independent variables together despite the combinatorial problem because:

  ○ Some variables are related in some way, even though they're independent under our definition. For example, the variables might have a joint effect on some other variable.

  ○ Some variables are supposed to be independent but they're not. (The program does have bugs, after all.) You might run a few combination tests of supposed-to-be-independent variables as a quick check for a problem.

This Example doesn't provide anything of interest for this analysis. **FirstNumber** and **SecondNumber** might be independent and might be interesting to analyze together, but we're going to look at them next, as part of the analysis of **Sum**.

For more on testing variables together, see *Chapters N. Analyze Independent Variables that Should Be Tested Together* on page 181, *O. Analyze Variables that Hold Results* on page 191 and *P. Analyze Non-Independent Variables. Deal with Relationships and Constraints* on page 201.

O. ANALYZE VARIABLES THAT HOLD RESULTS

The result variable is **Sum**, a result of **FirstNumber** + **SecondNumber**.

What could go wrong with **Sum**?

Probably the most interesting things that can go wrong with **Sum** are involved with how the program uses **Sum**. The Example's description doesn't provide any information about how the program will use **Sum**, so there aren't many interesting risks to consider. Here's what comes to mind:

---

7   Mathematicians would call this an example of a *three-tuple*. Programmers would often call the data structure that holds these three values a *record*.

- *Calculation error?* It takes talent to write a program that can return the wrong sum of two small Integers, but some programmers are very talented.

- *Divide by zero?* Maybe. Murphy's Law, applied to testing, says that if **Sum** takes the value 0, some part of the program will divide by it. However, the program description doesn't provide information about how or where **Sum** might be used, so there is no way to test for this risk at this time.

- *Overflow?* Probably not. The range of possible values for **Sum** is 0 to 198.

- *Invalid data type?* This can happen only if **FirstNumber** and **SecondNumber** have invalid values. The program should have rejected these.

Risk involving Sum	Valid case equivalence class	Invalid case equivalence class	Value of Sum	FirstNumber	SecondNumber	Notes
Calculation error	0 to 198		0	0	0	
			198	99	99	
		< 0	-1	0	-1	should be impossible
			-1	−1	0	should be impossible
		> 198	199	99	100	should be impossible
			199	100	99	should be impossible
Overflow		> > 198	999999			should be impossible

There are a few more Tasks in the Schema, but this Example has run out of interesting details, so we'll stop here.

A MORE DETAILED LOOK AT DOMAIN TESTING

The essence of domain testing is that you **partition a domain** *into subdomains* **(equivalence classes)** *then select* **representatives** *of each subdomain for your tests.*

Domain testing (Clarke, 1976; Clarke, Hassel & Richardson, 1982; Copeland, 2004; Elmendorf, 1967; Ostrand & Balcer, 1988; Weyuker & Jeng, 1991; White, 1981) is also known as equivalence partitioning and boundary analysis. It is probably the most widely described (and one of the most widely practiced) software testing technique. Some books (*e.g.*, Burnstein, 2003) present test design as if domain testing was the only test technique. According to Rick Craig, a well known software testing teacher, "equivalence partitioning is … intuitively used by virtually every tester we've ever met." (Craig & Jaskiel, 2002, p. 162)

Domain testing is a type of functional testing (Elmendorf, 1967; Howden, 1980a, 1987; Ostrand & Balcer, 1988). The tester views the program as a function, feeds it interesting inputs and evaluates its outputs. This approach focuses attention on the data (the inputs and the outputs).

DOMAINS

Functions have input domains (the set of possible input values) and output domains.

- Many discussions focus on *input domains* (Beizer, 1995; Binder, 2000; Jorgensen, 2008; Myers, 1979; White, 1981).

- The same analysis applies to *output domains* (Burnstein, 2003; Jorgensen, 2008; Kaner, et al., 1993), including typically-considered outputs (such as reports) and output to devices or file systems (Whittaker, 2003). Whittaker also emphasized the value of analyzing intermediate results of calculations. These results might be stored in variables that you don't see from the user interface, but that doesn't make them any less likely to be overflowed or corrupted in the same ways as more visible outputs.

PARTITIONING

Partitioning a set means splitting it into subsets (partitions) that are *nonoverlapping* (no values in common).

Disjunction (nonoverlapping) is important for some models, but testers often work with overlapping sets (Kaner, et al., 1993; Weyuker & Jeng, 1991). For our purposes, in practice, partitioning means dividing a set of possible values of a variable into subsets that either don't overlap at all or don't overlap much.

Partitioning usually splits a set into equivalence classes.

EQUIVALENCE CLASSES

How you define *equivalence class* carries implications for theoretical interpretation and practical application of domain testing.

In principle, the definition is straightforward: "All elements within an equivalence class are essentially the same for the purpose of testing" (Ostrand & Balcer, 1988, p. 676). However, the notion of "essentially the same" has evolved in different ways.

- *Intuitive or subjective equivalence:* Intuitive definitions (*e.g.*, Craig & Jaskiel, 2002; Kit, 1995) appear obvious. For example:

  "Basically we are identifying inputs that are treated the same way by the system and produce the same results." (Craig & Jaskiel, 2002, p. 162)

  "If you expect the same result from two tests, you consider them equivalent. A group of tests forms an equivalence class if you believe they all test the same thing … Two people analyzing a program will come up with a different list of equivalence classes. This is a subjective process." (Kaner, 1988, p. 81)

  In other words, as you get to know the program or as you get more familiar with this type of testing, it becomes obvious what is equivalent to what.

  These books and courses provide examples and often list heuristics for identifying easy-to-analyze variables and picking test cases (Burnstein, 2003; Kaner, et al., 1993; Kit, 1995; Myers, 1979).

  We've managed testers trained this way and we've trained them this way ourselves. In retrospect, we think the training was too vague. Testers trained this way lack guidance for finding (or abstracting from natural language) information needed to partition variables. They often don't know how to generalize to new variables or to the testing of several variables together.

- *Specified equivalence:* Under another common approach, variables' values are valid (according to the specification) or invalid. The tester chooses cases from the valid set and each invalid set (Burnstein, 2003; DeMillo, McCracken, Martin & Passafiume, 1987; Myers, 1979). Kaner *et al.* (1993) note that detailed specifications of commercial software often don't exist. Without a specification, there can be no specified equivalence.

In our experience, testers trained to rely primarily on specifications when they design tests often find it hard to adapt to less formal environments.

- *Analysis of the code that defines or uses the variables:* The intuitive and specified-equivalence approaches focus on the program's variables, primarily from a black-box perspective. Some authors (*e.g.,* Howden, 1980a, 1980b) suggest ways to partition data or identify boundary values by reading the code.

- *Path-based equivalence:* Descriptions that appear primarily in the research literature say that two values of a variable are equivalent if they cause the program to take the same branch or the same (sub)path. (Beizer, 1995; Clarke, et al., 1982; Tian, 2005; White, 1981) This makes sense for testers familiar with the source code. It depends on information that is usually unavailable to the black-box tester.[8]

- *Risk-based equivalence*: Several early authors pointed out that domain tests target specific types of errors (Binder, 2000; Boyer, 1975; Clarke, 1976; White, 1981).

  - Weyuker & Ostrand (1980; *see also* Jeng & Weyuker, 1989, p. 38) proposed that the ideal partitioning should be *revealing*, meaning that it:

    "divides the domain into disjoint subdomains with the property that within each subdomain, either the program produces the correct answer for every element or the program produces an incorrect answer for every element."

  - Whittaker (2003) describes domain testing as an attack (essentially a pattern) for exposing a class of commonly occurring faults.

  - Myers (1979) illustrated risk analysis with a program that interprets three inputs as sides of a triangle and then decides whether the triangle is scalene, isosceles, equilateral or not a triangle.

    Myers' tests included numeric inputs that were appropriate for the different types of triangles and other numeric inputs that did not yield triangles. (For example, try to draw a triangle with one side that is 3 inches and two sides that are 1 inch each.) Myers also included non-numeric input and the wrong number of inputs.

    Many (many, many) authors have presented their own analyses of the same triangle program. For example, Binder (2000) listed 65 triangle tests. He considered several additional risks, including for example, the potential failure from running the same test more than once. Collard (2003) listed 4 tests that might be sufficient and noted Kent Beck's claim that 6 tests would suffice for Beck's triangle program implementation, Collard (2003, p. 4) said:

    "This sounds like a bad joke – ask four different experts, get four different answers which range from four to 140 (*see* Jorgensen, 2008) test cases – and four consulting bills."

    Analyses of the triangle vary because they consider risks beyond mishandled numeric input. They consider dimensions different from the number line that shows which inputs are too large or small. Each dimension requires a different analysis. Examples:

    (a) The valid number of sides of a triangle is three. Two and four sides are members of the too-few-sides and too-many-sides equivalence classes.

---

8   Black-box testers will often find it useful to ask the programmers about implementation details. However, to base a series of tests on path-based equivalence, you will need ongoing access to the code and time to build a detailedc understanding of it.

(b) For ASCII encoded input, the valid range (digits) runs from 48 ("0") to 57 ("9"). Characters 47 ("/") and 58 (":") are the interesting boundary values for non-digit input.

(c) Delays between entries of numbers might trigger a ***timeout***. At that point, the system will stop accepting data and do something else. A delay just briefer than the timeout limit and one just longer are in different equivalence classes.

Consider the following three test cases:

(i) Side 1 = 1, side 2 = 2, side 3 = 3, delay between entries = 1 second

(ii) Side 1 = 2, side 2 = 2, side 3 = 3, delay between entries = 1 hour

(iii) Side 1 = <space>2, side 2 = 2, side 3 = 3, delay between entries = 1 second.

Cases (i) and (ii) are equivalent with respect to risks that the program won't process digits correctly or won't accept three entries as the right number. However, they aren't equivalent relative to the risk that the program (Case i) would accept three sides that don't define a triangle or (Case ii) won't recognize the inputs because of timeout.

Similarly, Cases (ii) and (iii) are equivalent with respect to the size of the numbers entered. However, they're in different classes relative to the risk that the program will not sensibly interpret a leading space.

This workbook adopts a subjective, risk-based definition of equivalence.

Under this definition[9], two tests are ***equivalent*** *relative to a potential error*:

- Given the same variable under analysis, two testers are likely to imagine different lists of potential errors because of their different experience history. (This is why we say equivalence is subjective.)
- A test is ***error-revealing*** if it can reveal a specific type of error. Two tests are equivalent if both are error-revealing for the same type of error or neither is error-revealing for that type of error (Weyuker & Ostrand, 1980).
- The same test might be error-revealing relative to one potential error and not revealing relative to another.

---

9   Iain McCowatt's comments on this definition of equivalence will probably clarify the definition for several readers:

"I initially struggled with this definition of equivalence, in that it introduces a contradiction to the heart of this chapter: if a subdomain is indeed equivalent with regards to a potential error then doesn't every representative of that subdomain have the same potential to reveal that error? This would seem to contradict the statement, later in the chapter that "If one member of the class would reveal an error, will all the others? No." This is likely to be lost on the casual reader. For others it might sow confusion.

It seems to me that there are two important yet distinct notions of equivalence that testers need to deal with:

1. ***Equivalence relative to potential errors*** is the one that really /matters/, in that we want to select the tests that are most likely to reveal problems.

Unfortunately, we're not blessed with foreknowledge of where the bugs will be, so we're forced to use a proxy:

2. ***Equivalent relative to some idea as to how the software will behave***

When you talk about identifying a dimension, and partitioning the domain based on that dimension, you're using the second notion of equivalence. A special case is when you do risk based partitioning, which draws on both: your ideas as to how the software will behave IS a potential error. Interestingly, the act of selecting a best representative can be seen as a second act of partitioning: first you partition the domain based on an idea as to how the software will behave and THEN you partition the subdomains based on the power of each member to reveal a problem."

When we call a set an equivalence class, we're making a working assumption that the program will respond to all the values in the set the same way. That assumption is not entirely correct. We must pick from "equivalent" values with care.

SELECTING REPRESENTATIVES

Are all members of an equivalence class equivalent in all respects? If one member of the class would reveal an error, can we be sure that all the others will too? *No.* (Hamlet, 2010; Myers, 1979; Ostrand & Balcer, 1988). Random sampling from equivalence classes is often ineffective (Hamlet & Taylor, 1990).

Consider numeric input fields: programs tend to fail more at boundaries because some errors (off-by-one errors) are specific to boundaries. Several discussions of domain testing stress optimal choice of test values within equivalence classes (Beizer, 1995; Kaner, et al., 1993; Kit, 1995).

Boundaries are representatives of the equivalence classes you sample them from. Boundary values are more likely to expose a classification error than other class members, so they're *better* representatives (Foster, 1980, 1984; Howden, 1980b; Reid, 1997a, 1997b; Whittaker & Jorgensen, 1999).

In case you're not familiar with the terminology (***classification errors***), consider *Example 1: Integer Input* on page 229. The program should accept numbers between -999 to 999. It has a classification error if it accepts numbers outside this range or rejects numbers within it. This error is typically the result of a mistake in the inequality.

For example, the code might accept numbers > 999.

- The equivalence class for this includes everything bigger than 999. All of these are error-revealing for that error.
- But what if the error is narrower? For example, suppose the programmer makes a very small mistake, writing code that rejects any value > 1000 instead of ≥ 1000. This will still accept a value > 999, but only one value (1000). Only one test for this is error-revealing (test with 1000).

Therefore, the best representative of the set of values > 999 is 1000 because it is error-revealing against the general misclassification error (accept anything bigger than 999) and against the boundary-value error (accept 1000).

Boundary errors are common. Programmers sometimes mistype an inequality. Specifiers sometimes misunderstand what *should* happen at a boundary and mistakenly *decide* to accept an inappropriate boundary value instead of rejecting it.

Boundaries are interesting, but they aren't the only points of interest.

- Sometimes there are special cases, such as 0. If you can think of a reason the program is more likely to fail with a specific value, test with that value.
- Sometimes there is no boundary value. Rather than a single most-extreme value of interest, several values in the set might be equally likely to reveal an error. In this case, you sample (arbitrarily or randomly) from that set.

In the ideal case, you'll select a single value (like a boundary) that is more likely to cause a failure than the others. If that's not possible, the goal is to select a value that is at least as good as the others. Rather than describing the search for test values as boundary-value analysis, we say we're looking for the best representatives of each set.

> "A ***best representative*** of an equivalence class is a value that is at least as likely as any other value in the class to expose an error." (Kaner, Bach & Pettichord, 2002, p. 37)

Generalizing from boundaries to best representatives is useful for analyzing nonordered domains, such as printers (Kaner, Falk & Nguyen, 1993).[10]

Imagine testing application-software compatibility with printers. Failure with a printer causes dissatisfaction even if the underlying error is more fairly attributed to the printer than the software under test. There are so many types of printers that it's impractical to test them all.

Suppose you group as equivalent all printers advertised as Postscript Level 3 compatible. In theory, all of them print the same input the same way.

There is no smaller-to-larger ordering within or between groups of printers, so how can you decide which specific printers to test? What is the boundary case for the set of Postscript-compatible printers?

- A printer prone to memory management problems might be a best representative (most likely to fail) for tests that consume memory or run long sequences of tasks.
- A printer prone to timing bugs might be a best representative for tests that push the printer into multitasking. (Timing bugs sometimes lead to paper jams, unexpectedly-blank lines or an unexpected failure to print a page the printer has been able to print before).

Different risks yield different best representatives.

AUTOMATING DOMAIN TESTS

Domain tests can be automated in several ways:

- The obvious approach is regression automation. As the program changes in new builds, retest already-tested areas of the product to see if you can find new problems. Regression testing reuses old tests to check the program can still pass the tests it passed before. Boundary values are often hard-coded into regression tests because of the assumption (not always correct) that boundary values tend to be stable in a program.

- A more interesting approach automatically creates the tests. If you know the characteristics of the variable under test (the data type, the intended boundaries), it is a routine matter to generate the input values for most (or all) of the tests you would create. Why create these by hand?

- Similarly, automated creation of domain tests is common when testing a protocol that specifies the structure of messages from one process to another. The protocol will specify the variables that can appear in a valid message, the permissible values of each variable and the permissible ordering of variables in the message. From here, test design can be made routine.

- What is harder to automate is assessment of the *impact* of the test. What are the *effects* of entering boundary values into a variable? You can check whether the program accepted

---

10 This is an old example. The reason we use it is that Kaner, Falk & Nguyen worked through it in a LOT of detail and explained the analysis in a way that we think generalizes well to other types of devices. Replicating that type of analysis for a different device class will take an enormous amount of research into the details of incompatibilities of different devices within the same class (e.g., Android phones or dashboard-mountable GPS units or Bluetooth keyboards) and a 20-30 page writeup that, not long from now, will look as dated as our analysis of printers. Our hope is that you can see past the oldness of the details to the current value of the analytical method.

the right values and rejected the wrong ones, but what other variables depend on this variable? Which variables hold the results of calculations that involve this variable?

You aren't likely to write a program that figures out what variables use a particular variable and whether they use it well. ***Program slicing*** is an approach to identifying and testing variables that use values entered into other variables (*see* Binkley & Gallagher, 1996; Binkley & Harman, 2004; Gallagher & Lyle, 1991; Horowitz & Reps, 2013; Jorgensen, 2008; Tip, 1995; Weiser, 1984). However, this technique is too complex for this workbook. It is not yet widely used. In current practice, figuring out impact is a creative, human task.

DOCUMENTING AND EXPLORING

Because this is a book, we documented our examples fairly heavily. Some readers have misinterpreted this as a recommendation that you heavily document your work when you test.

Like all test techniques, domain testing can be done in a way that emphasizes preplanning and thorough documentation or it can be done as needed, tests designed just as you're about to run them, with little or no documentation (this is sometimes called ***exploratory testing***):

- You can do a domain analysis without creating any paperwork whatever. After we've done domain analysis of a type of variable (or relationship) several times, we rarely need to create charts for a new instance of that type of variable. Analyzing this type of variable becomes straightforward to us. We can just do it. Unless there is some other reason to keep these charts, we'll skip creating them and just run the tests.[11]

- We have sometimes written detailed test documentation, adding detailed descriptions to tables like the ones we present here.

  ○ The tables have often been useful tools for explaining what tests we were going to run and why.

  ○ The tables have been excellent training tools. When we want to train a tester to design these types of tests, these tables give the tester a clear structure for their work. It helps them organize their thinking. It helps us evaluate their work and give feedback.

  ○ Added detail (rationale or how-to) was sometimes helpful, especially when explaining an unusual, difficult or complex application of the technique.

  ○ Added detail was sometimes helpful for explaining work to someone who doesn't know much about testing. However, creating this type of documentation and keeping it up-to-date can be very expensive. Detailed test documentation is sometimes necessary,

---

11 Paul Gerrard expresses a different view:

"The 18 step process looks daunting. It feels like it's cumbersome and bureaucratic. But a general purpose technique requires a systematic approach. That's just the way it has to be. So far so good.

An eighteen step process (although not all steps are used all the time), being systematic and comprehensive, shouts out for a documentation process too. If you really are taking the trouble to follow the process, then it makes sense to keep track of what you produce in terms of intermediate workings, and eventual tests in a tool or a document. It seems too comprehensive to incorporate into an exploratory testing session, I would say.

So my query is, how would you convince an exploratory tester this is an appropriate approach for them to use? Personally, having a lousy short term memory, I could not follow the process without keeping at least some notes to keep me on track."

Paul's comments are well-taken. We should note that nothing in the test design guidance that we provide in this book determines how much documentation you should create. Our intuition is that less is, generally, better. Many other people in the field consider it more appropriate to work from a much higher baseline.

but if it is not required, we're unlikely to provide it. Usually, a table is good enough to provide a good historical record and clear instructions to another tester.

- We have often scribbled tables onto whatever piece of paper was handy, to help us work through our analysis and keep track of our work as we explored a program. Sometimes we kept those notes, sometimes not.

- We have often found domain analysis useful for helping us understand how programs use their data. Rather than comparing the test results to expected results, we run the tests to find out what will happen when we try different boundaries. The *style of thinking* that domain testing teaches us is *at least* as helpful to us when we're first learning the program as later, when we're checking expectations.

SECTION 1. PART 2. SUMMARIES OF KEY TECHNICAL CONCEPTS

- **Black-box software testing**
- **BBST®**
- **Goals of testing**
- **Domain**
  - **Input and output domains**
  - **Specified domain**
- **Specification**
- **Variable**
  - **Input, result, output, and configuration variables**
  - **Stored data**
- **Variable types**
  - **Record**
  - **Data entry field**
  - **User Interface Control**
- **Dimension**
  - **Primary dimension**
  - **Secondary dimension**
- **Notional variable**
- **Multidimensional variable**
  - **Explicit versus implicit**
  - **N-tuple**
  - **Combinatorial explosion**
- **Risk**
- **Theory of error**
  - **Similarity of tests**
  - **Test idea**
  - **Risk/equivalence table**
- **Power of a test**
  - **Error-revealing**
  - **Best representative**
  - **Corner case**
- **Oracle**
  - **Filters**
- **Analogy to opinion polling**
  - **Stratified sampling**
- **Linearizable variable**
- **Coverage**

This Chapter presents our terminology. We're mindful of two very different groups of readers (we heard plenty from both groups during the book's review cycles):

- Some of you will find this Chapter dry and theoretical. We encourage you to skim this Chapter quickly—just to notice what's here—and to come back when one of these terms (later in the book) confuses you. At that point, we think the attention to detail in some of this Chapter's presentations will be helpful.

- Others will feel that some of the writing of this book is oversimplified or nonstandard. We hope the presentations here can clarify our usage and thinking for you.

In our experience, the essentials of domain testing are intuitively clear to most testers. They understand quickly that it addresses two important real-world problems:

- How to limit the number of tests
- How to pick tests that are likely to find bugs.

In our experience, most testers find it reasonable, even obvious, to group tests by similarity, to run only a few tests from each group and to choose tests (like boundary cases) that might be a little more powerful than the average member of a group.

However, the technical underpinnings of domain testing often run deeper than the knowledge of the average tester.

Over the years, we've had to develop ways of explaining the concepts and applications of domain testing that our students and trainees can understand.

This chapter presents those ways.

BLACK-BOX SOFTWARE TESTING

Before computers and software existed, people talked about studying devices as black boxes. The notion of a "black box" is the notion of a closed thing. You can't look inside it to see how it works. Instead, you give it inputs (like, pressing its buttons) and watch what happens.

Black-box software testing is usually defined in much the same way. When you test this way, you don't know, and don't learn, what's inside the box (the code and the data). You just know what the software does. The contrast with black-box testing is *glass-box testing*: when you do this, you look into the box. You design tests based on the characteristics of the code.

Put this way, the difference between black box and glass box is captured by a negative. You *don't know* something when you do black-box testing that you *do know* when you do glass-box testing.

That's the wrong way to look at it. It misses the essence of black-box testing.

In our view, what distinguishes black box from glass box is not what black-box testers **don't** *pay attention to. It's what black-box testers* **do** *pay attention to.*

WHAT'S SPECIAL ABOUT BLACK-BOX TESTING

Black-box testing is the study of:

- What the program should do.
- What the program should not do.
- What the program actually does do and whether that is acceptable.

To do this well, you have to discover:

- Who will use this program or depend on it in some other way?
- What makes this program valuable to these people? What benefits does it provide to these people? (Note: Different people will enjoy different benefits.)
- What would change the value? (Note: What makes the program better for some people might make it worse for others.)
- What do these people expect of the program and why do they expect that? Many expectations are set by things separate from this program's code. For example by:
  - The usual practices of lawyers, bankers, salespeople and others who use software to help them do their professional activities.
  - The capabilities of competing programs, and how they do things.
  - The laws of physics (think of how objects move in a game).
  - The laws that govern an activity (think of software that calculates tax returns).
  - The requirements and capabilities of other devices, programs or systems that the software under test interacts with.

You can't learn much about these from the code. If you bury your nose in the code, you won't learn what you need to know to do competent black-box testing.[12, 13]

SOMETIMES YOU WILL BE STUCK WITH BLACK-BOX TESTING

One of the most common objections from the early readers/reviewers of this book is that we write, throughout the book, as if:

- You don't have access to the code (or you wouldn't have time or skill to understand the source code if you did have access)

- You don't have access to a specification that will tell you all the necessary things about the software's design

- You don't have access to programmers who will answer all your questions.

Yes, we do know that some companies write thorough, formal specifications. If you have them, use them!

No analysis of any example in this book would be harmed by adding a little more (and a little more trustworthy) information.

We also know that many companies are more agile. They don't have formal specifications but they have lots of useful informal documentation, like story cards. Again, use them if you have them. But our experience is that many story cards describe a concept and don't get into the fine details, like what variables should have what boundaries.

We know, too, that many companies foster a close working relationship between testers and programmers, which makes it much easier for testers to ask programmers detailed questions about the design and implementation of the program. Having worked as programmers ourselves, we agree that when you have them available and cooperative, programmers can be informative and entertaining.

---

12 One interesting problem in glass-box testing involves discovery of missing code. It is relatively easy to recognize errors in code that you can read. It is harder to recognize, when reading the code or writing tests based on the code, that something is missing. Coverage measures, for example, won't tell you that you haven't tested something that isn't there. Brian Marick (2000) summarized seven studies that reported coding errors (not the absence of desirable features) that resulted from missing code. Between 22% and 54% of the reported errors were faults of omission. Eldh (2011) reported an additional replication. In her research classifying coding errors, faults of omission were the most common type of error and accounted for 38% of her sample.

13 In an early meeting of the Los Altos Workshops on Software Testing, James Whittaker and Alan Jorgensen presented their approach to testing using constraint-based attacks. This approach to test design considers many kinds of limits (constraints) in the program and tries to break those with selected data values and sequences of actions. Whittaker described four classes of constraints: input, output, calculation and storage. He drew a diagram of his model that looked a little like a turtle.

During the meeting, we had the inevitable black-box-versus-glass-box debate (my box is testier than your box). Whittaker pointed out that glass boxes aren't so glassy. Source code written in a modern programming language, will be translated by an optimizing compiler that might add branches and special cases not visible in the source code. In addition, the program probably calls many library functions. The source code for those is not necessarily available. The program probably also relies on libraries that are loaded at run-time and that are frequently updated (changed). Because people don't necessarily apply updates when they should, any particular machine today combines an unpredictable mix of past and present run-time library functions.

Thus, when you look at source code, you don't *really* see what is going on in the machine. What you see is the programmer's model of what should be going on. It's still a model. You are still working with notional variables that may have surprising constraints. (*See* Hyde, 2006.)

As Whittaker eloquently put it, no matter how low a level you test the code at, "It's turtles all the way down!"

However,

- When people tell us that any company that values the quality of its products or the professionalism of its staff will have detailed formal specifications, that doesn't match our experience. We have seen wonderful products that sold well, had great customer-support track records, but their "specifications" (some written on napkins at local bars) were incomplete, inconsistent, inaccurate and out of date.

- When people tell us we should assume that programmers are always available, we know that this happens in many more companies than before, but we also know testers who work in distributed work environments on a different continent from their projects' programmers. And we know testers working in independent test labs who have no access to the technical staff of some of their lab's client companies or who have to funnel questions through a company liaison. And we know testers working in companies who subcontract some of their development to third parties and have limited or no access to the subcontractors' programmers. And we also know testers who work in companies that have traditional views about separating programmers and testers and the traditional intracompany politics that tag along with those views.

Serious organizations working with serious software face these challenges. As we write this, in July 2013, we think of a request for research proposals that was just published by the United States' National Aeronautics and Space Administration (NASA, 2013). Here's what they say (Subtopic AFCS—1.2):

> "More and more, design and implementation of software systems used in aviation is contracted out to external companies. For example, the FAA rarely develops its air traffic software systems internally; it usually acquires them from contractors who develop new systems in accordance with the FAA's requirements. The delivered products usually do not include intermediate products (e.g., design models or source code), which would allow the FAA to take advantage of advanced verification techniques (e.g., formal methods or abstract interpretation); it thus leaves black-box testing as the only means of verification. Similarly, most of the aviation industry has shifted from developing software systems entirely in house to integrating sub-systems developed in house with Commercial Off-The-Shelf (COTS) developed by sub-contractors and delivered as black boxes. Again testing, despite its shortcomings, is the only solution left for verifying the entire system."

If you can easily get all the information you need, use it! But when you can't, you still have a program to test. It can be useful to have tactics for dealing with that possibility.

You can use domain testing for black-box or glass-box testing. The logic of the technique is the same—the differences between black box and glass box domain analysis lie in the nature of the information that is readily available and the sources of information you will consult to gather more information.

BBST®

BBST is the registered trademark associated with a series of courses on Black-box Software Testing. For more information, *see* http://bbst.info.

GOALS OF TESTING

Traditionally, software testing has been described as bug-hunting. Testers test in order to find bugs (Burnstein, 2003; Myers, 1979; Kaner, Falk & Nguyen, 1993). The more modern view is that testing is an empirical investigation, conducted to provide stakeholders with quality-related information about the product or service under test.

You might test software to characterize its behavior (e.g. performance testing), to predict its future support costs, to assess its value for doing a type of task, or for many other reasons beyond bug hunting.

We advocate the modern view. (See the BBST courses, for example.)

However, domain testing is a technique that hammers a program with extreme cases in order to expose bugs quickly and efficiently.

Domain testing is all about bug hunting. Because this book is focused on domain testing, this book will consistently describe testers as if their mission in life is to find bugs.

DOMAIN

To testers, a common meaning of the word *domain* is a *domain of knowledge*. For example, someone testing banking software is considered a domain expert if they know a lot about how banks (and banking software) work.

---

*Domain **testing** is not about domain knowledge. In domain testing, a **domain** is a **set**.*

In mathematics:

- An *input domain* is the set of possible inputs to a function.
- An *output domain* (often called the *range* of the function) is the set of possible outputs of the function.

In black-box software testing, you don't necessarily know what function you're testing because you don't see the code. You know the program:

- Accepts input data (for example, from a user via a user interface or from other programs or from storage).
- Does calculations using the data.
- Outputs results (to the user via a user interface or to other programs or to storage).

When the program accepts data, it puts the data in a variable. We're going to call this an *input variable*.

> (Yes, the program will do things with this variable, but for as long as we're thinking about a place in memory that receives input data, we're referring to it as an input variable.)

When the program outputs data, it is copying out the value of a variable (or of a calculation, but for our purposes, we can pretend the calculation is temporarily stored in a variable--see the discussion of *notional variables* later in this Chapter). We're going to call this an *output variable*.

> (Yes, this is artificial. We're using a terminology of convenience. A program can accept data, store it in a variable, then save that value. In cases like this, the same variable is both

an input variable and an output variable. In this book, it is useful to think in functional terms. A variable is an input variable when it is receiving data and an output variable when it is a source for output.)

INPUT AND OUTPUT DOMAINS

In black-box testing:

- The *input domain* of an input variable is the set of values that you can imagine entering into that variable.

- The *output domain* of a variable is the set of values that you can imagine the output variable can have.

SPECIFIED DOMAIN

The *valid* subset of the input domain is the set of values the program is supposed to accept and process normally. This subset is also called the *specified domain*.

Consider this task:

"An Integer variable can take values in the range -999 and 999, the endpoints being inclusive. Develop a series of tests by performing equivalence class analysis and boundary value analysis on this variable."

The *specified domain* is { -999, ... , 999 } [14]

Specified domain means: *the program should accept these values*.

Of course, people can provide other inputs too, including so-called *invalid values*. If people can input a value, the program should process it in an orderly way. Even if the program's response is an error message, this is an orderly response. Thus, all these values, valid and invalid, are members of an input domain the program must handle.

SPECIFICATION

We define *specification* loosely, as any document that describes the product.

- The "document" might be a formal writing, a story card, a videotaped demonstration, a competing program or a tape of an interview. What makes it a document is that you can get the same information from it repeatedly over a long period of time.

- The "description" doesn't have to be detailed and it doesn't have to address the whole product. It has to provide some information about the product (even if it is just a little) that will be taken as credible by members of the project team or other people with project-relevant power or influence.

VARIABLE

A variable in a computer program is a labelled area of memory. You can access the contents of the area of memory by referring to the label (the variable's name).

---

14 When mathematicians specify a range of numbers, they often use a different notation. For example, [999, ..., 999] would show a range that runs from -999 to 999. The square bracket means the range includes the endpoints. A parenthesis indicates the range includes everything up to but not including the endpoint. For example, [-999, ..., 999) includes everything from -999 up to (but not including) 999. We have chosen not to use this notation, preferring simple set notation for all domains.

From a functional point of view, a *variable* is something that can have different values.

In this book, we're particularly interested in five kinds of variables: input variables, result variables, output variables, configuration variables and variables whose data are stored over a long period of time.

INPUT VARIABLE

If you can enter data into the variable, it is an *input variable.*

- You might enter data into the variable:
  - By typing into a data entry field in a dialog.
  - By selecting a value from a list (in a listbox) or by pressing a button or moving a slider or indicating the value using some other type of user interface *control.*
- The program might enter data into a variable without direct human input. We will often treat this as an input variable too. For example:
  - Load the variable from storage (such as reading it from disk).
  - Load the value from a message sent from another program or another part of this program.

RESULT VARIABLE

A *result variable* gets its values from a calculation that uses other variables. For example, consider three variables: v_1, v_2 and v_3, related to each other as follows:

$$v_3 = v_1 \times v_2$$

In this equation, v_3 is a result variable.

Here's another example. Imagine testing a checkbook application. Enter deposits and withdrawals.[15] After a transaction, you have a new bank balance.[16] The *inputs* are the deposits and the withdrawals. The balance is the *result.*

- One class of results includes all positive balances.
- The bank probably handles your account differently when you're overdrawn, so you could treat all negative balances as a separate class.

You haven't adequately tested this program until you work with inputs that test both output classes (positive and negative balances) and the boundary (zero balance) that separates them.

Here's a third example (*see Example 17: Joan's Pay on page 343*): Joan works at a store, under the following contract:

- Her normal pay rate is $8 per hour.
- For hours worked beyond 40 hours per week, her normal rate is $12 per hour.

---

15 The starting balance (the balance before a test's deposit or withdrawal) is an example of what we're calling a *configuration* variable.

16 Morven Gentleman notes this simplification. "Note the unstated assumption that deposits and withdrawals are sequentializable. Actually, the bank I use does not operate that way. Although there is exception-handling for excessive withdrawals, normally transactions are accumulated over the banking day, and only resolved at banking day end. This facilitates simultaneous transactions, as well as post-withdrawal transfers from other accounts in order to cover unanticipatedly large withdrawals. That is, momentary overdrafts are acceptable."

This balance is still a result—but it might be a result of several transactions rather than just one. In addition, look at all these additional *consequences.* A withdrawal in one account might impact several others.

- For work between midnight and 6 a.m. on any day, she gets $16 per hour.
- For work between 6 a.m. and noon on Sunday, she gets $16 per hour.
- If she earns $500 or less in a week, 10% of her pay is deducted for taxes.
- If she earns more than $500, the tax deducted is $50 plus 20% of earnings greater than $500 that week. (So, if she earns $600, the tax deducted is $70.)

We'll work through this Example later. What's important here is to recognize that all these conditions and calculations lead to a single result variable, Joan's take-home pay.

To analyze a result variable, you must determine the partitions and best representatives of that variable (such as partitions and boundaries of take-home pay).

But how can you test these? You can't set the value of the result directly. To set the value of the result, you must choose values of the input variables that yield a calculation with the result you want.

When an input variable (like, how many hours worked) leads to a result (take-home pay), you must work the problem both ways:

- Focus on the input variable: what are the consequences when you change its value?
- Focus on the result variable: what values of the input variable(s) are of greatest interest in terms of their impact on this result?

OUTPUT VARIABLE

When the program displays or prints or stores a value or sends it to some other program, we call this the value of an *output variable*.

Most output variables are also result variables, but an output carries an additional set of risks.

What is interesting about an output variable is that the value's validity is determined by whatever receives it.

For example, an output is invalid if it is:

- Too long to be printed.
- Too large to be stored in the data file.
- The wrong type for the receiving variable, such as a date that the program will try to interpret as a price.

Theoretical discussions of domain testing rarely discuss result or output variables. Ammann & Offutt (2008) discuss the academic literature (and the practical recommendations arising out of that literature) associated with "input domain testing" in detail. They don't mention the idea of partition-analysis of variables that hold results (the words "result", "output" and "outcome" don't even appear in their index.) Tian (2005) says, in his chapter on Input Domain Partitioning and Testing, that:

> "Output variables are not explicitly specified. But, we assume that there are ways to check if the expected output is obtained for any input" (p. 128)

"Corresponding to these terms and definitions for the input, we can define output variable, space, vector, point, range (corresponding to input domain), etc. Since the output is only implicitly specified in most domain testing strategies, we omit the corresponding definitions." (p. 129).

We see this as a serious blind spot.

No one (but testers) (and hackers) would enter data into a program just to see if it can filter its **inputs.** *Users care about the inputs because they want the program to* **use** *those inputs, to generate results.*

To check the information that is valuable to the user, you have to check what happens when you drive the results (the outputs) to their extreme values.

Testing of outputs is discussed by Jorgensen (2008); Kaner et al. (1993); Whittaker & Jorgensen (1999) and Whittaker (2003).

CONFIGURATION VARIABLE

A *configuration variable* holds information about the hardware and software environment that the software is running on or interacting with:

- What operating system are you running? What are your country or language settings? What time zone is your clock set to? Generally, what are the settings of the system and of the program?
- What printers, mice, video cards, keyboards, speakers, cameras, disk drives or other peripherals are connected?
- What other software is your program trading data with? What version? What communications protocol?

Some of these configuration variables aren't traditional variables (labelled areas of memory that can store data) or they aren't variables on your system.

- For example, if your program receives data from another program running on another computer, your program might not store any information about the version of the other program, but your program will be impacted if the new version has a new message structure or additional message codes (e.g., new error messages that it can send you).
- However, as a tester, you can change the configuration that you're testing with. From a functional point of view, if you can change it, it's a variable somewhere. And if changing it impacts the software under test, you can model it (for testing purposes) *as if* it is a variable of that software. (See our discussion of notional variables.)

Many people say *environment variable* or an *environmental input* for what we call a *configuration variable*.

STORED DATA

This is quite different from input, result output and configuration variables. Reviewers Tom Delmonte and Curtis Pettit convinced us to address long-stored data *somewhere* in our discussion of variables. This seems like the best place for it.

Suppose that a program defines an input variable that will take its values from a database that has been added to over many years. Call this the *variable under test*.

- If you don't know what the specified domain is for the variable under test, you can get a first approximation from the set of values stored in the database. The assumption is that stored values were checked before they were saved and are therefore probably valid values.

- If you believe that you know the specified domain but some stored values are invalid, then it must be that:

  ○ Your specification is incorrect (a not infrequent problem).

  ○ There are errors in the database.

  ○ The present range of valid values has changed from a previous range.

- Sometimes, changes to the valid range of a variable happen without anyone making conscious decisions to change anything. For example, not so long ago, it would have been reasonable to assume the age of a person who had a valid driving license could fit in 2 digits (0 to 99 years old). Now, however, it is conceivable that some people with valid driving licenses are older than 99. Thus the field must accept 3-digit values. Any input variable, calculation, result or output that assumes all valid drivers' age must be ≤ 99 years old should probably be seen as defective.[17]

- If the specified domain has changed:

  ○ Previously-created domain tests for the variable under test are all suspect. (It is time to review your regression tests for boundary errors in the tests).

  ○ Check the impact of the change on variables that depend on (*e.g.,* use) the variable under test. These variables might still be expecting the variable under test to operate within the old limits.

VARIABLE TYPES

In a computer program, a variable has a name and (typically) a *type*. The type is the type of data the variable can hold. For example, a variable might hold Integers.

For more on variable types (including Records), see *Chapter D. Determine Type and Scale of the Variable's Primary Dimension* on page 71.

RECORD

A *Record* is a variable that contains other variables. You've probably run into Records when working with databases. Each entry (Record) in the database has the same Fields. (A *Field* is an individual variable within a Record.)

For example, in a bug tracking database, each bug report is a Record. Within the Record, typical fields include the bug number, the date, the name of the person who reported the bug, a String that describes the bug, etc.

An important thing to remember about a Record is that all of its Fields belong together for some reason. For example, all Fields of a bug report are about the same bug.

---

17 These types of changes to boundaries are not uncommon. They are often side effects of improvements to other software (such as a programming library). In these cases, the programmers might not even intend to make the changes—they just happen. Ron Pihlgren (personal communication) provides another everyday example of this kind of change in consumer products: "One day I went to my local gas station and found a sticker on the pump saying that when paying with a credit card you could not have a single transaction of $100.00 or more. After a while (I assume there was a program update/fix) that sticker was removed."

DATA ENTRY FIELD

When the program displays a dialog box that includes controls for setting the values of several variables, a *data entry field* is a box where you can type a value. That value gets copied to a variable. In the old days, a typical dialog box presented a set of data entry fields and each field corresponded to a different Field of the same Record.

USER INTERFACE CONTROL

A control is an element of the user interface that you (the user) use to enter data or that the programmer can use to display data. Examples of controls for input include data entry fields, pull-down menus, spinners and sliders.

DIMENSIONS

Think of a *dimension* as an axis along which a variable can vary. For example,

- If you measure how long someone takes to run a race, the dimension is time.

- If you enter an amount of money that you want to withdraw at an ATM, the dimension is money.

For lack of a better word, we also use *dimension* to refer to a set of all possible values of a variable even if the set can't be ordered. For example, there is no natural ordering of the set of all possible Android phones, but if you're compatibility-testing your software, each phone is a different element of this large and diverse set.

PRIMARY VERSUS SECONDARY DIMENSIONS

Secondary dimensions have more to do with the program's implementation details than with the purpose of the variable.[18]

---

18 Scott Allman (personal communication) wrote an exceptional explanation of secondary dimensions:

"During the May, 2013 BBST Test Design class there were many questions about the concept of a secondary dimension. Here are some thoughts I had when helping with that class and some more that came to me after reading the sections in the workbook.

In an algorithm, there is only the primary dimension.

Sometimes programmers will select an algorithm from a reference instead of using their own design. For example, Don Knuth wrote a book on different algorithms for sorting and searching. By itself, an algorithm can be proven to be correct when variables are in a specified domain. In the 1970s and 1980s a promising line of research in computer science was to prove the correctness of algorithms. The claims of the algorithm could be checked solely on logical grounds. These proofs are a kind of test but not the kind discussed in the workbook.

An implementation of the algorithm, introduces the secondary dimension.

Domain testing shifts the testing task from being a logical exercise to being an empirical one. Testing, and not formal proofs, demonstrate the flaws and warts of a program that were not in the algorithm. There was a lengthy debate about this matter in the computer science literature between C.A.R. Hoare and James Fetzer (see Fetzer,1988). Since a program expands an algorithm beyond the logical realm and into the empirical realm other factors which can potentially affect the outcome are introduced. Collectively these are the secondary dimensions. The workbook notes all the perils awaiting an executing program when the inputs are garbled, time delays introduced, and word boundaries violated. Most algorithms don't consider these dimensions. Fetzer begins with a quote from Hoare which should pique the interest of every software tester, "I hold the opinion that the construction of computer programs is a mathematical activity like the solution of differential equations, that programs can be derived from their specifications through mathematical insight, calculation, and proof, using algebraic laws as simple and elegant as those of elementary arithmetic". And then Fetzer states his position, "Algorithms, as logical structures, are appropriate subjects for deductive verification. Programs, as causal models of those structures, are not". The causal effects of time and the assumptions of all supporting software introduce the secondary dimensions."

- You can usually determine the primary dimension by asking what the program is designed to learn from the variable.

- You can imagine secondary dimensions by asking *how else* the variable could change.

For example, when you withdraw money from an ATM:

- You enter a money amount at an ATM.

  This is the primary dimension.

- The machine will probably allow you a limited amount of time to enter your number. If you take too long, it will probably cancel the transaction and require you to swipe your card again if you want to start over.

  Time is NOT the primary dimension. The ATM isn't there to measure how fast you are, it is there to give you money when you ask for it. It might be necessary to program a timeout deadline into the user interface, but if so, that deadline runs on a secondary dimension (time).

For lack of a better term, we also label as "dimensions" some sets of possible values that are hard to order from smallest to largest, such as the set of all characters that could be entered at the keyboard.

NOTIONAL VARIABLE

A notional variable reflects the tester's "notion" of what is in the code. The tester analyzes the program as if this variable was part of the code.

The notional variable is part of a model, created by the tester, to describe how the program behaves or should behave. The model won't be perfect. That exact variable is probably not in the code. However, the notional variable is probably functionally equivalent to (works the same way as) a variable that *is* in the code or functionally equivalent to a group of variables that interact to produce the same behavior as this variable.

The model is usefully close to the real program if you can design tests for the model that are appropriate for the actual program.

Testers' models have inaccuracies. Testers will discover inaccuracies as they observe the program's responses to their experiments (tests), as they get guidance from stakeholders and as they study how a program like this *should* behave. Over time, they can revise their models (including the models' notional variables), creating better new tests.[19]

WHY DO YOU NEED NOTIONAL VARIABLES?

Domain testing can be done as a black-box testing activity or as a glass-box activity.

- When you test *glass box*, you can look at the code and see its variables. For this, you don't need notional variables.

- When you test *black box*, you don't see any variables. Instead, if you want to use an analysis that is driven by variables and their possible values, you have to work with notional variables.

---

19 Some test groups limit their ability to learn from experience. They choose to spend most of their testing time documenting a set of tests (the **regression tests**) and running these tests over and over. We see value in doing **some** regression testing, but test managers must think carefully about how they balance time among old tests, improvement of tests and creation of new ones.

In this book, we're doing black-box analysis, so discussions of "the variable" in our analyses almost always refer to notional variables.

MULTIDIMENSIONAL VARIABLES

Many variables are explicitly multidimensional.

For example, consider a pay record for hours worked. The record includes the person's name, the number of hours she worked and the pay rate. From this, you can calculate the amount due this person. (For simplicity, we're ignoring taxes and overtime pay.)

You can represent the payment record as a 4-tuple, a variable that is made of 4 parts:

(**Name, HoursWorked, PayRate, AmountDue**)

The **AmountDue** is **HoursWorked** × **PayRate**. The other variables are independent of each other in the sense that the range of possible values for one does not depend on the specific value of any other.

Every pay record will have all 4 parts and therefore every test will involve a value for each part. It wouldn't work to test **AmountDue** without specifying *some* value for **HoursWorked**.

In a multidimensional variable, it makes no sense to call one dimension the primary dimension and the others secondary. You might temporarily focus on only one dimension, but to test the values of any dimension, you must specify values for all others.

PRIMARY AND SECONDARY DIMENSIONS

Many variables *appear* one-dimensional. For example, "What is the price of that toy?" The "price" is a one-dimensional variable. The dimension is an amount of money.

What we're pointing out in this book is that even variables that look one-dimensional are in fact multidimensional. When you enter "price" into a computer program, you're not just entering an amount of money. The string you enter (and the way you enter it) vary in many other ways beyond the amount of money.

Just as the pay record has 4 dimensions:

(**Name, HoursWorked, PayRate, AmountDue**)

You can imagine "price of that toy" as having many dimensions too, such as

(Amount of money, length of the input string, number of leading spaces)

Similarly, when some other part of the program uses the variable later, that use might involve more than one dimension.

EXPLICIT VERSUS IMPLICIT MULTIDIMENSIONALITY

Many reviewers were confused by the way we speak of dimensions and of multidimensional variables.

We have not seen other descriptions of domain testing (and boundary value / equivalence analysis) that speak directly to this underlying multidimensionality of variables. Several give examples of variation in a secondary dimension, but they don't explain their analysis. (Calling it *exploring* or *error guessing* gives it a name, but the names are just names, not explanation or analysis.)

For us, it was a clarifying insight that variables could look one-dimensional but, as they were being entered into the program or being used by the program, the variables could be modeled as if they were multidimensional and we could pick interestingly different test values by looking along each dimension that we could imagine.

It might be helpful to think in terms of **explicit dimensions** and **implicit dimensions**.

EXPLICIT DIMENSIONS

The pay record is an example of a variable with 4 explicit dimensions:

> `(Name, HoursWorked, PayRate, AmountDue)`

These dimensions are stated (explicitly) as part of the description of the variable. They're stable. A pay record always has all four, they're the same four all the time and everyone will agree on what they are. (In a given record, a value might not be filled in, but we call that an incomplete record.)

IMPLICIT DIMENSIONS

In contrast, the "price of that toy" has only one explicit dimension, the amount of money.

The other dimensions aren't mentioned in the description of "price of that toy." Only the price is mentioned. These other dimensions are also not stable:

> (Amount of money,   length of the input string,   number of leading spaces)

- They are not stable over time:

   The length of the input string and the number of leading spaces are only interesting when the program is processing the input. Once the input is processed—once the program has interpreted the input as an amount of money and stored the result some-where—the secondary dimensions that were associated with the input are no longer relevant.

- They are not stable in their content:

   The number of leading spaces is potentially interesting, but what about the number of trailing zeros (at the end of the number, after the decimal point)? Isn't that a dimension too? The answer is yes, of course it is. There are plenty of secondary dimensions. You will probably not analyze any variable in terms of all of its secondary dimensions. You might use test values from some secondary dimensions one week and then switch to other secondary dimensions when you test the variable again a few weeks later.

However, for that period of time when the program is receiving and interpreting the amount of money, all input-related secondary dimensions are in play. During that short time, the "price of that toy" variable is every bit as multidimensional as the pay record.

There is no need to memorize this distinction between explicit and implicit dimensions. We won't use it again in the book. We raised it here as a way of:

- acknowledging the differences between variables that most people would call multidimen-sional (the variables like pay record) and variables that seem to be one-dimensional (like, "price of that toy"),

- while asserting that it is useful to model one-dimensional variables *as if* they were multidimensional.

N-TUPLES

You have probably seen n-tuple notation when you studied geometry. Suppose you draw a graph with an **x**-axis and a **y**-axis. The 2-tuple (1, 3) represents a point on this graph that is drawn at **x**=1, **y**=3. Similarly, (6, 2) specifies **x**=6 and **y**=2. If we don't know the values of **x** and **y**, but want to refer generally to a point on this graph, we often write it as (x, y).

On a three-dimensional graph (we'll call the axes **x**, **y** and **z**), (3, 6, 9) specifies the point drawn at **x**=3, **y**=6, **z**=9. If we don't know the values of **x** and **y** and **z**, but want to refer generally to a point on this graph, we often write it as (x, y, z).

In general, an n-tuple is a point on an n-dimensional graph. If we don't know how many dimensions there are (or if there are a lot of them), we can't easily label the axes with letters and so we call them Axis-1, Axis-2 and so on. Thus (3, 6, 9) becomes the point with Axis-1 = 3, Axis-2 = 6 and Axis-3 = 9. If we don't know the values of Axis-1, Axis-2 and Axis-3, but want to refer generally to a point on this graph, we often write it as (x_1, x_2, x_3).

---

*Consider a variable, **V**, with N dimensions (we aren't specifying exactly how many N is).*

If we want to describe a single value of this variable (a single point on the graph of this variable), we will use this notation:

$$\mathbf{V} = (v_1, v_2, \ldots, v_n).$$

If we want to refer to several values of this variable (several points on the graph), we will use this notation:

$$\mathbf{V}_1 = (v_{1,1}, v_{1,2}, \ldots, v_{1,n}) \quad \text{and} \quad \mathbf{V}_2 = (v_{2,1}, v_{2,2}, \ldots, v_{2,n}).$$

Very detailed domain-test analyses have been published for variables that combine together to create a linear input domain (Beizer, 1995; Clarke et al. 1982; Tian, 2005 are three of many examples). Unfortunately, these analyses have regularly befuddled our students (and us, sometimes). We'll try our hand at a slightly different presentation at *Section 2: Part 3: Generalize To Multidimensional Variables* on page 171.

COMBINATORIAL EXPLOSION

Consider testing several variables together. If variable $\mathbf{V}_1$ has $\mathbf{N}_1$ possible values and $\mathbf{V}_2$ has $\mathbf{N}_2$ possible values and $\mathbf{V}_3$ has $\mathbf{N}_3$ possible values, the number of possible tests of $\mathbf{V}_1$, $\mathbf{V}_2$ and $\mathbf{V}_3$ together is $\mathbf{N}_1 \times \mathbf{N}_2 \times \mathbf{N}_3$. This can quickly grow to a huge number. (For more discussion and examples, of the hugeness, see *The Combinatorial Explosion* on page 173.

You can use domain testing principles to reduce the number of test items (the number of values to test from $\mathbf{V}_1$, $\mathbf{V}_2$ and $\mathbf{V}_3$). If you shrink the number of tests for $\mathbf{V}_1$ from $\mathbf{N}_1$ to $\mathbf{B}_1$ (the number of best representatives from the partitions) and do the same for $\mathbf{N}_2$ and $\mathbf{N}_3$, then $\mathbf{B}_1 \times \mathbf{B}_2 \times \mathbf{B}_3$ should be much less than $\mathbf{N}_1 \times \mathbf{N}_2 \times \mathbf{N}_3$.

You can also reduce the number of values of the $\mathbf{V}_i$'s that you use in combination tests by skipping out-of-bounds values. We normally prefer to test out-of-bounds values one variable at a time rather than combining them. When we suspect a possible interaction of out-of-bounds values, we design a specific test for that specific interaction rather than running several combinations of them. Some people think that combining out-of-bounds values for several variables makes a test powerful in the same way as combining several in-bounds boundary values is powerful. Their theory is that the program has to go through error handling for each bad value, so the combinations of error-handling activities might cause problems. However, these combinations of bad values are often unnecessary or impossible to actually test. If the program stops processing when it sees the first bad value, the combination actually tests only one out-of-bounds value at a time.

The differences in our treatment of in-bounds and out-of-bounds values of the v_i's illustrate three different approaches to combination testing:

- A *mechanical approach* to combination testing applies an algorithm (a procedure) to create the tests. Discussions of domain testing usually suggest mechanical approaches to combination testing (Beizer, 1995; Clarke, et al., 1982; Copeland, 2004; Howden, 1987; Jorgensen, 2008).

> *In general, when you use a mechanical approach to design combination tests, you will restrict the values of each variable to in-bound values.*

- A *risk-based approach* to combination testing starts from a suspicion that certain combinations are more likely to yield failures. There are many bases for suspicion. For example:

  ◦ A suspicion might come from historical data. For example, suppose previous versions of the program under test had trouble when run with less than a certain amount of available memory on systems with a particular central processing chip *and* a particular video chipset, running a specific operating system version. Based on the failure history, testers should check this version of the program with this configuration (and similar ones).

  ◦ A suspicion might come from knowledge of the code or of aspects of its design. For example, a system designed to be *fault-tolerant* is designed to cope with error conditions and keep processing. When testing fault-tolerant systems, it is appropriate to design a few tests that feed the program a steady stream of bad inputs (e.g., out-of-bounds values). Perhaps the program will overflow its stack or memory or some other resource involved in error handling.

> **In general, when you use a risk-based approach to designing combination tests, you will start with a theory of error (a suspicion of how or why the program might fail) and choose in-bound or out-of-bound values in whatever way maximizes failure according to that theory of error.**

- A *scenario-based approach* to combination testing starts from a plausible story about how someone might try to use the system under test. A good scenario involves a coherent story that is:

  ◦ Credible (people will believe it can happen).

  ◦ Complex (involving several variables and/or tasks and/or sequences of inputs and outputs).

  ◦ Motivating (if the program fails this test, someone who has influence over the project will want to see the bug fixed).

  ◦ Easy to evaluate.

You can combine several invalid values in a good scenario test if you can tell a coherent, credible, motivating story in which all of those variables get bad values at the same time.

In general, when you use a scenario-based approach to designing combination tests, you will choose variables and values that are relevant to the stories that are the foci of your tests.

For more on scenarios, see Carroll (1999) and Kaner (2003a).

Each approach to combination testing is sometimes useful. We'll explore them in more detail in *Section 2: Part 3: Generalize To Multidimensional Variables* on page 171.

RISK

All testing is based on risk. If products weren't subject to risk, you wouldn't have any reason to test them. However, as with most terminology in our field, the term has several incompatible definitions:

> "A risk is something that could go wrong... It is predictably ironic that there is no single, agreed-upon definition of risk in common use. We have seen several dictionary definitions including 'the possibility of loss or injury' and 'exposure to mischance.' These definitions imply that a risk has two dimensions—an uncertain probability and a potential for loss or injury—which together determine its scale." Gerrard & Thompson (2002, p. 12).

Gerrard & Thompson raise three aspects underlying the idea of software risk:

(a) How the program could fail (also known as the *failure mode*).

(b) The probability that the program could fail that way.

(c) The consequence of such a failure.

Taken together, (b) and (c) let you quantify a risk. Thinking this way is helpful for *prioritizing* test-related work—an important task for test managers (Black, 2002; Schaefer, 2002). However, it doesn't help you *design* the tests.

In this book, we're more concerned with how the program could fail. A tester who has an idea about how the program can fail can design tests that are optimized to expose that failure.

- Prioritization of testing based on risk is called *risk-based test management.*

- Design of tests based on failure modes is called *risk-based test design.*

Depending on who is speaking, either of these might be called *risk-based testing.*

Domain Testing is a risk-based test design technique.

THEORY OF ERROR

We use the term *theory of error* to express together two ideas:

- A *failure mode* (a way the program can fail).

- Some idea of why the program might fail that way.

Our idea of "theory" is intentionally broad. Examples that meet our intent include hunches, elaborate mathematical models and patterns in historical data.

When we ask, *What's your theory of error?*, we expect an answer that describes a possible failure (what it would look like) and why you think it could happen.

For more on the application of failure mode analysis to software, we suggest FMEA Info Center (undated), SoftRel (undated) and Vijayaraghavan & Kaner (2003).

SIMILARITY OF TESTS

Domain testing is organized around theories of error. Two values of a variable are **similar** if both seem likely to lead the program to fail *in the same way*.

TEST IDEA

A **test idea** is a brief description of the design of a test that is focused on a theory of error.

- For example, suppose your *theory of error* is that the program could accept an input string without checking its length. The program will put this string somewhere in memory. If that area isn't big enough to hold all the characters, but the program copies them all into memory anyway, the excess characters will overwrite some other data or code. The program will fail next time it tries to access this overwritten memory. If it overwrote data, it will operate on incorrect data values; if it overwrote code, it will misbehave. The best known class of failures of this kind are **buffer overflow errors**. They're among the most common security-related bugs.

  Given that theory of error, the obvious *test idea* is to test with a very long string.

We learned the concept of the *test idea* from Brian Marick (2005). Edgren and his colleagues have been developing lists of sources for test ideas, that can be used to guide risk-based testing (Edgren, undated; Edgren, Jansson & Emilsson, 2012). Hendrickson (e.g. 2006) and Hunter (2010) are also widely-read collections. Every risk that you can imagine that involves a variable can be used as a basis for partitioning values of the variable and selecting representatives that have power to expose the program's vulnerability to that risk.

RISK/EQUIVALENCE TABLE

The risk/equivalence table makes the risk-based nature of domain testing explicit. In the first column, write your test idea (or some other summary of your theory of error). In the next columns, you describe the equivalence classes and representatives that are appropriate for that theory of error. The table makes it obvious that different theories of error yield different equivalence classes. For more discussion of the table, see *Chapter M. Summarize Your Analysis with a Risk / Equivalence Table* on page 151.

POWER OF A TEST

Statistical power refers to the ability of a statistical test to demonstrate that an incorrect statement is highly improbable. Statisticians compare tests in terms of their power. One statistical test is more powerful than another if it is more likely to show that the incorrect statement is wrong. See https://en.wikipedia.org/wiki/Statistical_power

The same concept has been imported into software testing. One software test is more powerful than another if it is more likely to expose a certain type of bug.

The power of a software test is always relative to a risk. One test can be much more effective than another for finding one type of bug but less effective for a different type of bug.

ERROR REVEALING

When you have a possible failure in mind, a test that can expose that failure is called *error-revealing* (Weyuker & Ostrand, 1980).

The same test might be error-revealing relative to one potential error and not revealing relative to another.

Two tests are equivalent (relative to a potential error) if both are error-revealing for that type of error or neither is error-revealing for it (Weyuker & Ostrand, 1980).[20]

Even if two tests are both error-revealing for the same error, one might be more powerful than the other. For example, if you're looking for a buffer-overflow bug, tests that give the program a *big string* might be error-revealing, but a test that gives the program a *huge string* might be more likely to cause the program to fail or to fail more obviously.

BEST REPRESENTATIVE

Domain testing involves two central tasks:

- Partition the domain into equivalence classes. Each class is composed of similar values.
- Select one or two representatives from each equivalence class. These serve as your test values.

The basis for selection of the representatives is power. The elements of an equivalence class are all similar to each other but they aren't the same as each other. If you can find an element of the class that is even slightly more likely to drive the program to failure than the others, that element yields a more powerful test. Under the logic of domain testing, that more powerful test is a better representative of the class.

The best representative of the class is the one that makes the most powerful test.

Sometimes, several elements of a class (maybe all of them) seem to have the same power. In these cases, there is no unique best representative. Instead, you can select any element that is at least as powerful as every other value in the set.

CORNER CASE

To be precise, a corner case is a test that uses boundary values of two variables. The name comes from the graph. If you plot the two variables on a graph and a test that uses both boundaries will appear as one of the corners of the graph.

In practice, when programmers describe a test (or a bug) as a corner case, they're making the point that the test is so extreme that it doesn't matter what the program does. They're dismissing the program's failure by saying the test is worthless (to them, not credible).

---

20   This is the same idea as *similarity* of two values of a variable.

Domain testing leads testers to use corner cases. We use them for efficiency. The theory is that if the program can pass tests with these extreme values, it will almost certainly pass with less extreme values.

Most programs will pass most corner-case tests. These extreme-value tests let you move quickly to other tests that hunt other bugs.

However, when you *do* make the program fail with a corner case, you shouldn't stop there. Now that you have a bug, you can afford to spend a little time investigating it. Try running a similar test that uses less extreme values.

- If the program still fails, your bug report won't be about a corner case.
- If the program fails only with extreme values, document that narrowness in the bug report.

SHOULD ALL TESTS BE POWERFUL?

All *domain tests* should be powerful.

Power is one of the desirable properties of tests. Another is **representativeness**: how well the conditions of the test represent what will happen in normal use of the program. Kaner (2003b) describes several other properties.

Domain testing is one technique among many. Every technique emphasizes different properties.

- Well-designed domain tests are powerful and efficient but aren't necessarily representative. Boundary values are suitable for domain testing even if those values would be rare in use.

- As a contrasting example, well-designed scenario tests are usually representative but they're often not powerful (Kaner, 2003a).

To test a program well, you'll use several different techniques, generating tests with several different desirable characteristics.

ORACLES

An **oracle** is a mechanism that helps a tester determine whether a program passed or failed a test.

Oracles don't always lead to correct decisions—passing a test is not a guarantee the program is working and failing a test is not a guarantee the program is misbehaving (Hoffman, 2009).

At first glance, the oracle is well-defined in domain testing. Partitioning a variable's values into equivalence classes creates the oracle. Some partitions hold valid values; others hold invalid values. If you can take a variable to an invalid value, the test fails.

But how do you do this partitioning and what behavior should you see when you give the program a value? When you do a domain test, you must consider:

- Whether it is possible to drive the variable of interest to an invalid value.

- Whether it is possible to make the program misbehave even though it classifies an input correctly.

- Whether it is possible to make the program misbehave when a result variable or output variable takes on a valid value.

- Whether it is possible to give the variable of interest a value that will drive something else to do an invalid operation or reach an invalid result.

FILTERS

It's common to focus on input fields and what you can put into them. For example, if a program accepts an input of 0 to 99 for a given field, you might test it with four cases: -1, 0, 99 and 100.

This mechanism that enforces the rule that inputs must be between 0 and 99 is an example of a *filter*. A filter rejects some data while allowing other data to reach the program. Tests of input filters should be done at the unit level (*see, e.g.,* Hunt & Thomas, 2004, for suggestions on how to do this).

TESTING PAST THE FILTER

The analysis of *result variables* illustrates how inappropriately narrow it is to focus system testing only on inputs and the input filter.

It is often necessary but rarely sufficient to enter some input values and confirm the program either accepts them or rejects them. This is too trivial an oracle to be of much value. You must also consider how the program will use the input and how a boundary-value input might be acceptable to the input filter but too small or too large for some other part of the program to cope with.

For example, if you enter the biggest valid number into a field and the program accepts it, you won't know whether the program can cope with this number until you learn how the program uses that number:

- Where it copies it.
- What it calculates with it.
- Where it prints it or displays it or stores it.

For each use, you can check whether the use fails. The failure might be a calculation error, corruption of data in memory or on disk, overflow as a result of calculation or from trying to store too much in too small a space, etc.

Thus, for each way the program uses an input, you must consider what oracle will help you assess the success of that use. This is a core part of test planning and execution in general (*How will you tell if the program failed the test?*). It is no less a core part of domain testing. The risk and the oracle play fundamental, complementary roles in test design.

In practice, domain tests you run early in the project will probably be input tests and, initially, you'll probably treat the input filter as your oracle.

However, as the program stabilizes and you get to know it better, you should extend the same tests of the same variables to take into account how the program will use those data. For example, suppose you transfer money from your bank account to pay bills. For each payment, there is an input (how much you'll pay). The input is subject to boundary evaluation (for example, you might not be able to make a payment for more than the amount you have in the bank). Now consider the set of payments that you make over a month. The program will add these together to give you a summary of your transactions. As a tester, you might consider whether you could enter a series of values that are individually acceptable but that, together, are too much for the bank to process. Perhaps the total violates a policy restricting the number of withdrawals or transfers from the account or perhaps you can generate a total that will have one too many digits for the printed statement's format.

- Every calculation takes inputs, processes them and generates outputs. For all the inputs, all the calculations and all the displays or uses of the outputs, we want to ask what is too little, too much or too strange.

- Every printed report, every saved file, every display gets data from somewhere, formats it and passes it to a device that has to cope with it. Anything that might look bad or corrupt a file will be a problem.

Sometimes, the best input values for confusing the calculations or messing up the output won't be boundary cases. Sometimes, it will be more effective to enter a series of easy-to-handle values that don't make any trouble until you put them all into the same calculation or the same file together.

When testing calculations or outputs, the question is not how to find the best representatives of the inputs. You want best-representative values of the calculations or the outputs. What inputs will yield those values?

AN ANALOGY: HOW DOMAIN TESTING IS LIKE OPINION POLLING

Domain testing is like stratified sampling for conducting opinion polls (Kaner, 1997; Ntafos, 2001; Podgurski & Yang, 1993; Podgurski, Masri, McCleese & Wolff, 1999). Many of the same cognitive challenges to domain-test designers also challenge the poll designer. So let's look at the task of designing and conducting public opinion polls.

Consider predicting the outcome of an election.

Organizations like Gallup telephone people and ask their opinion of the candidates. It is impractical to call all 200 million potential voters. Instead Gallup calls a smaller sample, about 3000 people. The challenge is to call the *right* 3000 people.

Gallup *could* simply call a randomly-selected subset of the population. A lot of statistical research has gone into this type of sampling. As long as we design our surveying method carefully to ensure that every person has an equal chance of being called, we can compute how many people Gallup would have to call in order to achieve what precision of result. For example, Gallup might say that if everyone were actually voting today, this candidate would win with 51% of the vote, *plus or minus* 3%. The 3% is the precision or level of uncertainty, of the poll.

The problem with random sampling is that if every person has an equal chance of being selected, and if you choose any 5 of them, sometimes you'll pick 5 people who belong to the same group, and who will vote the same way, even though the majority of the population might vote differently. To reduce the probability of accidentally overrepresenting some group, and thus to improve the precision, you have to call more people. The more you call, the more likely your sample is to be a good representative of the population at large.

Purely random sampling is well understood, but you have to call a lot of people.

Polling organizations can improve their efficiency (reduce the number of people they have to call) by using a process called *stratified random sampling*. Imagine dividing the population into 100 groups and then randomly sampling a fixed percentage of each group. Every person who belongs to the same group has the same chance of being called as every other person within that group, but a person who belongs to Group 1 will never receive a call intended for Group 2 (or any group other than Group 1).

If the polling organization classifies the population into subgroups skillfully, it can achieve the same level of accuracy as from a large random sample, but with many fewer phone calls.

Let's consider the analogy so far:

- Like the polling organization, software testers often need a sampling strategy because we (testers) have to choose a relatively small set of good tests from a vast pool of possible tests that we could run (but don't have enough time to run).

- Like the polling organization, we could sample randomly. However, many of our tests would be wasted. We might run 100 tests that are all sensitive to the same bug and no tests that are sensitive to some other bug.

- Thus, like the polling organization, we need a sampling strategy that is more efficient than purely random sampling.

- There is an important difference between pollsters and testers:

  ◦ Pollsters want to predict the outcome of elections. They want their sample to be representative of the whole population. Because many people are similar in their situations and views, the polling organization will intentionally include multiple members of a group that votes essentially the same way.

  ◦ In contrast, testers want to find bugs. We want to find more bugs faster, with fewer tests, at lower cost. For us, redundant tests (tests that would expose the same bug without providing other useful information) are undesirable. So are blind spots (bugs that none of the tests would expose, including bugs that will happen only occasionally in actual use of the product). Thus our sampling strategies will minimize redundancy and maximize coverage of potential problems.

Despite the difference in objectives, pollsters and testers have usefully similar challenges as they try to improve their sampling efficiency. We see this in the similarities and differences between *stratifying* and *partitioning*.

STRATIFIED SAMPLING

To do stratified sampling well, polling organizations model the population they're studying.

- If they think the amount of money people make might correlate with how they vote, they divide the population into subsets based on income. Suppose they partitioned the pool of registered voters into 10 groups, ranging from the poorest 10%, the next-poorest 10%, up through the wealthiest 10%. Pollsters call these groups *strata* or layers. Stratification is the process of dividing the pool of registered voters into strata. In a stratified sampling strategy, pollsters would call people from each of the 10 groups.

- A key assumption in stratified sampling is that two people within the same stratum should be treated as equally representative of the stratum. If subgroups are systematically different from each other, it is probably better to subdivide the stratum, sampling from the subgroups.

- Suppose a poll designer decides to stratify by religion. The designer can't create equally-sized strata because more people belong to some religions than others. However, he can still stratify (classify each person by religion) and call people from each group. Stratification is not always obvious. For example, consider starting with a division into Atheists, Buddhists, Christians, Hindus, Jews, Muslims, Others and Unknown. Is this good enough or should the poll designer subdivide further (for example, distinguishing Catholics from Protestants)?

- The poll designer will probably stratify along additional dimensions too. Common possibilities include gender, sexual preference, race, educational level, where people live (what part of the country, big city, small city, etc.) and even whether they consider themselves NASCAR racing fans.

- Note that each person belongs to several groups. For example, a person might be Catholic, female, left-handed, with a high income and a Ph.D. We're stratifying along several different dimensions. Each person has a value on each dimension.

In summary, when designing a polling strategy, the designer faces several critically important, cognitively challenging tasks, including:

- *Prioritizing*. Deciding what issues are important and what questions might help shed light on those issues.

- *Optimizing*. Deciding how to minimize the number of people who have to be called by working through the details of the stratification strategy:

  - Decide what dimensions might be informative (e.g., should we stratify on the basis of religion? race? income?)

  - For each dimension, decide how to subdivide it (e.g., should we classify all Jews as equivalent or subdivide further?)

  - Develop a method for determining which subgroup a person belongs to.

PARTITIONING COMPARED TO STRATIFYING

In testing, we have a different vocabulary but similar challenges:

- We call the process of dividing things into subsets *partitioning* instead of stratifying.

- We call the set of possible values of a variable the variable's *domain*. We partition the domain into *subsets* or *partitions* or *subgroups* or *subdomains* or *subranges*. (We'll make minor distinctions between subdomains and subranges later, but for almost all purposes in this book, all of these words mean the same thing). We also assume the members of a subdomain are equivalent—and so testers often call the subdomains *equivalence classes*.

- There are many dimensions for every variable, even the simple-looking ones. We can imagine many different types of failures. For each one, we can model at least one dimension and create tests along that dimension.

And so, in domain testing, we have tasks similar to polling:

a. Deciding what risks are interesting and which variables will help us set up experiments (tests) to assess those risks.

b. Deciding how to optimally choose values for those variables (minimize the number of tests) by working through the details of the partitioning strategy:

  i.   For each variable, decide what dimensions might be informative (e.g., time, data type, potential uses of the input).

  ii. For each dimension, decide how to subdivide it.

iii. Develop a method for determining which subgroup a value belongs to (as we will see, this is straightforward for linearizable or ordered variables but more difficult for unordered variables).

iv. Deal with the fact that in every test, when you enter a value into a variable, you're setting a value for each dimension associated with that variable.

There is one essential difference between stratified sampling (for polling) and domain testing.[21]

- *The pollster's goal is to create a highly representative sample of the full society, in order to accurately predict (from a small sample) the opinion of the large population.* Pollsters subdivide a group of people if they believe the subgroups have strongly different mixes of opinion, in order to more accurately sample the mix of opinions across the population as a whole. Pollsters select randomly within a stratum on the assumption that one person in the group is much like any other.

- *In contrast, the domain tester's goal is to create a highly powerful set of tests in order to expose bugs (with a small group of tests), in all of the program's testable variables.* Testers subdivide a variable's domain into subsets when they believe that different subsets could trigger different program failures. Domain testers don't select values randomly from equivalence classes (unless there is no basis for preferring one test over another). They select the values most likely to drive the program to failure.

LINEARIZABLE VARIABLES

Some authors apply domain testing only to linear input domains (*e.g.*, Beizer, 1995; Clarke, et al., 1982; White, 1981).

A *linearizable variable's* values can be mapped to a number line.[22] A linear domain has boundaries that can all be drawn on a graph as points on lines or as edges of surfaces. In the sense of the term used by the authors, you can divide equivalence classes by a simple inequality. A value might be in one equivalence class if it is greater than 5; in a different class if less than or equal to 5.

Suppose you work with a program that treats even numbers differently from odd ones. All the even numbers (2, 4, 6, 8, ...) will be in one equivalence class; the odd numbers are in the other class. You *could* draw one line to connect all the even numbers and another line to connect all the odd numbers, but you couldn't use those lines to show the separation of the evens from the

---

21 One of the repeatedly-studied research questions is whether partitioning is a better sampling strategy for software testing than simple random sampling (for example, see Arcuri, Iqbal & Brand, 2012; Chen & Yu, 1994, 1996; Duran & Ntafos, 1984; Gutjahr, 1999; Hamlet, 1996; Hamlet & Taylor, 1990; Reid, 1997a, 1997b; Weyuker & Jeng, 1991). If errors are distributed randomly throughout the program, then random sampling is probably equivalent to stratified sampling. Under several other statistical assumptions, random sampling and partitioning are probably equally effective (and partitioning takes more work to do, therefore costs more). However, in this book, we work from a different assumption. We partition based on a theory of error—we group tests that we consider likely to expose the same problem. We select specific tests from the partition not randomly but again on a theory of error, asking whether any member of the "equivalence" class is even slightly more likely to expose a problem than the others. If so, we choose that as the test (the best representative of the set). If our risk analysis is correct, our sampling system will almost certainly be more powerful (more likely to find more bugs with fewer tests) than random sampling.

22 As with so much terminology in testing, this is an imprecise use of a more precisely-defined mathematical term and both definitions show up in our field's publications. We use this definition because, for domain-testing purposes, it is more general (it includes everything that meets the narrower definition and we think we've seen it used more often.) In practice, we don't think that whether a variable is linearizable will matter when you use domain testing in your work, so we aren't going to drag you through the definitional distinctions.

odds. You can't separate odds from evens by showing that all the odds are bigger than all the evens. Therefore, we would not call evens or odds a linearizable set.

Domain analysis is easier when a variable can be linearized, but several authors relax this restriction. Ostrand & Balcer (1988) described a method for any type of input parameter or environmental condition associated with any function. Jeng & Weyuker (1994) developed an approach that skips linear domain assumptions while still sensitive to the types of errors in describing input specifications (such as "boundary shifts") that are most often discussed in the theoretical literature.

Kaner, Falk & Nguyen (1993) generalized domain testing far beyond this. Working through a detailed analysis of device compatibility testing, they showed that the same principles that underlie domain testing (risk-based stratified sampling) can be used to group devices, such as printers, even though they cannot be put into a meaningful smallest-to-largest order. For more detail on this, see *Where Can You Apply Domain Analysis?* on page 402.

In this book, we follow Kaner, Falk & Nguyen and reject the restriction of domain testing to linearizable (or even ordinal) variables. We don't care whether a domain is linear or not, whether a variable is continuous or not or whether the variable maps to the number line or not. We think stratified sampling is such a useful idea that we'll use it wherever we can, with the most powerful few tests that we can find, to represent each stratum.

There is a limit to how far we can take this analogy. If there is no theory of error that allows you to reasonably divide classes, if your partitioning would have to be arbitrary, if no representatives are predictably better than any others, then you're better off doing random sampling (Hamlet, 2006). This illustrates a general rule for using test techniques.

No technique is applicable to every possible situation. If you run into a situation that is not a good fit for one technique, use something else.

COVERAGE

The *coverage* of a testing effort is the proportion of a set of possible tests that actually were run.

STRUCTURAL COVERAGE

Most programming books and courses mean some kind of **structural coverage** (also known as **code coverage**) when they talk about coverage.[23]

- The program's structures include its statements, branches, loops, methods—anything you can think of as a building block of a program.

- If you can think of a type of structure, and if you have access to the underlying code, then you can count all the occurrences of that type of structure. With the right tools, you can count how many of them you have tested and that's your coverage measure.

- For example, the most common mentioned structural coverage is **statement coverage**. If your program has 100,000 statements and your tests execute 75,000 of those, you have achieved 75% statement coverage.

See Amman & Offutt (2008) for a thorough review of many types of structural coverage.

---

23 Sadly, many of these seem unable to even imagine a kind of coverage that is not structural coverage. For example, https://en.wikipedia.org/wiki/Code_coverage is blind to non-structural measures.

Plenty of coverage monitors are available for programmers. These can measure many different types of structural coverage. For example, at Florida Tech, our software engineering students learn EMMA as they write Java code using the Eclipse development environment (see https://en.wikipedia.org/wiki/Java_Code_Coverage_Tools). Developers in the Microsoft ecosystem find coverage support in Visual Studio.

IT IS EASY TO IMAGINE MORE COVERAGE THAN YOU CAN (OR SHOULD) TEST

Path coverage is another type of structural coverage. Think of the sequence of statements the program executes from an entry point (where it starts) to an exit point: that's one path. Consider the set of all possible sequences from all entry points of a program to all exits: that's what you must test for complete path coverage.

For any nontrivial program, there is an impossibly large number of paths. In many programs, the number of paths is infinite. Myers (1979) provides a clear example involving about a simple program with about 20 statements, one entry point, one exit point and one simple loop. The program has about 100,000,000,000,000 paths.

Even for the simpler types of coverage, it might be possible to achieve 100% of that kind of coverage, but that doesn't necessarily make it desirable. If you focus your efforts on achieving high coverage (of any kind), you're likely to create a bunch of tests that meet that criterion but aren't particularly good by any other criterion (such as power). Marick (1997) is probably the most widely cited presentation of this issue.

THERE IS MORE TO COVERAGE THAN CODE COVERAGE

In a leading textbook written for graduate-level university Computer Science courses in software testing, Tian (2005) includes a chapter on "Coverage ... Based on Checklists and Partitions".

- If you partition the possible values of a variable, and run tests from each partition, you have achieved complete partition coverage for that variable.

- If you list all the input variables, partition them, run a test from each partition, you have achieved complete partition coverage for all input variables.

Hoffman, Strooper & White (1997) discuss the use of partitioning and boundary values to achieve data coverage.

Kaner (1996) listed 100 types of coverage, most of them involving sets of tests that black-box testers could run. For example:

- You can cover every error message.

- You can cover every Android phone (check the compatibility of your software with every phone that runs this operating system).

- You can create a big list of risks. For each risk, design a test that is powerful for proving the program can fail in this specific way. You can count the percentage of risks from this list that your tests cover. We can call this *risk coverage* or *failure mode coverage*.

COVERAGE CRITERION

A *coverage criterion* specifies an acceptable coverage level. For example:

- A project team might decide they must achieve at least 90% input-variable coverage. That is, they won't agree that the tasks of testing are complete unless they have run (and the program has passed) a full set of domain tests for at least 90% of the known input variables.

- A project coverage criterion might specify coverage levels across several dimensions, such as X% input variable coverage, Y% coverage of the big list of risks, etc.

- Some test techniques are built around coverage criteria. For example, see the coverage criteria for combinatorial test techniques in *Chapter N. Analyze Independent Variables that Should Be Tested Together* on page 181.

COVERAGE-FOCUSED TEST TECHNIQUES

Kaner, Bach & Pettichord (2002) described test techniques as being focused on (one or more of) testers, coverage, potential problems, activities and evaluation.

A coverage-focused technique is primarily organized around achieving some type of coverage. For example, many people use domain testing as a coverage-focused technique:

IF

- You can model some aspect of the program as a variable, and

- The variable can have many values, and

- You think the program will deal with similar values in similar ways

THEN

- Call it a variable, and

- Give it some domain tests.

TRY TO DOMAIN TEST EVERY VARIABLE

If you think that trying to domain test every variable (or most variables) is an important part of domain testing, then you think that domain testing is a coverage-focused technique. (For a little more on this, see the *Afterword: Domain Testing as Part of a Testing Strategy* on page 417.

SECTION 2: WORKING THROUGH THE SCHEMA'S TASKS

The rest of the book is organized in terms of a structure that we think captures the key domain testing tasks and orders them in a natural way. This *Schema for Domain Testing* lists 18 tasks. This Section[24] works through the tasks one by one: a chapter for each. The chapters are numbered A through R to correspond to the task list. Each chapter illustrates its task by applying it to a set of examples.

The Schema is a checklist, not a script:

- You won't do all the tasks in every analysis. (Nor do we, in the examples.)
- You won't do the tasks in the same order every time.
- You have to supply your own thinking. This just reminds you of the main ideas.

Section 3 flips the analysis. Each chapter focuses on one example and works that example through the tasks from start to finish.

Section 2 divides the Schema into four parts:

- Part 1: Characterize the variable

  What variable are you testing, what is the nature of the variable, how does the program use it and how are the program's other variables related to it?

- Part 2: Analyze the variable and create tests.

  Apply the classical domain analysis and create the classical table. Then apply the risk-based approach and create the risk/equivalence table.

- Part 3: Generalize to multidimensional variables

  Analyze this variable as part of a group of variables that can be tested together.

- Part 4: Prepare for additional testing

  Look forward to tests that you might run in the future, perhaps domain tests of other variables or other types of risk-based tests.

We strongly recommend that you work through the examples and exercises yourself, using our solutions as explanatory feedback on your work. The more actively you work with this material, the more you'll learn.

---

24 If you haven't read *How to Use This Book* on page xvii (in the Preface), we recommend that you read it now.

SECTION 2. PART 1: CHARACTERIZE THE VARIABLE

Every time you notice the program is asking for input or providing output, you can apply the tasks of Part 1. You can list all the variables involved, decide which of these to focus your attention on and then learn enough about them to apply a domain analysis.

A. Identify the potentially interesting variables.

B. Identify the variable(s) you can analyze now. This is the variable(s) of interest.

C. Determine the primary dimension of the variable of interest.

D. Determine the type and scale of the variable's primary dimension and what values it can take.

E. Determine whether you can order the variable's values (from smallest to largest).

F. Determine whether this is an input variable or a result.

G. Determine how the program uses this variable.

H. Determine whether other variables are related to this one.

These tasks help you identify and characterize many variables, but they don't include creating any equivalence class tables or designing any tests. (For that, see *Section 2. Part 2: Analyze The Variable And Create Tests* on page 113.

In our practice, we don't stick rigidly to this list, always doing tasks in this order. For example:

- We often start filling in equivalence class tables early in our analyses, using them as convenient places to jot down information about the variables as we discover it.

- We also often run tests during this basic analysis. For example:

  - If the boundaries of a variable aren't specified, we make a first estimate empirically, by testing to see what boundaries the program enforces.

  - We try boundaries and invalid values to see what the program does with them, whether there are unexpected vulnerabilities or whether there seem to be effects on unexpected parts of the program.

However, even if you follow this less formal approach, you probably won't *complete* the Part 2 analysis of a variable until you know the types of information in the Part 1 list.

A SCHEMA FOR DOMAIN TESTING

1. CHARACTERIZE THE VARIABLE

A. Identify the potentially interesting variables.

B. Identify the variable(s) you can analyze now. This is the variable(s) of interest.

C. Determine the primary dimension of the variable of interest.

D. Determine the type and scale of the variable's primary dimension and what values it can take.

E. Determine whether you can order the variable's values (from smallest to largest).

F. Determine whether this is an input variable or a result.

G. Determine how the program uses this variable.

H. Determine whether other variables are related to this one.

2. ANALYZE THE VARIABLE AND CREATE TESTS

I. Partition the variable (its primary dimension).

   - If the dimension is ordered, determine its sub-ranges and transition points.
   - If the dimension is not ordered, base partitioning on similarity.

J. Lay out the analysis in a classical boundary/equivalence table. Identify best representatives.

K. Create tests for the consequences of the data entered, not just the input filter.

L. Identify secondary dimensions. Analyze them in the classical way.

M. Summarize your analysis with a risk/equivalence table.

3. GENERALIZE TO MULTIDIMENSIONAL VARIABLES

N. Analyze independent variables that should be tested together.

O. Analyze variables that hold results.

P. Analyze non-independent variables. Deal with relationships and constraints.

4. PREPARE FOR ADDITIONAL TESTING

Q. Identify and list unanalyzed variables. Gather information for later analysis.

R. Imagine and document risks that don't necessarily map to an obvious dimension.

A. IDENTIFY POTENTIALLY INTERESTING VARIABLES

It's up to you to discover what variables you can test.[25] A specification fragment often mentions several variables, but provides test-supporting information about only one or two. Sometimes the spec describes the other variables in more detail elsewhere.

Note that when we say "specification," we really mean any document that describes the program. It could be a formal specification, a user story, a user manual, an advertisement, a video tutorial, a prototype or an email from a knowledgeable person.

Many programs come with no specifications or with incomplete, inaccurate information. You must still test the program. For domain testing, you have to find variables to test and decide which ones might be interesting to test now. In effect, we're recommending a thoughtful *tour* of the program (Bolton, 2009; Kelly, 2005):

- Make a note of every variable that you read about or see.
- Having a list of the "full" set of variables will help you ensure that you cover all of them in your testing.

For a demonstration of a tour through a program, watch the first set of videos on Test Design at http://www.testingeducation.org/BBST (Kaner & Fiedler, 2011).

Here are some examples of this type of analysis.

FROM EXAMPLE 3: SUNTRUST VISA

SunTrust issues Visa credit cards with credit limits in the range of $400 to $40000. A customer is not to be approved for credit limits outside this range. A customer can apply for the card using an online application form in which one of the fields requires that the customer type in his/her desired credit limit.

This description mentions only one input field:

- `DesiredCreditLimit`

The example mentions or implies other variables but does not describe them as input fields. Many tests are likely to collect values for these variables:

- `CreditLimit` (to be assigned to this account)
- `CustomerName`

Notice the potential relationship among these variables. The credit limit to be assigned to the account should probably not exceed the desired credit limit.

The description also mentions an online application form, which probably has lots of other fields. However, beyond noting that there should be details about this somewhere, there is not enough information about the form to be useful.

FROM EXAMPLE 5: UNDERGRADUATE GRADES

The passing score for any undergraduate course at Florida Tech is 60/100. A student who scores less than 60 receives an 'F' on her transcript.

This specification (problem description) mentions one input field:

---

25 Ajay Bhagwat (personal communication) writes, "The process of analyzing a program using a domain analysis *reveals* many of the variables and helps you understand what they are. This in itself is actually a very important finding for a tester whether you go further in the domain analysis for each variable or not.."

- **StudentScore** in a particular course

The problem description mentions one output based on the input field

- **LetterGrade** on the transcript, computed from the numeric grade

The problem description suggests other variables but doesn't provide information about them. For example:

- **StudentName**
- **CourseID**

Our general rule for deciding whether to include a variable in this list is that if we think the variable is probably in the program or should be, we're likely to include it. The goal behind this is to create a list of every variable that should be tested. Some won't appear in any specification and might not be obvious on any input screen. If a variable is already on your master list, there might not be any additional value in listing it here.

FROM EXAMPLE 27: OPENOFFICE IMPRESS GRID OPTIONS

Here is a dialog from the OpenOffice Impress product:

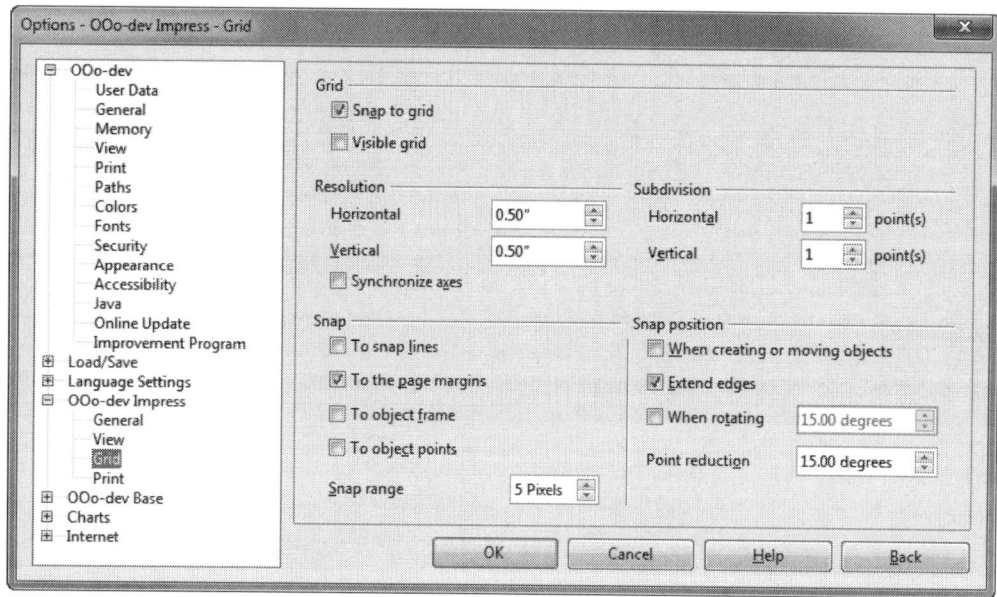

Note: OpenOffice is abbreviated as OOo.

This dialog shows a huge number of variables. The list on the left are pointers to dialogs. Click an entry on the list and get a dialog like the one on the right. Let's focus on the dialog that's currently displayed.

All variables in the dialog are input fields.

The following are typical variables for domain analysis. Each accepts a range of numbers:

- **HorizontalResolution**
- **VerticalResolution**
- **HorizontalSubdivision**
- **VerticalSubdivision**

- `SnapPositionWhenRotating`
- `SnapRangeNumberOfPixels`
- `PointReduction`

The purposes of these variables aren't obvious from the dialog. For example, what does `Point-Reduction` do? Does it interact with `SnapPositionWhenRotating`, which is also entered in degrees? We haven't found an explanation in OpenOffice's Help documentation. To learn about undocumented variables, we would run tests to see how the program responds when we change their values. We would look at descriptions of comparable variables in competing products' documentation (PowerPoint's docs are helpful here.) And, if possible, talk with developers or experienced users.

For now these variables would go on every list of variables in this dialog, but not on the list of variables to analyze today.

The following are binary variables. ***Binary variables are not suitable for domain analysis*** because you have to test both values of each variable. However, these binaries might interact with or constrain other variables that are suitable for domain analysis.

- `SnapToGrid`
- `VisibleGrid`
- `SynchronizeAxes`
- `SnapToSnapLines`
- `SnapToPageMargins`
- `SnapToObjectFrame`
- `SnapToObjectPoints`
- `SnapPositionWhenCreatingOrMovingObjects`
- `SnapPositionExtendEdges`

For example, does the `SnapRange` interact with the type of thing (grid, lines, etc.) that you snap to?

RECORD-KEEPING

The examples have distinguished between four types of variables:

- Variables explicitly described in the specification (or obvious on the screen) as input variables.
- Variables mentioned or implied in the specification but that can't yet be analyzed as input variables.
- Variables that are calculated from the input variable (for example, the *F* on the transcript, calculated from the input grade).
- Binary variables.

If you create an equivalence class table that analyzes all the variables for a given dialog, it's common to list the related variables that you're not analyzing on the same table. For each variable, create a row with the name of the variable but no information (or brief notes) on its possible values.

Some people add a column to the table that lists the document(s) or specification section that mentions the variable (probably with a page or section reference). Others write this on the table below the name of the variable.

EXERCISES: PART 1-A

Please identify the potentially interesting variables in these questions:

A.1. *Example 1: Integer Input* **on page 229**

A data entry field will accept Integers from -999 to 999.

A.2. *Example 10: The Circle* **on page 293**

Consider a circle defined by $x_1^2 + x_2^2 = 100$. Some of the points on this circle are (0, 10), (6, 8), (8, 6), (10, 0), (8, -6), (6, -8), (0, -10), (-6, -8), (-8, -6), (-10, 0), (-8, 6) and (-6, 8).

Consider these sets:

> (a) $\{ (x_1, x_2) \mid x_1^2 + x_2^2 = 100 \}$ (the circle)
>
> (b) $\{ (x_1, x_2) \mid x_1^2 + x_2^2 < 100 \}$ (the points inside the circle)
>
> (c) $\{ (x_1, x_2) \mid x_1^2 + x_2^2 > 100 \}$ (the points outside the circle)
>
> (d) $\{ (x_1, x_2) \mid x_1^2 + x_2^2 \leq 100 \}$ (the circle & points inside it)
>
> (e) $\{ (x_1, x_2) \mid x_1^2 + x_2^2 \geq 100 \}$ (the circle & points outside it)

A.3. *Example 15: Mailing Labels* **on page 325**

A program prints mailing labels. The first line of the label is the person's name. The program builds the name from three fields, `FirstName`, `MiddleName` and `LastName`. Each field can hold up to 30 characters. The label can be up to 70 characters wide.

A.4. *Example 17: Joan's Pay* **on page 343**

Joan works at a store under the following contract:

- Her normal pay rate is $8 per hour.

- For hours worked beyond 40 hours per week, her normal rate is $12 per hour.

- For work between midnight and 6 a.m. on any day, she gets $16 per hour.

- For work between 6 a.m. and noon on Sunday, she gets $16 per hour.

- If she earns $500 or less in a week, 10% of her pay is deducted for taxes.

- If she earns more than $500, the tax deducted is $50 plus 20% of earnings greater than $500 that week. (So, if she earns $600, the tax deducted is $70.)

A.5. *Example 25: Moodle Assign User Roles* **on page 395**

Moodle is a program that manages online courses. Here is one of its dialogs. The user can assign participants in a class to one or more roles in the course, such as student or teacher.

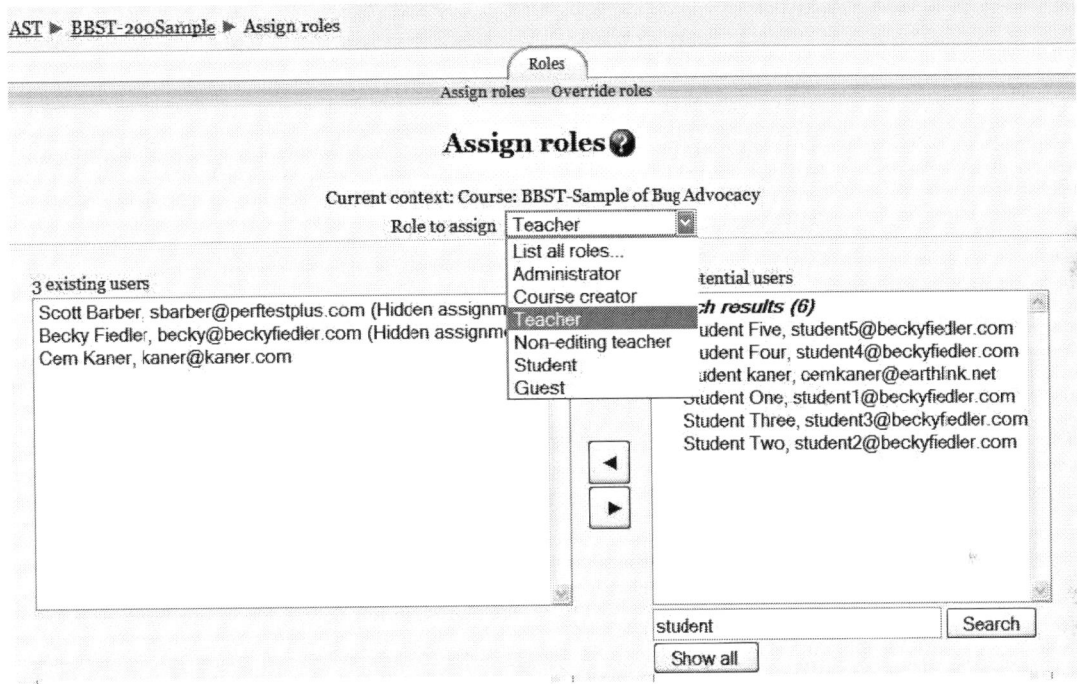

A SCHEMA FOR DOMAIN TESTING

1. CHARACTERIZE THE VARIABLE

    A. Identify the potentially interesting variables.

    B. Identify the variable(s) you can analyze now. This is the variable(s) of interest.

    C. Determine the primary dimension of the variable of interest.

    D. Determine the type and scale of the variable's primary dimension and what values it can take.

    E. Determine whether you can order the variable's values (from smallest to largest).

    F. Determine whether this is an input variable or a result.

    G. Determine how the program uses this variable.

    H. Determine whether other variables are related to this one.

ANALYZE THE VARIABLE AND CREATE TESTS

    I. Partition the variable (its primary dimension).

       – If the dimension is ordered, determine its sub-ranges and transition points.

       – If the dimension is not ordered, base partitioning on similarity.

    J. Lay out the analysis in a classical boundary/equivalence table. Identify best representatives.

    K. Create tests for the consequences of the data entered, not just the input filter.

    L. Identify secondary dimensions. Analyze them in the classical way.

    M. Summarize your analysis with a risk/equivalence table.

3. GENERALIZE TO MULTIDIMENSIONAL VARIABLES

    N. Analyze independent variables that should be tested together.

    O. Analyze variables that hold results.

    P. Analyze non-independent variables. Deal with relationships and constraints.

4. PREPARE FOR ADDITIONAL TESTING

    Q. Identify and list unanalyzed variables. Gather information for later analysis.

    R. Imagine and document risks that don't necessarily map to an obvious dimension.

B. IDENTIFY VARIABLE(S) YOU CAN ANALYZE NOW

This task starts in Part *A. Identify potentially interesting variables.* When doing that task, you build a list of input or output variables that are listed in specifications, other documents or are visible on the screen.

These sources often provide enough information to make you aware of a variable and its general purpose, but not enough for you to do much analysis. For example, they might fail to mention:

- The variable's data type.
- Its range of valid values.
- Subranges of valid values that are treated differently.
- Response(s) to invalid values.
- Special-case values that are treated differently.
- Other variables that depend on the value of this variable.
- How other variables constrain the value of this variable.

It's common to start testing without all of this information, learning it as you go. However, you can't learn everything about everything all at the same time. Pick a few variables that you think you can learn enough about *now*, that are interesting to study *now*, and get back to the rest later.

FROM EXAMPLE 4: PAGE SETUP OPTIONS

The page setup function of a text editor allows a user to set the width of the page in the range of 1 to 56 inches. The **PageWidth** input field accepts (and remembers) up to 30 places after the decimal point.

The page setup function probably includes several variables, but the only one described here is **PageWidth**. The description gives you plenty of information to start testing.

FROM EXAMPLE 6: TAX TABLE

In 1993, the Internal Revenue Service calculated taxes based on this table (Beizer, 1995, p. 151):

Income Range	Tax
$0 <$ **TaxableIncome** $\leq \$22100$	$0.15 \times$ **TaxableIncome**
$\$22100 <$ **TaxableIncome** $\leq \$53500$	$\$3315 + 0.28 \times ($ **TaxableIncome** $- 22100)$
$\$53500 <$ **TaxableIncome** $\leq \$115000$	$\$12107 + 0.31 \times ($ **TaxableIncome** $- 53500)$
$\$115000 <$ **TaxableIncome** $\leq \$250000$	$\$31172 + 0.36 \times ($ **TaxableIncome** $- 115000)$
$\$250000 <$ **TaxableIncome**	$\$79772 + 0.396 \times ($ **TaxableIncome** $- 250000)$

There are two variables: **TaxableIncome** and **Tax**, how much of tax to pay. **Tax** is computed from **TaxableIncome**, so you might want to start testing **TaxableIncome**. However:

- The problem description says very little about **TaxableIncome**. It mentions **TaxableIncome** as something you need in order to calculate another variable (**Tax**).

- Like **Tax**, **TaxableIncome** is probably a computed result rather than a variable you enter directly. What do you have to enter to get a value into **TaxableIncome**? You probably have to calculate **Income**, which might involve dozens of variables. Until you know how to enter data into **TaxableIncome** (directly or indirectly), you can't domain-test it.

Thus, the description of Example 6 might not provide enough information about any variable for you to start an analysis.

FROM EXAMPLE 23: FREQUENT FLYER MILES

An airline awards frequent-flyer miles according to the following table (Black, 2007, p. 218):

Status Level	None	Silver	Gold	Platinum
Trip bonus	0%	25%	50%	100%
Distance traveled	d	d	d	d
Points awarded	d	$1.25 \times d$	$1.5 \times d$	$2 \times d$
Miles required to reach this level	0	25,000	50,000	100,000

Your status is determined before you fly. The number of miles flown on this trip does not affect your status on this trip, though a long trip might result in elevating your status before your next trip. Determine whether the system awards the correct number of points for a given trip.

There are four interacting variables:

- `DistanceTraveled` (in the table, **d**): The distance traveled on the current trip
- `TotalMiles`: The number of miles traveled this year (or whatever the period is that counts for determining frequent flyer status).
- `PointsAwarded`: Number of points awarded for this trip.
- `StatusLevel`: Determined from `TotalMiles`.

The variable the program identifies as the one to test is the output variable, `PointsAwarded`. However, you can't test this without testing the input parameter (**d**). Therefore, these are variables to analyze together.

To test these, you must set the value of `StatusLevel`. At this point, plan to force values into `StatusLevel`. Use any values that help you work with `PointsAwarded` and distance (**d**). Focus your testing on `StatusLevel` itself later, when you're testing `TotalMiles`.

EXERCISES: PART 1-B

Please identify the variables that you can analyze now:

B.1. *Example 2: ATM Withdrawal* **on page 237**

An ATM allows withdrawals of cash in amounts of $20 increments from $20 to $200 (inclusive) (Craig & Jaskiel, 2002, p. 164).

B.2. *Example 9: Create Table (Max Cells)* **on page 289**

In OpenOffice (OOo) Impress, you can create a table. With this dialog, you set the starting numbers of rows and columns. Suppose the maximum number of cells in the table is 4095.

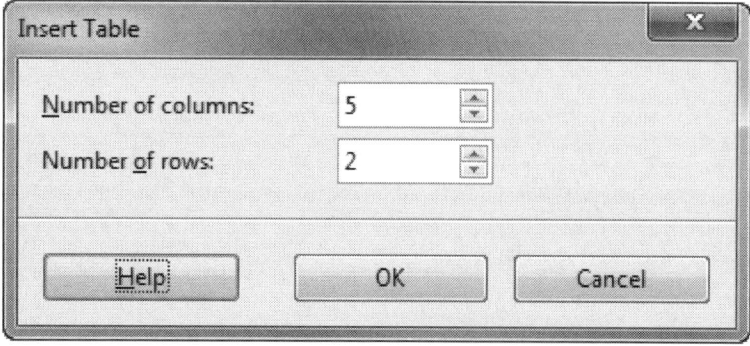

B.3. *Example 14: Result Of Calculations* **on page 319**

I, J and K are Unsigned Integers. You can enter values into I and J, but the program calculates the value of K = I × J. Treat K as the primary variable.

B.4. *Example 20: Sum Of Squares (MAX)* **on page 359**

$$SS = x_1^2 + x_2^2 + ... + x_n^2$$

(SS is the sum of squared values of the n variables, x_1 through x_n.)

The x_i's are all Floating Point.

SS ≤ 45.

B.5. *Example 21: Spreadsheet Sort Table* **on page 361**

In OpenOffice Calc, you can sort a table. The fields in the dialog are all **SortBy** fields. The first field is the primary sort key.

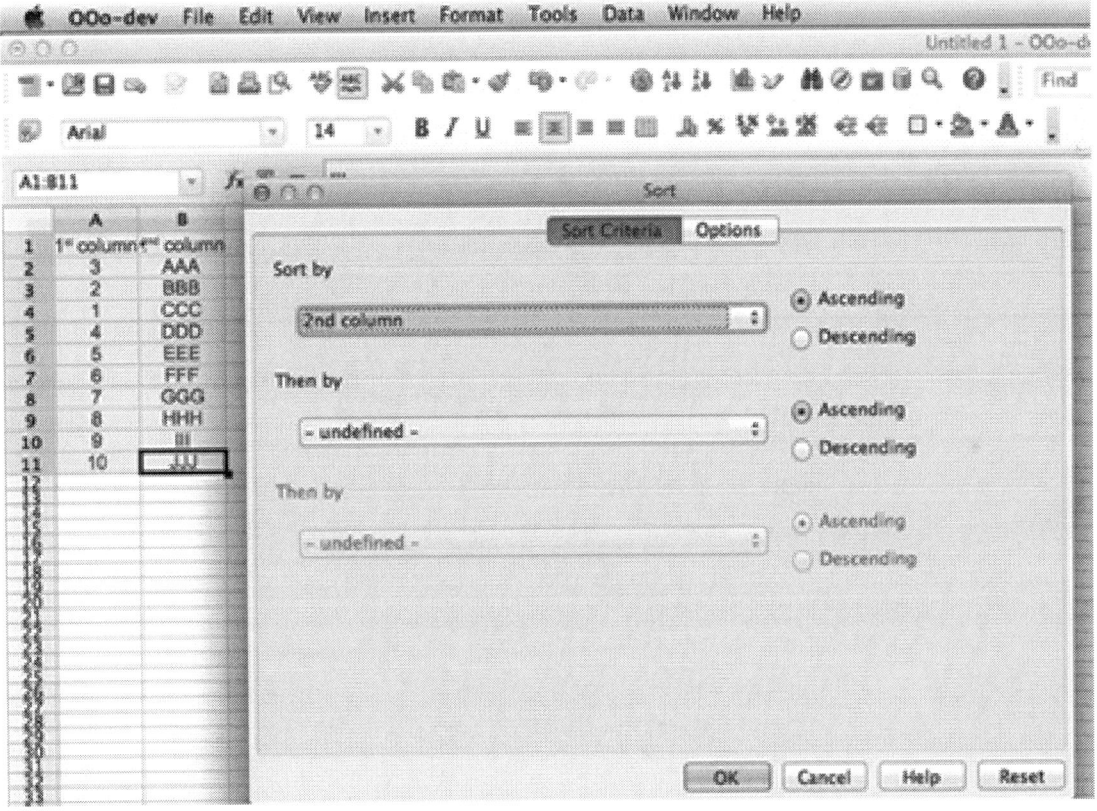

In this case, the table will be sorted by the values in the column labeled **SecondColumn**: AAA before BBB. Because this sorts the whole table, in the column labeled **FirstColumn**, 3 comes before 2 which comes before 1.

If you sort by **FirstColumn** instead, OpenOffice will sort the row with 1 before 2 before 3 but now you would see CCC before BBB before AAA in **SecondColumn**.

Note: OpenOffice is abbreviated as OOo.

A SCHEMA FOR DOMAIN TESTING

1. CHARACTERIZE THE VARIABLE

A. Identify the potentially interesting variables.

B. Identify the variable(s) you can analyze now. This is the variable(s) of interest.

C. Determine the primary dimension of the variable of interest.

D. Determine the type and scale of the variable's primary dimension and what values it can take.

E. Determine whether you can order the variable's values (from smallest to largest).

F. Determine whether this is an input variable or a result.

G. Determine how the program uses this variable.

H. Determine whether other variables are related to this one.

2. ANALYZE THE VARIABLE AND CREATE TESTS

I. Partition the variable (its primary dimension).

- If the dimension is ordered, determine its sub-ranges and transition points.
- If the dimension is not ordered, base partitioning on similarity.

J. Lay out the analysis in a classical boundary/equivalence table. Identify best representatives.

K. Create tests for the consequences of the data entered, not just the input filter. Identify secondary dimensions. Analyze them in the classical way.

L. Summarize your analysis with a risk/equivalence table.

3. GENERALIZE TO MULTIDIMENSIONAL VARIABLES

M. Analyze independent variables that should be tested together.

N. Analyze variables that hold results.

O. Analyze non-independent variables. Deal with relationships and constraints.

4. PREPARE FOR ADDITIONAL TESTING

P. Identify and list unanalyzed variables. Gather information for later analysis.

Q. Imagine and document risks that don't necessarily map to an obvious dimension.

C. DETERMINE THE PRIMARY DIMENSION OF THE VARIABLE OF INTEREST

A variable doesn't vary on only one dimension. The ***primary dimension*** is about the purpose of the variable. The others are incidental , having more to do with the implementation than with the purpose of the variable. If you're not sure, you can usually determine the ***primary*** dimension by considering what the program is trying to learn, achieve or control with the variable.

FROM EXAMPLE 3: SUNTRUST VISA

SunTrust issues Visa credit cards with credit limits in the range of $400 to $40000. A customer is not to be approved for credit limits outside this range. A customer can apply for the card using an online application form in which one of the fields requires that the customer type in his/her desired credit limit.

Consider the `DesiredCreditLimit`.

- `CreditLimit` can take on values from $400 to $40000. The limits for `DesiredCreditLimit` are probably the same.

- If 400 to 40000 are the limits, the number of characters you can enter runs from 3 to 5.

- The permissible characters in this variable run from 0 to 9 and might include "." or "," or "$" (but the list doesn't include letters).

These are three separate dimensions (amount of money, length of input and characters permitted). All three are involved in the entry and processing of this variable. The program might check each one separately from the others.

However, the *primary dimension* is the amount (in dollars) of `DesiredCreditLimit`:

- The point of the variable is to find out how big a credit limit the person wants. The reason someone will enter data into the variable is to tell the bank how much money they want.

- The limits on the number of characters and the type of data (numbers rather than letters) are implementation issues.

FROM EXAMPLE 5: UNDERGRADUATE GRADES

The passing score for any undergraduate course at Florida Tech is 60/100. A student who scores less than 60 receives an 'F' on her transcript.

The problem description says very little about these two variables. It tells you that if `StudentScore` is less than 60, then `LetterGrade` is F.

Note the ***implicit specification***. The author of the problem is relying on the reader's background knowledge instead of writing out every detail:

- `StudentScore` probably runs from 0 to 100.
- `LetterGrade` probably includes F, D, C, B, A.
- If 59 maps to an F, the grading scale probably follows a commonplace system in the United States that maps 0-59 to F, 60-69 to D, 70-79 to C, 80-89 to B and 90-100 to A. Note that in schools that assign only letter grades, the mapping from numbers to letters often varies from professor to professor.

The primary dimension of `LetterGrade` is probably an enumerated variable with letter values from F to A.

However, the implicit specification is ambiguous. The program could be dealing with a set of letter grades that includes only { F, D, C, B, A } or with a larger set, such as { F, D-, D, D+, C-, C, C+, B-, B, B+, A-, A, A+, A++ }. You have no way of knowing, from this specification, which of these sets is the "real" set. Therefore, you can't yet fully specify the letter grade's dimension. You'll have to try scores like 100 (A? A+? A++?). Or you can ask someone.

FROM EXAMPLE 27: OPENOFFICE IMPRESS GRID OPTIONS

The variable comes from this dialog:

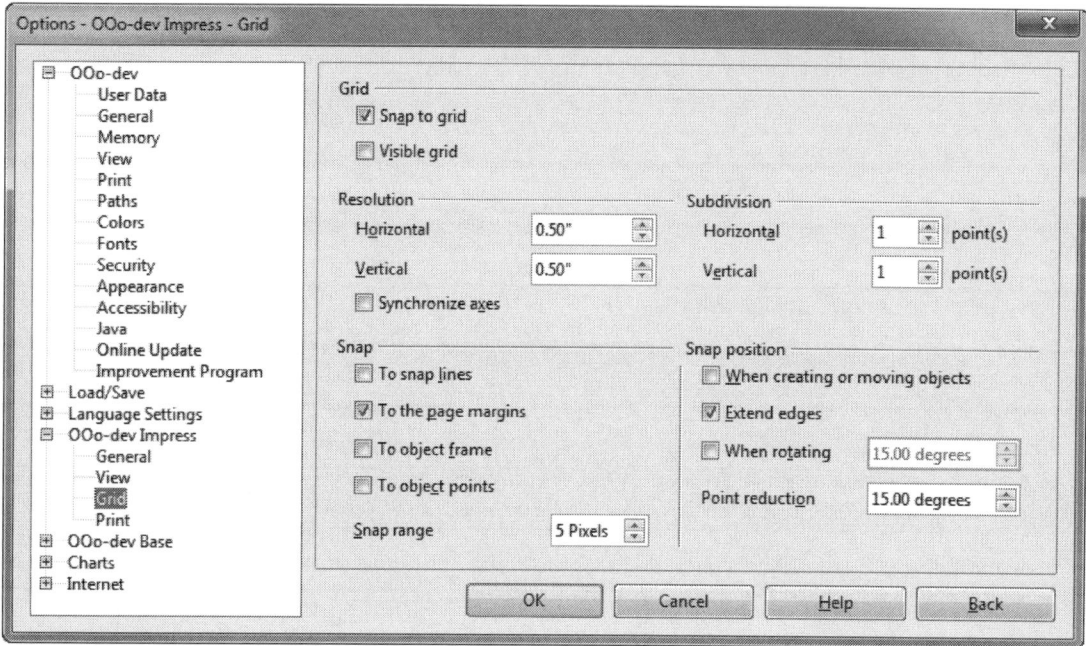

Note: OpenOffice is abbreviated as OOo.

Suppose you decide to work on `SnapRange`.

- `SnapRange` can take on values from 1 Pixel through 50 Pixels and it will go up and down by 1 pixel each time you click on an arrow.

- You can select the number (e.g., 5 from the 5 pixels value showing in this picture) and then overwrite it with a number, like 1.5 or 3.14159265. The length runs from 0 (erase the number) through many (we don't know the upper bound on the number of characters you can enter.)

- You can select any portion of "5 Pixels" and type whatever text you want, such as "Three Points" or "My dog likes you." (In either case, OpenOffice will ignore the text and stick with 5 Pixels. Other programs might respond more dramatically.)

The primary dimension is the number of pixels. The other ways in which the input can vary must be tested, but they don't have anything to do with why the user would enter data into this field or what the program was designed to do with such data.

EXERCISES: PART 1-C

Please determine the primary dimension of the key variable(s) in each question below:

C.1. *Example 7: Student Names* **on page 275**

A **StudentLastName** field must start with an alphabetic character (upper or lower case). Subsequent characters must be letters, numbers or spaces.

C.2. *Example 11: University Admissions* **on page 301**

Stateless University's admission standards use both high school grades and **ACT** test scores (Copeland, 2004, p. 121).

- **ACT** scores are Integers running between 0 and 36.
- **GPA** scores are Fixed-Point variables (always exactly one digit after the decimal point) running between 0.0 and 4.0.

Students are accepted if they meet any of these requirements:

- **ACT** = 36 and **GPA** ≥ 3.5
- **ACT** ≥ 35 and **GPA** ≥ 3.6
- **ACT** ≥ 34 and **GPA** ≥ 3.7
- **ACT** ≥ 33 and **GPA** ≥ 3.8
- **ACT** ≥ 32 and **GPA** ≥ 3.9
- **ACT** ≥ 31 and **GPA** = 4.0

The relationship between **ACT** and **GPA** is that students are admitted if

$$\textbf{ACT} + (10 \times \textbf{GPA}) \geq 71$$

C.3. *Example 16: Unemployment Insurance Benefits* **on page 337**

In the state of Domainia, every unemployed adult receives a benefit of 350. If that person has worked and is older than 40, the benefit is raised by 100. Alternatively (else), if the person has exactly 4 children, the benefit is raised by 50 (van Veenendaal & Seubers, 2002, p. 231).

C.4. *Example 25: Moodle Assign User Roles* **on page 395**

Moodle is a program that manages online courses. Here is one of its dialogs. The user can assign participants in a class to one or more roles in the course, such as student or teacher.

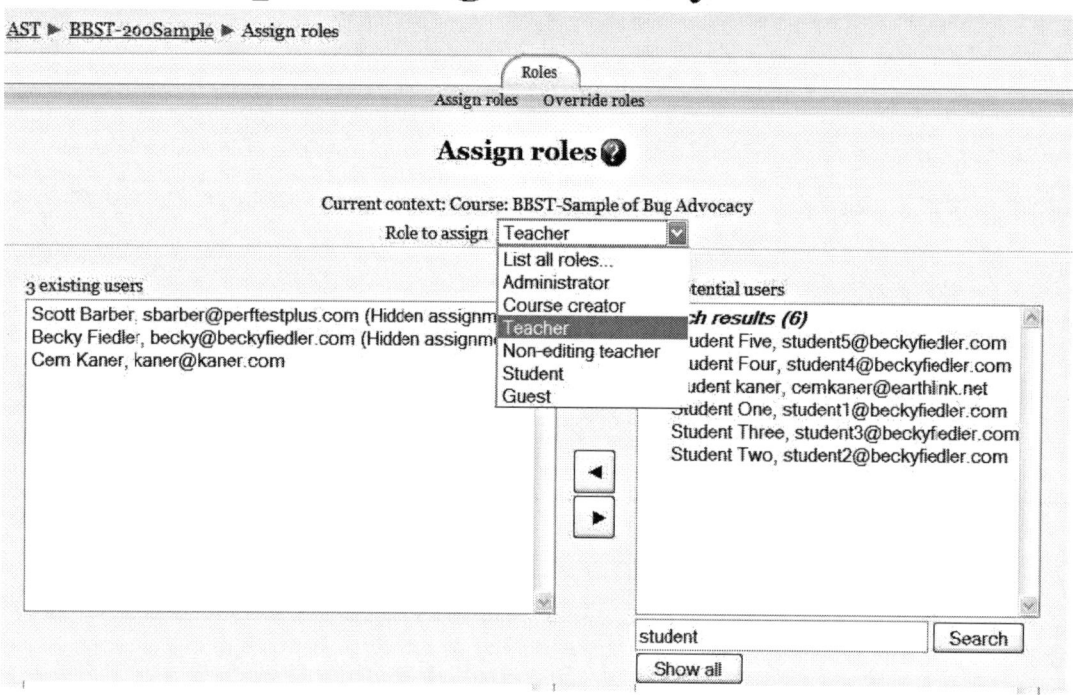

C.5. *Example 28: OpenOffice Printing Options* **on page 409**

Here is a printing-options dialog from a development build of OpenOffice 4.

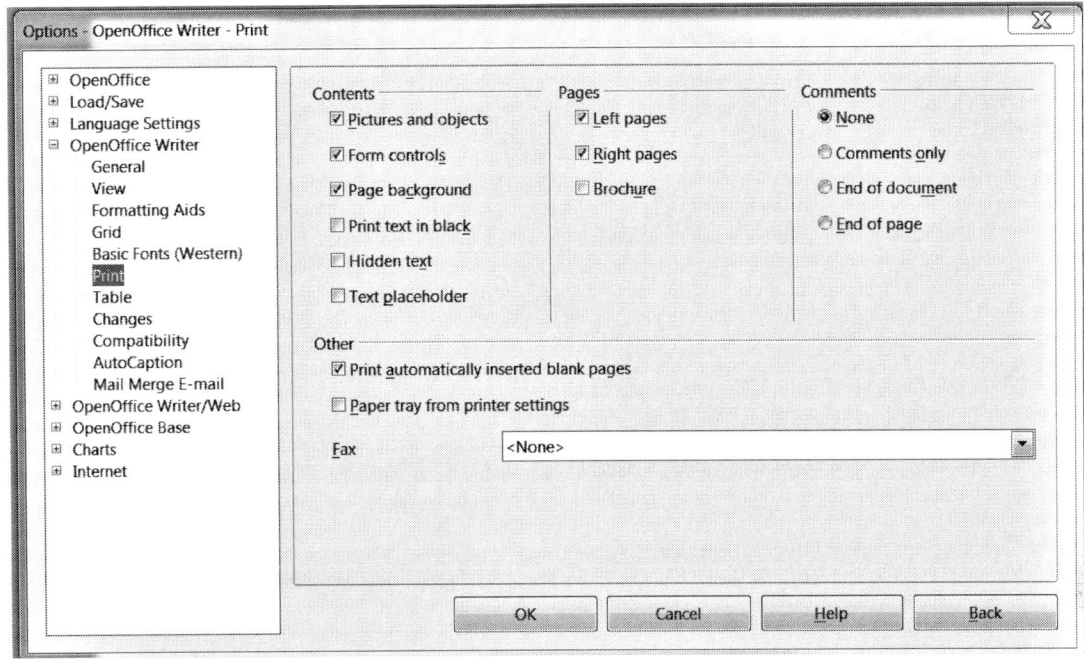

A SCHEMA FOR DOMAIN TESTING

1. CHARACTERIZE THE VARIABLE

A. Identify the potentially interesting variables.

B. Identify the variable(s) you can analyze now. This is the variable(s) of interest.

C. Determine the primary dimension of the variable of interest.

D. Determine the type and scale of the variable's primary dimension and what values it can take.

E. Determine whether you can order the variable's values (from smallest to largest).

F. Determine whether this is an input variable or a result.

G. Determine how the program uses this variable.

H. Determine whether other variables are related to this one.

2. ANALYZE THE VARIABLE AND CREATE TESTS

I. Partition the variable (its primary dimension).

- If the dimension is ordered, determine its sub-ranges and transition points.
- If the dimension is not ordered, base partitioning on similarity.

J. Lay out the analysis in a classical boundary/equivalence table. Identify best representatives.

K. Create tests for the consequences of the data entered, not just the input filter.

L. Identify secondary dimensions. Analyze them in the classical way.

M. Summarize your analysis with a risk/equivalence table.

3. GENERALIZE TO MULTIDIMENSIONAL VARIABLES

N. Analyze independent variables that should be tested together.

O. Analyze variables that hold results.

P. Analyze non-independent variables. Deal with relationships and constraints.

4. PREPARE FOR ADDITIONAL TESTING

Q. Identify and list unanalyzed variables. Gather information for later analysis.

R. Imagine and document risks that don't necessarily map to an obvious dimension.

D. DETERMINE TYPE AND SCALE OF THE VARIABLE'S PRIMARY DIMENSION

Equivalence class analysis is about similarity. Two values belong in the same class if they're so similar the program will treat them the same way.

One fundamental determiner of similarity is data type. Another determiner is scale.

DATA TYPE

Suppose **x** is a variable whose valid values range from 1 to 99. Which pair of values belong in the same equivalence class?

    (a) 9 and 10

    (b) 9 and 9.01

    (c) 9 and A

    (d) 9 and :

If **x** is an Integer variable, then only (a) holds an equivalent pair.

But if **x** is a Floating-Point variable, (a) and (b) both have equivalent pairs.

If the program is working with hexadecimal numbers, then (a) and (c) (and maybe (b)) are equivalent (the value of the hexadecimal digit A is the decimal number 10, which is clearly between 1 and 99).

If **x** is a string variable and "1" and "99" are character strings rather than numbers, then (d) might hold an equivalent pair. Computers typically store text in the ASCII encoding scheme (or the Unicode superset) . The code for "9" is 57. The code for ":" is 58. In terms of codes, "9" is more similar to ":" than to "1" (code is 49).

You can't tell valid from invalid, similar from dissimilar, if you don't know the variable's data type.

Most programming languages have several built-in or primitive data types. For example,

INTEGERS

An *Integer* can take on values between **MININT** and **MAXINT**.

- The values are whole numbers, like 25 or -14, but not 25.5.
- If the Integer is Unsigned, **MININT** is 0.
- If the Integer is Signed, **MININT** is generally -**MAXINT**-1. For example, if **MAXINT** is 32767, **MININT** is -32768.
- Integers can overflow. For example, the result of **MAXINT**+1 can't be an Integer, even though **MAXINT** and 1 are both valid Integer values.

Integer division truncates fractional results. For example, 3/2 = 1, not 1.5.

Integer arithmetic, other than division, does not have rounding errors. 5×5 is exactly 25, not 24.99999999 or 25.00000001.

MAXINT

MAXINT is the largest Integer. If you're not an experienced programmer, you're probably thinking this is absurd because in mathematics, there is no largest Integer. However, in computing, you store Integers in a fixed range of memory. Many languages reserve 32 bits for Integers. So the Unsigned Integer (an Integer that cannot be negative) can range from 0 to 2^{32}-1. In this case, **MAXINT** is 2^{32}-1. (Petzold, 2000, provides an approachable introduction to machine representations of data.)

We could consider a simpler example, storing all Integers in a byte (8 bits of memory). A byte can hold any pattern of 8 bits (binary digits), such as 00000000, 00000001 and 11111111. There are 2 x 2 x 2 x 2 x 2 x 2 x 2 x 2 = 2^8 = 256 possible values, ranging from 0 to 255. In this example, **MAXINT** is 255.

FIXED POINT

A *Fixed-Point* variable is like an Integer, but with a fixed number of digits after the decimal point.

- For example, a Fixed-Point variable with 1 digit after the fixed (constant-location) decimal point can take on values like 25.1 but not 25.11 (too many digits after the decimal point) or 25 (you need 1 digit after the decimal point, 25.0).

The same calculation rules apply to Fixed-Point and Integer variables, except the decimal is shifted. For example, 3.0/2.0 does yield 1.5. However, 0.3/2 = 0.1, not 0.15. Fixed-Point variables are also bound by a maximum and a minimum.

FLOATING POINT

A *Floating-Point* variable is like a Fixed-Point variable, except that different Floating Point numbers can have different numbers of digits after the decimal point. For example, 25.1 and 25.11 and 25.000000000001 are Floating-Point numbers.

You can represent Floating-Point numbers in four parts:

Number = **s** × **d** × **b**$^{\mathbf{e}}$

    s is the *sign bit*. Its values are -1 or 1.

    d is the *significand*.

    b is the *base*.

    ○ **e** is the *exponent*.

For the moment, let's set the sign of **Number** positive (**s** = 1) and the base to 10 (**b** = 10).

Here are some examples of Floating-Point numbers.

123

=	123×10^0	($10^0 = 1$)
=	12.3×10^1	($10^1 = 10$)
=	1.23×10^2	
=	0.123×10^3	
=	1230×10^{-1}	($10^{-1} = \frac{1}{10}$)
=	12300×10^{-2}	($10^{-2} = \frac{1}{100}$)

You might also have seen Floating-Point numbers represented in *Scientific Notation* (https://en.wikipedia.org/wiki/Scientific_notation):

$$1.23E2 \qquad \text{is the same as} \qquad 1.23 \times 10^2$$

The E in this notation means 10 raised to a power, like E2 means 10^2.

Floating-Point numbers are often written in a *normalized form*. In this form, you write `Number` with one non-zero digit before the decimal point and the remaining digits after. You adjust the value of the exponent to make this an accurate representation of `Number`.

- 1.23×10^2 is the normalized form of 123.0.
- In scientific notation, 1.23E2 is the normalized form.

This format makes it possible to show very small numbers in a readable way.

- The normalized form of 0.1 is 1.0×10^{-1}.
- The normalized form of 0.0000000000000001 is 1.0×10^{-16}. It is much easier to tell how big this number is. If you work only with numbers like 0.0000000000000001, you will waste a lot of time counting all the 0's.

A Floating-Point number has some number of *significant digits*. If you show a number in normalized form, you count the number of digits starting from the one to the left of the decimal point and ending at the last non-zero number. For example:

- 1.23×10^2 and 1.23000×10^2 and 1.23×10^{21} and 1.23×10^{-21} all have 3 significant digits.
- 1.0×10^{-16} has one significant digit, but $1.000000000000001 \times 10^{-16}$ has 16 significant digits.

Computers store numbers in a limited space.

- A number can have too many significant digits to store in the space reserved for the significand.
- A number can have an exponent that is too large or too small (-1 times a big number) to store in the space reserved for the exponent.

For example, the number ⅓ = 0.333333333... There is no end to the 3's after the decimal point. The number of significant digits is infinite. To store a number like ⅓, the software must round it (get rid of the digits that it can't store).

- If you round ⅓ to 3 significant digits, you get 0.333.
- 0.333 is an *approximation* of ⅓. It's value is close to ⅓, but not quite the same. 0.333 differs from ⅓ by 0.00033333333...
- That difference is called *rounding error*.
- Each time you add, subtract, multiply or divide an approximation by another number (especially another approximation), the result gets a little less accurate. This is the general problem of *rounding error* in Floating-Point Arithmetic.

When you work with Floating-Point numbers, you cannot not expect programs to give you exactly correct calculation results. Instead you should expect the results to be very close to the values that would be theoretically correct. Rather than testing whether a result **equals** *a value, you must test whether it is* **close enough** *to that value. The amount of error you're willing to tolerate (how close it has to be to be close enough) is your* **tolerance limit.**

The Relevance of Floating Point Math to Domain Testing

The main reason that we're going through all of this material *in this book on domain testing* is that testers have to think about small differences between numbers when they think about numbers that are near a boundary. Here are some specific questions that come up when people test Floating-Point variables:

- What are the smallest and the largest valid values of this variable?

- What value is just beyond the boundary? For example, what is the smallest number that is bigger than the upper bound?

- Many boundaries are far from the theoretical extremes (largest and smallest). For example, a boundary is defined by a circle with a radius of 10 in *Example 10: The Circle* on page 293. In this example, 10 isn't an extreme value, but it is a boundary. When testing, you want to look at values just inside the circle and just outside the circle. How close to the circle can your test points be?

- A result variable's value comes from calculations that involve other variables. Those calculations have rounding errors. Imagine a result that is supposed to be within a certain range but it is actually a little outside of that range. Should you interpret that result as a rounding error or as a bug in the program?

Many working programmers and testers have no idea how to answer these questions. They have incorrect expectations about the results of Floating-Point calculations. We have seen testers make fools of themselves by demanding greater precision (less rounding error) than the program is designed to achieve. We have seen programmers waste hours or days of debugging time trying to understand why the program isn't yielding a more accurate calculation than it *can* achieve. We have also heard of testers and programmers failing to recognize actual calculation errors in programs that were allegedly doing higher-precision calculations but were giving lower-precision results.

Different Types of Floating-Point Numbers

We are *intentionally simplifying this summary.* We're making a deliberate tradeoff between technical accuracy on the one hand and practical utility on the other. When we say practical utility, we mean:

- We think the statements about precision and tolerance levels are close enough to the theoretically correct values to serve most testers' needs when testing most programs.

- We think that more technical treatments will require a significant level of diligent study or will be incomprehensible to many testers and programmers (including programmers with undergraduate and graduate Computer Science or Software Engineering degrees from reputable universities).

MAXFLOAT is the largest Floating-Point value that can be stored by the software under test. **MINFLOAT** is the smallest value, the negative of **MAXFLOAT**. The size of **MAXFLOAT** will depend on the type (the precision) of the Floating-Point variable.

The basic representation of a Floating-Point number is as above:

Number = s × d × b^e

- **s** is the *sign bit*. Its values are -1 or 1.
- **d** is the *significand*.
- **b** is the *base*.
- **e** is the *exponent*.

However, rather than working in Base 10, programming languages work in Base 2 (binary).

Modern programming languages follow IEEE Standard 754 for Floating-Point Arithmetic (IEEE, 2008). This defines several types of Floating-Point variables. They differ in two ways:

- how many digits they can store for the significand
- how many digits they can store for the exponent

We refer to the following types in this book:

- *Single-Precision Floating-Point.* The significand can hold 23 binary digits (23 bits or in decimal numbers: 0 to 8388608). The exponent is between -126 and 127.

  - This corresponds to *approximately* 7 digits of decimal precision.

  - The difference between a Single-Precision number and the next one larger or smaller is approximately $\Delta(1)$ times the number.[26] For Single-Precision, $\Delta(1)$ is *approximately* 10^{-7}. In practice, we think you should do follow-up testing whenever you get a result that differs from the result you expected by more than 10^{-6} times the expected result.

  - **MAXFLOAT** (the largest value) is 2^{128} ($3.40282346638528860 \times 10^{38}$).

  - The smallest value greater than 0 is 2^{-149} ($1.40129846432481707 \times 10^{-45}$). The largest value less than 0 is -2^{-149}.[27]

- *Double-Precision Floating-Point.* The significand can hold 52 binary digits (in decimal numbers: 0 to 4.5×10^{15}). The exponent is between -1022 and 1023. This corresponds to *approximately* 16 digits of decimal precision. The difference between a Double-Precision number and the next one larger or smaller is approximately $\Delta(1)$ times the number. For Double-Precision, $\Delta(1)$ is *approximately* 10^{-16}. In practice, we think you should do follow-up testing whenever you get a result that differs from the result you expected by more than 10^{-14} times the expected result. **MAXFLOAT** is about 2^{1024}.

- *Quadruple-Precision Floating-Point.* The significand can hold 112 binary digits (in decimal numbers: 0 to 5.2×10^{33}). The exponent is between -16382 and 16383. This corresponds to *approximately* 34 digits of decimal precision. The difference between a Quadruple-Precision number and the next one larger or smaller is approximately $\Delta(1)$ times the number, where $\Delta(1)$ is *approximately* 10^{-34}. In practice, we think you should do follow-up testing whenever you get a result that differs from the result you expected by more than 10^{-32} times the expected result. **MAXFLOAT** is about 2^{16384}.

The more complex the calculation, the higher the tolerance you must have for rounding errors. For example,

- Suppose the program does a series of Single-Precision calculations that should yield a result 1234.567.

- If the tolerance limit is 10^{-6} times the expected result, the calculation will seem OK if the result is between 0.999999×1234.567 and 1.000001×1234.567.

- If the calculation is complex enough—if it contains many other calculations—then it is possible that a tolerance limit of 10^{-5} times the expected result or even 10^{-3} times the expected result is the best you can count on. If that's not accurate enough, the programmer will probably have to revise the code to use Double-Precision or Quadruple-Precision arithmetic.

---

26 We define $\Delta(1)$ in the next section.

27 Yes, the exponent is -149 even though the smallest value that you can store in the exponent byte is -126. IEEE's standard includes some clever rules for handling very small numbers.

TOLERANCE LEVELS, DELTA AND MACHINE EPSILON

For Integers and Fixed-Point numbers, we can (and will) talk about a constant, Δ (DELTA) that is the smallest representable difference between two numbers. This is a useful concept, but DELTA is not a constant for Floating-Point numbers.

- Languages often define a constant, EPSILON, that is the smallest difference between 1.0 and the next-largest Floating Point number.

  There are different EPSILONs for Single-Precision, Double-Precision and Quadruple-Precision Floating Points. See Wikipedia (https://en.wikipedia.org/wiki/Machine_epsilon) for values for different numeric types.

- If you're writing code, you can find (the number that should be) the value of EPSILON by using a *nextUp()* or *nextAfter()* function (one or both of these is available in most modern languages). For any Floating Point number **x**, nextUp(**x**) tells you the next-largest number that this language's implementation of Floating Point can represent on this computer.

The problem in Floating Point[28] is that:

- nextUp(0) is approximately 1.4E-45 (in other words 1.4×10^{-45}), whereas
- nextUp(1) is approximately 1 + 1.192092896E-7 (in other words, 1.0000001192092896).

As numbers get bigger, the smallest Floating-Point-representable difference between them gets bigger too. Let's continue to use Δ as the smallest representable number that is bigger than our current number. Thus $\Delta(\mathbf{x})$ means the same thing as nextUp(**x**) - **x**.

A common way to estimate the value of $\Delta(\mathbf{x})$ is:

$$\Delta(\mathbf{x}) \quad = \quad \mathbf{x} \times \Delta(1)$$
$$= \quad \mathbf{x} \times (\text{nextUp}(1) - 1)$$
$$= \quad \mathbf{x} \times 1.192092896E\text{-}7 \qquad \text{(Dawson 2012)}$$

The values of $\Delta(1)$ are much smaller for Double-Precision and Quadruple-Precision Floating-Point numbers (the greater the precision, the smaller the Δ).

A FEW MORE DETAILS ABOUT FLOATING POINT

You might decide that this last part of the Floating Point section is necessary or interesting or you might not. It's OK to skip it.

Rounding errors are studied in the field of *Numerical Analysis*. This is where you look when you want to learn how to estimate the probable and maximum rounding error from a given type of calculation and if you want to learn how to do the calculation in a way that minimizes these errors.

Venners (1996) provides a helpful tutorial on Floating-Point numbers, including an applet that demonstrates many calculations. Other helpful introductions are in Dawson (2012), Goldberg (1991), Harold (2009), Petzold (2000); Python Software Foundation (2009: Chapter 14: Floating point arithmetic: Issues and limitations) and Sun Microsystems (2000). We also provide a simplified overview for testers in the *BBST-Foundations* lectures at http://www.testingeducation.org/BBST.

---

28 These specific numbers are correct for Single-Precision Floating Point. The numbers are different for Double and Quad, but the problem is the same.

Gosling et al. (2013, Section 4.2.3) describe the IEEE-754 rules as they're implemented in the Java language at http://docs.oracle.com/javase/specs/jls/se7/html/jls-4.html#jls-4.2.3. Here are some details of the Java representation of *Single-Precision Floating Point*.

- We allocate 8 bits to the *exponent* (**e**) so that, in theory, it can run between 0 and 255. However, Java treats 255 as a flag that the result is not a number (for example, the result of divide by zero). It treats a bit pattern of 8 bits set to 0 as a flag that the significand is not normalized. (We'll cover normalization in a moment.) Thus, the values of the exponent that are handled normally run from 1 to 254. To allow for negative exponents, the bit pattern is interpreted as running from -126 to 127.

- In variables of type Float, we allocate 23 binary digits to the *significand* (**d**). Thus it can have 8388608 distinct values ($2^{23} = 8388608$). We can interpret these as if they were Integers (0 to 8388607) but it is more common to interpret them as fractions.

In binary arithmetic, interpret any digits after the decimal point as fractions. For example:

0.1000 is interpreted as ½.

0.0100 is interpreted as ¼.

0.1100 is interpreted as ½ + ¼ which equals ¾.

In a Floating-Point representation, when you show a fraction with a 1 in the most significant place after the decimal (1 × ½ instead of 0 × ½) this is call *normalized*. The decision to use a normalized representation is a matter of choice:

If you multiply ½ by 2^3 you get 4.

If you multiply ¼ by 2^4 you get 4.

Thus, you can trade off the size of the exponent, **e**, against the position of the first significant digit and get the same final number.

When the exponent is between -126 and 127, Java interprets d as a normalized 24-bit fraction whose first bit is always 1. Thus if **d** (as stored) is 00000000000000000000000, Java will interpret this as 100000000000000000000000 (1 followed by 23 zeros) and then interpret that as 0.100000000000000000000000, which is ½. Similarly, if **d** is stored as 10000000000000000000000 (1 and 22 0's here), Java interprets this as 110000000000000000000000 (11 and 22 0's)—that is, as ¾.

When the exponent is between -126 and 127, all values of **d** are interpreted as fractions between ½ and 1.

When the exponent is -127, don't interpret it as -127. Interpret it as -126 but interpret d as a non-normalized fraction. Java no longer adds a leading 1. A value in d of 00000000000000000000000 is taken as 0. A value of 10000000000000000000000 is taken as ½. A value of 00000000000000000000001 is $1 / 2^{23}$ and when you multiply that by the exponent, you have $2^{-23} \times 2^{-126}$, which is 2^{-149}.

Therefore:

- The largest Single-Precision Floating-Point value (in Java) is 2^{128}. ($3.40282346638528860 \times 10^{38}$). We will call this **MAXFLOAT**.
- The smallest Float that is greater than 0 is 2^{-149} ($1.40129846432481707 \times 10^{-45}$).
- The largest Float that is less than 0 is -2^{-149}.
- The smallest Float that is less than 0 is **-MAXFLOAT**. We will call this **MINFLOAT**.
- Because there are only 8388608 distinct values for **d**, ($2^{23} = 8388608$) Single-Precision Floating-Point calculations can be done only to about 7 significant digits of precision. No

matter how many digits you print, at most 7 of them are accurate. Sedgewick and Wayne (2007) provide a clear discussion of rounding error, with several interesting examples.

CHAR

A *Char* variable holds an individual character, which might fit in one byte (up to 255 different characters, usually mapped to the ASCII code) or two bytes (Unicode). These can be letters, numbers, punctuation symbols (comma, period, etc.) or anything else you could type at a keyboard.

ENUMERATED

An *Enumerated* variable can take any value from a (usually short) list. For example, consider a variable, `Month`, whose values are from {January, February, March, April, May, June, July, August, September, October, November, December}.

Programs often treat each value of an enumerated variable as a unique case, branching to different code for each one. If each value is processed separately, the variable is unsuitable for domain testing because you have to test each value. Imagining these as "equivalence classes" achieves no gain in efficiency. It just adds confusing jargon tol the analysis.

BOOLEAN (OR BINARY)

A *Boolean* variable has two values, typically 0 and 1 (or No and Yes).

Boolean variables are the simplest kind of enumerated variable. They are unsuitable for domain testing because the program will process the two values of the variable differently. There is no gain in efficiency from treating the two values as two equivalence classes.

ARRAY

An *Array* is a set of variables of the same type that are stored together and organized in a sequence (there is a first element, a second element, etc.). You can access the individual elements in the sequence by number. For example, a variable named `Salary` might be an Integer Array with 100 elements. `Salary` stores a list of employee salaries, with the first employee earning $1000, the second employee earning $1250 and so on until you reach the end of the list, with the company's 100th employee earning $950.

- The first element of the Array is Salary[0]. Salary[0] = 1000.
- The second element, Salary[1] = 1250.
- The 100th element, Salary[99] = 950.

For more on Arrays, see https://en.wikipedia.org/wiki/Array_data_type.

STRING

A *String* variable holds a sequence of characters. A string is like an array of char variables: "Hello" is a String, whose second element is "e".

A String is not exactly an array of characters. It typically stores information about its length, either with an actual count of the number of characters or with a special character (probably ASCII 0, the Null character) to mark the end of the characters.

For more on Strings, see https://en.wikipedia.org/wiki/String_(computer_science).

RECORD

A *Record* is a variable that contains other variables. You've probably run into Records when working with databases (such as a bug tracking database). Each entry (Record) in the database has the same Fields. (A *Field* is an individual variable within a Record.)

- A typical bug tracking system is made of Records that include these Fields:
  - The bug report number.
  - The name of the person who reported the bug.
  - The date the bug was reported.
  - The name of the program that has the bug.
  - The version number and/or build of the program.
  - The title (summary description) of the bug.
  - The description of the bug.
  - and so forth.

  In the database, each bug report is a separate Record.

- Another example you might have worked with is a database that stores credit card transactions (look at the statement you get from your credit card company). A typical transaction would be a purchase, a refund or a payment. A typical transaction record for a purchase includes such information as:
  - The date that you bought something.
  - The date the transaction was "posted" (officially recorded by the credit card company).
  - The name of the company that sold you something.
  - The amount of the purchase.
  - A transaction identifier (a transaction number or code).
  - Possibly even a graphic image of the purchase slip with your signature.

It is typical of Records that:

- The values of the Record's Fields are all related in some way.
  - In the bug tracking system, the values of every Field in the same Record refer to the same bug.
  - In the credit card system, the values of every Field in the same Record refer to the same purchase.
- The values of the Record's Fields are of different types:
  - The bug report number is an Integer, the bug report date is a Date, the title is a String.
  - The credit card purchase date is a Date, the vendor name is a String, the amount of the purchase is probably Fixed Point.

For more on Records, see https://en.wikipedia.org/wiki/Record_(computer_science).

PROGRAMMER-SPECIFIED TYPE, STRUCT OR CLASS

A *Record* is an example of a *Programmer-Specified* type. You might also have seen this named a *struct* or a *class*. (In this book, we are avoiding using the very common term, *class*, because of its confusability with *equivalence class*.) A programmer can establish any ordering on her own data type: Jones-5 can be smaller than Jones-4 but larger than Jones-3. Similarity is at the whim of the creator of the type.

LIST

A *List* is an ordered collection of values. The individual values are called the items, entries or elements of the list. Different elements of the list can have the same value. Depending on the type of list, the programmer can establish different orderings of the elements of the same list.

For more on Lists, see https://en.wikipedia.org/wiki/List_(computer_science).

SCALE

Along with knowing the type of the variable, testers often benefit from knowing the intended scale of a variable (*see* Crawford's (1997) Chapter 3, Levels of measurement & scaling; Stevens 1946, 1951; Trochim, 2006; Wikipedia: Level of measurement).

The following sections present different types of scales. In these, consider a variable, **v**, that can take on the values, A, B, C, D and F.

NOMINAL SCALE

Nominal values ("A" or "B") are like names. A variable whose value is "A" is no larger or smaller than another variable whose value is "B" or "C".

Most mathematical operations are meaningless on nominal data.

For example, it makes no sense to take an average of nominal data. What is the average of "Fred", "Susan" and "Pete"? Many people use numbers as names—they code data or events with 1, 2, 3, 4 and 5. Imagine recording the contents of a basket of fruit by coding every apple as a 1, every orange as a 2 and every peach as a 3. If a basket has 10 apples, 5 oranges and 5 peaches, does it make any sense to talk about a total of 35 (10 apples x 1, 5 oranges x 2, 5 peaches x 3) or an average fruit score of 35/20=1.75?

If this sounds too distant from practical situations, consider student numbers or Social Security Numbers in a database. These are numeric in form, but they're identifiers. You can't meaningfully add, multiply or divide them, or take an average of them.

For domain testing, the critical issue for nominal data is that it can't be put into an order. There is no biggest value and no smallest value. There are no boundary cases. It will take careful thinking to come up with equivalence classes, if that is possible at all.

ORDINAL SCALE

A variable, **v**, whose scale is *ordinal*, takes on values that can be ordered. "A" is larger (or better) than "B", which is larger than "C". If A, B and C are ordinal numbers, you won't know how much bigger "A" is than "B." It's just bigger. But A is closer to B than A is to C.

For example, suppose you have three pieces of fruit. Assign a 3 to the smallest one (a small orange), 4 to the next smallest one (a large apple) and 5 to the watermelon. You don't know how much bigger a size 3 fruit is than a 2. You just know that if you get a size 2 fruit, the 3 will be bigger.

Ordinal data can have boundaries. If variable **v** can take any ordinal value in the range of 3 to 10, the equivalence class (valid values) for **v** is {3, 4, 5, 6, 7, 8, 9, 10}. The smallest valid value of **v** is 3. The largest is 10. Two is too small and 11 is too big. The difference between 10 and 11 (two watermelons, almost the same size) might be much less than the difference between 2 and 3 (a grape and an orange), but any fruit with a size less than 3 is smaller than the lower bound of the permitted set and any fruit with a size bigger than 10 is larger than the upper bound of the permitted set.

INTERVAL SCALE

With an interval scale, you can compare the sizes of intervals. For example, if the distance between "A" and "B" is 5 and the distance between "C" and "D" is 5, then A is as far from B as C is from D.

Remember, you can't say this about ordinal data. If A is 10 and B is 5 and C is 6 and D is 1, the differences between A and B and between C and D might look the same (5), but you don't know how much bigger 10 is than 5 or how much bigger 6 is than 1. That makes the subtraction (A-B) of ordinal-scale numbers meaningless.

Temperature, as measured on a Fahrenheit or Celsius scale, is interval-scaled. If the high temperature of the day is 60° (Fahrenheit) on Monday, 70° on Tuesday and 80° on Wednesday, the temperature is rising by 10 degrees each day. The difference between Monday and Tuesday is the same as between Tuesday and Wednesday (10°). If you convert to Celsius, the numbers assigned to the temperatures change (15.6°, 21.1° and 26.7° for the same three days) but the differences are still constant: Monday is 5.6° cooler than Tuesday. Tuesday is the same amount (5.6°) cooler than Wednesday.

Subtraction of interval-scaled numbers yields meaningful results, but multiplication does not. For example,

- ∘ 10° Celsius is 50° Fahrenheit.
- If you multiply by 2, you get
  - ∘ 20° Celsius (which equals 68° Fahrenheit) or
  - ∘ 100° Fahrenheit (which equals. 37.8° Celsius).
- If you believe these results then:
  - ∘ 68° Fahrenheit (20° Celsius) must be twice as hot as 50 (10° Celsius), *and*
  - ∘ 37.8° Celsius (100° Fahrenheit) must be twice as hot as 10 (50° Fahrenheit).

Both of these are absurd. The example illustrates that even simple multiplication (multiply by 2) doesn't work when you multiply interval-scaled numbers.

RATIO SCALE

Ratio-scaled variables are interval-scaled, with additional properties. If values of **v** (A, B, C, D, F) are ratio scaled, you know how much bigger A is than B **and** you can speak meaningfully about the ratio of A to B (you can say that A is twice as big as B).

For a quantity to be ratio-scaled, there must be an absolute zero. Ratios compare the difference from zero. Many quantities in normal life are ratio scaled (such as distance, weight, profit, amount of money in the bank) and so people often generalize and assume that all numbers (all quantities) are ratio-scaled. This is a mistake. Numbers like degrees Fahrenheit are interval-scaled and have mathematically undefined ratios.

For domain testing, the critical question is whether you can put a set in an order. If a set has an unquestionably biggest value (anything bigger is too big), that biggest value is a boundary case and smaller values are members of an equivalence class.

FROM EXAMPLES 3, 5 AND 8

In Example 3 (SunTrust VISA), `DesiredCreditLimit` is probably a Fixed-Point variable (dollars and cents: two digits after the decimal point) or an Integer (dollars). `DesiredCreditLimit` is probably ratio-scaled.

In Example 5 (Undergraduate Grades), is `StudentScore` an Integer? Can you enter a score of 82.5? Assume for now that the program expects whole numbers (but ask the program what it thinks, when you have a chance). The *scale* poses a harder problem. In our experiences as graders, when we think of these numbers as measurements of the student's knowledge, there is a huge difference between the meaning of 60 (the student's knowledge is adequate) and 59 (the student's knowledge is inadequate). In terms of how graders assign numbers, the difference between 59 and 60 is a lot bigger than the difference between 94 and 95. This is inconsistent with the characteristics of interval and ratio scales.

In Example 8 (Create Table), the `NumberOfRows` is an Integer, ratio scaled. Knowing the scale is potentially useful because it tells you that you can (for example) set up tests with one table twice as tall as another.

FROM EXAMPLE 24: NOTEPAD OPEN FILE DIALOG

Example 24 presents the Notepad Open File dialog with a list of files.

- What is shown in the dialog is a list of file names. These are nominal.
- It might sometimes make sense to analyze these files on the basis of file *size,* which is, of course, ratio-scaled.

FROM EXAMPLE 25: MOODLE ASSIGN USER ROLES

Example 25's variable appears to be a simple string (a nominal-scale variable) but is actually a user-defined *record* (a variable with many fields).

The user interface lists all of the people who have accounts on the Moodle server. (Moodle is a course management system.)

This dialog allows the Course Instructor (or an administrator who has suitable privileges) to bring anyone with a Moodle account into the course and to assign them privileges. The Instructor can bring the person in as a guest, a student, a teaching assistant or as another instructor.

In the dialog, you first select a Role that you'll assign to people (for example, Student). Then select people to assign that Role to. The dialog shows a selection of Role in progress (Teacher is highlighted) and a list of people's names. Some (the ones on the left list) have already been assigned as teachers, others (the ones on the right list) can be assigned as teachers. Someone who has been assigned can be removed.

Each person who has an account on Moodle has a record containing a list of all the courses s/he has taken, a name, contact information, various preference settings, location (what country), etc. Selecting a person (from a list of names) brings all of that person's record into the course.

You probably won't be able to group these records into meaningful equivalence classes based on the names, but the other fields will provide several opportunities. For example, you could group everyone who is taking their first course, everyone from Germany, everyone who has never failed a course offered on this server, etc.

EXERCISES: PART 1-D

Please determine the type and scale of the key variable in each question below:

D.1. *Example 7: Student Names* **on page 275**

A `StudentLastName` field must start with an alphabetic character (upper or lower case). Subsequent characters must be letters, numbers or spaces.

D.2. *Example 14: Result Of Calculations* **on page 319**

`I`, `J` and `K` are Unsigned Integers. You can enter values into `I` and `J`, but the program calculates the value of `K = I × J`. Treat `K` as the primary variable.

D.3. *Example 28: OpenOffice Printing Options* **on page 409**

Here is a printing-options dialog from a development build of OpenOffice 4.

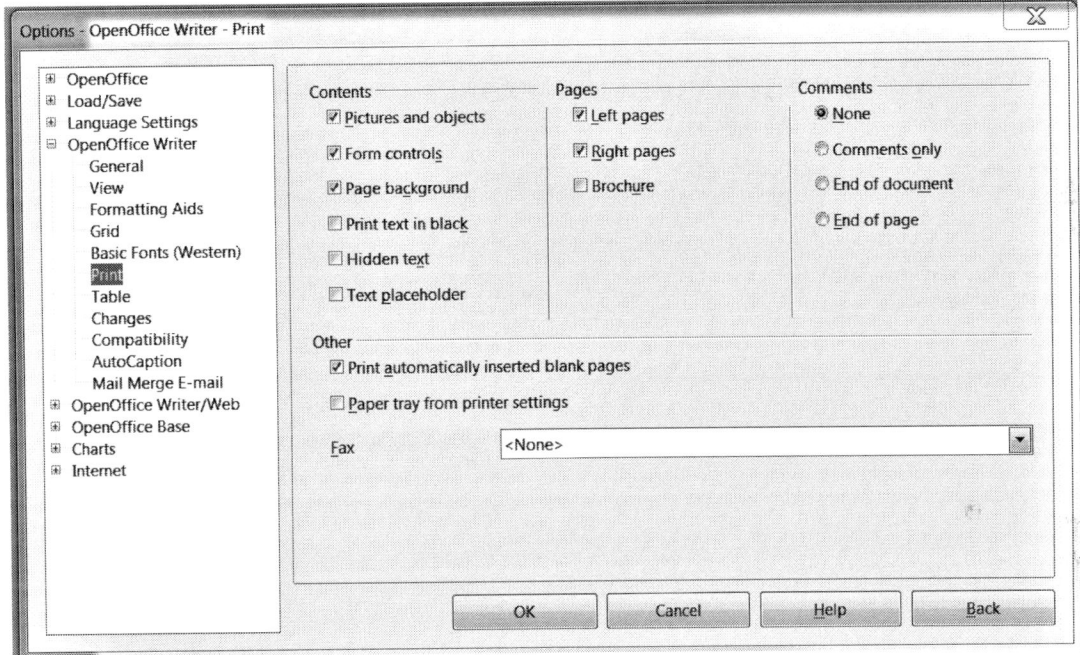

A SCHEMA FOR DOMAIN TESTING

1. CHARACTERIZE THE VARIABLE

A. Identify the potentially interesting variables.

B. Identify the variable(s) you can analyze now. This is the variable(s) of interest.

C. Determine the primary dimension of the variable of interest.

D. Determine the type and scale of the variable's primary dimension and what values it can take.

E. **Determine whether you can order the variable's values (from smallest to largest).**

F. Determine whether this is an input variable or a result.

G. Determine how the program uses this variable.

H. Determine whether other variables are related to this one.

2. ANALYZE THE VARIABLE AND CREATE TESTS

I. Partition the variable (its primary dimension).

   – If the dimension is ordered, determine its sub-ranges and transition points.

   – If the dimension is not ordered, base partitioning on similarity.

J. Lay out the analysis in a classical boundary/equivalence table. Identify best representatives.

K. Create tests for the consequences of the data entered, not just the input filter.

L. Identify secondary dimensions. Analyze them in the classical way.

M. Summarize your analysis with a risk/equivalence table.

3. GENERALIZE TO MULTIDIMENSIONAL VARIABLES

N. Analyze independent variables that should be tested together.

O. Analyze variables that hold results.

P. Analyze non-independent variables. Deal with relationships and constraints.

4. PREPARE FOR ADDITIONAL TESTING

Q. Identify and list unanalyzed variables. Gather information for later analysis.

R. Imagine and document risks that don't necessarily map to an obvious dimension.

E. DETERMINE WHETHER YOU CAN ORDER THE VARIABLE'S VALUES

If a variable is ordered, you can sort its possible values from smallest to largest. For example, the Introduction presented an ordered variable that ranged from -999 to 999.

The prototypic domain analysis partitions a variable into three categories:

- Too small (less than -999)
- Within the acceptable range (-999 to 999)
- And too large (greater than 999).

The analysis also determines boundary values. If Δ is the smallest possible difference between two numbers (between Integers, Δ is 1), the boundaries for this variable are:

- Too small (-999 - Δ) (in this case, -1000)
- Smallest acceptable value (-999)
- Largest acceptable value (999)
- Too large (999 + Δ) (in this case, 1000)

It is impossible to draw partitions and boundaries this way if you can't tell whether one value is larger or smaller than another.

EXAMPLES OF VARIABLES THAT CAN BE ORDERED

Most descriptions of domain testing present a simple numeric input field or a combination of a few number fields (for example, three sides of a triangle). This simplicity has led some testers to conclude that domain testing works only when you're analyzing a field that explicitly asks you for a numeric input. That is too narrow a view.

You can put many types of variables into an order, even if they aren't associated with an obvious numeric input field. Here are some examples (expanded from Kaner, 1987).

CHARACTER-BASED ENCODING

- Names that start with "A" come before names that start with "B."
- You can sort any other type of string in terms of its underlying character codes or in a modified sort order that treats capital letters and lower case letters and accented letters the same.

HOW MANY

- How many times you can run an evaluation copy before a program stops working.
- How many times you can do an operation before the program runs out of memory.
- How many names you can store in a mailing list, records in a database, variables in a spreadsheet, bookmarks in a browser, etc.
- How many spelling mistakes a spellchecker can flag in a document.
- How many devices can be connected, how many active.
- How many sessions can be open.
- How many processes can be running in memory.
- How many processes can access the database at the same time.

- How many interrupts can be stacked (process receives an interrupt while running. and another interrupt while servicing the first interrupt, etc.).
- How many devices of a certain type (e.g., how many printers) are connected or how many drivers for devices of a certain type have been loaded on the system.

HOW BIG

- Size of a number you enter (how many digits).
- Size of a sum of numbers (overflow or underflow the data type or the number of digits or characters the sum can hold).
- Size of a character string.
- Size of a concatenated string.
- Size of a path specification or a file name.
- Size (in characters, paragraphs or pages) of a document.
- Size of a file (in your testing, try some special values such as 2^n for various n's—256, 512, 1024 bytes, etc.).
- Size of a document on the page (compare it to page margins on different page sizes).
- Size of a document on a page in terms of memory limits for a formatted page.
- Input or output intensity (voltage levels to an analog-to-digital converter).
- Transition points for inputs that are handled differently because of an optimization. For example, Abramowitz & Stegun (1964, p. 941) provide different formulas for calculating the approximate value of the Chi-Square probability function. A program will use one formula for values of **DegreesOfFreedom** (an input variable) greater than 100 and a different formula for **DegreesOfFreedom** between 30 and 100. This transition won't be obvious at the user interface, but it splits the inputs into different equivalence classes and offers an interesting boundary question. What if you use the formula that is appropriate for the larger values on values slightly smaller than appropriate for this formula?

TIMING

- How much time is allowable between Event A and Event B.
- First event, most recent event, last event.
- Timeout: Suppose you have access to a remote server, but it logs you off if you don't enter a command within a period of time. How long is the period? What happens if you enter a command just after you are logged off? Is there a zone of vulnerability between the time the server decides to log you off and the time at which it stops listening to your commands? Does it operate correctly within this zone?
- Timeout: generalize to any two processes, A and B, where A will deny B access if B does not send A a message before the timeout period expires. What are the tolerance limits on "before", "same time" and "after"? Can the program cope with a case in which B's message comes just a little before or a little after A's timeout?
- Race conditions: generalize timeout to any case in which a program expects Event A (or Task A) to complete before B. What are the tolerance limits on "before", "same time" and "after"?
- Resource availability: if the program expects to be able to use a certain resource (free memory, free disk space, free printer), how long will the program keep trying if the resource is unavailable? What happens if you make it partially available (free up some, but not enough, memory) during the keep-trying period?
- Dates and timestamps.

SPEED

- Time between keystrokes. Time between commands, entered menu after menu or at a dialog that accepts multiple commands or on a command line.
- Time between requests from other processes, especially in a system that can handle concurrent tasks.
- Speed / extent of a voltage transition (e.g., from a very soft to a very loud sound).

CONFIGURATION

The following examples might or might not be orderable. Even if you can impose a smallest-to-largest ranking, that might be the least informative way of grouping them.

- Video resolution, number of colors.
- Operating system version.
- How much system memory; available memory.
- System resources consumed compared to resources available (memory, handles, stack space, other devices).

VARIATION BETWEEN THINGS THAT SHOULD BE EQUIVALENT

- Variation within a group of operating system versions that should be compatible (such as Version 7 with different updates applied).
- Variations within a group of "compatible" printers, sound cards, video cards, network cards, etc.
- Pages to be printed, sounds to be played, more generally: outputs that will go to the same device that could be classified as essentially the same in terms of how the software should process them.

MEMBERSHIP IN THE SAME GROUP

A variable's values might cluster in a way that gives all elements in each subset the same value. Perhaps you can order the subsets, but not the elements within the subsets. For example:

- In calculating employment benefits, all full-time employees might get the same benefits, all part-time employees might get a lower level of benefits and independent contractors might get none. You can order these groups in terms of their benefit status, but any two members of the same group get the same treatment.
- If you have to enter a country name, the valid equivalence class includes all countries' names. The invalid class includes all inputs that aren't country names. What about abbreviations, almost-correct spellings, native-language spellings or names that are now out of date but were once country names? Do you have a similarity metric that partially orders the invalid class?
- Clustering might be forced by the application. For example, American taxpayers file as single, married, filing a joint return, married filing separate returns, head of household or qualifying widow(er) with dependent child. Some people refuse to describe their marital status, which is also legal. There are plenty of people in each category, but there is nothing (in this categorization) to differentiate them.

LEAD TO THE SAME CONSEQUENCE

A program uses the values of variables when it makes decisions or does actions. If two values lead it to make the same decision (simplest example: take the same branch) or take the same action, then in this respect, they have the same consequence. However, when the program does make a decision or take an action, the specific value of the variable might lead to success in some cases and failure in other cases. For example:

- The employee-benefits example (Membership in the Same Group) illustrates this when someone wants to use their benefits. To test the benefits, you start by selecting an employee who is entitled to the benefits.

- Consider a variable holds a URL. Several URLs redirect to the same page or to a page that has the same (relevant) content as the other pages. Some URLs might redirect to a different category of pages.

- In double-sided printing, odd-numbered pages print on the front of the page and even-numbered pages print on the back of the page.

EXPOSURE TO THE SAME RISK

All of the previous categorizations are examples of this one, but sometimes thinking directly about risk can suggest groupings that you might have missed.

- Imagine a program that executes remote procedures (the code that will be executed is stored somewhere else and execution is triggered via a link to that other server). Now imagine the risk that one of the procedures has been compromised and redirects to malware.

  ◦ Can you list all the remote procedures and all the places that point to each procedure?

  ◦ Do all the links that point to (what is supposed to be) the same procedure actually point to exactly the same place?

    ▪ If so, select any one of them to check for malware at the link.

    ▪ If not, then even if all links point to almost-the-same place and are supposed to eventually execute the same code, you should probably test each unique link separately.

FROM EXAMPLE 26: INSTALL PRINTER SOFTWARE

Some variables simply can't be put into an order. For example, consider testing printers for compatibility with OpenOffice. Here is a dialog that illustrates the set of Windows-compatible printers: Note that in this dialog, selecting the manufacturer brings up a list of printers made by that manufacturer.

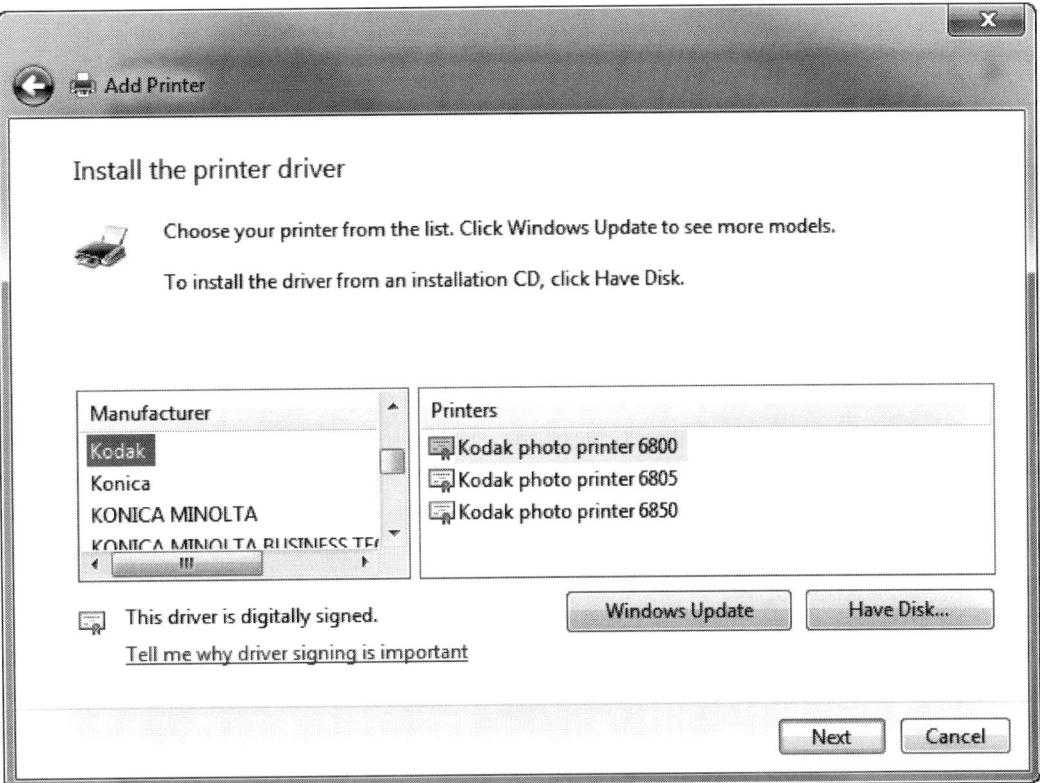

There is no natural ordering for these printers (or their drivers).

- Grouping by manufacturer is obvious, but manufacturers make many printers. How do you order them within such grouping? Some of these printers are very different from each other; some might be more similar to printers made by other companies than to some of the others made by their own company.

- You could order by name: the name of the HP LaserJet 2410 printer comes before Kodak 1392 in the alphabet. Or you could order by file sizes of the drivers. However, neither name nor file size has any relevance to whether the printer will actually work when an application, like OpenOffice, sends it data to print.

SOME THEORISTS RESERVE DOMAIN TESTING FOR INTERVAL AND RATIO VARIABLES

We started this Chapter by asserting that variables must be ordered (ordinal scale) for traditional domain testing (partitioning into equivalence classes separated at boundary values).

Some authors apply domain testing only to linear domains (*e.g.*, Beizer, 1995; Clarke, et al., 1982; White, 1981). Tian (2005, p. 129) lays out the assumptions for linear domains particularly clearly. Beizer (2005) notes that old research on COBOL programs found that 85% of the domains specified in the program were linear.

You can *linearize a variable* if you can map its values to a number line. (Such a variable is either interval-scaled or ratio-scaled.)

In a *linear domain,* all the boundaries can be described as *linear inequalities*.

Consider a variable $\mathbf{X} = (\mathbf{x}_1, \mathbf{x}_2, \dots, \mathbf{x}_n)$ and constants $\mathbf{C} = (\mathbf{c}_1, \mathbf{c}_2, \dots, \mathbf{c}_n)$ and $\mathbf{k}$. An inequality is linear if it is of the form:

$$\mathbf{k} + \mathbf{c}_1\mathbf{x}_1 + \mathbf{c}_2\mathbf{x}_2 + \dots \mathbf{c}_n\mathbf{x}_n \geq 0.$$

With a linear domain, you can apply a simple one-on-and-one-off heuristic for developing tests (Beizer, 1995). That is, choose one point on the boundary and one point off (below the low boundary or above the high one).

However, some variables can't be linearized. For example, you might decide that two printers are equivalent if they work the same way and run the same software, but you won't be able to map them to a number line. If you can't map a variable to the number line, you can't meaningfully calculate the value of a linear expression that includes that variable and so you can't have a linear domain.

- For purposes like configuration testing, when working with printers, we apply a sampling strategy that is properly called domain testing under the definitions in this book. We would group the printers by similarity (and risk) into equivalence classes and choose our printers to test from each class.

- Some other reputable authors who have considered domain testing deeply would probably not treat our approach to configuration testing as domain testing. For example, we think Boris Beizer might consider our printer-sampling strategy *reasonable*, but he would probably suggest that we call it something else, not domain testing.

FROM EXAMPLE 12: PIECEWISE BOUNDARY

The input domain of a function is the set of all points $(\mathbf{x}, \mathbf{y})$ that meet these criteria (Binder, 2000, p. 404):

- $\mathbf{x}$ and $\mathbf{y}$ are Floating-Point variables
- $1 < \mathbf{x} \leq 10$
- $1 \leq \mathbf{y} \leq 10$
- $\mathbf{y} \leq 14 - \mathbf{x}$

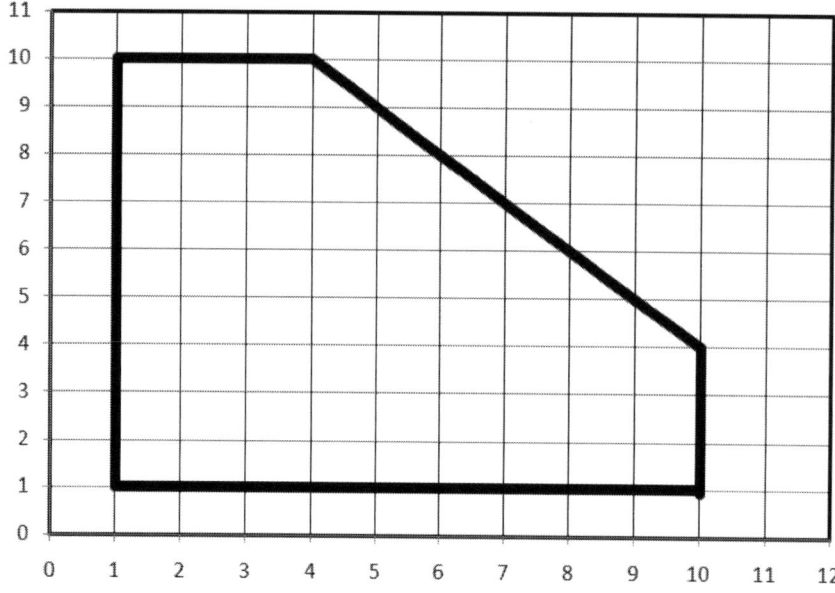

This example shows a classic linear domain.

FROM EXAMPLE 10: THE CIRCLE

Consider a circle defined by $x_1^2 + x_2^2 = 100$.

The individual variables (x_1 and x_2) can be ordered (they look like simple numeric variables). However, the relationships that define their values aren't easily converted to linear ones. As you can see in Chapter P's discussion of *Example 12: Piecewise Boundary (Linear Relationships)* on page 203, there are still boundaries and you can work with values just on and just off the boundary.

FROM EXAMPLE 24: NOTEPAD OPEN FILE DIALOG

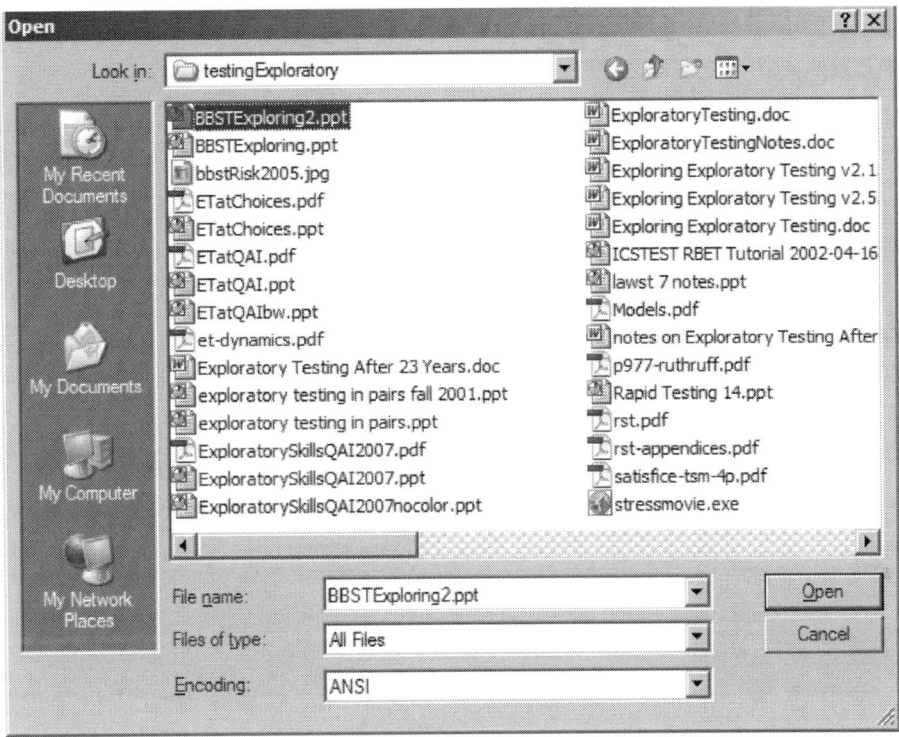

Consider Notepad's Open File dialog. There are several ways to order the values in this dialog (you can set preferences to show any of these attributes of the files):

- Alphabetical (file name)
- Length of the file name
- Size of the file
- Date the file was last saved

Whether these are *useful* orderings depends on what kind of error you're trying to discover.

In addition to establishing an ordering, you could consider distances between some of the values. But be cautious about how you interpret these numbers:

- Is it relevant that one file is twice the size of another?
- Is it relevant that one file was saved twice as long ago as another?

For most testing purposes, exact distances and ratios don't matter. As long as you can put the variable's values in order and tell whether a value is above or below a boundary, you often know enough.[29]

EXERCISES: PART 1-E

Please determine whether the key variable in each question below can be ordered:

E.1. *Example 11: University Admissions* **on page 301**

Stateless University's admission standards use both high school grades and **ACT** test scores (Copeland, 2004, p. 121).

- **ACT** scores are Integers running between 0 and 36.
- **GPA** scores are Fixed-Point variables (always exactly one digit after the decimal point) running between 0.0 and 4.0.

Students are accepted if they meet any of these requirements:

- **ACT** = 36 and **GPA** ≥ 3.5
- **ACT** ≥ 35 and **GPA** ≥ 3.6
- **ACT** ≥ 34 and **GPA** ≥ 3.7
- **ACT** ≥ 33 and **GPA** ≥ 3.8
- **ACT** ≥ 32 and **GPA** ≥ 3.9
- **ACT** ≥ 31 and **GPA** = 4.0

We can represent this relationship by stating that students are admitted if

$$\textbf{ACT} + 10 \times \textbf{GPA} \geq 71$$

E.2. *Example 15: Mailing Labels* **on page 325**

A program prints mailing labels. The first line of the label is the person's name. The program builds the name from three fields, `FirstName`, `MiddleName` and `LastName`. Each field can hold up to 30 characters. The label can be up to 70 characters wide.

---

29 Morven Gentleman says, "I would say something weaker: As long as you can identify whether a test is is within or outside a test set, especially if you can recognize when a test case is on the boundary of the test set, it doesn't matter whether the variable is ordered. It doesn't even matter whether two arbitrary values of the variable can be compared at all!"

E.3. *Example 25: Moodle Assign User Roles* **on page 395**

Moodle is a program that manages online courses. Here is one of its dialogs. The user can assign participants in a class to one or more roles in the course, such as student or teacher.

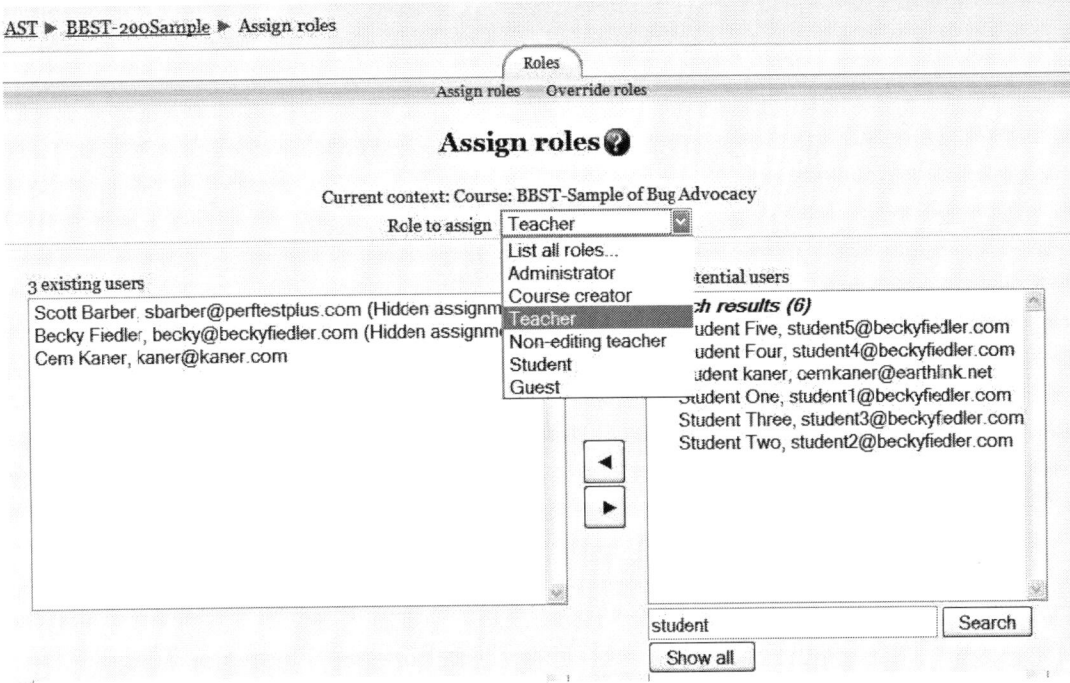

A SCHEMA FOR DOMAIN TESTING

1. CHARACTERIZE THE VARIABLE

A. Identify the potentially interesting variables.

B. Identify the variable(s) you can analyze now. This is the variable(s) of interest.

C. Determine the primary dimension of the variable of interest.

D. Determine the type and scale of the variable's primary dimension and what values it can take.

E. Determine whether you can order the variable's values (from smallest to largest).

F. Determine whether this is an input variable or a result.

G. Determine how the program uses this variable.

H. Determine whether other variables are related to this one.

2. ANALYZE THE VARIABLE AND CREATE TESTS

I. Partition the variable (its primary dimension).

- If the dimension is ordered, determine its sub-ranges and transition points.

- If the dimension is not ordered, base partitioning on similarity.

J. Lay out the analysis in a classical boundary/equivalence table. Identify best representatives.

K. Create tests for the consequences of the data entered, not just the input filter.

L. Identify secondary dimensions. Analyze them in the classical way.

M. Summarize your analysis with a risk/equivalence table.

3. GENERALIZE TO MULTIDIMENSIONAL VARIABLES

N. Analyze independent variables that should be tested together.

O. Analyze variables that hold results.

P. Analyze non-independent variables. Deal with relationships and constraints.

4. PREPARE FOR ADDITIONAL TESTING

Q. Identify and list unanalyzed variables. Gather information for later analysis.

R. Imagine and document risks that don't necessarily map to an obvious dimension.

F. DETERMINE WHETHER THIS IS AN INPUT VARIABLE OR A RESULT

If you can enter data into a variable, it's an ***input variable***. Input might come from the keyboard, from values saved on disk or from another process somewhere on the network.

Other variables aren't input variables. Perhaps they're constants, set in the program itself. If not, they're probably ***result variables.*** Result variables get their values from other variables, not from direct input.

For example, consider three variables: v_1, v_2 and v_3, related to each other as follows:

$$v_3 = v_1 \times v_2$$

In this equation, v_3 is a result variable.

As a practical example, consider using a program to track your banking activities. When you write a check, you enter the details into the program and the program calculates your current balance. The check amount is the input variable, the balance is the result variable.

Suppose you're writing a memo using a wordprocessor. You insert a table. The program brings up a dialog asking how many rows and how many columns. It then inserts an empty table on the page with that many rows and columns. The variables holding the number of rows and the number of columns are the input variables. Every aspect of the object that you see on the screen (the table) is a result. For example, the height of the rows is determined by a calculation that takes into account the number of rows, the height of the page and its margins and a preference setting for the default height. The placement of the dots that make up the display of the table on the screen is also a result.

Most variables that users are interested in are result variables. They enter data in order to learn things (like, "What's my bank balance?") or to create things (like, the table or the document).

Because those variables are important to the user, it's important to analyze them and test them. If a result variable can take on many possible values, use domain testing to limit the number of tests.

The analysis will be very similar to the analysis of an input variable:

- Figure out what values the variable *can* take.
- Divide that set of values into equivalence classes (at this point, there might be only one class, the valid values).
- Identify boundaries or other best representatives.

However, you also have to figure out how to enter values into this variable and what values you should enter into them.

- Because you're working with a result variable, you must enter values into some other variables that are, in turn, used in calculations that determine the value of your result.
- Can you enter values into the input variables that yield calculated values outside the valid range for the result variable? If so, can you create equivalence classes. For example, create a set of values that will drive the result too low and another set that will drive the result too high?

In this Chapter, we're not doing the full analysis. The only question we're asking here is whether the variable is an input, a result or both. We continue the analysis of results in the next Chapter and in *O. Analyze Variables that Hold Results* on page 191.

FROM EXAMPLE 2: ATM WITHDRAWAL

An ATM allows withdrawals of cash in amounts of $20 increments from $20 to $200 (inclusive) (Craig & Jaskiel, 2002, p. 164).

The obvious input variable is `AmountRequested` (the amount the customer asks for at the ATM).

Here are two examples of variables that will hold results of this transaction:

- `AmountReceived` (how much the customer actually gets)
- `UpdatedBalance` (the balance in the customer's bank account after the withdrawal)

FROM EXAMPLE 4: PAGE SETUP OPTIONS

The page setup function of a text editor allows a user to set the width of the page in the range of 1 to 56 inches. The `PageWidth` input field accepts (and remembers) up to 30 places after the decimal point.

The input variable is `PageWidth`. An example of a result based on `PageWidth` is the width of a printout of the document.

FROM EXAMPLE 14: RESULT OF CALCULATIONS

`I`, `J` and `K` are Unsigned Integers. You can enter values into `I` and `J`, but the program calculates the value of `K = I × J`. Treat `K` as the primary variable.

The input variables are `I` and `J`. The primary variable, `K`, is a result variable.

FROM EXAMPLE 23: FREQUENT-FLYER MILES

An airline awards frequent-flyer miles according to the following table (Black, 2007, p. 218):

Status Level	None	Silver	Gold	Platinum
Trip bonus	0%	25%	50%	100%
Distance traveled	d	d	d	d
Points awarded	d	1.25 × d	1.5 × d	2 × d
Miles required to reach this level	0	25,000	50,000	100,000

Your status is determined before you fly. The number of miles flown on this trip does not affect your status on this trip, though a long trip might result in elevating your status before your next trip.

Determine whether the system awards the correct number of points for a given trip.

The number of points awarded is a result variable. Your Status Level and accumulated points toward your next Status Level are also result variables. The input variables are all the things you enter to specify the trip (who are you, what's your frequent flyer number, where are you flying, what specific flight, etc.).

EXERCISES: PART 1-F

Please determine whether the variables in these exercises are input variables or result variables.

F.1. *Example 13: Sum of Two Integers* **on page 315**

A program adds two Integer numbers, which you enter. Each number should be one or two digits. Analyze this in terms of the paired inputs (**FirstNumber**, **SecondNumber**) or in terms of the output (**Sum**). The **sum** will also be an Integer.

F.2. *Example 15: Mailing Labels* **on page 325**

A program prints mailing labels. The first line of the label is the person's name. The program builds the name from three fields, **FirstName**, **MiddleName** and **LastName**. Each field can hold up to 30 characters. The label can be up to 70 characters wide.

F.3. *Example 21: Spreadsheet Sort Table* **on page 361**

In OpenOffice Calc, you can sort a table. The fields in the dialog are all **SortBy** fields. The first field is the primary sort key.

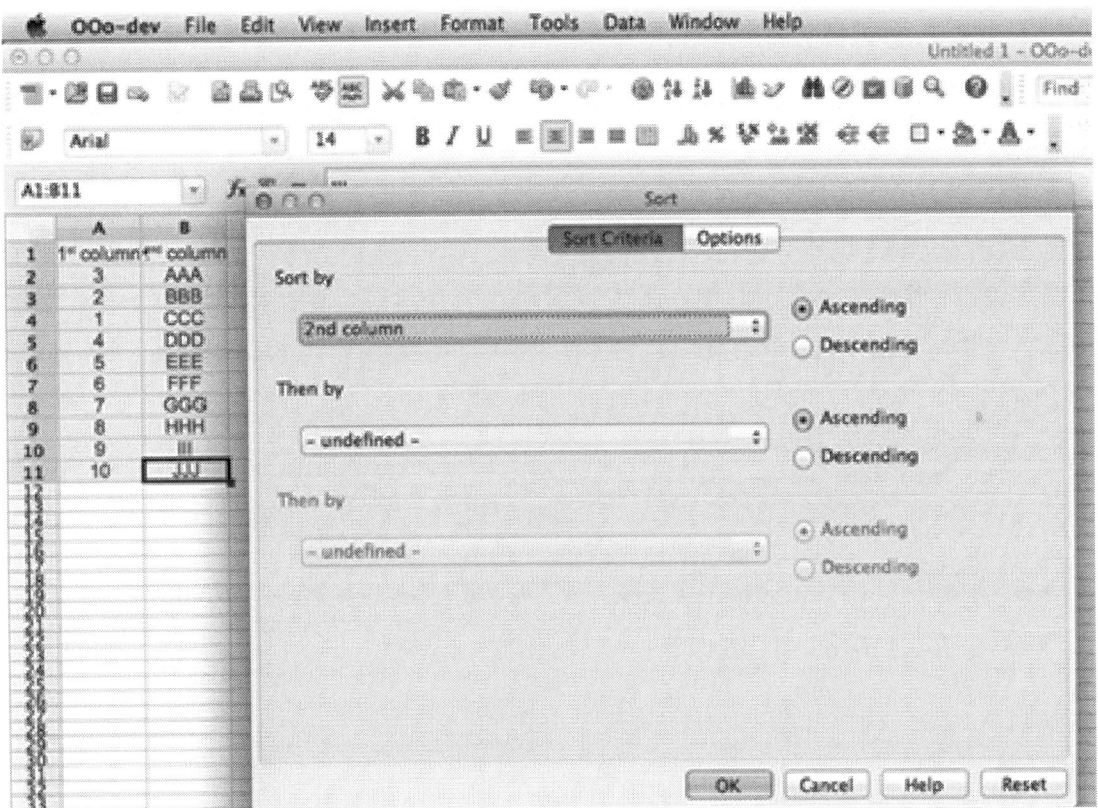

In this case, the table will be sorted by the values in the column labeled **SecondColumn**: AAA before BBB. Because this sorts the whole table, in the column labeled **FirstColumn**, 3 comes before 2 which comes before 1.

If you sort by **FirstColumn** instead, OpenOffice will sort the row with 1 before 2 before 3 but now you would see CCC before BBB before AAA in **SecondColumn**.

Note: OpenOffice is abbreviated as OOo.

A SCHEMA FOR DOMAIN TESTING

1. CHARACTERIZE THE VARIABLE

A. Identify the potentially interesting variables.

B. Identify the variable(s) you can analyze now. This is the variable(s) of interest.

C. Determine the primary dimension of the variable of interest.

D. Determine the type and scale of the variable's primary dimension and what values it can take.

E. Determine whether you can order the variable's values (from smallest to largest).

F. Determine whether this is an input variable or a result.

G. Determine how the program uses this variable.

H. Determine whether other variables are related to this one.

2. ANALYZE THE VARIABLE AND CREATE TESTS

I. Partition the variable (its primary dimension).

- If the dimension is ordered, determine its sub-ranges and transition points.
- If the dimension is not ordered, base partitioning on similarity.

J. Lay out the analysis in a classical boundary/equivalence table. Identify best representatives.

K. Create tests for the consequences of the data entered, not just the input filter.

L. Identify secondary dimensions. Analyze them in the classical way.

M. Summarize your analysis with a risk/equivalence table.

3. GENERALIZE TO MULTIDIMENSIONAL VARIABLES

N. Analyze independent variables that should be tested together.

O. Analyze variables that hold results.

P. Analyze non-independent variables. Deal with relationships and constraints.

4. PREPARE FOR ADDITIONAL TESTING

Q. Identify and list unanalyzed variables. Gather information for later analysis.

R. Imagine and document risks that don't necessarily map to an obvious dimension.

G. DETERMINE HOW THE PROGRAM USES THIS VARIABLE

We're still characterizing the variable, figuring out how to describe it and what its properties are. We aren't yet figuring out how to test it.

The question for this Chapter is, *What does the program DO with this variable?*

For example, imagine placing an order for stocks in an online brokerage program. The variable is the order. Suppose the order is to buy 100 shares of Intel stock for $20 per share.

- **The program will start by applying its input filters (check input validity).** It will reject orders with invalid prices, invalid quantities or invalid stock names.

    - The program might question (request confirmation) for a price significantly lower or higher than the last price paid for the stock. The program might reject (refuse even after confirmation) a price *very* far from the last price paid.

    - The program will reject a price that is not in dollars and cents. For example, $12.074 is invalid (it should be $12.07). For some types of equities, the program will reject prices that aren't divisible by 5 cents or by 10 cents.

    - For some equities, the program will require quantities in the hundreds of shares. An order of 100 or 200 shares is OK, but 150 is not.

    - The program will reject an order if it doesn't recognize the stock name (for Intel, it is INTC)

- **The program will also reject some orders based on its knowledge of what it will do with those orders.**

    - For example, if you order 100 shares of a $20 stock, the program will reject the order if you don't have enough cash or credit in your account to pay the $2000.

- **If the program accepts the order, it will do some things with it.**

    - Suppose your order seeks to buy the stock at a lower price than its current price. Your order won't be completed yet, but the program will probably reduce the amount of money you can allocate to your next order.

    - After you buy the stock, the program will change the value of your portfolio, display a new line in the table that shows your current holdings and their values, reduce the amount of cash in your account, update your purchase history records for your year-end tax report, add this to the list of stocks that it sends you emails about when significant corporate events happen and trigger a message to the corporation whose stock it is so that it can send you messages and send the broker dividends for your account.

Consider another example. Fidelity (a brokerage) gives clients extra privileges if their account has at least $25,000 and they place at least 30 trades in a quarter. They can use additional research tools and place trades from the tools. Some brokers change the amount of commission they charge as trading volume goes up and change the types of trades that their tools will let you perform. Both of these contingencies illustrate a class of cases in which an input not only has its immediate effect; it also changes your privileges and with that, the visible capabilities and options of the software you're using.

The key thing to realize is that you will probably imagine new potential impacts of changes to a variable's value when you think about how the program uses the variable, why it's doing that with the variable and what is the ultimate benefit of that action to the user.

FROM EXAMPLE 4: PAGE SETUP OPTIONS

The page setup function of a text editor allows a user to set the width of the page in the range of 1 to 56 inches. The **PageWidth** input field accepts (and remembers) up to 30 places after the decimal point.

Certainly you should test whether the program can receive input into this field and filter inappropriate values. However, only an amateur would stop here. *What happens when you change the width?*

- When you change width in some versions of PowerPoint, the program also makes a proportional change to the table dimensions and the graphics on the slide. (In earlier versions, it also changed the text dimensions.)

Here is a PowerPoint 2007 slide that has not yet been rescaled. Original dimensions are 10 inches wide by 7.5 inches tall.

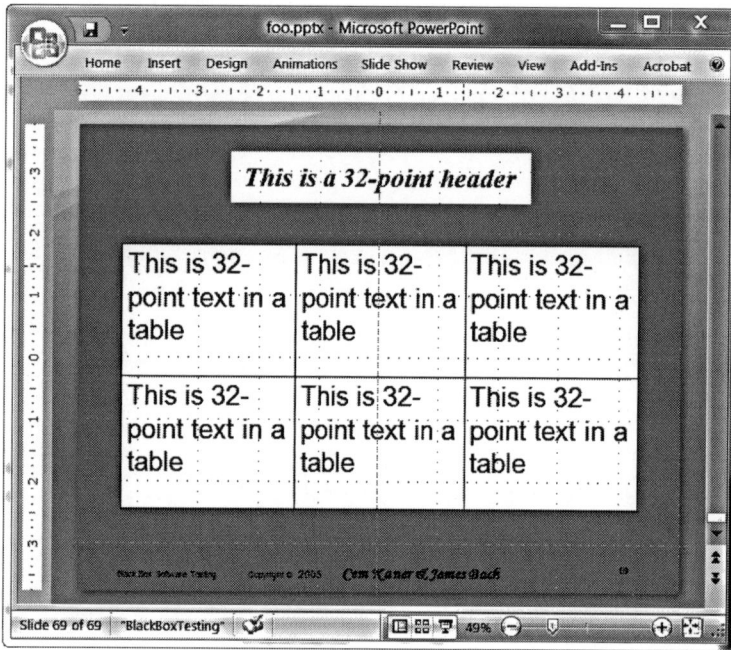

Here is the same slide rescaled to 56 inches wide and 7.5 inches tall.

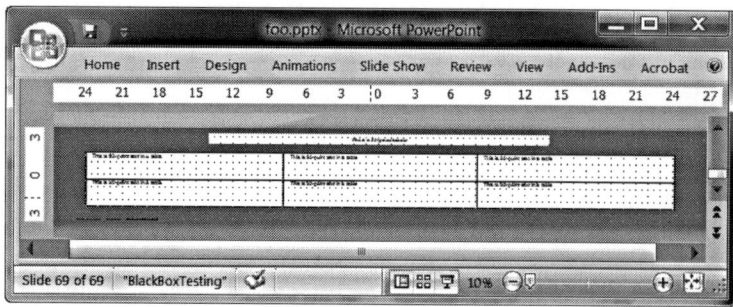

Is that a bug or a feature?

What if you add a graphic? For example, paste a 1-inch x 1-inch picture of your favorite insect at normal width. Now scale the slide to maximum width. If the program scales the graphic, the insect becomes 1" high and about 5" wide. Then paste the same insect beside the first one. Does it come in as 1"x1" or 1"x5"? Does it look the same as the first one? Should it?

What if you change the slide from a normal width (like 11 inches wide) to minimum, then maximum, then minimum, and then normal? Does anything get distorted in the process?

What happens if you try to print slides at these extreme widths? What if the printer driver is set to use printer fonts instead of downloading bitmaps of the fonts? Do the stretched (or shrunken) characters cause any problems?

- This field will change the shape/size of the region where you enter text. When you print, you'll print a document that (presumably) has the designated width. What happens if your page width is wider than the printer's page width? Some programs will "tile" to the printer (print multiple pages that will replicate this one page if you lay the pages side by side). Other programs will give an error message at print time.

- Why does the program accept and remember a page width to a precision of 30 digits after the decimal place? Is this essentially an accident of implementation or is the programmer going to use this value in calculations that actually require great accuracy? What calculations are those? If they exist, you should test them.

FROM EXAMPLE 6: TAX TABLE

In 1993, the Internal Revenue Service calculated taxes based on this table (Beizer, 1995, p. 151):

Income Range	Tax
$0 < $ `TaxableIncome` $\leq \$22100$	$0.15 \times$ `TaxableIncome`
$\$22100 < $ `TaxableIncome` $\leq \$53500$	$\$3315 + 0.28 \times ($ `TaxableIncome` $- 22100)$
$\$53500 < $ `TaxableIncome` $\leq \$115000$	$\$12107 + 0.31 \times ($ `TaxableIncome` $- 53500)$
$\$115000 < $ `TaxableIncome` $\leq \$250000$	$\$31172 + 0.36 \times ($ `TaxableIncome` $- 115000)$
$\$250000 < $ `TaxableIncome`	$\$79772 + 0.396 \times ($ `TaxableIncome` $- 250000)$

The program uses `TaxableIncome` to compute `Tax`.

The example's description provides no information about how (or if) the program uses `Tax`.

FROM EXAMPLE 23: FREQUENT-FLYER MILES

An airline awards frequent-flyer miles according to the following table (Black, 2007, p. 218):

Status Level	None	Silver	Gold	Platinum
Trip bonus	0%	25%	50%	100%
Distance traveled	d	d	d	d
Points awarded	d	$1.25 \times d$	$1.5 \times d$	$2 \times d$
Miles required to reach this level	0	25,000	50,000	100,000

Your status is determined before you fly. The number of miles flown on this trip does not affect your status on this trip, though a long trip might result in elevating your status before your next trip.

Determine whether the system awards the correct number of points for a given trip.

The primary variable in this example is the number of points awarded. How will the program use this?

The example description doesn't say directly how this variable will be used. But you probably know some things about frequent-flyer miles:

- The program will add the number of points awarded for this flight to the customer's current number of points. A customer with enough points can buy flights or other merchandise with points.

- The program will add the number of points (or some portion of them) to a total used to calculate status level. A customer with a higher status level gets more points per flight, better seating and other privileges.

EXERCISES: PART 1-G

Please evaluate how the program uses the values of its variables in each example below. If the example description doesn't provide the relevant information, either say that no information is available or use what you know about the world to supplement what the example's description does provide.

G.1. *Example 11: University Admissions* **on page 301**

Stateless University's admission standards use both high school grades and **ACT** test scores (Copeland, 2004, p. 121).

- **ACT** scores are Integers running between 0 and 36.
- **GPA** scores are Fixed-Point variables (always exactly one digit after the decimal point) running between 0.0 and 4.0.

Students are accepted if they meet any of these requirements:

- **ACT** = 36 and **GPA** ≥ 3.5
- **ACT** ≥ 35 and **GPA** ≥ 3.6
- **ACT** ≥ 34 and **GPA** ≥ 3.7
- **ACT** ≥ 33 and **GPA** ≥ 3.8
- **ACT** ≥ 32 and **GPA** ≥ 3.9
- **ACT** ≥ 31 and **GPA** = 4.0

You can represent this relationship by stating that students are admitted if

$$ACT + 10 \times GPA \geq 71$$

G.2. *Example 9: Create Table (Max Cells)* **on page 289**

In OpenOffice (OOo) Impress, you can create a table. With this dialog, you set the starting numbers of rows and columns. Suppose the maximum number of cells in the table is 4095.

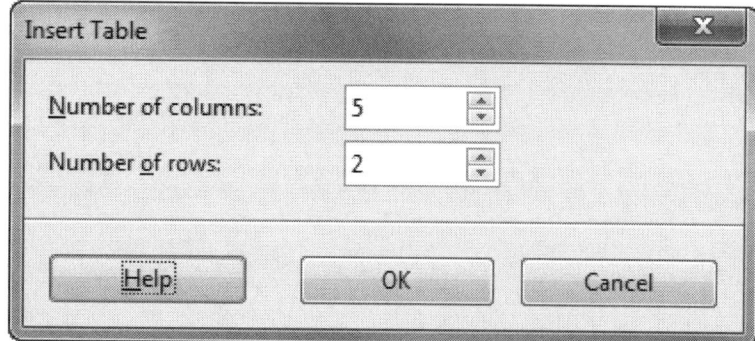

Design Notes: The difference between this and Example 8 is the additional constraint (maximum number of cells is 4095). Otherwise, the analysis here and in Example 8 is the same.

The input values must be Integers. The program will round fractional amounts, so that 8.4 rows is changed to 8 when you press Tab or Enter to exit an input field and 8.5 rows is changed to 9. The program also ignores non-numeric characters: for example, it interprets 2a3 as 23.

G.3. *Example 20: Sum Of Squares (MAX)* **on page 359**

$$SS = x_1^2 + x_2^2 + ... + x_n^2$$

(**SS** is the sum of squared values of the **n** variables, x_1 through x_n.)

The x_i's are all Floating Point.

SS ≤ 45.

G.4. *Example 21: Spreadsheet Sort Table* **on page 361**

In OpenOffice Calc, you can sort a table. The fields in the dialog are all **SortBy** fields. The first field is the primary sort key.

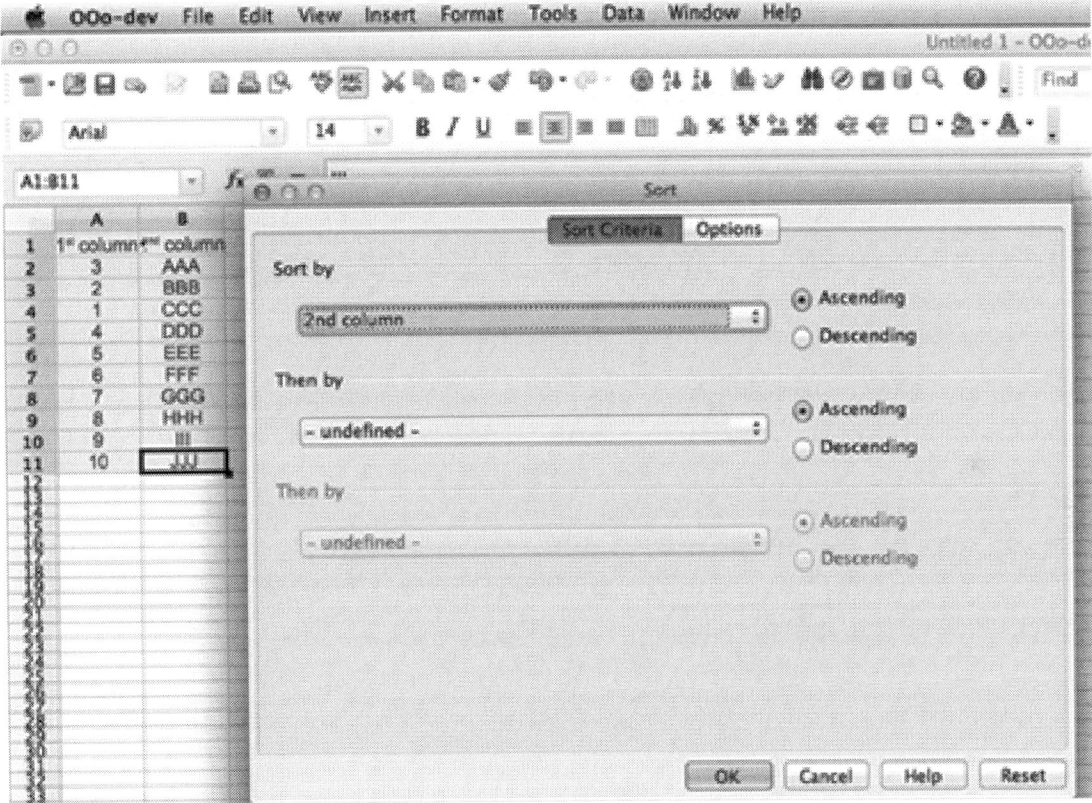

In this case, the table will be sorted by the values in the column labeled **SecondColumn**: AAA before BBB. Because this sorts the whole table, in the column labeled **FirstColumn**, 3 comes before 2 which comes before 1.

If you sort by **FirstColumn** instead, OpenOffice will sort the row with 1 before 2 before 3 but now you would see CCC before BBB before AAA in **SecondColumn**.

Note: OpenOffice is abbreviated as OOo.

A SCHEMA FOR DOMAIN TESTING

1. CHARACTERIZE THE VARIABLE

A.   Identify the potentially interesting variables.

B.   Identify the variable(s) you can analyze now. This is the variable(s) of interest.

C.   Determine the primary dimension of the variable of interest.

D.   Determine the type and scale of the variable's primary dimension and what values it can take.

E.   Determine whether you can order the variable's values (from smallest to largest).

F.   Determine whether this is an input variable or a result.

G.   Determine how the program uses this variable.

H. Determine whether other variables are related to this one.

2. ANALYZE THE VARIABLE AND CREATE TESTS

I.   Partition the variable (its primary dimension).

   - If the dimension is ordered, determine its sub-ranges and transition points.

   - If the dimension is not ordered, base partitioning on similarity.

J.   Lay out the analysis in a classical boundary/equivalence table. Identify best representatives.

K.   Create tests for the consequences of the data entered, not just the input filter.

L.   Identify secondary dimensions. Analyze them in the classical way.

M.   Summarize your analysis with a risk/equivalence table.

3. GENERALIZE TO MULTIDIMENSIONAL VARIABLES

N.   Analyze independent variables that should be tested together.

O.   Analyze variables that hold results.

P.   Analyze non-independent variables. Deal with relationships and constraints.

4. PREPARE FOR ADDITIONAL TESTING

Q.   Identify and list unanalyzed variables. Gather information for later analysis.

R.   Imagine and document risks that don't necessarily map to an obvious dimension.

H. DETERMINE WHETHER OTHER VARIABLES ARE RELATED TO THIS ONE

Another way to characterize a variable is to determine what variables it's related to and how those relationships work. Later, we'll figure out how to test those relationships (see *Section 2: Part 3: Generalize To Multidimensional Variables* on page 171). For now, the goal is simply to identify the related variables.

HOW CAN YOU IDENTIFY POTENTIALLY-RELATED VARIABLES?

Some variables are obviously related:

- The value of one influences the value of another or
- The values of two jointly influence the value of a third or
- The values of two jointly determine a decision (the path the program will follow).

Most variables are unrelated. When variables are completely unrelated, there's little reason to test them together. However, sometimes variables that seem unrelated actually are related. Sometimes the relationship is an emergent property of the software's design. Other times, the relationship arises out of a coding error.

For example:[30]

- An early version of Quicken would crash if you searched its database for a nonexistent cheque, but only if your system was running the Microsoft Intellisense keyboard driver.

- In the early 1990's, 1600x1200 was high resolution for a display and 600 dpi was high resolution for a printer. We tested a program called Calendar Creator with each of these settings and found no problem. In the field, however, the program crashed when customers set their default printer to high resolution, their display resolution to 1600×1200 and then attempted print preview. Both the printer driver and the video driver were attempting to store temporary data in the same area of memory.

Both of these illustrate unexpected (bug-caused) combinations of variables.

You won't know about unexpected relationships early in testing. You'll discover them as you test. These discoveries illustrate something that is easy to misunderstand about this approach.

---

*Our sequence from A to R looks very organized. We made it look like a step-by-step sequence because that was our best way to make a coherent description of our approach. However, in practice, you'll skip back and forth through these tasks, adding new ideas as you think of them and information as you discover it. The list **looks** linear, but the process, in practice, is not.*

---

30 Morven Gentleman describes an excellent example of dependencies among elements in an array or a linked list:
"The example that comes to my mind, from use in a class of students exactly like your target audience, is an array where the rows form a sequence in time of directives. Each directive specifies what time to allocate a specific resource or what time to de-allocate a specific resource. A resource can only be de-allocated once and must have been allocated previously. The intended computation on the array is to produce a histogram of how many resources are allocated what percentage of the time. As I recall, none of my students coded this correctly the first time, although they did seem to comprehend the task and the dependency."

Identifying variables that are supposed to be related (and some that are related even though they're not supposed to be) is a straightforward task *if you have the source code and the time to analyze it.* If you can read the code, you can identify a variable (call it Variable **A**), you can see where the program sets the value of **A**, where it uses **A** in calculations, where it compares other variables to **A**, where it passes **A** to a method and where it displays, prints or saves **A**.

However, most testers don't have the code or have only some of it or don't have the time to read it. If that's your situation, you'll be working with incomplete information. As a result, your evaluation will be incomplete. It will probably have errors. It will evolve over time.

We can present some heuristics for spotting variables that are probably related to each other or probably worth testing together. Heuristics are useful, but they're never perfect decision rules (Koen, 1985). When relying on heuristics:

- You will sometimes identify combinations that yield little information of interest when you test the variables together, and
- You will sometimes miss combinations that cause the program to fail.

Heuristics are imperfect, but this is the best we can offer. We suggest that you test variables together when:

- The value of one is passed to the other.
- One constrains the other.
- The value of one is causally affected by the other.
- Variables operate together to have a joint effect.
- The variables are subject to a common risk, including loss of access to a common resource.
- The variables (or the functions that are driven by them) compete for a common resource.
- There is a historical relationship among the variables.
- Some values of the variables are commonly combined in the marketplace and so failure would carry serious market risk.
- You have a hunch that it might be interesting to look at them together.

VALUE OF ONE PASSED TO THE OTHER

Most programs are written as a collection of methods (you might have learned to call them subroutines or functions). When the program calls the method, it passes data to it. For example, imagine a function that calculates the square of a value. Suppose you pass Variable **A** to this method. If **A** = 3, the method will return 9. The method defines its own variables. It has a variable (call it **B**) that receives its value from **A**. The method does what it does with **B** to achieve its result.

Suppose the method changes the value of **B** while doing its calculations:

- After copying the value of **A** into **B**, the program might treat these as independent variables (this is called *passing by value*).
- The program might keep **A** and **B** linked, so that any change in **B** effects the same change in **A** (this can be described and implemented in several ways, but the most common is *passing by reference*).

CONSTRAINT RELATIONSHIPS

We'll consider four classes of constraints in *Chapter P. Analyze Non-Independent Variables. Deal with Relationships and Constraints* on page 201. Those classes are:

- *Constrained to a range.* The value of one variable limits the range of values of the second. For example, Variable **B** might have to be always less than Variable **A**.

- *Must calculate to a constant value.* The result of a calculation involving all of the variables must be a constant. For example:

  > This paragraph is set with fully-justified margins. That means that every line (except the last) starts and ends at the same distance from the page's right and left margins. The widths of all the characters on the line and the distances between all of them have to be adjusted to keep the total length of the line constant.

- *Variables must be equal.* Once the value of one variable is specified, the other variable must match it. For example, in an accounting system, the values of several calculated variables are checked against each other. If they don't match, there's a problem. Typically the problem is a data entry error, but if the entered data are correct, the program has an error.

- *Selection from a list.* One variable might restrict the list of options available to the next. For example, the program might specify that **B** must be in the same list as **A** or must be in a different list from **A** or (as we'll see in the discussion of Example 26), the choice of **A** might determine which list you pick **B** from.

CAUSAL EFFECT

You have a causal relationship if a change in the value of one variable results in a change in the value(s) of the other(s). We discussed these types of relationships in *Chapters F. Determine Whether this is an Input Variable or a Result* on page 95, *K. Create Tests for the Consequences of the Data Entered* on page 133 and *O. Analyze Variables that Hold Results* on page 191.

JOINT EFFECT

In this case, two (or more) variables, operating together, have a larger or different impact than they would have operating alone. For example:

- Adding a column to a table increases the number of cells by the current `NumberOfRows`. Adding a row to a table increases the number of cells by the current `NumberOfColumns`. Both of these are linear increases: add 5 rows and the number of cells increase by 5 times what you get if you add 1 row.

  If you add a row *and* a column, the effect is multiplicative. You are multiplying more rows times more columns.

  Together, these consume memory and time. The program takes longer to recalculate the values of the cells. If any other processes are attempting to run concurrently, they will have to deal with a busier processor.

- 2009 was a bad year for corporate travel. There were several intriguingly complex deals available. At one point, if you used a specific credit card at a specific brand of hotel, you could get a discount from the hotel, a rebate from the credit card company, a reward-point bonus from the specific travel agency that you used to book the hotel and, if you had already registered for this on the hotel company's website, you would be entered into a contest. Just using the credit card (at other hotels) would not yield these benefits, nor would booking at this hotel without this credit card.

- If you order several things at Amazon.com, how does that affect your shipping options and your shipping costs? Does it matter if some of these are books and others are other types of merchandise? Does it matter whether the goods come from Amazon's warehouses directly or from a fully separate vendor? How much (number of items, types of items) can you roll into the same shipment?

RISK IN COMMON

Two features might be subject to the same risks. For example:

- They might depend on the same code library. If the code is updated and the update brings a new bug, what features will fail because of that bug?

- They might be vulnerable to the same data distortions. Imagine having a connection to a stream of data from a remote source (such as real-time trading data from a brokerage). What applications in your system use that data? What features in those applications use that data? What gets corrupted by the corruption in that data?

Two features might require use of the same resource. If the resource becomes unavailable, both fail. "Resource" could include memory, time, money, a printer, disk space, etc. For example:

- What will be affected if you slow a system by 90%? Which features might fail? What variables should you check to notice these failures?

- Suppose the bank freezes access to your checking account and several applications deposit money, withdraw money, pay bills and create cash flow records using that account. What features will fail? What data will be outdated or corrupted?

We're writing in terms of features, but every feature uses data. It has inputs and outputs. If the feature makes errors, some of its outputs will be wrong. Some of those might be invisible for the moment (such as memory leaks or temporary variables that won't have their effect until some later calculation is made, to produce a later output) but every failure has an impact and every impact is visible in some data (an erroneous value of some variable) somewhere at some time.

COMPETITION FOR A COMMON RESOURCE

Sometimes two features (and their associated variables) compete for the same resources. For example:

- They might both be attempting to send data to the printer at the same time or to the database or to an external application.

- They might both need more processing time now, so they can send a result to a remote process before it times them out.

- The Calendar Creator bug illustrated a classic competition for resources. Both settings (high-resolution video, high-resolution print) caused the system to store temporary data in a seemingly-available area of memory. Both used the same area, clobbering each other's data.

You could think of this as a special case of a common risk, but we find it helpful to think of cases in which a lack of resources will cause hardship for both features (common risk) as different from cases in which one feature's grabbing of the resource creates a problem for the other. These might not be different in principle, but they lead us to different ideas when brainstorming.

HISTORICAL RELATIONSHIP

If the program has a history of bugs that involve several variables, you should test them together in its subsequent versions.

It is useful to understand the relationships among these variables, to have a theory about why they would be involved together in these failures. However, whether you have that understanding or not, the historical pattern makes this testing imperative.

We've been shocked at the number of times we've seen test groups ignore help desk data or external-technical support data because the failure patterns coming from the field didn't map to the test group's theories about what was important to test. There's a different way to look at this—if the program is failing in the field in ways the test group didn't imagine during testing, the problem is with the test group's theories, not with the defective use of the product by the customers.

FROM EXAMPLE 6: TAX TABLE

In 1993, the Internal Revenue Service calculated taxes based on this table (Beizer, 1995, p. 151):

Income Range	Tax
$0 < \texttt{TaxableIncome} \leq \$22100$	$0.15 \times \texttt{TaxableIncome}$
$\$22100 < \texttt{TaxableIncome} \leq \$53500$	$\$3315 + 0.28 \times (\texttt{TaxableIncome} - 22100)$
$\$53500 < \texttt{TaxableIncome} \leq \$115000$	$\$12107 + 0.31 \times (\texttt{TaxableIncome} - 53500)$
$\$115000 < \texttt{TaxableIncome} \leq \$250000$	$\$31172 + 0.36 \times (\texttt{TaxableIncome} - 115000)$
$\$250000 < \texttt{TaxableIncome}$	$\$79772 + 0.396 \times (\texttt{TaxableIncome} - 250000)$

This example illustrates a causal relationship. The value of `Tax` is determined by the value of `TaxableIncome`.

FROM EXAMPLE 10: THE CIRCLE

Consider a circle defined by $x_1{}^2 + x_2{}^2 = 100$. Some of the points on this circle are (0, 10), (6, 8), (8, 6), (10, 0), (8, -6), (6, -8), (0, -10), (-6, -8), (-8, -6), (-10, 0), (-8, 6) and (-6, 8).

Consider these sets:

(a) $\{ (x_1, x_2) | x_1{}^2 + x_2{}^2 = 100 \}$ (the circle)

(b) $\{ (x_1, x_2) | x_1{}^2 + x_2{}^2 < 100 \}$ (the points inside the circle)

(c) $\{ (x_1, x_2) | x_1{}^2 + x_2{}^2 > 100 \}$ (the points outside the circle)

(d) $\{ (x_1, x_2) | x_1{}^2 + x_2{}^2 \leq 100 \}$ (the circle and points inside it)

(e) $\{ (x_1, x_2) | x_1{}^2 + x_2{}^2 \geq 100 \}$ (the circle and points outside it)

In each case, x_1 and x_2 constrain each other. For example:

- In set (a), the value of x_1 is constrained to two values by x_2 (and vice-versa). For example, if $x_2 = 6$, then x_1 must be 8 or -8.

- In set (b), the value of x_1 is constrained to a range by x_2 (and vice-versa). For example, if $x_2 = 6$, then x_1 must be between $-8 + \Delta$ and $8 - \Delta$.

  Notation reminder: Δ is the smallest difference between two numbers that can be recognized in this type of data. For Single-Precision Floating-Point numbers like the ones we're working with (in a range from 1 to 100 or -1 to -100), Δ is about 0.0000001. For higher-precision numbers, Δ is smaller. For more information, see *Floating Point* on page 72.

- The analyses for the inequalities in sets (c), (d) and (e) are essentially the same as for set (b).

FROM EXAMPLE 26: INSTALL PRINTER SOFTWARE

The Microsoft Install Printer Software dialog installs the driver for the printer you select. There are a few thousand Windows-compatible printers. In this dialog, selecting the manufacturer brings up a list of printers made by that manufacturer.

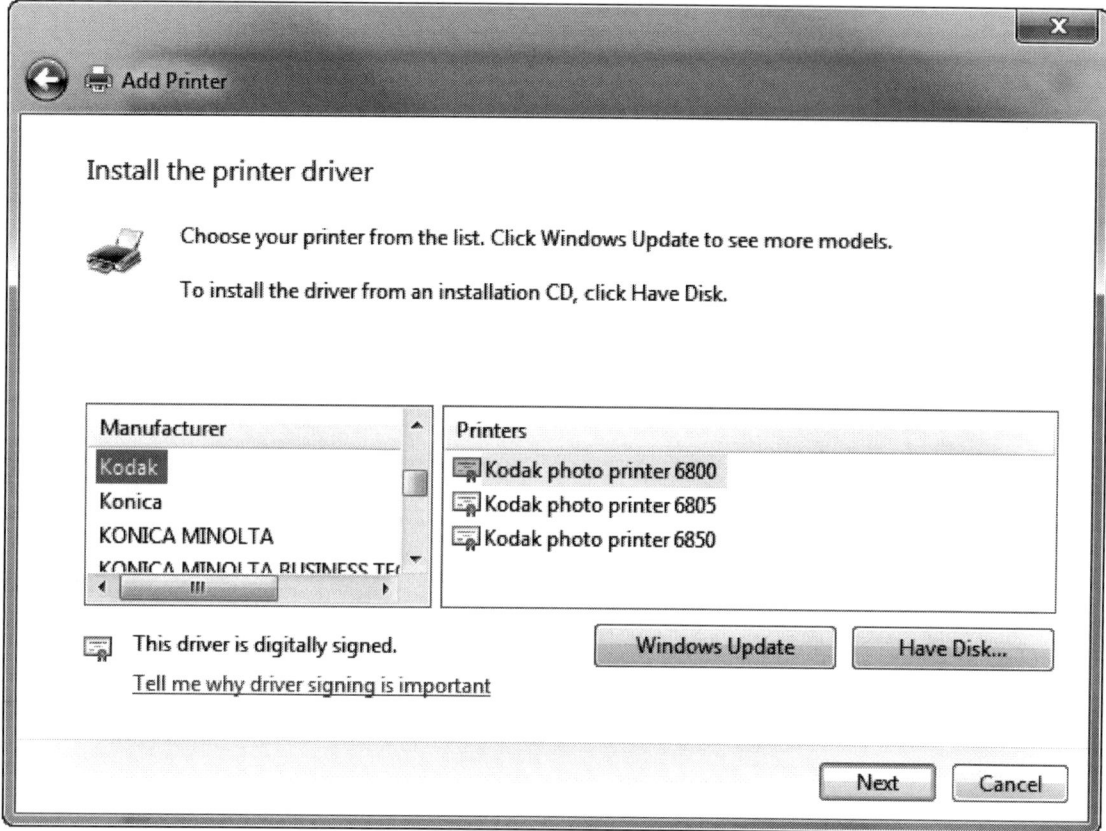

In this example, the selection of the printer manufacturer constrains the displayed printers to a range. The program displays only the printers made by that manufacturer.

EXERCISES: PART 1-H

Please identify the variables and describe any relationships among them.

H.1. *Example 13: Sum of Two Integers* **on page 315**

A program adds two Integer numbers, which you enter. Each number should be one or two digits. Analyze this in terms of the paired inputs (**FirstNumber, SecondNumber**) or in terms of the output (**Sum**). The **Sum** will also be an Integer.

H.2. *Example 9: Create Table (Max Cells)* **on page 289**

In OpenOffice (OOo) Impress, you can create a table. With this dialog, you set the starting numbers of rows and columns. Suppose the maximum number of cells in the table is 4095.

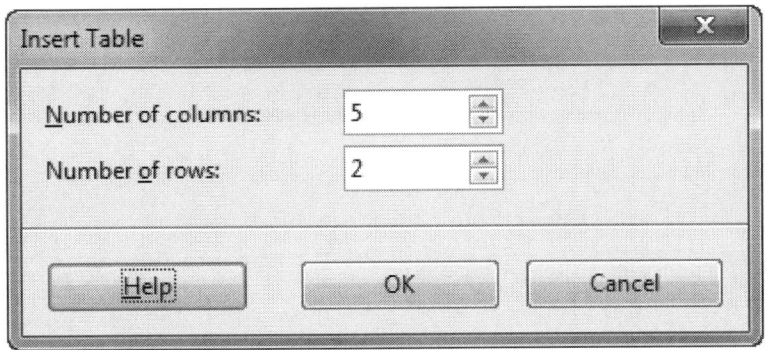

H.3. *Example 22: NextDate* **on page 373**

"**NextDate** is a function of three variables: month, day and year. It returns the date of the day after the input date." (Jorgensen, 2008, p. 22).

Jorgensen limits the year to the range $1812 \leq year \leq 2012$ and of course $1 \leq day \leq 31$ and $1 \leq month \leq 12$. If the user enters a bad date, the program rejects it with a "bad date" message.

SECTION 2. PART 2: ANALYZE THE VARIABLE AND CREATE TESTS

The Part 1 tasks characterized the variable. Now you know what the variable is, what the program does with it and what other variables interact with it.

Now it's time to figure out how to test it.

The tasks of this Part are:

I. Partition the variable (its primary dimension).

    — If the dimension is ordered, determine its sub-ranges and transition points.

    — If the dimension is not ordered, base partitioning on similarity.

J. Lay out the analysis in the classical boundary/equivalence table. Identify best representatives.

K. Create tests for the consequences of the data entered, not just the input filter.

L. Identify secondary dimensions. Analyze them in the classical way.

M. Summarize your analysis with a risk/equivalence table.

You're not going to be able to do all of these for every variable. For example, if you don't know how the program uses the variable, you can't do Task K.

PRACTICAL CONSIDERATIONS IN WORKING WITH SECONDARY DIMENSIONS

We provide examples of lists of secondary dimensions at:

- *Secondary Dimensions for Integers* on page 153.
- *Secondary Dimensions for Fixed-Point Variables* on page 157.
- *Secondary Dimensions for Floating-Point Variables* on page 160.
- *Secondary Dimensions for Strings* on page 166.

In practice, we often skip the classical analysis of secondary dimensions and move directly to the risk/equivalence table (combine Task L with Task M). We separate tasks L and M in this book because we've found that inexperienced testers and students find it hard to jump directly to the risk/equivalence table.

- Task L helps them gain experience identifying secondary dimensions and understanding their range and equivalence classes.
- When they have that information, moving them to the new table (Task M) is easier.

CREATING THESE LISTS

The examples we provide are very long. If these inspire you to create secondary-dimension lists for other types of data, set some time aside for it. These were the products of several brainstorming sessions among different groups of people. They evolved over time. If you are working alone or in a small, time-pressed group, it is handy to write a short list or concept map on a flipchart page (leave most of the page empty) and add new ideas as you think of them or as visitors suggest them. A few months later, you'll probably have a great list.

PRIORITIZING YOUR TESTS

We suggest that you consider a critical question of scope:

With so many possible tests, should you really run them all?

Maybe.

If you consider it important to run all (or most) of these, we suggest that you adopt an iterative method, running some tests on each build of the software until you have covered the full set.

Imagine creating a table to structure manual testing of a variable, that lists tests for each secondary dimension. For example, see *The Risk/Equivalence Table (Integers)* on page 155.

- In the first build of the software, run a few of these tests. Mark the ones you tested.

- In your second iteration of testing, run a few of the other tests.

- In the third iteration, choose a few more tests.

In this way, you do regression testing every build (you retest the same area of the program) but you test for different risks. If you test enough builds, you cover all the cases, at least once each.

However, there are a lot of *other* possible tests of this program. Maybe it would be interesting to learn whether the program can actually do what it is supposed to do.

For example, if you're testing a computer game, you want the program to correctly process your offer of 100 pieces of silver for that special sword. But maybe you should also spend time trying out the program's feel when you duel. How's the animation? Sound effects? What happens when another swordsman joins the fight?

Which would stop you from ever playing the game again?

- The program crashes if you offer a00 pieces of silver for the sword (that is, it crashes on an invalid input), or

- Distortions in the graphics create a situation in which you duck under the other guy's sword, you see the sword pass over your avatar's head, but the game says the other guy chopped your head off and killed you.

If you would be grumpier about losing the sword fight, maybe you should spend more time testing things like that even if that leaves less time for testing input filters.[31]

USING STANDARD LISTS FOR SECONDARY DIMENSIONS

In practice, domain testing is applicable when you're writing the code or later, when you're running system tests of the code.

- ***If you're writing the code,*** consider creating a collection of filtering methods that you can call any time you deal with data of a certain type. For example, create a standard structure for processing Integers that includes code to check for many types of bad input and call this whenever you deal with Integer input. You can also create a standard battery of unit tests to try out the filter's effectiveness. Good unit testing will significantly reduce the need for the simple, but time-consuming, tests at the system level.

---

31 See Black (2007) for analysis of the hypothetical Grays and Blues game that also raises these types of tradeoffs.

- *If you're doing system testing after the programmers have done extensive unit testing of their variables,* it will be unnecessary and wasteful to do thorough testing of secondary dimensions. You should do basic testing of each variable (the simple boundary tests from the Classical Analysis). Suppose you're testing a program with 100 visible variables. For any given secondary dimension, perhaps test it with 1 or 2 of these 100 variables. The goal is to spot-check the programmers' testing, to see whether they have missed a category of test.

- *If you're doing system testing and the programmers have not done extensive unit testing,* you have to do more testing. You still can't afford to test every value of potential interest of every variable. However, you will test more secondary dimensions of more variables.

An individual programmer's errors tend to be consistent. If you know who wrote what, try to teach each secondary dimension at least once per programmer. For example, if there are five programmers, you might check whether a program can handle 1000 leading spaces in front of an Integer input on five variables, each selected from the code of one programmer.

A SCHEMA FOR DOMAIN TESTING

1. CHARACTERIZE THE VARIABLE

A. Identify the potentially interesting variables.

B. Identify the variable(s) you can analyze now. This is the variable(s) of interest.

C. Determine the primary dimension of the variable of interest.

D. Determine the type and scale of the variable's primary dimension and what values it can take.

E. Determine whether you can order the variable's values (from smallest to largest).

F. Determine whether this is an input variable or a result.

G. Determine how the program uses this variable.

H. Determine whether other variables are related to this one.

2. ANALYZE THE VARIABLE AND CREATE TESTS

I. Partition the variable (its primary dimension).

- If the dimension is ordered, determine its sub-ranges and transition points.
- If the dimension is not ordered, base partitioning on similarity.

J. Lay out the analysis in a classical boundary/equivalence table. Identify best representatives.

K. Create tests for the consequences of the data entered, not just the input filter.

L. Identify secondary dimensions. Analyze them in the classical way.

M. Summarize your analysis with a risk/equivalence table.

3. GENERALIZE TO MULTIDIMENSIONAL VARIABLES

N. Analyze independent variables that should be tested together.

O. Analyze variables that hold results.

P. Analyze non-independent variables. Deal with relationships and constraints.

4. PREPARE FOR ADDITIONAL TESTING

Q. Identify and list unanalyzed variables. Gather information for later analysis.

R. Imagine and document risks that don't necessarily map to an obvious dimension.

I. PARTITION THE VARIABLE

The essence of *domain testing* is that you:

- *partition* a domain (a set of values) into subdomains (*equivalence classes*) and then
- select *representatives* of each subdomain for your tests.

We consider how to partition variables in this Chapter.

Partitioning a set involves dividing it into subsets. In mathematics, partitions don't overlap. In testing, this criterion is sometimes too strict. Sometimes, with multidimensional variables, you won't have a clear and unambiguous dividing line between classes. A subdivision can be useful even if it isn't perfect.

Example 1 presents a simple introduction. We'll review it here:

> "An Integer variable can take values in the range -999 and 999, the endpoints being inclusive. Develop a series of tests by performing equivalence class analysis and boundary value analysis on this variable."

The specified domain is { -999, ... , 999 }

Specified domain means, the program should accept these values. The program will (or should) reject all other values.

Domain testers typically partition the possible values for this variable into three sets:

- *Invalid values*: all Integers less than -999 (too small)
- *Valid values*: all Integers from -999 to 999 (the specified domain)
- *Invalid values*: all Integers greater than 999 (too large)

You can map these invalid values to the same dimension as the valid values. In other words, you can create a graph that shows the valid values and these invalid values on the same line.

In this Chapter, we're focusing on the variable's primary dimension. We'll come back to non-primary (secondary) dimensions in *Chapter L. Identify Secondary Dimensions. Analyze them in the Classical Way* on page 141.

In order to partition the variable, you must determine whether it's ordered along its primary dimension. A variable is *ordered* if you can compare any two possible values of the variable and determine whether the first is smaller, larger or equal to the other. We've discussed this in *Chapter E. Determine Whether You Can Order the Variable's Values* on page 85.

- If the dimension is ordered, partition by determining the variable's sub-ranges and transition points. (*These sets are typically non-overlapping.*)
- If the dimension is not ordered, base partitioning on similarity. (*These sets might overlap.*)

ANALYZING ORDERED DIMENSIONS

The variable that runs from -999 to 999 is typical of textbook examples used to illustrate partitioning. Because the variable is ordered, you can create three non-overlapping sets:

- A set of values that are too small.
- An intermediate set of acceptable values.
- A set of values that are too big.

Here are more examples that involve ordered variables.

FROM EXAMPLE 4: PAGE SETUP OPTIONS

The page setup function of a text editor allows a user to set the width of the page in the range of 1 to 56 inches. The `PageWidth` input field accepts (and remembers) up to 30 places after the decimal point.

The classic partitioning is:

- Too small: less than 1 inch
- Acceptable: 1-56
- Too big: greater than 56

We would add two more sets:

- Negative values
- Extremely large values

FROM EXAMPLE 6: TAX TABLE

In 1993, the Internal Revenue Service calculated taxes based on this table (Beizer, 1995, p. 151):

Income Range	Tax
$0 < $ `TaxableIncome` $\leq \$22100$	$0.15 \times$ `TaxableIncome`
$\$22100 < $ `TaxableIncome` $\leq \$53500$	$\$3315 + 0.28 \times ($ `TaxableIncome` $- 22100)$
$\$53500 < $ `TaxableIncome` $\leq \$115000$	$\$12107 + 0.31 \times ($ `TaxableIncome` $- 53500)$
$\$115000 < $ `TaxableIncome` $\leq \$250000$	$\$31172 + 0.36 \times ($ `TaxableIncome` $- 115000)$
$\$250000 < $ `TaxableIncome`	$\$79772 + 0.396 \times ($ `TaxableIncome` $- 250000)$

Consider the variable, `TaxableIncome`. The table gives this partitioning:

- Negative income
- 0 to 22100
- 22101 to 53500
- 53501 to 115000
- 115001 to 250000
- More than 250000

FROM EXAMPLE 19: SUM OF SQUARES

$$SS = x_1^2 + x_1^2 + \dots + x_n^2$$

(`SS` is the sum of squared values of the **n** variables, x_1 through x_n.)

The x_i's are all Floating Point.

The ranges for `SS` are:

- *Too small*: less than 0
- *Acceptable*: 0 through `MAXFLOAT`
- *Too large*: greater than `MAXFLOAT`

FROM EXAMPLE 28: OPENOFFICE PRINTING OPTIONS

As a contrast, here is a printing-options dialog from OpenOffice 4.

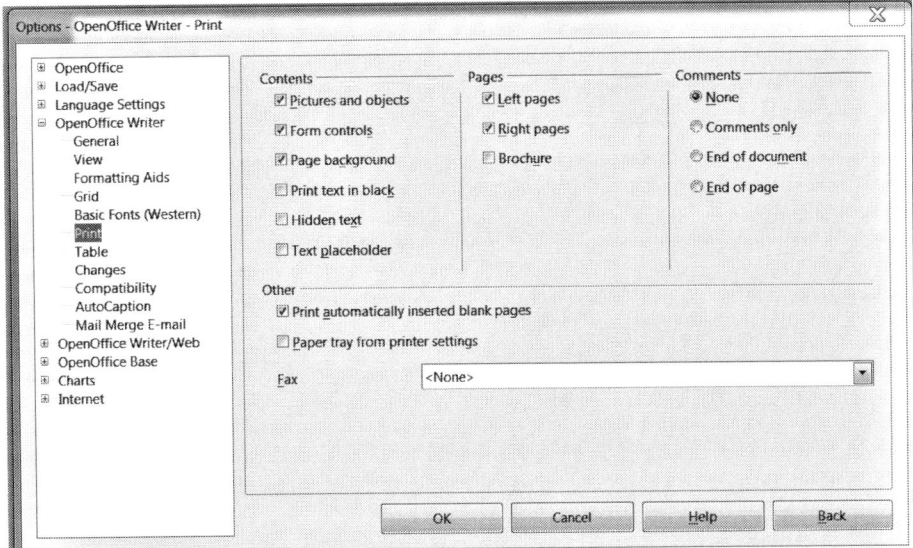

Setting aside the Fax field, these are all binary variables. There is nothing to partition here. The values are either checked or unchecked, on or off. Each partition has one and only one value.

There's no benefit to analyzing these with a domain analysis.

ANALYZING NON-ORDERED DIMENSIONS

When variables can't be ordered, partitioning involves grouping them by similarity.

Many variables are multidimensional. Ordering them can be difficult because one variable can be smaller than another on one dimension but larger than the other on a different dimension. So which is bigger than the other?

As a first example, consider laws that divide people into minors (below a threshold age) and adults (at or above the age). This could provide one fundamental partition of the population, but both sets are very large. How can you partition this further?

There are plenty of ways to subdivide the population: You could order them by income, height or weight, group them by race, gender, religious preference, sexual preference or whether they had outstanding parking tickets. *Are any of these relevant?*

The challenge with grouping by similarity is that you need to know more about the context (what the program will do with this variable, what the user will do with this program) to know what similarities are useful. If you understand the variables well, your similarities will map to specifiable risks.

FROM EXAMPLE 26: INSTALL PRINTER SOFTWARE

To test OpenOffice's compatiblity with printers, you have to install some printers.

The Microsoft Install Printer Software dialog installs the driver for the printer you select. There are a few thousand Windows-compatible printers. In this dialog, selecting the manufacturer brings up a list of printers made by that manufacturer.

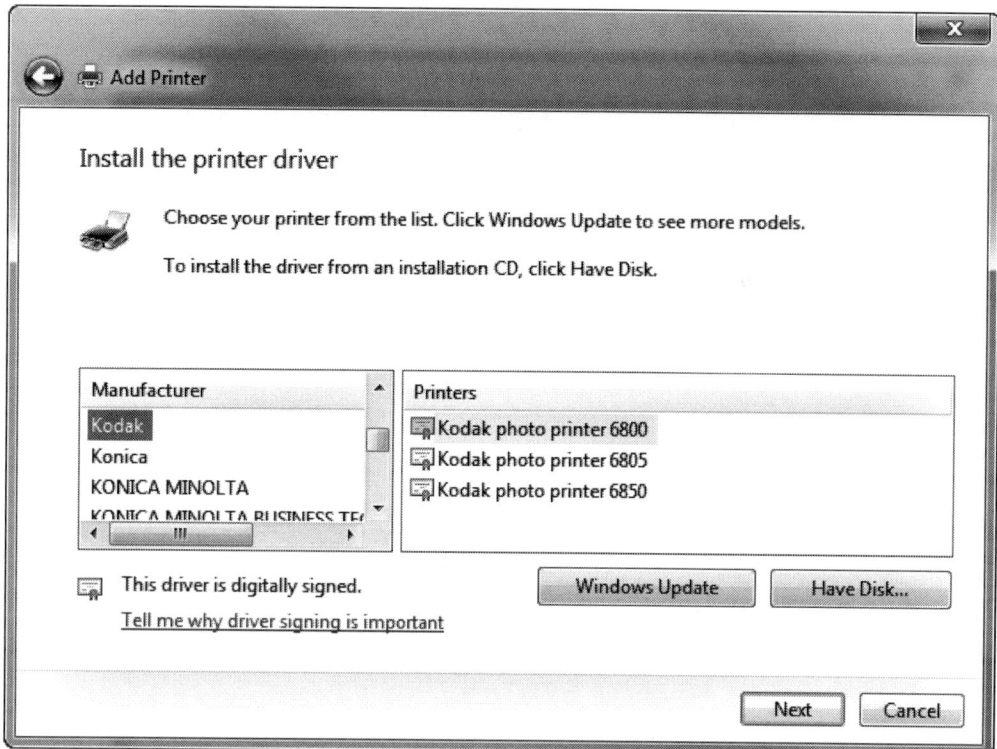

There is no natural ordering for these printers (or their drivers). For example, neither the name nor the file size has any relevance to whether the printer will work when an application, like OpenOffice, sends it data to print.

Instead, you can group printers by similarity, testing only one printer (or a few) from each group.

Kaner, Falk & Nguyen (1993) discussed this type of analysis in 25 pages of detail, laying out a strategy for organizing compatibility testing with printers, video cards, mice, network cards, scanners and any other type of peripheral.

In summary, they recommended:

- Test for device-independent, functionality errors first, then
- Test for device-class-specific errors, then
- Test for driver-class specific errors, then
- Test for errors that arise only with a specific (e.g., printer) model, then
- Test for errors that arise when this device is used in conjunction with another one (such as high-resolution print preview to a high-resolution display).

A key lesson from the discussion of printers is that the more you know about the variable you're analyzing (in this case, printers and their drivers), the better you'll be at recognizing similarities, partitioning, and picking best representatives.

We discuss this in more detail in the main presentation of Example 26.

FROM EXAMPLE 24: NOTEPAD OPEN FILE DIALOG

The Open File dialog from Notepad:

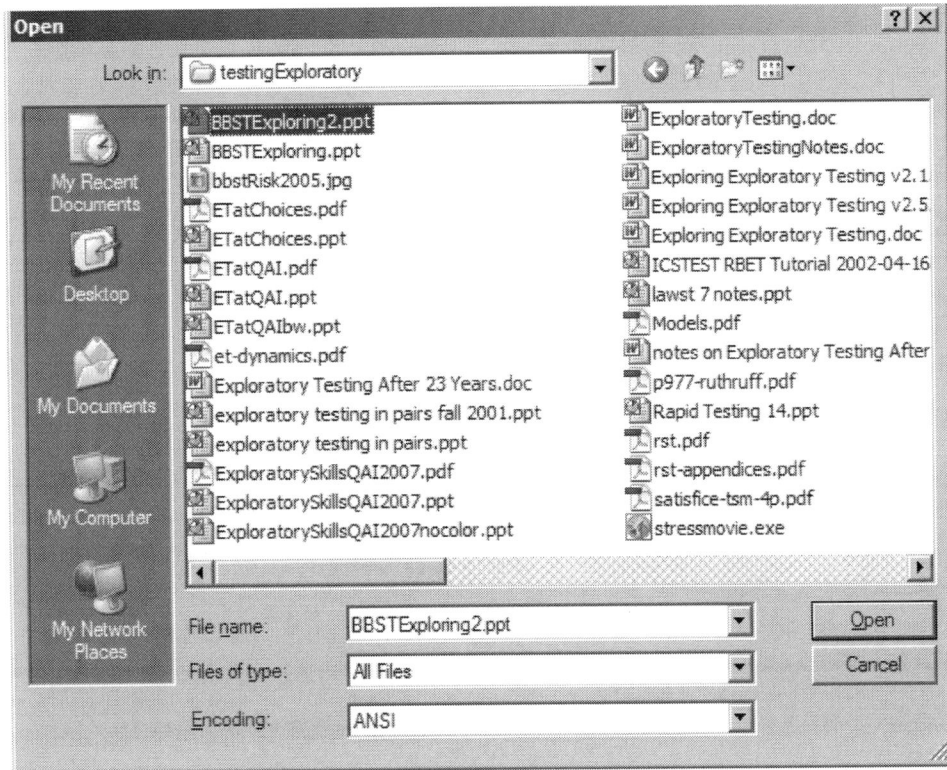

A common initial reaction is that there is no obvious way to create equivalence classes and pick useful boundaries and tests on the basis of file names.

- However, if you understand how the operating system processes file name strings, groupings based on characters in the file name string are possible. See Rollison 2007a-c, which we will study in *Example 24: Notepad Open File Dialog* on page 381.

- On further thinking, you might also consider that the file name often carries information about how data are stored in the file. It might make sense to create an equivalence class of all files in pdf format and another class for all the files in plain text format. To the extent that file names can be counted on as specifiers of file types, you can subdivide on the basis of this aspect of the name.

Notice two things about categorizing on the basis of file name/type:

1. The file names are nominal-scaled but by convention they carry information about the way their contents are organized. You can group pdf files together and say that pdfs are different from txts are different from docs, but there is no obvious system by which you could say that pdfs are bigger or better or in some other way more or less than txts or docs. There is grouping, but no ordering.

2. The mapping from file name to file type is imperfect. You can name any file with an extension .pdf. That doesn't *make* its internal format a Portable Document Format. All the name

does is create an *expectation* that the internal format is a certain kind. (Of course, creating a mismatch between the expected format and the actual format might be an excellent tactic for exposing failures in programs that assume perfect correspondence between file names and types.)

You can partition on the basis of file types. Imagine a set of 10 pptx files. Which would be the best representative?

EXERCISES: PART 2-I

Please partition the key variable(s) in each question below:

I.1. *Example 15: Mailing Labels* **on page 325**

A program prints mailing labels. The first line of the label is the person's name. The program builds the name from three fields, **FirstName**, **MiddleName** and **LastName**. Each field can hold up to 30 characters. The label can be up to 70 characters wide.

I.2. *Example 29: Select And Flip Picture* **on page 411**

In OpenOffice Impress (3.0), you can select a picture on a slide and then flip it vertically or horizontally.

This photo by Marc St. Gil is part of the Environmental Protection Agency's DOCUMERICA series. The National Archives identifier is 207/27/012387.

A SCHEMA FOR DOMAIN TESTING

1. CHARACTERIZE THE VARIABLE

    A. Identify the potentially interesting variables.

    B. Identify the variable(s) you can analyze now. This is the variable(s) of interest.

    C. Determine the primary dimension of the variable of interest.

    D. Determine the type and scale of the variable's primary dimension and what values it can take.

    E. Determine whether you can order the variable's values (from smallest to largest).

    F. Determine whether this is an input variable or a result.

    G. Determine how the program uses this variable.

    H. Determine whether other variables are related to this one.

2. ANALYZE THE VARIABLE AND CREATE TESTS

    I. Partition the variable (its primary dimension).

       – If the dimension is ordered, determine its sub-ranges and transition points.

       – If the dimension is not ordered, base partitioning on similarity.

J. Lay out the analysis in a classical boundary/equivalence table. Identify best representatives.

    K. Create tests for the consequences of the data entered, not just the input filter.

    L. Identify secondary dimensions. Analyze them in the classical way.

    M. Summarize your analysis with a risk/equivalence table.

3. GENERALIZE TO MULTIDIMENSIONAL VARIABLES

    N. Analyze independent variables that should be tested together.

    O. Analyze variables that hold results.

    P. Analyze non-independent variables. Deal with relationships and constraints.

4. PREPARE FOR ADDITIONAL TESTING

    Q. Identify and list unanalyzed variables. Gather information for later analysis.

    R. Imagine and document risks that don't necessarily map to an obvious dimension.

J. LAY OUT THE ANALYSIS IN THE CLASSICAL TABLE. IDENTIFY BEST REPRESENTATIVES

The essence of domain testing is that you

- *partition* a domain (a set of values) into subdomains (*equivalence classes*), then
- select *representatives* of each subdomain for your tests.

In this Chapter, we're looking at the variable's primary dimension. We've partitioned the variable. Now it's time to select best representatives (the boundary cases and other interesting special cases) of each partition. We also discussed this in the Introduction, at *I. Partition the variable (its primary dimension)* on page 7 and *An Analogy: How Domain Testing is Like Opinion Polling* on page 44.

In the course of this analysis, we're working with many related items: a variable, its equivalence classes, their boundaries and other special values and perhaps notes on the types of bugs to look for when testing this variable. We find it useful to organize this information into a table that shows the items and their relationships:

- For a straightforward analysis of the primary dimension of a single ordered variable, we prefer the classical boundary/equivalence table. This provides a clear structure that is easy to understand and easy to teach.

- As we add secondary dimensions to the analysis or work with multidimensional variables, the classical table can become confusing. With greater complexity, we prefer the risk/ equivalence class table.

The next two examples show the simple analysis on both tables. To our eyes, the classical table presents the information more clearly and more concisely. We'll look at examples where the risk/equivalence table shines in *Chapter M. Summarize Your Analysis with a Risk / Equivalence Table* on page 151.

FROM EXAMPLE 3: SUNTRUST VISA

SunTrust issues Visa credit cards with credit limits in the range of $400 to $40000. A customer is not to be approved for credit limits outside this range. A customer can apply for the card using an online application form in which one of the fields requires that the customer type in his/her desired credit limit.

The primary variable is the `DesiredCreditLimit`, whose potential valid values are $400 to $40000. These are money values, so we suppose that 401.50 is as valid as 401 or 402, but we'll do the analysis both ways (Integer or Fixed-Point):

THE CLASSICAL BOUNDARY/EQUIVALENCE TABLE

Variable	Valid case equivalence class	Invalid case equivalence class	Boundaries and special cases	Notes
`DesiredCreditLimit`	400 to 40000		400	
			40000	
		< 400	399.99	If Fixed-Point variables are accepted
			399	If only Integers are accepted
		> 40000	40000.01	If Fixed-Point variables are accepted
			40001	If only Integers are accepted

The classical table shows the three equivalence classes and their boundaries with one test (one boundary) per line:

- The first two lines show the valid class (the specified domain) and its lower and upper boundaries.
- The next lines show two invalid classes and boundary tests associated with each.

Now, look at the same thing with the risk-focused table:

THE RISK/EQUIVALENCE TABLE

Variable	Risk (potential failure)	Classes that should not trigger failure	Classes that might trigger failure	Test cases (best representatives)	Notes
DesiredCreditLimit	misclassifies valid values	< 400	400-40000	400	
		> 40000		40000	
	mishandles values that are too small	≥ 400	< 400	399.99	
				399	
	mishandles values that are too large	≤ 40000	> 40000	40000.01	
				40001	

The risk/equivalence table adds another column: Risk.

- Each entry in the risk column identifies a way the program could fail.
- For each risk, you can identify two types of equivalence classes:
  - One type includes values of the variable that can't cause this type of failure.
  - The other type includes values that might cause this type of failure. When you have a possible failure in mind, a test that can expose that failure is called ***error-revealing***. This class is the set of error-revealing tests for this type of failure.

The risk-equivalence table shows tests only from the error-revealing classes. Thus:

- For the risk that the program will mishandle values that are too small, test values less than 400.
- For the risk that the program will mishandle values that are too large, test values greater than 40000.
- For the risk that the program will misclassify valid values, test values in the specified domain (between 400 and 40000).

Both analyses lead to the same tests. We believe both analyses yield the same tests when working with the primary dimension of an ordered variable.

The risk/equivalence table adds a column but the risks listed here are the obvious ones. For this simple case, we think the table adds complexity without offering added value.

Here's another example. It's a little more complex but as long as you focus on the primary dimension, this is arguably still easier to analyze using the classical table.

FROM EXAMPLE 6: TAX TABLE

In 1993, the Internal Revenue Service calculated taxes based on this table (Beizer, 1995, p. 151):

Income Range	Tax
$0 < $ `TaxableIncome` $\leq \$22100$	$0.15 \times$ `TaxableIncome`
$\$22100 < $ `TaxableIncome` $\leq \$53500$	$\$3315 + 0.28 \times ($ `TaxableIncome` $- 22100)$
$\$53500 < $ `TaxableIncome` $\leq \$115000$	$\$12107 + 0.31 \times ($ `TaxableIncome` $- 53500)$
$\$115000 < $ `TaxableIncome` $\leq \$250000$	$\$31172 + 0.36 \times ($ `TaxableIncome` $- 115000)$
$\$250000 < $ `TaxableIncome`	$\$79772 + 0.396 \times ($ `TaxableIncome` $- 250000)$

THE CLASSICAL BOUNDARY/EQUIVALENCE TABLE

Variable	Valid case equivalence classes	Invalid case equivalence class	Boundaries and special cases	Notes
`TaxableIncome (TI)`		$TI < 0$	-1	Can you force a negative income?
	0		0	Probably treated as a special case
	$0 < TI \leq 22100$		0.01	If it accepts Floating Point
			1	
			22100	
`TaxableIncome (TI)`	$22100 < TI \leq 53500$		22100.01	
			22101	
			53500	
	$53500 < TI \leq 115000$		53500.01	
			53501	
			115000	
	$115000 < TI \leq 250000$		115000.01	
			115001	
			250000	
	$250000 < TI$		250000.01	
			250001	
		no upper bound is specified. Uh oh!	99999-lots-of-9999's?	Is there a limit?
			2^{32}	use the actual value of `MAXINT` $+ 1$
			2^{64}	use the value of `MAXLONG` $+ 1$

Thinking within the box, we ignore values below the lower bound (negative numbers) and any data type other than Integer or Currency (Fixed Point: two digits after the decimal)

We can show the same analysis (same restrictions) on the risk-focused table:

THE RISK/EQUIVALENCE TABLE

Variable	Risk (potential failure)	Classes that should not trigger failure	Classes that might trigger failure	Test cases (best representatives)	Notes
Taxable-Income (TI)	mishandles values that are too small	> 0	≤ 0	-1	If they're possible, use values < 0
				0	
	misclassifies valid values	$TI < 0$	$0 < TI \leq 22100$	0.01	
				1	
				22100	
			$22100 < TI \leq 53500$	22100.01	
				22101	
				53500	
			$53500 < TI \leq 115000$	53500.01	
				53501	
				115000	
			$115000 < TI \leq 250000$	115000.01	
				115001	
				250000	
			$250000 < TI$	250000.01	
				250001	
	mishandles values that are too large			99999-lots-of-9999's?	Is there a limit?
				2^{32}	use the actual value of **MAXINT** + 1
				2^{64}	**MAXLONG** + 1

If you stick to the primary dimension and ignore other types of errors than you'd find with a basic boundary analysis, the old and new forms of the table present the same information and the same tests. The next two examples present the classical table.

We return to the risk/equivalence table in *M. Summarize Your Analysis with a Risk / Equivalence Table* on page 151.

FROM EXAMPLE 8: CREATE TABLE (COLUMNS, ROWS)

In OpenOffice (OOo) Impress, you can create a table. With this dialog, you set the starting numbers of rows and columns.

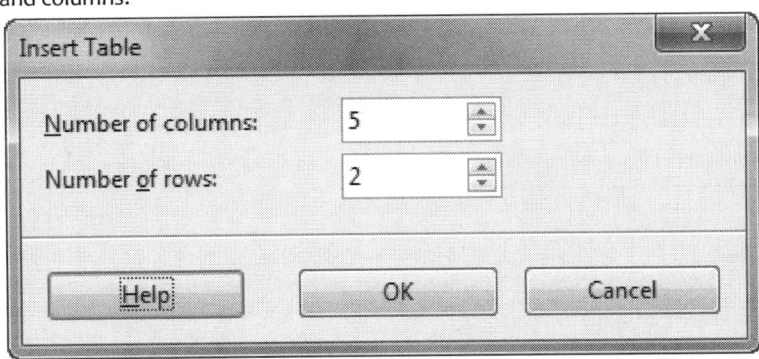

Design Notes: The input values must be Integers. The program will round fractional amounts, so that 8.4 rows is changed to 8 when you press Tab or Enter to exit an input field and 8.5 rows is changed to 9. The program also ignores non-numeric characters: for example, it interprets 2a3 as 23.

The variables of interest are **NumberOfColumns** and **NumberOfRows**. In the version of OpenOffice we tested, the valid range for both variables was 0 to 75. The program is also designed to accept out-of-bounds inputs but convert them to the valid boundary cases. Thus, an input of 76 is too big, but OpenOffice accepts it and changes it to 75.

Here is the classical table for **NumberOfRows**. Table entries for **NumberOfColumns** will be the same:

Variable	Valid case equivalence class	Invalid case equivalence class	Boundaries and special cases	Notes
NumberOfRows	1 to 75		1	
			75	
		< 1	0	converted to 1 by OpenOffice
		< 0	-1	converted to 1
		> 75	76	converted to 75
	0.500 to 75.499		0.500	OOo rounds inputs. Check Floating-Point values that should round to the valid equivalence class. 0.500 should round to 1
			75.499	should round to 75
		< 1	0.4999	will round to 0
		> 75	75.500	OOo is designed to truncate this to 75.

FROM EXAMPLE 9: CREATE TABLE (MAX CELLS)

In OpenOffice (OOo) Impress, you can create a table. With this dialog, you set the starting numbers of rows and columns. Suppose the maximum number of cells in the table is 4095.

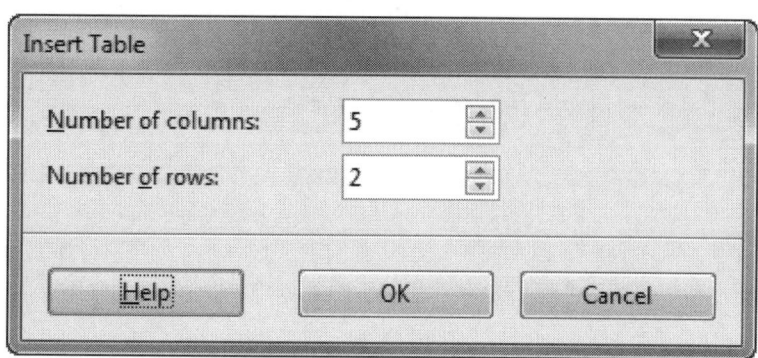

The input values must be Integers. The program will round fractional amounts, so that 8.4 rows is changed to 8 when you press Tab or Enter to exit an input field and 8.5 rows is changed to 9. The program also ignores non-numeric characters: for example, it interprets 2a3 as 23.

Example 9 is *almost* the same as Example 8. The difference is the upper limit on the number of cells. If you set both **NumberOfRows** and **NumberOfColumns** to their upper limit (75), you get 75 × 75 = 5625 cells. That's too many. Therefore, in this example, the value of **NumberOfRows** can limit the range of valid values for **NumberOfColumns** and the value of **NumberOfColumns** can limit the range of valid values for **NumberOfRows**.

Variable	Valid case equivalence class	Invalid case equivalence class	Boundaries and special cases	Notes
NumberOfRows	1 to 75		1	
			75	
			54	max when NumberOfColumns is 75. Test (rows, columns) = (54,75)
			(63,65)	4095 cells when NumberOfColumns is 65
		< 1	0	converted to 1 by OpenOffice
		< 0	-1	converted to 1
		> 75	76	converted to 75
		NumberOfRows × NumberOfColumns > 4095	(64,64)	64 rows × 64 columns = 4096 cells
	0.500 to 75.499		0.500	should round to 1
			75.499	should round to 75
		< 1	0.4999	will round to 0
		> 75	75.500	OOo will truncate this to 75

The classical table for **NumberOfRows** in Example 9 is more complex because it has to take into account the boundaries created by the **NumberOfColumns**. For example:

- If **NumberOfColumns** takes its maximum value, 75, then the maximum for **NumberOfRows** is 54.

- To test the maximum number of cells (4095), you have to add a test with 63 for one variable and 65 for the other.
- To test just beyond the maximum number of cells (4095+1), you have to test with both variables set to 64.

These tests don't show up automatically when you do a basic partitioning. You have to think about the two variables together, how they interact and what problems these interactions might raise. These tests certainly fit in the table. But if these values were missing, nothing in the structure of the table would alert you to that.

As you consider more variables and more risks, the classical table shows your tests but it *doesn't guide you to create them.* As you increase complexity, the risk/equivalence table provides more cognitive support for your work.

EXERCISES: PART 2-J

Please lay out the analysis in the boundary/equivalence table for each question below:

J.1. *Example 2: ATM Withdrawal* **on page 237**

An ATM allows withdrawals of cash in amounts of $20 increments from $20 to $200 (inclusive) (Craig & Jaskiel, 2002, p. 164).

J.2. *Example 7: Student Names* **on page 275**

A `StudentLastName` field must start with an alphabetic character (upper or lower case). Subsequent characters must be letters, numbers or spaces.

Focus your analysis on the input filter that determines whether a character is valid or invalid.

J.3. *Example 11: University Admissions* **on page 301**

Stateless University's admission standards use both high school grades and **ACT** test scores (Copeland, 2004, p. 121).

- **ACT** scores are Integers running between 0 and 36.
- **GPA** scores are Fixed-Point variables (always exactly one digit after the decimal point) running between 0.0 and 4.0.

Students are accepted if they meet any of these requirements:

- **ACT** = 36 and **GPA** $\geq$ 3.5
- **ACT** $\geq$ 35 and **GPA** $\geq$ 3.6
- **ACT** $\geq$ 34 and **GPA** $\geq$ 3.7
- **ACT** $\geq$ 33 and **GPA** $\geq$ 3.8
- **ACT** $\geq$ 32 and **GPA** $\geq$ 3.9
- **ACT** $\geq$ 31 and **GPA** = 4.0

We can represent this relationship by stating that students are admitted if

$$\textbf{ACT} + 10 \times \textbf{GPA} \geq 71$$

J.4. *Example 14: Result Of Calculations* **on page 319**

`I`, `J` and `K` are Unsigned Integers. You can enter values into `I` and `J`, but the program calculates the value of `K` = `I` × `J`. Treat `K` as the primary variable.

A SCHEMA FOR DOMAIN TESTING

1. CHARACTERIZE THE VARIABLE

    A. Identify the potentially interesting variables.

    B. Identify the variable(s) you can analyze now. This is the variable(s) of interest.

    C. Determine the primary dimension of the variable of interest.

    D. Determine the type and scale of the variable's primary dimension and what values it can take.

    E. Determine whether you can order the variable's values (from smallest to largest).

    F. Determine whether this is an input variable or a result.

    G. Determine how the program uses this variable.

    H. Determine whether other variables are related to this one.

2. ANALYZE THE VARIABLE AND CREATE TESTS

    I. Partition the variable (its primary dimension).

       – If the dimension is ordered, determine its sub-ranges and transition points.

       – If the dimension is not ordered, base partitioning on similarity.

    J. Lay out the analysis in a classical boundary/equivalence table. Identify best representatives.

K. Create tests for the consequences of the data entered, not just the input filter.

    L. Identify secondary dimensions. Analyze them in the classical way.

    M. Summarize your analysis with a risk/equivalence table.

3. GENERALIZE TO MULTIDIMENSIONAL VARIABLES

    N. Analyze independent variables that should be tested together.

    O. Analyze variables that hold results.

    P. Analyze non-independent variables. Deal with relationships and constraints.

4. PREPARE FOR ADDITIONAL TESTING

    Q. Identify and list unanalyzed variables. Gather information for later analysis.

    R. Imagine and document risks that don't necessarily map to an obvious dimension.

K. CREATE TESTS FOR THE CONSEQUENCES OF THE DATA ENTERED

*One of the distinguishing characteristics of a skilled domain tester is that she designs tests that focus on what the program will **do** with the data she is testing.*

The basic filters (the routines that reject values that are too big, too small, not numbers, etc.) are easy to imagine, easy to code, easy to test and easy to fix.

The skilled tester goes beyond these to ask whether values that are acceptable to the input function will cause problems later, as those values are processed by other functions.

We started this analysis in *Chapters G. Determine How the Program Uses this Variable* on page 99 and *H. Determine Whether Other Variables are Related to this One* on page 105. In those Chapters, our goal was simply to understand and describe the variable—to find *opportunities* to do some testing. Now we have to figure out how to design the tests.

This process is a lot easier if you have the source code (and have the time to read it). If you can read the code, you can identify a variable (call it Variable **A**), you can see where the program sets the value of **A**, where it uses **A** in calculations, where it compares other variables to **A**, where it passes **A** to a method and where it displays, prints or saves **A**.

- Any place that the program sets the value of **A**, you can test it with the usual boundaries (barely too small, minimum, 0, maximum, barely too big).

- When the program uses **A** in calculations, set the values of **A** to drive the calculated values to their extremes (too big, too small, etc.). These tests look to the boundaries of the *calculations* (the variables that hold intermediate and final results of the calculations). The values of **A** needed to produce those boundaries-of-calculations might or might not be boundaries of **A**.

- Consider another variable, **B**. When the program uses **A** to set the value of **B** or constrain the value of **B**, set **A** to values that push **B** to its limits or to special values that might pose problems for whatever uses **B**.

- When the program passes **A** to a method, set **A** to values that will change the calculation values or the flow of control (the sequence of steps executed) in the method. Try to determine which values of **A** will yield boundary cases for decisions or variables in the method and use those.

- When the program displays, prints or saves **A**, set **A** to values that might not print, display or save properly. As above look for values of **A** that reach boundaries. For example, what value might be barely too wide for the area available to display **A**?

In doing this testing, you're looking at everywhere in the program that is affected by A. This might include a lot of the program or not so much, but taken together, these are all the places you'd want to look to discover the consequences of setting **A** to any particular value.

This type of analysis is called *program slicing* (Binkley & Gallagher, 1996; Binkley & Harman, 2004; Gallagher & Lyle, 1991; Horowitz & Reps, 2013; Jorgensen, 2008; Tip, 1995; Weiser, 1984). This is the subject of a fair bit of academic research. It is still highly skilled work, not yet a task that can be done well with a routine use of a tool. But if you have access to the code and want to apply domain testing thoroughly, you'll find it useful to learn more about slicing and about the static source code analysis tools that can help you do it.

Most testers don't have access to the code or the time to read it. If that's your situation, then slicing is not for you. If you don't have the code, then when you work with Variable **A**, you won't be able to see where in the code **A** constrains or changes the value of some other variables or what values of A cause the program to take one branch instead of another. You will be working with incomplete information, sometimes making guesses. Your analysis will be incomplete, sometimes incorrect and it will evolve over time.

Black-box analysis is not as precise as glass-box slicing, but it can reveal things that you would not notice with slicing (at least, the simpler forms of it). In slicing, you'll typically look at how a change in one variable affects each other variable. You might not notice that changing one variable affects another variable that affects another variable that constrains another variable that determines the value of another variable that the program uses to calculate a value that it will display. Long chains can be too hard to trace (there are too many of them) for slicing. But if that final displayed value is important enough and if the input is conceptually related to it, then a black-box analysis is likely to encourage you to test the two variables together.

When the program uses a variable, it either displays it, prints it, saves it or uses this variable to influence the value of some other variable. In *Chapter H. Determine Whether Other Variables are Related to this One* on page 105, we described several types of influences. This list is a reminder. Consult Chapter H if you need to review the details:

- The value of one is passed to the other.
- One constrains the other.
- The value of one is causally affected by the other.
- Variables operate together to have a joint effect.
- The variables are subject to a common risk, including loss of access to a common resource.
- The variables (or the functions that are driven by them) compete for a common resource.
- There is a historical relationship among the variables.
- Some values of the variables are commonly combined in the marketplace and so failure carries serious market risk.
- You have a hunch that it might be interesting to look at them together.

Whenever you spot a relationship like this, you can change values of the variable under test to see how it affects the other variable and what the program does with that other variable.

CALCULATE THE AMOUNT TO PAY AN EMPLOYEE

Consider a program that determines how much to pay an employee for a week's work and prints the paycheck. Suppose the input variables are the number of hours worked and the hourly rate of pay. Several other variables determine the amount to be paid, such as deductions for taxes and employee benefits. If you can't read the code, you won't know exactly how those calculations are implemented or where the program makes which decisions. However, you do know a fair bit about how the program uses these variables, so you can still run tests. For example:

- You know that, for each employee, more hours worked will yield more pay.

  ○ How much pay is too much to print on a check? How much is too little? You might not know in advance exactly how many hours it will take to push a specific employee's pay to the limit, but you can test with different hours worked until you reach that limit. Is the number of hours worked reasonable for that limit? Does the program behave reasonably at the limit?

- ○ Does the program recognize partial hours? Will the program pay someone more if they work 10 hours and 1 minute than if they work 10 hours? What about 10 hours and 29 minutes? 10 hours and 31?

- You know that as income rises, tax rates change. For a given employee, you can test with different hours worked and trace the change in tax rates. You might not know exactly where the rates should change, but you can notice patterns of change that are unreasonable.

ADD COLUMNS TO A SPREADSHEET

Consider another example. Add some columns to a spreadsheet:

- This changes how wide the spreadsheet is. Add columns until the sheet becomes barely wider than a page

  - ○ What happens when you try to print the spreadsheet? Does the program spread the printout to split the columns across two pages? If so:

    - Does the formatting make sense?
    - Can you tell by looking at the printout which pages should be looked at side by side?
    - Does the program skip printing the last column?

  - ○ Can you set the program to resize the sheet (and its contents) so that it fits on one page? If so:

    - Put some long words and some wide graphics in the spreadsheet. Add columns. As the column widths shrink, what happens to them? Can the column width become too narrow to display them? What happens?

- Adding columns changes how much memory the spreadsheet takes and how long the program will take to recalculate the contents of the cells:

  - ○ As you add columns, can you run the program out of memory? How will you tell how much memory the program consumes?

  - ○ Can you set the spreadsheet to automatically recalculate its cells whenever there's a change? As you add columns, do the recalculations take longer? Do they ever get unacceptably long?

  - ○ If adding empty columns has only a small effect, what happens if you add full columns (copy filled columns and insert the copies) instead?

These ideas are incomplete, but they illustrate following the impact of a variable as the program uses it. All of these tests can be done with any value of the variable under test. That's too many possible tests. Sampling is necessary. Domain analysis can guide the selection of tests just as well here as when you test the variable's input filter.

SOLVING A SYSTEM OF LINEAR EQUATIONS

When a program does routine calculations after accepting a combination of non-boundary input data, the program might still make serious calculation errors. It is the relationship among the data, not their nearness to boundaries, that causes the trouble.

In this example, the input data are parameters that specify a system of linear equations (Holistic Numerical Methods Institute, 2010). The program will represent the linear equations as a matrix. It will then solve the equations or (if the matrix is invertible) invert the matrix. The solution to the system of equations is the set of result variables.

For an easy-to-use example of a JavaScript program that illustrates and explains this type of functionality, *see* Arsham (2010).

In our example, each equation will be defined by three numbers. We'll restrict the input fields to any Floating Point between 0 and 1000. Numbers like 1, 1.001, 2, 3.999 and 4 are clearly within this range.

A system of equations is ***ill-conditioned*** if a small change in the data results in a large change in the solution. (Kaw, 2008).

Consider the system:

$$1\mathbf{x} \quad + \quad 2\mathbf{y} \qquad = \qquad 4$$
$$2\mathbf{x} \quad + \quad 3.999\mathbf{y} \qquad = \qquad 7.999$$

The input parameters are three-tuples, in this case (1, 2, 4) and (2, 3.999, 7.999).

The solution to the system is $x = 2$ and $y = 1$.

To see that this is a solution, plug $x = 2$ and $y = 1$ into the equation:

$$1 \times \mathbf{x} + 2 \times \mathbf{y} \quad = \quad 1 \times 2 + 2 \times 1 \quad = \quad 4$$
$$2 \times \mathbf{x} + 3.999 \times \mathbf{y} = \quad 2 \times 2 + 3.999 \times 1 = \quad 7.999$$

Next, consider the almost identical equations:

$$1\mathbf{x} \quad + \quad 2\mathbf{y} \qquad = \qquad 4.001$$
$$2\mathbf{x} \quad + \quad 3.999\mathbf{y} \qquad = \qquad 7.998$$

The solution for these is very different: $\mathbf{x} = -3.999$ and $\mathbf{y} = 4.000$

Here's another small variation:

$$1.001\mathbf{x} \quad + \quad 2.001\mathbf{y} \qquad = \qquad 4$$
$$2.001\mathbf{x} \quad + \quad 3.998\mathbf{y} \qquad = \qquad 7.999$$

The solution is $\mathbf{x} = 3.994$ and $\mathbf{y} = 0.001388$. The result variables are $\mathbf{x}$ and $\mathbf{y}$.

As a result of very small changes to the multipliers of $\mathbf{x}$ and $\mathbf{y}$, you get large differences in the solved values for $\mathbf{x}$ (2, -3.999 and 3.994) and $\mathbf{y}$ (1, 4 and 0.001388). (Kaw, 2008, Chapter 4.09, p. 3).

The individual values all look fine. You aren't pushing against any *input* boundaries here. There's nothing alarming about 1.001 or 3.998.

When you're dealing with ill-conditioned systems of equations:

- Even a slight error in calculating or entering the parameters (the input values) can change the resulting calculations enormously.

- Small rounding errors in the calculations, errors that you would normally consider tolerable, can have huge consequences.

The underlying variable of interest for the system of equations is the ***condition number*** (Kaw, 2008, Chapter 4.09). A system with a condition number of 1 is said to be perfectly conditioned (National Institute of Science & Technology, 2007, Glossary) and an ill-conditioned matrix has a high condition number. Mathematicians and software engineers have worked for several decades to create collections of test-matrices, including matrices with high condition numbers (Boisvert et al., 1997; Gregory & Karney, 1969; National Institute of Science & Technology, 2007).

Matrix operations (such as solving systems of equations) are common tasks, such as in financial or medical software that report statistical analyses of business-critical or life-critical datasets. Ill-conditioned systems exist in the real world—it would be inappropriate to block users from entering them. However, by testing this software with matrices that have very high condition numbers, you can see whether the software under test reports significantly incorrect results. If so, your bug reports should lead the programmers to reimplement these functions using:

- Higher-precision arithmetic or

- Calculation heuristics that minimize rounding errors or

- Error messages that check the condition number of the matrix and warn the user that a given calculation is untrustworthy.

In the terminology of this book, the primary dimension of the input variables is the one that runs from 0 to 1000. The condition number is a secondary variable whose value depends the relationship of the three inputs. It is a result of the three inputs, but it is this result that sets the power of the test. Higher values are better representatives. The (possibly-miscalculated) matrix inverse is another result variable.

FROM EXAMPLE 15: MAILING LABELS

A program prints mailing labels. The first line of the label is the person's name. The program builds the name from three fields, **FirstName**, **MiddleName** and **LastName**. Each field can hold up to 30 characters. The label can be up to 70 characters wide.

The program might appear to be working correctly if it accepts maximum-length strings for all three names individually but it will probably overflow the mailing label when it tries to print the full name. You don't see the bug until you actually use the data that you entered. *In this case, the input boundaries aren't tightly enough coordinated to prevent a full-name string that is too long.*

Note how, in these cases, you delve into the underlying subject matter of the program. For example, you have to understand linear algebra to recognize that some equations pose more risk of error than others. You have to understand how the program uses the names to recognize the risk that the first-plus-middle-plus-last name can overflow a label.

When the skilled tester analyzes incoming data, she asks why the program needs this data, how the program will use it and what combinations of the incoming data might be especially challenging for those uses. In practical terms, it is those challenging combinations that are the best representatives of the input-data space.

FROM EXAMPLE 4: PAGE SETUP OPTIONS

For one more example, look back at the treatment of Example 4 in *Chapter G. Determine How the Program Uses this Variable* on page 99.

EXERCISES: PART 2-K

You worked with Examples 9, 11, 20 and 21 in *Chapter G. Determine How the Program Uses this Variable* on page 99. Now extend your analysis. How will you *test* these uses?

K.1. *Example 11: University Admissions* **on page 301**
Stateless University's admission standards use both high school grades and **ACT** test scores (Copeland, 2004, p. 121).

- **ACT** scores are Integers running between 0 and 36.
- **GPA** scores are Fixed-Point variables (always exactly one digit after the decimal point) running between 0.0 and 4.0.

Students are accepted if they meet any of these requirements:

- **ACT** = 36 and **GPA** ≥ 3.5
- **ACT** ≥ 35 and **GPA** ≥ 3.6
- **ACT** ≥ 34 and **GPA** ≥ 3.7
- **ACT** ≥ 33 and **GPA** ≥ 3.8
- **ACT** ≥ 32 and **GPA** ≥ 3.9
- **ACT** ≥ 31 and **GPA** = 4.0

We can represent this relationship by stating that students are admitted if

ACT + 10 × **GPA** ≥ 71

K.2. *Example 9: Create Table (Max Cells)* **on page 289**

In OpenOffice (OOo) Impress, you can create a table. With this dialog, you set the starting numbers of rows and columns. Suppose the maximum number of cells in the table is 4095.

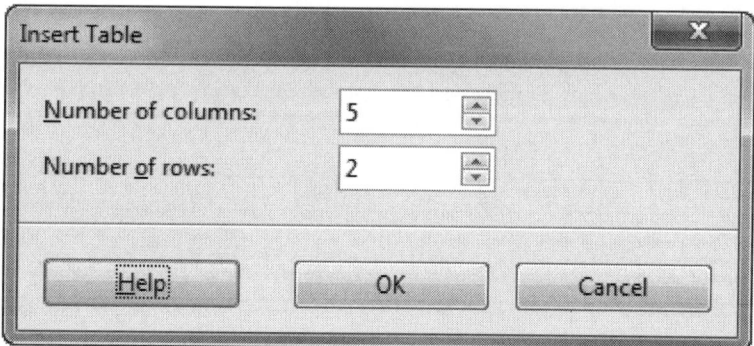

Design Notes: The difference between this and Example 8 is the additional constraint (maximum number of cells is 4095). Otherwise, the analysis here and in Example 8 is the same.

The input values must be Integers. The program will round fractional amounts, so that 8.4 rows is changed to 8 when you press Tab or Enter to exit an input field and 8.5 rows is changed to 9. The program also ignores non-numeric characters: for example, it interprets 2a3 as 23.

K.3. *Example 20: Sum Of Squares (MAX)* **on page 359**

$$SS = x_1^2 + x_2^2 + ... + x_n^2$$

(**SS** is the sum of squared values of the **n** variables, x_1 through x_n.)

The x_i's are all Floating Point.

SS ≤ 45.

K.4. *Example 21: Spreadsheet Sort Table* **on page 361**

In OpenOffice Calc, you can sort a table. The fields in the dialog are all **SortBy** fields. The first field is the primary sort key.

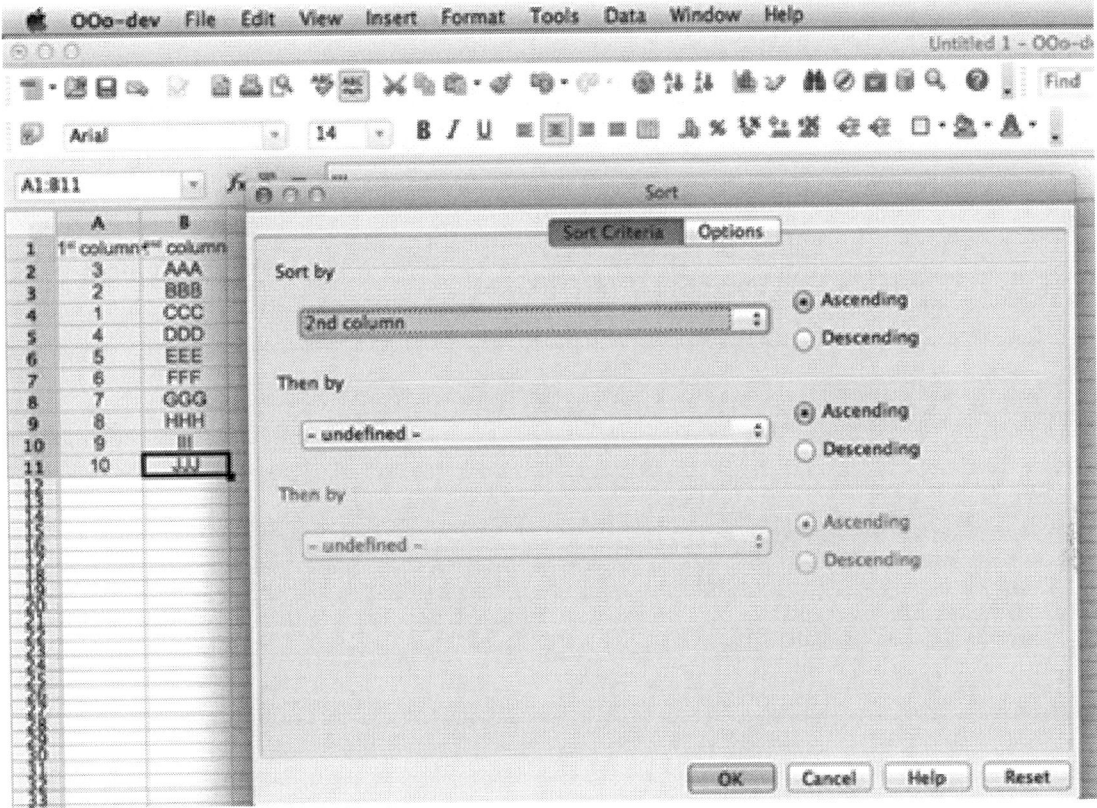

In this case, the table will be sorted by the values in the column labeled **SecondColumn**: AAA before BBB. Because this sorts the whole table, in the column labeled **FirstColumn**, 3 comes before 2 which comes before 1.

If you sort by **FirstColumn** instead, OpenOffice will sort the row with 1 before 2 before 3 but now you would see CCC before BBB before AAA in **SecondColumn**.

A SCHEMA FOR DOMAIN TESTING

1. CHARACTERIZE THE VARIABLE

A. Identify the potentially interesting variables.

B. Identify the variable(s) you can analyze now. This is the variable(s) of interest.

C. Determine the primary dimension of the variable of interest.

D. Determine the type and scale of the variable's primary dimension and what values it can take.

E. Determine whether you can order the variable's values (from smallest to largest).

F. Determine whether this is an input variable or a result.

G. Determine how the program uses this variable.

H. Determine whether other variables are related to this one.

2. ANALYZE THE VARIABLE AND CREATE TESTS

I. Partition the variable (its primary dimension).

  – If the dimension is ordered, determine its sub-ranges and transition points.

  – If the dimension is not ordered, base partitioning on similarity.

J. Lay out the analysis in a classical boundary/equivalence table. Identify best representatives.

K. Create tests for the consequences of the data entered, not just the input filter.

L. **Identify secondary dimensions. Analyze them in the classical way.**

M. Summarize your analysis with a risk/equivalence table.

3. GENERALIZE TO MULTIDIMENSIONAL VARIABLES

N. Analyze independent variables that should be tested together.

O. Analyze variables that hold results.

P. Analyze non-independent variables. Deal with relationships and constraints.

4. PREPARE FOR ADDITIONAL TESTING

Q. Identify and list unanalyzed variables. Gather information for later analysis.

R. Imagine and document risks that don't necessarily map to an obvious dimension.

L. IDENTIFY SECONDARY DIMENSIONS. ANALYZE THEM IN THE CLASSICAL WAY

Most people who organize their domain tests with a table use some version of the classical table.

As you saw in *Chapter J. Lay Out the Analysis in the Classical Table. Identify best Representatives* on page 125, the classical table is an excellent tool for showing analysis of a variable's primary dimension.

If your analysis looks only at a few secondary dimensions, it probably makes sense to stick with the classical table. This Chapter describes that use of the table.

We prefer to switch to the risk/equivalence table as our analysis expands to include more secondary dimensions and result variables based on a variable you're analyzing. **The next** *Chapter M. Summarize Your Analysis with a Risk / Equivalence Table* on page 151, **considers a broader set of secondary dimensions.**

For any given variable, you'll probably show secondary dimensions on the classical table OR the risk/equivalence table, but not both.

Because the classical table and the risk/equivalence table are alternatives that substitute for each other, we are writing the next Chapter and this one in parallel ways, discussing the same issues and working through the same examples. In this Chapter, we add a few secondary dimensions to the classical table.

In the next Chapter, we will consider a much broader set of secondary dimensions.

SECONDARY DIMENSIONS

Secondary dimensions have more to do with the program's implementation details than with the purpose of the variable.

- You can usually determine the *primary* dimension by asking what the program is designed to learn from the variable.
- You can imagine *secondary* dimensions by asking how *else* the variable could change.

Myers' (1979) classic presentation of equivalence classes instructs the reader to enter three Integers, which the program interprets as lengths of the sides of a triangle. The program determines whether these specify a scalene, isosceles or equilateral triangle:

- If they're equal, the triangle is equilateral.
- If only two sides are equal, isosceles.
- If all three sides are different (and they form a triangle), it is scalene.

The decision the program is making is what type of triangle is specified by three sides. This decision is the result variable. It's an enumerated variable. If you consider its domain, Myers' description specifies a set of three values: {scalene, isosceles, equilateral}. There is an implicit fourth value: **IsATriangle**, which can be True or False.

The input variables are the three sides of the triangle and the primary dimension of each is their length.

Myers included several tests that addressed other dimensions than length. For example, he recommended testing with:

- Non-Integers (Floating Points or letters).
- The wrong number of values (two sides or no sides or four, instead of three).
- Different orderings of the sides (try 1,2,4 then 2,1,4, then 4,1,2, etc.).

The purpose of this program is to classify triangles, not to tell the difference between entries that are Integers, Floating-Point numbers or letters. However, the data that you can enter can be non-Integer and therefore the program has to cope with this type of bad input. ***These are examples of secondary dimensions.***

Myers' example begs further analysis:

(a) What is the length in relationship to the other two sides?

(b) And therefore, which response should the program give?

These are important, but they aren't examples of secondary dimensions. They're examples of:

(a) The relationships among variables. See *Chapters H. Determine Whether Other Variables are Related to this One* on page 105 and *P. Analyze Non-Independent Variables. Deal with Relationships and Constraints* on page 201.

(b) How the program deals with result variables. See *Chapters K. Create Tests for the Consequences of the Data Entered* on page 133 and *O. Analyze Variables that Hold Results* on page 191.

The classical boundary/equivalence table handles the primary dimension very well, as you have seen in the last few chapters. The table is also useful if you want to add a few cases for a few more dimensions. Here are some examples:

FROM EXAMPLE 1: INTEGER INPUT

A data entry field will accept Integers from -999 to 999.

The stated domain of the primary dimension is {-999, 999}. The classic analysis says the interesting tests are -1000, -999, 999 and 1000.

The classical table shows this as:

Variable	Valid case equivalence class	Invalid case equivalence class	Boundaries and special cases	Notes
The input value	-999 to 999		-999	
			0	Some domain testers would skip 0. Because 0 is sometimes troublesome, test it.
			999	
		< -999	-1000	
		> 999	1000	

Testers often extend the classical table to include invalid values that aren't on the primary dimension. Common examples are:

- Letters
- Letters that can be interpreted as hexadecimal digits
- Empty input field
- Whitespace (leading or trailing spaces, tabs, etc.)

These go into the table as new rows with invalid values, like this:

Variable	Valid case equivalence class	Invalid case equivalence class	Boundaries and special cases	Notes
The input value	-999 to 999		-999	
			0	
			999	
		< -999	-1000	
		> 999	1000	
		a to z	a	misinterpret as hexadecimal?
			g	non-hexadecimal
		non-alphanumeric	/	ASCII character 47 — "0" is 48
			:	ASCII character 58 — "9" is 57
		no input	empty field	
		whitespace	<space>999	4 characters. Does it ignore spaces?
			<space>	no number, just a space
			lots of <spaces>	overflow? or ignored?

FROM EXAMPLE 3: SUNTRUST VISA

SunTrust issues Visa credit cards with credit limits in the range of $400 to $40000. A customer is not to be approved for credit limits outside this range. A customer can apply for the card using an online application form in which one of the fields requires that the customer type in his/her desired credit limit.

The primary variable is the `DesiredCreditLimit`.

The stated valid range is $400 to $40,000. Is this an Integer, a Fixed Point variable with 2 digits after the decimal point or Floating Point (any number of digits after the decimal)?

For now, suppose this is Fixed Point. Here's the classical table for the primary dimension:

Variable	Valid case equivalence class	Invalid case equivalence class	Boundaries and special cases	Notes
`DesiredCreditLimit`	400 to 40000		400.00	
			40000.00	
		< 400	399.99	
		> 40000	40000.01	

Add a secondary dimension into the mix: the number of digits after the decimal point. The classical table looks like this:

Variable	Valid case equivalence class	Invalid case equivalence class	Boundaries and special cases	Notes
Desired- CreditLimit	400.00 to 40000.00		400.00	
			40000.00	
		< 400	399.99	
		> 40000	40000.01	
		no digits after decimal point	400	The program probably handles these as valid
			40000	
		only 1 digit after the decimal point	400.1	You could try 400.0 and 40000.0 but how many times do you want to do almost exactly the same test. This tests essentially the same risk, with a new value
			39999.9	
		too many digits	400.009	If the program accepts cents, this is a boundary invalid case
			40000000etc000	Paste 1000000 digits

Now consider several secondary dimensions:

- The number of digits in the number.
- The number of digits after the decimal point.

    Let **NUMBEROFDIGITSAFTERDECIMAL** be the number of digits that are supposed to be stored after the decimal point. For example, it would be 2 for a dollars-and-cents variable. For other data, it might be larger. What does the program do when someone enters fewer or more than **NUMBEROFDIGITSAFTERDECIMAL** digits? The important thing to recognize for Fixed-Point is that this describes a maximum number of digits (maximum after the decimal point) that is distinct from the variable's overall maximum number of digits.

- **DesiredCreditLimit** is a numeric variable. Consider non-numerics:
  - Non-digits.
  - Hexadecimal numbers.
  - Upper ASCII characters.
  - Unicode values beyond traditional ASCII (UTF-8, UTF-16 and UTF-32) (*See* http://www. utf-8.com/).
  - Leading spaces.
- How many characters in **DesiredCreditLimit**:
  - 400 is 3 characters.
  - 400.00 is 6 characters (5 digits and a decimal point).
  - 40000.00 is 8 characters (7 digits and a decimal point) or 5 characters if 40000 is acceptable.
  - What about leading or trailing zeros or spaces that take the length beyond its limits?
- What about negative numbers?
- What about numbers that include characters that are normally accepted as numeric, but with a problem:

- ◦ Numbers with two or more decimal points?
- ◦ Numbers with one or more leading + signs?
- ◦ Numbers with spaces between the digits (rather than leading or trailing)?

- How many numbers can you fit in this field? (For example 1 in the field is one number and 1 2 3 is 3 numbers.)

  - ◦ Suppose 400 is an acceptable input.

    - Can you enter it twice into the field? For example, try 400<space>400 or 400<tab>400 or 400<comma>400.
    - What about values that would be valid if the variable ignored the embedded spaces? For example, try 4<space>4<space>4.

- Expressions that compute to valid inputs:

  - ◦ 399+1   Expressions that include a value (399) that is invalid on its own.
  - ◦ 400+0   Expressions that are valid whether the + is executed or ignored.
  - ◦ 4000+1   Expressions that would be valid if the + is executed but invalid if the + is ignored (interpreted as 40001).

THE CLASSICAL BOUNDARY/EQUIVALENCE TABLE

Variable	Valid case equivalence class	Invalid case equivalence class	Boundaries and special cases	Notes
Desired-CreditLimit	400.00 to 40000.00		400.00	
			40000.00	
		< 400	399.99	
		> 40000	40000.01	
		no digits after decimal point	400	The program will probably handle these as valid inputs
			40000	
		only 1 digit after the decimal point	400.1	You could try 400.0 and 40000.0 but how many times do you want to do almost exactly the same test. This tests essentially the same risk, with a new value
			39999.9	
		too many digits	400.009	If the program accepts cents, this is a boundary invalid case
			40000000etc000	Paste 1000000 digits!
		non-digits	/400	In ASCII code, **/** and **:** are the boundary non-numbers. *See* http://www.asciitable.com
			400:	
		hex	0x400	They *are* numbers
			0xA12	
			A12	

Variable	Valid case equivalence class	Invalid case equivalence class	Boundaries and special cases	Notes
	6 (or 3) to 8 (or 5) characters		400, 400.00, 40000, 40000.00	Already tested
		2 characters	40	(or 40.00)
		0 characters	press <enter> for an empty field	
		huge number		You did this already (40000000etc000)
		leading 0	040000	6 digits
		leading 0	0000etc40000	Lots of leading 0's
		leading spaces	_400000	
		negatives	-400	
			-1	

We haven't filled in all the secondary dimensions, but this table illustrates the analysis and the problem. The first four rows of the table are straightforward, but what about the others? If you didn't have the list of secondary dimensions in front of you, would you understand what all these additional test rows were about?

FROM EXAMPLE 7: STUDENT NAMES

A **StudentLastName** field must start with an alphabetic character (upper or lower case). Subsequent characters must be letters, numbers or spaces.

This is a string:

- The first character is constrained to be only letters (upper or lower).
- Subsequent characters can be letters, numbers or spaces.

Partitioning:

- **FirstLetter**:
  - ASCII 65-90 and 97-122 (A-Z and a-z).
  - We'll treat anything out of the set {65-90, 97-122} as invalid.
- Subsequent characters:
  - ASCII 32, 48 to 57, 65-90 and 97-122 (space, 0-9, A-Z and a-z).
  - Anything out of the set {32, 48-57, 65-90, 97-122} is invalid.

The classical table looks like this:

Variable	Valid case equivalence class	Invalid case equivalence class	Boundaries and special cases	Notes
FirstLetter	65 - 90 (A - Z)		65 (A)	
			90 (Z)	
		< 65	64 (@)	

Variable	Valid case equivalence class	Invalid case equivalence class	Boundaries and special cases	Notes
		91 - 96	91 ([ )	
			96 (`)	
	97 - 122 (a - z)		97 (a)	
			122 (z)	
		> 122	123 ({)	ignore upper ASCII and Unicode beyond first 127 chars
All other letters		0 - 31	0 (null byte)	non-printing character
			31 (us)	non-printing character
	32		32 (space)	
		33 - 47	33 (!)	
			47 (/)	
	48 - 57		48 (0)	
			57 (9)	
		58 - 64	58 (:)	
			64 (@)	
	65 - 90 (A - Z)		65 (A)	
			90 (Z)	
		91 - 96	91 ([ )	
			96 (`)	
	97 - 122 (a - z)		97 (a)	
			122 (z)	
		> 122	123 ({)	

Now consider secondary dimensions.

The most important one is probably `length` of the string.

No maximum length was specified, but the system will enforce *some* maximum. Otherwise there will be interesting problems in formatting reports and in allocating storage for the unbounded name field, which is probably the key field of this database. We'll call this limit **MAXNAME**. Probably it's 30 characters or less.

That adds the following tests:

Variable	Valid case equivalence class	Invalid case equivalence class	Boundaries and special cases	Notes
String length	1 to **MAXNAME**		1 character	
			MAXNAME	
		Too short	0 characters	is an empty name invalid?
		> Too long	**MAXNAME** + 1	

Variable	Valid case equivalence class	Invalid case equivalence class	Boundaries and special cases	Notes
			127	common buffer maximum. 127, 128, 255, 256 are interesting cases (but maybe not invalid) no matter what value in **MAXNAME**
			128	
			255	common buffer maximum
			256	2^8 (8-bit word + 1) boundary
			65536	2^{16}
			16777216	2^{24} if there's going to be an overflow, 16 million characters will probably do it.
			4294967296	2^{32}

This is just one secondary dimension (string `length`). The table shows it clearly, but what happens when you add others? If you didn't have the list of secondary dimensions in front of you, would you understand what all those additional test rows were about?

EXERCISES: PART 2-L

For each question below, please identify the primary dimension and a few secondary dimensions and show them on the classical boundary/equivalence table:

L.1. *Example 2: ATM Withdrawal* **on page 237**

An ATM allows withdrawals of cash in amounts of $20 increments from $20 to $200 (inclusive) (Craig & Jaskiel, 2002, p. 164).

Analyze the variable **AmountRequested**.

L.2. *Example 5: Undergraduate Grades* **on page 265**

The passing score for any undergraduate course at Florida Tech is 60/100. A student who scores less than 60 receives an 'F' on her transcript.

Analyze the input grade as an Integer.

L.3. *Example 15: Mailing Labels* **on page 325**

A program prints mailing labels. The first line of the label is the person's name. The program builds the name from three fields, **FirstName**, **MiddleName** and **LastName**. Each field can hold up to 30 characters. The label can be up to 70 characters wide.

In your analysis of the three fields, don't forget their relationship to the total string length of the full name (the key result variable).

A SCHEMA FOR DOMAIN TESTING

1. CHARACTERIZE THE VARIABLE

    A. Identify the potentially interesting variables.

    B. Identify the variable(s) you can analyze now. This is the variable(s) of interest.

    C. Determine the primary dimension of the variable of interest.

    D. Determine the type and scale of the variable's primary dimension and what values it can take.

    E. Determine whether you can order the variable's values (from smallest to largest).

    F. Determine whether this is an input variable or a result.

    G. Determine how the program uses this variable.

    H. Determine whether other variables are related to this one.

2. ANALYZE THE VARIABLE AND CREATE TESTS

    I. Partition the variable (its primary dimension).

        – If the dimension is ordered, determine its sub-ranges and transition points.

        – If the dimension is not ordered, base partitioning on similarity.

    J. Lay out the analysis in a classical boundary/equivalence table. Identify best representatives.

    K. Create tests for the consequences of the data entered, not just the input filter.

    L. Identify secondary dimensions. Analyze them in the classical way.

    M. Summarize your analysis with a risk/equivalence table.

3. GENERALIZE TO MULTIDIMENSIONAL VARIABLES

    N. Analyze independent variables that should be tested together.

    O. Analyze variables that hold results.

    P. Analyze non-independent variables. Deal with relationships and constraints.

4. PREPARE FOR ADDITIONAL TESTING

    Q. Identify and list unanalyzed variables. Gather information for later analysis.

    R. Imagine and document risks that don't necessarily map to an obvious dimension.

M. SUMMARIZE YOUR ANALYSIS WITH A RISK / EQUIVALENCE TABLE

Most people who organize their domain tests with a table use some version of the classical table.

As you saw in *Chapter J. Lay Out the Analysis in the Classical Table. Identify best Representatives* on page 125, the classical table is an excellent tool for showing analysis of a variable's primary dimension.

If your analysis looks only at a few secondary dimensions, it probably makes sense to stick with the classical table. The previous Chapter described the classical table.

We prefer to switch to the risk/equivalence table as our analysis expands to include:

- **more secondary dimensions**
- **result variables based on a variable you're analyzing**
- **consequences associated with the variable you're analyzing**
- **constraints imposed on the variable you're analyzing by other variables** (Modification to the table: add columns for the related variables. For example, see *Risk/Equivalence Table Showing Multiple Related Variables* on page 304.)

That's what we're working on in this Chapter.

For any given variable, you'll probably show secondary dimensions on the classical table OR the risk/equivalence table, but not both.

Because the classical table and the risk/equivalence table are alternatives that substitute for each other, we wrote the last Chapter and this one in parallel ways, discussing the same issues and working through the same examples. In this Chapter, we consider a broader set of secondary dimensions.

SECONDARY DIMENSIONS

Secondary dimensions have more to do with the program's implementation details than with the purpose of the variable.

- You can usually determine the *primary* dimension by asking what the program is designed to learn from the variable.
- You can imagine *secondary* dimensions by asking how else the variable could change.

Myers' (1979) classic presentation of equivalence classes instructs the reader to enter three Integers, which the program interprets as lengths of the sides of a triangle. The program determines whether these specify a scalene, isosceles or equilateral triangle:

- If they're equal, the triangle is equilateral.
- If only two sides are equal, it is isosceles.
- If all three sides are different (and they form a triangle), it is scalene.

The decision the program is making is what type of triangle is specified by three sides. This decision the result variable. It's an enumerated variable. If you consider its domain, Myers' description specifies a set of three values: {scalene, isosceles, equilateral}. There is an implicit fourth value: `IsATriangle`, which can be True or False.

The input variables are the three sides of the triangle and the primary dimension of each is their length.

Myers included several tests that did not address either dimension. For example, he recommended testing with:

- Non-Integers (Floating Points or letters)
- The wrong number of values (two sides, no sides or four, instead of three)
- Different orderings of the sides (try 1,2,4 then 2,1,4, then 4,1,2, etc.).

The purpose of this program is to classify triangles, not to tell the difference between entries that are Integers, Floating-Point numbers or letters. However, the data that you can enter can be non-Integer and therefore the program has to cope with this type of bad input. *These are examples of secondary dimensions.*

Myers' example begs further analysis:

(a) What is the length in relationship to the other two sides?

(b) And therefore, which response should the program give?

These are important, but they aren't examples of secondary dimensions. They're examples of:

(a) The relationships among variables. See *Chapters H. Determine Whether Other Variables are Related to this One* on page 105 and *P. Analyze Non-Independent Variables. Deal with Relationships and Constraints* on page 201.

(b) How the program deals with result variables. See *Chapters K. Create Tests for the Consequences of the Data Entered* on page 133 and *O. Analyze Variables that Hold Results* on page 191.

As you saw in the last chapter, the classical boundary/equivalence table handles the primary dimension and a small number of tests based on secondaries well. However, if you do a more thorough analysis of secondary dimensions, the risk/equivalence table brings those dimensions out more explicitly. To our eyes, that makes it clearer, easier to understand and easier to assess in terms of coverage. Here are some examples:

FROM EXAMPLE 1: INTEGER INPUT

A data entry field will accept Integers from -999 to 999.

The stated domain of the primary dimension is {-999, 999}. The classic analysis says the interesting tests are -1000, -999, 999 and 1000. The classical table shows this as:

Variable	Valid case equivalence class	Invalid case equivalence class	Boundaries and special cases	Notes
the input value	-999 to 999		-999	
			0	
			999	
		< -999	-1000	
		> 999	1000	

Testers often extend the classical table to include invalid values that aren't on the primary dimension. Common examples are:

- Letters.
- Letters that can be interpreted as hexadecimal digits.
- Empty input field.
- Whitespace (leading or trailing spaces, tabs, etc.).

These go into the table as new rows with invalid values, like this:

Variable	Valid case equivalence class	Invalid case equivalence class	Boundaries and special cases	Notes
the input value	-999 to 999		-999	
			0	
			999	
		< -999	-1000	
		> 999	1000	
		a to z	a	misinterpret as hexadecimal?
			g	non-hexadecimal
		non-alphanumeric	/	ASCII character 47 — "0" is 48
			:	ASCII character 58 — "9" is 57
		no input	empty field	
		whitespace	\<space\>999	4 characters. Does it ignore spaces?
			\<space\>	no number, just a space
			lots of \<spaces\>	overflow? ignored?

To the extent that a secondary dimension is identified, the description is in the Notes column. It is not obvious which secondary dimensions are covered or how well or what the best tests are for those dimensions. These are the types of concerns that led us to design a new table to show our equivalence classes, the risk/equivalence table.

SECONDARY DIMENSIONS FOR INTEGERS

Hung Quoc Nguyen, President of LogiGear, creates lists of standard testing issues for variables of a given type. The following list merges test ideas from Nguyen et al., (2003, p. 619) with a few more from Kaner et al. (2002). Depending on the range of values of the variable under test, some of these tests might not be useful for the particular variable that you're testing:

- Nothing
- Emptied field (clear the default value)
- Whitespace only (tab, space)
- 0
- Valid value
- At lower bound of range - 1
- At lower bound of range
- At upper bound of range
- At upper bound of range + 1

- Far below the lower bound of range
- Far above the upper bound of range
- Far below the lower bound number of digits or characters
- At lower bound minus 1 number of digits or characters
- At lower bound number of digits or characters
- At upper bound number of digits or characters
- At upper bound plus 1 number of digits or characters
- Far above the upper bound number of digits or characters (can you create an overflow?)
  - with digits or printing characters
  - with leading 0's (are they ignored?)
  - with leading spaces (are they ignored?)
  - with leading minus signs
- Leading spaces
- Many leading spaces
- Leading zeros
- Many leading zeros
- Leading space or zero plus a sign (+ or -)
- Negative values
- Non-digits (especially / (ASCII 47) and : (ASCII character 58)
- Uppercase characters
- Lowercase characters
- Upper ASCII (128-254) and Unicode values beyond traditional ASCII (UTF-8, UTF-16 and UTF-32) (*See* http://www.utf-8.com/)
- Modifiers (e.g., Ctrl, Alt, Shift-Ctrl, etc.)
- Function key (F2, F3, F4, etc.)
- Nonprinting characters (such as control characters)
- Operating system file name reserved characters (such as "*.:)
- ASCII 255 (0 and 255 are often interpreted as end of file)
- *See* Whittaker (2003, p. 29-33) for many other ideas on troublesome characters
- Wrong data type (e.g., Floating Point into Integer)
- Decimal point (or no decimal point)
- Number of digits after the decimal
- Decimal comma
- Contains one or more commas (thousands separators)
- Contains one or more points (thousands separators)
- Expressions
- Background activity / competition for resource
- Enter nothing but wait for a long time before pressing or clicking whatever signals completed input for the field. Is there a timeout?
- Enter one digit and wait a long time before entering the next
- Enter digits and then (a) erase them and enter new digits or (b) backspace and type over them with new digits. Are all these keystrokes accumulated until you press <Enter> (or however you signal that your input is complete) or are erased characters discarded imme-

diately? If the program waits until it receives the full string before processing it, there must be a limit on the number of characters (including <Backspace> characters). What happens at the limit?

- Enter digits while you click the mouse or turn the printer on and off or create other types of interrupts

Marick (1995) calls lists like this *catalogs* of test ideas.

It would be a mistake to run all of these tests on every variable.

- If the programmers consistently use libraries that guard against some of these errors, you don't need to check for those errors.

- If the programmers have done good unit testing, they'll have already found and fixed these kinds of bugs.

In either case, perhaps you should run a few tests to spot-check for inconsistency, but if you don't find any problems with these, spend the rest of your testing time looking for problems that are more likely to be in the code.

THE RISK/EQUIVALENCE TABLE (INTEGERS)

The following table implements the list above, with cross-references to the test ideas in the last column. We would normally not fill the "Notes" column with these comments. We do it here simply to show the mapping from one to the other.

Variable	Risk (potential failure)	Classes that should not trigger failure	Classes that might trigger failure	Test cases (best representatives)	The tests are based on these entries in Nguyen's list
the input value	misclassifies valid inputs	anything out of bounds	-999 to 999	-999	Valid value Negative values At lower bound of range At upper bound number of digits or characters
				0	0 At lower bound number of digits or characters
				999	At upper bound of range At upper bound number of digits (no minus sign)
	mishandles values that are too small	≥ -999	< -999	-1000	At lower bound of range - 1
	mishandles values that are too large	≤ 999	> 999	1000	At upper bound of range + 1
				999...999 (16384 nines)	Far above the upper bound of range
	too few characters	any input value	empty field	enter nothing	Enter nothing At lower-bound-minus-1 number of digits or characters
				clear the field	Empty the field (clear the default value)

Variable	Risk (potential failure)	Classes that should not trigger failure	Classes that might trigger failure	Test cases (best representatives)	The tests are based on these entries in Nguyen's list
				space character	Whitespace only (tab, space)
	too many characters	≤ 4 characters	> 4 characters	-1000	Repeats the "too small" test At upper-bound-plus-1 number of digits or characters
				+999	At upper-bound-plus-1 number of digits
				<space>999	Leading spaces
				<space>-999	Leading space plus a sign (+ or -)
				<space> <space> ... <space>999	Many leading spaces
				0999	Leading zeros
				-0999	Leading space plus a sign (+ or -)
				000...000999	Many leading zeros
				- -999	Two leading minus signs
				-- ... - -999	Many leading minus signs
	confused by wrong data type	Integers	non-Integers	9.0	Wrong data type (e.g., decimal point into Integer) Decimal point (or no decimal point)
				9.000	Number of digits after the decimal
			non-digits	/	Non-digits (especially / (ASCII 47)
				:	and : (ASCII character 58)
				ASCII 255	ASCII 255 (may be interpreted as end of file)
				*	Operating system file name reserved characters (such as "*.:)
				9-9	Arithmetic expressions
				We're treating these as irrelevant to the problem statement for this example, so we're skipping them	Uppercase and lowercase characters, upper ASCII (128-254) and Unicode. Modifiers (e.g., Ctrl, Alt, Shift-Ctrl, etc.), function keys (F2, F3, F4, etc.) and nonprinting characters (such as control characters) *See* Whittaker (2003, p. 29-33) for many other ideas on troublesome characters Background activity / competition for resource Enter nothing. Wait a long time before signaling completed input for the field. Is there a timeout? Enter one digit. Wait a long time before entering the next Enter digits. Erase them. Enter new digits Enter digits while you click the mouse, turn the printer off or create other interrupts

FROM EXAMPLE 3: SUNTRUST VISA

SunTrust issues Visa credit cards with credit limits in the range of $400 to $40000. A customer is not to be approved for credit limits outside this range. A customer can apply for the card using an online application form in which one of the fields requires that the customer type in his/her desired credit limit.

The primary variable is the `DesiredCreditLimit`.

The stated valid range is $400 to $40,000, but is this Integer, Fixed Point with 2 digits after the decimal point or a Floating Point (any number of digits after the decimal)?

For now, suppose this is Fixed Point. Here's the classical table for the primary dimension:

Variable	Valid case equivalence class	Invalid case equivalence class	Boundaries and special cases	Notes
DesiredCreditLimit	400 to 40000		400.00	
			40000.00	
		< 400	399.99	
		> 40000	40000.01	

Add a secondary dimension into the mix: the number of digits after the decimal point. The classical table looks like this:

Variable	Valid case equivalence class	Invalid case equivalence class	Boundaries and special cases	Notes
Desired-CreditLimit	400.00 to 40000.00		400.00	
			40000.00	
		< 400	399.99	
		> 40000	40000.01	
		no digits after decimal	400	The program probably handles these as valid
			40000	
		only 1 digit after the decimal point	400.1	You could try 400.0 and 40000.0 but how many times do you want to do almost exactly the same test. This tests essentially the same risk, with a new value
			39999.9	
		too many digits	400.009	If the program accepts cents, this is a boundary invalid case
			40000000etc000	Paste 1000000 digits

SECONDARY DIMENSIONS FOR FIXED-POINT VARIABLES

Example 1 presented Hung Quoc Nguyen's list of standard testing issues for Integer variables. The list that follows adapts Nguyen's list for Floating-Point variables.

You might find it useful to refer to *Floating Point* on page 72. However, unlike Floating-Point numbers, there is a true Δ for Fixed-Point numbers. For example, if **NUMBEROFDIGITSAFTERDEC-IMAL** = 2 (2 digits are allowed after the decimal point), then Δ = 0.01.

- Nothing
- Emptied field (clear the default value)
- Whitespace only (tab, space)
- 0
- Valid value
- At lower bound of range - Δ
- At lower bound of range
- At upper bound of range
- At upper bound of range + Δ
- Far below the lower bound of range, such as at **MINFLOAT**
- Far above the upper bound of range, such as at **MAXFLOAT**
- Far below the lower bound number of digits or characters
- At lower bound minus 1 number of digits or characters
- At lower bound number of digits or characters
- At upper bound number of digits or characters
- At upper bound plus 1 number of digits or characters
- Far above the upper bound number of digits or characters (try to overflow the buffer)
  - with digits or printing characters
  - with leading 0's (are they ignored?)
  - with leading spaces (are they ignored?)
  - with leading minus signs
- Number of digits before the decimal point (lower and upper bounds)
- Number of digits after the decimal point (lower and upper bounds)
- Leading space
- Many leading spaces
- Leading zero
- Many leading zeros
- Leading space or zero plus a sign (+ or -)
- Currency sign before or after the digits
- Negative values
- Hexadecimal digits
- Non-digits (especially / (ASCII 47) and : (ASCII character 58)
- Non-digits embedded in the number, such as 1a3 (some programs will interpret this as 13)
- Uppercase characters
- Lowercase characters
- Upper ASCII (128-254) and Unicode values beyond traditional ASCII (UTF-8, UTF-16 and UTF-32) (*See* http://www.utf-8.com/)
- Modifiers (e.g., Ctrl, Alt, Shift-Ctrl, etc.)
- Function key (F2, F3, F4, etc.)
- Nonprinting characters (such as control characters)
- Operating system file name reserved characters (such as "\ *.:)
- ASCII 255 (0 and 255 are often interpreted as end of file)

- *See* Whittaker (2003, p. 29-33) for many other ideas on troublesome characters
- Wrong data type (e.g., a variable defined as a Double-Precision Floating-Point constant)
- No decimal point (probably acceptable and interpreted properly, but test it once)
- Two decimal points
- Decimal comma
- Contains one or more commas (thousands separators)
- Contains one or more points (thousands separators)
- Commas in appropriate places within the number
- Commas in inappropriate places within the number
- Scientific notation
- Scientific notation with an invalid exponent
- Scientific notation with an exponent that will cause an overflow
- Scientific notation with an exponent that implies too many digits after the decimal point
- Scientific notation with a significand that has too many digits
- Scientific notation with a significand/exponent combination that will cause an overflow
- Fraction
- Special mathematical constants, such as π
- Expressions, including expressions that resolve to a valid value for input
- Background activity / competition for resource
- Enter nothing but wait for a long time before pressing or clicking whatever signals completed input for the field. Is there a timeout?
- Enter one digit and wait a long time before entering the next
- Enter digits and then (a) erase them and enter new digits or (b) backspace and type over them with new digits. Are all these keystrokes accumulated until you press <Enter> (or however you signal that your input is complete) or are erased characters discarded immediately? If the program waits until it receives the full string before processing it, there must be a limit on the number of characters (including <Backspace> characters). What happens at the limit?
- Enter digits while you click the mouse or turn the printer on and off or create other types of interrupts

As with the other test idea catalogs, good unit testing and consistent use of error-aware programming libraries will reduce the need for many of these tests at the system level. Before deciding how many of these tests to run, if you can, check with the programmers.

THE RISK/EQUIVALENCE TABLE (FIXED POINT)

Here we illustrate the Fixed-Point table with a few test ideas. Note how the table is structured to highlight the test ideas.

Variable	Risk (potential failure)	Classes that should not trigger failure	Classes that might trigger failure	Test cases (best representatives)	Notes
Desired-CreditLimit	mishandles values that are too small	≥ 400	< 400	399	
	mishandles values that are too large	≤ 40000	> 40000	40001	

Variable	Risk (potential failure	Classes that should not trigger failure	Classes that might trigger failure	Test cases (best representatives)	Notes
	misclassifies valid values	< 400	400-40000	400	
		> 40000		40000	
	doesn't cope with Floating-Point values	Integers	Floats, including Currency	400.	decimal, no digits
				400.1	10 cents?
				400.10	10 cents
				400.101	not cents
				400.11111111	
	fails on nondigits	digits	ASCII chars other than digits	/ or /400 or 400/	boundary non-digit
				: or :400 or 400:	
			expression includes nondigit	500+2	
	too few characters	3 to 5 chars	< 3	20	
	too many characters	3 to 5 chars	>5	123456	
				012345	leading zero
				000000etc12345	lots of leading zeros

When you're dealing with many different ways of analyzing the same variable, this table structure lets you record and communicate more of your thinking, in a more convenient way.

FROM EXAMPLE 4: PAGE SETUP OPTIONS

The page setup function of a text editor allows a user to set the width of the page in the range of 1 to 56 inches. The `PageWidth` input field accepts (and remembers) up to 30 places after the decimal point.

`PageWidth` might be a Fixed-Point variable, but we're going to treat it as if it is a Quadruple-Precision Floating Point. This type of variable will hold 34 significant digits.

SECONDARY DIMENSIONS FOR FLOATING-POINT VARIABLES

The list that follows is almost the same as the Fixed-Point list. As with that list, you might find it useful to refer to *From Example 28: OpenOffice Printing Options* on page 119.

When you use it, your Floating-Point table will be a little more complex than the Fixed-Point table because its Δ varies with the size of the number under test and the numbers (and their exponents) can vary over an enormously larger range.

As we explained in the discussion of Floating Point, the smallest recognizable difference between two numbers (Δ) is not a constant.

- We use the notation $\Delta(\mathbf{x})$ to represent the smallest value that you can add to $\mathbf{x}$ to obtain a number recognizably larger than $\mathbf{x}$.
- When dealing with Quadruple Precision, the value of $\Delta(1.0) =$ is 2^{-112} (which is about $1.93E^{-34}$). (See https://en.wikipedia.org/wiki/Machine_epsilon.)
- In general, $\Delta(\mathbf{x}) = x \times \Delta(1.0)$.

Here are the test ideas:

- Nothing
- Emptied field (clear the default value)
- Whitespace only (tab, space)
- 0
- Valid value
- At lower bound of range - Δ
- At lower bound of range
- At upper bound of range
- At upper bound of range + Δ
- Far below the lower bound of range, such as at **MINFLOAT**
- Far above the upper bound of range, such as at **MAXFLOAT**
- Far below the lower bound number of digits or characters
- At lower bound minus 1 number of digits or characters
- At lower bound number of digits or characters
- At upper bound number of digits or characters
- At upper bound plus 1 number of digits or characters
- Far above the upper bound number of digits or characters (try to overflow the buffer)
  - with digits or printing characters
  - with leading 0's (are they ignored?)
  - with leading spaces (are they ignored?)
  - with leading minus signs
- Number of digits before the decimal point (lower and upper bounds)
- Number of digits after the decimal point (lower and upper bounds)
- Leading space
- Many leading spaces
- Leading zero
- Many leading zeros
- Leading space or zero plus a sign (+ or -)
- Negative values
- Hexadecimal digits
- Non-digits (especially / (ASCII 47) and : (ASCII character 58)
- Non-digits embedded in the number, such as 1a3 (some programs will interpret this as 13)
- Uppercase characters
- Lowercase characters
- Upper ASCII (128-254) and Unicode values beyond traditional ASCII (UTF-8, UTF-16 and UTF-32) (*See* http://www.utf-8.com/)

- Modifiers (e.g., Ctrl, Alt, Shift-Ctrl, etc.)
- Function key (F2, F3, F4, etc.)
- Nonprinting characters (such as control characters)
- Operating system file name reserved characters (such as "\ *.:)
- ASCII 255 (0 and 255 are often interpreted as end of file)
- *See* Whittaker (2003, p. 29-33) for many other ideas on troublesome characters
- Wrong data type (e.g., a variable defined as a Fixed-Point constant)
- No decimal point
- Two decimal points
- Decimal comma
- Contains one or more commas (thousands separators)
- Contains one or more points (thousands separators)
- Commas in appropriate places within the number
- Commas in inappropriate places within the number
- Scientific notation
- Scientific notation with an invalid exponent
- Scientific notation with a significand that has too many digits
- Scientific notation with an exponent that will cause an overflow
- Scientific notation with a significand/exponent combination that will cause an overflow
- Fraction
- Special mathematical constant, such as π
- Expressions, including expressions that resolve to a valid value for input
- Background activity / competition for resource
- Enter nothing but wait for a long time before pressing or clicking whatever signals completed input for the field. Is there a timeout?
- Enter one digit and wait a long time before entering the next
- Enter digits and then (a) erase them and enter new digits or (b) backspace and type over them with new digits. Are all these keystrokes accumulated until you press <Enter> (or however you signal that your input is complete) or are erased characters discarded immediately? If the program waits until it receives the full string before processing it, there must be a limit on the number of characters (including <Backspace> characters). What happens at the limit?
- Enter digits while you click the mouse or turn the printer on and off or create other types of interrupts

As with the other test idea catalogs, good unit testing and consistent use of error-aware programming libraries will reduce the need for many of these tests at the system level. Before deciding how many of these tests to run, if you can, check with the programmers.

A RISK/EQUIVALENCE TABLE FOR A FLOATING-POINT VARIABLE

This table is not focused only on the input values. This type of table is organized in terms of the risks associated with this variable.

- Some of the risks involve how the program receives your inputs to `PageWidth`.
- Other risks involve the consequences of the value you give to `PageWidth`.

There are many other risks than you can list in this table. You can probably easily imagine more tests associated with the risks that we listed in the table, more potential consequences of the value of `PageWidth` and other variables that `PageWidth` could interact badly with.

Here we illustrate the Floating Point table with a few test ideas.

Variable	Risk (potential failure	Classes that should not trigger failure	Classes that might trigger failure	Test cases (best representatives)	Notes
Page-Width	misclassifies valid inputs	anything out of bounds	1.0 to 56.0	1	Valid value At lower bound of range At lower bound of number of digits after decimal (zero digits)
				1.0	lowest non-zero number of digits after decimal
				1.00...0	30 zeros. Max number of digits after decimal
				55.99...9	30 nines. Max number of digits after decimal
				56.00...0	30 zeros, most digits before and after decimal, biggest valid value. This has a total of 33 characters.
				56.	decimal point but no digits after decimal
	mishandles values that are too small	≥ 1	< 1	0.99...9	30 nines. Can it really tell this is not 1.0?
				0	
	mishandles negative values	≥ 0	< 0	-0	some programs distinguish positive from negative zero. Does this make a difference here?
				-1	negative mirror of valid value
	mishandles values that are too large	≤ 56	> 56	56.00...01	29 zeros, then 1
				57	probably unnecessary.
				5599...999	huge number (30 nines, no decimal point) but within the length of string it can process: 32 digits
	too few characters	> 0 chars	maybe 0	empty field	If a default value shows in dialog, erase it and then try to get the program to accept the empty value. Probably it will treat this as zero and reject it.
				space character	Whitespace only (tab, space). Probably it will treat this as zero and reject it.
	too many chars before decimal	< 3	≥ 3	100	smallest 3-digit entry
				100...0	1 then 33 zeros.
				<space>56	3 characters but the value is within bounds
				<spaces>56	If it likes <space>56, try 31 spaces. What about 100 spaces?

Variable	Risk (potential failure	Classes that should not trigger failure	Classes that might trigger failure	Test cases (best representatives)	Notes
				+56	does it treat +56 same as 56?
				056	leading zero
				000...0056	LOTS of leading zeros
				++++++56	how many plus signs will it take?
				--56	minus-minus 56 is 56, right?
				56<space>	trailing space
				56<spaces>	LOTS of trailing spaces
	too many chars after decimal	< 31	≥ 31	1.00...09	30 zeros, then 9. Smallest too-big case. The width is within bounds, only the number of digits after the decimal is bad.
				1.00...09	LOTS of zeros.
				1.00...09<space>	29 zeros, then 9, then a trailing space
				1.00...09<spaces>	29 zeros, then 9, then LOTS of trailing spaces
	confused by wrong data type		strings		
			non-digits	/	Non-digits (especially / (ASCII 47)
				:	and : (ASCII character 58)
				ASCII 255	ASCII 255 (may be interpreted as end of file)
				*	Operating system file name reserved characters (such as "*.:)
				9-9	Algebraic expressions
	Takes an unreasonable time to process the page	small page size	large page size	56	56" wide page. We want to run this test with tall page height, fill the page and see how long it takes to do basic editing or repainting or repaginating tasks. If the delay is unacceptable, simplify the test (for example, with a much shorter page height).
	Out of memory	small page size	large page size	56	How does the editor store data? Does page size matter or is the important issue the amount of text/graphic in the story or document being edited? If the editor stores more data in memory (or in an area it reserves as "working memory") when the page is larger, we want to try complex designs on big pages. `PageWidth` is one of the variables in this multidimensional extreme-value (memory stress) test
	Unprintable	small page	big page	56	max width page, what happens when you try to print it? Try with a few different types of printers.

FROM EXAMPLE 7: STUDENT NAMES

A `StudentLastName` field must start with an alphabetic character (upper or lower case). Subsequent characters must be letters, numbers or spaces.

`StudentLastName` is a string:

- The first character is constrained to be only letters (upper or lower).
- Subsequent characters can be letters, numbers or spaces.

Partitioning:

- `FirstLetter`:
  - ASCII 65-90 and 97-122 (A-Z and a-z)
  - We'll treat anything out of the set {65-90, 97-122} as invalid.

- Subsequent characters:
  - ASCII 32, 48 to 57, 65-90 and 97-122 (space, 0-9, A-Z and a-z)
  - Anything out of the set {32, 48-57, 65-90, 97-122} is invalid.

The classical table looks like this:

Variable	Valid case equivalence class	Invalid case equivalence class	Boundaries and special cases	Notes
`FirstLetter`	65 - 90 (A - Z)		65 (A)	
			90 (Z)	
		< 65	64 (@)	
		91 - 96	91 ([ )	
			96 (`)	
	97 - 122 (a - z)		97 (a)	
			122 (z)	
		> 122	123 ({)	ignore upper ASCII and Unicode beyond first 127 chars
All other letters		0 - 31	0 (null byte)	non-printing character
			31 (us)	non-printing character
	32		32 (space)	
		33 - 47	33 (!)	
			47 (/)	
	48 - 57		48 (0)	
			57 (9)	
		58 - 64	58 (:)	
			64 (@)	
	65 - 90 (A - Z)		65 (A)	
			90 (Z)	
		91 - 96	91 ([ )	
			96 (`)	
	97 - 122 (a - z)		97 (a)	

Variable	Valid case equivalence class	Invalid case equivalence class	Boundaries and special cases	Notes
			122 (z)	
		> 122	123 ({)	

To consider secondary dimensions, you can use a test idea catalog (Marick, 2005). Here is the same kind of generic test list, for Strings, that you've just seen for Integers and Floating Point variables. Thanks to Elisabeth Hendrickson (2006) for additional ideas.

SECONDARY DIMENSIONS FOR STRINGS[32]

- Nothing
- Emptied field (clear the default value)
- Null character (ASCII 0)
- Whitespace only (tab, space, CR (ASCII 13), ASCII 127)
- Nonprinting characters, such as ASCII 0 to 31. *See* Whittaker (2003, p. 29-33) for a discussion of these.
- Character codes that have not been assigned to a character (see Page et al., 2009, p. 93)
- End of file (ASCII 0 or 255)
- One valid character long. (A "valid" character might be alpha only, alphanumeric, printable lower ASCII (ASCII 32-126), printable characters of any kind (including extended ASCII or Unicode: UTF-8 or UTF-16) or any subset of these depending on the needs of the application.)
- For variables that accept only alpha characters, try @ (ASCII 64; A is 65), [(ASCII 91), ` (ASCII 97) and { (ASCII 123).
- For variables that accept only alpha characters, try accented characters, such as à, â, á, ã, ä, å, ç and letters in non-Western-Latin character sets (such as Arabic, Cyrillic, Devanāgarī, Hebrew)
- Strings that include common delimiters, such as space, tab, comma, dot, en dash (–), em dash (—), hyphen, " ' " ' ", ( ), < >, { }, [ ], / | \, !, @, #, ^, &, *, +, ~ and =
- Strings that include string operators, such as +, ==, !=, <, <=, [], etc.
- Strings that include numbers and operators that are valid in expressions, such as * / + - ()
- Non-alpha characters that are legitimately grouped with alpha strings, such as ©, ® and ™
- Modifiers (e.g., Ctrl, Alt, Shift-Ctrl, etc.)
- Function key (F2, F3, F4, etc.)
- Command strings, such as SQL commands (SQL injection attacks)
- Wildcard characters, such as * and ?
- Lower bound number of (valid) characters - 1
- Lower bound number of (valid) characters
- Byte boundary numbers of characters (255, 256, 1023, 1024, etc.)
- Upper bound number of (valid) characters
- Upper bound number of (valid) characters + 1
- Far below the lower bound number of (valid) characters
- Far above the upper bound number of (valid) characters (try to overflow the buffer)
- Leading or trailing spaces

---

32 For more discussion of this, see Johnson (2007). and Page, Johnston & Rollison (2009).

- Leading or trailing spaces that take the string up to the lower bound number of characters
- Leading or trailing spaces that take the string beyond the maximum number of characters
- Identical to another string except that one string's characters are uppercase and the other's are lowercase
- Background activity / competition for resource
- Enter nothing but wait for a long time before pressing or clicking whatever signals completed input for the field. Is there a timeout?
- Enter one character and wait a long time before entering the next
- Enter characters and then erase them and enter new characters or backspace and type over them with new characters—are all these keystrokes accumulated (in which case, there is a limit, so what happens at the limit?) until you press <Enter> (or however you signal that your input is complete) or are erased characters discarded immediately?
- Enter characters while you click the mouse or turn the printer on and off or create other types of interrupts

THE RISK/EQUIVALENCE TABLE (STRINGS)

The following table is only an approximation of what we would do in real practice. The characters with ASCII codes 0 to 31 (and many others) aren't really equivalent because each has (if it is not ignored) a different effect. These were old codes to control your teletype. One rings a bell. Delete and backspace are in this group. So are vertical tab and formfeed. They have characters for handshaking (on-signal, off-signal), end of text and so on. If we were concerned about these, we would sample different ones in different regression runs (if we were doing manual testing) or we would consider programming tests for all of them.

Note that we have assumed that this program accepts only lower ASCII text, so non-English characters aren't supposed to be accepted. Many other programs will accept these and process them properly.

As with the other test idea catalogs, good unit testing and consistent use of error-aware programming libraries will reduce the need for many of these tests at the system level. Before deciding how many of these tests to run, if you can, check with the programmers.

Variable	Risk (potential failure)	Classes that should not trigger failure	Classes that might trigger failure	Test cases (best representatives)	Notes
Student's last name	Allows empty or blank field		0 characters	Enter nothing, leave the field blank	Lower bound number of chars -1
				Erase default string to empty the field	
			No name	Null (ASCII 0)	
				Space character	
				Tab character	
				ASCII 127	DEL
				ASCII 255	might be end of file
	Rejects valid non-alpha characters		embedded space or dot	St. John	one period, one space
		embedded spaces		Van Heusen	Two spaces

Variable	Risk (potential failure)	Classes that should not trigger failure	Classes that might trigger failure	Test cases (best representatives)	Notes
		embedded dots		St.. John	Two dots
		dot w/o space		St.John	No space
	Rejects valid alpha	traditional capitalization	unusual capitalization	smith	lower case first letter
				CamelCase	interior capital letter
	Accepts invalid characters		ASCII 1 to 31	ASCII 3	may generate a program interrupt
				ASCII 4	end of text
				ASCII 26	end of text
					The others are interesting too. Sample from them
			Numbers	0	Names (probably) don't have numbers in them
				9	
			Delimiters or other special text characters	letters + tab + letters	whitespace like space, but invalid
				letters + delimiter + letters	space, tab, comma, dot, en dash (–), em dash (—), hyphen, " ' " ' ", ( ), < >, { }, [ ], /	\, !, @, #, ^, &, *, +, ~, ? and =
			boundary non-alpha	@	ASCII 64
				]	ASCII 91
				`	ASCII 96
				}	ASCII 123
			Other non-alpha	©	™ ® ©
				%	For example, %20 is interpreted as a space in a URL
			Accented letters	à	à, â, á, ã, ä, å, ç, etc.
				Jàne	The program might check the first character and assume later ones are acceptable
			Foreign alphabets	Д	Unicode 0414 Cyrillic
				Я	Unicode 042F Cyrillic
					Additional letters in non-Western-Latin character sets (such as Arabic, Cyrillic, Devanāgarī, Hebrew).
	Processes wildcard		any string with * or ?	John*	If it accepts John*, what does it store?
				John1 and John?	what does it store for John?

Variable	Risk (potential failure)	Classes that should not trigger failure	Classes that might trigger failure	Test cases (best representatives)	Notes
				search for John?	Does it find John1 or John? when you try to retrieve John?
	Executes commands embedded in strings		strings with string operators	James+Brown	==, !=, <, <=, [], +=
				Brown[1]	
			SQL commands	SELECT	
			File commands	Delete	names and syntax depend on your OS
			strings that look like arithmetic expressions	2+3	
	too short	≥ 1 nonwhite-space printing characters	empty	empty	we covered this already (Lower bound number of chars - 1)
	too short after filtering whitespace	≥ 1 nonwhite-space printing characters	non-empty strings that have only whitespace (enough to take us to the string's minimum length)	1 space or tab	whitespace might be OK for strings in general but leading and trailing whitespace will almost certainly be stripped from names
				MAXNAME spaces	should be rejected as 0-length name
	rejects valid as too short		≥ 1 nonwhite-space printing character	1 alpha character (e.g., "a")	Lower bound number of (valid) characters
	rejects valid as too long			**MAXNAME** characters	
	accepts character string that is too long			**MAXNAME** + 1	
				127	common buffer maximum. 127, 128, 255, 256 are interesting cases (but maybe not invalid) no matter what value in **MAXNAME**
				128	
				255	common buffer maximum
				256	2^8 (8-bit word + 1) boundary
				65536	2^{16}
				16777216	2^{24} if there's going to be an overflow, 16 million characters will probably do it.
				4294967296	2^{32}

Variable	Risk (potential failure)	Classes that should not trigger failure	Classes that might trigger failure	Test cases (best representatives)	Notes
	rejects a valid name that has irrelevant whitespace that makes the string too long	≤ **MAXNAME**	total string length > **MAXNAME**	1 leading space plus a valid **MAXNAME**-length name	
				256 leading spaces plus a valid **MAXNAME**-length name	

EXERCISES: PART 2-M

For each question below, please use one of the test idea catalogs (or create your own) to develop a risk/equivalence table.

M.1. *Example 2: ATM Withdrawal* **on page 237**

An ATM allows withdrawals of cash in amounts of $20 increments from $20 to $200 (inclusive) (Craig & Jaskiel, 2002, p. 164).

Analyze the variable **AmountRequested**.

M.2. *Example 5: Undergraduate Grades* **on page 265**

The passing score for any undergraduate course at Florida Tech is 60/100. A student who scores less than 60 receives an 'F' on her transcript.

Analyze the input grade as an Integer.

M.3. *Example 15: Mailing Labels* **on page 325**

A program prints mailing labels. The first line of the label is the person's name. The program builds the name from three fields, **FirstName, MiddleName** and **LastName**. Each field can hold up to 30 characters. The label can be up to 70 characters wide.

In your analysis of the three fields, don't forget their relationship to the total string length of the full name (the key result variable).

SECTION 2: PART 3: GENERALIZE TO MULTIDIMENSIONAL VARIABLES

The tasks of this Part are:

    N. Analyze independent variables that should be tested together.

    O. Analyze variables that hold results.

    P. Analyze non-independent variables. Deal with relationships and constraints.

Many variables are inherently multidimensional.[33] Other variables are distinct, but after testing the individual variables on their own, you might test them together, treating them as if they were one multidimensional variable.

We test variables (dimensions of a variable) together to expose errors that only a combination of their values will trigger.

In this book, *multivariable testing, multidimensional testing* and **combination testing** mean the same thing. As we see it, any test of two variables together is equivalent to testing one variable that has two dimensions: one dimension is the value of the first variable, the other dimension is the value of the second variable. Any test that sets values of two or more variables (dimensions) is testing a combination of values. All three terms are commonplace and we will use them interchangeably.

Multidimensional analysis is a complex area in its own right. A workbook on multidimensional testing would be longer and more complex than this workbook on domain testing. We will *not* cover multidimensional testing in depth here. We will often present suggestions, ways to think about a problem or ideas on how to approach it, rather than methods and worked examples.

Our intent is to highlight a few interesting intersections of domain testing and multidimensional testing:

- When you test several variables together (or equivalently, several dimensions of a multi-dimensional variable), the number of possible tests is enormous. It makes the number of possible tests for single variables look small and manageable by comparison. (This is often called the **combinatorial explosion**, which will be described shortly.)This is natural territory for domain analysis: *Any time that you see a huge number of possible tests, you should consider domain analysis as an intelligent sampling strategy that can bring down the number of tests needed to a manageable size.*

- Some variables are so closely related that you will naturally see them together when doing a domain analysis of either one. Determining what set of tests are useful for testing them together is a natural extension of the domain analysis for either on its own.

For example:

- Chapter L (Identify Secondary Dimensions) describes the triangle problem. You must analyze the three sides together to determine what type of triangle you have.

---

33 We have already shown that all variables are multidimensional because they all have secondary dimensions. As you read the next few Chapters, **temporarily forget about the secondary dimensions**. That's not what this Chapter is about. Think of a rectangle: to describe its size, you have to specify its length and its width. Those are the two dimensions of the rectangle. Those are the kinds of dimensions we are writing about here, the ones we have been calling primary dimensions. If you find this at all confusing, we suggest that you read about our distinction between implicit and explicit dimensions in *Multidimensional Variables* on page 35.

- Example 9 presents a table that can have at most 4095 cells. A table with 4095 rows can have only one column. A table with 4095 columns can have only one row. To this point, we have analyzed variables like **NumberOfRows** and **NumberOfColumns** separately. In this case, you must analyze them together because they constrain each other.

- Example 10 presents a circle. To know whether a point lies on, in or outside the circle, you must consider the two variables that define the coordinates of the point.

- Example 11 presents a decision. A university admits students based on two scores. A good score of one type can counterbalance a less-good score of the other type.

- Example 12 presents a region of a graph that is defined by several lines.

- Example 15 presents a situation in which three variables constrain each other's possible values.

In a multidimensional variable, it makes no sense to call one dimension the primary dimension and the others secondary. You might temporarily focus on one dimension, but to test the values of any dimension, you must specify values for all of the others.

We have to cover a few items that are common to the next few chapters, primarily some core terminology, notation and a few design concepts before proceeding to the Chapters:

- An overview of three design traditions that underlie multivariable testing

- Notation for multidimensional variables (N-tuple notation)

- The combinatorial explosion

- An overview of the four basic questions in the design of any combination test:

    (a) What variables should you test together?
    (b) What values of those variables should you test?
    (c) How should you combine them?
    (d) What coverage criterion should you use to establish your minimum set of combination tests?

MULTIDIMENSIONAL DESIGN TRADITIONS

We see three broad traditions in designing combination tests:

- *Mechanical (or procedural) combination*: The tester uses a routine procedure to design the tests. This procedure can probably be automated.

- *Risk-based combination*: When we say, *risk*, we mean a way the program could fail. We often use the term *risk* as a synonym for *failure mode*. Given that you can imagine the program failing in a certain way, the goal in *risk-based testing* is to design a test that *makes it* fail that way.

- *Scenario-based combination*: A scenario is a story about how the program can be used. Scenario tests typically involve several variables and several tasks. We see scenario testing as an important area, worthy of detailed study in its own right. We will only briefly consider scenarios in this book.

The next chapters illustrate all three approaches, emphasizing mechanical and risk.

N-TUPLE NOTATION

This section is a summary of the presentation of *N-Tuples* on page 37.

Consider a pay record for hours worked. The record includes the person's name, the number of hours she worked and the pay rate. From this, you can calculate the amount due this person. (For simplicity, ignore taxes and overtime pay.)

You can represent the payment record as a 4-tuple, a variable that is made of 4 parts:

(`Name`, `HoursWorked`, `PayRate`, `AmountDue`)

An n-tuple is a notation for showing an n-dimensional variable. Geometrically, it is a point on an n-dimensional graph. Suppose you have a variable with **n** dimensions (we aren't specifying exactly how many **n** is).

- To describe a single value of this variable (a single point on the graph of this variable), we use this notation:

$$X = (x_1, x_2, ..., x_n)$$

- To refer to several values of this variable (several points on the graph), we use this notation:

$$X_1 = (x_{1,1}, x_{1,2}, ..., x_{1,n}) \text{ and } X_2 = (x_{2,1}, x_{2,2}, ..., x_{2,n})$$

THE COMBINATORIAL EXPLOSION

Start by considering four classes of variables:

- Input variables
- Output variables
- Configuration variables
- Internal variables

A test could specify any combination of values of any of these types of variables. For example, we define three variables, $K = I \times J$, in *Example 14: Result Of Calculations* on page 319. A test of K will typically be a test of all three variables, the two input variables I and J and the output variable K.

INPUT VARIABLES

These are the variables that you can enter data into, directly from a user interface, from a database or from another application.

Notation: To show **m** input variables: $(I_1, I_2, ..., I_m)$.

OUTPUT VARIABLES

These are the variables that you display, print or save the values of, or send in messages to other applications.

Notation: To show **n** output variables: $(O_1, O_2, ..., O_n)$.

Sometimes you directly output an input variable. For counting purposes, let's ignore these variables.

CONFIGURATION VARIABLES

These include:

- Persistent option settings within the program (for example, in a word processor, whether the program will automatically check your spelling as you type). These are variables that you might set once when you first use the program and never reset.

- Transient option settings within the program. (For example, in a word processing program, you might be able to tell the spell checker to "ignore" an oddly-spelled word. During this editing session, the checker ignores every instance of that word in the document. However, next time you open the document, the spell checker resets and flags the word again.)

- System configuration choices, such as the amount of memory or the types of printers connected.

Notation: To show **p** configuration variables: $(C_1, C_2, \dots, C_p)$.

INTERNAL VARIABLES

These are variables not visible in any external interface. For example, a programmer might create a variable to hold interim results of calculations. Some programmers rely on huge numbers of internal variables (this is often associated with very buggy code) while others use almost none. If you're testing at the black-box level, these are hidden from you. But if you're testing your own code or doing maintenance on someone else's code, you'll be able to see them.

Notation: To show **q** internal variables: $(H_1, H_2, \dots, H_q)$

In total, you have $m + n + p + q$ *variables.*

TESTING 2 VARIABLES TOGETHER

If you test two independent variables together, the number of possible tests is the number of possible values of variable 1 times the number of possible values of variable 2. For example, if the possible values of Variable 1 are **A** and **B** and the possible values of Variable 2 are **X**, **Y** and **Z**, there are $2 \times 3 = 6$ possible tests:

(A, X),	(A, Y),	(A, Z)
(B, X),	(B, Y),	(B, Z)

TESTING M+N+P+Q VARIABLES TOGETHER

Any test of the program actually involves all of the Input, Output, Configuration and Internal variables together, whether you set a value deliberately or leave the variable with a default (or other unspecified) value. You can thus represent any test as a point:

Test = $(I_1, I_2, \dots, I_m, O_1, O_2, \dots, O_n, C_1, C_2, \dots, C_p, H_1, H_2, \dots, H_q)$.

The number of possible tests is

number-of-values-of-I_1 × number-of-values-of-I_2 × ... × number-of-values-of-I_m ×
number-of-values-of-O_1 × number-of-values-of-O_2 × ... × number-of-values-of-O_n ×
number-of-values-of-P_1 × number-of-values-of-P_2 × ... × number-of-values-of-P_p ×
number-of-values-of-H_1 × number-of-values-of-H_2 × ... × number-of-values-of-H_q.

That's a lot of tests!

Many variables have thousands of possible values. For example, a variable with valid values from -999 to 999 has 1999 possible results. If you test three variables like this together, you will have 1999 × 1999 × 1999 possible tests. That works out to 7,988,005,999 possible tests. Many variables have lots more than 1999 possible values and you might test more than 3 variables together. When you test variables together, there are a lot of possible tests.

As you increase the number of variables or the number of values to test per variable, you quickly reach a point where you can't hope to cover all the possible combination tests. You must choose combinations with care.

The first and most obvious tactic to reduce the number of tests is to pick boundary values for each variable.

Suppose that for each variable, you consider only two valid values (lower, upper bounds) and two out-of-bounds values of interest (too low, too high). If you test only these four values of each variable, the number of possible tests will be only $4^{n+m+p+q}$. For example, testing 3 variables together, you should have only $4^3 = 64$ tests. That's still a lot of tests, but it's a lot less than 7,988,005,999.

If you test a variable that allows positive and negative values, you'll probably also test with 0. Suppose you test 3 variables with 5 values each. Now there are $5^3 = 125$ tests. That's a lot more than 64, but still better than 7,988,005,999.

We can simplify this further. We don't recommend testing out-of-bounds values together. If the program rejects the test as invalid, you won't know whether its rejection was based on the first, second, third or Nth bad value. Typical code will reject on seeing the first bad value and ignore the rest of the input, so a test that is out of bounds several times is no more powerful or informative than a test with only one out-of-bounds value. Therefore, in most cases, all of our out-of-bounds tests will be single-variable tests rather than combination tests.

If your combination tests include only the valid boundaries (low value and high value) for each variable, the total number of combination tests will be $2^{n+m+p+q}$. This can still be a lot of tests. Imagine a program with (only) 10 input variables, 10 output variables, 10 configuration variables and no hidden, internal variables. Testing only two valid boundaries, there are $2^{10+10+10} = 1,073,741,824$ tests.

Most programs have many more variables than this, so the real number of possible tests makes 1,073,741,824 look small.

The more variables you test together, the more tests. Therefore, you'll probably run combination tests with only a few variables at a time, ignoring the possibility of interactions between variables that you confidently (if not always accurately) believe are unrelated.

Let's summarize this:

If you design tests to check **k** variables at a time and each variable has **v** values of interest (perhaps boundary values and special cases like 0), then the number of possible tests of those **k** variables is **v^k**.

For example:

- If you test 5 variables and 2 values of each, there are $5^2 = 32$ tests.
- If you test 5 variables and 3 values of each, there are $5^3 = 243$ tests.
- If you test 5 variables and 4 values of each, there are $5^4 = 1024$ tests.
- If you test 5 variables and 5 values of each, there are $5^5 = 3125$ tests.

If you don't test the same number of values for each variable, the calculation is slightly different but the principle is the same. For example:

- If you test one variable with 3 values, another with 4 values and another with 5 values, there are $3 \times 4 \times 5 = 60$ possible tests of the three of them together.

The rapid rise in the number of tests is called the **combinatorial explosion**. The number of combinations to be tested can quickly explode to a huge, impossibly-large-to-test number. Managing this is the fundamental challenge in combination testing.

DESIGNING COMBINATION TESTS

Once you identify variables to test with the variable you're focused on, it's time to design the combination tests.

We'll represent our set of **N** variables as $\{ v_1, v_2, \ldots, v_N \}$.

When we write of "designing" the test in this Chapter, what we mean is

- selecting the variables to include in the test and
- selecting the values for those variables.

We aren't concerned, *here*, with how the test will be run, what test results to look at, how the test results will be evaluated or how often (or when) the test should be run.

For purposes of this Chapter, the design of a specific test must answer four questions:

(a) What variables should you test together?
(b) What values of those variables should you test?
(c) How should you combine them?
(d) What coverage criterion should you use to establish your minimum set of combination tests?

(A) WHAT VARIABLES SHOULD YOU TEST TOGETHER?

In a sense, every test involves all N variables. However, in combination testing, you explicitly decide to set the values of some variables and leave the others with their defaults (or whatever other value they happen to have). The ones you intentionally change are the ones you're "testing together."

We haven't found a technique that tells you exactly which variables to test together. Our suggestion is subjective—test those variables together that you think make sense to test together.

In general:

- Independent variables are typically easier to test together, but you might not learn much from these tests
- Non-independent variables typically require you to think more carefully about what values to test.

The most widely-used mechanical approaches (such as all-pairs combination testing) assume the variables are independent. However, except for configuration testing, you're probably more often interested in testing variables that aren't independent.

INDEPENDENT VARIABLES

An important factor driving test design is the independence (or non-independence) of the variables. We say that two variables are independent if the value of one variable has no effect on the range of valid values of the other variable.

There are other definitions of independence. For example, statistical independence requires the variables to be uncorrelated. We do not. Two variables might be highly correlated, so that if one has a large value, the other is very likely to have a high value and very unlikely to have a small value. However, when testing, our concern is with which tests are *possible*, not which are *probable*. If (high value, small value) is a valid pair, we see it as a valid test even if it is improbable.

- Testing variables together (testing them in combination) when you know they're independent is an expensive use of time. There's almost no limit on the number of combination tests you could run (remember the discussion of the combinatorial explosion). What will you learn from testing lots and lots of combinations that you wouldn't learn from testing the variables on their own? Where do you stop?

- Test independent variables together despite the combinatorial problem because:

  ○ Some variables are related in some way, even though they're independent under our definition. For example, the variables might have a joint effect on some other variable.

  ○ Some variables are supposed to be independent but they are not. (The program does have bugs, after all.) You might run a few combination tests of supposed-to-be-independent variables as a quick check for a problem.

  ○ Configuration variables (what printer, how much memory, what video card, etc.) *should be* independent, but too often in practice they interact. This interaction is an example of a joint effect—taken one at a time, the devices create no problems, but together, they destabilize the system. Configuration-related bugs have been the most expensive category of technical support problems at many software publishing companies.

NON-INDEPENDENT VARIABLES

For dealing with non-independent variables, the most widely recommended mechanical technique is cause-effect graphing (Elmendorf, 1973; Myers et al., 2004; Paradkar, Tai & Vouk,1997). This is an advanced technique—not everyone who attempts to understand it succeeds. It is beyond the scope of this workbook. If you decide to learn this technique well enough to actually use it, the best training that we're aware of is with Richard Bender (http://www.benderrbt.com/menu.htm).

(B) WHAT VALUES OF THOSE VARIABLES SHOULD YOU TEST?

Imagine testing the Integer variable that ranges between -999 and 999 with other variables. Which values of the Integer should you test? We can't tell you exactly what to do. We can tell you how we usually think about problems like this.

Consider invalid values of this variable:

- We *might* include out-of-bounds (invalid) values (-1000 or 1000) in combination tests, but if we did, we would combine them with valid values of all of the other variables.

  ○ The program should reject these tests on the basis of the invalid value of this variable and so the values of the other variables probably won't matter. We would choose the values of these variables arbitrarily or randomly (selection using a random number generator).

- Some programs will attempt to cope with an invalid value and keep doing the rest of the task. In this case, giving the program several bad values in the same task causes it to reject-the-bad-value-and-recover then reject-the-next-bad-value-and-recover and so on. This is not the usual situation. We almost always test one bad value at a time, not in combination with other bad values.

- We don't recommend including tests of secondary dimensions, such as checking letters or empty fields or ultra-long inputs. Normally, we test filtering for invalid values in tests that focus on the individual variable, not in combination with tests of other variables.

Now consider the valid values. Which ones should you include?

- We *would* test both within-bounds extreme values (-999 and 999). We are always tempted to test with 0, but we would be cautious about testing with any value not at the edges, even 0. The problem is combinatorial explosion.

If you're going to combination-test an additional value of any variable, you're going to have a multiplicative effect on the total number of combination tests that you run. If you have a good reason to include the value, include it. Perhaps, though, you should just add a few tests that include this value in a combination, to see if these tests are fruitful before running the full set.

(C) HOW SHOULD YOU COMBINE VALUES OF VARIABLES INTO TESTS?

Under the risk-based and scenario-based approaches, pick the combinations that fit your criteria. For example:

- If historical data suggests some combinations are troublesome, test them.

- If market data suggests some configurations are particularly common or are heavily used by important customers, test those configurations because the cost of failure on those is extremely high.

- If you think a particular combination might overflow memory or corrupt storage in some other way, test it.

- If you think that running a group of combinations several times might overflow memory or storage, run the group.

- However, if you have only a vague disquiet about several variables as a group and don't know which specific combinations would be interesting, use a mechanical approach for selecting the combinations.

Under a mechanical approach, combine according to an algorithm. The two most common approaches are:

- Random combination.
- Combinatorial testing, including:
  - All singles.
  - All n-tuples.
  - All pairs.

For more discussion of combinatorial testing, read Cohen, Dalal, Parelius & Patton (1996) or the papers at Czerwonka (2011). We lecture on this and provide some worked examples in the BBST Test Design Course (Kaner & Fiedler, 2011). We'll discuss this further in *Chapter N. Analyze Independent Variables that Should Be Tested Together* on page 181.

(D) COVERAGE CRITERIA

Risk-based testing and scenario-based testing don't have inherent coverage criteria:

- For risk-based testing, test the combinations that explore your list of potential failure modes, until you run out of failure modes or run out of time.

- For scenario-based testing, test the combinations that explore the program's benefits, the ways a person would use the program or the other stories you can create about the program that might give you insight into its quality. For a discussion of several approaches to generating scenarios, *see* Kaner (2003a). There is no end to the possible scenarios. Stop when they stop giving you insight or when you run out of time.

As to mechanical approaches:

- There is no coverage criterion inherent in random combination testing. Different testing objectives might lead you to different statistical models for coverage sufficiency (for example, *see* Hamlet & Taylor, 1990).

- Combinatorial testing methods are distinguished by their coverage criterion. All-singles testing includes enough tests to cover every value of every variable. All-pairs testing covers every pairing of values of one variable with values of each other variable. All-n-tuples testing covers every combination of values of all the variables.

We'll present these in a bit more detail in the next Chapter.

A SCHEMA FOR DOMAIN TESTING

1. CHARACTERIZE THE VARIABLE

A. Identify the potentially interesting variables.

B. Identify the variable(s) you can analyze now. This is the variable(s) of interest.

C. Determine the primary dimension of the variable of interest.

D. Determine the type and scale of the variable's primary dimension and what values it can take.

E. Determine whether you can order the variable's values (from smallest to largest).

F. Determine whether this is an input variable or a result.

G. Determine how the program uses this variable.

H. Determine whether other variables are related to this one.

2. ANALYZE THE VARIABLE AND CREATE TESTS

I. Partition the variable (its primary dimension).

- If the dimension is ordered, determine its sub-ranges and transition points.
- If the dimension is not ordered, base partitioning on similarity.

J. Lay out the analysis in a classical boundary/equivalence table. Identify best representatives.

K. Create tests for the consequences of the data entered, not just the input filter.

L. Identify secondary dimensions. Analyze them in the classical way.

M. Summarize your analysis with a risk/equivalence table.

3. GENERALIZE TO MULTIDIMENSIONAL VARIABLES

N. Analyze independent variables that should be tested together.

O. Analyze variables that hold results.

P. Analyze non-independent variables. Deal with relationships and constraints.

4. PREPARE FOR ADDITIONAL TESTING

Q. Identify and list unanalyzed variables. Gather information for later analysis.

R. Imagine and document risks that don't necessarily map to an obvious dimension.

N. ANALYZE INDEPENDENT VARIABLES THAT SHOULD BE TESTED TOGETHER

This Chapter and Example 30 are as far as we go with combinatorial testing. We provide some description and a few worked examples of combinatorial test design, but probably not enough to help you get good at it.

Cohen et al. (1996) provided an early description of the combinatorial approach and the all-pairs coverage criterion. *See* Czerwonka (2011) for extensive discussion of all-pairs testing, all-triples testing, etc. and tools (including free tools). Kaner and Fiedler (2011) provide some worked examples with a step-by-step description on video.

We use (and recommend):

- Microsoft's *Pairwise Independent Combination Testing (PICT)* tool (available at http://download.microsoft.com/download/f/5/5/f55484df-8494-48fa-8dbd-8c6f76cc014b/pict33.msi). Czerwonka (2008) describes the tool in some detail.

- National Institute of Science & Technology's *Automated Combinatorial Testing for Software (ACTS)* tool, available at http://csrc.nist.gov/groups/SNS/acts/index.html. For theoretical background, *see* National Institute of Science & Technology (2013a).

We address combinatorial testing in a book on domain testing because, like domain testing, testers use combinatorial testing to guide their sampling of a few tests from an unmanageably large set of available tests. However, there is an essential difference between the approaches:

- Domain testing selects tests with the goal of maximizing the power of each test by relying on best representatives.

- Combinatorial testing focuses on meeting a coverage criterion (such as all-pairs) rather than risk. The combinatorial approach doesn't specify what values of each variable you should test. It treats those as a given and tells you how to combine the given values of each variable.

We study all pairs because it is an important application of domain testing. You will typically use domain analysis (best representatives) to choose the specific values of each variable that you will then test in combination using all pairs.

TESTING INDEPENDENT VARIABLES

When we say that two variables are independent, we mean the value of one variable has no effect on the range of valid values of the other variable.

This is not the only definition of independence:

- Many people equate *independent* with *unrelated*. For two variables to be unrelated, neither could have any type of effect on the other and they wouldn't have a joint effect on other variables.

- Other people think of *statistical independence*. For two variables to be statistically independent, no value of either variable would change the probability of the other variable's taking on any value.

People test independent variables together because:

- Some variables are related in some way, even though they're independent under our definition. For example, variables might have a joint effect on some other variable.

- Configuration variables are often supposed to be independent. In practice, they often interact unexpectedly. Configuration-related bugs have been the most expensive category of technical support problems at many software publishing companies.

- Some variables should be independent but are not (because of a bug). You might run a few combination tests of supposed-to-be-independent variables as a quick check for a problem.

This Chapter focuses on mechanical combination tests of independent variables. We noted two other approaches to combination testing—risk-based testing and scenario testing—in *Section 2: Part 3: Generalize To Multidimensional Variables* on page 171.

Under a mechanical approach, testers combine the values of variables according to an algorithm. The two most common approaches are:

- Random combination.

- Combinatorial testing, including:
  - All singles.
  - All n-tuples.
  - All pairs.

RANDOM COMBINATIONS

Start with some notation.

- We represent N variables as v_1, v_2, ... , v_N.
- We represent the individual test values for variable v_i as v_{i1}, v_{i2} and so forth.
- If v_i is the ith variable, then v_{ij} is the jth test value of the ith variable.
  - For example, if the 2rd variable is the one that runs from -999 to 999 and if the test values are -999, 0 and 999, then v_{21} is -999, v_{22} is 0 and v_{23} is -999.
- T_i is the number of test values for variable v_i.
  - In this example, v_2 has $T_2 = 3$ possible test values.

To create a random combination, select the test values for each variable randomly.

Bach & Schroeder (2004) reported that random selection of test values achieved almost the same pair-coverage as all-pairs testing. Kuhn, Kacker & Lei (2009) reported that random generation exposed *more* bugs than all-pairs in their tests of a network simulator. However, they exposed *fewer* bugs (with substantially less coverage) compared to all-quadruples and all-quintuples testing. For additional research comparing bug-finding with all-pairs, all-triples, all-quadruples, etc., see the resources linked in National Institute of Science & Technology (2013a). In general, we would expect better results from combinatorial generation of tests of independent variables than random generation.

When v_i and v_j aren't independent, the possible values of v_j depend on the value of v_i.

Direct application of all-pairs to non-independent variables will generate invalid pairs and miss valid pairs.

To deal with non-independence:

- We would check whether the test-case generator (PICT, ACTS or some other one) would allow us to specify the relationships among the variables and create tests that stayed within these constraints. If so, we would use the tool.

- We would consider using cause-effect graphing because it is designed to deal with sets of related variables.

- We would typically program the random combination generator to select within a valid range. If the set of valid values for v_j changes for different values of v_i, pick the value for v_i first, then limit the values available to the generator for v_j.

  - To test at an all-pairs level, we would generate $T_1 \times T_2$ combination tests randomly (constraining the selection process to generate only valid pairs).

  - To test at an all-triples level, we would generate $T_1 \times T_2 \times T_3$ combination tests randomly (again, constraining selection so that it produces only valid triples). Similarly for all-quadruples.

If we found combination bugs, we would increase the number of tests.

ALL SINGLES

Use the same notation as in *Multidimensional Variables* on page 35. Use T_i to represent the number of test values for variable v_i. For example, if v_2 can take on the values {4, 5, 6} then T_2 is 3.

To satisfy the all-singles coverage criterion, create tests that set a value for every variable and ensure that every value of every variable is included in at least one test.

Consider three variables, v_1, v_2 and v_3, with test values:

- v_1 is drawn from {1, 2, 3}
- v_2 is drawn from {4, 5, 6}
- v_3 is drawn from {7, 8}

You can draw a *combination test table* as follows:

	v_1	v_2	v_3
Test 1	1	4	7
Test 2	2	5	8
Test 3	3	6	7

In this table, every row is a test case. Every column shows values of a different variable.

If you are creating a combination test table by hand, reorder the variables so that:

- v_1 has the largest number of possible values.
- v_2 has the next-largest number of possible values.
- v_3 has the smallest number of possible values.

That is, sort the v_i's so that $T_1 \geq T_2 \geq T_3$.

This will help you reduce the number of mistakes you make creating the table.

If you sort the variables this way, then the number of tests needed to achieve all-singles coverage is always T_1 (in this case, 3).

Notice that in the last column, the values {7, 8} are covered in the first two tests. The third test can take either value (7 or 8).

ALL N-TUPLES

Use the same notation as in *Multidimensional Variables* on page 35 and the same example as in All Singles. As above, T_i is the number of test values for variable v_i.

To satisfy the all-n-tuples coverage criterion, generate tests that set a value for every variable and ensure that every value of each variable is combined with every combination of the values of the other variables. The number of tests you need is $T_1 \times T_2 \times T_3$, in this case 3 x 3 x 2 = 18.

Here's the combination table, assuming the variables are independent:

	v_1	v_2	v_3
Test 1	1	4	7
Test 2	1	4	8
Test 3	1	5	7
Test 4	1	5	8
Test 5	1	6	7
Test 6	1	6	8
Test 7	2	4	7
Test 8	2	4	8
Test 9	2	5	7
Test 10	2	5	8
Test 11	2	6	7
Test 12	2	6	8
Test 13	3	4	7
Test 14	3	4	8
Test 15	3	5	7
Test 16	3	5	8
Test 17	3	6	7
Test 18	3	6	8

In this example, the variables are independent. *If the variables were not independent,* some values of one variable would block values of other variables and require substitution of other boundary tests.

For example, suppose that:

- v_3 is drawn from {7, 8} if v_1 is 1 or 2
- v_3 is drawn from {9, 10} if v_1 is 3

The resulting table looks like this:

	V_1	V_2	V_3
Test 1	1	4	7
Test 2	1	4	8
Test 3	1	5	7
Test 4	1	5	8
Test 5	1	6	7
Test 6	1	6	8
Test 7	2	4	7
Test 8	2	4	8
Test 9	2	5	7
Test 10	2	5	8
Test 11	2	6	7
Test 12	2	6	8
Test 13	3	4	9
Test 14	3	4	10
Test 15	3	5	9
Test 16	3	5	10
Test 17	3	6	9
Test 18	3	6	10

For a similar analysis, see *Example 12: Piecewise Boundary* on page 309.

ALL PAIRS, ALL TRIPLES, ETC.

Use the same notation as in *Multidimensional Variables* on page 35 but add a few variables:

- V_1 is drawn from {1, 2, 3}
- V_2 is drawn from {4, 5, 6}
- V_3 is drawn from {7, 8, 9}
- V_4 is drawn from {10, 11, 12}
- V_5 is drawn from {13, 14, 15}
- V_6 is drawn from {16, 17, 18}

As above, T_i is the number of test values for variable V_i.

To meet the all-pairs coverage criterion (Cohen et al., 1996):

- Generate tests that set a value for every variable.
- Ensure that every value of each variable is paired with every value of every other variable.

Consider the first three variables. Here's a combination table.

	v_1	v_2	v_3
Test 1	1	4	7
Test 2	1	5	8
Test 3	1	6	9
Test 4	2	4	8
Test 5	2	5	9
Test 6	2	6	7
Test 7	3	4	9
Test 8	3	5	7
Test 9	3	6	8

Check the table: it includes every possible pair of values. For example:

- Consider $v_1 = 1$: tests pair v_1 with $v_3 = 7$ (test 1), with $v_3 = 8$ (test 2) and with $v_3 = 9$ (test 3).
- Consider $v_2 = 5$: tests pair v_2 with $v_3 = 7$ (test 8), with $v_3 = 8$ (test 2) and with $v_3 = 9$ (test 5).

Notice that this does not cover all possible combinations. For example, there is no test (1, 4, 8). Instead:

- the pair (1, 4) is included in (1, 4, 7).
- the pair (1, 8) is included in the test (1, 5, 8).
- the pair (4, 8) is included in the test (2, 4, 8).

When you combine relatively few variables, there are $T_1 \times T_2$ tests and the method for filling in the table is very mechanical. (For more step-by-step discussions of the process, *see* Kaner, Bach & Pettichord, 2002 and Kaner & Fiedler, 2011.)

When you add more variables, the table needs more rows. Here's an example with all 6 variables:

	v_1	v_2	v_3	v_4	v_5	v_6
Test 1	1	4	7	10	13	16
Test 2	1	5	8	11	14	16
Test 3	1	6	9	12	15	17
Test 4	2	4	8	12	15	17
Test 5	2	5	9	10	14	17
Test 6	2	6	7	11	13	18
Test 7	3	4	9	11	14	18
Test 8	3	5	7	12	13	18
Test 9	3	6	8	10	15	16
Test 10	1	4	8	10	15	18
Test 11	2	5	9	12	14	16
Test 12	3	6	7	11	13	17

To check the table, pick a pair of values and see where it exists in the table. (They're all there.)

The table has 12 tests, from a pool (all n-tuples) of $3 \times 3 \times 3 \times 3 \times 3 \times 3 = 729$ tests.

All-triples is like all-pairs except that you must ensure that every triple is included in the table (a triple is a combination of three values, like (2, 4, 8)). When you combine relatively few variables, there are $T_1 \times T_2 \times T_3$ tests. In this case $3 \times 3 \times 3 = 27$ tests will yield all triples for these 6 variables, compared to 729 tests for all n-tuples.

As we noted in *(A) What Variables Should You Test Together?* on page 176, it is commonplace to test independent variables together, but not necessarily very valuable.

With independent variables, the most common recommendation for testing the variables together is combinatorial test design, such as all pairs. Configuration testing is a typical example of the value of the combinatorial approach. We'll illustrate this with *Example 30: Configuration Testing* on page 413.

Configuration testing is often (but not always) quite straightforward. Set up a machine with the appropriate operating system, memory, video card, printer, hard drive, etc., and run the program.

(a) It's common to run the same set of tests on every configuration.[34]

(b) The tests often explore the basic operation of the program.

(c) Some skilled testers will add a few tests for any configuration they find interesting, exploring specific tasks they think might be more likely to fail under some configurations than others. For example, you might find greater vulnerability to memory leaks (or to running out of memory when doing slightly-complex tasks) on a system with relatively little memory and a video card that displays high-resolution images but doesn't provide dedicated graphic RAM.

Combinatorial testing helps you with tests (a) and (b). Tests (c) are risk-based. In general, we favor a risk-based approach for testing whether variables have a collective effect—they don't constrain each other, but together they yield an unacceptable value for some other variable or cause the program to attempt to do something inappropriate.

FROM EXAMPLE 30: CONFIGURATION TESTING

We want to test our software with some or all of the following equipment:

- Operating system: Linux, Windows XP, Windows Vista, Windows 7
- RAM: 1 gByte, 2 gByte, 3 gByte, 4 gByte, 8 gByte
- Printer: Brother multifunction, Canon Laser, HP InkJet, Xerox Color Laser
- Video card: Nvidia GeForce, ATI Radeon, Diamond Stealth
- Disks: 1 hard drive, 2 hard drives, 3 hard drives

These variables are enumerated. The problem lists 4 operating systems, 5 levels of memory, 4 types of printers, 3 types of video cards and 3 numbers of hard drives. None of these is equivalent to the others.

---

34 Some of our reviewers noted that they used a different process, switching configurations as they ran different series of functional tests. The testers gained efficiency by integrating the functional and configuration testing. We've done that too, but what we describe here comes from our experiences in mass-market software companies that sometimes ran compatibility tests with 50 to 1000 configurations. In these cases, it made a lot of sense to set up a lab with multiple machines that we could test in parallel, using a test suite intentionally created to work through a list of known compatibility risks. You might do it either of these ways or a third way. The question we're exploring in this book is how to efficiently select configurations to test with whatever tests we're going to use.

If you test all combinations, there will be 4 x 5 x 4 x 3 x 3 tests = 720 tests. Testing with all-pairs coverage reduces the set to 5 x 4 = 20 tests. Here's a table that satisfies the all-pairs requirement.

	RAM	O/S	Printer	Video	Drives
1	1 gB	Linux	Brother	Nvidia	1 drive
2	1 gB	Windows XP	Canon	ATI	2 drives
3	1 gB	Windows Vista	HP	Diamond	3 drives
4	1 gB	Windows 7	Xerox	Nvidia	1 drive
5	2 gB	Linux	Xerox	ATI	3 drives
6	2 gB	Windows XP	Brother	Diamond	2 drives
7	2 gB	Windows Vista	Canon	Nvidia	1 drives
8	2 gB	Windows 7	HP	ATI	2 drives
9	3 gB	Linux	HP	Diamond	2 drives
10	3 gB	Windows XP	Xerox	Nvidia	1 drives
11	3 gB	Windows Vista	Brother	ATI	3 drives
12	3 gB	Windows 7	Canon	Diamond	3 drives
13	4 gB	Linux	Canon	Nvidia	3 drives
14	4 gB	Windows XP	HP	ATI	1 drives
15	4 gB	Windows Vista	Xerox	Diamond	2 drives
16	4 gB	Windows 7	Brother	Nvidia	2 drives
17	8 gB	Linux	Brother	ATI	1 drive
18	8 gB	Windows XP	Canon	Diamond	3 drives
19	8 gB	Windows Vista	HP	Nvidia	2 drives
20	8 gB	Windows 7	Xerox	Diamond	1 drive

Notice the implied equivalence analysis in the enumeration. Consider: *Which version of Linux* are you testing with? You can easily expand this set of operating systems to accept different versions of each operating system, but the total number of tests will get huge quickly. Instead, the configurations described here include one representative of each class (one Linux, one version of XP, one version of Windows 7, one type of Brother printer, etc.).

In practice, you'll probably have to decide which values of each variable to test. For example, rather than being told which specific 4 printers to test, you'll probably have to decide how many printers to test and which specific printers are needed. This is an example of picking best representatives of a variable that can't be ordered. We worked through this type of problem (selecting the specific printers from a huge set) in detail in Chapter 8 of *Testing Computer Software* (Kaner, Falk & Nguyen, 1993, pp. 143-168). We summarize their approach at *Example 26: Install Printer Software* on page 401.

EXERCISES: PART 3-N

There are no exercises in this Chapter.

A SCHEMA FOR DOMAIN TESTING

1. CHARACTERIZE THE VARIABLE

    A. Identify the potentially interesting variables.

    B. Identify the variable(s) you can analyze now. This is the variable(s) of interest.

    C. Determine the primary dimension of the variable of interest.

    D. Determine the type and scale of the variable's primary dimension and what values it can take.

    E. Determine whether you can order the variable's values (from smallest to largest).

    F. Determine whether this is an input variable or a result.

    G. Determine how the program uses this variable.

    H. Determine whether other variables are related to this one.

2. ANALYZE THE VARIABLE AND CREATE TESTS

    I. Partition the variable (its primary dimension).

       – If the dimension is ordered, determine its sub-ranges and transition points.

       – If the dimension is not ordered, base partitioning on similarity.

    J. Lay out the analysis in a classical boundary/equivalence table. Identify best representatives.

    K. Create tests for the consequences of the data entered, not just the input filter.

    L. Identify secondary dimensions. Analyze them in the classical way.

    M. Summarize your analysis with a risk/equivalence table.

3. GENERALIZE TO MULTIDIMENSIONAL VARIABLES

    N. Analyze independent variables that should be tested together.

    O. Analyze variables that hold results.

    P. Analyze non-independent variables. Deal with relationships and constraints.

4. PREPARE FOR ADDITIONAL TESTING

    Q. Identify and list unanalyzed variables. Gather information for later analysis.

    R. Imagine and document risks that don't necessarily map to an obvious dimension.

O. ANALYZE VARIABLES THAT HOLD RESULTS

Discussions of domain testing often focus on input variables. We think that's too narrow. Whenever you test an input variable, consider how the program uses the value of that variable. When you enter boundary values into a variable, check its impact on every other variables whose values depend, directly or indirectly on the input variable.

Very few programs are written simply to collect data. Sure, the program *collects* data, but it *uses* the data to provide new information or other benefits. Users are typically most interested in the uses, the results of working with those variables.

For example, consider a payroll program. Someone enters the hours you worked and your rate of pay. From this, the program calculates how much you should be paid and it sends a deposit to your checking account.

The amount of pay is a result variable. You don't provide it directly. The program calculates it from the inputs you provide. The only way to vary the values of this variable is to vary the inputs.

People are likely to be grumpy if a program pays them the wrong amount, so testing this result variable is very important.

EQUIVALENT RESULTS

You can't test the pay amount by entering values into it directly. You have to test it by entering values into hours-worked and pay-rate.

You can get $100 in pay by working for 1 hour at $100 per hour, 4 hours at $25 per hour or 10 hours at $10 per hour. In terms of the output ($100) these are equivalent inputs. The set of equivalent inputs can be described as:

$$\{ \, (\texttt{Hours, RateOfPay}) \mid \texttt{Hours} \times \texttt{RateOfPay} = 100 \, \}$$

(If you have forgotten your algebra lessons from years ago, this is read as "The set of all pairs of **Hours** and **RateOfPay** such that **Hours** times **RateOfPay** equals 100") .

Testing a result (or output) variable is always a multivariable combination test involving the result variable and the inputs needed to produce that desired value of the result.

Whenever you test a result variable:

- Start by picking the output value that you want to test.
- Identify the equivalence class of input values that jointly yield the desired output.
- Pick one or a few representatives from the set of inputs.

DATA FLOWS

Several authors discuss the concept of testing result variables in terms of *data flow* testing (*see, e.g.,* Ammann & Offutt, 2008; Binkley & Gallagher, 1996; Binkley & Harman, 2004; Gallagher & Lyle, 1991; Horowitz & Reps, 2013; Jorgensen, 2008; Tian, 2005; Tip, 1995; Weiser, 1984). A data flow starts when you *set* a variable with a value. The flow is complete when another variable *uses* that value. The two variables form a *set-use* pair. Suppose that you set:

- (a) $v_1 = 5$
- (b) $v_2 = v_1 \times v_1$

(c) $v_3 = 7$

(d) $v_4 = v_1 \times v_3$

(e) $v_5 = v_2 \times v_3$

(f) $v_6 = v_2 \times v_4$

The pair of variables, (v_1, v_2) is a set-use pair. The value of the second variable depends on the value of the first. Three other examples of set-use pairs are (v_1, v_4) and (v_3, v_4) and (v_3, v_5). These are *first-order* pairs (we can also call them first-order data flows)—the value of the second variable depends *directly* on the value of the first.

In contrast, consider v_5 and v_6. v_5 depends directly on the values of v_2 and v_3, but v_2 depends on the value of v_1 and therefore v_5 depends (via v_2) on v_1. There is a first-order data flow from v_2 to v_5 and a *second-order* data flow from v_1 to v_5. Similarly, you have second-order data flows from v_1 to v_6 and from v_3 to v_6.

Most discussions of data flow testing focus on first-order data flows. We don't restrict our focus in this way. *Any* relationship between two variables is of interest. Because of this, rather than using the language of data flows, we usually think (and speak) in terms of *impact*. Setting a value of one variable has an impact on a second variable if there is a data flow (of any order) from the first variable to the second.

FROM EXAMPLE 14: RESULT OF CALCULATIONS

I, J and K are Unsigned Integers. You can enter values into I and J, but the program calculates the value of K = I × J.

Let's start by assuming that you have done the basic testing of I and J and that they are in fact Unsigned Integers. Therefore their values range from 0 to **MAXINT**.

This simplifies the analysis of K:

- K can't be a letter or a negative number because it is an Unsigned Integer. (If I and J are both Unsigned Integers and K = I × J, how could you possibly get a negative number into K?)

- K can't exceed **MAXINT** because there is no room available in memory for any number larger than **MAXINT**. If you somehow store a larger number for K, you achieve an "overflow" and corrupt part of memory that is not allocated to storing a value for K. That would be a serious error.

- The absolutely biggest value we can imagine *trying* to store in K is **MAXINT** × **MAXINT** (I and J both **MAXINT**).

For a variable whose possible values are so tightly constrained, we recommend using the simpler domain analysis table.

Variable	Valid case equivalence class	Invalid case equivalence class	Boundaries and special cases	Notes
K	0 to **MAXINT**		0	
			MAXINT	
		< 0	can't do that	
		> **MAXINT**	**MAXINT**+1	
			MAXINT × **MAXINT**	

This table shows what values of K are interesting to try. Now you have to figure out what values of I and J to use in order to generate those values of K.

Because K is an Unsigned Integer, it runs from 0 to MAXINT. I and J can't both be MAXINT because MAXINT × MAXINT will cause an overflow value in K. More generally, we can describe the set of valid (I,J) pairs as:

{ (I, J) | I = 0 or J = 0 or

for nonzero I,J: I ≤ MAXINT / J and J ≤ MAXINT / I }

This set keeps K below MAXINT+1.

For the lower bound, K = 0:

Several (I,J) pairs will yield K = 0. The full set can be described like this:

{ (I, J) | I × J = 0 }

Continuing this analysis:

{ (I, J) | I × J = 0 }= { (I, J) | I = 0 or J = 0 }

This set is an equivalence set on the (I, J)'s. The set includes (0, 0), (1, 0), (MAXINT, 0), (0, 1), (0, MAXINT) as well as the many intermediate values, like (0, 2000).

The analysis for K = MAXINT is a little trickier. A common mistake is to write the set this way:

K = MAXINT for { (I, J) | I = MAXINT / J }

That works for J = 1 and J = MAXINT. However, Integer arithmetic truncates. So, for example, 2/3 = 0 and 3/2 = 1.

Instead, stick with:

K = MAXINT for { (I, J) | I × J = MAXINT }

This set includes at least two values, (1, MAXINT) and (MAXINT, 1). It will probably include a few other values. For example:

- Consider an 8-bit Unsigned Integer (ranges from 0 to 255).
- (2, MAXINT/2) might look like a good pair:
  - it might look like 2 × MAXINT/2 = MAXINT
  - but when you do Integer arithmetic, MAXINT/2 becomes 127, not 127.5
  - so 2 × MAXINT/2 = 254.

The equivalence set for MAXINT = I × J, when MAXINT = 255 is:

{ (1, 255), (3, 85), (5, 51), (15, 17), (17, 15), (51, 5), (85, 3) and (255, 1) }

Which values should you test?

There are debates about the best heuristics for selecting best representatives of multidimensional variables (like (I, J)) (*see* Beizer, 1995).

- As a general rule, we think the boundary cases are reasonable choices. Using boundaries is an easy heuristic to work with, so that's what we'll emphasize in this case. Thus, the tests (1, 255) and (255, 1) (that is, (1, MAXINT) and (MAXINT, 1)) are your choices.

- However, we aren't fond of repetition. If you're using 1 and 255 in several tests, choose other values for some (perhaps many) of those tests.

Finally, consider **MAXINT**+1.

The typical range of possible values for an Integer is 0 through 2^N-1, for example 2^{32}-1:

- **MAXINT** is 2^N-1
- **MAXINT**+1 is 2^N
- If **N** is even (such as 16 or 32 or 64), it is easy to find values for **I** and **J**:
  - **MAXINT** = $(2^{N/2} - 1)$ times $(2^{N/2} + 1)$.
  - **MAXINT**+1 = $2^{N/2}$ times $2^{N/2}$

Continuing the example of **N** = 8 (**K** ranges from 0 to 255), the test will be 2^4 times 2^4, which works out to 16 × 16 (which is 256 = **MAXINT**+1).

Here is how we lay out the full analysis:

Variable	Valid case equivalence class	Invalid case equivalence class	Boundaries and special cases	I	J	Notes
K = I × J	0 to **MAXINT**		0	0	0	$\{(I, J) \mid I = 0 \text{ or } J = 0\}$
				0	**MAXINT**	
				MAXINT	0	
			MAXINT	1	**MAXINT**	$\{(I, J) \mid I \times J = \text{MAXINT}\}$
				MAXINT	1	
		< 0	can't do that			
		> **MAXINT**	**MAXINT**+1	$2^{N/2}$	$2^{N/2}$	where **MAXINT** = 2^N-1
			MAXINT × **MAXINT**	**MAXINT**	**MAXINT**	

FROM EXAMPLE 17: JOAN'S PAY

Joan works at a store, under the following contract:

- Her normal pay rate is $8 per hour.
- For hours worked beyond 40 hours per week, her normal rate is $12 per hour.
- For work between midnight and 6 a.m. on any day, she gets $16 per hour.
- For work between 6 a.m. and noon on Sunday, she gets $16 per hour.
- If she earns $500 or less in a week, 10% of her pay is deducted for taxes.
- If she earns more than $500, the tax deducted is $50 plus 20% of earnings greater than $500 that week. (So, if she earns $600, the tax deducted is $70.)

Joan's take-home pay is a result variable.

The example doesn't specify the program's user interface. You can't know what the actual input variables are. We model the solution using notional input variables:

- **HoursWorked** (the total number of hours worked)
- **NightHours** (the number of hours worked between midnight and 6)
- **SundayHours** (the number of hours worked from 6 a.m. to noon Sunday)

From these, you can calculate:

- **TimeAndHalfHours** (the number of hours worked beyond 40 that aren't between midnight and 6 a.m. and not on Sunday morning) (If the calculated value is below 0, set it to 0.)

  = 0 or **HoursWorked** - **NightHours** - **SundayHours** - 40

- **NormalHours** (the number of hours worked, up to 40, that aren't between midnight and 6 a.m. and not on Sunday morning) (If the calculated value is below 0, set it to 0. If it is above 40, set it to 40.)

  = 0 or 40 or **HoursWorked** - **NightHours** - **SundayHours**

- **GrossPay**

  = 8 × **NormalHours** + 12 × **TimeAndHalfHours** + 16 × **NightHours** + 16 × **SundayHours**

- **TakeHomePay**

  = **GrossPay** × 0.9 if **GrossPay** ≤ 500 or

  GrossPay - 50 - (**GrossPay** -500) × 0.2

Partition the variables:

- **HoursWorked**: (input variable)
  - Too small: $\text{HoursWorked} < 0$
  - Valid: $0 \le \text{HoursWorked} \le 168$ (7 days x 24 hours)
  - Too large: $168 < \text{HoursWorked}$

- **NightHours**: (input variable)
  - Too small: $\text{NightHours} < 0$
  - Valid: $0 \le \text{NightHours} \le 42$ (7 days x 6 hours)
  - Too large: $42 < \text{NightHours}$

- **SundayHours**: (input variable)
  - Too small: $\text{SundayHours} < 0$
  - Valid: $0 \le \text{SundayHours} \le 6$
  - Too large: $6 < \text{SundayHours}$

- **TimeAndHalfHours**: (calculated)
  - Too small: $\text{TimeAndHalfHours} < 0$
  - Valid: $0 \le \text{TimeAndHalfHours} \le 80$ (168 - 42 - 6 - 40)
  - Too large: $80 < \text{TimeAndHalfHours}$

- **NormalHours**: (calculated)
  - Too small: $\text{NormalHours} < 0$
  - Valid: $0 \le \text{NormalHours} \le 40$
  - Too large: $40 < \text{NormalHours}$

- **GrossPay**: (calculated)
  - Too small: $\text{GrossPay} < 0$
  - Valid lower range: $0 \le \text{GrossPay} \le 500$
  - Valid: $500 < \text{GrossPay} \le 2048$

- ◦ Too large: $2048 < \texttt{GrossPay}$
- **TakeHomePay**: (calculated)
  - ◦ Too small: $\texttt{TakeHomePay} < 0$
  - ◦ Valid: $0 < \texttt{TakeHomePay} \leq 1688.40$
  - ◦ Too large: $1688.40 < \texttt{TakeHomePay}$

The question requests a domain analysis of take-home pay. The lower and upper bounds are clear, but there are other interesting values:

- If Joan worked only Sundays, the maximum **GrossPay** is $96 and the maximum **TakeHomePay** is $86.40.

- If Joan worked only regular hours, the maximum **GrossPay** is $320 and the maximum **TakeHomePay** is $288.00.

- If Joan worked only regular hours and Sundays, the maximum **GrossPay** is $416 and the maximum **TakeHomePay** is $374.40. If Joan worked only 40 regular hours and 3 overtime hours and 9 night hours, the maximum **GrossPay** is $500 and the maximum **TakeHomePay** is $450.00.

- If Joan worked only 40 regular hours and 3.0167 overtime hours and 9 night hours, the maximum **GrossPay** is $500 and the maximum **TakeHomePay** is $451.16. (If the program miscalculates the tax, deducting 10% from the added minute instead of 20%, the erroneous **TakeHomePay** will be $451.18).

- If Joan worked only night shifts, the maximum **GrossPay** is $672 and the maximum **TakeHomePay** is $587.60.

- If Joan worked only night shifts and Sundays, the maximum **GrossPay** is $768 and the maximum **TakeHomePay** is $664.40.

- If Joan worked only regular hours and nights, the maximum **GrossPay** is $992 and the maximum **TakeHomePay** is $843.60.

- If Joan worked only regular hours and time-and-a-half hours, the maximum **GrossPay** is $1280 and the maximum **TakeHomePay** is $1074.

- If Joan worked only regular hours and time-and-a-half hours and Sundays, the maximum **GrossPay** is $1376 and the maximum **TakeHomePay** is $1150.80.

- If Joan worked only regular hours and time-and-a-half hours and nights, the maximum **GrossPay** is $1952 and the maximum **TakeHomePay** is $1611.60.

The following table summarizes these cases. Abbreviations: **TH** TakeHomePay, **HW** HoursWorked, **NH** NightHours, **SH** SundayHours. The table doesn't distinguish overtime from regular hours because these can be derived from **HW**, **NH** and **SH**.

Variable	Valid case equivalence class	Invalid case equivalence class	Boundaries and special cases	HW	NH	SH	Notes
TH	0 to 1688.40		0	0	0	0	
			86.40	6	0	6	
			288	40	0	0	
			374.40	46	0	6	
			450	52	9	0	

Variable	Valid case equivalence class	Invalid case equivalence class	Boundaries and special cases	HW	NH	SH	Notes
			451.16	52.01	9	0	
			587.60	42	42	0	
			664.40	48	42	6	
			843.60	82	42	0	
			1074.00	120	0	0	
			1150.80	126	0	6	
			1611.60	162	42	0	
			1688.40	168	42	6	
	< 0						not possible
	> 1688.40			169	42	6.017	should be impossible
				169	42.017	6	should be impossible

We assume for this exercise that $\Delta = 1$ minute (0.0167 hours).

Going larger than $1688.40 will require an invalid input in the number of hours. Before running this combination test, you should already have tested the program with invalid inputs and it should have rejected them. Therefore, the combinations with too many hours should be impossible tests.

FROM EXAMPLE 20: SUM OF SQUARES (MAX)

$$SS = x_1^2 + x_2^2 + \ldots + x_n^2$$

(SS is the sum of squared values of the n variables, x_1 through x_n.)

The x_i's are all Floating Point.

$SS \leq 45$.

The ranges for the x_i^2s and SS are:

- *Too small*: less than 0
- *Acceptable*: 0 through 45
- *Too large*: greater than 45. The boundary case is $45 + \Delta$ (the smallest Floating-Point number larger than 45 that can be represented in this programming language).

ANALYSIS OF THE x_i'S.

Because no x_i^2 can exceed 45, no x_i can exceed $\sqrt{45}$.

It appears that values of x_i can be positive or negative: x_i^2 will be positive whether x_i is positive or negative.

Another constraint on each x_i is that the sum of the x_i^2s must be less than 45.

The example's description doesn't specify a value (or a maximum limit) for n, the number of x_i's. Assuming that n is an Integer, the absolute maximum on n is MAXINT.

ANALYSIS OF THE RESULT VARIABLE, ss.

The boundary values for **ss** are easy to determine. Finding values of the x_i's that yield boundary values for **ss** is the challenge. Here are some specific tests that fulfill this requirement:

ss is the sum of the x_i's.

- To set **ss** to 0, set all the x_i's to 0.
- To set **ss** to 45, set $x_1 = 2$, $x_2 = 4$ and $x_3 = 5$.
- To set **ss** to $45 + \Delta$, try $x_1 = 2$, $x_2 = 4$, $x_3 = 5$ and $x_4 = \sqrt{\Delta(45)}$.

If you don't recall the meaning of $\Delta(45)$, see *Floating Point* on page 72.

EXTREME INPUTS DON'T NECESSARILY YIELD EXTREME OUTPUTS

Dorothy Graham provides two lessons with a simple example:

> "A max or min for output may be in the middle of an input range. For example age and the cost of car insurance: at 17 (in this country) it is very high, then it goes down and rises again when you get old (over 70). So the minimum output is somewhere around respectable middle age." (Graham, personal communication.)

- First the relationship between input variables and results might not be simple. The values of the input might rise while the result goes up and down.

- Second, the result might not come from a simple calculation. In this example, the base insurance rate for a specific age might come from a lookup table or a more complex database.

EXERCISES: PART 3-O

Please identify and analyze the variables that hold results in each question below:

O.1. *Example 9: Create Table (Max Cells)* **on page 289**

In OpenOffice (OOo) Impress, you can create a table. With this dialog, you set the starting numbers of rows and columns. Suppose the maximum number of cells in the table is 4095.

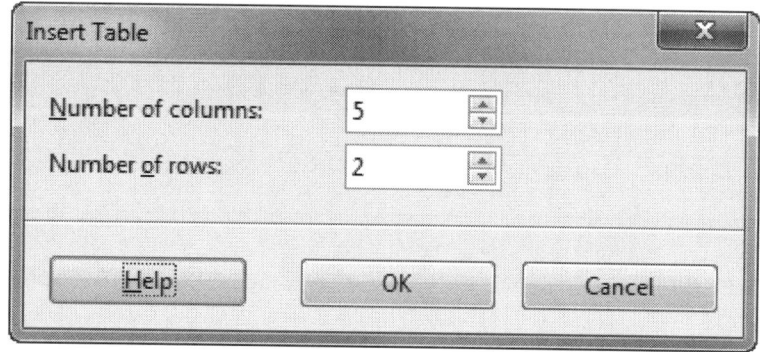

The input values must be Integers. The program will round fractional amounts, so that 8.4 rows is changed to 8 when you press Tab or Enter to exit an input field and 8.5 rows is changed to 9. The program also ignores non-numeric characters: for example, it interprets 2a3 as 23.

O.2. *Example 15: Mailing Labels* **on page 325**

A program prints mailing labels. The first line of the label is the person's name. The program builds the name from three fields, **FirstName**, **MiddleName** and **LastName**. Each field can hold up to 30 characters. The label can be up to 70 characters wide.

O.3. *Example 16: Unemployment Insurance Benefits* **on page 337**

In the state of Domainia, every unemployed adult receives a benefit of 350. If that person has worked and is older than 40, the benefit is raised by 100. Alternatively (else), if the person has exactly 4 children, the benefit is raised by 50 (van Veenendaal & Seubers, 2002, p. 231).

A SCHEMA FOR DOMAIN TESTING

1. CHARACTERIZE THE VARIABLE

A. Identify the potentially interesting variables.

B. Identify the variable(s) you can analyze now. This is the variable(s) of interest.

C. Determine the primary dimension of the variable of interest.

D. Determine the type and scale of the variable's primary dimension and what values it can take.

E. Determine whether you can order the variable's values (from smallest to largest).

F. Determine whether this is an input variable or a result.

G. Determine how the program uses this variable.

H. Determine whether other variables are related to this one.

2. ANALYZE THE VARIABLE AND CREATE TESTS

I. Partition the variable (its primary dimension).

- If the dimension is ordered, determine its sub-ranges and transition points.
- If the dimension is not ordered, base partitioning on similarity.

J. Lay out the analysis in a classical boundary/equivalence table. Identify best representatives.

K. Create tests for the consequences of the data entered, not just the input filter.

L. Identify secondary dimensions. Analyze them in the classical way.

M. Summarize your analysis with a risk/equivalence table.

3. GENERALIZE TO MULTIDIMENSIONAL VARIABLES

N. Analyze independent variables that should be tested together.

O. Analyze variables that hold results.

P. Analyze non-independent variables. Deal with relationships and constraints.

4. PREPARE FOR ADDITIONAL TESTING

Q. Identify and list unanalyzed variables. Gather information for later analysis.

R. Imagine and document risks that don't necessarily map to an obvious dimension.

P. ANALYZE NON-INDEPENDENT VARIABLES. DEAL WITH RELATIONSHIPS AND CONSTRAINTS

For our purposes, two variables are *independent* if the value of one variable has no effect *on the range* of valid values of the other variable.

There are other definitions of independence. For example, statistical independence requires the variables to be uncorrelated. Our definition is not this stringent. Consider this example with two variables, **X** and **Y**.

- In the statistical sense, **Y** is dependent on **X** if setting **X** to 5 *changes the probability* that **Y** can be 10.

- In the way we mean "independent",

  - **Y** might not be dependent on **X** if setting **X** to 5 *changes the probability* that **Y** can be 10.

  - We treat **X** and **Y** as dependent if setting **X** to 5 *makes it impossible* for **Y** to be 10.

We call the variables independent if all the pairs (**X**, **Y**) of valid values of **X** and valid values of **Y** are valid pairs. Our interest is whether all the combinations are *possible*, not whether they're more or less likely.

WAYS VARIABLES CONSTRAIN EACH OTHER

Here are some of the ways that variables can be non-independent, *i.e.*, some of the kinds of constraints that you can find among variables:

- *Constrained to a range.*

  The values of some variables limit the range of values of the second. Examples:

  - The width of a line you draw on a page must be less than the width of the page.
  - The width of a page margin has to be less than the width of the page.
  - A variable must not be zero if you'll divide something by it.
  - The product or sum (or other function) of a pair of variables must not overflow the data type. Example: **A** and **B** are Integers, **A+B** can't exceed **MAXINT**. Therefore A and B constrain each other.
  - A calculated result of two or more variables must not produce an invalid input to a function that will use that result. Example: in **log(A+B)**, **A+B** must be greater than 0.
  - In a Date field, the range of valid days (1-28, 1-29, 1-30 or 1-31) depends on the month (and if the month is February, also the year and the century).

- *Must calculate to a constant value.*

  For example:

  - The sum of the three angles of a triangle must be 180.
  - The product of a variable and its inverse must be 1; the sum of a variable and its inverse must be 0.

  Note that if you're doing Floating-Point calculations, these "must be" statements turn into "must be very close to" because of rounding error.

- *Variables must be equal.*

  Once the value of one variable is specified, another variable must match it. Examples:

- The inverse of a function should yield the original value (e.g., the square root of the square of 2 should be 2).

- Financial records often have to balance. Examples:

  - The new balance in your checking account must equal the old balance plus deposits and other credits minus checks, withdrawals and fees).

  - In any financial ledger, debits and credits must sum to the same value; also, the sums of the rows must equal the sums of the columns.[35]

A related concept that we group under this one is that of variables that must be proportional. For example, Variable 2 might have to be twice Variable 1 instead of equal to it.

As we noted above, "equal" doesn't really mean "equal" when you're dealing with Floating-Point calculations. "Equal" means almost the same, where the difference is no bigger than some (very small) maximum error, which we call the tolerance level. The higher the precision of your calculations, the smaller the tolerance level.

- *Selection from a list.*

  One variable might restrict the list of options available to the next. For example:

  - In the print driver dialog of Example 26, you select the manufacturer first and then you select among the printers that are made by that manufacturer.

  - When you do a search (e.g., Amazon, Bing, etc.), you end up selecting from the list of documents that results from the search.

  - Failure to consistently enforce such a constraint in the Therac-25 has killed people (Leveson, 1995; Leveson & Turner, 1993).

EXAMPLE 8: CREATE TABLE (COLUMNS, ROWS) (VARIABLES THAT MULTIPLY TO A MAXIMUM)

In OpenOffice (OOo) Impress, you can create a table. With this dialog, you set the starting numbers of rows and columns.

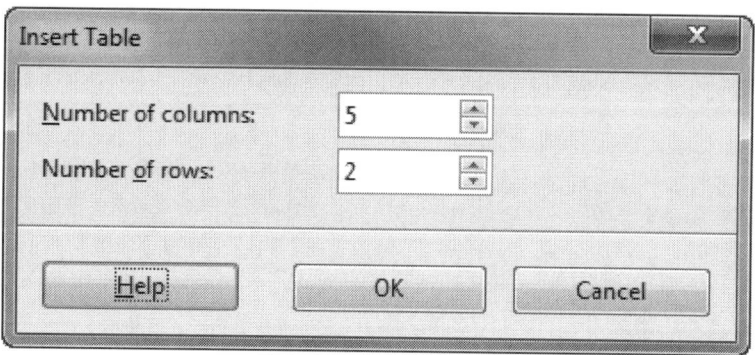

Notes: The input values must be Integers. The program will round fractional amounts, so that 8.4 rows is changed to 8 when you press Tab or Enter to exit an input field and 8.5 rows is changed to 9. The program also ignores non-numeric characters: for example, it interprets 2a3 as 23.

---

35 Michael Bolton notes the ledger is a widely used oracle. If the values don't match, we've made a calculation error or a data input error. This is true for many of the constraints—violation of the constraint points to an error that might be an input error or a basic calculation error or might reflect the program's inability to cope with an extreme value in one or more of the variables. That last case is the most interesting one from the point of view of domain testing.

OpenOffice will accept up to 75 rows and 75 columns. These appear to be independent. However, the more cells, the slower OpenOffice responds. Long before you hit the maximum, OpenOffice becomes unusably slow. So the empirical question is what the practical limit is on the number of cells in the table. From that you can determine the constraints on the number of rows and columns.

Before you tell us (as several people have) that "No one would make a table this big for a presentation," remember that PowerPoint is often used to create posters for academic presentations. Posters run up to 4 feet tall. We've seen a 12-foot wide poster. Imagine posting a large and complex set of data on one huge "page" on a wall so that you and a few colleagues could study it together. How many rows and columns of data would a 4 foot by 12 foot poster hold?

And before you tell us (as several people have) that "No one would want to look at that much data at one time," here are two specific types of examples we've seen repeatedly:

- Researchers obtained unexpected results and are scanning large sets of manually-entered data, looking for anomalously large or small or otherwise-strange (different from the others) values that might indicate data entry errors, other experimental errors or specific, genuine, results that merit close investigation.

- Investment modelers are looking for patterns in data associated with specific stocks that might distinguish between stocks that then went up by more than **x**% versus stocks that then went down by more than **x**%. Which groups of variables might be predictive?

Boundaries are funny things. When people say "No one would need a value that big," what they really mean is "I can't imagine why anyone would need a value that big." The world is often less constrained than the limits of our imagination.

EXAMPLE 12: PIECEWISE BOUNDARY (LINEAR RELATIONSHIPS)

Some commonplace relationships between variables are linear. That is, the individual variables can be graphed (mapped to the number line) and the relationship between any two variables, **x** and **y**, can be described in the form $y = a \times x + b$ (or $y > a \times x + b$), where **a** and **b** are numeric constants. Analyses of domain-testing selection rules have been widely published for linear boundaries (*see, e.g.*, Beizer, 1995; Clarke et al. 1982; Tian, 2005).

The input domain of a function is the set of all points (**x**, **y**) that meet these criteria (Binder, 2000, p. 404):

- **x** and **y** are Floating-Point variables

- $1 < x \leq 10$

- $1 \leq y \leq 10$

- $y \leq 14 - x$

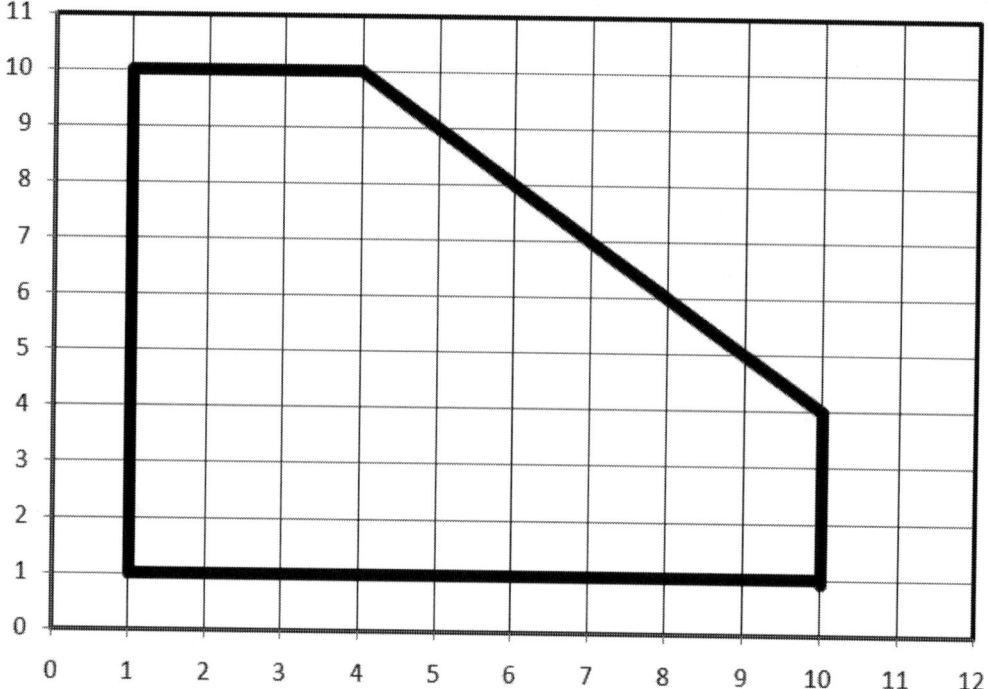

This example illustrates variables that aren't independent. For example, even though **x** can be 10 and **y** can be 10, a test with (10,10) makes no sense because this point is far outside the domain, nowhere near the domain's boundary.

Several academics use examples like this one to criticize naive testers who test with extreme-value combinations (like (0,0) and (10,0)) instead of testing on the domain's actual boundaries. (*See, e.g.,* Beizer, 1995, p. 161, "What's Wrong With Extreme Point Combinations?")

These tests are inappropriate when the input variables aren't independent. However, when variables are independent, combining extreme values will normally be the right approach because those combinations (those points) will be points *on* the boundary, not far from it.

The example defines a bounding area, set by 5 inequalities:

$$1 < \mathbf{x}$$
$$\mathbf{x} \leq 10$$
$$1 \leq \mathbf{y}$$
$$\mathbf{y} \leq 10$$
$$\mathbf{y} \leq 14 - \mathbf{x}$$

The 5 inequalities determine the 5 line segments shown on the graph.

To discuss domains shown with diagrams, we need a few definitions:

- *On point:* a point that is on the boundary
- *Off point:* a point that is not on the boundary
- *Inner point:* a point that is inside the specified domain (a member of the set that defines the domain)
- *Outer point:* a point that is outside the specified domain (not a member of the set that defines the domain)

- *Open boundary*: the boundary is not inside the specified range or area, For example, 1 is not inside $1 < x$
- *Closed boundary*: the boundary is inside the specified range or area. For example, 10 is inside $x \le 10$.

Here's the basic pattern for dealing with linear boundaries:

- You always need an Inner point and an Outer point. One of these will be an On point; the other will be an Off point.
- If the input domain is specified as *equal to* the boundary, pick three points, one on the boundary, one on one side of it and one on the other side.

Applying that to this example, for each line segment (for each inequality):

- When you have a closed boundary, a point on the boundary is an On point. For example, any point on the line $y = 1$ (when $1 < x \le 10$) is an On point because the boundary is specified as $1 \le y$.
- When you have an open boundary, a point on the boundary is an Off point. For example, any point on the line $x = 1$ (between $y = 1$ and $y = 10$) is an Off point because the boundary is defined as $1 < x$.
- Notice that we haven't yet specified what value the other variable will take. For example, if you choose $y = 1$, what value do you pick for x? Recommendations seem to vary, but the most common recommendation seems to be to pick a mid-range value. Thus the test might be ($x = 5.5$, $y = 1$). Alternatively:
  - For the Inner point, you might pick a more challenging case ($x = 1.00001$, $y = 1$)
  - But for Outer Off point, where you're forcing an error message, you might pick the non-error value to be mid-range, focusing attention on the variable that is out of bounds ($x = 5.5$, $y = 0.999999$).

Here are our tests. The Inner cases touch every corner, the Outer cases touch the middle of each line:

Inequality	Inner Points		Outer Points	
	x	y	x	y
$1 < x$	1.00001	1 $1 \le y \le 10$	1	5.5 midrange
$x \le 10$	10	4 $1 \le y \le 4$	10.0001	2.5 midrange
$1 \le y$	10 $1 < x \le 10$	1	5.5 midrange	0.999999
$y \le 10$	1 $1 < x \le 4$	10	2.5 midrange	10.0001
$y \le 14 - x$	$x = 4$	$y = 10$	$x = 7$ midrange	$y = 7.00001$ midrange

This analysis is straightforward once you get used to the definitions. However, what if the domain's definition is nonlinear?

EXAMPLE 10: THE CIRCLE (NONLINEAR RELATIONSHIPS)

Consider a circle defined by $x_1^2 + x_2^2 = 100$.

Some of the points on this circle are (0, 10), (6, 8), (8, 6), (10, 0), (8, -6), (6, -8), (0, -10), (-6, -8), (-8, -6), (-10, 0), (-8, 6) and (-6, 8).

Consider these sets:

(a) $\{ (x_1, x_2) \mid x_1^2 + x_2^2 = 100 \}$ (the circle)
(b) $\{ (x_1, x_2) \mid x_1^2 + x_2^2 < 100 \}$ (the points inside the circle)
(c) $\{ (x_1, x_2) \mid x_1^2 + x_2^2 > 100 \}$ (the points outside the circle)
(d) $\{ (x_1, x_2) \mid x_1^2 + x_2^2 \leq 100 \}$ (the circle and points inside it)
(e) $\{ (x_1, x_2) \mid x_1^2 + x_2^2 \geq 100 \}$ (the circle and points outside it)

In each of these cases, the set (a) defines the boundary (the set of points *on* the circle).

Let's work through these one at a time. We'll leave (e) as an exercise for you because it's so similar to the others. We provide a little more detail at *Example 10: The Circle* on page 293.

(A) THE CIRCLE $\{ (x_1, x_2) \mid x_1^2 + x_2^2 = 100 \}$

Only the points on the circle are in the "valid" equivalence class.

Any point inside or outside (but not on) the circle is an:

- *Off point* and an
- *Outer point* (even the ones inside the circle)

because "Outer" means outside of the set that specifies the class. The inside of the circle is not part of the class.

If you follow the heuristics for linear cases, you will pick one point on the circle and two off, one that you can plot inside the circle ($x_1^2 + x_2^2 < 100$) and one that you can plot outside ($x_1^2 + x_2^2 > 100$).

We're not entirely comfortable with using only three points.

We don't have a clear theory of error that demands more than one test with an On point, but we'd like to trace the shape in both dimensions. Therefore, we test one On point in each quadrant of the circle. In practice, if we found several functions like this in a program and found no indication that the program treated points in different quadrants differently, we would quickly reduce our test set, probably back to one On point, rather than one per quadrant.

We would probably run these tests:

Type of test point	x	y	Notes
On Inner	0	10	Table for Case A. Valid values are on the circle
On Inner	0	-10	
On Inner	10	0	
On Inner	-10	0	
Off Outer	0	0	We usually test zero. Note that if the circle shifted so that (0,0) was not the center, we would still be interested in (0,0).
Off Outer	.001	10	barely outside the circle
Off Outer	0	-9.99	barely inside the circle

Alternatively, you might consider points away from the axes because:

a. there is no rounding error on the square of zero, so you might be missing a potential problem and

b. if the programmer tested any points on the circle, she probably tested these, so why repeat the same tests?

Under that view, we would still try 4 On points, one per quadrant of the circle, but they would be at different relative places.

Type of test point	x	y	Notes
On Inner	6	8	This is another table for Case A. This one tests On points that aren't on the graph's axes.
On Inner	$\sqrt{50}$	$-\sqrt{50}$	
On Inner	-3	$-\sqrt{91}$	
On Inner	$-\sqrt{75}$	5	
Off Outer	0	0	We almost always test zero
Off Outer	.001	10	Barely outside the circle
Off Outer	0	-9.99	Barely inside the circle

We don't have a basis for preferring one of these sets of tests over the other. We would choose our strategy based on our experiences testing this program or our history with code from these programmers.

(B) INSIDE THE CIRCLE { $(x_1, x_2) \mid x_1^2 + x_2^2 < 100$ }

The input domain includes only the points inside the circle. The points on the boundary (on the circle) and the points outside the circle are both outside of the input domain. At a minimum, you should include one point inside the circle (inside the domain) and one point on the circle (on the boundary but outside the domain).

As above, our inclination is to include one Inner point for each quadrant and two On points (these are our Outer points), each in separate quadrants.

Type of test point	x	y	Notes
Off Inner	6	7.99	Table for Case B. Valid values are inside the circle.
Off Inner	0	-9.99	
Off Inner	2.99	$-\sqrt{91}$	
Off Inner	$-\sqrt{74.9}$	5	
Off Inner	0	0	
On Outer	$\sqrt{50}$	$-\sqrt{50}$	
On Outer	0	10	

(C) OUTSIDE THE CIRCLE { $(x_1, x_2) \mid x_1^2 + x_2^2 > 100$ }

The input domain includes only the points outside the circle. The points on the boundary (on the circle) and the points *inside* the circle are *outside* of the input domain. At a minimum, include one Inner point (points outside the circle are inner to the specified domain) and one point on the circle (because it is on the boundary but outside the domain).

Normally, we include one Inner point for each quadrant and two On points (these are our Outer points), each in separate quadrants.

Type of test point	x	y	Notes
Off Inner	6	8.01	Table for Case C. Valid values are outside the circle.
Off Inner	0	-10.01	
Off Inner	3.01	$-\sqrt{91}$	
Off Inner	$-\sqrt{75.1}$	5	
Off Inner	0	0	
On Outer	$\sqrt{50}$	$-\sqrt{50}$	
On Outer	0	10	

(D) THE CIRCLE & POINTS INSIDE IT $\{ (x_1, x_2) \mid x_1^2 + x_2^2 \leq 100 \}$

The input domain includes all the points inside the circle, plus the circle. At a minimum, include a point on the boundary (the circle is inside the input domain) and a point outside the circle. Normally, we include one On point for each quadrant and two Off points (points outside the circle are our Outer points), each in separate quadrants.

Type of test point	x	y	Notes
On Inner	6	8	Table for Case D. Valid values are on the circle or inside it.
On Inner	$\sqrt{50}$	$-\sqrt{50}$	
On Inner	-3	$-\sqrt{91}$	
On Inner	$-\sqrt{75}$	5	
Off Inner	0	0	
Off Outer	$\sqrt{50.1}$	$-\sqrt{50}$	
Off Outer	0.001	10	

EXAMPLE 3: SUNTRUST VISA (COMPLEX RELATIONSHIPS)

SunTrust issues Visa credit cards with credit limits in the range of $400 to $40000. A customer is not to be approved for credit limits outside this range. A customer can apply for the card using an online application form in which one of the fields requires that the customer type in his/her desired credit limit.

The problem description mentions only one input field—`DesiredCreditLimit`. However, in the real world, we would want to test this in combination with several other variables such as:

- The customer name and whatever credit history that name pulls up.

- Whether the customer already has another SunTrust Visa card and how much their credit limit is on that card. (Does the total of that card and the new one exceed $40,000?)

Whether the customer will get credit, and how much, will depend on these variables and probably several others that reflect policies of the bank.

The relationships among some of these variables might be deterministic and linear, easy to test in combination. Other relationships might involve human judgment. Your tests might check whether the software restricts judgment-based decisions to a range that is derived from the values of the inputs.

ADDITIONAL EXAMPLES

SELECTION FROM A LIST

Michael Bolton gave us this example of the relationship described above as *selection from a list*:

> "My favorite example of this: I'm filling out a Web page for, let's say, a car rental in the U.S. I'm filling out the payment information. The state/province dropdown doesn't list any Canadian provinces. After futzing around for a while, I realize that the province isn't selectable until I've selected the country, which appears lower down in the form. Then when I select the country, the Web site takes me to the Canadian version of the site—and clears out everything that I've entered so far."

SOMETIMES RELATED, SOMETIMES NOT

Imagine writing a program to do comparison shopping. The total cost of an order is a function of the price of the individual items, the sales tax and the shipping cost. Some states don't charge sales tax.

- If the program considers only vendors like Amazon, that's all the information you need. The shipping price per unit is the same no matter how many units you buy.
- However, if you plan to buy many items from the same vendor on eBay, you can send a note to the vendor asking for a discount on shipping. In our experience, vendors will often agree to a discount because their shipping cost per item is lower (they can put several items in the same box).

The relationship between shipping costs and the number of units is linear at Amazon. It appears to be linear at eBay too, but if you ask for a discount, the relationship might be negotiable and nonlinear.

The possibility of a discount isn't posted on the vendor's website. It is undocumented. Modeling of a problem sometimes involves judgment, especially when variables come into play sometimes but are invisible most of the time. These situations often call for scenario tests rather than mechanical combinations.

EXERCISES: PART 3-P

Please analyze these non-independent variables. Deal with relationships and constraints in each question below:

P.1. *Example 10: The Circle* **on page 293**
Continue this Chapter's analysis by working through Case (e).

P.2. *Example 18: Volume Discounts* **on page 349**
Consider the following pricing system:

- For the first 10 units, the price is $5.
- For the next 10 units (11 to 20), the price is $4.75.

- For the next 10 units (21 to 30), the price is $4.50.
- For more than 30 units, the price is $4.00.

Do a domain analysis that partitions according to the number of units purchased or according to the **Total-PricePaid** (Desikan & Ramesh, 2006).

P.3. *Example 22: NextDate* **on page 373**

"**NextDate** is a function of three variables: month, day and year. It returns the date of the day after the input date." (Jorgensen, 2008, p. 22).

Jorgensen limits the year to the range $1812 \leq year \leq 2012$ and of course $1 \leq day \leq 31$ and $1 \leq month \leq 12$. If the user enters a bad date, the program rejects it with a "bad date" message.

P.4. *Example 23: Frequent-Flyer Miles* **on page 377**

An airline awards frequent-flyer miles according to the following table (Black, 2007, p. 218):

Status Level	None	Silver	Gold	Platinum
Trip bonus	0%	25%	50%	100%
Distance traveled	d	d	d	d
Points awarded	d	$1.25 \times d$	$1.5 \times d$	$2 \times d$
Miles required to reach this level	0	25,000	50,000	100,000

Your status is determined before you fly. The number of miles flown on this trip does not affect your status on this trip, though a long trip might result in elevating your status before your next trip.

Determine whether the system awards the correct number of points for a given trip.

SECTION 2. PART 4: PREPARE FOR ADDITIONAL TESTING

Parts 1 to 3 covered the tasks that we think make up domain testing.

However, domain testing is just one of many test techniques. While you're designing and running domain tests, you're likely to see things that aren't relevant to the testing you're doing *right now* but that can later help you design new domain tests or new tests of other types.

We often find it useful to record that other information, the other facts that we notice and the ideas and insights that don't neatly fit with the tests at hand.

This Part is about noticing and keeping that information:

    Q. Identify and list unanalyzed variables. Gather information for later analysis.

    R. Imagine and document risks that don't necessarily map to an obvious dimension.

These tasks are open-ended. If you spend too much time on them or pay too much attention to them, they might distract you from the work at hand. We can't tell you how to set your priorities—they will, and they should, vary from context to context.

A SCHEMA FOR DOMAIN TESTING

1. CHARACTERIZE THE VARIABLE

A. Identify the potentially interesting variables.

B. Identify the variable(s) you can analyze now. This is the variable(s) of interest.

C. Determine the primary dimension of the variable of interest.

D. Determine the type and scale of the variable's primary dimension and what values it can take.

E. Determine whether you can order the variable's values (from smallest to largest).

F. Determine whether this is an input variable or a result.

G. Determine how the program uses this variable.

H. Determine whether other variables are related to this one.

2. ANALYZE THE VARIABLE AND CREATE TESTS

I. Partition the variable (its primary dimension).
    - If the dimension is ordered, determine its sub-ranges and transition points.
    - If the dimension is not ordered, base partitioning on similarity.

J. Lay out the analysis in a classical boundary/equivalence table. Identify best representatives.

K. Create tests for the consequences of the data entered, not just the input filter.

L. Identify secondary dimensions. Analyze them in the classical way.

M. Summarize your analysis with a risk/equivalence table.

3. GENERALIZE TO MULTIDIMENSIONAL VARIABLES

N. Analyze independent variables that should be tested together.

O. Analyze variables that hold results.

P. Analyze non-independent variables. Deal with relationships and constraints.

4. PREPARE FOR ADDITIONAL TESTING

Q. Identify and list unanalyzed variables. Gather information for later analysis.

R. Imagine and document risks that don't necessarily map to an obvious dimension.

Q. IDENTIFY AND LIST UNANALYZED VARIABLES. GATHER INFORMATION FOR LATER ANALYSIS

The first two steps in the Schema for domain testing are:

A. Identify the potentially interesting variables.

B. Identify the variable(s) you can analyze now.

To find these variables, you might use an explicit variable-hunting process, such as a variable-identification tour (Kelly, 2005). But that's beyond the scope of this book.

Here, we'll point out that you're likely to run into variables in many ways in the normal course of designing and running domain tests. For example, when you're testing one variable, you might:

- See other variables in the dialog box(es) where you enter data into this variable.

- Consider how the variable gets its value. Even if it's an input value, how does the user decide what value it should have? Are other variables or other decisions (based on other variables) influential? Maybe you don't know the names of those variables yet or where they appear in the program, but if you understand their function in the overall system, you can describe them. Once you know, conceptually, what you're looking for, you can identify the actual variables later.

- Consider how the program uses the variable. What variables depend on this one? What variables are constrained by it? Again, you might not know the details of those variables, but if you know what to look for, you'll eventually find them.

For example, imagine entering a credit card purchase into a credit transaction system. Right now, you might know only the amount of the purchase, but you can probably figure out that the purchase will change the balance due on the card, the amount of interest the customer will have to pay on the credit card balance, the amount of credit available to the customer, the amounts that will be printed on the credit card statement. If the purchase is big enough, it might even affect the customer's credit rating. This loan by the bank will also reflect on the bank's finances, such as how much money it has loaned and therefore how much it has left for lending to others.

You might also notice (or decide to find out):

- What variables it is stored with.

- What reports it appears in and what variables it is printed or displayed with.

- What external systems the system under test communicates with and how the value of this variable is communicated to them (and thus, what variables in those systems interact with this one).

FROM EXAMPLE 24: NOTEPAD OPEN FILE DIALOG

This is Notepad's file open dialog.

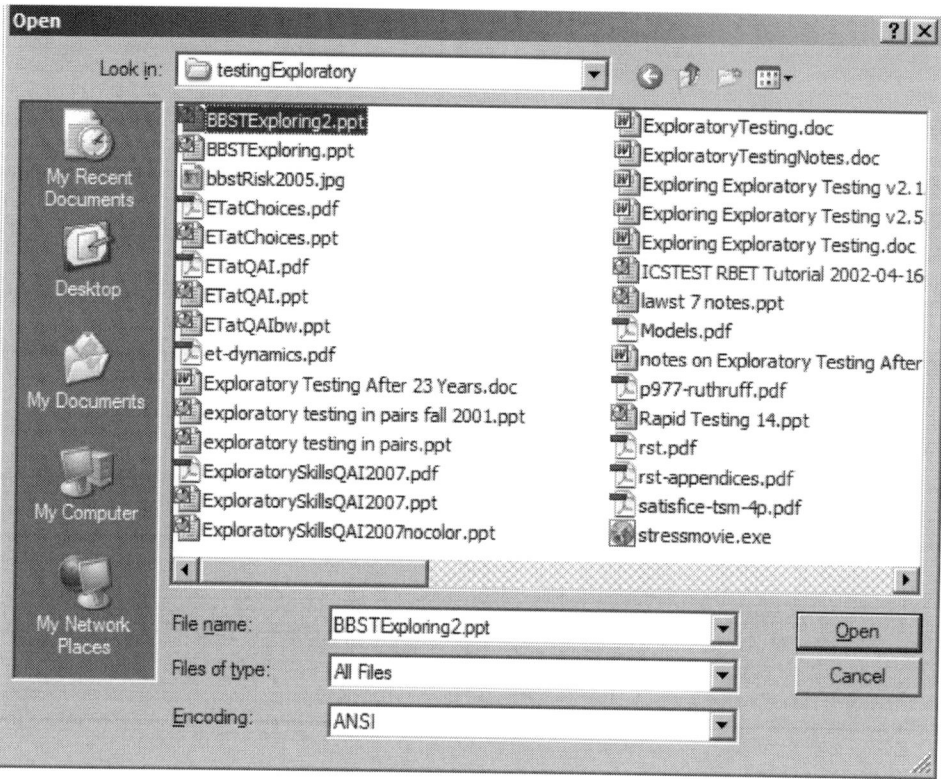

What *are* the variables here?

- **FileName**: full name of the file, including extension (last 3 chars)
- **FileType**: filters the files that appear in the file name window
- **Encoding**: what mapping between characters and the underlying numeric codes, such as ASCII or Unicode

In addition, you have several things you can vary. Here are a few:

- What type of data are actually stored in the file? For example, a file might actually include plain text no matter what extension it has.
- How long is the file name?
- How dissimilar are two file names? If both are the same for the first **N** characters, is there a value of N so big that even if the two names differ in the **N+1**th character, the program won't be able to tell the difference?
- How long is the full path to the document?

FROM EXAMPLE 3: SUNTRUST VISA

SunTrust issues Visa credit cards with credit limits in the range of $400 to $40000. A customer is not to be approved for credit limits outside this range. A customer can apply for the card using an online application form in which one of the fields requires that the customer type in his/her desired credit limit.

The example describes only one input field:

- `DesiredCreditLimit`

The example mentions other variables but does not describe them as input fields. Many tests are likely to collect values for these variables:

- `CreditLimit` (the limit to be assigned to this account)
- `CustomerName`

In addition:

- Is there a variable that holds the decision (application accepted or rejected)?
- What other fields does the application include:
  - Customer income, address and other demographic data?
  - Other credit cards, other loans and other income and credit data?

EXERCISES: PART 4-Q

Please identify and describe unanalyzed variables in each question below:

Q.1. *Example 18: Volume Discounts* **on page 349**

Consider the following pricing system:

- For the first 10 units, the price is $5.
- For the next 10 units (11 to 20), the price is $4.75.
- For the next 10 units (21 to 30), the price is $4.50.
- For more than 30 units, the price is $4.00.

Do a domain analysis that partitions according to the number of units purchased or according to the `TotalPricePaid` (Desikan & Ramesh, 2006).

Q.2. *Example 22: NextDate* **on page 373**

"`NextDate` is a function of three variables: month, day and year. It returns the date of the day after the input date." (Jorgensen, 2008, p. 22).

Jorgensen limits the year to the range $1812 \leq year \leq 2012$ and of course $1 \leq day \leq 31$ and $1 \leq month \leq 12$. If the user enters a bad date, the program rejects it with a "bad date" message.

Q.3. *Example 29: Select And Flip Picture* **on page 411**

In OpenOffice Impress (3.0), you can select a picture on a slide and then flip it vertically or horizontally.

This photo by Marc St. Gil is part of the Environmental Protection Agency's DOCUMERICA series. The National Archives identifier is 207/27/012387.

What variables (for example, what attributes of the picture or the document) do you think would be relevant to how well this feature works?

A SCHEMA FOR DOMAIN TESTING

1. CHARACTERIZE THE VARIABLE

    A. Identify the potentially interesting variables.

    B. Identify the variable(s) you can analyze now. This is the variable(s) of interest.

    C. Determine the primary dimension of the variable of interest.

    D. Determine the type and scale of the variable's primary dimension and what values it can take.

    E. Determine whether you can order the variable's values (from smallest to largest).

    F. Determine whether this is an input variable or a result.

    G. Determine how the program uses this variable.

    H. Determine whether other variables are related to this one.

2. ANALYZE THE VARIABLE AND CREATE TESTS

    I. Partition the variable (its primary dimension).

        – If the dimension is ordered, determine its sub-ranges and transition points.

        – If the dimension is not ordered, base partitioning on similarity.

    J. Lay out the analysis in a classical boundary/equivalence table. Identify best representatives.

    K. Create tests for the consequences of the data entered, not just the input filter.

    L. Identify secondary dimensions. Analyze them in the classical way.

    M. Summarize your analysis with a risk/equivalence table.

3. GENERALIZE TO MULTIDIMENSIONAL VARIABLES

    N. Analyze independent variables that should be tested together.

    O. Analyze variables that hold results.

    P. Analyze non-independent variables. Deal with relationships and constraints.

4. PREPARE FOR ADDITIONAL TESTING

    Q. Identify and list unanalyzed variables. Gather information for later analysis.

R. Imagine and document risks that don't necessarily map to an obvious dimension.

R. IMAGINE AND DOCUMENT RISKS THAT DON'T MAP TO AN OBVIOUS DIMENSION

In domain testing, you focus on the possible values of a variable. You organize them along a dimension, partitioning them into equivalence classes. You start with the variable's primary dimension and then imagine other ways that a variable's value could cause a problem—these reveal secondary dimensions.

While you're focused on one variable, you might notice or imagine other risks that don't map neatly to specific values and so don't fit into a framework that seeks to focus your testing onto a small subset of values of the variable (such as boundary values).

    (a) You might follow up the ideas immediately.

    (b) You might ignore them, treating them as distractions.

    (c) You might note the ideas, keeping them to follow up later.

These options are all sometimes appropriate.

- Option (a) is typical of exploratory testing. The key advantage is that you always run the tests that you consider most promising at the moment. The key disadvantage is that after doing a lot of domain testing, you might not know (and might significantly overestimate) how much you've actually done.

- Option (b) is the reaction to (a). The key advantage is that you get done what you planned to do. The key disadvantage is that you probably won't remember any of these ideas when you need them (after you've finished your domain testing and started designing other types of tests). This is often a poor choice.

- Option (c) is the middle ground. Stopping frequently to make notes can still be distracting, especially if the notes are detailed. Writing notes that aren't very detailed can be quick, but they might be useless later. Writing detailed notes can be time-consuming and much of what you're noting might have been obvious anyway once you start doing a risk analysis.

We can't guide you on how to prioritize your time. The best answer depends too much on your circumstances. However, we suspect that too many testers treat Options (a) and (c) as the primary choices and don't include (b) as part of their process. Even if you aren't a fan of detailed test documentation (we think it is often wasteful), we strongly recommend that you carry a notebook to fill with test ideas, describing them to whatever level of formality and detail that you'll personally find useful later.

FROM EXAMPLE 3: SUNTRUST VISA

SunTrust issues Visa credit cards with credit limits in the range of $400 to $40000. A customer is not to be approved for credit limits outside this range. A customer can apply for the card using an online application form in which one of the fields requires that the customer type in his/her desired credit limit.

Here are a few risks that we imagined while doing a domain analysis of this problem. These don't map directly to the input field(s) but they would be involved in the processing the application that these input fields are part of.

- What if this applicant already has a credit card with SunTrust? Will that be caught as part of the credit evaluation?

  - If the applicant has a credit limit of $35,000 on that first card, should his credit on this new card be kept below $5000 (to keep the total below $40,000)?

- ○ Is it within the intended scope of the system you're testing to notice issues like this?
- What if this applicant has applied for this card previously and been rejected? Should the system detect this?
- What if this applicant has a huge savings account here? Should someone with $10 million in assets with the bank be restricted to a $40,000 credit card limit?
- Can the system offer an amount greater than the amount requested? Should this be possible?
- If the applicant is rejected for this card, does this system alert him to other card offers for which he would be approved? For example, does the system propose that he accept a card with higher interest rate? Should it?
- Is there a limit on how many credit cards SunTrust can approve? Suppose the applicant meets SunTrust's acceptance criteria, but granting this credit puts SunTrust's loan-to-asset ratios just over a limit? Should this system detect this problem?
- What if there are content errors in the application (wrong street address, for example) Does this system check for these and, if it finds an error, what should it do?
- Can the amount offered be greater than the amount requested? Should this be possible?

FROM EXAMPLE 25: MOODLE ASSIGN USER ROLES

Moodle is a program that manages online courses. Here is one of its dialogs. The user can assign participants in a class to one or more roles in the course, such as student or teacher.

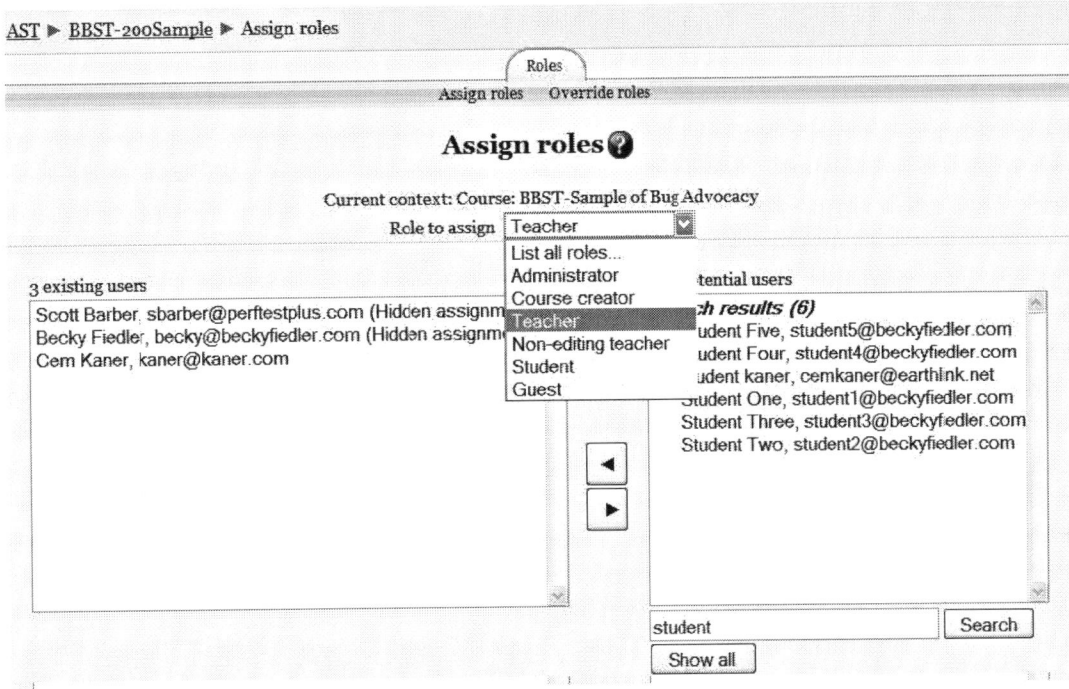

Here are some of the questions that come to us when we consider this dialog:

- What happens if you assign someone to every role?

- What happens if you have a long list of students and you assign all of them to every role? Is there a memory limit somewhere?

- What if you assign someone to a role (like, teacher) that gives them special privileges, they do things in that role and then you remove that role? For example, in Moodle, there is a course announcements forum that teachers can use to send messages to every student. Teachers can see and edit their posts to any forum. Students can't post messages to this forum. Suppose you make Joe a teacher, he posts messages to the forum and then you demote his privilege level from teacher to student. With this privilege level, can he access and edit one of his old posts?

- If you remove someone from a role, does Moodle add their name back to the Potential users list for that role?

These questions arise from considering the variables we're studying and how they're used in the program, but they don't map easily to the kinds of variation in values of these variables that we would try as part of domain testing. They're still interesting and important questions.

FROM EXAMPLE 30: CONFIGURATION TESTING

We want to test our software with some or all of the following software and equipment:

- Operating system: Linux, Windows XP, Windows Vista, Windows 7
- RAM: 1 gByte, 2 gByte, 3 gByte, 4 gByte, 8 gByte
- Printer: Brother multifunction, Canon Laser, HP InkJet, Xerox Color Laser
- Video card: Nvidia GeForce, ATI Radeon, Diamond Stealth
- Disks: 1 hard drive, 2 hard drives, 3 hard drives

First, the variables named here aren't completely specified. For example, which version of Linux do you want to test? And which of Brother's multifunction printers?

Also, there are other potentially interacting variables. For example, what resolutions should you test the video card at? How many screens should you connect to the card? How much activity (changes in display) should happen on the screens and how rapidly should it change? How much memory is free? What about disk space?

What happens if you change one of these variables mid-test? For example, what if you change how much memory is available to the application while the software under test is doing something.

What should the software under test be doing? What tests will reveal potential configuration problems?

EXERCISES: PART 4-R

Please imagine and document risks that don't necessarily map to an obvious dimension in each question below:

R.1. *Example 2: ATM Withdrawal* **on page 237**

An ATM allows withdrawals of cash in amounts of $20 increments from $20 to $200 (inclusive) (Craig & Jaskiel, 2002, p. 164).

R.2. *Example 8: Create Table (Columns, Rows)* **on page 283**

In OpenOffice (OOo) Impress, you can create a table. With this dialog, you set the starting numbers of rows and columns.

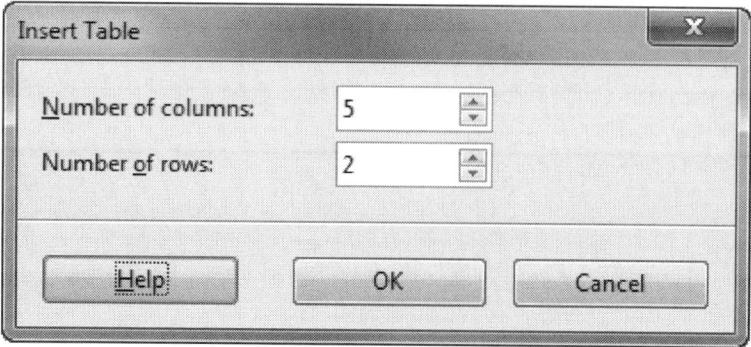

Design Notes: The input values must be Integers. The program will round fractional amounts, so that 8.4 rows is changed to 8 when you press Tab or Enter to exit an input field and 8.5 rows is changed to 9. The program also ignores non-numeric characters: for example, it interprets 2a3 as 23.

R.3. *Example 29: Select And Flip Picture* **on page 411**

In OpenOffice Impress (3.0), you can select a picture on a slide and then flip it vertically or horizontally.

What risks would you associate with flipping an image that aren't tied to whether you flip it horizontally or vertically?

SECTION 3: WORKED EXAMPLES

Section 3 works through the book's 30 examples.[36] Each chapter applies a domain analysis to a single example. Section 3 is the inverse of Section 2.

- Section 2's chapters each focused on a single Task (A through R) and called on several examples to illustrate the Task.

- Section 3's chapters each focus on a single example and work through that example by applying all of the necessary Tasks.

In the first chapters of Section 3 (Part 3.1), we explicitly consider each Task as we work through each example. We don't do every Task in every example:

- The 24 Chapters of this Part take about 200 pages. Many Tasks are redundant: the analysis is the same for several examples. Rather than adding over 100 more pages, we cross-reference to the example that shows the relevant application of the Task.

- Some Tasks are inapplicable to some examples. Sometimes this is because the example description doesn't provide the information you will need to do the Task. Other times, it is because the Task is simply not very interesting for a problem of this type. We have emphasized throughout the book that parts of this Schema apply more naturally to some variables than others. When they don't apply, don't do them.

We show the Tasks in a standard sequence. However, in doing these examples (and in our real-life work), we don't always do the tasks in the same sequence. For example, if we're working primarily with a result variable, we are likely to start our work more like this:

- A. Identify the potentially interesting variables
- N. Analyze independent variables that should be tested together
- O. Analyze variables that hold results

We drew many of these examples from other authors, often from classic presentations of domain testing. We encourage you to compare our solutions with their approaches. We make no claim that our Schema is The Right One. We just think it is useful. In the work of the other authors, you're likely to find other ideas that can help you modify our Schema to create one that is more useful to you.

We have found the examples (and analytical progressions to solutions) particularly understandable in Jorgensen (2008), Kaner et al. (1993), Myers (1979) and Spillner, Linz & Shaefer (2007). We recommend that you look these over for further practitioner-oriented presentation.

---

36 If you haven't read *How to Use This Book* on page xvii (in the Preface), we recommend that you read it now.

SECTION 3. PART 1: EXAMPLES THAT ILLUSTRATE THE SCHEMA

In this Part, we work through examples Task by Task, showing how to apply the Schema to each example.

The next Part is more conceptual, working with examples that are less directly suited to domain analysis. There, we consider how to stretch domain testing so that it can be useful as a part of a different testing approach.

EXAMPLE 1: INTEGER INPUT

A data entry field will accept Integers from -999 to 999.

A. IDENTIFY THE POTENTIALLY INTERESTING VARIABLES

There's only the one variable (the one that receives its value from the data entry field).

B. IDENTIFY THE VARIABLE YOU CAN ANALYZE NOW. THIS IS THE VARIABLE OF INTEREST

The input value.

C. DETERMINE THE PRIMARY DIMENSION OF THE VARIABLE OF INTEREST

The primary dimension, in this case, is the only one mentioned—the one that runs from -999 through 999.

D. DETERMINE THE TYPE AND SCALE OF THE VARIABLE'S PRIMARY DIMENSION AND WHAT VALUES IT CAN TAKE

Integers -999 through 999.

E. DETERMINE WHETHER YOU CAN ORDER THE VARIABLE'S VALUES (FROM SMALLEST TO LARGEST)

Yes.

F. DETERMINE WHETHER THIS IS AN INPUT VARIABLE OR A RESULT

This is an input variable.

G. DETERMINE HOW THE PROGRAM USES THIS VARIABLE

The problem description provides no information about how the variable is used.

H. DETERMINE WHETHER OTHER VARIABLES ARE RELATED TO THIS ONE

There is only one variable. The problem description does not provide information to identify relationships between this variable and any others.

I. PARTITION THE VARIABLE (ITS PRIMARY DIMENSION)

The dimension is ordered. The sub-ranges and transition points are:

-∞ to -1000	too small
-999 to 999	within-range
1000 to ∞	too big

J. LAY OUT THE ANALYSIS IN A CLASSICAL BOUNDARY/EQUIVALENCE TABLE. IDENTIFY BEST REPRESENTATIVES

Variable	Valid case equivalence class	Invalid case equivalence class	Boundaries and special cases	Notes
the input value	-999 to 999		-999	
			0	Some domain testers would skip 0 because it is in the middle of the domain. Our heuristic is that divide-by-zero is as common an error as a boundary misspecification, so we test it
			999	
		< -999	-1000	
		> 999	1000	

The tests use the values in the "Boundaries and special cases" column.

K. CREATE TESTS FOR THE CONSEQUENCES OF THE DATA ENTERED, NOT JUST THE INPUT FILTER

The problem description does not provide information about how the variable is used or what it can interact with. Therefore we can't create tests for consequences.

L. IDENTIFY SECONDARY DIMENSIONS. ANALYZE THEM IN THE CLASSICAL WAY

Testers often extend the classical table to include invalid values that aren't on the primary dimension. Common examples are:

- Letters
- Letters that can be interpreted as hexadecimal digits
- Empty input field
- Whitespace (leading or trailing spaces, tabs, etc.)

These go into the table as new rows with invalid values, like this:

Variable	Valid case equivalence class	Invalid case equivalence class	Boundaries and special cases	Notes
the input value	-999 to 999		-999	
			0	
			999	
		< -999	-1000	
		> 999	1000	
		a to z	a	misinterpret as hexadecimal?
			g	non-hexadecimal
		nonalphanumeric	/	/ is ASCII character 47 — "0" is 48
			:	: is ASCII character 58 — "9" is 57
		no input	empty field	
		whitespace	<space>999	4 characters. Does it ignore spaces?
			<space>	no number, just a space
			lots of <spaces>	overflow? or ignored?

It's convenient to record ideas like this in the classical table, but it can be confusing and unintentionally incomplete.

The table is designed to make the tester's reasoning about the primary dimension obvious. It shows the ranges of valid and invalid values and the tests for the boundaries of each set.

However, the table doesn't provide an organizing structure for secondary dimensions. Why include lower case but not uppercase? Which letters should you test with? Which whitespace tests should you run? Why? All of these are in the Invalid Case column. Boundaries between these and the Valid Case values aren't obvious (and so the tests are often just interesting tests, not boundary values). The tester can describe the reasoning behind the test in the Notes column, but there's not *very much* room for that description.

The classical table is handy for highlighting a few extra tests, but if you want to analyze a variable thoroughly and show your analysis clearly, use the Risk/Equivalence table.

TEST IDEA CATALOG FOR INTEGERS

Hung Quoc Nguyen, President of LogiGear, creates lists of standard testing issues for variables of a given type. Marick (1995) calls lists like this *catalogs* of test ideas. The following list merges test ideas from Nguyen et al., (2003, p. 619) with a few more from Kaner et al. (2002.) Depending on the range of values of the variable under test, some of these tests might not be useful for the particular variable that you're testing:

- Nothing
- Emptied field (clear the default value)
- Whitespace only (tab, space)
- 0
- Valid value
- At lower bound of range - 1
- At lower bound of range
- At upper bound of range
- At upper bound of range + 1
- Far below the lower bound of range
- Far above the upper bound of range
- Far below the lower bound number of digits or characters
- At lower bound minus 1 number of digits or characters
- At lower bound number of digits or characters
- At upper bound number of digits or characters
- At upper bound plus 1 number of digits or characters
- Far above the upper bound number of digits or characters (try to overflow the buffer)
  - with digits or printing characters
  - with leading 0's (are they ignored?)
  - with leading spaces (are they ignored?)
  - with leading minus signs
- Leading spaces
- Many leading spaces
- Leading zeros

- Many leading zeros
- Leading space or zero plus a sign (+ or -)
- Negative values
- Non-digits   (especially / (ASCII 47) and : (ASCII character 58)
- Uppercase characters
- Lowercase characters
- Upper ASCII (128-254) and Unicode values beyond traditional ASCII (UTF-8, UTF-16 and UTF-32) (*See* http://www.utf-8.com/)
- Modifiers (e.g., Ctrl, Alt, Shift-Ctrl, etc.)
- Function key (F2, F3, F4, etc.)
- Nonprinting characters (such as control characters)
- Operating system file name reserved characters (such as "*.:)
- ASCII 255 (0 and 255 are often interpreted as end of file)
- *See* Whittaker (2003, p. 29-33) for many other ideas on troublesome characters
- Wrong data type (e.g., Floating Point into Integer)
- Decimal point (or no decimal point)
- Number of digits after the decimal
- Decimal comma
- Contains one or more commas (thousands separators)
- Contains one or more points (thousands separators)
- Expressions
- Background activity / competition for resource
- Enter nothing but wait for a long time before pressing or clicking whatever signals completed input for the field. Is there a timeout?
- Enter one digit and wait a long time before entering the next
- Enter digits and then (a) erase them and enter new digits or (b) backspace and type over them with new digits. Are all these keystrokes accumulated until you press <Enter> (or however you signal that your input is complete) or are erased characters discarded immediately? If the program waits until it receives the full string before processing it, there must be a limit on the number of characters (including <Backspace> characters). What happens at the limit?
- Enter digits while you click the mouse or turn the printer on and off or create other types of interrupts.

It would be a mistake to run all of these tests on every variable.

- If the programmers consistently use libraries that guard against some of these errors, you don't need to check for those errors.

- If the programmers have done good unit testing, they will have already found and fixed these kinds of bugs.

In either case, perhaps you should run a few tests to spot-check for inconsistency, but if you don't find any problems with these, spend the rest of your testing time looking for problems that are more likely to be in the code.

M. SUMMARIZE YOUR ANALYSIS WITH A RISK/EQUIVALENCE TABLE

The following table implements the test idea catalog above, with cross-references to the test ideas in the last column. We would not normally fill the "Notes" column with comments like these. We do it here simply to show the mapping from one to the other.

GENERIC RISK/EQUIVALENCE TABLE FOR INTEGERS

Variable	Risk (potential failure)	Classes that should not trigger the failure	Classes that might trigger the failure	Test cases (best representatives)	The tests are based on these entries in Nguyen's list
The input value	misclassifies valid inputs	anything out of bounds	-999 to 999	-999	Valid value Negative values At lower bound of range At upper bound number of digits or characters
				0	0 At lower bound number of digits or characters
				999	At upper bound of range At upper bound number of digits (no minus sign)
	mishandles values that are too small	≥ -999	< -999	-1000	At lower bound of range - 1
	mishandles values that are too large	≤ 999	> 999	1000	At upper bound of range + 1
				999 ... 999 (16384 nines)	Far above the upper bound of range
	too few characters	any input value	empty field	enter nothing	Enter nothing At lower-bound-minus-1 number of digits or characters Far below the lower bound of range (this is as far below as it gets)
				clear the field	Empty the field (clear the default value)
				space character	Whitespace only (tab, space)
	too many characters	≤ 4 characters	> 4 characters	-1000	Repeats the "too small" test At upper-bound-plus-1 number of digits or characters
				+999	At upper-bound-plus-1 number of digits
				<space>999	Leading spaces
				<space>-999	Leading space plus a sign (+ or -)
				<space><space> <space> ... <space>999	Many leading spaces
				0999	Leading zeros
				-0999	Leading space plus a sign (+ or -)

Variable	Risk (potential failure)	Classes that should not trigger the failure	Classes that might trigger the failure	Test cases (best representatives)	The tests are based on these entries in Nguyen's list
				000 ... 000999	Many leading zeros
				- - 999	Two leading minus signs
				- - ... - - 999	Many leading minus signs
	confused by wrong data type	Integers	non-Integers	9.0	Wrong data type (e.g., decimal point into Integer)
					Decimal point (or no decimal point)
				9.000	Number of digits after the decimal
			non-digits	/	Non-digits (especially / (ASCII 47)
				:	and : (ASCII character 58)
				ASCII 255	ASCII 255 (might be interpreted as end of file)
				*	Operating system file name reserved characters (such as "*.:)
				9-9	Arithmetic expressions
				We're treating these as irrelevant to the problem statement for this example, so we're skipping them	Uppercase and lowercase characters
					Upper ASCII (128-254) and Unicode
					Modifiers (e.g., Ctrl, Alt, Shift-Ctrl, etc.)
					Function key (F2, F3, F4, etc.)
					Nonprinting characters (such as control characters)
					See Whittaker (2003, p. 29-33) for many other ideas on troublesome characters
					Background activity / competition for resource
					Enter nothing. Wait a long time before signaling completed input for the field. Is there a timeout?
					Enter one digit. Wait a long time before entering the next
					Enter digits. Erase them. Enter new digits
					Enter digits while you click the mouse, turn the printer off or create other interrupts

N. ANALYZE INDEPENDENT VARIABLES THAT SHOULD BE TESTED TOGETHER

The problem description provides no information for identifying other variables.

O. ANALYZE VARIABLES THAT HOLD RESULTS

This is an input variable. It doesn't hold results.

P. ANALYZE NON-INDEPENDENT VARIABLES. DEAL WITH RELATIONSHIPS AND CONSTRAINTS

The problem description gives information about only one variable.

Q. IDENTIFY AND LIST UNANALYZED VARIABLES. GATHER INFORMATION FOR LATER ANALYSIS

This Task goes beyond what we're trying to teach with this example.

R. IMAGINE AND DOCUMENT RISKS THAT DON'T NECESSARILY MAP TO AN OBVIOUS DIMENSION

The problem description provides no information about the application. Therefore, the only risks to note are the generic ones and these were documented in the risk/equivalence table.

EXAMPLE 2: ATM WITHDRAWAL

An ATM allows withdrawals of cash in amounts of $20 increments from $20 to $200 (inclusive) (Craig & Jaskiel, 2002, p. 164).

A. IDENTIFY THE POTENTIALLY INTERESTING VARIABLES

- `AmountRequested`
- `AmountReceived`
- `PreviousBalance`
- `UpdatedBalance`
- `AccountNumber`

The obvious input field is the **AmountRequested**.

It seems obvious that these other variables will be also involved in the transaction. Therefore, they will come up in tests of this feature.

B. IDENTIFY THE VARIABLE YOU CAN ANALYZE NOW. THIS IS THE VARIABLE OF INTEREST

- `AmountRequested`

C. DETERMINE THE PRIMARY DIMENSION OF THE VARIABLE OF INTEREST

Money, from $0 to $200.

D. DETERMINE THE TYPE AND SCALE OF THE VARIABLE'S PRIMARY DIMENSION AND WHAT VALUES IT CAN TAKE

This is an enumerated list (20, 40, 60, 80, 100, 120, 140, 160, 180, 200). Zero might also be acceptable. All other values should be rejected.

E. DETERMINE WHETHER YOU CAN ORDER THE VARIABLE'S VALUES (FROM SMALLEST TO LARGEST)

Yes.

F. DETERMINE WHETHER THIS IS AN INPUT VARIABLE OR A RESULT

`AmountRequested` is an input variable.

G. DETERMINE HOW THE PROGRAM USES THIS VARIABLE

The program accepts an entry into **AmountRequested**. If enough money is available, the ATM gives the customer the **AmountReceived** (same as **AmountRequested**) and the software updates the relevant results variables (**UpdatedBalance** and maybe an overdraft balance and service charges if the customer asks for more money than is in the account.)

H. DETERMINE WHETHER OTHER VARIABLES ARE RELATED TO THIS ONE

- `AmountRequested` should determine `AmountReceived`. (`AmountReceived` will be 0 if `AmountRequested` is too big.)
- `AmountRequested` probably can't exceed `PreviousBalance`. (See risks)
- `AmountReceived` and `PreviousBalance` will jointly determine **UpdatedBalance**

I. PARTITION THE VARIABLE (ITS PRIMARY DIMENSION)

The dimension is ordered, so determine the sub-ranges and transition points.

< 0 is probably not possible or testable	(A negative withdrawal is a deposit.)
0	Probably not valid
20, 40, ... , 200	These 10 values are the permissible set
> 200	Too big
not divisible by 20	These are all invalid inputs

J. LAY OUT THE ANALYSIS IN A CLASSICAL BOUNDARY/EQUIVALENCE TABLE. IDENTIFY BEST REPRESENTATIVES

Variable	Valid case equivalence class	Invalid case equivalence class	Boundaries and special cases	Notes
Amount-Requested	maybe 0	maybe 0	0	If this is valid, the machine will operate very differently. On the other entries, the machine gives you cash.
	20, 40, 60, 80, 100, 120, 140, 160, 180, 200		20	Check amount of cash received
			200	Check amount of cash received
		< 0	-20	Depending on the keyboard, this might be impossible to enter
		not divisible by 20	21	
			30	Divisible by 10, perhaps this is more likely to be accepted than 21.
		> 200	220	The appropriate case is 220, not 201 because 201 will also be rejected as not divisible by 20

The tests use the values in the "Boundaries and special cases" column.

K. CREATE TESTS FOR THE CONSEQUENCES OF THE DATA ENTERED, NOT JUST THE INPUT FILTER

Some of the likely consequences that we would test are:

- The machine should give the right amount of money.
- The machine should give an appropriate error message whenever the user enters an invalid request.
- The bank account should be correctly updated.
- If the user attempts to withdraw more than the amount in the bank account, the system should respond appropriately. Depending on the bank's policies, this might involve:
  - A warning and a request for confirmation or
  - The right amount of money, but the account is charged with an overdraft fee or

- An offer to change the amount to the amount available (and then a correct update to the account and delivery of the correct amount of money).

- If the user attempts to withdraw more than the daily ATM withdrawal maximum, the system should respond appropriately. Depending on the bank's policies, this might involve:

  - A warning and a refusal to pay the amount or
  - The machine captures the card.

Most (all?) ATMs will collect input from the user and then send a message to another computer. The message holds the ATM's interpretation of the user input. Can you access these messages? For example, are they logged anywhere?

- Are invalid inputs filtered out at the ATM or do they go back to the main system? (If they go back to the main system, can you create any mischief for that system with especially bad values? What is the class of interesting values for these messages?)

- How complex is the message traffic when the user requests more money than he has or tries to access an account that he doesn't have (or has closed)?

As you come to know the system, you'll recognize many additional potential consequences of any test. You haven't completed the test if you don't peek at its later effects.

These tests of consequences don't look like typical boundary tests, but the boundary values (and all the other values) that you enter while doing your domain testing will affect the full system, not just the parts most tightly linked to looking at your inputs.

L. IDENTIFY SECONDARY DIMENSIONS. ANALYZE THEM IN THE CLASSICAL WAY

The typical ATM keypad allows only digits or arrow keys. However, some ATM keypads look like telephone keypads and accept text. Some kiosks (general-purpose computers available for public use) have full computer keyboards but can function as ATMs. A search with Bing Images shows a variety of other layouts. Without knowing what keypad is available for use, you can't know what unacceptable characters the user can try to enter. In general, we would work from the list of ideas for secondary dimensions that we provided in Example 1, *L. Identify secondary dimensions. Analyze them in the classical way* on page 230.

Thinking specifically of a simple ATM keyboard, the most obvious secondary dimensions to us are length and time.

- *Length:* The user can try to enter numbers that are too big, too long, too short (0 or 1 digit), etc.

- *Time:* Start entering data into one of the fields and wait before completing the entry. How long before the system times out and cancels the transaction? The user can delay (for example) for a short time, for almost too long, for barely too long and for a really long time.

It might be fun to try a few other tests that emphasize the length of the input:

- *Book test:* Put a book on the keypad (hit all the keys at the same time).
- *Extended book test*: Hold the book on the keypad for a while, holding all the keys down for a long time.
- *Sticky finger test*: Hold down a single key for a long time.

The tests in the table show a slightly more systematic approach to testing for long digits. In theory, you could run infinitely many tests (with infinitely many digits). Assuming the ATM will actually allow you to enter many digits, what are the practical limits?

We would try tests like these:

- a number that is 1 digit longer than the maximum

- a number that is many digits longer, enough to tax a storage boundary (such as **MAXINT**+1)

- a number that is many more digits longer. Did it take the software longer to process this long number?
    - If not, perhaps try one much longer number and if there is no processing time change, stop.
    - If so, then the program is probably not truncating inputs that are too long. It is probably reading the whole input and trying to interpret it. This creates opportunities for failures based on buffer overflow. Keep trying numbers that are orders of magnitude longer than the last until the system fails or you're confident that adding more digits won't change the result.

You can show the added tests on the classical table:

Variable	Valid case equivalence class	Invalid case equivalence class	Boundaries and special cases	Notes
Amount-Requested	0		0	This may be valid, but the machine won't give you any money.
	20, 40, 60, 80, 100, 120, 140, 160, 180, 200		20	Check amount of cash received
			200	Check amount of cash received
		< 0	-20	Depending on the keyboard, this might be impossible to enter
		not divisible by 20	19	
			21	
			30	Divisible by 10, perhaps this is more likely to be accepted than, say, 21.
		> 200	220	The appropriate case is 220, not 201 because 201 will also be rejected as not divisible by 20
	1 to 3 digits		0, 20 and 200	You've already tested these
		0 digits		In effect, this is a timeout test.
		> 3 digits	1000	Many systems will make entry of 4 or more digits impossible, so the next cases might be infeasible
			= **MAXINT**	perhaps 4294967295 (10 digits)
			MAXINT+1	10 digits
		way too many:	127 digits	common buffer maximum. 127, 128, 255, 256 are interesting cases
			128 digits	
			255 digits	

Variable	Valid case equivalence class	Invalid case equivalence class	Boundaries and special cases	Notes
			256 digits	2^8 (8-bit word + 1) boundary
			1024 digits	See if there is a difference in processing time as the number of characters increases. If so, keep increasing digits by orders of magnitude until the system (probably) crashes.
			65536 digits	2^{16}
			16777216 digits	2^{24} if there's going to be an overflow, 16 million characters will probably do it.
			4294967296 digits	2^{32}
	MinTime to MaxTime		MinTime	MinTime is the shortest time between keystrokes that the ATM can cope with
			MaxTime	MaxTime is either the longest time between keystrokes before the system times out the user or the longest total time allowed to enter the AmountRequested into the system
		< MinTime		This may be impossible (MinTime near 0)
		> MaxTime		

M. SUMMARIZE YOUR ANALYSIS WITH A RISK/EQUIVALENCE TABLE

There is little basis for analyzing secondary dimensions of the input field until you know more about the keyboard.

Until you have a way of working with the other variables (**AmountReceived**, etc.), we think a risk/equivalence table adds little value. We would stick with the classical table for now.

N. ANALYZE INDEPENDENT VARIABLES THAT SHOULD BE TESTED TOGETHER

The problem description does not provide information for this.

O. ANALYZE VARIABLES THAT HOLD RESULTS

Two obvious result variables are:

- **AmountReceived**
- **UpdatedBalance**

There are result variables beyond this. For example, in Task K above, we considered message fields that convey information about the transaction from the ATM to a connected computer. If you can log traffic between the ATM and the server behind it, all echoes and interpretations of the user inputs and the responses to them are result variables.

Note that when you *do* test **UpdatedBalance**, you'll be dealing with equivalence classes. You can test for an **UpdatedBalance** of (for example) 0 with any pair of **AmountRequested** and **PreviousBalance** that have equal values. Therefore, the set of pairs

$$\{ (\texttt{AmountRequested, PreviousBalance}) \mid \texttt{UpdatedBalance} = 0 \}$$

is an equivalence class.

P. ANALYZE NON-INDEPENDENT VARIABLES. DEAL WITH RELATIONSHIPS AND CONSTRAINTS

The user enters `AmountRequested`.

- `AmountRequested` is constrained by `PreviousBalance` (and by the bank's overdraft limits, daily withdrawal limits, security policies and the amount of money in the ATM).
- `AmountReceived` should be `AmountRequested` or 0.
- `PreviousBalance` is not constrained by any of the variables in this problem.
- `UpdatedBalance` should equal `PreviousBalance` - `AmountReceived`, unless fees are applied or overdraft is permitted.

Q. IDENTIFY AND LIST UNANALYZED VARIABLES. GATHER INFORMATION FOR LATER ANALYSIS

At this point in the analysis, the task is to identify what you don't know, making notes for things you have to find out later.

- The problem description has given no information about `AmountReceived`, `PreviousBalance` and `UpdatedBalance`, but you were able to do a small amount of work with them anyway.
- The analysis should also have made you aware of the possible existence of overdraft-related variables and of transaction-message fields (from the ATM to the server). The next task (risks) will also suggest some security-related variables.

R. IMAGINE AND DOCUMENT RISKS THAT DON'T NECESSARILY MAP TO AN OBVIOUS DIMENSION

- What happens if customer terminates the request before completing the transaction?
- What if the customer's card is invalid?
- Can the customer make multiple withdrawal requests? Is there a minimum wait time between requests? What is the daily limit and how is it enforced?
- For an ATM, this is an unlikely risk but as you analyze other multiuser systems consider this: If there is no minimum wait time between requests, can you create a Denial of Service attack by flooding the system with rapid requests?
- Suppose withdrawals are attempted in different locations, too close together in time for the same user to have personally attempted both transactions. The system might detect this. Depending on the bank's policies, responses might include:
  - refusal to pay the amount
  - calling the customer's phone
  - capturing the card
  - accepting the transaction because multiple cards are linked to the same account
- If multiple cards are authorized against the account, is there a locking system in place to prevent multiple users from withdrawing the same money? If so, can it be deadlocked? *Notice the dimension and the boundary here. The dimension is time. The system might not be able to handle it when two transactions happen sufficiently close to simultaneously,*
- Suppose the customer requests more than the available balance. Will the system reject the request or allow an overdraft? If overdrafts are allowed, what new variables come into play?
- Is there an overdraft fee? Is it subtracted correctly from the balance?

- Suppose the balance is 0 and the system allows overdrafts. What if the overdraft-allowable amount is $100 and the customer requests $200. Does the system tell him there is $100 available?
- Is the overdraft recorded as a negative balance in this account or as a loan from an overdraft account?
- Are race conditions possible between ATM withdrawals and electronic transfers? Can both be approved on the basis of money apparently present? What other races are possible?
- What if there isn't enough money in the ATM machine?
- Some machines allow the customer to select the payment's denominations. For example, rather than getting $100 as five $20 bills, the customer could ask for two $50 bills. What if the machine has more than enough total cash, but not enough to pay the customer in the way requested? Another problem on the same lines: Suppose the customer requests $210, but the ATM has run out of $5 and $10 bills, so only $200 and $220 are possible.
- Is there a service charge for using the ATM? Could this cause the account to go overlimit? Is it subtracted correctly from the balance?
- What kinds of problems can arise between the ATM and the system it is connected to? Is there any thing the user can do at the ATM that will increase the likelihood of a problem in the communications?

EXAMPLE 3: SUNTRUST VISA

SunTrust issues Visa credit cards with credit limits in the range of $400 to $40000. A customer is not to be approved for credit limits outside this range. A customer can apply for the card using an online application form in which one of the fields requires that the customer type in his/her desired credit limit.

A. IDENTIFY THE POTENTIALLY INTERESTING VARIABLES

This description mentions only one input field:

- `DesiredCreditLimit`

The example mentions other variables but does not describe them as input fields. Many tests are likely to collect values for these variables:

- `CreditLimit` (to be assigned to this account)
- `CustomerName`

B. IDENTIFY THE VARIABLES YOU CAN ANALYZE NOW. THESE ARE THE VARIABLES OF INTEREST

- `DesiredCreditLimit` is the value the customer enters.
- The customer almost certainly enters `CustomerName` somewhere, but the problem description doesn't say anything about that field.
- The bank may assign a `CreditLimit`, but the problem description doesn't say how or where this will be reported. You only know what the customer has requested.

C. DETERMINE THE PRIMARY DIMENSION OF THE VARIABLE OF INTEREST

The primary dimension is the amount (in dollars) of `DesiredCreditLimit`. This is what the program is designed to process. Other dimensions, such as the number of digits and the set of permissible characters, are merely aspects of an implementation that makes it possible for you to enter an amount of money.

D. DETERMINE THE TYPE AND SCALE OF THE VARIABLE'S PRIMARY DIMENSION AND WHAT VALUES IT CAN TAKE

`DesiredCreditLimit` is primarily a money variable. It is probably a Fixed-Point variable (dollars and cents: two digits after the decimal point) or an Integer (dollars). `DesiredCreditLimit` is ratio scaled.

`CreditLimit` can take on values from $400 to $40000. The limits for `DesiredCreditLimit` are probably the same.

The permissible characters of `DesiredCreditLimit` run from 0 to 9 and might include "." or "," or "$" (but the list doesn't include letters).

All three of these dimensions (amount of money, length of input and characters permitted) are involved in the entry and processing of this variable. The program might check each one separately from the others.

E. DETERMINE WHETHER YOU CAN ORDER THE VARIABLE'S VALUES (FROM SMALLEST TO LARGEST)

Yes

F. DETERMINE WHETHER THIS IS AN INPUT VARIABLE OR A RESULT

This is an input variable.

The problem description also implies a result variable, the size of the credit limit granted, but that probably depends on other variables as well, such as the customer's credit rating.

G. DETERMINE HOW THE PROGRAM USES THIS VARIABLE

The program probably uses `DesiredCreditLimit` as one factor in the evaluation of customer's request for credit.

H. DETERMINE WHETHER OTHER VARIABLES ARE RELATED TO THIS ONE

Nothing appears to constrain `DesiredCreditLimit`, the amount of money the customer can *ask for*. However, the `CreditLimit` granted will be between $400 and $40,000 so the program might reject values of `DesiredCreditLimit` outside this range.

In addition:

- Probably, `CreditLimit` ≤ `DesiredCreditLimit`.
- Probably, `CreditLimit` is limited by the customer's credit history in many ways.

I. PARTITION THE VARIABLE (ITS PRIMARY DIMENSION)

The dimension is ordered, so determine the sub-ranges and transition points.

- *Too small*: less than $400
- *Acceptable*: $400 to $40,000
- *Too much*: more than $40,000

The problem description doesn't say these are the actual limits on `DesiredCreditLimit`, but at a minimum, these are interesting boundaries because the program won't grant credit outside of these limits.

The description doesn't specify whether the amounts are to the nearest dollar or to the penny. You don't know whether $399 or $399.99 is the boundary below $400.

J. LAY OUT THE ANALYSIS IN A CLASSICAL BOUNDARY/EQUIVALENCE TABLE. IDENTIFY BEST REPRESENTATIVES

The stated valid range is $400 to $40,000, but is the variable an Integer, a Fixed-Point variable with 2 digits after the decimal point or a Floating-Point (any number of digits after the decimal)?

For now, suppose it is Integer or Fixed Point. Here is the classical table for the primary dimension:

Variable	Valid case equivalence class	Invalid case equivalence class	Boundaries and special cases	Notes
DesiredCreditLimit	400 to 40000		400	
			40000	
		< 400	399.99	If Fixed-Point variables are accepted
			399	If only Integers are accepted

Variable	Valid case equivalence class	Invalid case equivalence class	Boundaries and special cases	Notes
			0	We like 0
		> 40000	40000.01	If Fixed-Point variables are accepted
			40001	If only Integers are accepted

The tests use the values in the "Boundaries and special cases" column.

K. CREATE TESTS FOR THE CONSEQUENCES OF THE DATA ENTERED, NOT JUST THE INPUT FILTER

The problem description doesn't say how the bank will use the `DesiredCreditLimit` or what other variables are affected by it.

L. IDENTIFY SECONDARY DIMENSIONS. ANALYZE THEM IN THE CLASSICAL WAY

Here are several secondary dimensions:

- How many digits in the number.
- How many digits after the decimal point.

  Let **NUMBEROFDIGITSAFTERDECIMAL** be the number of digits that are supposed to be stored after the decimal point. For example, it will be 2 for a dollars-and-cents variable. For other data, it might be larger. What does the program do when someone enters fewer or more than **NUMBEROFDIGITSAFTERDECIMAL** digits? The important thing to recognize for Fixed-Point is that this describes a maximum number of digits (maximum after the decimal point) that is distinct from the variable's overall maximum number of digits.

- `DesiredCreditLimit` is a numeric variable. Consider non-numeric characters:
  - Non-digits
  - Hexadecimal numbers
  - Upper ASCII characters
  - Unicode values beyond traditional ASCII (UTF-8, UTF-16 and UTF-32) (*See* http://www.utf-8.com/)
  - What about leading spaces?
- How many characters the variable has (including permissible non-digits such as commas or leading or trailing zeroes or spaces):
  - 400 is 3
  - 40000.00 is 8 characters (7 digits and a decimal point)
  - Is the permissible range of characters 3-to-7 or can leading or trailing zeros or spaces extend the permissible length? To what limits?
- What about negative numbers?
- What about numbers that include characters that are normally accepted as numeric, but with a problem:
  - Numbers with two or more decimal points?
  - Numbers with one or more leading + signs?
  - Numbers with spaces between the digits (rather than leading or trailing)?

- How many numbers can you fit in this field? (For example, if you enter "1" in the field, you have entered one number. If you enter "1 2 3" in the field, that is 3 numbers.)
  - Suppose that 400 is an acceptable input.
    - Can you enter it twice into the field, for example with 400<space>400 or 400<tab>400 or 400<comma>400?
    - What about values like 4<space>4<space>4, which would be valid if the variable ignored the embedded spaces?
- Expressions that compute to valid inputs:
  - 399+1   Expressions that include a value (399) that is invalid on its own.
  - 400+0   Expressions that are valid whether the + is executed or ignored.
  - 4000+1   Expressions that would be valid if the + is executed but invalid if the + is ignored (interpreted as 40001).

Putting these on the classical table, you get:

Variable	Valid case equivalence class	Invalid case equivalence class	Boundaries and special cases	Notes
Desired-CreditLimit	400.00 to 40000.00		400.00	
			40000.00	
		< 400	399.99	
			0	We like 0
		> 40000	40000.01	
		no digits after decimal	400	The program probably accepts these as valid
			40000	
		only 1 digit after the decimal point	400.1	You could try 400.0 and 40000.0 but how many times do you want to do almost exactly the same test. This tests essentially the same risk, with a new value
			39999.9	
		too many digits	400.009	If the program accepts cents, this is a boundary invalid case
			40000000etc000	Paste 1000000 digits!
		non-digits	/400	In ASCII code, / and : are the boundary non-numbers. *See* http://www.asciitable.com
			400:	
		hex	0x400	They *are* numbers
			0xA12	
			A12	
	6 (or 3) to 8 (or 5) characters		400, 400.00, 40000, 40000.00	Already tested
		2 characters	40	(or 40.00)

Variable	Valid case equivalence class	Invalid case equivalence class	Boundaries and special cases	Notes
		0 characters	press <enter> for an empty field	
			<space>	This is an innocuous character. After the program strips it, there are no more characters.
		huge number		You did this already (40000000etc000)
		leading 0	040000	6 digits
		leading 0	0000etc40000	Lots of leading 0's
		leading spaces	_400000	
		negatives	-400	
			-1	

This table doesn't show all the secondary dimensions, but it illustrates the analysis and the problem. The first four rows of the table are straightforward, but what about the others? If you didn't have the list of secondary dimensions in front of you, would you understand what all these additional test rows were about?

M. SUMMARIZE YOUR ANALYSIS WITH A RISK/EQUIVALENCE TABLE

TEST IDEA CATALOG FOR FIXED-POINT VARIABLES

Our discussion of Example 1 presented Hung Quoc Nguyen's list of standard testing issues for Integer variables. Marick (1995) calls lists like this *catalogs* of test ideas. The list that follows adapts Nguyen's list for Floating Point.

You might find it useful to refer to *Floating Point* on page 72. However, unlike Floating-Point numbers, there is a true Δ for Fixed-Point numbers. For example, if **NUMBEROFDIGITSAFTERDECIMAL** = 2 (2 digits are allowed after the decimal point), then $\Delta = 0.01$.

- Nothing
- Emptied field (clear the default value)
- Whitespace only (tab, space)
- 0
- Valid value
- At lower bound of range - Δ
- At lower bound of range
- At upper bound of range
- At upper bound of range + Δ
- Far below the lower bound of range, such as at **MINFLOAT**
- Far above the upper bound of range, such as at **MAXFLOAT**
- Far below the lower bound number of digits or characters
- At lower bound minus 1 number of digits or characters
- At lower bound number of digits or characters
- At upper bound number of digits or characters
- At upper bound plus 1 number of digits or characters

- Far above the upper bound number of digits or characters
  - with digits or printing characters
  - with leading 0's (are they ignored?)
  - with leading spaces (are they ignored?)
  - with leading minus signs
- Number of digits before the decimal point (lower and upper bounds)
- Number of digits after the decimal point (lower and upper bounds)
- Leading space
- Many leading spaces
- Leading zero
- Many leading zeros
- Leading space or zero plus a sign (+ or -)
- Currency sign before or after the digits
- Negative values
- Hexadecimal digits
- Non-digits (especially / (ASCII 47) and : (ASCII character 58)
- Non-digits embedded in the number, such as 1a3 (some programs will interpret this as 13)
- Uppercase characters
- Lowercase characters
- Upper ASCII (128-254) and Unicode values beyond traditional ASCII (UTF-8, UTF-16 and UTF-32) (*See* http://www.utf-8.com/)
- Modifiers (e.g., Ctrl, Alt, Shift-Ctrl, etc.)
- Function key (F2, F3, F4, etc.)
- Nonprinting characters (such as control characters)
- Operating system file name reserved characters (such as "*.:)
- ASCII 255 (0 and 255 are often interpreted as end of file)
- *See* Whittaker (2003, p. 29-33) for many other ideas on troublesome characters
- Wrong data type (e.g., a variable defined as a Double-Precision Floating-Point constant)
- No decimal point (this is probably acceptable and interpreted properly, but it should be tested once)
- Two decimal points
- Decimal comma
- Contains one or more commas (thousands separators)
- Contains one or more points (thousands separators)
- Commas in appropriate places within the number
- Commas in inappropriate places within the number
- Scientific notation
- Scientific notation with an invalid exponent
- Scientific notation with an exponent that will cause an overflow
- Scientific notation with an exponent that implies too many digits after the decimal point
- Scientific notation with a significand that has too many digits
- Scientific notation with a significand/exponent combination that will cause an overflow.
- Fraction

- Special mathematical constant, such as π
- Expressions, including expressions that resolve to a valid value for input
- Background activity / competition for resource
- Enter nothing but wait for a long time before pressing or clicking whatever signals completed input for the field. Is there a timeout?
- Enter one digit and wait a long time before entering the next
- Enter digits and then (a) erase them and enter new digits or (b) backspace and type over them with new digits. Are all these keystrokes accumulated until you press <Enter> (or however you signal that your input is complete) or are erased characters discarded immediately? If the program waits until it receives the full string before processing it, there must be a limit on the number of characters (including <Backspace> characters). What happens at the limit?
- Enter digits while you click the mouse or turn the printer on and off or create other types of interrupts

It would be a mistake to run all of these tests on every variable.

- If the programmers consistently use libraries that guard against some of these errors, you don't need to check for those errors.
- If the programmers have done good unit testing, they will have already found and fixed these kinds of bugs.

In either case, perhaps you should run a few tests to spot-check for inconsistency, but if you don't find any problems with these, spend the rest of your testing time looking for problems that are more likely to be in the code.

GENERIC RISK/EQUIVALENCE TABLE FOR FIXED-POINT VARIABLES

Here we illustrate the structure of the table, showing how it highlights the test ideas. This analyzes `DesiredCreditLimit` as a Fixed-Point variable.

Variable	Risk (potential failure	Classes that should not trigger failure	Classes that might trigger failure	Test cases (best representatives)	Notes
Desired-CreditLimit	mishandles values that are too small	≥ 400	< 400	399	
				0	
	mishandles values that are too large	≤ 40000	> 40000	40001	
	misclassifies valid values	< 400	400-40000	400	
		> 40000		40000	
	doesn't cope with Floating-Point values	Integers	Floats, including Currency	400.	decimal, no digits
				400.1	10 cents?
				400.10	10 cents
				400.101	not cents
				400.11111111	

Variable	Risk (potential failure	Classes that should not trigger failure	Classes that might trigger failure	Test cases (best representatives)	Notes
	fails on nondigits	digits	ASCII chars other than digits	/ or /400 or 400/	boundary nondigit
				: or :400 or 400:	
			expression includes nondigit	500+2	
	too few characters	3 to 5 chars	< 3	20	
				<space>	no numeric characters
				press <enter> for an empty field	no characters at all
	too many characters	3 to 5 chars	>5	123456	
				012345	leading zero
				000000etc12345	lots of leading zeros

N. ANALYZE INDEPENDENT VARIABLES THAT SHOULD BE TESTED TOGETHER

This Task goes beyond what we're trying to teach with this example.

O. ANALYZE VARIABLES THAT HOLD RESULTS

The only result variable mentioned is `CreditLimit`. The only tests directly suggested by the problem description are out-of-bounds values of `DesiredCreditLimit`. If the program accepts these values, what happens to `CreditLimit`?

P. ANALYZE NON-INDEPENDENT VARIABLES. DEAL WITH RELATIONSHIPS AND CONSTRAINTS

This Task goes beyond what we're trying to teach with this example.

Q. IDENTIFY AND LIST UNANALYZED VARIABLES. GATHER INFORMATION FOR LATER ANALYSIS

So far, we've identified three variables and analyzed one. We know about, but don't know enough to analyze:

- `CreditLimit` (the limit to be assigned to this account)
- `CustomerName`

In addition:

- Is there a variable that holds the decision (application accepted or rejected)?
- What other fields does the application include:
  - Customer income, address and other demographic data?
  - Other credit cards, other loans and other income and credit data?

R. IMAGINE AND DOCUMENT RISKS THAT DON'T NECESSARILY MAP TO AN OBVIOUS DIMENSION

Here are a few risks that we would want to check while working with this input. These don't map directly to the input field(s) but they would be involved in the processing of the application that these input fields are part of.

- What if this applicant already has a credit card with SunTrust? Will that be caught as part of the credit evaluation?
  - If the applicant has a credit limit of $35,000 on that first card, should his credit on this new card be kept below $5000 (to keep the total below $40,000)?
  - Is it within the intended scope of the system you're testing to notice issues like this?
- What if this applicant has applied for this card previously and been rejected? Should the system detect this?
- What if this applicant has a huge savings account here? Should someone with $10 million in assets with the bank be restricted to a $40,000 credit card limit?
- If the applicant is rejected for this card, does this system alert him to other card offers for which he would be approved? For example, does the system propose that he accept a card with higher interest rate? Should it?
- Is there a limit on how many credit cards SunTrust can approve? Suppose the applicant meets SunTrust's acceptance criteria, but granting this credit puts SunTrust's loan-to-asset ratios just over a limit? Should this system detect this problem?
- What if there are content errors in the application (wrong street address, for example) Does this system check for these? If it finds an error, what should it do?
- Can the amount offered be greater than the amount requested? Should this be possible?

EXAMPLE 4: PAGE SETUP OPTIONS

The page setup function of a text editor allows a user to set the width of the page in the range of 1 to 56 inches. The `PageWidth` input field accepts (and remembers) up to 30 places after the decimal point.

A. IDENTIFY THE POTENTIALLY INTERESTING VARIABLES

`PageWidth` (input value).

B. IDENTIFY THE VARIABLES YOU CAN ANALYZE NOW. THESE ARE THE VARIABLES OF INTEREST

The page setup function probably includes several variables, but the only one described here is `PageWidth`. The description gives you plenty of information to start testing.

C. DETERMINE THE PRIMARY DIMENSION OF THE VARIABLE OF INTEREST

Width of the page (in inches).

D. DETERMINE THE TYPE AND SCALE OF THE VARIABLE'S PRIMARY DIMENSION AND WHAT VALUES IT CAN TAKE

This appears to be a Quadruple-Precision Floating-Point variable in the range of 1 to 56. Variables of this type can hold 34 significant digits: https://en.wikipedia.org/wiki/Machine_epsilon). For more on Floating-Point variables, see *Floating Point* on page 72.

As you consider the possible values of this variable, you might marvel at the apparent precision. When 2400 dots per inch is exceptionally high resolution, what is the practical difference between 1 inch and 1.000000000000000000000000000001 inches?

A specification like this looks a little crazy to us, but it's based on a real case. Some programs let you specify page sizes, slide sizes and image sizes with high-precision variables.

Our task is to test the program in front of us. It is certainly appropriate to question a silly-looking design decision, but until the design changes, the tests have to reflect what is there.

E. DETERMINE WHETHER YOU CAN ORDER THE VARIABLE'S VALUES (FROM SMALLEST TO LARGEST)

Yes.

F. DETERMINE WHETHER THIS IS AN INPUT VARIABLE OR A RESULT

This is an input variable.

G. DETERMINE HOW THE PROGRAM USES THIS VARIABLE

The editor will treat this value as the width of the editable page. It will determine, for example:

- How many characters can fit on a line before the editor wraps to a new line.
- How wide the page will appear onscreen.
- If the editor shows the full width of the page in the editing window, the width of the page and the width of the window constrain how wide the displayed characters can be. (As

a side-effect, it probably changes the displayed height of the characters when it changes their displayed width.)

- Whether the document can fit on a printed page. The printing algorithm might have to shrink a wide-page-width page to fit it on a physical page or spread an editor page across several physical pages.

In some cases, changing the width of the page changes the size of the text or graphics on the page. PowerPoint 2007 does this, for example, when you change the width of the slide.

H. DETERMINE WHETHER OTHER VARIABLES ARE RELATED TO THIS ONE

The problem description doesn't provide any directly relevant information. However, this variable might constrain the page's height. (If you set the width of a letter-size page to 11", you know the height will be 8.5".) It will also affect the dimensions of the printable area on the page and the length of a multi-page document.

I. PARTITION THE VARIABLE (ITS PRIMARY DIMENSION)

The classic partitioning is:

- Too small: less than 1 inch
- Acceptable: 1-56
- Too big: greater than 56

We would probably consider two more sets

- negative numbers
- extremely large numbers

These will show up soon, in the risk/equivalence table.

J. LAY OUT THE ANALYSIS IN A CLASSICAL BOUNDARY/EQUIVALENCE TABLE. IDENTIFY BEST REPRESENTATIVES

If this were a *Fixed-Point* variable, we could start by defining a constant:

$$\textbf{DELTA} = 0.000000000000000000000000000001$$

This value of **DELTA** (Δ) is the smallest difference you can have between two numbers in a Fixed-Point system that accepts (and remembers) 30 digits after the decimal point.

As we explained in *Floating Point* on page 72. the smallest recognizable difference between two *Floating-Point* numbers is not a constant.

- We use the notation $\Delta(\textbf{x})$ to represent the smallest value that you can add to **x** to obtain a number recognizably larger than **x**.
- When dealing with Quadruple Precision, the value of $\Delta(1.0) =$ is 2^{-112} (which is about $1.93E^{-34}$. *See* https://en.wikipedia.org/wiki/Machine_epsilon.
- In general, $\Delta(\textbf{x}) = x \times \Delta(1.0)$.

Variable	Valid case equivalence class	Invalid case equivalence class	Boundaries and special cases	Notes
`PageWidth`	1 to 56 inches		1	
			56	
		< 1	$1 - \Delta(1.0)$	0. and thirty 9's after the decimal point. Can it really distinguish this from 1.0?
			0	
		> 56	$56 + \Delta(56.0)$	Can it really distinguish this from 56?

The tests use the values in the "Boundaries and special cases" column.

K. CREATE TESTS FOR THE CONSEQUENCES OF THE DATA ENTERED, NOT JUST THE INPUT FILTER

Our tests would check anything associated with the width of the page. For example:

- How the page is displayed.
- How it's printed.
- How much text (or graphic if the editor accepts graphics) can fit on a line.
- How wide the characters can be. (Imagine a big W on a narrow page. Can the single character be too wide for the page?)
- How long does it take to scroll through the document or to repaint the page?
- Can the program run out of memory trying to display a huge page?
- What happens to large graphics if you narrow the page (narrower than the graphic)?
- What happens to the length of the document? Does the program reduce the number of pages or leave the last pages blank?

L. IDENTIFY SECONDARY DIMENSIONS. ANALYZE THEM IN THE CLASSICAL WAY

There are many possible secondary dimensions. The following list of test ideas for Floating-Point variables is almost the same as the *Test Idea Catalog for Fixed-Point Variables* on page 249.

TEST IDEA CATALOG FOR FLOATING-POINT VARIABLES

- Nothing
- Emptied field (clear the default value)
- Whitespace only (tab, space)
- 0
- Valid value
- At lower bound of range - Δ
- At lower bound of range
- At upper bound of range
- At upper bound of range + Δ
- Far below the lower bound of range, such as at **MINFLOAT**
- Far above the upper bound of range, such as at **MAXFLOAT**
- Far below the lower bound number of digits or characters
- At lower bound minus 1 number of digits or characters
- At lower bound number of digits or characters

- At upper bound number of digits or characters
- At upper bound plus 1 number of digits or characters
- Far above the upper bound number of digits or characters
  - with digits or printing characters
  - with leading 0's (are they ignored?)
  - with leading spaces (are they ignored?)
  - with leading minus signs
- Number of digits before the decimal point (lower and upper bounds)
- Number of digits after the decimal point (lower and upper bounds)
- Leading space
- Many leading spaces
- Leading zero
- Many leading zeros
- Leading space or zero plus a sign (+ or -)
- Negative values
- Hexadecimal digits
- Non-digits (especially / (ASCII 47) and : (ASCII character 58)
- Non-digits embedded in the number, such as 1a3 (some programs will interpret this as 13)
- Uppercase characters
- Lowercase characters
- Upper ASCII (128-254) and Unicode values beyond traditional ASCII (UTF-8, UTF-16 and UTF-32) (*See* http://www.utf-8.com/)
- Modifiers (e.g., Ctrl, Alt, Shift-Ctrl, etc.)
- Function key (F2, F3, F4, etc.)
- Nonprinting characters (such as control characters)
- Operating system file name reserved characters (such as "*.:)
- ASCII 255 (0 and 255 are often interpreted as end of file)
- *See* Whittaker (2003, p. 29-33) for many other ideas on troublesome characters
- Wrong data type (e.g., a variable defined as a Fixed-Point constant)
- No decimal point
- Two decimal points
- Decimal comma
- Contains one or more commas (thousands separators)
- Contains one or more points (thousands separators)
- Commas in appropriate places within the number
- Commas in inappropriate places within the number
- Scientific notation
- Scientific notation with an invalid exponent
- Scientific notation with a significand that has too many digits
- Scientific notation with an exponent that will cause an overflow
- Scientific notation with a significand/exponent combination that will cause an overflow.
- Fraction

- Special mathematical constant, such as π
- Expressions, including expressions that resolve to a valid value for input
- Background activity / competition for resource
- Enter nothing but wait for a long time before pressing or clicking whatever signals completed input for the field. Is there a timeout?
- Enter one digit and wait a long time before entering the next
- Enter digits, then (a) erase them and enter new digits or (b) backspace and type over them with new digits. Are these keystrokes accumulated until you press <Enter> (or however you signal that your input is complete) or are erased characters discarded immediately? If the program waits and processes the full input string, there must be a limit on the number of characters (including <Backspace> characters). What happens at the limit?
- Enter digits while you click the mouse, turn the printer off or create other interrupts

It would be a mistake to run all of these tests on every variable.

- If the programmers consistently use libraries that guard against some of these errors, you don't need to check for those errors.
- If the programmers have done good unit testing, they will have already found and fixed these kinds of bugs.

In either case, perhaps you should run a few tests to spot-check for inconsistency, but if you don't find any problems with these, spend the rest of your testing time looking for problems that are more likely to be in the code.

SECONDARY DIMENSIONS IN THE CLASSICAL TABLE

The following table includes two secondary dimensions to illustrate what they look like in the classical analysis:

- Number of digits before the decimal point
- Number of digits after the decimal point

Variable	Valid case equivalence class	Invalid case equivalence class	Boundaries and special cases	Notes
PageWidth	positive numbers			1, 56 already tested
		negative	-1	negative mirror of the valid input, 1
	1-2 digits before decimal	too few digits		empty field
		too many	100	
	0 to 30 digits after decimal		empty	You can't have -1 digits. You've already tested with 0 digits after the decimal
			1.0, 1.9, 55.9	1 digit
			1.00...9	29 zeros after the decimal, then the 9
			55.00...9	2-digits before the decimal, then 29 zeros after the decimal, then the 9. This test maximizes the total allowable digits before and after decimal.
		> 30	1.00...9	thirty zeros after the decimal, then the 9

M. SUMMARIZE YOUR ANALYSIS WITH A RISK/EQUIVALENCE TABLE

This table is like Example 3's *Generic Risk/Equivalence Table for Fixed-Point Variables* on page 251 except that you're working with a Quadruple-Precision Floating-Point number instead of a Fixed-Point number. Most of the test ideas are the same.

A RISK/EQUIVALENCE TABLE FOR A FLOATING-POINT VARIABLE

This table is not focused only on the input values. This type of table is organized in terms of the risks associated with this variable.

- Some of the risks involve how the program receives your inputs to `PageWidth`.
- Other risks involve the consequences of the value you give to `PageWidth`.

There are many other risks than you can list in this table. You can probably easily imagine more tests associated with the risks that we listed in the table, more potential consequences of the value of `PageWidth` and of other variables that `PageWidth` could interact badly with.

Variable	Risk (potential failure)	Classes that should not trigger failure	Classes that might trigger failure	Test cases (best representatives)	Notes
Page-Width	misclassifies valid inputs	anything out of bounds	1.0 to 56.0	1	Valid value At lower bound of range At lower bound of number of digits after decimal (zero digits)
				1.0	lowest non-zero number of digits after decimal
				1.00...0	30 zeros. Max number of digits after decimal
				55.99...9	30 nines. Max number of digits after decimal
				56.00...0	30 zeros, most digits before and after decimal, biggest valid value. This has a total of 33 characters.
				56.	decimal point but no digits after decimal
	mishandles values that are too small	≥ 1	< 1	0.99...9	30 nines. Can it really tell this is not 1.0?
				0	
	mishandles negative values	≥ 0	< 0	-0	some programs distinguish positive from negative zero. Does this make a difference here?
				-1	negative mirror of valid value
	mishandles values that are too large	≤ 56	> 56	56.00...01	29 zeros then 1
				57	probably unnecessary.
				5599...999	huge number (30 nines, no decimal point) but within the length of string it can process: 32 digits

Variable	Risk (potential failure)	Classes that should not trigger failure	Classes that might trigger failure	Test cases (best representatives)	Notes
	too few characters	> 0 chars	maybe 0	empty field	If a default value shows in dialog, erase it and then try to get the program to accept the empty value. Probably it will treat this as zero and reject it.
				space character	Whitespace only (tab, space). Probably it will treat this as zero and reject it.
	too many chars before decimal	< 3	≥ 3	100	smallest 3-digit entry
				100...0	1 then 33 zeros.
				<space>56	3 characters but the value is within bounds
				<spaces>56	If it likes <space>56, try 31 spaces. What about 100 spaces?
				+56	does it treat +56 same as 56?
				056	leading zero
				000...0056	LOTS of leading zeros
				++++++56	how many plus signs will it take?
				--56	minus-minus 56 is 56, right?
				56<space>	trailing space
				56<spaces>	LOTS of trailing spaces
	too many chars after decimal	< 31	≥ 31	1.00...09	30 zeros, then 9. Smallest too-big case. The width is within bounds, only the number of digits after the decimal is bad.
				1.00...09	LOTS of zeros.
				1.00...09<space>	29 zeros, then 9, then a trailing space
				1.00...09<spaces>	29 zeros, then 9, then LOTS of trailing spaces
	confused by wrong data type		strings		
			non-digits	/	Non-digits (especially / (ASCII 47)
				:	and : (ASCII character 58)
				ASCII 255	ASCII 255 (might be interpreted as end of file)
				*	Operating system file name reserved characters (such as "*.:)
				9-9	Arithmetic expressions
	Takes an unreasonable time to process the page	small page size	large page size	56	56" wide page. We want to run this test with tall page height, fill the page and see how long it takes to do basic editing or repainting or repaginating tasks. If the delay is unacceptable, simplify the test (for example, with a much shorter page height).

Variable	Risk (potential failure)	Classes that should not trigger failure	Classes that might trigger failure	Test cases (best representatives)	Notes
	Out of memory	small page size	large page size	56	How does the editor store data? Does page size matter or is the important issue the amount of text/graphic in the story or document being edited? If the editor stores more data in memory (or in an area it reserves as "working memory") when the page is larger, we want to try complex designs on big pages. `PageWidth` is one of the variables in this multidimensional extreme-value (memory stress) test
	Unprintable	small page	big page	56	max width page, what happens when you try to print it? Try with a few different types of printers.

The risks shown here are common to many variables. We probably wouldn't check all these risks on every variable (and we certainly wouldn't check them all in every build).

For example, we might not check how the program handles leading spaces across all of those variables, but we might check this with a few variables. If we found a problem, we'd look more closely. If not, we'd drop this line of investigation and go looking for other bugs instead.

N. ANALYZE INDEPENDENT VARIABLES THAT SHOULD BE TESTED TOGETHER

The problem description describes only one variable.

If you use the editor, you will quickly discover several other variables that should be tested with `PageWidth`. However, many of these will be constrained by `PageWidth` or that will constrain it. Therefore, we'll consider these in Task P, below.

O. ANALYZE VARIABLES THAT HOLD RESULTS

Plenty of things will depend on `PageWidth`, but we don't have any specific result variables at this time.

P. ANALYZE NON-INDEPENDENT VARIABLES. DEAL WITH RELATIONSHIPS AND CONSTRAINTS

The problem description describes only one variable, but you will probably quickly encounter the following when you started testing.

- `PageHeight`. Is this independent of `PageWidth` or is there a constraint? Does the value of `PageWidth` limit the range of values for `PageHeight`?
  - Is (`MaxHeight`, `MaxWidth`) a permissible height/width pair?
  - Does (`MaxHeight`, `MaxWidth`) define a page that will be impossible to print? (For example, can you print an 11" x 11" page on physical pages of 8.5" x 11"?)
- What type of printer is connected to the computer? Is this independent of `PageWidth` or does it introduce constraint?

- ◦ Different printers accept pages of different sizes. Does this limit the permissible values of `PageWidth`?
- Page margins. Right and left margins must be constrained by `PageWidth` and by each other.
  - ◦ The right margin (distance from the right edge of the page to the right edge of the text) can't be wider than `PageWidth`.
- Width of an object you want to place on the page:
  - ◦ A graphic might be too wide to place on the page.
  - ◦ A large-font letter might be too wide to place on the page.
- Length of the document. Does `PageWidth` constrain the number of pages?
  - ◦ Does the program explicitly limit the number of characters in the document?
  - ◦ Will the program run out of memory if the document is too long?

Now, consider how to test these together.

Start by giving the variables short labels so that you can refer to them easily:

- `W` = page width (as entered into the program)
- `H` = page height (as entered into the program)
- `L` = left margin (as entered into the program)
- `R` = right margin (as entered into the program)
- `WO` = width of an object you will place on the page
- `PW` = width of the physical page in the printer

Testing these together involves a fundamental constraint:

$$L + R + WO \leq W$$

Now consider the relationship between `PW` and `W`. Some programs can tile output (print an over-width page onto two physical pages that a person will tape together). For this example, assume the program can't do that. Therefore:

$$W \text{ must be} \leq PW.$$

You can represent these variables together as a 5-tuple, (`L`, `R`, `WO`, `W`, `PW`).

A *mechanical approach* to combining these variables will create combinations algorithmically.

- One mechanical approach will apply an algorithm analogous to all-pairs. However, dealing with non-independent variables that way is challenging.
- We would instead generate random 5-tuples that either satisfy the constraint:

$$L + R + WO \leq W \leq PW$$

  or fail to satisfy it in a way that we consider interesting.

  For example, consider a set of boundary tests that satisfy these criteria:

  $$W = PW \quad \text{and}$$

  $$L + R + WO = W$$

  - ◦ For `L`, generate a random number between 0 and `W`.
  - ◦ For `R`, generate a random number between 0 and `W` - `L`.
  - ◦ Set `WO` = `W` - `L` - `R`.

When using a random number generator to create a set of tests, we normally add a few specific boundary cases such as:

- Set $L = R = 0$ and $WO = W$
- Set $L = W$ and $R = 0 = WO$
- Set $L = 0$ and $R = W$ and $WO = 0$

Often, we create a small set of tests that will satisfy all-singles and use the random number generator for the rest of the combinations.

- We would probably supplement this set with a few invalid combinations:
  - $L + R + WO > W$ where $W \le PW$ and
  - $L + R + WO \le W$ where $W > PW$

A *risk-based* approach starts by asking how the program could fail. Then design tests to expose those (potential) failures. For example:

- Given a very small page specification (such as W and $H = 1$ inch each), try printing one of these pages onto a normal size page.

- Test values of the margins that are just barely too big to fit the object:

  $W - L - R$ is barely $< WO$

- Test values that are just barely too big to fit the page width:

  $L + R + WO$ barely $> W$

- Test a page width just barely too big for the printer width:

  $L + R + WO \le W$ where W barely $> PW$

The risk-equivalence table earlier in this Chapter suggests several other tests that might be interesting.

Q. IDENTIFY AND LIST UNANALYZED VARIABLES. GATHER INFORMATION FOR LATER ANALYSIS.

The problem description doesn't list any additional variables. The analysis to this point has suggested several possibilities, such as page height and the margins. You would create this list as you work with the program, noting variables as you see them or think of them.

R. IMAGINE AND DOCUMENT RISKS THAT DON'T NECESSARILY MAP TO AN OBVIOUS DIMENSION

What mischief can you make with a variable that accepts too many digits after the decimal?

- What if you subtract one value from another that is the same until the 29th or 30th digit? For most practical purposes, the result is 0, but the program won't see it as zero. What can you do with the result?

- Can you make the program display or print one thing on top of another? What if the program is not designed to allow overlapping objects?

- Imagine creating vertical stripes (such as columns of tables or side-by-side graphics) that are so narrow that many will fit within a printable-width of 1/2400th of an inch. Give each stripe a different color. What gets displayed or printed?

EXAMPLE 5: UNDERGRADUATE GRADES

The passing score for any undergraduate course at Florida Tech is 60/100. A student who scores less than 60 receives an 'F' on her transcript.

A. IDENTIFY THE POTENTIALLY INTERESTING VARIABLES

The problem description mentions one field that is probably an input field:

- **StudentScore** in a particular course.

The problem description mentions one output, based on the input field

- **LetterGrade** on the transcript, computed from the numeric grade.

The problem description suggests other variables but does not provide details:

- **StudentName**.
- **StudentID** (on the transcript).
- **CourseID**.

Our general rule for deciding whether to include a variable in this list is that if you think the variable is probably in the program or should be, include it.

B. IDENTIFY THE VARIABLES YOU CAN ANALYZE NOW. THESE ARE THE VARIABLES OF INTEREST

- **StudentScore**
- **LetterGrade** probably includes A, B, C, D, F, but what about A+ and A-? And is the mapping rigid or can an instructor override it to give a student whose grade is 59 a D? Is the program designed to allow different schools to decide these questions as option settings? You need more information (which might be a working program to experiment with) before you can proceed.

C. DETERMINE THE PRIMARY DIMENSION OF THE VARIABLE OF INTEREST

The problem description says little about these two variables. It says that if **StudentScore** is less than 60, then **LetterGrade** is an F.

Note the *implicit specification*. The author of the problem is relying on the reader's background knowledge instead of writing out every detail:

- **StudentScore** probably runs from 0 to 100.
- **LetterGrade** probably includes F, D, C, B, A.
- If 59 maps to an F, the grading scale probably follows a commonplace system in the United States that maps 0-59 to F, 60-69 to D, 70-79 to C, 80-89 to B and 90-100 to A.

The primary dimension of **LetterGrade** is probably an enumerated variable with letter values from F to A.

However, the implicit specification is ambiguous. The program could be dealing with a set of letter grades that includes only { F, D, C, B, A } or with a larger set, such as { F, D-, D, D+, C-, C, C+, B-, B, B+, A-, A, A+, A++ }. You have no way of knowing, from this specification, which of these sets is the "real" set and so you can't yet fully specify the letter grade's dimension. You'll have to run some tests to see what happens or ask someone.

D. DETERMINE THE TYPE AND SCALE OF THE VARIABLE'S PRIMARY DIMENSION AND WHAT VALUES IT CAN TAKE

Is `StudentScore` an Integer? Can you enter a score of 82.5? Let's assume for now that it expects whole numbers (but ask the program what it thinks, when you have a chance).

The *scale* poses a harder problem. In our experiences as graders, if we think of these numbers as measurements of the student's knowledge, there is a huge difference between the meaning of 60 (the student's knowledge is adequate) and 59 (the student's knowledge is inadequate). In terms of how graders assign numbers, the difference between 59 and 60 is a lot bigger than the difference between 94 and 95. This is inconsistent with the characteristics of interval and ratio scales.

As testers, we might ask about the meaning of these numbers. But for data processing purposes, we would normally treat this as interval-scaled data.

E. DETERMINE WHETHER YOU CAN ORDER THE VARIABLE'S VALUES (FROM SMALLEST TO LARGEST)

Yes.

F. DETERMINE WHETHER THIS IS AN INPUT VARIABLE OR A RESULT

- `StudentScore` is definitely an input variable.
- `LetterGrade` is a result.

G. DETERMINE HOW THE PROGRAM USES THIS VARIABLE

The student's letter grade is based on the numeric score and the grade is stored in the transcript. The problem description provides no additional information.

H. DETERMINE WHETHER OTHER VARIABLES ARE RELATED TO THIS ONE

`LetterGrade` is calculated from `StudentScore`.

These aren't mentioned in the problem description but are probably also inputs:

- `StudentName`
- `StudentID`
- `CourseID`

These are probably also results, but based on more data than this one input:

- `LetterGrade`
- `GPA` (grade point average)
- The student's transcript

The problem description provides no information about other variables.

I. PARTITION THE VARIABLE (ITS PRIMARY DIMENSION)

If `StudentScore` < 60, then `LetterGrade` is an F. From this, there are only two partitions:

- `StudentScore` < 60
- `StudentScore` ≥ 60

However, grades almost always run from 0 to 100, so you can guess there is probably a better partition:

- $StudentScore < 0$ invalid
- $0 \leq StudentScore < 60$ valid, yielding F
- $60 \leq StudentScore \leq 100$ valid, yielding some other letter grade
- $100 < StudentScore$ probably invalid

J. LAY OUT THE ANALYSIS IN A CLASSICAL BOUNDARY/EQUIVALENCE TABLE. IDENTIFY BEST REPRESENTATIVES

Variable	Valid case equivalence class	Invalid case equivalence class	Boundaries and special cases	Notes
StudentScore	0 to 59		0	Expect F
			59	Expect F
	60 to 100		60	Probably a D
			100	Probably an A
		< 0	-1	
		> 100	101	
				The table needs cases for A, B, C, D but there is insufficient information for it at this time.

The tests use the values in the "Boundaries and special cases" column.

K. CREATE TESTS FOR THE CONSEQUENCES OF THE DATA ENTERED, NOT JUST THE INPUT FILTER

The grade determines whether the student passes or fails the course. The system probably creates several consequences for this, but the problem description doesn't say anything about the system.

L. IDENTIFY SECONDARY DIMENSIONS. ANALYZE THEM IN THE CLASSICAL WAY

Assuming StudentScore is an Integer, you can use the same analysis as Example 1's *Test Idea Catalog for Integers* on page 231.

It is premature to identify secondary dimensions for LetterGrade because the description provides no information about how the program calculates its value.

M. SUMMARIZE YOUR ANALYSIS WITH A RISK/EQUIVALENCE TABLE

Assuming StudentScore is an Integer, the table will probably look much like the one in Example 1.

We wouldn't create more than a skeleton of this table until we knew more about the data type (can the score take values like 80.5?) and the mapping from score to letter-grade.

N. ANALYZE INDEPENDENT VARIABLES THAT SHOULD BE TESTED TOGETHER

This Task goes beyond what we're trying to teach with this example.

O. ANALYZE VARIABLES THAT HOLD RESULTS

It's premature to do this analysis for `LetterGrade` or the transcript.

P. ANALYZE NON-INDEPENDENT VARIABLES. DEAL WITH RELATIONSHIPS AND CONSTRAINTS

It's premature to analyze relationships among `StudentScore`, `LetterGrade` and any other variables.

Q. TASKS Q & R ARE BEYOND WHAT WE'RE TRYING TO TEACH WITH THIS EXAMPLE.

EXAMPLE 6: TAX TABLE

In 1993, the Internal Revenue Service calculated taxes based on this table (Beizer, 1995, p. 151):

Income Range	Tax
$0 < $ `TaxableIncome` $\leq \$22100$	$0.15 \times$ `TaxableIncome`
$\$22100 <$ `TaxableIncome` $\leq \$53500$	$\$3315 + 0.28 \times ($ `TaxableIncome` $- 22100)$
$\$53500 <$ `TaxableIncome` $\leq \$115000$	$\$12107 + 0.31 \times ($ `TaxableIncome` $- 53500)$
$\$115000 <$ `TaxableIncome` $\leq \$250000$	$\$31172 + 0.36 \times ($ `TaxableIncome` $- 115000)$
$\$250000 <$ `TaxableIncome`	$\$79772 + 0.396 \times ($ `TaxableIncome` $- 250000)$

A. IDENTIFY THE POTENTIALLY INTERESTING VARIABLES

- `TaxableIncome`: This is probably a computed result, not an input variable. The inputs are probably amounts of income and expense and tax deductions.
- `Tax`: How much tax to pay (This is a result variable).

B. IDENTIFY THE VARIABLES YOU CAN ANALYZE NOW. THESE ARE THE VARIABLES OF INTEREST

There are two variables: `TaxableIncome` and `Tax`, the amount of tax to pay. The value of `Tax` is computed directly from `TaxableIncome`, so you might want to start testing `TaxableIncome`. However:

- The problem description says very little about `TaxableIncome`. It mentions `TaxableIncome` only as the input to the calculation of `Tax`.
- Like `Tax`, `TaxableIncome` is probably a computed result rather than a variable you enter directly.

You can analyze both variables now, but the analysis will be limited until you understand how `TaxableIncome` gets its value.

C. DETERMINE THE PRIMARY DIMENSION OF THE VARIABLE OF INTEREST

- `TaxableIncome`'s primary dimension is a dollar amount, running from 0 to a big number.
- `Tax`'s primary dimension is a dollar amount, running from 0 to a large number.

D. DETERMINE THE TYPE AND SCALE OF THE VARIABLE'S PRIMARY DIMENSION AND WHAT VALUES IT CAN TAKE

- Integer or
- Fixed point, with two digits after the decimal (dollars and cents). Thus:
  - Values like 10.25 are accepted but 10.251 is probably rejected or rounded to 10.25.
  - The program will probably convert 10 and 10.2 to 10.00 and 10.20.

E. DETERMINE WHETHER YOU CAN ORDER THE VARIABLE'S VALUES (FROM SMALLEST TO LARGEST)

Yes.

F. DETERMINE WHETHER THIS IS AN INPUT VARIABLE OR A RESULT

- The problem description doesn't identify any input variables.

- **TaxableIncome** is probably a result, computed on the basis of some other inputs.
- **Tax** is a result.

G. DETERMINE HOW THE PROGRAM USES THIS VARIABLE

The program uses **TaxableIncome** to compute **Tax**. **Tax** is a stepwise linear function of **TaxableIncome**.

The problem description provides no information about how (or if) the program uses **Tax**.

H. DETERMINE WHETHER OTHER VARIABLES ARE RELATED TO THIS ONE

TaxableIncome and **Tax** are related: The value of **Tax** is determined by the value of **TaxableIncome**.

The problem description doesn't list any other variables.

I. PARTITION THE VARIABLE (ITS PRIMARY DIMENSION)

The tax table specifies all the partitions and transition points (boundary values of the partitions) except for negative income:

- **TaxableIncome** < 0
- 0 ≤ **TaxableIncome** ≤ 22100
- 22100 < **TaxableIncome** ≤ 53500
- 53500 < **TaxableIncome** ≤ 115000
- 115000 < **TaxableIncome** ≤ 250000
- 250000 < **TaxableIncome**

J. LAY OUT THE ANALYSIS IN A CLASSICAL BOUNDARY/EQUIVALENCE TABLE. IDENTIFY BEST REPRESENTATIVES

The problem description doesn't specify whether **TaxableIncome** is an Integer or a Fixed Point (dollars and cents) variable that accepts two digits after the decimal.

SHOWING MULTIPLE VALID EQUIVALENCE CLASSES ON THE SAME TABLE

For **TaxableIncome** the table is:

Variable	Valid case equivalence classes	Invalid case equivalence class	Boundaries and special cases	Notes
TaxableIncome (TI)		TI < 0	-1	Is this possible?
	0 ≤ TI ≤ 22100		0	Probably treated separately as a special case
			0.01	If it accepts Floating Point
			1	
			22100	
	22100 < TI ≤ 53500		22100.01	

Variable	Valid case equivalence classes	Invalid case equivalence class	Boundaries and special cases	Notes
			22101	
			53500	
	$53500 <$ TI ≤ 115000		53500.01	
			53501	
			115000	
	$115000 <$ TI ≤ 250000		115000.01	
			115001	
			250000	
	$250000 <$ TI		250000.01	
			250001	
		no upper bound is specified. Uh oh!	99999-lots-of-9999's?	Is there a limit?
			2^{32}	Use the actual value of **MAXINT** + 1
			2^{64}	**MAXLONG** + 1

The tests use the values in the "Boundaries and special cases" column.

K. CREATE TESTS FOR THE CONSEQUENCES OF THE DATA ENTERED, NOT JUST THE INPUT FILTER

This Task goes beyond what we're trying to teach with this example.

L. IDENTIFY SECONDARY DIMENSIONS. ANALYZE THEM IN THE CLASSICAL WAY

- If `TaxableIncome` is an input field, it's either an Integer or Fixed Point. See *Test Idea Catalog for Integers* on page 231 and *Test Idea Catalog for Fixed-Point Variables* on page 249 for ideas.

- If `TaxableIncome` is a computed result, most of the identified risks in the generic test idea catalogs are inapplicable. For example, the program (probably) won't compute `Taxable-Income` in a way that turns it into a string and it will (probably) format it reasonably (for example, without hundreds of leading spaces). So these secondary-dimension risks are irrelevant.

In either case, it would be interesting to try to overflow `TaxableIncome` or make it negative.

M. SUMMARIZE YOUR ANALYSIS WITH A RISK/EQUIVALENCE TABLE

Here's a starting point for the table. This sticks to the primary dimension, without thinking about the other types of errors you could imagine (secondary dimensions).

The challenge is that the description doesn't say whether `TaxableIncome` is an input variable.

- If `TaxableIncome` is an input variable, the test idea catalogs for Integers and Floating Points will yield many additional tests.

- If not, the rest of the analysis has to wait until you know more about the program.

Variable	Risk (potential failure)	Classes that should not trigger failure	Classes that might trigger the failure	Test cases (best representatives)	Notes
Taxable-Income (TI)	mishandles values that are too small	> 0	≤ 0	0	If negative income is possible, add negative-value cases
	misclassifies valid values	$TI < 0$	$0 < TI \le 22100$	0.01	
				1	
				22100	
			$22100 < TI \le 53500$	22100.01	
				22101	
				53500	
			$53500 < TI \le 115000$	53500.01	
				53501	
				115000	
			$115000 < TI \le 250000$	115000.01	
				115001	
				250000	
			$250000 < TI$	250000.01	
				250001	
	mishandles values that are too large			99999-lots-of-9999's?	Is there a limit?
				2^{32}	Use the actual value of **MAXINT** $+ 1$
				2^{64}	**MAXLONG** $+ 1$

For **Tax**, there isn't enough information to support a risk/equivalence table yet. There is no user input to **Tax**, so there can't be user-error inputs.

N. ANALYZE INDEPENDENT VARIABLES THAT SHOULD BE TESTED TOGETHER

The problem description lists only two variables. Neither is multidimensional.

O. ANALYZE VARIABLES THAT HOLD RESULTS

For **Tax**, the classical table is:

Variable	Valid case equivalence classes	Invalid case equivalence class	Boundaries and special cases	Notes
Tax		$Tax \le 0$	$TI = 0$	TI is **TaxableIncome**
			$TI = -1$	What happens if the taxpayer (e.g., a business) shows a loss?
	$0 < Tax \le 3315$		$TI = 0.01$	If it accepts Floating Point
			$TI = 1$	

Variable	Valid case equivalence classes	Invalid case equivalence class	Boundaries and special cases	Notes
			TI = 22100	
	$3315 < \text{Tax} \le 12107$		TI = 22100.01	
			TI = 22101	
			TI = 53500	
	$12107 < \text{Tax} \le 31172$		TI = 53500.01	
			TI = 53501	
			TI = 115000	
	$31172 < \text{Tax} \le 79772$		TI = 115000.01	
			TI = 115001	
			TI = 250000	
	$79772 < \text{Tax}$		TI = 250000.01	
			TI = 250001	
		no upper bound is specified. Uh oh!	TI = 99999-lots-of-9999's?	Is there a limit?
			$\text{TI} = 2^{32}$	use the actual value of **MAXINT** + 1
			$\text{TI} = 2^{64}$	**MAXLONG** + 1

P. ANALYZE NON-INDEPENDENT VARIABLES. DEAL WITH RELATIONSHIPS AND CONSTRAINTS

This Task goes beyond what we're trying to teach with this example.

Q. IDENTIFY AND LIST UNANALYZED VARIABLES. GATHER INFORMATION FOR LATER ANALYSIS

Any tax return provides pages of forms that ask for data for **TaxableIncome**. There isn't enough information in this Example to decide which of these to cover. If this was Real Life and not just an Example, you'd be making a list of every variable you could find in all those forms.

R. IMAGINE AND DOCUMENT RISKS THAT DON'T NECESSARILY MAP TO AN OBVIOUS DIMENSION

Working only from the information in the Example, there isn't enough information to do much of this. But here are a few ideas:

- What happens if your deductions exceed your income (for example, if you lose money in your business)? Can you make your **TaxableIncome** negative?

- If **TaxableIncome** is calculated from a list, can you make a list that is too long?

EXAMPLE 7: STUDENT NAMES

A **StudentLastName** field must start with an alphabetic character (upper or lower case). Subsequent characters must be letters, numbers or spaces.

A. IDENTIFY THE POTENTIALLY INTERESTING VARIABLES

- **StudentLastName**.

B. IDENTIFY THE VARIABLE YOU CAN ANALYZE NOW. THIS IS THE VARIABLE OF INTEREST

- **StudentLastName**.

C. DETERMINE THE PRIMARY DIMENSION OF THE VARIABLE OF INTEREST

StudentLastName is a string:

- The first character is constrained to be only letters (upper or lower).
- Subsequent characters can be letters, numbers or spaces.
- Presumably, there is some limit on the length of the name.

So what is the *primary dimension* here? We don't think the answer is absolutely clear and certain.

Our heuristic is to ask what is the nature of the information the person is trying to enter into the variable. We treat *that* as what determines the primary dimension.

In this case, the user is entering a name. A name is made up of characters and the characters have to be valid for a name (letters appear in a valid name; question marks do not). On that basis, we tentatively treat character value as the primary dimension and length of the string as a secondary dimension. Your analysis (or more information about how the variable is used) might emphasize length more heavily.

D. DETERMINE THE TYPE AND SCALE OF THE VARIABLE'S PRIMARY DIMENSION AND WHAT VALUES IT CAN TAKE

- TYPE: String (any collection of alphanumeric characters)
- SCALE: Nominal (for most purposes, one name is not lesser or greater than any other). However, you could treat this as an ordinal variable ordered by spelling (A's before B's) or by length of the string.

Note that this definition will exclude some perfectly reasonable names. What if your name is O'Toole or Garcia-Mendez?

If a variable definitions are too restrictive, send a note or file a bug report that gives examples of reasonable inputs that the program rejects as invalid. If possible, delay the domain analysis until you learn whether the variable will be redefined.

This is a textbook example. Allowing more characters (such as ' and - and accented characters) will make the example more realistic but will also increase the complexity of the answer without teaching you much new. Therefore, we proceed as if the development group stayed with the original design decision.

E. DETERMINE WHETHER YOU CAN ORDER THE VARIABLE'S VALUES (FROM SMALLEST TO LARGEST)

You can order the names by the ASCII values of characters in a string, but that only tells part of the story. To separate valid from invalid values, you have to separate the ASCII ordering into valid and invalid subranges.

- ASCII codes for numbers run from 48 to 57.
- ASCII codes for upper case letters run from 65 to 90.
- ASCII codes for lower case letters run from 97 to 122.
- There are more letters (non-English characters) in the upper ASCII set (and in UTF-8 and UTF-16), but for purposes of this exercise, we'll ignore these.

Consider the first letter:

- The first character in the string must be a letter. Anything below 65 is invalid, anything in the ranges 65-90 and 97 to 122 is valid, 91-96 and above 122 is invalid.

Consider subsequent characters:

- ASCII codes for numbers run from 48 to 57. These are valid.
- ASCII 65-90 and 97-122 are valid.
- The Space character is encoded 32. It's valid.
- Anything out of the set {32, 48-57, 65-90, 97-122} is invalid.

As you work with these groupings, you should recognize that the ordering imposed by ASCII encoding is artificial. Why should a <space> have a lower code value than a number (32 vs 48)? Why should upper case letters have lower codes than lower case? The codes are numbers, but they don't have the usual properties of numbers. For example, if you add 32 (ASCII) and 32 (ASCII), you get two spaces, not 64.

F. DETERMINE WHETHER THIS IS AN INPUT VARIABLE OR A RESULT

This Task goes beyond what we're trying to teach with this example.

G. DETERMINE HOW THE PROGRAM USES THIS VARIABLE

This Task goes beyond what we're trying to teach with this example.

H. DETERMINE WHETHER OTHER VARIABLES ARE RELATED TO THIS ONE

The problem description provides little information relevant to this. Presumably, there are fields for the student's first name, middle name, etc.

I. PARTITION THE VARIABLE (ITS PRIMARY DIMENSION)

The dimensions are ordered, so determine the sub-ranges and transition points.

- `FirstLetter`:
  - ASCII 65-90 and 97-122 are valid. The rest are not.
- `Subsequent characters`:
  - ASCII 32, 48 to 57, 65-90 and 97-122 are valid. Everything else is not.
- `Final character`:
  - This is a subsequent character, but perhaps trailing spaces are allowed.

J. LAY OUT THE ANALYSIS IN THE CLASSICAL BOUNDARY/EQUIVALENCE TABLE. IDENTIFY BEST REPRESENTATIVES

Variable	Valid case equivalence class	Invalid case equivalence class	Boundaries and special cases	Notes
FirstLetter	65 - 90 (A - Z)		65 (A)	
			90 (Z)	
		< 65	64 (@)	
		91 - 96	91 ([ )	
			96 (`)	
	97 - 122 (a - z)		97 (a)	
			122 (z)	
		> 122	123 ({)	ignore upper ASCII and Unicode beyond first 127 chars
All other letters		0 - 31	0 (null byte)	non-printing character and possibly end of string
			31 (us)	non-printing character
	32 (space)		32 (space)	
		33 - 47	33 (!)	
			47 (/)	
	48 - 57		48 (0)	
			57 (9)	
		58 - 64	58 (:)	
			64 (@)	
	65 - 90 (A - Z)		65 (A)	
			90 (Z)	
		91 - 96	91 ([ )	
			96 (`)	
	97 - 122 (a - z)		97 (a)	
			122 (z)	
		> 122	123 ({)	

The tests use the values in the "Boundaries and special cases" column.

K. CREATE TESTS FOR THE CONSEQUENCES OF THE DATA ENTERED, NOT JUST THE INPUT FILTER

This Task goes beyond what we're trying to teach with this example.

L. IDENTIFY SECONDARY DIMENSIONS. ANALYZE THEM IN THE CLASSICAL WAY

The most important one is probably **length** of the string.

The description doesn't specify a maximum, but the system probably enforces one. Call this limit **MAXNAME**. Otherwise there will be interesting problems in formatting reports and allocating storage for the (probably-key) field in this database. **MAXNAME** is probably 30 characters or less.

Variable	Valid case equivalence class	Invalid case equivalence class	Boundaries and special cases	Notes
String length	1 to **MAXNAME**		1 character	
			MAXNAME	
		Too short	0 characters	is an empty name invalid?
		Too long	**MAXNAME**+1	
			127	common buffer maximum. 127, 128, 255, 256 are interesting cases (but maybe not invalid) no matter what value in **MAXNAME**
			128	
			255	common buffer maximum
			256	2^8 (8-bit word + 1) boundary
			65536	2^{16}
			16777216	2^{24} if there's going to be an overflow, 16 million characters will probably do it.
			4294967296	2^{32}

We'll consider a longer list of secondary dimensions in the next Section.

M. SUMMARIZE YOUR ANALYSIS WITH A RISK/EQUIVALENCE TABLE

This is our first example with a String variable, so we copy the generic string-test list from Chapter M's, *Secondary Dimensions for Strings* on page 166 and map it to the table.

TEST IDEA CATALOG FOR STRINGS[37]

- Nothing
- Emptied field (clear the default value)
- Null character (ASCII 0)
- Whitespace only (tab, space, LF (ASCII 10), CR (ASCII 13), ASCII 127)
- Nonprinting characters, such as ASCII 0 to 31. *See* Whittaker (2003, p. 29-33) for a discussion of these.
- Character codes for that have not been assigned to a character (*see* Page et al., 2009, p. 93)
- End of file (ASCII 0 or 255)
- One valid character long. (A "valid" character might be alpha only, alphanumeric, printable lower ASCII (ASCII 32-126), printable characters of any kind (including extended ASCII or Unicode: UTF-8 or UTF-16 or UTF-32) or any subset of these).
- For variables that accept only alpha characters, try @ (ASCII 64; A is 65), [(ASCII 91), ` (ASCII 97) and { (ASCII 123).
- For variables that accept only alpha characters, try accented characters, such as à, â, á, ã, ä, å, ç and letters in non-Western-Latin character sets (e.g., as Arabic, Cyrillic, Devanāgarī, Hebrew)
- Strings that include common delimiters, such as space, tab, comma, dot, en dash (–), em dash (—), hyphen, " ' " ' ' ", ( ), < >, { }, [ ], / | \, !, @, #, ^, &, *, +, ~ and =

---

37   For more ideas, see Johnson (2007) and Page, Johnston & Rollison (2009).

- Strings that include string operators, such as +, ==, !=, <, <=, [], etc.
- Strings that include numbers and operators that are valid in expressions, such as * / + - ()
- Non-alpha characters that are legitimately grouped with alpha strings, such as ©, ® and ™
- Modifiers (e.g., Ctrl, Alt, Shift-Ctrl, etc.)
- Function key (F2, F3, F4, etc.)
- Command strings, such as SQL commands
- Wildcard characters, such as * and ?
- Lower bound number of (valid) characters - 1
- Lower bound number of (valid) characters
- Byte boundary numbers of characters (255, 256, 1023, 1024, etc.)
- Upper bound number of (valid) characters
- Upper bound number of (valid) characters + 1
- Far below the lower bound number of (valid) characters
- Far above the upper bound number of (valid) characters
- Leading or trailing spaces
- Leading or trailing spaces that take the string up to the lower bound number of characters
- Leading or trailing spaces that take the string beyond the maximum number of characters
- Identical to another string except that one string's characters are uppercase and the other's are lowercase
- Background activity / competition for resource
- Enter nothing but wait for a long time before pressing or clicking whatever signals completed input for the field. Is there a timeout?
- Enter one character and wait a long time before entering the next
- Enter characters, then erase them and enter new characters or backspace and type over them with new characters—are all these keystrokes accumulated (in which case, there is a limit, so what happens at the limit?) until you press <Enter> (or however you signal that your input is complete) or are erased characters discarded immediately?
- Enter characters while you click the mouse or turn the printer on and off or create other types of interrupts

This table is only an approximation of what we would do in real practice. The characters with ASCII codes 0 to 31 (and many others) aren't really equivalent because each has (if it is not ignored) a different effect. These were old codes to control your teletype. One rings a bell. Delete and backspace are in this group. So are vertical tab and formfeed. We have characters for handshaking (on-signal, off-signal), end of text and so on. If we were concerned about these, we would sample different ones in different regression runs (if we were doing manual testing) or we would consider programming tests for all of them.

Note that we have assumed that this program accepts only lower ASCII text, so non-English characters aren't supposed to be accepted. Many programs will accept these and process them appropriately. English characters (characters encoded in ASCII) fit in a Byte, but other characters might be encoded in two Bytes, so calculations based on length of the String might not map well to space it occupies.

As with the other test idea catalogs, good unit testing and consistent use of error-aware programming libraries will reduce the need for many of these tests at the system level. Before deciding how many of these tests to run, if you can, check with the programmers.

GENERIC RISK/EQUIVALENCE TABLE FOR STRINGS

Variable	Risk (potential failure)	Classes that should not trigger failure	Classes that might trigger failure	Test cases (best representatives)	Notes
Student's last name	Allows empty or blank field		0 characters	Enter nothing, leave the field blank	Lower bound number of chars -1
				Erase default string to empty the field	
			No name	Null (ASCII 0)	
				Space character	
				Tab character	
				ASCII 127	DEL
				ASCII 255	might be end of file
	Reject valid non-alpha characters		embedded space or dot	St. John	one period, one space
		embedded spaces		Van Heusen	Two spaces
		embedded dots		St.. John	Two dots
		dot w/o space		St.John	No space
	Rejects valid alpha	traditional capitalization	unusual capitalization	smith	lower case first letter
				CamelCase	interior capital letter
	Accepts invalid characters		ASCII 1 to 31	ASCII 3	may generate a program interrupt
				ASCII 4	end of text
				ASCII 26	end of text
					The others are interesting too. Sample from them
			Numbers	0	Names (probably) don't have numbers in them
				9	
			Delimiters or other special text characters	letters + tab + letters	whitespace like space, but invalid
				letters + delimiter + letters	space, tab, comma, dot, en dash (–), em dash (—), hyphen, "'"'", ( ), < >, { }, [ ], / \, !, @, #, ^, &, *, +, ~, ? and =
			boundary non-alpha	@	ASCII 64
				]	ASCII 91
				`	ASCII 96
				}	ASCII 123
			Other non-alpha	©	™ ® ©

Variable	Risk (potential failure)	Classes that should not trigger failure	Classes that might trigger failure	Test cases (best representatives)	Notes
			Accented letters	à	à, â, á, ã, ä, å, ç, etc.
				Jàne	The program might check the first character and assume later ones are acceptable
			Foreign alphabets	Д	Unicode 0414 Cyrillic
				Я	Unicode 042F Cyrillic
					Additional letters in non-Western-Latin character sets (such as Arabic, Cyrillic, Devanāgarī, Hebrew).
	Processes wildcard		any string with * or ?	John*	If it accepts John*, what does it store?
				John1 and John?	what does it store for John?
				search for John?	Does it find John1 or John? when you try to retrieve John?
	Executes commands embedded in strings		strings with string operators	James+Brown	==, !=, <, <=, [], +=
				Brown[1]	
			SQL commands	SELECT	
			File commands	Delete	names and syntax depend on your OS
			strings that look like arithmetic expressions	2+3	
	too short	≥ 1 nonwhite-space printing character	empty	empty	you covered this already (Lower bound number of chars - 1)
	too short after filtering whitespace	≥ 1 nonwhite-space printing character	non-empty strings that have only whitespace (enough to take us to the string's minimum length)	1 space or tab	whitespace might be OK for strings in general but leading and trailing whitespace will almost certainly be stripped from names
				MAXNAME spaces	should be rejected as 0-length name
	rejects valid as too short		≥ 1 nonwhite-space printing character	1 alpha character (e.g., "a")	Lower bound number of (valid) characters
	rejects valid as too long			**MAXNAME** characters	
	accepts too long			**MAXNAME** + 1	

Variable	Risk (potential failure)	Classes that should not trigger failure	Classes that might trigger failure	Test cases (best representatives)	Notes
				127	common buffer maximum. 127, 128, 255, 256 are interesting cases (but maybe not invalid) no matter what value in **MAXNAME**
				128	
				255	common buffer maximum
				256	2^8 (8-bit word + 1) boundary
				65536	2^{16}
				16777216	2^{24} if there's going to be an overflow, 16 million characters will probably do it.
				4294967296	2^{32}
	rejects a valid name with irrelevant whitespace that makes the string too long	≤ **MAXNAME**	total string length > **MAXNAME**	1 leading space plus a valid **MAXNAME**-length name	
				256 leading spaces plus a valid **MAXNAME**-length name	

N. ANALYZE INDEPENDENT VARIABLES THAT SHOULD BE TESTED TOGETHER

The problem description provides no information about this. We look at the full name (a combination of first name, middle name, last name) in *Example 15: Mailing Labels* on page 325.

O. ANALYZE VARIABLES THAT HOLD RESULTS

This Task goes beyond what we're trying to teach with this example.

P. ANALYZE NON-INDEPENDENT VARIABLES. DEAL WITH RELATIONSHIPS AND CONSTRAINTS

This Task goes beyond what we're trying to teach with this example.

Q. IDENTIFY AND LIST UNANALYZED VARIABLES. GATHER INFORMATION FOR LATER ANALYSIS

First name, middle name, salutation (Dr., Mr., Ms., etc.), postfixes (II, III, Ph.D., etc.)

R. IMAGINE AND DOCUMENT RISKS THAT DON'T NECESSARILY MAP TO AN OBVIOUS DIMENSION

- What if the name is misspelled?
- What if the name doesn't map to any student in the database?
- What if two students have the same last name?

EXAMPLE 8: CREATE TABLE (COLUMNS, ROWS)

In OpenOffice (OOo) Impress, you can create a table. With this dialog, you set the starting numbers of rows and columns.

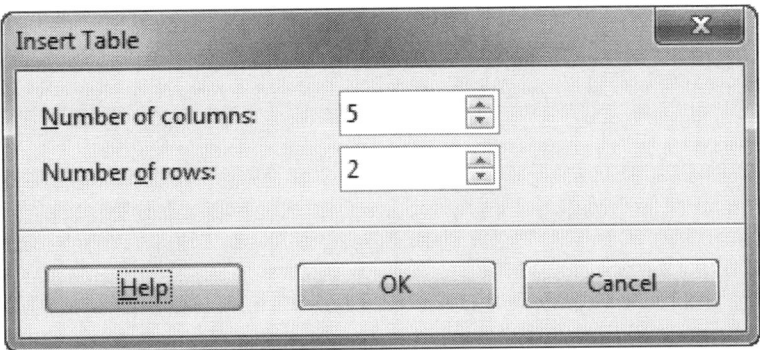

Design Notes: The input values must be Integers. The program will round fractional amounts, so that 8.4 rows is changed to 8 when you press Tab or Enter to exit an input field and 8.5 rows is changed to 9. The program also ignores non-numeric characters: for example, it interprets 2a3 as 23.

A. IDENTIFY THE POTENTIALLY INTERESTING VARIABLES

- `NumberOfColumns`
- `NumberOfRows`

B. IDENTIFY THE VARIABLES YOU CAN ANALYZE NOW. THESE ARE THE VARIABLES OF INTEREST

- `NumberOfColumns`
- `NumberOfRows`

The analysis is the same for NumberOfRows and NumberOfColumns, so you'll typically work on one or the other, rather than saying the same thing twice.

C. DETERMINE THE PRIMARY DIMENSION OF THE VARIABLE OF INTEREST

The primary dimension is the number of rows (columns).

D. DETERMINE THE TYPE AND SCALE OF THE VARIABLE'S PRIMARY DIMENSION AND WHAT VALUES IT CAN TAKE

In the version of OOo we tested, both variables run from 1 to 75.

Both variables are Integers. You can enter non-Integers, such as 64.123 but OOo rounds them to Integer values. OOo ignores non-digits. For example, it interprets both 5a2 and 5-2 as 52. `NumberOfRows` and `NumberOfColumns` are ratio scaled. We can speak meaningfully about a table having twice as many rows (or columns) as another.

E. DETERMINE WHETHER YOU CAN ORDER THE VARIABLE'S VALUES (FROM SMALLEST TO LARGEST)

Yes.

F. DETERMINE WHETHER THIS IS AN INPUT VARIABLE OR A RESULT

These are both input variables.

G. DETERMINE HOW THE PROGRAM USES THIS VARIABLE

The program will create a table with the specified number of rows and columns. It might fit the table on one page, squeezing the width and height of the cells to fit.

H. DETERMINE WHETHER OTHER VARIABLES ARE RELATED TO THIS ONE

- `NumberOfCells` is the product of the rows and columns.

- The amount of memory used by the table and the amount of free memory are probably driven by `NumberOfCells`, perhaps in conjunction with formatting.

- How big is the page you're going to print this table on? What about a table that will just barely fit (or just barely not fit) on a page formatted for output on a specific printer?

- How do the print margins interact with the size of the table?

I. PARTITION THE VARIABLE (ITS PRIMARY DIMENSION)

The dimension is ordered, so determine the sub-ranges and transition points.

- negative inputs
- $0 \le$ `NumberOfColumns` < 1
- $1 \le$ `NumberOfColumns` ≤ 75
- $75 \le$ `NumberOfColumns`

The partition is the same for `NumberOfRows`.

J. LAY OUT THE ANALYSIS IN THE CLASSICAL BOUNDARY/EQUIVALENCE TABLE. IDENTIFY BEST REPRESENTATIVES

Variable	Valid case equivalence class	Invalid case equivalence class	Boundaries and special cases	Notes
NumberOfRows	1 to 75		1	
			75	
		< 1	0	converted to 1 by OpenOffice
		< 0	-1	converted to 1
		> 75	76	converted to 75
	0.500 to 75.499		0.500	should round to 1
			75.499	should round to 75
		< 1	0.4999	will round to 0
		> 75	75.500	OOo is designed to truncate this to 75. Design tests and expectations around OOo's standard behavior.

K. CREATE TESTS FOR THE CONSEQUENCES OF THE DATA ENTERED, NOT JUST THE INPUT FILTER

Create a big table (for example max rows and max columns). Now work with the table. Are there any problems with a table so large?

- Try inserting pictures in the cells.
- Try inserting significant amounts of text in the tables.

- The columns will have to be very thin and the rows very short (assuming the program tries to fit them on one page). Format the text to be too tall for the row or too wide for the column.
- Try anything that might stress memory, output size, display or output formatting or time to complete the task.

L. IDENTIFY SECONDARY DIMENSIONS. ANALYZE THEM IN THE CLASSICAL WAY

Some secondary dimensions include:

- Length of the input
- Number of decimal points in the input
- Characters (non-numeric) allowed in the input

The set of characters that you can enter into **NumberOfColumns** seems unlimited. For example, move the cursor into the field and right-click. The context menu shows:

- **Paste**: It appears that you can paste anything into this field. Here's a paste the field accepts:

  64.12345678901234567890abcdefghijkl-64.12345678901234567890abcdefghijkl64.12345678901234567890abcdefghijkl64.12345678901234567890abcdefghijkl64.12345678901234567890abcdefghijkl64.12345678901234567890abcdefghijkl64.12345678901234567890abcdefghijkl

  We verified that the version of OpenOffice we were testing accepted all these characters into the field. OOo then replaced the long input with 64 when we pressed TAB to move out of the field.

- **Special Character**: Clicking Special Character brings up a menu that allows you to select any printable character and insert it into the **NumberOfColumns** or **NumberOfRows** field. Sometimes, it appears to follow the usual rule (round the input, ignoring non-numeric characters) and other times, it interprets the input as a big number and substitutes 75.

M. SUMMARIZE YOUR ANALYSIS WITH A RISK/EQUIVALENCE TABLE

Variable	Valid case equivalence class	Invalid case equivalence class	Boundaries and special cases	Notes
`NumberOfRows`	1 to 2 characters	no chars	backspace over the default value to get a 0-length input	OpenOffice restores the default value (such as, 2 rows)
	1 char		0	OpenOffice replaces this with 1
			a	You can try all the different types of non-numbers. If you decide to do that, see the table in Example 1 for test ideas.
	2 characters		10	This is the smallest 2-digit Integer. We don't think this boundary is of much interest for this variable.
			75	Largest acceptable 2-digit Integer
			76	Two digits but too big anyway
		> 2 chars	7a5	3 characters but only two are digits. OOo ignores non-digits and should accept this as 75. A different program would treat this differently.
			100	3 digits, converted to 75
			0.499999...	
			huge number of digits	
Number of Decimal Points in `NumberOfRows`	0 or 1			You already know that OOo handles Integers and simple rounding, so the valid cases are redundant
		2	1..2	OOo will probably ignore the second digit and round 1.2

N. ANALYZE INDEPENDENT VARIABLES THAT SHOULD BE TESTED TOGETHER

You are entering two values together. Think of this as a two-dimensional variable (**R,C**), where **R** is the number of rows and **C** is the number of columns.

There are no constraints between `NumberOfColumns` and `NumberOfRows`. The obvious combinations use the boundaries of the two variables:

$$(1, 1) \qquad (1, 75) \qquad (75, 1) \qquad (75, 75)$$

As we explain in *The Combinatorial Explosion* on page 173, common to test invalid boundaries individually rather than in combination. Therefore, the out-of-bounds values aren't part of our analysis here.

O. ANALYZE VARIABLES THAT HOLD RESULTS

`NumberOfCells` is the number of rows and columns that actually appear in the table. It's the product of the rows and columns. The valid values are Integers from 1 to 75^2.

The widths and heights of the cells are probably also changed as a result of setting these variables. However, the description of this example doesn't provide enough information for further analysis.

P. ANALYZE NON-INDEPENDENT VARIABLES. DEAL WITH RELATIONSHIPS AND CONSTRAINTS

OpenOffice will accept up to 75 rows and 75 columns. These appear to be independent. However, the more cells, the slower OpenOffice responds. Long before you hit the maximum, OpenOffice becomes unusably slow. So the empirical question is what is the practical limit on the number of cells in the table. From that you can determine the constraints on the number of rows and columns.

Q. IDENTIFY AND LIST UNANALYZED VARIABLES. GATHER INFORMATION FOR LATER ANALYSIS

We don't have any suggestions beyond the ones we've raised already.

R. IMAGINE AND DOCUMENT RISKS THAT DON'T NECESSARILY MAP TO AN OBVIOUS DIMENSION

- How much time will it take to display the table or refresh display of the slide on the table or to print the slide that contains the table?

- In a word processor or a spreadsheet, tables can spread across several pages. What mischief could you create around the page breaks?

In a word processor, the user can create tables for many purposes. If you don't consider how or why the user is creating tables, your test designs will be simpler and more generic. If you are taking this approach, consider designing tests that combine other variables with values of the variable under test, such as these:

- How much memory the platform has.
- How much memory is in use.
- How big the page is, compared to the size of a page in the table.

EXAMPLE 9: CREATE TABLE (MAX CELLS)

In OpenOffice (OOo) Impress, you can create a table. With this dialog, you set the starting numbers of rows and columns. Suppose the maximum number of cells in the table is 4095.

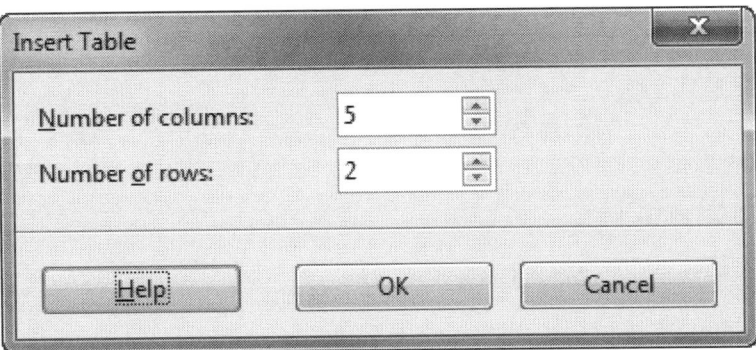

Design Notes: The difference between this and Example 8 is the additional constraint (maximum number of cells is 4095). Otherwise, the analysis here and in Example 8 is the same.

The input values must be Integers. The program will round fractional amounts, so that 8.4 rows is changed to 8 when you press Tab or Enter to exit an input field and 8.5 rows is changed to 9. The program also ignores non-numeric characters: for example, it interprets 2a3 as 23.

A. IDENTIFY THE POTENTIALLY INTERESTING VARIABLES

- `NumberOfRows`
- `NumberOfColumns`
- `NumberOfCells` (`NumberOfRows` × `NumberOfColumns`) is not on the dialog but it is implied by the dialog.

B. IDENTIFY THE VARIABLES YOU CAN ANALYZE NOW. THESE ARE THE VARIABLES OF INTEREST

- `NumberOfRows`
- `NumberOfColumns`
- `NumberOfCells`

Our discussion is focused on the two input variables (`NumberOfRows` and `NumberOfColumns`). `NumberOfCells` is a result variable, more interesting in this example than the last because you have a boundary value for it (4095).

The analysis is the same for NumberOfRows and NumberOfColumns, so you'll typically work on one or the other, rather than saying the same thing twice.

C. DETERMINE THE PRIMARY DIMENSION OF THE VARIABLE OF INTEREST

The primary dimension is the number of rows (columns).

D. DETERMINE THE TYPE AND SCALE OF THE VARIABLE'S PRIMARY DIMENSION AND WHAT VALUES IT CAN TAKE

Both variables are Integers. You can enter non-Integers into the fields, such as 64.123 (or numbers with many more digits) but the program rounds these to Integer values.

The version of OOo we tested restricted both variables to the range from 1 to 75, subject to the constraint that **NumberOfRows** times **NumberOfColumns** has a maximum value of 4095.

The program ignores non-digits. For example, it interprets both 5a2 and 5-2 as 52.

NumberOfRows and **NumberOfColumns** are ratio scaled. We can speak meaningfully about a table having twice as many rows (or columns) as another.

E. DETERMINE WHETHER YOU CAN ORDER THE VARIABLE'S VALUES (FROM SMALLEST TO LARGEST)

Yes.

F. DETERMINE WHETHER THIS IS AN INPUT VARIABLE OR A RESULT

- **NumberOfRows** and **NumberOfColumns** are both input variables.
- **NumberOfCells** is a result.

G. DETERMINE HOW THE PROGRAM USES THIS VARIABLE

The program will create a table with the specified number of rows and columns. It might fit the table on one page, squeezing the width and height of the cells to fit.

H. DETERMINE WHETHER OTHER VARIABLES ARE RELATED TO THIS ONE

- **NumberOfCells** is the product of **NumberOfRows** and **NumberOfColumns**, to a maximum of 4095.
- The amount of memory used by the table and the amount of free memory are probably driven by **NumberOfCells**, perhaps in conjunction with formatting.
- How big is the page you're going to print this table on? What about a table that will just barely fit (or just barely not fit) on a page formatted for output on a specific printer?
- How do the print margins interact with the size of the table?

I. PARTITION THE VARIABLE (ITS PRIMARY DIMENSION)

The dimension is ordered, so determine the sub-ranges and transition points:

- Negative inputs
- $0 \leq$ **NumberOfColumns** < 1
- $1 \leq$ **NumberOfColumns** $\leq$ **NumberOfRows**$/4095 \leq 75$
- $75 \leq$ **NumberOfColumns**

The partition is the same for **NumberOfRows**.

J. LAY OUT THE ANALYSIS IN THE CLASSICAL BOUNDARY/EQUIVALENCE TABLE. IDENTIFY BEST REPRESENTATIVES

Variable	Valid case equivalence class	Invalid case equivalence class	Boundaries and special cases	Notes
NumberOfRows	1 to 75		1	
			75	
			54	max when NumberOfColumns is 75

Variable	Valid case equivalence class	Invalid case equivalence class	Boundaries and special cases	Notes
			63	4095 cells when NumberOfColumns is 65
		< 1	0	converted to 1 by OpenOffice
		< 0	-1	converted to 1
		> 75	76	converted to 75
		NumberOfRows × NumberOfColumns > 4095	(64, 64)	64 rows × 64 columns = 4096 cells
	0.500 to 75.499		0.500	should round to 1
			75.499	should round to 75
		< 1	0.4999	will round to 0
		> 75	75.500	OOo will truncate this to 75.

The tests use the values in the "Boundaries and special cases" column.

K. CREATE TESTS FOR THE CONSEQUENCES OF THE DATA ENTERED, NOT JUST THE INPUT FILTER

Create a big table (for example max rows and max columns). Now work with the table. Are there any problems with a table so large?

- Try inserting pictures in the cells.
- Try inserting significant amounts of text in the tables.
- The columns will have to be very thin and the rows very short (assuming the program tries to fit them on one page). Format the text to be too tall for the row or too wide for the column.
- Try anything that might stress memory, output size, display or output formatting or time to complete the task.

L. IDENTIFY SECONDARY DIMENSIONS. ANALYZE THEM IN THE CLASSICAL WAY

These are the same as the previous example.

M. SUMMARIZE YOUR ANALYSIS WITH A RISK/EQUIVALENCE TABLE

This is the same as the previous example.

N. ANALYZE INDEPENDENT VARIABLES THAT SHOULD BE TESTED TOGETHER

`NumberOfColumns` and `NumberOfRows` aren't independent, so they and `NumberOfCells` are analyzed in the next section.

O. ANALYZE VARIABLES THAT HOLD RESULTS

You are entering two values together. Think of this as a two-dimensional variable (`R`,`C`), where `R` is `NumberOfRows` and `C` is `NumberOfColumns`.

The constraint between `NumberOfColumns` and `NumberOfRows` is that `R` × `C` can't exceed 4095. The constraints make the boundaries of the two variables a bit complex:

(1, 1) , (1, 75), and (75, 1) are the lower-bound tests.

(75, 75) is invalid because 75 × 75 = 5625, which exceeds 4095.

The boundary values on the upper end are these:

(54, 75) (55, 74) (56, 73) (56, 72) (57, 71) (58, 70) (59, 69) (60, 68)

(61, 67) (62, 66) (63, 65) (63, 64) (64, 63) (65, 63) (66, 62) (67, 61)

(68, 60) (69, 59) (70, 58) (71, 57) (72, 56) (73, 56) (74, 55) (75, 54)

You probably won't want to test all of these. Think of this as another equivalence class to sample from.

Regarding the cases that are out of bounds, we suggest in *The Combinatorial Explosion* on page 173, that it's common to test invalid boundaries individually rather than in combination. Therefore, most of the out-of-bounds values aren't part of our analysis here.

The one out-of-bounds case that we think you should test is (64, 64). The inputs are valid. It is the product (64 × 64 = 4096) that is 1 beyond the maximum of `NumberOfCells`.

Four other variables hold results:

- The number of rows that actually appear in the table and the heights of these rows.
- The number of columns that actually appear in the table and the widths of these columns.

P. ANALYZE NON-INDEPENDENT VARIABLES. DEAL WITH RELATIONSHIPS AND CONSTRAINTS

We've already considered the constraint that `NumberOfColumns` × `NumberOfRows` can't exceed 4095.

Q. IDENTIFY AND LIST UNANALYZED VARIABLES. GATHER INFORMATION FOR LATER ANALYSIS

We don't have any suggestions beyond the ones we've raised already.

R. IMAGINE AND DOCUMENT RISKS THAT DON'T NECESSARILY MAP TO AN OBVIOUS DIMENSION

- How much time will it take to display the table or refresh display of the slide on the table or to print the slide that contains the table?
- In a word processor or a spreadsheet, tables can spread across several pages. What mischief could you create around the page breaks?

In a word processor, the user can create tables for many purposes. If you don't consider how or why the user is creating tables, your test designs will be simpler and more generic. If you are taking this approach, consider designing tests that combine other variables with values of the variable under test, such as these:

- How much memory the platform has.
- How much memory is in use.
- How big the page is, compared to the size of a page in the table.

EXAMPLE 10: THE CIRCLE

Consider a circle defined by $x_1{}^2 + x_2{}^2 = 100$. Some of the points on this circle are (0, 10), (6, 8), (8, 6), (10, 0), (8, -6), (6, -8), (0, -10), (-6, -8), (-8, -6), (-10, 0), (-8, 6) and (-6, 8).

Consider these sets:

(a) $\{ (x_1, x_2) | x_1{}^2 + x_2{}^2 = 100 \}$ (the circle)

(b) $\{ (x_1, x_2) | x_1{}^2 + x_2{}^2 < 100 \}$ (the points inside the circle)

(c) $\{ (x_1, x_2) | x_1{}^2 + x_2{}^2 > 100 \}$ (the points outside the circle)

(d) $\{ (x_1, x_2) | x_1{}^2 + x_2{}^2 \le 100 \}$ (the circle and points inside it)

(e) $\{ (x_1, x_2) | x_1{}^2 + x_2{}^2 \ge 100 \}$ (the circle and points outside it)

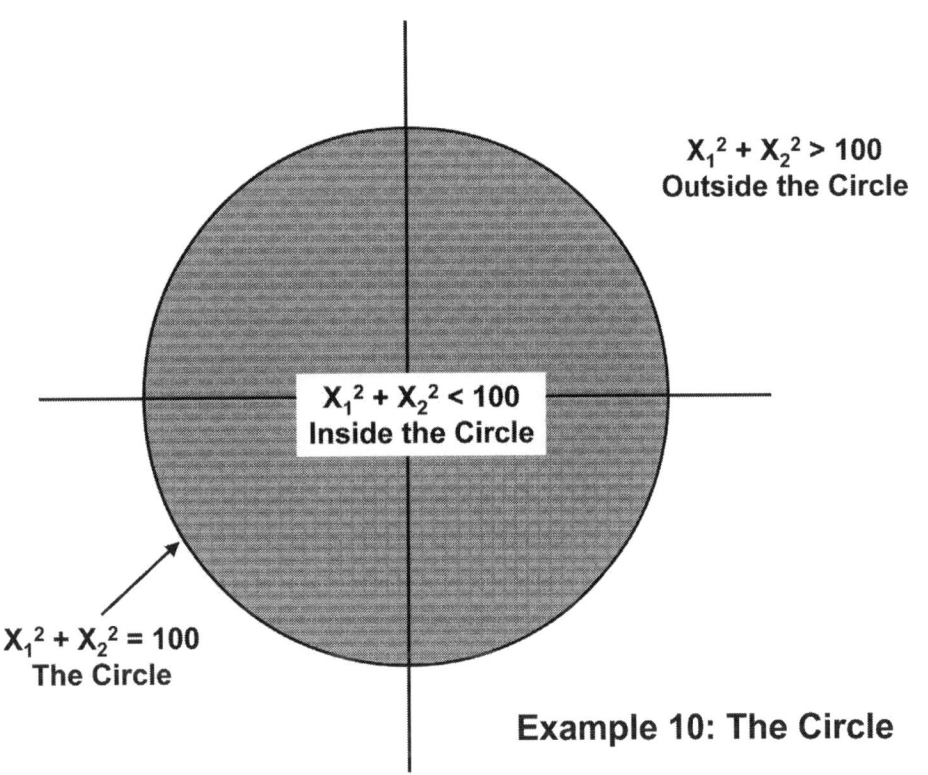

$X_1{}^2 + X_2{}^2 > 100$
Outside the Circle

$X_1{}^2 + X_2{}^2 < 100$
Inside the Circle

$X_1{}^2 + X_2{}^2 = 100$
The Circle

Example 10: The Circle

A. IDENTIFY THE POTENTIALLY INTERESTING VARIABLES

There are only two variables, x_1 and x_2.

There is also an odd constant, 100. Why is this 100? Will it never change?

B. IDENTIFY THE VARIABLES YOU CAN ANALYZE NOW. THESE ARE THE VARIABLES OF INTEREST

x_1 and x_2.

C. DETERMINE THE PRIMARY DIMENSION OF THE VARIABLE OF INTEREST

Both variables appear to be simple numeric variables with positive and negative values.

D. DETERMINE THE TYPE AND SCALE OF THE VARIABLE'S PRIMARY DIMENSION AND WHAT VALUES IT CAN TAKE

The description doesn't specify whether these are Integers or Floating Point. Assume (until you learn otherwise) the variable is a Float, stored with 6 digits of decimal precision.

E. DETERMINE WHETHER YOU CAN ORDER THE VARIABLE'S VALUES (FROM SMALLEST TO LARGEST)

Yes. The individual variables can be ordered (they look like simple numeric variables). However, the *relationships* that constrain their values aren't easily converted to linear ones.

F. DETERMINE WHETHER THIS IS AN INPUT VARIABLE OR A RESULT

The description doesn't say where the values of x_1 and x_2 come from. For now, assume they're input variables.

G. DETERMINE HOW THE PROGRAM USES THIS VARIABLE

The problem description gives no information about this.

H. DETERMINE WHETHER OTHER VARIABLES ARE RELATED TO THIS ONE

In each of the five cases, x_1 and x_2 constrain each other. For example:

- In set (a), the value of x_1 is constrained to two values by x_2 (and vice-versa). For example, if $x_2 = 6$, then x_1 must be 8 or -8.

- In set (b), the value of x_1 is constrained to a range by x_2 (and vice-versa). For example, if $x_2 = 6$, then x_1 must be between $-8+\Delta$ and $8-\Delta$.

  Notation reminder: Δ is the smallest difference between two numbers that can be recognized in this type of data. For Single-Precision Floating-Point numbers of the magnitude of this example (think of numbers between 1 and 100), Δ is about 0.0000001. For small numbers or higher-precision numbers, Δ is smaller.

- The analyses for the inequalities in sets (c), (d) and (e) are essentially the same as for set (b).

I. PARTITION THE VARIABLE (ITS PRIMARY DIMENSION)

The dimensions are ordered, so determine the sub-ranges and transition points.

The partitions of x_1 considered on its own, are:

$$x_1 < -10 \qquad \text{(too small)}$$

$$-10 \leq x_1 \leq 10 \qquad \text{(valid)}$$

$$10 < x_1 \qquad \text{(too large)}$$

The same partitioning applies to x_2.

Because x_1 and x_2 constrain each other, this single-variable analysis is only good for testing the input filters. Our main analysis for this example will be in the discussion of non-independent variables.

J. LAY OUT THE ANALYSIS IN A CLASSICAL BOUNDARY/EQUIVALENCE TABLE. IDENTIFY BEST REPRESENTATIVES

The analysis for the individual variables is the same for x_1 and x_2.

Variable	Valid case equivalence class	Invalid case equivalence class	Boundaries and special cases	Notes
x_1	$-10 \leq x_1 \leq 10$		$x_1 = -10$	
			$x_1 = 0$	
			$x_2 = 0$	
			$x_1 = 10$	
		$x_1 < -10$	$x_1 = -10 - \Delta$	$\Delta(10) \approx 0.0001$ for 6 Floating Point digits precision
		$x_1 > 10$	$x_1 = 10 + \Delta$	
			$x_1 = \sqrt{\mathtt{MAXFLOAT+1}}$	Overflows when you calculate $x_1{}^2$

The tests use the values in the "Boundaries and special cases" column.

K. CREATE TESTS FOR THE CONSEQUENCES OF THE DATA, NOT JUST THE INPUT FILTER

This Task goes beyond what we're trying to teach with this example.

L. IDENTIFY SECONDARY DIMENSIONS. ANALYZE THEM IN THE CLASSICAL WAY

For the individual input variables, this is a routine analysis of a Floating Point variable. Follow the analysis in *Secondary Dimensions for Floating-Point Variables* on page 160.

Tests for secondary-dimension problems (such as input string too long) should be done as part of testing the individual inputs, not as part of testing the pairs, (x_1, x_2). This simplification helps you avoid an unnecessary explosion of combination tests.

Tests of the pairs are discussed in Task P (Analyze Non-Independent Variables) below. In addition to the boundary tests, we would consider a few more possible errors, such as:

- Overflow error: $x_1{}^2 + x_2{}^2 > \mathtt{MAXFLOAT}$

- Rounding error: a pair of values is misclassified because of rounding error in the calculation of x^2. These types of error will happen only at the boundary, but the values we would pick to maximize the risk of rounding error would be different from the usual round-number cases like (10, 0). For example, the sum of:

$$9.99999^2 + 0.14143^2$$

$$= \quad 99.9998000001 + 0.000200024449$$

$$= \quad 100.000000024549$$

This result exceeds 100. Therefore, if the specified domain includes all points on the circle or inside it (Case (d)), then (9.99999, 0.14143) should be invalid.

However, with rounding error, 99.9998000001 + 0.000200024449 = 100 and the pair appears to be a point on the circle.

Rounding errors are inevitable in Floating Point calculations. In practice, this misclassification might be acceptable (not a bug) in an application you're testing. Check with the development team before spending too much time on finding or reporting small rounding errors.

M. SUMMARIZE YOUR ANALYSIS WITH A RISK/EQUIVALENCE TABLE

For the individual input variables, this is a routine analysis of a Floating Point variable. Follow the analysis in *From Example 4: Page Setup Options* on page 160.

Because we have only a few added risk/equivalence tests, we'll add these to the basic equivalence table.

N. ANALYZE INDEPENDENT VARIABLES THAT SHOULD BE TESTED TOGETHER

The problem description does not mention any independent variables.

O. ANALYZE VARIABLES THAT HOLD RESULTS

The problem description does not mention or suggest any variables that hold results or at least none beyond whatever holds the calculated value of $x_1^2 + x_2^2$.

P. ANALYZE NON-INDEPENDENT VARIABLES. DEAL WITH RELATIONSHIPS AND CONSTRAINTS

This Example describes a multidimensional domain defined by a mathematical relationship among the variables. You can show it on a graph. In this case, the relationship is nonlinear. We described heuristics for choosing tests for linearly-related multidimensional domains at *Example 12: Piecewise Boundary (Linear Relationships)* on page 203. Our analysis for a nonlinear relationship is similar to this.

CHOOSING ON POINTS AND OFF POINTS FOR TESTING NONLINEAR RELATIONSHIPS

The relationship between the variables is defined by a circle ($x_1^2 + x_2^2 = 100$). You can partition the set of values of (x_1, x_2) into four ranges:

1. Values on the circle itself.
2. Values inside the circle.
3. Values outside the circle, where $-10 \leq x_1 \leq 10$ and $-10 \leq x_2 \leq 10$.
4. Values outside the circle, where $x_1 \leq -10$ or $x_1 \geq 10$ or $x_2 \leq -10$ or $x_2 \geq 10$. If you draw a square on your graph, the smallest square that contains the circle (this is sometimes called a bounding box), this is the set of all points outside of that square.

We can describe these points in four groups:

- *On point:* The circle defines the boundary. Any point on the circle (any point on the line or curve that defines the boundary) is an *On point*.

- *Off point:* Any point that is not on the line or curve that defines the boundary is an *Off point*.

- *Inner point*: a point that is inside the specified equivalence class (a member of the set that defines the class).

- *Outer point*: Any point that is outside of an equivalence class is *Outer* relative to that class. If someone doesn't specify the class, an *Outer* point is outside the valid class. As a particular example, consider Case (c): the valid values are outside the circle and therefore the *Outer points* are inside the circle.

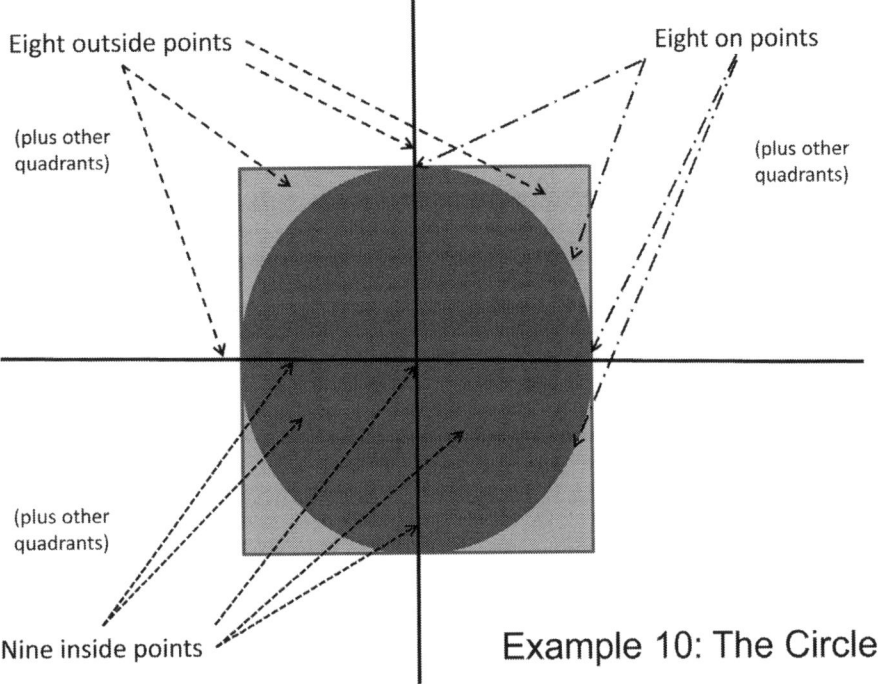

Eight outside points

Eight on points

(plus other quadrants)

(plus other quadrants)

(plus other quadrants)

Nine inside points

Example 10: The Circle

Set (1) is the set of *On* points. Sets (2), (3) and (4) are all Off points. They are sometimes Inner points and sometimes Outer points, depending on the definition of the valid class (Cases (a), (b), (c), (d) or (e)).

Consider each of the Cases in turn:

(A) THE CIRCLE $\{ (x_1, x_2) \mid x_1{}^2 + x_2{}^2 = 100 \}$

Only the points on the circle are in the "valid" equivalence class (Set 1).[38]

Any point inside or outside (but not on) the circle is an:

- *Off point* and an
- *Outer point* (even the ones inside the circle).

If you follow the heuristics for linear cases, pick:

- One point on the circle.
- Two off:
  - One that you plot inside the circle ($x_1{}^2 + x_2{}^2 < 100$).
  - One that you plot outside ($x_1{}^2 + x_2{}^2 > 100$).

---

38 Note that for a pair, (x_1, x_2), to be valid, you have to be able to plot it on the circle. However, some points on the circle will require values of x_1 or x_2 that have many more significant digits than you can represent in a finite-precision Floating-Point number. A program that uses Floating-Point numbers will always generate points that are on the circle or off it, but it will not be able to reach every point on the circle.

We're not entirely comfortable with using only three points.

We don't have a clear theory of error that demands more than one test with an On point, but we'd like to trace the shape in both dimensions. Therefore, we test one On point in each quadrant of the circle. In practice, if we found several functions like this in a program and found no indication that the program treated points in different quadrants differently, we would quickly reduce our test set, probably back to one On point, rather than one per quadrant.

We would probably run these tests:

Type of test point	x_1	x_2	Notes
On Inner	0	10	Table for Case A. Valid values are on the circle.
On Inner	0	-10	
On Inner	10	0	
On Inner	-10	0	
Off Outer	0	0	We like to test zero. Note that even if the circle shifted so that (0,0) was not the center, we would still be interested in (0,0).
Off Outer	.00001	10	barely outside the circle
Off Outer	0	-9.99999	barely inside the circle

We have no theoretical basis for testing one On point per quadrant of the circle. This might be excessively cautious. We would probably drop to fewer On points per circle (probably just one per circle) if we were testing several circles and we didn't see any indication the program treated points in different quadrants differently.

Alternatively, you might consider points away from the axes because:

a. there is no rounding error on the square of zero, so you might be missing a potential problem and

b. if the programmer tested any points on the circle, she probably tested these, so why repeat the same tests?

Under that view, we would still try four On points, one per quadrant of the circle, but they would be at different relative places, like these:

Type of test point	x_1	x_2	Notes
On Inner	6	8	This is another table for Case A. This one tests On points that aren't on the graph's axes.
On Inner	$\sqrt{50}$	$-\sqrt{50}$	
On Inner	-3	$-\sqrt{91}$	
On Inner	$-\sqrt{75}$	5	
Off Outer	0	0	We usually test zero
Off Outer	.00001	10	Barely outside the circle
Off Outer	0	-9.99999	Barely inside the circle

We don't have a basis for preferring one of these sets of tests over the other. We would choose our strategy based on our experiences testing this program or our history with code from these programmers.

(B) INSIDE THE CIRCLE $\{ (x_1, x_2) \mid x_1^2 + x_2^2 < 100 \}$

The input domain includes only the points inside the circle (Set 2).

The points on the boundary (on the circle) and the points outside the circle are both outside of the input domain. At a minimum, you should include one point inside the circle (inside the domain) and one point on the circle (on the boundary but outside the domain).

As above, our inclination is to include one Inner point for each quadrant and two On points (these are our Outer points), each in separate quadrants.

Type of test point	x_1	x_2	Notes
Off Inner	6	7.99	Table for Case B. Valid values are inside the circle.
Off Inner	0	-9.99	Inside and near the circle
Off Inner	2.99	$-\sqrt{91}$	
Off Inner	$-\sqrt{74.9}$	5	
Off Inner	0	0	
On Outer	$\sqrt{50}$	$-\sqrt{50}$	
On Outer	0	10	

(C) OUTSIDE THE CIRCLE $\{ (x_1, x_2) \mid x_1^2 + x_2^2 > 100 \}$

The input domain includes only the points outside the circle (Sets 3 and 4).

The points on the boundary (on the circle) and the points *inside* the circle are *outside* of the input domain. At a minimum, include one Inner point (points outside the circle are inner to the specified domain) and one point on the circle (because it is on the boundary but outside the domain).

Normally, we include one Inner point for each quadrant and two On points (these are our Outer points), each in separate quadrants.

Type of test point	x_1	x_2	Notes
Off Inner	7	8.01	Table for Case C. Valid values are outside the circle.
Off Inner	0	-10.01	Outside and near the circle
Off Inner	3.01	$-\sqrt{91}$	
Off Inner	$-\sqrt{75.1}$	5	
Off Inner	9.99999	0.014143	$x1^2 + x2^2 = 100.000000024549$ but might be rounded to 100, making the pair appear to be an invalid value (on the circle) instead of a valid one (should be outside the circle)
Off Inner	0	0	
On Outer	$\sqrt{50}$	$-\sqrt{50}$	
On Outer	0	10	

(D) THE CIRCLE & POINTS INSIDE IT { $(x_1, x_2) \mid x_1^2 + x_2^2 \leq 100$ }

The input domain includes all the points inside the circle, plus the circle (Sets 1 and 2).

At a minimum, include a point on the boundary (the circle is inside the input domain) and a point outside the circle. Normally, we include one On point for each quadrant and two Off points (points outside the circle are our Outer points), each in separate quadrants.

Type of test point	x_1	x_2	Notes
On Inner	6	8	Table for Case D. Valid values are on the circle or inside it.
On Inner	$\sqrt{50}$	$-\sqrt{50}$	
On Inner	-3	$-\sqrt{91}$	
On Inner	$-\sqrt{75}$	5	
Off Inner	0	0	Inside the circle
Off Outer	$\sqrt{50.1}$	$-\sqrt{50}$	Outside and near the circle
Off Outer	0.001	10	

(E) THE CIRCLE & POINTS OUTSIDE IT { $(x_1, x_2) \mid x_1^2 + x_2^2 \geq 100$ }

The input domain includes all the points outside the circle, plus the circle (Sets 1, 3 and 4).

At a minimum, include a point on the boundary (the circle is inside the input domain) and a point inside the circle. Normally, we include one On point for each quadrant and two Off points (points outside the circle are our Outer points), each in separate quadrants.

Type of test point	x_1	x_2	notes
On Inner	6	8	Table for Case E. Valid values are on the circle or outside it.
On Inner	$\sqrt{50}$	$-\sqrt{50}$	
On Inner	-3	$-\sqrt{91}$	
On Inner	$-\sqrt{75}$	5	Outside and near the circle
Off Inner	$\sqrt{50.1}$	$-\sqrt{50}$	
Off Outer	0	0	
Off Outer	$\sqrt{49.9}$	$-\sqrt{50}$	Inside and near the circle

C. TASKS Q & R ARE BEYOND WHAT WE'RE TRYING TO TEACH WITH THIS EXAMPLE.

EXAMPLE 11: UNIVERSITY ADMISSIONS

Stateless University's admission standards use both high school grades and **ACT** test scores (Copeland, 2004, p. 121).

- **ACT** scores are Integers running between 0 and 36.
- **GPA** scores are Fixed-Point variables (always exactly one digit after the decimal point) running between 0.0 and 4.0.

Students are accepted if they meet any of these requirements:

- **ACT** = 36 and **GPA** ≥ 3.5
- **ACT** ≥ 35 and **GPA** ≥ 3.6
- **ACT** ≥ 34 and **GPA** ≥ 3.7
- **ACT** ≥ 33 and **GPA** ≥ 3.8
- **ACT** ≥ 32 and **GPA** ≥ 3.9
- **ACT** ≥ 31 and **GPA** = 4.0

We can represent this relationship by stating that students are admitted if:

$$\textbf{ACT} + 10 \times \textbf{GPA} \geq 71.$$

For example, if **ACT** = 33 and **GPA** = 3.9, then

$$\textbf{ACT} + 10 \times \textbf{GPA} \quad = \quad 33 + 10 \times 3.9 \quad = \quad 72.$$

A. IDENTIFY THE POTENTIALLY INTERESTING VARIABLES

- **ACT**[39]
- **GPA**[40]
- `AdmissionCalculation` (the value of **ACT** + 10 × **GPA**)
- `AdmissionDecision` (Yes, if `AdmissionCalculation` ≥ 71. Otherwise, No.).

The program may not have a specific variable that holds `AdmissionCalculation`, but if we interpret the problem description as stating the program will do this calculation, then the program will store the result at least temporarily in order to make the admission decision. `AdmissionCalculation` is the name we're giving to whatever the program uses to store that result.

B. IDENTIFY THE VARIABLES YOU CAN ANALYZE NOW. THESE ARE THE VARIABLES OF INTEREST

- `ACT`
- `GPA`
- `AdmissionCalculation`
- `AdmissionDecision`

C. DETERMINE THE PRIMARY DIMENSION OF THE VARIABLE OF INTEREST

- **ACT** is a test score (numeric). Bigger numbers are better scores.
- **GPA** is a weighted average of course grades. Bigger numbers are better.
- `AdmissionCalculation` is a linear function of **ACT** and **GPA**. Bigger numbers are better.
- `AdmissionDecision` is Binary (Yes / No).

---

39 If you are curious about ACT scores, see http://www.actstudent.org/

40 To see how GPA (grade point average) is calculated, see http://academicservices.berkeley.edu/advising/gpa/

D. DETERMINE THE TYPE AND SCALE OF THE VARIABLE'S PRIMARY DIMENSION AND WHAT VALUES IT CAN TAKE

- `ACT` is an Integer running from 0 to 36.
- `GPA` is Fixed Point, with 1 digit after the decimal, running from 0.0 to 4.0.
- `AdmissionCalculation` might be Fixed or Floating Point. It ranges from 0.0 to 76.0 in steps of 1.0.
- `AdmissionDecision` is Binary (Yes / No).

E. DETERMINE WHETHER YOU CAN ORDER THE VARIABLE'S VALUES (FROM SMALLEST TO LARGEST)

`ACT`, `GPA` and `AdmissionCalculation` are ordered.

F. DETERMINE WHETHER THIS IS AN INPUT VARIABLE OR A RESULT

- `ACT` and `GPA` are input variables.
- `AdmissionCalculation` and `AdmissionDecision` are result variables.

G. DETERMINE HOW THE PROGRAM USES THIS VARIABLE

The program uses `ACT` and `GPA` to determine whether a student should be admitted to the university.

The problem description doesn't specify clearly how the program uses these values *internally*, to reach that decision. Here are two of the possibilities:

(a) The program accepts `ACT` and `GPA`, uses them to calculate `AdmissionCalculation` and from that sets the value of `AdmissionDecision`.

(b) The program puts the test scores into an ordered pair (`ACT`, `GPA`). For example, a student who earns 29 on the `ACT` and a `GPA` of 3.1 has the pair (29, 3.1). The program then checks the student's pair against a reference set that holds all the pairs that are good enough for admission.

{ (31, 4.0), (32, 3.9), (32, 4.0), (33, 3.8), (33, 3.9), (33, 4.0), (34, 3.7), (34, 3.8), (34, 3.9), (34, 4.0), (35, 3.6), (35, 3.7), (35, 3.8), (35, 3.9), (35, 4.0), (36, 3.5), (36, 3.6), (36, 3.7), (36, 3.8), (36, 3.9), (36, 4.0) }

This is a manageably-short list. Many languages have well-optimized functions for checking whether a value is a member of a set and so this might be much faster than calculating $ACT + 10 \times GPA \geq 71$.

In this case, there is no need for `AdmissionCalculation`. In practice, we might actually implement the decision this second way.

This distinction illustrates the significance of having knowledge of the code. As you'll see, if we test on the basis of the implementation, the two implementations steer us toward different sets of tests.

H. DETERMINE WHETHER OTHER VARIABLES ARE RELATED TO THIS ONE

Thinking broadly, we can imagine many potentially-related variables. For example, the applicant's name and whether she gets a scholarship. However, the problem description mentions no other variables.

I. PARTITION THE VARIABLE (ITS PRIMARY DIMENSION)

The dimensions are ordered, so determine the sub-ranges and transition points.

		ACT	<	0	(too small)
0	≤	ACT	≤	36	(valid)
36	<	ACT			(too large)
		GPA	<	0	(too small)
0.0	≤	GPA	≤	4	(valid)
4.0	<	GPA			(too large)
		AdmissionCalculation	<	0	(too small)
0.0	≤	AdmissionCalculation	≤	76.0	(valid)
76.0	<	AdmissionCalculation			(too large)
		AdmissionDecision	Yes or No		(Anything else is invalid.)

J. LAY OUT THE ANALYSIS IN A CLASSICAL BOUNDARY/EQUIVALENCE TABLE. IDENTIFY BEST REPRESENTATIVES

The table that follows considers only the primary dimension of the input variables. Secondary dimensions come in Task L. The two result variables are in Task O.

Variable	Valid case equivalence class	Invalid case equivalence class	Boundaries and special cases	Notes
ACT	0 to 36		0	
			36	
		< 0	-1	
		> 36	37	
GPA	0.0 to 4.0		0	should be acceptable with no decimal point
			4.0	
		< 0	-0.1	
		> 4	4.1	

The tests use the values in the "Boundaries and special cases" column.

K. CREATE TESTS FOR THE CONSEQUENCES OF THE DATA ENTERED, NOT JUST THE INPUT FILTER

The program uses (ACT, GPA) to decide whether to admit the student to the university. That usage is analyzed in Task O.

L. IDENTIFY SECONDARY DIMENSIONS. ANALYZE THEM IN THE CLASSICAL WAY

ACT is an Integer, with the usual data entry risks—how does it deal with non-digits, numbers that aren't Integers, inputs that have too many digits, etc. The main discussion of secondary-dimension issues for Integers is at *Example 1: Integer Input* on page 229.

GPA is a Fixed-Point variable with 1 digit after the decimal point. See *Example 3: SunTrust VISA* on page 245.

M. SUMMARIZE YOUR ANALYSIS WITH A RISK/EQUIVALENCE TABLE

The tables for the two input variables, ACT and GPA, will be essentially the same as the tables in *Generic Risk/Equivalence Table for Integers* on page 233 and *Generic Risk/Equivalence Table for Fixed-Point Variables* on page 251.

There *are* interesting additional risks to consider. See Task O.

N. ANALYZE INDEPENDENT VARIABLES THAT SHOULD BE TESTED TOGETHER

ACT and GPA are independent, but they have a collective effect on AdmissionCalculation and AdmissionDecision, so this analysis is deferred to Task O.

O. ANALYZE VARIABLES THAT HOLD RESULTS

The two result variables are AdmissionCalculation and AdmissionDecision.

TESTS BASED ON A BLACK-BOX MODEL MAY DIFFER FROM TESTS BASED ON THE CODE

The program will probably set a value for AdmissionDecision in one of two ways:

> *(a) Calculate a function that uses the values of ACT and GPA.* Based on the problem description, the function will probably calculate $ACT + 10 \times GPA$ and set AdmissionDecision if the result is 71 or larger. We have labeled the result of the calculation as AdmissionCalculation and are treating it as a variable.

> *(b) Check the pair of values of ACT and GPA against a list of values that yield acceptance or rejection.* The implementation will probably be equivalent to checking whether the ordered pair (ACT, GPA) belongs to this set of acceptance values: { (31, 4.0), (32, 3.9), (32, 4.0), (33, 3.8), (33, 3.9), (33, 4.0), (34, 3.7), (34, 3.8), (34, 3.9), (34, 4.0), (35, 3.6), (35, 3.7), (35, 3.8), (35, 3.9), (35, 4.0), (36, 3.5), (36, 3.6), (36, 3.7), (36, 3.8), (36, 3.9), (36, 4.0) }

Therefore:

- AdmissionDecision is a binary variable with values equivalent to Yes or No.
- AdmissionCalculation exists only in (a). If the program sets AdmissionDecision as in (b), by checking against a list, then there is no AdmissionCalculation. In case (a), AdmissionCalculation takes values from 0 to 76. The variable type might be Fixed Point or Floating Point—there might be a decimal point and a 0 after the number—but the values will be equivalent to the Integers {0, 1, 2, ... , 76} (no fractional values).

ANALYSIS ON THE ASSUMPTION THE IMPLEMENTATION IS EQUIVALENT TO CASE A

You can't enter values directly into AdmissionCalculation or AdmissionDecision. To obtain boundary values for these, you must input appropriate values to ACT and GPA.

RISK/EQUIVALENCE TABLE SHOWING MULTIPLE RELATED VARIABLES

This risk/equivalence table uses additional columns to show multiple variables.

Risk (potential failure)	Admission-Calculation	Admission-Decision	Equivalence Class	ACT	GPA	Notes
Decision value inconsistent with the calculated value	Calculated value < 71	No	Any (**ACT**, **GPA**) that yields a score < 71	33	3.7	Score is 70. Decision should be No.
	Calculated value ≥ 71	Yes	Any (**ACT**, **GPA**) that yields a score ≥ 71	33	3.8	Score is 71. Decision should be Yes.
Confusion at the extreme score values	0	No	(**0, 0**)	0	0.0	Lower bound
Confusion at the extreme score values	76	Yes	(36, 4.0)	36	4.0	Upper bound
A sloppy filter might set **Admission-Calculation** to a fractional value	70.6	???	(**ACT**, **GPA**) such that calculated value is < 71 AND has non-zero digits after the decimal	30.6	4.0	Should be impossible to enter 30.6 into **ACT**. **GPA** should be allowed only 1 digit after decimal
				31	3.96	If it handles 70.6 correctly, it will probably handle values below 70 and above 71
	76.1	???	(**ACT**, **GPA**) such that calculated value > 76	36.1	4.0	Should be impossible to enter this into **ACT**.
				36	4.01	Should be impossible to enter this into **GPA**.
A sloppy filter might set **Admission-Calculation** to an out-of-bounds value	-1	???	(**ACT**, **GPA**) such that calculated value < 0	-1	0	You already tested 76.1, which exceeds upper limit. This tests the lower limit (below 0)
				0	-0.1	Negatives into **ACT** and **GPA** should be impossible
	> **MAXINT**			MAX-INT	1	
	> **MAXFLOAT**			36	MAX-FLOAT	

ANALYSIS ON THE ASSUMPTION THE IMPLEMENTATION IS EQUIVALENT TO CASE B

In this case, there is no **AdmissionCalculation** variable. Instead, the program checks the pair of values (ACT, GPA) against a list. If a pair is in the list, the AdmissionDecision is Yes. Otherwise it is No.

What could go wrong with this?

- The program might implement the decision incorrectly, deciding No even though values are in the list or deciding Yes even though values aren't in the list.

- The list might be wrong. It might have some extra values or it might be missing some values.
- If the input filter was written sloppily, it might allow some values that round to valid values but aren't valid as accepted because they contain too many digits after the decimal point.

As a reminder, here is the list:

{ (31, 4.0), (32, 3.9), (32, 4.0), (33, 3.8), (33, 3.9), (33, 4.0), (34, 3.7), (34, 3.8), (34, 3.9), (34, 4.0), (35, 3.6), (35, 3.7), (35, 3.8), (35, 3.9), (35, 4.0), (36, 3.5), (36, 3.6), (36, 3.7), (36, 3.8), (36, 3.9), (36, 4.0) }

Risk (potential failure)	Admission-Decision	Equivalence Class	ACT	GPA	Notes
Wrong decision	Yes	(ACT, GPA) is in the list	31	4.0	The correct value for `AdmissionDecision` is Yes
	No	(ACT, GPA) is not in the list	31	3.9	You could test these first 2 tests with non-boundary values. They check basic logic: how the list as a whole is handled, not how specific values are handled.
Error in the list	Yes	(ACT, GPA) is in the list but at a boundary	31	4.0	
			32	3.9	
			33	3.8	
			34	3.7	
			35	3.6	
			36	3.5	
	No	(ACT, GPA) is not in the list but at a boundary	30	4.0	
			31	3.9	
			32	3.8	
			33	3.7	
			34	3.6	
			35	3.5	
			36	3.4	
			36	4.1	
Unrecognized values	Yes	ACT or GPA has too many digits after decimal	33.1	3.8	The correct action would probably be to say Yes, but these values aren't in the list.
			33	3.81	
Confused by negative values	No	ACT or GPA has a negative number	-1	3.6	
			34	-0.1	

We show different sets of tests for Case A and Case B. Which should you actually use?

- If the code is designed as in Case B and if you're writing the code yourself or maintaining someone else's code, the Case B tests will be useful. These will help you understand whether the code behaves the way your understanding of the implementation says it should behave. Testing this way will often reveal to you that your understanding of the implementation is incorrect—this is *especially* valuable when you're trying to understand someone else's code or code that you wrote a long time ago.

- If you don't know how the code is designed or you know that today it is designed like Case B but you believe the design might change in the future and you want a test suite that will be useful even if the implementation changes, then we think the Case A tests are the better choice.[41]

You can do a domain analysis that takes into account specific low-level design or implementation details of the code under test. These tests will help you check your understanding of the code and help you ensure the code does what you intend with the implementation. However, tests that are specific to a design or implementation become uninformative when the design changes. A set of tests that make generic assumptions about the implementation, focusing instead on the product's capabilities, will maintain its value over time as the implementation evolves.

P. ANALYZE NON-INDEPENDENT VARIABLES. DEAL WITH RELATIONSHIPS AND CONSTRAINTS

See Task O, above.

Q. IDENTIFY AND LIST UNANALYZED VARIABLES. GATHER INFORMATION FOR LATER ANALYSIS

Variables related to test scores probably include the student's name and demographic information and any data in the student transcript. The scores probably also influence decisions about scholarships.

R. IMAGINE AND DOCUMENT RISKS THAT DON'T NECESSARILY MAP TO AN OBVIOUS DIMENSION

Some schools report GPA scores on a scale of 0 to 5. Other schools refuse to report GPA scores. A few refuse to report any grade beyond pass or fail. How will this system cope with that?

---

41 This is an example of a case in which you make a choice about the design of your tests based on an explicit assumption about the underlying architecture, design or implementation of the program. If you keep archival notes about your testing, this is the type of information that belongs in those notes.

EXAMPLE 12: PIECEWISE BOUNDARY

The input domain of a function is the set of all points (**x**, **y**) that meet these criteria (Binder, 2000, p. 404):

- **x** and **y** are Floating-Point variables
- $1 < \mathbf{x} \le 10$
- $1 \le \mathbf{y} \le 10$
- $\mathbf{y} \le 14 - \mathbf{x}$

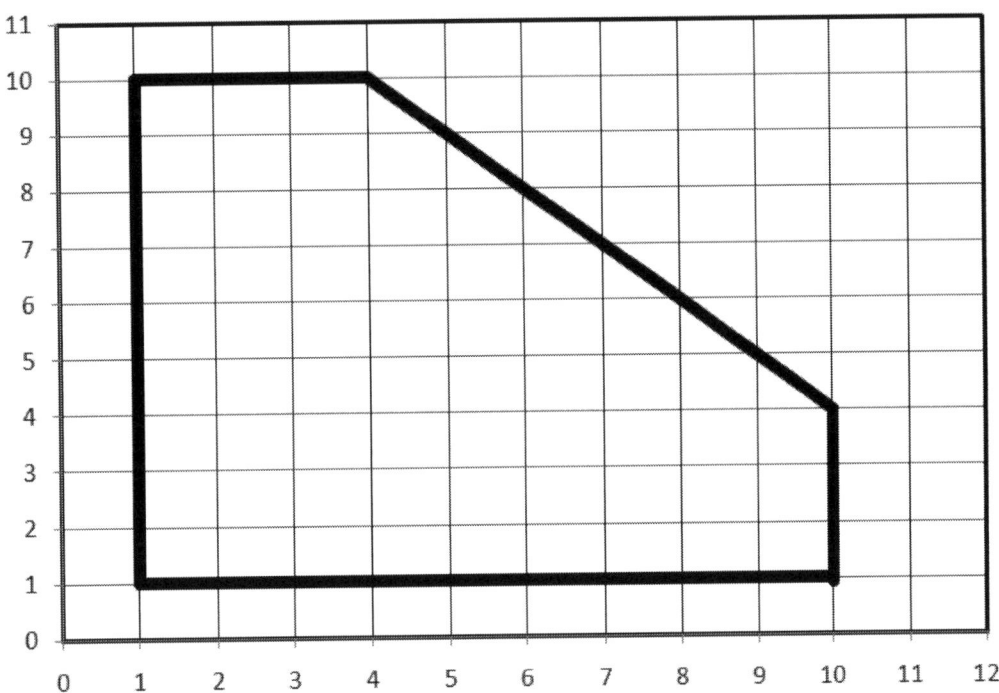

A. IDENTIFY THE POTENTIALLY INTERESTING VARIABLES

x and **y**

B. IDENTIFY THE VARIABLES YOU CAN ANALYZE NOW. THESE ARE THE VARIABLES OF INTEREST

x and **y**

C. DETERMINE THE PRIMARY DIMENSION OF THE VARIABLE OF INTEREST

Basic numeric variables

D. DETERMINE THE TYPE AND SCALE OF THE VARIABLE'S PRIMARY DIMENSION AND WHAT VALUES IT CAN TAKE

These are Single-Precision Floating-Point variables. Binder (2000) specified they have 6 decimal digits of precision.

E. DETERMINE WHETHER YOU CAN ORDER THE VARIABLE'S VALUES (FROM SMALLEST TO LARGEST)

Yes.

F. DETERMINE WHETHER THIS IS AN INPUT VARIABLE OR A RESULT

These are input variables to a function. The problem description provides no information about how the variables got their value. The user might input the values directly or they might be calculated or retrieved from storage—we don't know.

For purposes of this example, we will treat these variables as if they were input variables (variables whose values are set from a user interface).

G. DETERMINE HOW THE PROGRAM USES THIS VARIABLE

A not-otherwise-specified function takes the values as inputs and does something with them.

H. DETERMINE WHETHER OTHER VARIABLES ARE RELATED TO THIS ONE

The graph shows the relationship between **x** and **y**. Every point on or inside the geometric figure is a valid input point (valid pair of values (**x**, **y**)).

The function that uses (**x**, **y**) probably sets the values of some variables. Those variables are probably calculated using (**x**, **y**).

I. PARTITION THE VARIABLE (ITS PRIMARY DIMENSION)

The dimension is ordered, so determine the sub-ranges and transition points.

The basic partitioning of x and y examines the variables separately. From this:

$$\texttt{MINFLOAT} \leq \quad \textbf{x} \quad \leq \quad 1 \qquad \text{(too small)}$$
$$1 \quad < \quad \textbf{x} \quad \leq \quad 10 \qquad \text{(valid)}$$
$$10 \quad < \quad \textbf{x} \quad < \quad \texttt{MAXFLOAT} \qquad \text{(too big)}$$
$$\texttt{MINFLOAT} \leq \quad \textbf{y} \quad \leq \quad 1 \qquad \text{(too small)}$$
$$1 \quad < \quad \textbf{y} \quad \leq \quad 10 \qquad \text{(valid)}$$
$$10 \quad < \quad \textbf{y} \quad < \quad \texttt{MAXFLOAT} \qquad \text{(too big)}$$

The description also specifies that $\textbf{y} \leq 14 - \textbf{x}$. We'll come back to this relationship in Task P, below.

J. LAY OUT THE ANALYSIS IN A CLASSICAL BOUNDARY/EQUIVALENCE TABLE. IDENTIFY BEST REPRESENTATIVES

The basic analysis is the same for **x** and **y**, so the table shows only **x**.

Variable	Valid case equivalence class	Invalid case equivalence class	Boundaries and special cases	Notes
x	$1 < \textbf{x} \leq 10$		1.00001	
			10	
		$\texttt{MINFLOAT} \leq \textbf{x} \leq 1$	1	$\texttt{MINFLOAT} = \texttt{-MAXFLOAT}$
		$10 < \textbf{x} < \texttt{MAXFLOAT}$	10.0001	

The tests use the values in the "Boundaries and special cases" column.

K. CREATE TESTS FOR THE CONSEQUENCES OF THE DATA ENTERED, NOT JUST THE INPUT FILTER

This Task goes beyond what we're trying to teach with this example.

L. IDENTIFY SECONDARY DIMENSIONS. ANALYZE THEM IN THE CLASSICAL WAY

The usual secondary dimensions for Floating-Point variables are listed at *Test Idea Catalog for Floating-Point Variables* on page 257.

M. SUMMARIZE YOUR ANALYSIS WITH A RISK/EQUIVALENCE TABLE

The usual secondary dimensions for Floating-Point variables are tabled at *A Risk/Equivalence Table for a Floating-Point Variable* on page 260.

N. ANALYZE INDEPENDENT VARIABLES THAT SHOULD BE TESTED TOGETHER

The problem description does not include any independent variables.

O. ANALYZE VARIABLES THAT HOLD RESULTS

There is not enough information about the function that uses (x, y) to do this analysis yet.

P. ANALYZE NON-INDEPENDENT VARIABLES. DEAL WITH RELATIONSHIPS AND CONSTRAINTS

The variables x and y are non-independent. They constrain each other according to the rule, $y \leq 14 - x$. Under this rule, any pair (x, y) that does not satisfy $y \leq 14 - x$ is not a valid input pair to the function.

The set of valid pairs can be drawn as points on a graph. The five line segments on the graph show:

*   the upper bound on x, $x = 10$
*   the upper bound on y, $y = 10$
*   the interaction of x and y $y = 14 - x$
*   the lower bound on y, $y \geq 1$
*   the lower bound on x, $x > 1$

These segments graph as a ***bounding figure***. Any point inside this bounding figure or on one of its first four line segments is a valid input.

CHOOSING ON POINTS AND OFF POINTS FOR TESTING LINEAR RELATIONSHIPS

The objective of Task P (analyze non-independent variables) is to determine what tests to use to check that the program accepts only valid pairs (x, y).

To consider the possible tests, we need a few definitions:

*   *On point:* a point that is on the boundary.[42]
*   *Off point*: a point that is not on the boundary.

---

42 Note that for some x or y, there may be no Floating-Point values that are On points. As represented in the computer, the set of On points is not continuous.

- *Inner point*: a point that is inside the specified domain (a member of the set that defines the domain).
- *Outer point*: a point that is outside the specified domain (not a member of the set that defines the domain)
- *Open boundary*: the boundary is not inside the specified range or area, For example, 1 is not inside $1 < \mathbf{x}$.
- *Closed boundary*: the boundary is inside the specified range or area. For example, 10 is inside $\mathbf{x} \leq 10$.

The bounding area is defined by 5 inequalities. ($1 < \mathbf{x} \leq 10$ has two inequalities: $\mathbf{x} > 1$ and $\mathbf{x} \leq 10$). The 5 inequalities determine the 5 line segments shown on the graph.

Here's the basic pattern for dealing with linear boundaries:

- You always need an Inner point and an Outer point. One of these will be an On point; the other will be an Off point.
- If the input domain is specified as *equal to* the boundary, pick three points, one on the boundary, one on one side of it and one on the other side.

Applying that to this example, for each line segment (for each inequality):

- When you have a closed boundary, a point on the boundary is an On point. For example, any point on the line $\mathbf{y} = 1$ (when $1 < \mathbf{x} \leq 10$) is an On point because the boundary is specified as $1 \leq \mathbf{y}$.

- When you have an open boundary, a point on the boundary is an Off point. For example, any point on the line $\mathbf{x} = 1$ (between $\mathbf{y} = 1$ and $\mathbf{y} = 10$) is an Off point because the boundary is defined as $1 < \mathbf{x}$.

- Notice that we haven't yet specified what value the other variable will take. For example, if you choose $\mathbf{y} = 1$, what value do you pick for $\mathbf{x}$? Recommendations seem to vary, but the most common recommendation seems to be to pick a mid-range value. Thus the test might be ($\mathbf{x} = 5.5$, $\mathbf{y} = 1$). Alternatively:
  - For the Inner point, you might pick a more challenging case ($\mathbf{x} = 1.00001$, $\mathbf{y} = 1$)
  - But for Outer Off point, where you're forcing an error message, you might pick the non-error value to be mid-range, focusing attention on the variable that is out of bounds (x = 5.5, y = 0.999999).

Here are our tests:

The Inner cases touch every corner, the Outer cases touch the middle of each line.

Inequality	Inner Points		Outer Points	
	x	y	x	y
1 < x	1.00001	1 $1 \leq y \leq 10$	1	5.5 midrange
x ≤ 10	10	4 $1 \leq y \leq 4$	10.0001	2.5 midrange
1 ≤ y	10 $1 < x \leq 10$	1	5.5 midrange	0.999999
y ≤ 10	1 $1 < x \leq 4$	10	2.5 midrange	10.0001
y ≤ 14 - x	x = 4	y = 10	x = 7 midrange	y = 7.00001 midrange

Q. TASKS Q & R ARE BEYOND WHAT WE'RE TRYING TO TEACH WITH THIS EXAMPLE.

ADDITIONAL NOTES

Beizer (1990, 1995) made a significant effort to explain this approach to testers who were just beginning to study it. Copeland (2004) also provides an introductory presentation.

EXAMPLE 13: SUM OF TWO INTEGERS

A program adds two Integer numbers, which you enter. Each number should be one or two digits. Analyze this in terms of the paired inputs (`FirstNumber, SecondNumber`) or in terms of the output (`Sum`). The `sum` will also be an Integer.

A. IDENTIFY THE POTENTIALLY INTERESTING VARIABLES

- `FirstNumber`
- `SecondNumber`
- `Sum`

B. IDENTIFY THE VARIABLES YOU CAN ANALYZE NOW. THESE ARE THE VARIABLES OF INTEREST

- `FirstNumber`
- `SecondNumber`
- `Sum`

C. DETERMINE THE PRIMARY DIMENSION OF THE VARIABLE OF INTEREST

These are all basic numeric variables (Integers).

D. DETERMINE THE TYPE AND SCALE OF THE VARIABLE'S PRIMARY DIMENSION AND WHAT VALUES IT CAN TAKE

These are Integers.

- `FirstNumber` and `SecondNumber` have one or two digits. The description does not say whether they can take negative values as well as positive ones. The domain for each variable is either:

    -99 to 99   or   0 to 99.

    For this Example, assume the specified domains should be -99 to 99.
- `Sum` runs from -198 to 198 (assuming the inputs run from -99 to 99).

E. DETERMINE WHETHER YOU CAN ORDER THE VARIABLE'S VALUES (FROM SMALLEST TO LARGEST)

Yes.

F. DETERMINE WHETHER THIS IS AN INPUT VARIABLE OR A RESULT

- `FirstNumber` and `SecondNumber` are input variables.
- `Sum` is a result.

G. DETERMINE HOW THE PROGRAM USES THIS VARIABLE

The description provides little information about this. It says the program uses `FirstNumber` and `SecondNumber` to compute `Sum`. Beyond that, nothing.

H. DETERMINE WHETHER OTHER VARIABLES ARE RELATED TO THIS ONE

There is no information beyond the relationship between `Sum` and the two inputs.

I. PARTITION THE VARIABLE (ITS PRIMARY DIMENSION)

We'll analyze `Sum` in Task O (result variables).

The two inputs are ordered, so determine their sub-ranges and transition points:

`MININT`	≤	`FirstNumber`	<	-99	(too small)
-99	≤	`FirstNumber`	≤	99	(valid)
99	<	`FirstNumber`	≤	`MAXINT`	(too big)
`MININT`	≤	`SecondNumber`	<	-99	(too small)
-99	≤	`SecondNumber`	≤	99	(valid)
99	<	`SecondNumber`	≤	`MAXINT`	(too big)

J. LAY OUT THE ANALYSIS IN A CLASSICAL BOUNDARY/EQUIVALENCE TABLE. IDENTIFY BEST REPRESENTATIVES

Variable	Valid case equivalence class	Invalid case equivalence class	Boundaries and special cases	Notes
`FirstNumber`	-99 to 99		-99	
			0	
			99	
		< 99	-100	
		> 99	100	
`SecondNumber`	-99 to 99		-99	
			0	
			99	
		< 99	-100	
		> 99	100	

The tests use the values in the "Boundaries and special cases" column.

K. CREATE TESTS FOR THE CONSEQUENCES OF THE DATA ENTERED, NOT JUST THE INPUT FILTER

See Task O (result variables) below.

L. IDENTIFY SECONDARY DIMENSIONS. ANALYZE THEM IN THE CLASSICAL WAY

These are garden-variety Integer variables (nothing special about them). The analysis is the same as *Test Idea Catalog for Integers* on page 231.

M. SUMMARIZE YOUR ANALYSIS WITH A RISK/EQUIVALENCE TABLE

The input variables are garden-variety Integer variables (nothing special about them). The analysis *of the input filter* is the same as *Generic Risk/Equivalence Table for Integers* on page 233. For risks associated with the sum, see Task O.

N. ANALYZE INDEPENDENT VARIABLES THAT SHOULD BE TESTED TOGETHER

The independent variables described in this example are `FirstNumber` and `SecondNumber`. They've already been analyzed.

O. ANALYZE VARIABLES THAT HOLD RESULTS

The result variable is Sum, a result of `FirstNumber` + `SecondNumber`.

What could go wrong with `Sum`?

- *Calculation error?* This is such a simple calculation that errors are unlikely (but not impossible).

- *Divide by zero?* Maybe. Murphy's Law, applied to testing, says that if `Sum` takes the value 0, some part of the program will divide by it. However, the program description doesn't provide information about how or where `Sum` might be used, so there is no way to test for this risk at this time.

- *Overflow?* Probably not. The range of possible values for `Sum` is -198 to 198. As long as the input filters for `FirstNumber` and `SecondNumber` are doing their jobs—*Remember: Test your input filters <u>before</u> testing combinations of input data*—the possible values of `Sum` aren't close to the limits on Integers. If the input filters are working, testing for overflow of the sum will be impossible.

- *Invalid data type?* If the inputs are bad (e.g., letters or non-Integer numbers) and they get past the input filter, `Sum` will probably be bad. If the input filters are working, testing for overflow of the sum will be impossible.

The most efficient way to check for the effect of a broken input filter on the sum combines this with tests of the secondary dimensions of the input variable(s). These are the tests that will show that an input filter is letting bad values through. If you find that some type of bad data can be accepted into the input variable, enter it and then ask the program for Sum. *Putting all the input filter tests into the table that checks input pairs' effect on the* Sum *will be wasteful because the tests will either be impossible or they'll be redundant with the input-filter tests that you should already have run.*

Risk involving Sum	Valid case equivalence class	Invalid case equivalence class	Value of Sum	First-Number	Second-Number	Notes
Calculation error	-198 to 198		-198	-99	-99	
			0	0	0	Equivalence class of inputs: any pair that sums to 0
			198	99	99	
Overflow		< -198	-199	-100	-99	error message, if it gets past the input filter
			???	`MININT`	-1	overflow, if this gets past the input filter
		> 198	199	99	100	error message, if it gets past the input filter
			???	1	`MAXINT`	overflow, if this gets past the input filter

P. ANALYZE NON-INDEPENDENT VARIABLES. DEAL WITH RELATIONSHIPS AND CONSTRAINTS

See Task O.

Q. TASKS Q & R ARE BEYOND WHAT WE'RE TRYING TO TEACH WITH THIS EXAMPLE.

EXAMPLE 14: RESULT OF CALCULATIONS

I, J and K are Unsigned Integers. You can enter values into I and J, but the program calculates the value of $K = I \times J$. Treat K as the primary variable.

A. IDENTIFY THE POTENTIALLY INTERESTING VARIABLES

I, J and K.

B. IDENTIFY THE VARIABLES YOU CAN ANALYZE NOW. THESE ARE THE VARIABLES OF INTEREST

I, J and K.

C. DETERMINE THE PRIMARY DIMENSION OF THE VARIABLE OF INTEREST

All three are basic numeric variables.

D. DETERMINE THE TYPE AND SCALE OF THE VARIABLE'S PRIMARY DIMENSION AND WHAT VALUES IT CAN TAKE

All three variables are Unsigned Integers. They run from 0 to **MAXINT**. For Unsigned Integers, the value of **MAXINT** is $2^N - 1$, where N is the number of bits allocated to store each Integer. For example, if Integers are stored in 32-bit words, **MAXINT** for Unsigned Integers is $2^{32} - 1$ (4,294,967,295).

E. DETERMINE WHETHER YOU CAN ORDER THE VARIABLE'S VALUES (FROM SMALLEST TO LARGEST)

Yes.

F. DETERMINE WHETHER THIS IS AN INPUT VARIABLE OR A RESULT

- I and J are input variables.
- K is a result variable.

G. DETERMINE HOW THE PROGRAM USES THIS VARIABLE

There's no information beyond the statement that I and J are used to create K.

H. DETERMINE WHETHER OTHER VARIABLES ARE RELATED TO THIS ONE

K is the primary variable. I and J are related to it. See Task O for details.

I. PARTITION THE VARIABLE (ITS PRIMARY DIMENSION)

The example's description asks you to treat K as the primary variable, so we could partition it here. However, K is a result variable. You have to analyze I and J to get to K anyway, so we will partition those two here and K in Task O.

I and J are ordered, so we determine their sub-ranges and transition points. We analyze them here as standalone input variables. They do constrain each other. We'll work on that in Task P.

$$I < 0 \qquad \text{(too small)}$$
$$0 \leq I \leq \textbf{MAXINT} \qquad \text{(valid)}$$

$$\text{MAXINT} \le \text{I} \qquad \text{(too big)}$$

$$\text{J} < 0 \qquad \text{(too small)}$$

$$0 \le \text{J} \le \text{MAXINT} \qquad \text{(valid)}$$

$$\text{MAXINT} \le \text{J} \qquad \text{(too big)}$$

J. LAY OUT THE ANALYSIS IN A CLASSICAL BOUNDARY/EQUIVALENCE TABLE. IDENTIFY BEST REPRESENTATIVES

This table shows only the primary dimension of I and J, ignoring secondary dimensions and the constraint between I and J. These are boundary tests of the input filter.

Variable	Valid case equivalence class	Invalid case equivalence class	Boundaries and special cases	Notes
I	0 to MAXINT		0	
			MAXINT	
		< 0	-1	impossible for Unsigned Integer
		> MAXINT	MAXINT+1	
J	0 to MAXINT		0	
			MAXINT	
		< 0	-1	
		> MAXINT	MAXINT+1	

The tests use the values in the "Boundaries and special cases" column.

K. CREATE TESTS FOR THE CONSEQUENCES OF THE DATA ENTERED, NOT JUST THE INPUT FILTER

See Task O.

L. IDENTIFY SECONDARY DIMENSIONS. ANALYZE THEM IN THE CLASSICAL WAY

I and J are Unsigned Integers. The only difference between them and regular Integers is that they can't take negative values (and therefore their MAXINT is twice as large). For secondary dimensions of Integers, see *Test Idea Catalog for Integers* on page 231.

M. SUMMARIZE YOUR ANALYSIS WITH A RISK/EQUIVALENCE TABLE

See *Generic Risk/Equivalence Table for Integers* on page 233.

N. ANALYZE INDEPENDENT VARIABLES THAT SHOULD BE TESTED TOGETHER

This example doesn't include any independent variables.

O. ANALYZE VARIABLES THAT HOLD RESULTS

K is the variable that the problem description tells you to analyze. K is a result variable, the product of I and J.

This analysis starts by assuming you have done the basic testing of I and J and they are in fact Unsigned Integers. Therefore their values range from 0 to MAXINT.

Sticking to valid values for I and J simplifies the analysis of K:

- K can't be a letter or a negative number because it is an Unsigned Integer. (If I and J are both Unsigned Integers and K = I × J, how could you possibly get a negative number or a letter into K?)

- K can't exceed **MAXINT** because there is no room available in memory for any number larger than **MAXINT**. If you somehow store a larger number for K, you achieve an "overflow" and corrupt part of memory that is not allocated to storing a value for K. That would be a serious error.

- The absolutely biggest value we can imagine *trying* to store in K is **MAXINT** × **MAXINT** (I and J both **MAXINT**).

For a variable whose possible values are so tightly constrained, we recommend using the simpler boundary/equivalence table.

Variable	Valid case equivalence class	Invalid case equivalence class	Boundaries and special cases	Notes
K	0 to **MAXINT**		0	
			MAXINT	
		< 0	can't do that	
		> **MAXINT**	**MAXINT**+1	
			MAXINT × **MAXINT**	

This table shows what values of K are interesting to try. Now you have to figure out what values of I and J to use in order to generate those values of K.

Because K is an Unsigned Integer, it runs from 0 to **MAXINT**.

Therefore, I × J must run from 0 to **MAXINT**.

For the lower bound, K = 0:

Several (I,J) pairs will yield K = 0. The full set can be described like this:

$$\{ (I, J) \mid I \times J = 0 \}$$

Continuing this analysis:

$$\{ (I, J) \mid I \times J = 0 \} = \{ (I, J) \mid I = 0 \text{ or } J = 0 \}$$

This is an equivalence set on the (I, J)'s. The set includes (0, 0), (1, 0), (**MAXINT**, 0), (0, 1), (0, **MAXINT**) as well as the many intermediate values, like (0, 2000).

For the upper bound, K = **MAXINT**:

The analysis for K = **MAXINT** is a little trickier. A common mistake is to write the set this way:

$$K = \textbf{MAXINT} \text{ for } \{ (I, J) \mid I = \textbf{MAXINT} / J \}$$

That works for J = 1 and J = **MAXINT**. However, Integer arithmetic truncates. So, for example, 2/3 = 0 and 3/2 = 1.

Instead, stick with:

$$K = \textbf{MAXINT} \text{ for } \{ (I, J) \mid I \times J = \textbf{MAXINT} \}$$

This set includes at least two values, (1, **MAXINT**) and (**MAXINT**, 1). It will probably include a few other values. For example, consider an 8-bit Unsigned Integer (ranges from 0 to 255).

- ◦ (2, **MAXINT**/2) might look like a good pair:
  - ▪ It might look like 2 × **MAXINT**/2 = **MAXINT**.
  - ▪ But when you do Integer arithmetic, **MAXINT**/2 becomes 127, not 127.5.
  - ▪ So 2 × **MAXINT**/2 = 254.
- ◦ The equivalence set for **MAXINT** = **I** × **J**, when **MAXINT** = 255 is:

$$\{ (1, 255), (3, 85), (5, 41), (15, 17), (17, 15), (41, 5), (85, 3) \text{ and } (255, 1) \}$$

To test above the upper bound, **K** = **MAXINT**:

I and **J** can't both be **MAXINT** because **MAXINT** × **MAXINT** will cause an overflow value in **K**.

More generally, we can describe the set of valid (**I**,**J**) pairs as:

$$\{ (\textbf{I}, \textbf{J}) \mid \textbf{I} = 0 \text{ or } \textbf{J} = 0 \text{ or (for nonzero } \textbf{I},\textbf{J}) \ \textbf{I} \leq \textbf{MAXINT} / \textbf{J} \text{ and } \textbf{J} \leq \textbf{MAXINT} / \textbf{I} \}$$

This will keep **K** below **MAXINT**+1.

Thus, the equivalence set of values of (**I**, **J**) that drive **K** above **MAXINT** is:

$$\{ (\textbf{I}, \textbf{J}) \mid \textbf{I} > 0 \text{ and } \textbf{J} > 0 \text{ and } \textbf{I} > \textbf{MAXINT} / \textbf{J} \text{ or } \textbf{J} > \textbf{MAXINT} / \textbf{I} \}$$

Which values should you test?

There are debates about the best heuristics for selecting best representatives of multidimensional variables (like (**I**, **J**)) (*see* Beizer, 1995).

- • As a general rule, we think the boundary cases are reasonable choices. Using boundaries is an easy heuristic to work with, so that's what we'll emphasize.
- • Continuing the illustration using **MAXINT** = 255:
  - ◦ The obvious tests for **K** = 0 are (0, 0), (0, 255) and (255, 0).
  - ◦ The obvious tests for **K** = **MAXINT** are (1, 255) and (255, 1).
  - ◦ However, we aren't fond of repetition. Don't use 1 and 255 in all (or even most) tests. Choose other values from the equivalence class for some tests.
- • To test **MAXINT**+1:
  - ◦ The possible values for an Unsigned Integer is 0 through 2^N-1, for example 2^8-1, which is 255:
    - ▪ **MAXINT** is 2^N-1
    - ▪ **MAXINT**+1 is 2^N
    - ▪ **N** is almost certainly even (such as 8, 16 or 64). The obvious test for **MAXINT**+1 is $2^{N/2} \times 2^{N/2}$
    - ▪ Continuing the example of **N** = 8 (**K** ranges from 0 to 255), the test would be 2^4 times 2^4, which works out to 16 × 16 (which is 256 = **MAXINT**+1).
- • To test **MAXINT** × **MAXINT**:
  - ◦ Use **I** = **MAXINT** and **J** = **MAXINT**.

Here is how we lay out the full analysis:

Variable	Valid case equivalence class	Invalid case equivalence class	Boundaries and special cases	I	J	Notes
K = I × J	0 to MAXINT		0	0	0	$\{(I, J) \mid I=0 \text{ or } J=0\}$
				0	MAXINT	
				MAXINT	0	
			MAXINT	1	MAXINT	$\{(I, J) \mid I \times J = MAXINT\}$
				MAXINT	1	
		<0	can't do that			
		>MAXINT	MAXINT+1	$2^{N/2}$	$2^{N/2}$	where MAXINT = 2^N-1
			MAXINT × MAXINT	MAXINT	MAXINT	

P. ANALYZE NON-INDEPENDENT VARIABLES. DEAL WITH RELATIONSHIPS AND CONSTRAINTS

I and J constrain each other. Because K must not exceed MAXINT, I × J must not exceed MAXINT. Therefore, as we explained in Task O, the set of valid pairs (I, J) is:

$$\{ (I, J) \mid I = 0 \text{ or } J = 0 \text{ or (for nonzero I,J) } I \le MAXINT / J \text{ and } J \le MAXINT / I \}$$

How should this constraint change testing of the input filter? The filter should not allow values of I and J outside this set.

Variable	Valid case equivalence class	Invalid case equivalence class	Boundaries and special cases	Notes
I	0 to MAXINT		0	
			MAXINT	
		<0	-1	
		>MAXINT / J	I = (MAXINT+1)/2 J = 2	If MAXINT = 255, I is 128
		>MAXINT	MAXINT+1	
J	0 to MAXINT		0	
			MAXINT	
		<0	-1	
		>MAXINT / I	I = 2 J = (MAXINT+1)/2	If MAXINT = 255, J is 128
		>MAXINT	MAXINT+1	

Q. TASKS Q & R ARE BEYOND WHAT WE'RE TRYING TO TEACH WITH THIS EXAMPLE.

EXAMPLE 15: MAILING LABELS

A program prints mailing labels. The first line of the label is the person's name. The program builds the name from three fields, **FirstName**, **MiddleName** and **LastName**. Each field can hold up to 30 characters. The label can be up to 70 characters wide.

A. IDENTIFY THE POTENTIALLY INTERESTING VARIABLES

- **FirstName**
- **MiddleName**
- **LastName**
- **PrintedName** (the name printed on the label)

Because the lengths of the names are important, we're going to name some length variables:

- **FL** will be the length of the **FirstName**
- **ML** will be the length of the **MiddleName**
- **LL** will be the length of the **LastName**
- **PL** will be the total length of the **PrintedName**

B. IDENTIFY THE VARIABLES YOU CAN ANALYZE NOW. THESE ARE THE VARIABLES OF INTEREST

- **FirstName** and **FL**
- **MiddleName** and **ML**
- **LastName** and **LL**
- **PrintedName** and **PL**

C. DETERMINE THE PRIMARY DIMENSION OF THE VARIABLE OF INTEREST

The primary dimension appears to be the length of the string.

D. DETERMINE THE TYPE AND SCALE OF THE VARIABLE'S PRIMARY DIMENSION AND WHAT VALUES IT CAN TAKE

Each variable is a String. Their lengths are Integers.

- The maximum length of each input name is 30 characters.
- The minimum length of each input is unspecified. We'll return to this after considering the content of the names.
- The strings hold printable characters.

  The most traditional name strings start with an uppercase letter and continue with lower-case letters. However, this is too restrictive. People might attempt to enter a person's or company's "real" name (the name most appropriate for mailing) and that might not fit this model. For example:

  (a) *III* (pronounced "three," this is the complete name of a friend of ours).

  (b) *John O'Neill* (the apostrophe isn't a letter).

  (c) *Professor Dr. John Jay Joe-Bob Sid Hörst-Garcia 3rd, Ph.D., ASQ-CQE* (This ficti-tious name is 67 characters. Some people like to see their name with all their titles and honors. Someone who writes Dr. Joe-Bob a letter asking for a favor will want the mailing label to print Dr. Joe-Bob's name the way he likes it.)

    (**d**) **R2D2** (Would you want your *mailing program* to tell your child that it won't let him send a letter to his favorite robot?)

    (**e**) **The \$\$-Gold-4-Life-\$\$!! Company** (Just because it's a tacky name doesn't mean they can't name their business with it.)

- From the examples, it appears the minimum length of an input name might be 0. For example, III has a `FirstName` = III (3 characters), but no `MiddleName` or `LastName`.

- We therefore describe the values of the primary dimension (string length) as follows:

  - $0 \le \text{FL} \le 30$

  - $0 \le \text{ML} \le 30$

  - $0 \le \text{LL} \le 30$

  - $1 \le \text{PL} \le 70$ (At least one input character or there is no name)

Note that lengths of input names constrain each other. If `FL` and `ML` are 30, then `LL` can't exceed 10. (Actually, `LL` can't exceed 8 in this case, but we'll explain that later.)

E. DETERMINE WHETHER YOU CAN ORDER THE VARIABLE'S VALUES (FROM SMALLEST TO LARGEST)

Yes, the lengths of the variables can be ordered. You could also order them alphabetically, but the task that this example emphasizes is putting together a name string that can be printed (≤ 70 characters).

F. DETERMINE WHETHER THIS IS AN INPUT VARIABLE OR A RESULT

- `FirstName, MiddleName` and `LastName` are input variables.

- `FL, ML` and `LL` are probably calculated from the input names. We consider these as convenient labels for an attribute of the name variables, rather than as variables in their own right. However, if you prefer, you could consider them to be result variables.

- `PrintedName` is a result variable and `PL` is the label for its length.

G. DETERMINE HOW THE PROGRAM USES THIS VARIABLE

The program prints the names on a mailing label. It probably does other things with the name too, but the problem description doesn't say anything about that.

H. DETERMINE WHETHER OTHER VARIABLES ARE RELATED TO THIS ONE

Lots of other variables are probably related to this one, but the problem description gives no hints about what those variables might be.

I. PARTITION THE VARIABLE (ITS PRIMARY DIMENSION)

`FL, ML` and `LL` are ordered, so determine their sub-ranges and transition points. We analyze them here as standalone input variables. They do constrain each other. We'll work on that in Task O. We'll also work on `PL` in Task O.

	$\text{FL} < 0$	(too small)
$0 \le$	$\text{FL} \le 30$	(valid)
$30 <$	FL	(too big)
	$\text{ML} < 0$	(too small)

$$0 \leq \text{ML} \leq 30 \quad \text{(valid)}$$
$$30 < \text{ML} \quad \text{(too big)}$$
$$\text{LL} < 0 \quad \text{(too small)}$$
$$0 \leq \text{LL} \leq 30 \quad \text{(valid)}$$
$$30 < \text{LL} \quad \text{(too big)}$$

J. LAY OUT THE ANALYSIS IN A CLASSICAL BOUNDARY/EQUIVALENCE TABLE. IDENTIFY BEST REPRESENTATIVES

Variable	Valid case equivalence class	Invalid case equivalence class	Boundaries and special cases	Notes
FL	$0 \leq \text{FL} \leq 30$		0	
			30	
		FL < 0	-1	impossible
		30 < FL	31	
ML	$0 \leq \text{ML} \leq 30$		0	
			30	
		ML < 0	-1	
		30 < ML	31	
LL	$0 \leq \text{LL} \leq 30$		0	
			30	
		LL < 0	-1	
		30 < LL	31	

The tests use the values in the "Boundaries and special cases" column.

K. CREATE TESTS FOR THE CONSEQUENCES OF THE DATA ENTERED, NOT JUST THE INPUT FILTER

The program uses `FirstName`, `MiddleName` and `LastName` to create `PrintedName`. It will then print `PrintedName`. We analyze the *length* of `PrintedName` in Task O. However, there is another risk in the use of the names.

When the program tries to print `PrintedName`, what if it can't print a character that was accepted into one of the input names? To test for this:

- Create a set of test strings that, together, include all the characters that should (or might) be accepted as valid input characters.
- Report bugs for any characters that should be accepted but are rejected.
- Try to print the test strings to an appropriate sample of printers. Report bugs for any characters that are accepted by the input filter but are unprintable.

L. IDENTIFY SECONDARY DIMENSIONS. ANALYZE THEM IN THE CLASSICAL WAY

These are ordinary strings. See *From Example 7: Student Names* on page 165.

M. SUMMARIZE YOUR ANALYSIS WITH A RISK/EQUIVALENCE TABLE

These are ordinary strings. See *The Risk/Equivalence Table (Strings)* on page 167.

N. ANALYZE INDEPENDENT VARIABLES THAT SHOULD BE TESTED TOGETHER

No independent variables are mentioned in this example.

O. ANALYZE VARIABLES THAT HOLD RESULTS

`PrintedName` holds the results of concatenating `FirstName`, `MiddleName` and `LastName`.

The analysis starts from the assumption that `FirstName`, `MiddleName` and `LastName` are proper strings of appropriate lengths. The input filter has been tested and it works. The risk we're concerned about is that `PrintedName` might be too short or too long to print on a mailing label.

What could go wrong with the length?

- The first puzzle is the 70-character limit. In most typefaces, a string of 70 W's would be a lot wider than a string of 70 i's. The example description must be assuming the characters are printed in a fixed-width font. Is that assumption correct? If not, the rest of our length calculations are all wrong.

- For `PrintedName` to be 70 characters, all three input names must have some text. This is because each name has at most 30 characters. Two 30-character names can't add up to a 70-character `PrintedName`.

- Between every two names, there will be a space character. If $FL = 30$ and $ML = 30$, then a name string made up of `FirstName` and `MiddleName` will have 61 characters because it will add a space between `FirstName` and `MiddleName`.

- Because of the added space characters, if `PrintedName` has 70 characters, then $FL + ML + LL$ will be 68.

Represent the lengths of the input-name strings as a three-tuple, (FL, ML, LL). In this notation (5, 10, 15) means that `FirstName` is 5 characters long, `MiddleName` is 10 characters long and `LastName` is 15 characters long. `PrintedName` will be 32 characters long because of the spaces between the names.

You can create a set of valid three-tuples. It contains all the input-name lengths that yield a `PrintedName` length between 1 and 70 characters.

You can plot the three-tuples as points on a graph (see below). The result will be a three-dimension figure (like a box, but its surfaces won't all be the same size). In a three-dimensional figure, the boundary is not just a line. It is a surface (like the side of a box). On one side of the surface, all the points are outside the set. On the other side of the surface (or on the surface), all the points are in the set. The bounding surface is itself bounded by lines.

Testing whether a set of lengths is valid is equivalent to testing whether the corresponding three-tuple belongs to the valid set, which is equivalent to testing whether the three-tuple would be plotted in the valid figure.

To create a set of boundary tests for a figure like this, we find it useful to start with a bounding cube. A *bounding cube* is the smallest cube that fits around a figure of interest. In this example, the bounding cube is defined by these 12 lines:

1.	(0, 0, 0)	to	(0, 0, 30), where (0, 0, 30) means FL=0, ML=0, LL=30
2.	(0, 0, 0)	to	(0, 30, 0)
3.	(0, 0, 0)	to	(30, 0, 0)
4.	(0, 30, 0)	to	(0, 30, 30)
5.	(0, 30, 0)	to	(30, 30, 0)

6.	(0, 0, 30)	to	(0, 30, 30)
7.	(0, 0, 30)	to	(30, 0, 30)
8.	(30, 0, 0)	to	(30, 0, 30)
9.	(30, 0, 0)	to	(30, 30, 0)
10.	(30, 0, 30)	to	(30, 30, 30)
11.	(30, 30, 0)	to	(30, 30, 30)
12.	(0, 30, 30)	to	(30, 30, 30)

Some of the points on the cube will be outside the figure. Any point on the cube that adds up to **FL** + **ML** + **LL** > 68 is outside the figure. (Remember, it's 68, not 70, because of the spaces between the words).

Thus (30, 30, 30) is on the cube but outside of the figure because it adds up to 30 + 30 + 30 = 90.

On the line that goes from (30, 30, 0) to (30, 30, 30), the valid points go from (30, 30, 0) to (30, 30, 8). The nearest valid points to (30, 30, 8) are (29, 30, 8), (30, 29, 8) and (30, 30, 7), not the invalid (30, 30, 9).

A graph of all of the points that add up to 68, yields a triangle running from (8, 30, 30) to (30, 8, 30) to (30, 30, 8).

The valid figure (the graph of the set of all valid points) is the bounding cube with one corner sliced off by the triangle. Here is a picture of it.

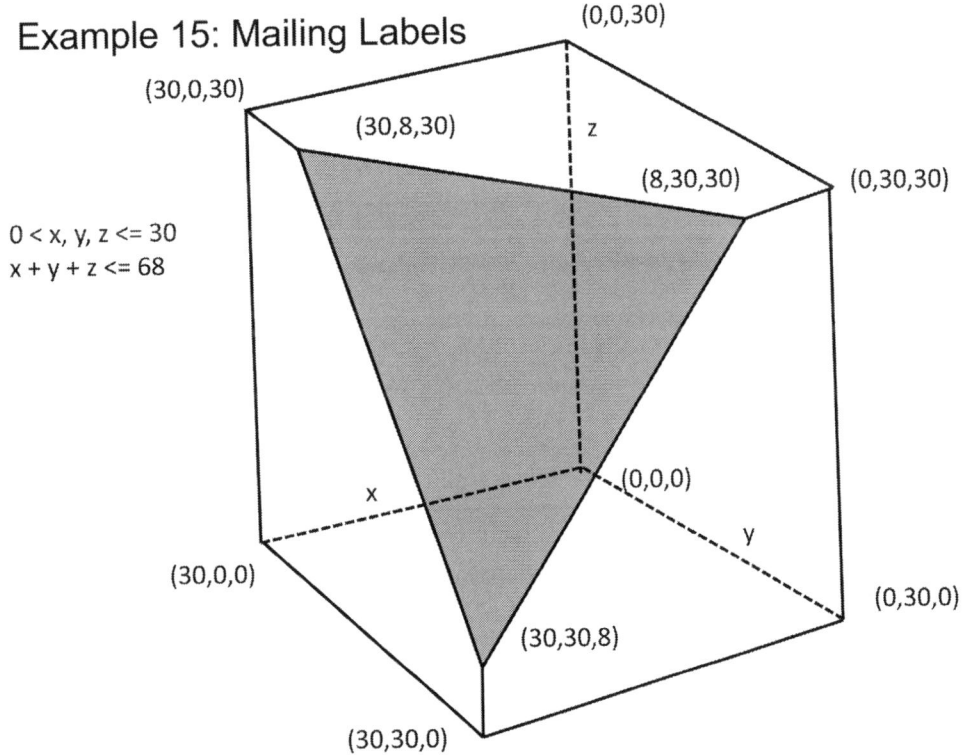

Next is a picture that emphasizes the bounding cube. (The first picture cuts off the cube to show the triangle. The second one shows the cube's extension on top of the triangle.)

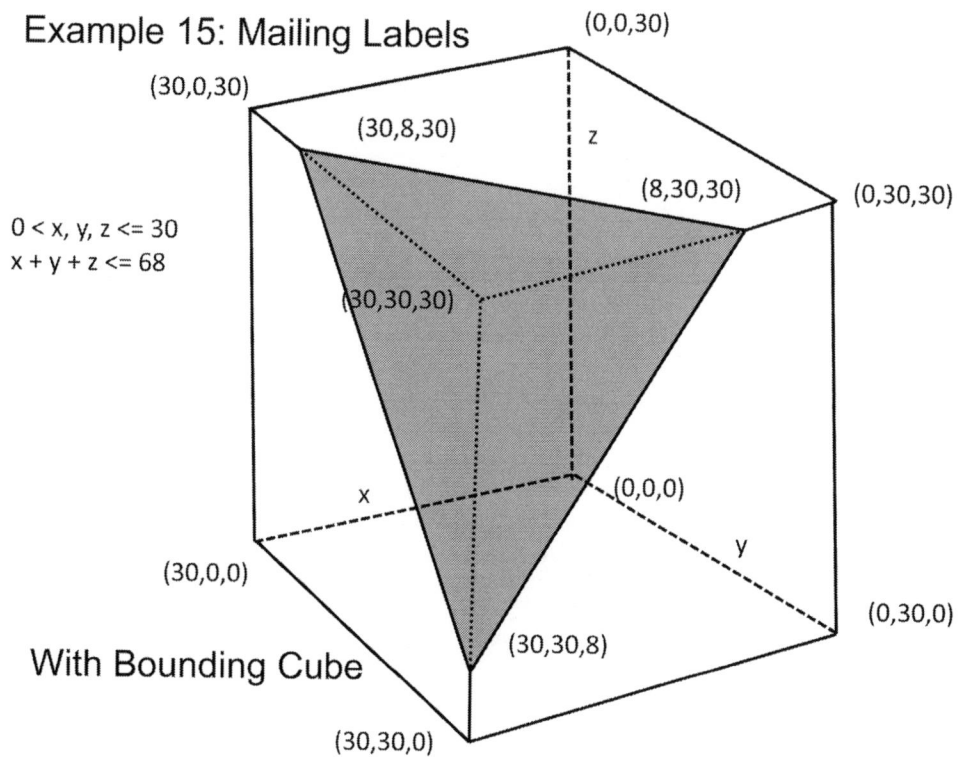

Example 15: Mailing Labels

0 < x, y, z <= 30
x + y + z <= 68

With Bounding Cube

Our final set of boundary lines is:

(1)	(0, 0, 0)	to	(0, 0, 30)
(2)	(0, 0, 0)	to	(0, 30, 0)
(3)	(0, 0, 0)	to	(30, 0, 0)
(4)	(0, 30, 0)	to	(0, 30, 30)
(5)	(0, 30, 0)	to	(30, 30, 0)
(6)	(0, 0, 30)	to	(0, 30, 30)
(7)	(0, 0, 30)	to	(30, 0, 30)
(8)	(30, 0, 0)	to	(30, 0, 30)
(9)	(30, 0, 0)	to	(30, 30, 0)
(10)	(0, 30, 30)	to	(8, 30, 30)
(11)	(30, 0, 30)	to	(30, 8, 30)
(12)	(30, 30, 0)	to	(30, 30, 8)
(13)	(30, 30, 8)	to	(8, 30, 30)
(14)	(8, 30, 30)	to	(30, 8, 30)
(15)	(30, 8, 30)	to	(30, 30, 8)

From here, the analysis is essentially the same as in *Choosing On Points and Off Points for Testing Linear Relationships* on page 311. We use the same definitions:

- *On point:* a point that is on the boundary (the bounding surface)
- *Off point:* a point that is not on the boundary
- *Inner point:* a point that is inside th (a member of the set that defines the domain)
- *Outer point:* a point that is outside the specified domain (not a member of the set that defines the domain)
- *Open boundary:* the boundary is not inside the specified range or area, For example, 1 is not inside $1 < x$
- *Closed boundary:* the boundary is inside the specified range or area. For example, 10 is inside $x \leq 10$.

The basic pattern for dealing with linear boundaries is:

- You always need an Inner point and an Outer point. One of these will be an On point; the other will be an Off point.

- If the input domain is specified as *equal to* the boundary, pick three points, one on the boundary, one on one side of it and one on the other side.

Consider the box that runs:

from $(0, 0, 0)$ to $(30, 0, 0)$
from $(30, 0, 0)$ to $(30, 30, 0)$
from $(30, 30, 0)$ to $(0, 30, 0)$
from $(0, 30, 0)$ to $(0, 0, 0)$.

All of the points on this box are on the surface of the valid-domain figure.

- Test an On point on the line from $(0, 0, 0)$ to $(30, 0, 0)$ (for example, test $(5, 0, 0)$) and test two Off points.

  - One Off point should be an Inner point that is very close to the On point—just inside the boundary. $(1, 5, 0)$ would work. (Or $(\Delta(1), 5, 0)$ if you're working with Floating-Point variables rather than Integers).

  - The other Off point should be an Outer point that is very close to the On point—just outside the boundary $(-1, 5, 0)$ would work.

- Test another On point and two Off points for another line. For example, test the line from $(30, 0, 0)$ to $(30, 30, 0)$

  - with the On point $(30, 20, 0)$
  - with the Inner Off point $(29, 20, 0)$
  - and with the Outer Off point $(31, 20, 0)$.

- Test the other two lines this way and you have boundary-tested the box.

- You can reduce the number of tests, in this case, by testing the corners $(0, 0, 0)$ as an On point for two lines.

Now extend this testing. You have tested the four sides of a two-dimensional figure, just like *Example 12: Piecewise Boundary* on page 309. Add tests for the other 11 lines and you'll have tested all the boundaries of the figure.[43]

CONSTRAINT SATISFACTION PROBLEMS

We have just completed analysis of the boundaries of a fairly simple 3-dimensional object. For example, our analysis will be more complex if we change the limits on the input names from:

$0 \leq$ **Name** ≤ 30

to

$0 \leq$ **Name** ≤ 60

while still keeping the limit:

PrintedName ≤ 70.

(We'll leave the discovery of the added issues as an exercise for the reader. ☺)

Add a few more constraints or a few more variables, and the analysis becomes *much* more complex.

Analyses like these are examples of Constraint Satisfaction Problems.

There's a good (free) introductory tutorial on this type of problem (Cork Constraint Computation Centre, 2005). They introduce the topic this way:

> "Problems often consist of choices. Making a choice that is compatible with all other choices made and optimal is difficult. Constraint Programming (CP) is the branch of Artificial Intelligence (AI), where computers help us to make these choices.
>
> "A constraint program consists of a set of variables, a set of values for each variable and a set of constraints. For example, the problem might be to fit components (values) to circuit boards (variables), subject to the constraint that no two components can be overlapping. A solution to a CP is an allocation of values to variables such that none of the constraints are violated. The goal of CP is to find one solution, all solutions or a good (optimal) solution to a problem."

They continue:

> "The formal definition of a CSP involves variables and their domains, and constraints. Suppose we have a set of variables, $X_1, X_2, ..., X_n$, all with domains $D_1, D_2, ..., D_n$ such that all variables X_i have a value in their respective domain D_i. There is also a set of constraints, $C_1, C_2, ..., C_m$, such that a constraint C_i restricts (imposes a constraint on) the possible values in the domain of some subset of the variables. A solution to a CSP is an assignment of every variable some value in its domain such that every constraint is satisfied. Therefore, each assignment (a state change or step in a search) of a value to a variable must be consistent: it must not violate any of the constraints."

What we're doing in domain testing is finding values of the x_i's that just barely violate one or more constraints or that just barely don't violate one or more constraints. We check whether the

---

43 To check your understanding, try this exercise. Consider a surface bounded by (30, 30, 8), (30, 8, 30) and (8, 30, 30). What is the shape of the surface? Is (23, 25, 20) an On point on this surface? Identify two Off points near (23, 25, 20) that are inside the valid range and two Off points outside the range. Identify two more points on this surface.

program classifies the value correctly (as a value that does or does not violate a constraint) and whether the program can successfully use a value that is at the limit but does not quite violate any constraints.

As an area of computer science, the systematic study of constraint satisfaction problems is still emerging. Many people consider the area quite difficult. (It will get easier as people come to understand it better and then figure out how to teach it better.)

Another starting point, if you want to follow up on this, is Wikipedia's article, "Constraint satisfaction problem".

WHY SHOULD **YOU** CARE ABOUT GEOMETRIC BOUNDARY PROBLEMS?

The problems most often discussed in testing textbooks that involve several variables and relatively simple-to-describe linear relationships (often cause-and-effect relationships) usually involve some type of scoring (assigning values to variables) and decision-making.

For example, we use programs to make decisions about whether to give someone a scholarship or a raise, how long to send someone to jail, how many frequent flyer miles to award for a trip, whether someone is qualified to receive a discount or a rebate, whether to sell them an insurance policy (with what coverage and at what price), whether an unfortunate event is covered by the insurance policy (and how much to pay them) and whether a school's lunches meet nutritional standards.

Here's an example that might feel a little less mathematical (or a little less theoretical). Suppose you're testing World of Warcraft. One character punches another in the face. Did the punch connect?

- The fist is a 3-dimensional object. It has a surface (an outer boundary). It moves in time (a 4th dimension).

- The face is a 3-dimensional object with a surface and it moves in time.

If the 4-dimensional boundary of the fist crosses the boundary of the face (right place, right time), the character gets whacked.

We aren't experts in this area of computing or in this type of testing. Our understanding is that the collision detection problem in games is a constraint satisfaction problem, that it's quite challenging to find and test the relevant boundaries and that people often simplify the testing (as testers and as programmers telling their code how to decide whether the character got whacked or not). They simplify it by working with a simpler enclosing cube or sphere (or even a bounding plane) to represent the fist (car, pinball, bird) and checking whether any points on the boundary of *that* simplified object overlapped with the bounding cube or sphere that approximates the location of the face (other car, pinball flipper, tree branch). For some additional introductions and tutorials, *see* Baker (2012a, 2012b), Cristopoulos (2012) and Jaegers (2012).

WHAT SHOULD YOU DO WITH PROBLEMS LIKE THIS?

If you see a problem that is expressed as a set of linear inequalities or that you can rewrite as a set of linear inequalities, you can follow the approach that we've been showing in Example 12 and this one.

In real-life practice, the problem won't be laid out as neatly as we do it in the book. Here are some suggestions:

- Try to identify all the variables that are involved in the problem (all the variables you're going to test together).

- For each variable, figure out its lower and upper limits.

- For each variable, look for other variables that constrain it. We discuss types of constraints in *Chapter P. Analyze Non-Independent Variables. Deal with Relationships and Constraints* on page 201. We're especially interested in limiting constraints—one variable limits the values of another.

  ○ For example, if you know that $x + y = 5$, then knowing x tells you y. If you know that $x + y < 5$, knowing x tells you a firm limit on the maximum value of y. You can draw this type of inequality on a graph as a line.

    ▪ Information like this might not be expressed in a tidy equation. Instead, you might know that *this* is bigger than *that*. Or you might know the program will do something if *this* is bigger than *that* or bigger than *that* by *this much*.

  ○ The constraint relationship might involve more variables than 2. For example, the equation, $x + y + z = 5$ shows up on a graph as a plane (a 2-dimensional figure) rather than a line.

- Once you have a list of variables, figure out how to represent all of them together as an n-tuple (x, y, z, a, b, c). If you prefer, do this in a table, one column per variable (one row per test)

- Create a simple, symmetrical bounding object. If there are two dimensions, it is a bounding square. If there are three dimensions, it is a bounding cube. In n dimensions, it is a hypercube (https://en.wikipedia.org/wiki/Hypercube). The corners of this object will be the extreme points of each variable. For example, suppose:

  ○ The minimum values of x, y, z, a, b and c are 1, 2, 3, -1, -2 and -3.

  ○ The maximum values of x, y, z, a, b and c are 3, 12, 14, 6, 8 and 1.

  Three of the corners of the 6-dimensional hypercube are (1, 2, 3, -1, -2, -3), (3, 12, 14, 6, 8, 1) and (1, 2, 3, 6, 8, 1).

- The constraint relationships will tell you that some of these corners are outside the set of valid values. For example, if you know that $x + y \leq 13$, then you know that:

  ○ If $x = 3$, then y must be ≤ 10 and so the point (3, 12, 14, 6, 8, 1) is outside of valid domain as is every other point that contains (3, 12, z, a, b, c) for every value of z, a, b and c.

  ○ You can use $x + y \leq 13$ to establish a new boundary (like side of the triangle in the mailing label program). That boundary is along the line $x + y = 13$. You might work with end points of that boundary ($x = 1$, $y = 12$) and ($x = 3$, $y = 10$).

  ○ The more we feel uncertain about whether $x + y = 13$ is a true boundary of the object, the more likely we are to generate random values and test with those. For example, we could randomly generate a value for x that is between 1 and 3 (within its limits). Then we would set $y = 13\text{-}x$. Then we would test with the same value for x but with $y + \Delta$ and $y - \Delta$, and with the same value for y, but with $x + \Delta$ and $x - \Delta$.

- The same idea applies if you have a constraint that involves more variables, such as $x + y + z + a = 22$.

  ○ Generate random values for x, y and z that are within their limits and then set:

    $A = 22 - x - y - z.$

> **A** is an On point. (At least, it is On your bounding surface for the problem, which might not be a perfectly accurate representation of the valid-domain under test.)

- ○ Generate Off-point tests by adding or subtracting Δ to each variable in turn (one at a time).

- ○ If you're not confident that $X + Y + Z + A = 22$ is a perfectly accurate edge of the domain under test, add more random tests (On points and Off points near the edge).

- ○ In each case, look at how the program responds to it. For example, if a bounding surface is the edge of the character's fist, (a) *Should* the fist hit the jaw? and (b) *Does* the fist hit the jaw? Watch the play (probably in slow motion). Every time the program responds differently than your bounding-surface model says it should do, you're either seeing a bug or an opportunity to improve the model. Find out what the program should do (ask someone, if you have to). Then add new variables or new constraints or tighten the ones you have.

This process is iterative and imprecise. You start with incomplete information, use it to approximate a boundary, and run tests as if your boundary was correct. Refine your boundary (and thus your tests) until you're satisfied that your approximation is good enough.

If we were actually testing games or testing other systems that required a lot of constraint satisfaction analysis involving several variables, we would do more reading on constraint satisfaction and collision detection, possibly take some courses and look for tools. This is a rapidly evolving area. The writings, courses and tools available tomorrow will be more capable and easier to understand than those available yesterday.

We would probably look closely at materials and tools on game design / development, even if our problem was not part of a game, because those materials and tools will often be presented at a more practical, less computer-science-theoretical level. Of course, if you already know a lot about artificial intelligence and computer graphics, you might not need a gentle introduction to this work.

P. ANALYZE NON-INDEPENDENT VARIABLES. DEAL WITH RELATIONSHIPS AND CONSTRAINTS

This analysis was covered in the preceding Task.

Q. IDENTIFY AND LIST UNANALYZED VARIABLES. GATHER INFORMATION FOR LATER ANALYSIS

Is every mailing label 70 characters wide? Even the narrow ones and the wide ones?

R. IMAGINE AND DOCUMENT RISKS THAT DON'T NECESSARILY MAP TO AN OBVIOUS DIMENSION

What happens if the program prints in a proportional-width font instead of a fixed-width font?

What happens if the program abbreviates names that are too long? For example, the program might reduce John Quincy Adams to John Q. Adams.

EXAMPLE 16: UNEMPLOYMENT INSURANCE BENEFITS

In the state of Domainia, every unemployed adult receives a benefit of 350. If that person has worked and is older than 40, the benefit is raised by 100. Alternatively (else), if the person has exactly 4 children, the benefit is raised by 50 (van Veenendaal & Seubers, 2002, p. 231).

A. IDENTIFY THE POTENTIALLY INTERESTING VARIABLES

This Example refers to an individual's employment record. We only see fragments of the record here. Obviously, the person has a name, probably an insurance number.

The function computes `BenefitAmount`.

The input fields identified as relevant to the calculation of `BenefitAmount` are:

- `Employed`: Whether the person is employed (Y / N)
- `HasWorked`: Whether the person has worked (Y / N)
- `Age`
- `NumberOfChildren`

B. IDENTIFY THE VARIABLES YOU CAN ANALYZE NOW. THESE ARE THE VARIABLES OF INTEREST

- `Employed`
- `HasWorked`
- `Age`
- `NumberOfChildren`
- `BenefitAmount`

C. DETERMINE THE PRIMARY DIMENSION OF THE VARIABLE OF INTEREST

Any of these could be analyzed as the variable of interest. The names we've picked for the variables name their primary dimensions.

D. DETERMINE THE TYPE AND SCALE OF THE VARIABLE'S PRIMARY DIMENSION AND WHAT VALUES IT CAN TAKE

- `Employed` (Boolean :Y / N)
- `HasWorked` (Boolean: Y/N)
- `Age` (probably Integer, in years, probably 0 to 3 digits)
- `NumberOfChildren` (Integer, probably 0 to 2 digits)
- `BenefitAmount` (Integer, but only three possible amounts: 350, 400, 450)

E. DETERMINE WHETHER YOU CAN ORDER THE VARIABLE'S VALUES (FROM SMALLEST TO LARGEST)

Yes (except for the Booleans).

F. DETERMINE WHETHER THIS IS AN INPUT VARIABLE OR A RESULT

- `Employed`, `HasWorked`, `Age` and `NumberOfChildren` are probably input variables.
- `BenefitAmount` is a result.

G. DETERMINE HOW THE PROGRAM USES THIS VARIABLE

It uses the input variables to calculate the unemployment benefit amount.

H. DETERMINE WHETHER OTHER VARIABLES ARE RELATED TO THIS ONE

The relationships have already been stated.

I. PARTITION THE VARIABLE (ITS PRIMARY DIMENSION)

- **HasWorked** and **Employed**

  The two values are Yes and No (has worked, has not worked). Normally we would not consider these for a domain analysis, but the variable is important for analysis of **BenefitAmount**. There is no partitioning for a Boolean. You must test both values.

- **Age**

< 0	too small
0 - 40	benefit will be 350 or 400
40 - **MAXAGE**	**MAXAGE** is unspecified so name a constant to hold the value
> **MAXAGE**	too big

- **NumberOfChildren**

< 0	too small
0 - 3	no benefit impact
4	if the person is younger than 40, raise benefit to 400
5 to **MAXCHILDREN**	
> **MAXCHILDREN**	too big

- **BenefitAmount**

0, 350, 400, 450	the only valid values

J. LAY OUT THE ANALYSIS IN A CLASSICAL BOUNDARY/EQUIVALENCE TABLE. IDENTIFY BEST REPRESENTATIVES

Variable	Valid case equivalence class	Invalid case equivalence class	Boundaries and special cases	Notes
Age	0 ≤ Age < 40		0	
			MINAGE − 1	What about the person who worked only when they were underage? Or who worked but is not yet an adult?
			MINAGE	Age of adulthood
			40	
	41 ≤ Age ≤ MAXAGE		41	
			MAXAGE	
			MAXAGE + 1	What IS MAXAGE? What if someone lives past that age?
NumberOf-Children	0 ≤ children < 4		-1	

Variable	Valid case equivalence class	Invalid case equivalence class	Boundaries and special cases	Notes
			0	
			1	
			3	
	4 children		4	
	4 < children ≤ **MAXCHILDREN**		5	
			MAXCHILDREN	
			MAXCHILDREN + 1	
Benefit-Amount	0			employed or non-adult
	350			**Age** < 40 and children ≠ 4
	400			**Age** < 40 and children = 4
	450			40 ≤ **Age**

The tests use the values in the "Boundaries and special cases" column.

K. CREATE TESTS FOR THE CONSEQUENCES OF THE DATA ENTERED, NOT JUST THE INPUT FILTER

The primary consequence that we can see in the description is that the person will (or won't) get a benefit check.

Here is a table of conditions for generating the values of **BenefitAmount**. Creating the tests from this will be straightforward use of the boundary cases.

BenefitAmount	Employed	HasWorked	Age	NumberOf Children	Notes
0	Yes	any value	any value	any value	
	No	Yes	< **MINAGE**	< 4	
				4	
				> 4	
350	No	No	≥ **MINAGE** and ≤ 40	< 4	
				> 4	
		No	> 40	< 4	
				> 4	
		Yes	≥ **MINAGE** and ≤ 40	< 4	
				> 4	
400	No	No	≥ **MINAGE** and ≤ 40	4	
			> 40	4	
		Yes	≥ **MINAGE** and ≤ 40	4	
450	No	Yes	> 40	< 4	
				4	
				> 4	

L. IDENTIFY SECONDARY DIMENSIONS. ANALYZE THEM IN THE CLASSICAL WAY

There's nothing special about these variables. For generic treatment of Integers, see *Test Idea Catalog for Integers* on page 231.

M. SUMMARIZE YOUR ANALYSIS WITH A RISK/EQUIVALENCE TABLE

The analysis of the Integer variables will look like the *Generic Risk/Equivalence Table for Integers* on page 233.

The other main risks involve the relationships among the variables (miscalculation of the `BenefitAmount`.) Those are tested from the table in Task K, above.

N. ANALYZE INDEPENDENT VARIABLES THAT SHOULD BE TESTED TOGETHER

See Task K, above.

O. ANALYZE VARIABLES THAT HOLD RESULTS

`BenefitAmount` is analyzed in Task K.

P. ANALYZE NON-INDEPENDENT VARIABLES. DEAL WITH RELATIONSHIPS AND CONSTRAINTS

Much of this Task is dealt with already in Tasks J and K. However, we would design tests for some additional questions:

- What does "employed" mean? Is there a criterion number of hours or amount of pay that divides employed from unemployed? Is it the same for all of the interactions with the other variables?

- Can someone be employed even if they aren't adult? If so:

  ○ Suppose a person who is under age works and loses their job, while still under age. Are they eligible for unemployment benefits? (Apparently not, from the rules in the description, but is that a bug in the description or an intended result?)

  ○ Suppose a person who is unemployed and under age has 4 children. (Imagine a country with the age of adulthood at 21 and the situation of a 20-year old who either has 4 natural children or who has taken over the care of 3 young siblings after the parents died or abandoned the children.) Is the benefit 400 or nothing? (Or something else?) What should it be?

- Under what circumstances will the software accept someone as having previously worked?

  ○ Suppose a person works pre-adult and never works again. (For example, imagine being permanently disabled on your first job.) Will this count as having been employed for the 450 benefit?

  ○ Suppose someone worked in another country, but never in Domainia. Have they worked previously or not?

  ○ Suppose someone worked full-time but at a job that paid them nothing or less than minimum wage. (Salespeople who are paid on a pure commission basis can have this problem. So can people who provide products or services on a piecework basis (for example a testing company that pays testers by the bug.) While they're doing this, are they employed? After they abandon this job, can this experience be classified as having worked?

- How should we count children?
    - Do foster children count? If someone has three natural children and a foster child, is that 4 (therefore a 400 benefit) or 3 (350 benefit)?
    - If the children are emancipated (no longer dependent on the parents), do they count among the 4 (for a 400 benefit)?
    - If the children aren't emancipated but they're adults (the 35-year old unemployed son living at home) do they count among the 4 children or not?
    - Do deceased children count?

Q. IDENTIFY AND LIST UNANALYZED VARIABLES. GATHER INFORMATION FOR LATER ANALYSIS

This Task goes beyond what we're trying to teach with this example.

R. IMAGINE AND DOCUMENT RISKS THAT DON'T NECESSARILY MAP TO AN OBVIOUS DIMENSION

See the notes in Tasks J, K and P.

EXAMPLE 17: JOAN'S PAY

Joan works at a store, under the following contract:

- Her normal pay rate is $8 per hour.
- For hours worked beyond 40 hours per week, her normal rate is $12 per hour.
- For work between midnight and 6 a.m. on any day, she gets $16 per hour.
- For work between 6 a.m. and noon on Sunday, she gets $16 per hour.
- If she earns $500 or less in a week, 10% of her pay is deducted for taxes. If she earns more than $500, the tax deducted is $50 plus 20% of earnings greater than $500 that week. (So, if she earns $600, the tax deducted is $70.)

Do a domain analysis of her take-home pay.

A. IDENTIFY THE POTENTIALLY INTERESTING VARIABLES

- `HoursWorked`   Total hours worked
- `HoursNight`   Total hours worked between midnight and 6 a.m.
- `HoursSunday`   Total hours worked 6 a.m. to noon Sunday
- `GrossPay`   Total pay before taxes deducted
- `TaxDeducted`   Total amount of taxes deducted
- `TakeHomePay`   Net pay (after taxes deducted)

The rates of pay and the time bounds appear to be constant.

B. IDENTIFY THE VARIABLES YOU CAN ANALYZE NOW. THESE ARE THE VARIABLES OF INTEREST

The problem description doesn't identify what data the user inputs to the program, so you don't actually know what variables you have available to work with. We're going to trust that we can map the input variables to these notional variables:

- `HoursWorked`
- `HoursNight`
- `HoursSunday`

From those, we can compute the result variables:

- `GrossPay`
- `TaxDeducted`
- `TakeHomePay`

C. DETERMINE THE PRIMARY DIMENSION OF THE VARIABLE OF INTEREST

The primary dimension of all the hours-worked variables is time.

The primary dimension of the result variables is money.

D. DETERMINE THE TYPE AND SCALE OF THE VARIABLE'S PRIMARY DIMENSION AND WHAT VALUES IT CAN TAKE

The problem description provides little guidance on this:

- The time variables could be Integers (whole hours worked) or they could include partial hours. For this analysis, we will assume that times are rounded to the nearest hour.

- We will treat the money variables as Fixed-Point (dollars and cents) rather than Integers (dollars).

E. DETERMINE WHETHER YOU CAN ORDER THE VARIABLE'S VALUES (FROM SMALLEST TO LARGEST)

Yes.

F. DETERMINE WHETHER THIS IS AN INPUT VARIABLE OR A RESULT

The time variables are inputs. The money variables are results.

G. DETERMINE HOW THE PROGRAM USES THIS VARIABLE

The obvious use of these variables in the problem description is to determine Joan's pay. In practice, these data would be used for many other purposes, such as providing information for assessment of her performance on the job.

H. DETERMINE WHETHER OTHER VARIABLES ARE RELATED TO THIS ONE

There are several obvious relationships:

- Hours worked at regular pay =

    40 or

    `HoursWorked - HoursNight - HoursSunday`,

    whichever is smaller.

- Overtime hours ($12 hours) =

    0 or

    `HoursWorked - 40 - HoursNight - HoursSunday`,

    whichever is greater.

We haven't identified "hours worked at regular pay" and "overtime hours" as variables. They might not be variables. That is, there might not be any variable designated in the program to hold these values. However, the program will probably calculate these values. These are examples of *intermediate variables*—they're like result variables except the program keeps their values only long enough to use them.

- `GrossPay` =

	8 * hours worked at regular pay
+	12 * overtime hours
+	16 * `HoursNight`
+	16 * `HoursSunday`

- `TaxDeducted` =

    0.10 * `GrossPay`, if `GrossPay` ≤ $500 or

    $50 + 0.20 * `GrossPay`, if `GrossPay` > $500

- `TakeHomePay` = `GrossPay` - `TaxDeducted`

I. PARTITION THE VARIABLE (ITS PRIMARY DIMENSION)

Each of these dimensions is ordered, so determine the sub-ranges and transition points.

The basic partitioning of the variables is straightforward. Here are the valid ranges. Values below are too small, values above are too big (and therefore get tested in the invalid-value partitions):

- `HoursWorked` can run from 0 to 168 $(168 = 7 * 24)$
- `HoursNight` can run from 0 to 42
- `HoursSunday` can run from 0 to 6
- Hours worked at regular pay can run from 0 to 40
- Hours worked overtime ($12) can run from 0 to 80 $(80 = 168\text{-}42\text{-}40\text{-}6)$
- Hours worked overtime must be 0 until regular pay hours reaches 40.
- `GrossPay` can run from 0 to 2048
- `TaxDeducted` can run from 0 to 359.60 $(359.6 = 50 + 0.2 * 1548)$
- `TakeHomePay` can run from 0 to 1688.40

J. LAY OUT THE ANALYSIS IN A CLASSICAL BOUNDARY/EQUIVALENCE TABLE. IDENTIFY BEST REPRESENTATIVES

In this part, focus on the input variables. The interesting variables in this problem are the result variables and we'll get to them, but first test the input variables individually. Once you confirm that invalid inputs are impossible (by testing them), you don't have to create combination tests with impossible values.

Variable	Valid case equivalence class	Invalid case equivalence class	Boundaries and special cases	Notes
`HoursWorked`	0 to 168		0	
			168	
		< 0	-1	
		> 168	169	
`HoursNight`	0 to 42		0	
			42	
		< 0	-1	
		> 42	43	
`HoursSunday`	0 to 6		0	
			6	
		< 0	-1	
		> 6	7	

The tests use the values in the "Boundaries and special cases" column.

K. CREATE TESTS FOR THE CONSEQUENCES OF THE DATA ENTERED, NOT JUST THE INPUT FILTER

What does the program (and the rest of the company's Human Resources systems) *do* with these variables? Probably many things and, if you were testing a real program, you'd be able to find them out. However, the problem description only mentions the transformations of the inputs to the result variables (how much Joan gets paid).

Task O will focus on those variables.

L. IDENTIFY SECONDARY DIMENSIONS. ANALYZE THEM IN THE CLASSICAL WAY

The input variables are Integers. See the *Test Idea Catalog for Integers* on page 231.

M. SUMMARIZE YOUR ANALYSIS WITH A RISK/EQUIVALENCE TABLE

See the *Generic Risk/Equivalence Table for Integers* on page 233.

N. ANALYZE INDEPENDENT VARIABLES THAT SHOULD BE TESTED TOGETHER

`HoursNight` and `HoursSunday` are independent. `HoursWorked` is a total of `HoursNight`, `HoursSunday`, regular hours and overtime hours.

In this example, we have assumed that regular and overtime hours aren't input directly but are calculated from the value of `HoursWorked`.

That calculation of regular and overtime hours should be tested. For purposes of this example, suppose that it has been tested elsewhere and it works. Therefore, invalid relationships between regular and overtime hours are impossible. In particular, overtime can't accumulate until regular hours are 40.

O. ANALYZE VARIABLES THAT HOLD RESULTS

`GrossPay`, `TaxDeducted`, hours worked at regular pay and hours worked overtime are all result variables. Because `TaxDeducted` and `TakeHomePay` are easily computed from `GrossPay`, this analysis will focus on `GrossPay`.

`GrossPay` depends on the values of:

- `HoursNight`
- `HoursSunday`
- regular hours and overtime hours, which are derived from `HoursWorked`.

Because the pay rates for nights ($16), Sundays ($16), regular time ($8) and overtime ($12) are different, the selection of tests of `GrossPay` is most readily shown in terms of these four variables. This table checks the valid combinations of boundary values:

Variable: Gross Pay	Night Hours	Sunday Hours	Regular Hours	Overtime Hours	Notes
0	0	0	0	0	
320	0	0	40	0	
1280	0	0	40	80	
96	0	6	0	0	
416	0	6	40	0	
1376	0	6	40	80	
672	42	0	0	0	
992	42	0	40	0	

Variable: Gross Pay	Night Hours	Sunday Hours	Regular Hours	Overtime Hours	Notes
1952	42	0	40	80	
768	42	6	0	0	
1088	42	6	40	0	
2048	42	6	40	80	

Note that no tests with 0 regular hours and 80 overtime hours are in the table. That's because it is impossible to have overtime hours if there are fewer than 40 regular hours.

P. ANALYZE NON-INDEPENDENT VARIABLES. DEAL WITH RELATIONSHIPS AND CONSTRAINTS

This Task goes beyond what we're trying to teach with this example.

Q. IDENTIFY AND LIST UNANALYZED VARIABLES. GATHER INFORMATION FOR LATER ANALYSIS

This Task goes beyond what we're trying to teach with this example.

R. IMAGINE AND DOCUMENT RISKS THAT DON'T NECESSARILY MAP TO AN OBVIOUS DIMENSION

- The variables are probably more tightly restricted than the values listed in this analysis. For example, it is unlikely the company will allow the worker to work (or bill) for all 168 hours in a week. Is there a company policy? Is it possible to violate the policy? How should the software deal with that?

- It is common to see minimum-duration shifts. For example, if a person comes to work at all, the company might pay them for 3 hours because of policy, contract or regulation. How will this affect the boundaries?

EXAMPLE 18: VOLUME DISCOUNTS

Consider the following pricing system:

- For the first 10 units, the price is $5.
- For the next 10 units (11 to 20), the price is $4.75.
- For the next 10 units (21 to 30), the price is $4.50.
- For more than 30 units, the price is $4.00.

Do a domain analysis that partitions according to the number of units purchased or according to the `Total-PricePaid` (Desikan & Ramesh, 2006).

A. IDENTIFY THE POTENTIALLY INTERESTING VARIABLES

- `NumberOfUnits`
- `TotalPricePaid`

B. IDENTIFY THE VARIABLES YOU CAN ANALYZE NOW. THESE ARE THE VARIABLES OF INTEREST

- `NumberOfUnits`
- `TotalPricePaid`

C. DETERMINE THE PRIMARY DIMENSION OF THE VARIABLE OF INTEREST

- `NumberOfUnits`: How many units are sold.
- `TotalPricePaid`: How much someone paid for the units.

D. DETERMINE THE TYPE AND SCALE OF THE VARIABLE'S PRIMARY DIMENSION AND WHAT VALUES IT CAN TAKE

- `NumberOfUnits`: Integers from 0 to an arbitrarily large number.
- `TotalPricePaid`: Fixed-Point (dollars and cents) from 0 to an arbitrarily large number.

E. DETERMINE WHETHER YOU CAN ORDER THE VARIABLE'S VALUES (FROM SMALLEST TO LARGEST)

Yes.

F. DETERMINE WHETHER THIS IS AN INPUT VARIABLE OR A RESULT

- `NumberOfUnits`: Input variable.
- `TotalPricePaid`: Result variable.

G. DETERMINE HOW THE PROGRAM USES THIS VARIABLE

The program uses `NumberOfUnits` sold to determine the `TotalPricePaid`. The problem description gives no information about how else the program uses number of units or how it uses the amount paid.

H. DETERMINE WHETHER OTHER VARIABLES ARE RELATED TO THIS ONE

The problem description doesn't provide information about any other variables. See Task Q below.

I. PARTITION THE VARIABLE (ITS PRIMARY DIMENSION)

We'll partition the input variable here and the result variable later. The dimension is ordered, so determine the sub-ranges and transition points. The problem description identifies 4 internal boundaries:

- For the first 10 units, the price is $5.
- For the next 10 units (11 to 20), the price is $4.75.
- For the next 10 units (21 to 30), the price is $4.50.
- For more than 30 units, the price is $4.00.

There must be a value that is too big, but the problem description doesn't specify it. Call that maximum value **MAXUNITS**. This might be an arbitrarily large value or it might vary day to day. Without further information, start by representing it as a constant.

Thus the partitions we see are:

< 0	too small
0 - 10	$5
11 - 20	$4.75
21 - 30	$4.50
31 - **MAXUNITS**	$4.00
> **MAXUNITS**	too big

J. LAY OUT THE ANALYSIS IN A CLASSICAL BOUNDARY/EQUIVALENCE TABLE. IDENTIFY BEST REPRESENTATIVES

Variable	Valid case equivalence class	Invalid case equivalence class	Boundaries and special cases	Notes
NumberOf Units	0 - 10		0	
			10	
	11 - 20		11	
			20	
	21 - 30		21	
			30	
	31 - **MAXUNITS**		31	
			MAXUNITS	
		< 0	-1	
		> **MAXUNITS**	**MAXUNITS + 1**	

K. CREATE TESTS FOR THE CONSEQUENCES OF THE DATA ENTERED, NOT JUST THE INPUT FILTER

Beyond setting the result variable, the problem description doesn't hint at any consequences.

L. IDENTIFY SECONDARY DIMENSIONS. ANALYZE THEM IN THE CLASSICAL WAY

- The input variable is an Integer. See the *Test Idea Catalog for Integers* on page 231.

- The output variable is Fixed-Point. See the *Test Idea Catalog for Fixed-Point Variables* on page 249.

M. ANALYZE INDEPENDENT VARIABLES THAT SHOULD BE TESTED TOGETHER

The problem description identifies only two variables. One is a result of the other. There are no identified variables to test with these.

N. SUMMARIZE YOUR ANALYSIS WITH A RISK/EQUIVALENCE TABLE

See the *Generic Risk/Equivalence Table for Integers* on page 233 and the *Generic Risk/Equivalence Table for Fixed-Point Variables* on page 251.

O. ANALYZE VARIABLES THAT HOLD RESULTS

`TotalPricePaid` is the result variable.

This table shows the relationship between `NumberOfUnits` and `TotalPricePaid`.

NumberOfUnits	TotalPricePaid	Notes
0 - 10	$5 \times$ `NumberOfUnits`	
11 - 20	$50 + 4.75 \times ($`NumberOfUnits`$- 10)$	
21 - 30	$97.50 + 4.50 \times ($`NumberOfUnits`$- 20)$	
31 - `MAXUNITS`	$142.50 + 4.00 \times ($`NumberOfUnits`$- 30)$	

And from that, you can create the classical table (as modified to show that the variable under test is a result variable)

TotalPricePaid	Valid case equivalence class	Invalid case equivalence class	Associated values of NumberOfUnits	Boundaries and special cases: (NumberOfUnits, TotalPricePaid)	Notes
	0 - 50.00		0 - 10	(0, 0.00)	
				(10, 50.00)	
	54.75 - 97.50		11 - 20	(11, 54.75)	
				(20, 97.50)	
	102.00 - 142.50		21 - 30	(21, 102.00)	
				(30, 142.50)	
	$146.5 - (142.5 + 4 \times ($`MAXUNITS`$- 30))$		31 - `MAXUNITS`	(31, 146.50)	
				(`MAXUNITS`, $142.5 + 4 \times ($`MAXUNITS`$- 30))$	
		< 0			Should be eliminated by single-variable testing on `NumberOfUnits`
		value associated with sales > `MAXUNITS`			Should be eliminated by single-variable testing on `NumberOfUnits`

P. ANALYZE NON-INDEPENDENT VARIABLES. DEAL WITH RELATIONSHIPS AND CONSTRAINTS

No other variables or relationships have been identified beyond the relationship between `NumberOfUnits` and `TotalPricePaid`.

Q. IDENTIFY AND LIST UNANALYZED VARIABLES. GATHER INFORMATION FOR LATER ANALYSIS

- Customer information (who bought all this stuff)
- Information about other sales made at the same time / same day / same month
- Inventory of the units offered for sale (can't sell a million if you have only 100)
- Availability to order additional units (you can sell a million if you have only 100 if you can order another million for immediate delivery for resale). How many units are available for immediate delivery?
- Lots of other variables associated with sales, such as who sold it, whether they're on commission, how much profit there is for these items, terms of the sale (cash, purchase order, etc.).

R. IMAGINE AND DOCUMENT RISKS THAT DON'T NECESSARILY MAP TO AN   SION

This Task goes beyond what we're trying to teach with this example.

EXAMPLE 19: SUM OF SQUARES

$$SS = x_1^2 + x_2^2 + \dots + x_n^2$$

(**SS** is the sum of squared values of the **n** variables, x_1 through x_n.)

The x_i's are all Floating Point (Single Precision).

A. IDENTIFY THE POTENTIALLY INTERESTING VARIABLES

- $x_1, x_2, \dots, x_n$
- SS

B. IDENTIFY THE VARIABLES YOU CAN ANALYZE NOW. THESE ARE THE VARIABLES OF INTEREST

- $x_1, x_2, \dots, x_n$
- SS

C. DETERMINE THE PRIMARY DIMENSION OF THE VARIABLE OF INTEREST

The "primary dimension" describes the purpose of the variable, but the problem description doesn't give any hint of what these variables are *for*.

D. DETERMINE THE TYPE AND SCALE OF THE VARIABLE'S PRIMARY DIMENSION AND WHAT VALUES IT CAN TAKE

The variables are Single-Precision Floating Point. For more on the characteristics of Floating-Point numbers, see *Floating Point* on page 72.

E. DETERMINE WHETHER YOU CAN ORDER THE VARIABLE'S VALUES (FROM SMALLEST TO LARGEST)

Yes.

F. DETERMINE WHETHER THIS IS AN INPUT VARIABLE OR A RESULT

The x_i's are probably input variables and will be treated as inputs in this example. **SS** is a result variable.

G. DETERMINE HOW THE PROGRAM USES THIS VARIABLE

This Task goes beyond what we're trying to teach with this example.

H. DETERMINE WHETHER OTHER VARIABLES ARE RELATED TO THIS ONE

The x_i's constrain each other because the sum of the squares of all of them can't exceed **MAXFLOAT**. So, if $x_1 = \sqrt{\text{MAXFLOAT}}$, then all of the other x_i's must be 0.

The problem description doesn't say whether the typical x_i would be large or small or how many x_i there are likely to be. Thus we don't know whether **MAXFLOAT** is a difficult constraint or a trivially easy one to meet.

I. PARTITION THE VARIABLE (ITS PRIMARY DIMENSION)

The ranges for the x_i's are:

- *Too small*: less than $-\sqrt{\text{MAXFLOAT}}$
- *Acceptable*: $-\sqrt{\text{MAXFLOAT}}$ to $\sqrt{\text{MAXFLOAT}}$
- *Too large*: greater than $\sqrt{\text{MAXFLOAT}}$

The ranges for **ss** are:

- *Too small*: less than 0 (But this is impossible—squared values can't be negative)
- *Acceptable*: 0 through **MAXFLOAT**
- *Too large*: greater than **MAXFLOAT**

where

- **MAXFLOAT** is the largest Floating-Point value that can be stored by the software under test.
- **MAXFLOAT** $+ \Delta$ is the smallest number bigger than **MAXFLOAT**.

J. LAY OUT THE ANALYSIS IN A CLASSICAL BOUNDARY/EQUIVALENCE TABLE. IDENTIFY BEST REPRESENTATIVES

For individual variables,

Variable	Valid case equivalence class	Invalid case equivalence class	Boundaries and special cases	Notes
x_i	$-\sqrt{\text{MAXFLOAT}}$ to $\sqrt{\text{MAXFLOAT}}$		$-\sqrt{\text{MAXFLOAT}}$	
			$\sqrt{\text{MAXFLOAT}}$	Could the sum of the squared x's cause an overflow?
			0	we always test with 0
		$> \sqrt{\text{MAXFLOAT}}$	$1 + \sqrt{\text{MAXFLOAT}}$	overflows x_i^2

The tests use the values in the "Boundaries and special cases" column.

For x_i's tested together, see Task P.

K. CREATE TESTS FOR THE CONSEQUENCES OF THE DATA ENTERED, NOT JUST THE INPUT FILTER

This Task goes beyond what we're trying to teach with this example.

L. IDENTIFY SECONDARY DIMENSIONS. ANALYZE THEM IN THE CLASSICAL WAY

The usual secondary dimensions that apply to most (or all) Floating-Point variables apply to the x_i's as well. See *Test Idea Catalog for Fixed-Point Variables* on page 249.

A number with more than 7 significant digits (http://en.wikipedia.org/wiki/Significant_figures) is readily converted to a Floating-Point number with 7 digits (round the least significant digits). However, you might be able to overflow an input buffer that stores such a number before it is interpreted as a Float and converted by the program (Jorgensen, 2003; Whittaker & Jorgensen, 2000; Whittaker, 2003).

Variable	Valid case equivalence class	Invalid case equivalence class	Boundaries and special cases	Notes
x_i	1 - 7 digits		8388607	biggest value of the significand
		too many	99999999	8 digits. Must be rounded
			$=$ **MAXFLOAT**	39 digits
			$>$ **MAXFLOAT**	39 digits, but the first one is greater than 3
		way too many: $>$ **MAXFLOAT**	127 digits	common buffer maximum. 127, 128, 255, 256 are interesting cases (but maybe not invalid) no matter what value in **MAXNAME**
			128 digits	
			255 digits	common buffer maximum
			256 digits	2^8 (8-bit word + 1) boundary
			65536 digits	2^{16}
			16777216 digits	2^{24} if there's going to be an overflow, 16 million characters will probably do it.
			4294967296 digits	2^{32}

M. SUMMARIZE YOUR ANALYSIS WITH A RISK/EQUIVALENCE TABLE

Variable	Risk (potential failure	Classes that should not trigger failure	Classes that might trigger failure	Test cases (best representatives)	Notes
x_i	Too many digits	1 - 7 digits		8388607	biggest value of the significand
			$>$ 7 digits	99999999	8 digits. Must be rounded
				$=$ **MAXFLOAT**	39 digits
				$>$ **MAXFLOAT**	39 digits, but the first one is greater than 3
				127 digits	common buffer maximum. 127, 128, 255, 256 are interesting (but maybe not invalid) no matter what value in **MAXNAME**
				128 digits	
x_i	Too many digits			255 digits	common buffer maximum
				256 digits	2^8 (8-bit word + 1) boundary
				65536 digits	2^{16}
				16777216 digits	2^{24} if there's going to be an overflow, 16 million characters will probably do it.
				4294967296 digits	2^{32}

N. ANALYZE INDEPENDENT VARIABLES THAT SHOULD BE TESTED TOGETHER

There are no independent variables.

O. ANALYZE VARIABLES THAT HOLD RESULTS

The ranges for **ss** are:

- *Too small*: less than 0 (But this is impossible—squared values can't be negative)

- *Acceptable*: 0 through MAXFLOAT
- *Too large*: greater than MAXFLOAT

Variable	Valid case equivalence class	Invalid case equivalence class	Boundaries and special cases	Notes
SS	0 to MAXFLOAT		0	
			MAXFLOAT	
		Negative	0	x_i^2 can't take a negative value, so negative values of SS are untestable
		> MAXFLOAT	MAXFLOAT + 0.00001	For a more precise boundary, use Δ(MAXFLOAT) instead of .00001

The value of SS is a function of the values of the x_i's. In a table that shows SS as a result variable, we would include a column for each x_i (x_1 through x_n).

It appears that n, could be any number up to MAXINT. We don't recommend creating x-many tables and analyzing each one. Instead, in practice, we would find out what values of n are reasonable and create tables (or a list that has the same data as the table) for:

- The smallest valid **n** (probably 1)
- A very common-in-practice, but relatively small **n** (perhaps 3)
- The largest "reasonable" value of **n** (we have no idea what this would be)
- The largest possible value of **n** allowed in this program.

Here's an example of our analysis, using **n** = 3.

Remember that Δ(0) = nextUp(0) and Δ(MAXFLOAT) = nextUp(MAXFLOAT) - MAXFLOAT. For the definition of nextUp(), see *Floating Point* on page 72. For a Single-Precision Floating-Point variable, nextUp(0) is approximately 10^{-45}.

Variable	Valid case equivalence class	Invalid case equivalence class	Test value of SS	x_1	x_2	x_3
SS	0 to MAXFLOAT		0	0	0	0
			Δ(0)	$-\sqrt{Δ(0)}$	0	0
				0	$\sqrt{Δ(0)}$	0
				0	0	$\sqrt{Δ(0)}$
			MAXFLOAT	$\sqrt{MAXFLOAT}$	0	0
				0	$-\sqrt{MAXFLOAT}$	0
				0	0	$-\sqrt{MAXFLOAT}$
		> MAXFLOAT	MAXFLOAT + Δ(MAXFLOAT)	$\sqrt{MAXFLOAT}$	$\sqrt{Δ(0)}$	0
				0	$\sqrt{MAXFLOAT}$	$\sqrt{Δ(0)}$
				$-\sqrt{Δ(0)}$	0	$-\sqrt{MAXFLOAT}$
			3 × MAXFLOAT	$\sqrt{MAXFLOAT}$	$\sqrt{MAXFLOAT}$	$\sqrt{MAXFLOAT}$

In practice, we might test fewer combinations of x_i's for each value of **ss**. In a set of regression tests, we might test only one combination in each run of the regression tests.

P. ANALYZE NON-INDEPENDENT VARIABLES. DEAL WITH RELATIONSHIPS AND CONSTRAINTS

The non-independent variables to test together are the x_i's. However, we already tested the combinations of these in Task O, so we're skipping this section as redundant.

Q. IDENTIFY AND LIST UNANALYZED VARIABLES. GATHER INFORMATION FOR LATER ANALYSIS

This Task goes beyond what we're trying to teach with this example.

R. IMAGINE AND DOCUMENT RISKS THAT DON'T NECESSARILY MAP TO AN OBVIOUS DIMENSION

An example of a real-life computation of **ss** involves computing the square of a sum of differences. Represent the *sample mean* (the average value) of a set of values (x_i's) as $\bar{x}$. That is, calculate $\bar{x}$ as:

$$\bar{x} = 1/N \sum_{(i=1)}^{N} x_i$$

Use this to calculate the *variance* of a set of numbers as:

$$VAR = 1/N \sum_{(i=1)}^{N} (x_i - \bar{x})^2$$

This calculation squares what's left after you subtract off the most significant digits. For example, (123456789 - 123456787) = 2. The lower-order digits are the most likely to be affected by rounding error. In low-precision arithmetic, these calculations can produce badly incorrect results (*see* Sedgewick & Wayne, 2007 for further discussion).

By demonstrating significant rounding errors in their calculations, you can encourage the programmers to switch to higher-precision arithmetic.

Higher precision takes a little more time and a little more space, so several programmers use low-precision calculations as a matter of course:

- Single-precision calculations were habitually done back when memory was tightly constrained and computers were much slower (Kaner and Hoffman still remember working with computers that had only 8K of memory—8000 words, compared to 2013's mass-market laptops that normally sell with 4 billion words of memory.)

- Double-precision calculations are routinely used in programming classes today.

Single-precision calculations are very prone to significant rounding errors. For calculations with any level of complexity (if you add a few numbers and multiply or divide once or twice, you have hit the danger-level of complexity), the risk of rounding errors must be managed—unless you don't care whether your answer is correct (or reasonably close to it).

Double-precision calculations also come with risk of significant rounding errors if the calculations are a little more complex. For example, see the discussion of *ill-conditioned equations* in *Solving a System of Linear Equations* on page 135.

These habits (using low precision to optimize for speed or space) have been passed down from experienced programmers to younger ones who don't realize the extent to which old systems demanded risky tradeoffs. Sometimes, optimizations that threaten the accuracy of calculations are still necessary. Often, however, they are no longer essential and some bug reports that demonstrate the risks can have a fundamental impact on a system's accuracy by motivating an upgrade from Float to Double or to higher precision data types that are readily available.[44]

---

44 On reading this chapter, Geordie Keitt offered the following experience report:

"I found a significant bug in the program that ran the Federal Communications Commissions's multi-round auctions which are used to sell licenses to broadcast in particular bands of the electromagnetic spectrum. The starting price for any license in any round had to be exactly 10% higher than the highest bid on that license in the previous round. (It was slightly more complicated than that in certain types of auctions, but never mind...)

I found that the opening price was consistently too low by up to 1%, which over the course of 1000 licenses and 100 rounds could lower the resulting price of licenses by millions of dollars.

The culprit was an intermediate data field specified in the database as a "currency" field type, which enforced double precision and truncated the value.

The fix was to allow higher precision in that field, which was never displayed, and only convert the value to currency at the end of all required processing.

I found the bug by simply doing the math in Excel and comparing the value to the one given by the SUT."

EXAMPLE 20: SUM OF SQUARES (MAX)

$$SS = x_1^2 + x_2^2 + \dots + x_n^2$$

(SS is the sum of squared values of the n variables, x_1 through x_n.)

The x_i's are all Floating Point (Single Precision).

$SS \leq 45$.

Design Notes: The difference between this Example and Example 19 is the additional constraint (maximum SS is 45). Otherwise, the analyses here and in Example 19 are the same.

ANALYSIS OF EXAMPLE 20

Because this example is largely redundant with Example 19, we won't repeat the standard Tasks here. Look at Example 19 for those.

The reason we're presenting this example is that it presents a limit on a result variable that is far below the maximum for that data type. How should you deal with such a boundary on a result (rather than on an input)?

The tests that are necessary for this type of limit depend on the relationship or the risk that this limit is being used to manage. For example:

- In the United States, the Federal Deposit Insurance Corporation (FDIC) will insure a person's deposit in a bank account of up to $250,000. The person can have more than $250,000 in the account, but if the bank fails, all they get back is $250,000.

    If the boundary on SS is like this, then values of SS beyond 45 won't pose any particular risk to the system. There is no need for the software to ensure that SS never exceeds 45. It can process values between 45 and MAXFLOAT as valid values that carry different consequences than values ≤ 45.

- Suppose that a limit like the FDIC limit is involved (values of SS above 45 would be valid but processed differently) but there is also some other limit on how the value of SS is stored, displayed or used in another calculation. For example:

    ◦ The value of SS might be rounded to an Integer and displayed in a 2-digit-wide field. Values ≥ 99.5 would cause a display overflow.

    ◦ The value of SS might be rounded and stored in a 1-byte Integer. Values above 127 (signed Int) or 255 (unsigned) would overflow the byte.

    ◦ The value of SS might be used in another calculation and cause it to overflow if SS was greater than some limit (or if SS times some other variable exceeded the limit).

    If the boundary on SS is like this, then it won't cause an overflow (or be a threat to the system in some other way) if the value of SS briefly exceeded 45. That is, there is no programmatic need to block SS from exceeding 45. What is needed is to check and, if necessary, reject SS before its value is used (displayed, saved, calculated, etc.) by the vulnerable part of the program.

- Suppose the most important limit is not on SS but on the component x_i's. That is, the program can detect values of SS that exceed 45 and reject them in an orderly way, but it will misbehave badly if any individual x_i exceeds $\sqrt{45}$.

    If the boundary on SS is like this, then the important boundary testing is on the individual x_i's, which you will probably have done before testing the more complex result variable.

- Finally, imagine The Limit That Must Not Be Reached. For example, the melting point of ice cream is about 33° Fahrenheit (or about 1° C). As we write this in the hot Florida summer, we know people who would consider it a Major Disaster if software controlling their refrigerator allowed their ice and (especially) their ice cream to melt.

> *If the boundary on SS is like this, then the code must be written to prevent SS from ever exceeding 45. How does the code do that? We would test this by creating random sequences of x_i's (each $\leq \sqrt{45}$), looking for a program response as watching as each x_i is entered. We would expect the program to do the equivalent of computing a sum of squares of all of the entered x_i's so far — call this SS_{TEMP} — and rejecting any value for the next x_i that exceeds $\sqrt{SS_{TEMP}-45}$.*

To understand how to test the limits of a result variable, when those limits are narrower than the limits of the data type, you'll have to learn:

- What this variable is for.
- Why its limits are in place—what risks those limits are designed to manage.
- What the consequences are if the variable goes outside its limits.

To learn this, you might have to talk with the programmers, with the authors of the requirements specifications or you might have to read the code.

EXAMPLE 21: SPREADSHEET SORT TABLE

In OpenOffice Calc, you can sort a table. The fields in the dialog are all **SortBy** fields. The first field is the primary sort key.

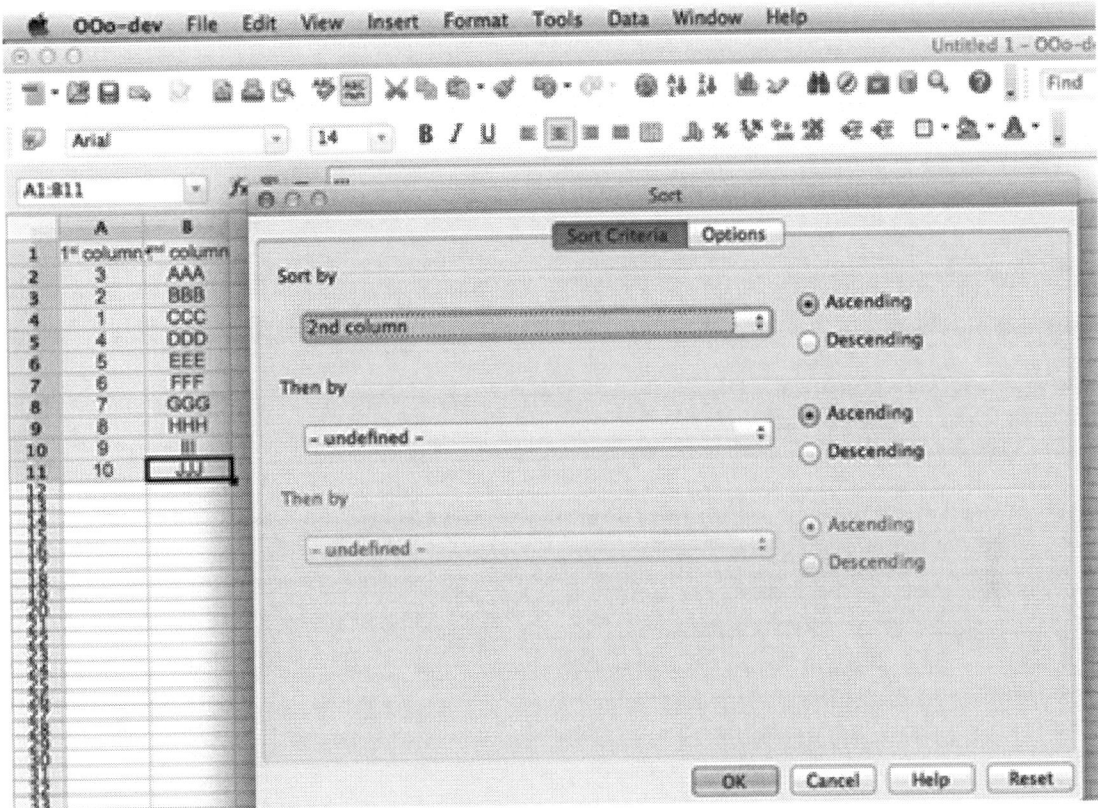

In this case, the table will be sorted by the values in the column labeled **SecondColumn**: AAA before BBB. Because this sorts the whole table, in the column labeled **FirstColumn**, 3 comes before 2 which comes before 1.

If you sort by **FirstColumn** instead, OpenOffice will sort the row with 1 before 2 before 3 but now you would see CCC before BBB before AAA in **SecondColumn**.

Note: OpenOffice is abbreviated as OOo.

A. IDENTIFY THE POTENTIALLY INTERESTING VARIABLES

This Example is packed with interesting variables. Here are just a few interesting examples.

- How many columns can you sort by? Are you limited to three? Can you add new selection row for additional criteria?
- Do the names of these columns matter?
- Can you specify the same **SortBy** column several times?
- What are you sorting? The characteristics of the list are relevant:
  - What types of data are you sorting?
  - Are the data unique or are ties allowed?
  - What is the initial order of the data, compared to the sort order that you want to achieve?

- How long (how many rows of data) can you sort?
- Is there a constraint on the number of cells of data (columns times rows) that you can sort?
- Is there a constraint on the number of columns you can sort? (When you move one row to be above another in the sort, do you move all columns or is there a limit on how many?)

For instructional purposes, we're going to focus on the characteristics of the list, with a particular emphasis on the order of items in the list to be sorted.

A *list* is a set of numbers (or other data) whose elements are arranged in an order. For example, the elements of the set might be {1, 2, 3}. One list with these elements is (1, 2, 3). Another list is (2, 3, 1). A third is (3, 2, 1). You could think of this as three separate lists or as one list that has been reordered twice.

You can treat a set of rows in a spreadsheet as a list. Each row is a multidimensional variable (x_1, x_2, ..., x_n). The component variables (x_i's) are the values of the row from each column. The first element of the list is the top row, the last element is the bottom row.

Sorting transforms the elements of a list from an initial order to a sorted order without adding any elements of the list, deleting any elements or changing any element values (apart from reordering them).

- The *initial order* of the list is the order before sorting.
- The *sort order* specifies the rule that will be used to sort elements of the list.
- The *sorted order* of the list is the order after sorting.

The variables to study are:

- The sort orders.
- The elements of the lists to be sorted.
- The initial orders of the elements of the lists.
- The result of sorting (the sorted order).

For example, suppose you're testing a numeric sort:

- You could test a 3-element list, with the *initial order* (3, 1, 2).
- If the sort order is numeric, running from smallest to largest, the *sorted order* should be (1, 2, 3).

B. IDENTIFY THE VARIABLES YOU CAN ANALYZE NOW. THESE ARE THE VARIABLES OF INTEREST

The variables associated with the list that we're studying include:

- The sort orders
  - In the OpenOffice spreadsheet, you specify this on the Options tab, which allows you to pick from a list or specify a Custom Sort Order.
- The elements of the lists to be sorted
  - You can focus on (and sort) only the values in a single column or
  - You can focus on (and sort) the values of all the columns together. In this case, each row moves together. For example, you can move all the values in the fifth row to the second row.

When the values in a row of a table are treated as dimensions of a single multidimensional variable, that variable is often called a *record*. (A database record is a set of values that are stored together. Relational databases can be represented as tables with each record being a row in one of the database's tables.) Other common names for types like records are struct and class. (While *class* is very common in object-oriented programming, we will avoid it here because of its confusability with *equivalence class*.)

- The initial order of the elements of the list.

  ○ A *list* is a set of numbers (or other data) whose elements are arranged in an order. For example, the elements of the set might be {1, 2, 3}. One list with these elements is (1, 2, 3). Another list is (2, 3, 1). A third is (3, 2, 1). You could think of these as three separate lists or as one list that has been reordered twice.

- The sorted order is a result variable.

C. DETERMINE THE PRIMARY DIMENSION OF THE VARIABLE OF INTEREST

- Cells in a spreadsheet can hold anything you can type. (Or, perhaps, graphics.)

  OpenOffice enumerates some types of variables (formats of values within cells) that you can specify. You can associate any one of these types with any cell:

  ○ Number
  ○ Percent
  ○ Currency
  ○ Date
  ○ Time
  ○ Scientific
  ○ Fraction
  ○ Boolean
  ○ Text
  ○ User-defined

  In addition, a specified type can be represented differently in different cells. For example, one Date cell might be formatted for dates like "Friday, December 31, 1999" while another might be formatted for dates like "12/31/99".

  There is no requirement that all of the cells in a column (including the column being sorted) be of the same type.

- A record (a row) in a spreadsheet is a multidimensional variable that holds a value from each column—these can be of many types.

Given this generality, the only thing we can say about the primary dimension is that it is whatever would cause you to decide that one member of the list should be higher in the list than another.

D. DETERMINE THE TYPE AND SCALE OF THE VARIABLE'S PRIMARY DIMENSION AND WHAT VALUES IT CAN TAKE

See the answer to Task C (primary dimension).

E. DETERMINE WHETHER YOU CAN ORDER THE VARIABLE'S VALUES (FROM SMALLEST TO LARGEST)

Most types of data can be ordered. Even if you're dealing with data for which there is no natural order (think of a set of boxes that differ only in color or only in smell), the development team might have imposed an ordering.

For example, the *sort order* (the order that elements of the list should be sorted into) could be:

- Numeric

- Numeric but in terms of the absolute value of the number. (Example: An absolute-value sort treats 8 as less than -9). If this seems like a strange ordering rule, imagine the next step after sorting is squaring. 8^2 is only 64, while $(-9)^2$ is 81. Which is bigger?

- Alphabetic (A and a both come before B)

- ASCII (A comes before B which comes before a. 1 and 11 both come before 9.)

- Date (December 31, 2003 comes before January 1, 2004 comes before December 31, 2004. When the year is not present, January always comes before December.)

- Custom (Example: an informal preference poll sorted these from least disfavored to most disfavored: Zombies, Vampires, Werewolves, U.S. Congressmen, Frozen Alien Slime Creatures.)

If there is no ordering for a list of data, then the data are already "sorted" no matter what order they're in.

What are the implications of this for testing?

- You must determine what all of the possible sort orders are.

  ◦ Because you can create custom orders, you'll have to sample from an infinite number of possible sort orders.

- For each sort order that you're going to test:

  ◦ You must create a suitable collection of lists of data:

    ▪ There is probably an infinite set of possible lists for any sort order, so you'll have to sample from these.

  ◦ You must arrange the elements of each list in a suitable way. That is, you must choose an *initial order*.

    ▪ If a list has n elements, those elements can be ordered in n! ways. (Read **n!** as "n-factorial"). **n!** = n × (n -1) × (n - 2) × ... × 1.

      (*See* https://en.wikipedia.org/wiki/Permutation)

      n! gets to be a big number very quickly. For example, 5! = 120 and 10! = 3628800 and 15! = 1307674368000. The number of orderings of a spreadsheet with 100 rows is about 9.3×10^{157}. This is too many to test. You will have to sample from these.

  ◦ Then you must check whether the program correctly sorts that list.

F. DETERMINE WHETHER THIS IS AN INPUT VARIABLE OR A RESULT

The sort order, the elements of the list and the initial order are all input variables. The sorted order is a result variable.

G. DETERMINE HOW THE PROGRAM USES THIS VARIABLE

- It uses the sort order to determine how the list should be sorted.
- It sorts the list, which has a set of elements arranged in an initial order.

H. DETERMINE WHETHER OTHER VARIABLES ARE RELATED TO THIS ONE

Anything that is (or can be) related to the size of the spreadsheet (for example page size) or to the contents of the spreadsheet could play a role in sorting.

I. PARTITION THE VARIABLE (ITS PRIMARY DIMENSION)

First, some notation:

- **MAXROWS** is the largest number of rows you can have in the spreadsheet.
- **MAXCOLUMNS** is the largest number of columns you can have in the spreadsheet.
- **MAXCELLS** is the largest number of cells you can have in the spreadsheet. As shown in *Example 9: Create Table (Max Cells)* on page 289, **MAXCELLS** may be less than **MAXROWS** × **MAXCOLUMNS**.

From here, start with a relatively simple case and then increase the complexity:

CASE 1: ONE-COLUMN, HOMOGENEOUS ORDERABLE DATA

- The spreadsheet has only one column.
- The data in each cell are of the same type.
- There is a natural ordering for the data (smallest to largest).

There are arbitrarily-many rows. How many should you test?

- Empty spreadsheet (no values in any cell)
- Spreadsheet with 1 row
- Spreadsheet with several rows (even number)
- Several rows (odd number)
- **MAXROWS**
- Perhaps 256 rows (and/or 1024 rows or 16384 rows or 32768 rows or 65536 rows—if these are less than **MAXROWS**)
- Some sort routines divide lists differently, depending on the length of the list. Ask the programmers whether there are any lengths that would be interesting to their algorithm.

The elements are in some initial order. How? The initial order should be:

- In the same order as the sort order
- In exactly the opposite order to the sort order
- Perhaps alternating orders (lowest / highest / next-lowest / next-highest / etc.)
- Ask the programmers what ordering would cause their algorithm to make the maximum number of swaps during its sorting. (You are looking for errors like stack overflow.)
- Random orders

The elements are homogeneous, but what data type is in each element?

As noted above, in OpenOffice you can associate any one of these types with any cell:

- Number
- Percent
- Currency
- Date
- Time
- Scientific
- Fraction
- Boolean
- Text
- User-defined

All of these (except some types of user-defined variables) can be put into a largest-to-smallest order. However, as noted above, different types of data can have different sort orders. For example, text could be sorted alphabetically or in ASCII order or in a user-defined order.

Are any ordering rules different from the others?

We think there are at least three types of rules.

- In one case, the programming language that your program was written in probably has built-in ordering rules. For example, the program probably knows that 1 < 2.

- In the other cases, the ordering has to be defined by the programmer. To achieve this:

  - The programmer might create a whole new data type (a new "class") that has a built-in order. For example, she might create a DaysOfTheWeek class that can have values { Monday, Tuesday, Wednesday, ..., Sunday } with a specified order (for example, Monday < Tuesday). Done this way, the program can compare days of the week with the less-than operator (just like numbers) and sorting will (should) work the same as it does with numbers.

  - The programmer might accept a custom sort order as an input at run-time. This would be a list of values, such as (Zombie, Vampire, Werewolf, Congressman, Alien Slime). When it sorts by this order, it compares two values by determining which is earlier in the list (something not in the list is treated as beyond Alien Slime).

It would be good to test at least one of each type.

Some spreadsheets accept more complex data elements in individual cells, such as pictures or tables. Before even thinking about how to include these in our tests of sorting, we would ask the stakeholders how these things *should be* sorted and we would look for competing products to see how they sort these things.

CASE 2: ONE-COLUMN, HOMOGENEOUS ORDERABLE DATA, WITH TIES

Start with the tests from Case 1, but add tests with tied values:

- Two rows with the same data in each cell
- Three rows with the same data in two cells
- In some of the tests in Case 1, randomly substitute values that will cause ties for some of the unique values.

CASE 3: ONE-COLUMN, NON-HOMOGENEOUS DATA

Start with the tests from Case 1 or 2, but vary the data types within the columns. For example, what happens when you sort a column using a numeric order that is appropriate for most of the cells, but some of the cells are text?

CASES 4, 5 AND 6: MULTIPLE COLUMNS

Create spreadsheets with multiple columns. In these cases, sort by one (1) column, whose contents are like those in Cases 1 to 3.

- Do the elements in this column sort properly?
- Do all the cells in the row move correctly when the sorted cell moves?

How many columns?

- Two (we've already tested one)
- **MAXCOLUMNS**
- If **MAXCOLUMNS** × **MAXROWS** < **MAXCELLS**, then the largest number of columns that keeps the table within **MAXCELLS**.
- Perhaps a few other values, powers of 2, that are less than **MAXCOLUMNS** (such as 256, 1024, etc.).

Which column will you sort by?

- First
- Last
- Some interior columns (we aren't sure whether any interior column is a better representative than the rest).

What data belong in the other columns?

There are two types of columns:

- One column contains the values the program looks at when it sorts the rows.
- The *other columns* are ignored for purposes of sorting and are simply moved with the cell that is being sorted.

The contents of the other columns shouldn't matter.

- Try homogeneous data in all of cells in all the other columns, using each data type.
- Try non-homogeneous data. We would probably randomly mix data types within rows and within columns.

CASES 7, 8 AND 9: SORT BY MULTIPLE COLUMNS

Create spreadsheets with multiple columns and sort by a subset of these. In general, the contents are like those in Cases 4 to 6. (Start with homogeneous values within each column orderable, with no ties; add ties; eliminate homogeneity, then add homogeneous or non-homogeneous data to the other columns.)

J. LAY OUT THE ANALYSIS IN A CLASSICAL BOUNDARY/EQUIVALENCE TABLE. IDENTIFY BEST REPRESENTATIVES

We would make a specific, narrow use of this table. The table would show our partitioning of the individual variables. It would ignore the rules we would use to combine the variables (Cases 1 to 9).

Variable	Valid case equivalence class	Invalid case equivalence class	Boundaries and special cases	Notes
NumberOfRows	1 to MAXROWS		1	
			4	even number
			5	odd number
			256	2^8
			MAXROWS	
		0		A table with 0 rows is non-existent. How about a table whose row(s) are all empty?
			Integer part of (MAXCELLS / NumberOfColumns)	If MAXCELLS < MAXROWS × MAXCOLUMNS, use the largest valid number of rows
		> MAXROWS	Integer part of (MAXCELLS / NumberOfColumns) + 1	This is probably MAXROWS + 1
			MAXROWS + 1	Include this if the last test was not this value

K. CREATE TESTS FOR THE CONSEQUENCES OF THE DATA ENTERED, NOT JUST THE INPUT FILTER

The primary tests for the consequences are tests of whether the spreadsheet is properly sorted.

The program (or the user working with the spreadsheet program) can use the sorted data for some other purposes. For example, you could store addresses in the spreadsheet, sort it by Postal Code, then read the spreadsheet to print mailings (addressed letters and envelopes). The print-order should be grouped by Postal Code, ready for delivery to the Post Office as pre-sorted mail.

We would look for these types of consequences as part of a scenario-design process. We would think in terms of the set of benefits the program is supposed to provide and then consider whether any of those benefits require a sorted spreadsheet.

L. IDENTIFY SECONDARY DIMENSIONS. ANALYZE THEM IN THE CLASSICAL WAY

- We probably wouldn't look systematically at secondary dimensions as part of this process. There are too many values of too many variables already in play: To see (for example) how the program handles non-numbers in a number cell, we would try those tests on one cell or on a spreadsheet with only a few cells. We address these types of mismatches in Cases 3, 6 and 9 but only to the extent they might interfere with sorting.

- If we create an automaton to test sorting (as we recommend in Task N, below), we can use it to insert random data in tester-specified cells. This enables testing of several secondary dimensions.

M. SUMMARIZE YOUR ANALYSIS WITH A RISK/EQUIVALENCE TABLE

We think this table will be unmanageably complex and so we aren't going to create it. Instead, we would create a list of risks. Here are a few examples:

- The largest class of risks is: *It didn't sort correctly because ...* The long list of potential causes would include:
  - It is confused by ties in the data.
  - It doesn't work properly with custom sort orders.
- We would also consider storage risks, such as:
  - Memory overflow.
  - Stack overflow.
  - Overflow of storage for that data type (like the result of trying to store a number bigger than **MAXINT** in an Integer variable).
  - Disk space overflow (some of these spreadsheets are very big. What if you run out of storage space for them? What about virtual storage while sorting?)
- Time-related risks might be interesting:
  - Sorting a spreadsheet with **MAXROWS** rows might take an astonishingly long time. Does it take longer than the long time that it is supposed to take?

You can probably find more ways that OpenOffice Calc has failed while sorting (or otherwise reordering) its tables by looking in the OpenOffice bug tracking database.

N. ANALYZE INDEPENDENT VARIABLES THAT SHOULD BE TESTED TOGETHER

We suggested several variables that should be tested together in Cases 1 through 9 of the partitioning. The question is how to test these together. The challenge, of course, is combinatorial explosion. Even with the simplifications laid out in the partitioning, there is a huge number of potential tests.

If the variables were actually all independent, you could try to manage the combinatorial explosion with all-pairs combination testing. However, many of the variations outlined in Cases 1-9 involve systematically studying relationships among several variables, which (if you're going to use a combinatorial coverage criterion) calls for all-triples, all-quadruples or all-quintuples levels of test coverage. As another complexity, several of these variables are related, so you would have to create a modified all-k-of-n-tuples to handle the non-independence of those variables.

We would do this a different way. Write a program to do it:

- It is a relatively simple matter to write a program to generate a set of data in CSV format (*i.e.*, in a format readable by a spreadsheet). Several popular modern languages have readily-available, well-documented library commands for writing data to that format.
- It is trivially easy to generate an array (two-dimensions: rows, columns) with either a specified number of rows and columns or a random number (with constraints, like 1 to **MAXROWS**).

- Given the array, pick the column to sort by (either pick it with a constant, such as first column or last column or randomly choose the column)
- Fill the column with random data that meet certain restrictions:
  - Decide which is the primary data type for that column.
  - Decide whether ties are permitted or not.
  - Decide whether the data are homogeneous or not.
    - If they are, generate all the data with the primary type.
    - If not, generate some percentage (or random proportion) of data from the primary type and the rest of the data from the other types.
- Decide what the initial order for the column should be. Should they be sorted smallest to largest, largest to smallest, outside in (smallest in the middle, increasing to the start and end of the list), alternating, random or something else?
  - You might specify the initial order in order to create a set of tests with that particular order or you might select it randomly.
  - You might do this before generating the data and generate them in that order or
  - You might generate the data in a random order first, then reorder them to meet the initial order criterion.
- Generate the data in all of the other columns
  - Allow ties or don't.
  - Keep the data within each column homogeneous or don't.
  - Keep the data in the entire table homogeneous or don't.
- Once you've got all that working, add a function to determine how many columns you'll sort by at once and create tables that have at least that many columns, pick which ones will be the sort columns, populate them, then populate the others.

You can either use this program to generate a huge set of test tables (as many as you want to store) in advance or to generate them on the fly. Given a table:

- Feed a copy of it to OpenOffice Calc and sort it.
- Feed a copy of it to Excel and sort it

Sorting doesn't change the values within the cells, so the sorted tables should match in order and contents of the cells.

As you do this, you can create several variables to track whatever type of coverage you're interested in.

Note the critical enabler of this strategy: *Excel is available as an oracle.*

Domain analysis can help you reduce the number of tests needed, but multivariable situations (even with domain-reduced variables) will often drive the number of tests beyond anything you would want to design or execute by hand. We suggest:

- Look for a program that you can use to create comparison results along the primary dimension.
  - In this case, the sort order is the primary dimension.
- Sometimes that comparison program (also known as a **reference program** or a **reference oracle**) will also enable you to check some secondary-dimension values or other risks.

- ◦ In this case, the specific values in each cell should be the same in Excel and OpenOffice, so we can check this along with checking the sort order.

- Sometimes the reference oracle might not be a good source for comparison.

  - ◦ For example, if you're sorting a column of cells that sometimes have numbers, sometimes letters and sometimes graphics, there is no "best" sort order. Excel and OpenOffice might reasonably sort differently. The useful question here is whether the differences are consistent and can be characterized in a checkable way.

- Some secondary-dimension issues will be invisible to this oracle.

  - ◦ For example, comparing sort orders won't tell you whether OpenOffice takes too long to sort, whether the change in sort times (longer lists should take predictably longer) is unreasonable, whether memory is being used and released properly, whether the stack is being used and released properly, etc. Comparing OOo to Excel won't reveal any of these problems.

    However, once you have an automaton that can create and run all of these OpenOffice tests, consider using it to run a massive series of secondary-dimension tests. For example, run a long series of sorts and record such things as:

    - ▪ Time taken for each sort
    - ▪ Free memory (and largest contiguous amount of free memory) after every Nth sort
    - ▪ The results of other system diagnostics that you think might be useful.

    These are examples of long-sequence (high-volume) automated testing (Kaner, 2013; Kaner, Oliver & Fioravanti, 2013; and check the kaner.com blog for more as Oliver continues her dissertation research in this area).

O. ANALYZE VARIABLES THAT HOLD RESULTS

The sort order is the variable that holds results. See Task N for the analysis.

P. ANALYZE NON-INDEPENDENT VARIABLES. DEAL WITH RELATIONSHIPS AND CONSTRAINTS

This Task goes beyond what we're trying to teach with this example.

Q. IDENTIFY AND LIST UNANALYZED VARIABLES. GATHER INFORMATION FOR LATER ANALYSIS

This Task goes beyond what we're trying to teach with this example.

R. IMAGINE AND DOCUMENT RISKS THAT DON'T NECESSARILY MAP TO AN OBVIOUS DIMENSION

- Sorting with multiple data types within a cell (e.g., a link name different from the actual link or a graphic and a name associated with it).

- Sorting when cells have been merged (in the sort by column and in other columns that get reordered with the sort.

- Sorting and resorting, ultimately causing memory or stack problems.

- Adding new rows to a sorted list: Does the program automatically put them in the correct place or does the user need to resort?

EXAMPLE 22: NEXTDATE

"`NextDate` is a function of three variables: month, day, and year. It returns the date of the day after the input date." (Jorgensen, 2008, p. 22).

Jorgensen limits the year to the range 1812 ≤ year ≤ 2012 and of course 1 ≤ day ≤ 31 and 1 ≤ month ≤ 12. If the user enters a bad date, the program rejects it with a "bad date" message.

A. IDENTIFY THE POTENTIALLY INTERESTING VARIABLES

- `InputDay`
- `InputMonth`
- `InputYear`
- `NextDay`
- `NextMonth`
- `NextYear`

We're ignoring the combined date (such as 10/11/2013) because the problem description has already parsed this date into its three components (month, day, year).

B. IDENTIFY THE VARIABLES YOU CAN ANALYZE NOW. THESE ARE THE VARIABLES OF INTEREST

- `InputDay`
- `InputMonth`
- `InputYear`
- `NextDay`
- `NextMonth`
- `NextYear`

C. DETERMINE THE PRIMARY DIMENSION OF THE VARIABLE OF INTEREST

- The days are days of the month.
- The months are months of the year. They run here from 1-12 but could as easily run from January to December.
- The years are Gregorian Calendar years Years are A.D. (1813 comes after 1812, not before.)

D. DETERMINE THE TYPE AND SCALE OF THE VARIABLE'S PRIMARY DIMENSION AND WHAT VALUES IT CAN TAKE

- The days are Integers, running from 1 to 28, 29, 30 or 31.
- The months are Integers, running from 1 to 12.
- The years are Integers, running from 1812 to 2012.

E. DETERMINE WHETHER YOU CAN ORDER THE VARIABLE'S VALUES (FROM SMALLEST TO LARGEST)

Each variable can be ordered independently. For example, day 31 > day 30. However, there are interrelationships because of comparisons like this:

- Month 1 < Month 12 and Day 1 < Day 31, but
- 1/1/2011 > 12/31/2010.

F. DETERMINE WHETHER THIS IS AN INPUT VARIABLE OR A RESULT

- The `Input` date variables are inputs.
- The `Next` date variables are results.

G. DETERMINE HOW THE PROGRAM USES THIS VARIABLE

The particular use mentioned in the problem description is that the `NextDate` function uses the input date (plus 1) to determine the next date.

In general, dates are ubiquitous. The program might use the date for a vast number of different purposes. If it stores the date, other programs that have access to data that your program stores might use it for many other purposes. Talk with the other developers about possible uses in this program.

H. DETERMINE WHETHER OTHER VARIABLES ARE RELATED TO THIS ONE

Same answer as Task G above. The date is used so often for so much that many variables might be related to (affected by) it. Talk to the other developers for more information for this program.

Within the threesome of variables (day, month, year), there are relationships:

- Month and Year determine the range for Day:
  - If Month = 1, 3, 5, 7, 8, 10 or 12, then $1 \leq Day \leq 31$
  - If Month = 4, 6, 9 or 11, then $1 \leq Day \leq 30$
  - If Month = 2 then
    - If Year is evenly divisible by 4 and Year is not 1900, then $1 \leq Day \leq 29$
    - Otherwise, $1 \leq Day \leq 28$

    (Remember that $1812 \leq Year \leq 2012$, so years like 1800 and 2100 aren't relevant to this analysis.)
- The `Input` date variables determine the `Next` date variables. See Task O for more about `Next` date variables.

I. PARTITION THE VARIABLE (ITS PRIMARY DIMENSION)

If you consider the variables independently:

		InputDay	≤ 0	too small
1	$\leq$	InputDay	≤ 31	valid (except February, etc.)
31	$\leq$	InputDay		too large
		InputMonth	≤ 0	too small
1	$\leq$	InputMonth	≤ 12	valid
31	$\leq$	InputMonth		too large
		InputYear	≤ 0	too small
1	$\leq$	InputYear	≤ 2012	
31	$\leq$	InputYear		too large

J. LAY OUT THE ANALYSIS IN A CLASSICAL BOUNDARY/EQUIVALENCE TABLE. IDENTIFY BEST REPRESENTATIVES

This table covers the tests for basic checks of the input filters:

Variable	Valid case equivalence class	Invalid case equivalence class	Boundaries and special cases	Notes
InputDay	1-31		1	
			28	non-leap year February
			29	leap-year february
			30	Month 4, 6, 9, 11
			31	Month 1, 3, 5, 7, 8, 10, 12
		< 1	0	
		≥ 29	29	non-leap february
		≥ 31	31	Month 4, 6, 9, 11
		> 31	32	
InputMonth	1-12		1	
			12	
		< 1	0	
		> 12	13	
InputYear	1812-2012		1812	
			2012	
		< 1812	1811	
		> 2012	2013	12/31/2012 is the end of the world

The tests use the values in the "Boundaries and special cases" column.

K. CREATE TESTS FOR THE CONSEQUENCES OF THE DATA ENTERED, NOT JUST THE INPUT FILTER

See Task O, below.

L. IDENTIFY SECONDARY DIMENSIONS. ANALYZE THEM IN THE CLASSICAL WAY

These are Integers. See *Test Idea Catalog for Integers* on page 231.

M. SUMMARIZE YOUR ANALYSIS WITH A RISK/EQUIVALENCE TABLE

See *Generic Risk/Equivalence Table for Integers* on page 233.

N. ANALYZE INDEPENDENT VARIABLES THAT SHOULD BE TESTED TOGETHER

Day, month and year variables are related, not independent.

O. ANALYZE VARIABLES THAT HOLD RESULTS

The result variables are **NextDay**, **NextMonth** and **NextYear**.

The rules below assume that input filtering has already been done, so there are no dates like November 31 or like February 29, 2001. We determine the values of **NextDate(InputMonth, InputDay, InputYear)** as follows:

(a) If (**InputMonth**, **InputDay**, **InputYear**) = (12, 31, 2012),

According to the problem description, the world ends. Bye!

(b) Else if (`InputMonth`, `InputDay`, `InputYear`) = (12, 31, `InputYear`),

(`NextMonth`, `NextDay`, `NextYear`) = (1, 1, `InputYear` + 1)

(c) Else if (`InputMonth`, `InputDay`, `InputYear`) = (2, 29, `InputYear`),

(`NextMonth`, `NextDay`, `NextYear`) = (3, 1, `InputYear`)

(d) Else if (`InputMonth`, `InputDay`, `InputYear`) = (2, 28, 1900),

(`NextMonth`, `NextDay`, `NextYear`) = (3, 1, 1900)

(e) Else if (`InputMonth`, `InputDay`, `InputYear`) = (2, 28, `InputYear` evenly divisible by 4),

(`NextMonth`, `NextDay`, `NextYear`) = (2, 29, `InputYear`)

(f) Else if (`InputMonth`, `InputDay`, `InputYear`) = (`InputMonth`, 31, `InputYear`),

(`NextMonth`, `NextDay`, `NextYear`) = (`InputMonth` + 1, 1, `InputYear`)

(g) Else if (`InputMonth`, `InputDay`, `InputYear`) = (`InputMonth` is in {1, 3, 5, 7, 8, 10, 12}, 30, `InputYear`),

(`NextMonth`, `NextDay`, `NextYear`) = (`InputMonth`, 31, `InputYear`)

(h) Else if (`InputMonth`, `InputDay`, `InputYear`) = (`InputMonth`, 30, `InputYear`),

(`NextMonth`, `NextDay`, `NextYear`) = (`InputMonth` + 1, 1, `InputYear`)

Some readers will be confused by the structure. If you're not familiar with the "Else if" construct, consider Case (f).

> Case (f) does not include December 31 because Cases (a) and (b) took care of all the December 31's. "Else if" means here that December 31's are no longer considered after they're taken care of. Therefore, we ignore them when working with cases (c) through (h).

Also,

> Case (f) does not include any invalid 31's, like April 31 because the input filter tests (Task J) took care of all of those.

Given these relationships, how should you test them?

- We treat Days 1 to 27 as an equivalence class. Days 28, 29, 30 and 31 are special cases that must be treated individually.

- There is some argument for treating Months 1, 3, 5, 7, 8, 10 and 12 as one equivalence class (except for December 31) and Months 4, 6, 9 and 11 as another equivalence class. If we were very time-constrained or if we had already tested them individually once or a few times, we would treat them as equivalent too. However, if feasible, we prefer to test the months as an enumerated list (April is April, not equivalent to June) because any of them could have been misclassified.

- Years that aren't divisible by 4 are an equivalence class.

- Years divisible by 4 that aren't 1900 and not 2000 are an equivalence class.

- Years 1900 and 2000 are special cases.

I. TASKS P, Q & R ARE BEYOND WHAT WE'RE TRYING TO TEACH WITH THIS EXAMPLE.

EXAMPLE 23: FREQUENT-FLYER MILES

An airline awards frequent-flyer miles according to the following table (Black, 2007, p. 218):

Status Level	None	Silver	Gold	Platinum
Trip bonus	0%	25%	50%	100%
Distance traveled	d	d	d	d
Points awarded	d	$1.25 \times d$	$1.5 \times d$	$2 \times d$
Miles required to reach this level	0	25,000	50,000	100,000

Your status is determined before you fly. The number of miles flown on this trip does not affect your status on this trip, though a long trip might result in elevating your status before your next trip.

Determine whether the system awards the correct number of points for a given trip.

A. IDENTIFY THE POTENTIALLY INTERESTING VARIABLES

- `DistanceTraveled` (in the table, **d**): The distance traveled on the current trip.
- `TotalMiles`: The number of miles traveled this year (or whatever the period is that counts for determining frequent flyer status).
- `PointsAwarded`: Number of points awarded for this trip.
- `StatusLevel`: Determined from `TotalMiles`.

B. IDENTIFY THE VARIABLES YOU CAN ANALYZE NOW. THESE ARE THE VARIABLES OF INTEREST

- `DistanceTraveled`
- `PointsAwarded`

The problem description doesn't describe how `TotalMiles` is calculated:

- What time period is involved in calculation of `TotalMiles`?
- Suppose the traveler flies a 1000-mile trip and is awarded 1500 points. Does the software add 1000 or 1500 to `TotalMiles`?

C. DETERMINE THE PRIMARY DIMENSION OF THE VARIABLE OF INTEREST

- `DistanceTraveled` runs from 0 to many miles.
- `PointsAwarded` runs from 0 to many frequent-flyer points.

D. DETERMINE THE TYPE AND SCALE OF THE VARIABLE'S PRIMARY DIMENSION AND WHAT VALUES IT CAN TAKE

The problem description doesn't state the scale explicitly, but based on experience we know that `DistanceTraveled` and `PointsAwarded` are Integers (on a ratio scale). The values run from 0 to `MAXTRIP`.

- A trip around the world once might involve about 23000 miles. Based on this, perhaps `MAXTRIP` (the longest possible excursion that can be sold as 1 trip) could not exceed 100,000 miles and therefore perhaps the maximum of `PointsAwarded` is 200,000.
- Based on the rough estimates above, we doubt the program would attempt to store `DistanceTraveled` or `PointsAwarded` in a 16-bit variable. We assume instead that the

variables are typical Integers, which run from **MININT** = -2^{31} (-2147483648) to **MAXINT** = 2^{31} - 1 (2147483647).

StatusLevel is an enumerated ordinal value (the four status levels have a rank ordering).

E. DETERMINE WHETHER YOU CAN ORDER THE VARIABLE'S VALUES (FROM SMALLEST TO LARGEST)

Yes.

F. DETERMINE WHETHER THIS IS AN INPUT VARIABLE OR A RESULT

- **DistanceTraveled** is an input variable.
- **PointsAwarded** is a result variable whose value depends jointly on **DistanceTraveled** and **StatusLevel**.
- **TotalMiles** and **StatusLevel** are results of a previous calculation.

To test the values of **PointsAwarded**, you must be able to set the value of **StatusLevel**. Even though **StatusLevel** is normally calculated from **TotalMiles**, you'll probably be able to set **StatusLevel** directly in the software. This is because, in practice, airlines can adjust **Status-Level** directly (for example to entice someone who has high frequent flyer status on another airline to fly on their airline).

In the analysis that follows, we treat **StatusLevel** as an input variable with four possible values, { None, Silver, Gold, Platinum } and no possible invalid values. When you test the actual software, check whether invalid values of **StatusLevel** are possible. If they are possible, test the calculation of **PointsAwarded** after setting **StatusLevel** to an invalid level.

G. DETERMINE HOW THE PROGRAM USES THIS VARIABLE

- The program increments **PointsAwarded** based on **DistanceTraveled** and **StatusLevel**.
- The program increments **TotalMiles** based on **DistanceTraveled** or **PointsAwarded**.

H. DETERMINE WHETHER OTHER VARIABLES ARE RELATED TO THIS ONE

- **DistanceTraveled** is independent of the other variables.
- The values of **TotalMiles**, **PointsAwarded** and **StatusLevel** are all influenced by **DistanceTraveled**.
- **StatusLevel** is influenced by **TotalMiles**.
- **PointsAwarded** is influenced by **StatusLevel**.
- **TotalMiles** might be influenced by **PointsAwarded**.

I. PARTITION THE VARIABLE (ITS PRIMARY DIMENSION)

- **DistanceTraveled**:

  - *Too small:* **DistanceTraveled** must exceed -1.
  - *Maybe possible*: **DistanceTraveled** might be 0 (for example, the system might record 0 miles for a trip paid for with frequent flyer miles).
  - *Valid range*: **MINTRIP** ≤ **DistanceTraveled** ≤ **MAXTRIP**:
    - **MINTRIP**: the minimum miles the airline awards per flight segment, often 250 miles.
    - **MINTRIP**: the length of the longest possible excursion that can be sold as 1 trip or the largest direct sale or gift of miles the airline can award a customer in one transaction.
  - *Too big*: **DistanceTraveled** > **MAXTRIP**.

- `PointsAwarded`:
  - *Too small:* `PointsAwarded` must exceed -1.
  - *Maybe possible*: `PointsAwarded` might be 0 (for example, the system might award 0 miles for a trip paid for with frequent flyer miles).
  - *Valid range*: `MINTRIP` $\leq$ `PointsAwarded` $\leq$ $2 \times$ `MAXTRIP`.
  - *Too big*: `PointsAwarded` $> 2 \times$ `MAXTRIP`.
- `StatusLevel` one of { None, Silver, Gold, Platinum }. We would not partition the values of this enumerated variable. Instead, treat each level as its own equivalence class.

J. LAY OUT THE ANALYSIS IN A CLASSICAL BOUNDARY/EQUIVALENCE TABLE. IDENTIFY BEST REPRESENTATIVES

We treat `DistanceTraveled` and `StatusLevel` as input variables.

Variable	Valid case equivalence class	Invalid case equivalence class	Boundaries and special cases	Notes
Distance-Traveled	0		0	This value might or might not be valid
	MINTRIP to MAXTRIP		MINTRIP	
			MAXTRIP	
		< 0	-1	
		1 to MINTRIP - 1	1	
			MINTRIP - 1	
		> MAXTRIP	MAXTRIP + 1	
StatusLevel			None	This is a short, enumerated list. There are no equivalence classes
			Silver	
			Gold	
			Platinum	

The tests use the values in the "Boundaries and special cases" column.

K. CREATE TESTS FOR THE CONSEQUENCES OF THE DATA ENTERED, NOT JUST THE INPUT FILTER

Changing `DistanceTraveled` changes `PointsAwarded`, which changes `TotalMiles`, which changes `StatusLevel`, which changes how `PointsAwarded` is calculated, etc. See Task O.

Beyond this obvious set of relationships, there are probably other consequences in the system under test. For example, the value of `TotalMiles` (or the rate of change of `TotalMiles`) probably triggers marketing offers. The problem description doesn't provide relevant information for this.

L. IDENTIFY SECONDARY DIMENSIONS. ANALYZE THEM IN THE CLASSICAL WAY

`DistanceTraveled` is an Integer. See *Test Idea Catalog for Integers* on page 231.

M. SUMMARIZE YOUR ANALYSIS WITH A RISK/EQUIVALENCE TABLE

See *Generic Risk/Equivalence Table for Integers* on page 233.

N. ANALYZE INDEPENDENT VARIABLES THAT SHOULD BE TESTED TOGETHER

This Task goes beyond what we're trying to teach with this example.

O. ANALYZE VARIABLES THAT HOLD RESULTS

The variable of interest is `PointsAwarded`. In the table that follows, we ignore invalid values of `DistanceTraveled` and `StatusLevel`. However, if it is possible to enter invalid values for these and have them retained long enough to be used to calculate `PointsAwarded`, then you should include invalid values in the table.

PointsAwarded Valid case equivalence class	Status Level	DistanceTraveled	PointsAwarded	Notes
0	any	any	0	Award travel
`MINTRIP` to 2 × `MAXTRIP`	None	`MINTRIP`	`MINTRIP`	
	Silver		`1.25 × MINTRIP`	
	Gold		`1.5 × MINTRIP`	
	Platinum		`2 × MINTRIP`	
	None	`MAXTRIP`	`MAXTRIP`	
	Silver		`1.25 × MAXTRIP`	
	Gold		`1.5 × MAXTRIP`	
	Platinum		`2 × MAXTRIP`	

P. ANALYZE NON-INDEPENDENT VARIABLES. DEAL WITH RELATIONSHIPS AND CONSTRAINTS

This Task goes beyond what we're trying to teach with this example.

Q. IDENTIFY AND LIST UNANALYZED VARIABLES. GATHER INFORMATION FOR LATER ANALYSIS

This Task goes beyond what we're trying to teach with this example.

R. IMAGINE AND DOCUMENT RISKS THAT DON'T NECESSARILY MAP TO AN OBVIOUS DIMENSION

Michael Bolton adds interesting cases to this example:

> "As someone who flies a lot, I'd like to ask 'what's a trip?' An entire itinerary, including all legs of the outbound and the return flight? A flight from one city to another? Two flights (legs) on the same trip? Frequent flier programs sometimes account for code-share or allied-carrier trips very poorly. (I'm just after having that experience; Lufthansa didn't have my frequent flier number attached to my ticket, apparently because I had an Air Canada flight number. I just KNOW my account isn't going to get credited for that flight.) What happens when there's been an error in crediting your account, accumulated miles have to be adjusted, and bonus thresholds back-dated? At that point, dates influence the domain problem in a whole new way."

EXAMPLE 24: NOTEPAD OPEN FILE DIALOG

The Open File dialog from Notepad:

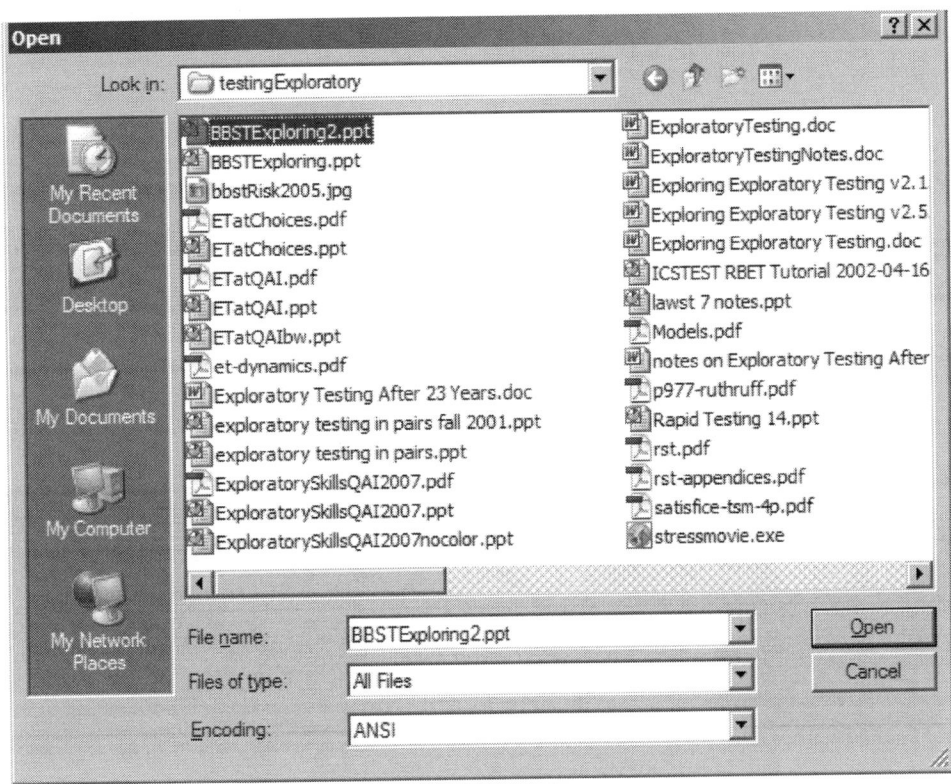

A. IDENTIFY THE POTENTIALLY INTERESTING VARIABLES

When you interview for a testing position, someone is likely to ask you to demonstrate your skill as a tester by testing something or designing tests for it. Interviewers often use the Open File dialog, showing a screen shot (or a rough sketch on the whiteboard) and saying, "Tell me how you would test this."

There are lots and lots and lots of things to test in the dialog. Which you choose and what you do with them reveals a lot about you.

We're going to focus on just one variable here, the `FileName` variable.

Notice that this is a Windows dialog, so Windows' rules apply.[45]

---

45 Morven Gentleman notes: "This illustrates a case in which the constraints are different for alternate environments in which the SUT should run. For instance, a variable of type string might be intended to hold a file pathname. For Unix, and its descendants, the constraint is that no component of the pathname can exceed a fixed length (which for Posix the maximum length of a pathname component), as well as the maximum name of a full pathname, can be different for every mounted file system. BSD supported full filenames up to 255 characters. Windows 3.11 only supported full filenames up to 63 characters. VMS had no limit on filename length, but only supported 8 pathname components."

B. IDENTIFY THE VARIABLES YOU CAN ANALYZE NOW. THESE ARE THE VARIABLES OF INTEREST

`FileName`

C. DETERMINE THE PRIMARY DIMENSION OF THE VARIABLE OF INTEREST

The purpose of the variable is to hold the name of a file. Because the variable doesn't have a natural ordering, we're not sure how to characterize "the primary dimension" more precisely.

D. DETERMINE THE TYPE AND SCALE OF THE VARIABLE'S PRIMARY DIMENSION AND WHAT VALUES IT CAN TAKE

The type of the variable is String. Actually, in Windows, it is a pair of Strings, the base filename and the Extension. (In the file name, ETatQAI.ppt, ETatQAI is the base filename and ppt is the extension.)

The scale of the variable is nominal. A variable that is "nominal scale" *is* a variable whose values are names. (That's the meaning of the word.)

It can contain any characters that a file name String can contain.

E. DETERMINE WHETHER YOU CAN ORDER THE VARIABLE'S VALUES (FROM SMALLEST TO LARGEST)

There is no primary ordering for a nominal-scale variable. You can *impose* an order on nominal variables, but the ordering is based on some aspect of the variable that you have decided to emphasize, not on the inherent meaning of the variable itself.

- The name Alphonso starts with an A, so maybe Alphonso comes before Joe.
- Joe is shorter than Alphonso, so maybe Joe comes before Alphonso.
- Alphonso is older than Joe, so maybe Joe comes before Alphonso.
- Alphonso has more money in the bank. Maybe on the bank's list, Alphonso comes before Joe.

Applying this to file names, you could sort them in these orders (and others):

- Alphabetical (file name)
- Length of the file name
- Size of the file
- Date the file was last saved

Whether these are *useful* orderings depends on what kind of error you're trying to discover.

Even though the variables don't have a natural order, you can group them and analyze them in terms of their groupings. We'll study Rollison's (2007a-c) groupings in Task I.

F. DETERMINE WHETHER THIS IS AN INPUT VARIABLE OR A RESULT

As entered in the `File name` field of the Open File dialog, `FileName` is an input variable.

G. DETERMINE HOW THE PROGRAM USES THIS VARIABLE

The program will attempt to find and open a file with this name in this directory.

H. DETERMINE WHETHER OTHER VARIABLES ARE RELATED TO THIS ONE

Lots of variables are related to this. Here are a few:

- The contents of the file.
- The format of the file (the way the contents are organized). This format *should be* consistent with the file extension. For example a file whose extension is pdf should be a Portable Document Format file. However, it might not be.
- The size of the file.
- The location of the file (specified by folder, path, URL, etc.).
- When the file was created.
- When it was last modified.
- Where the previous version of the file is and what the differences are between that one and this one.
- Who created the file.
- Who modified the file.
- Who owns the file.
- Whether the file is encrypted.
- Whether the file can be opened without a password (and if not, what password).
- Whether the file is already open in another application.
- Whether the file can be copied or printed or edited.

I. PARTITION THE VARIABLE (ITS PRIMARY DIMENSION)

- The dimension is not ordered, so determine what "similar" means for this variable and base partitioning on that.

Because the variable can't be ordered, the usual structure for partitioning (one set of values less than a boundary point, one set between the boundaries and one set above) won't work. Instead, group values by similarity.

Two values are similar if you expect the program to treat them the same way (see *Equivalence Classes* on page 15).

B.J. Rollison published a similarity analysis in 2007 and has graciously allowed us to quote extensively from it.

A TEST IDEA CATALOG FOR FILE NAME STRINGS

Equivalence Class Partitioning – Part 2: Character/String Data Decomposition

Bj Rollison, November 15, 2007

http://www.testingmentor.com/imtesty/2009/11/13/equivalence-class-partitioning-part-2-characterstring-data-decomposition/

Two weeks ago, I posted a challenge to decompose a set of character data (The ANSI Latin 1 Character Set) into valid and invalid equivalence class subsets in order to test the base filename parameter of a filename passed to COMDLG32.DLL on the Windows XP platform from the user interface using the File Save As... dialog of Notepad.

As illustrated below the filename on a Windows platform is composed of two separate parameters. Although the file name parameter of the Save As... dialog will accept a base filename, a base filename with an extension or a path with a filename with or without an extension, the purpose of the challenge was to decompose the limited set of characters into equivalence class subsets for the base filename component only. (Of course, complete testing will include testing with and without extensions, but let's first focus on building a foundation of tests to adequately evaluate the base filename parameter first, then we can expand our tests from there to include extensions.)

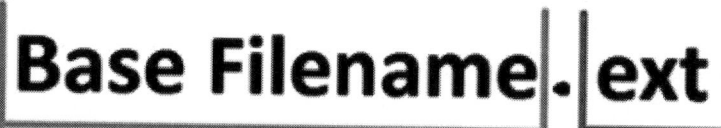

Base Filename.|ext

Windows filenames have 2 independent parameters.
The base filename parameter and the extension parameter.

As suggested in the earlier post, in order to adequately decompose this set of data within the defined, real world context (and not in alternate philosophical alternate universes) a professional tester would need to understand programming concepts, file naming conventions on a Windows platform, Windows XP file system, basic default character encoding on the Windows XP operating system (Unicode), some historical knowledge of the FAT file system, and even a bit of knowledge of the PC/AT architecture. The following is a table illustrating how I would decompose the data set into equivalence class subsets.

Valid Class Subsets

- V1 – escape sequence literal strings

  (STX, SOT, ETX, EOT, ENQ, ACK, BEL, BS, HT, LF, VT, FF, CR, SO, SI, DLE, DC1, DC2, DC3, DC4, NAK, SYN, ETB, CAN, EM, SUB, ESC, FS, GS, RS, US, DEL)

- V2 – space character (0×20) (but not as only, first or last character in the base file name)

- V3 – period character (0x2E) (but not as only character in the base file name)

- V4 – ASCII characters

  - punctuation (0×21, 0×23 – 0×29, 0x2B – 0x2D, 0x3B, 0x3D, 0×40, 0x5B, 0x5D, 0×60, 0x7B, 0x7D, 0x7E)

  - numbers (0×30 – 0×39)

  - alpha (0×41 – 0x5A, 0×61 – 0x7A)

- V5 – 0x80 through 0xFF

- V6 – 0×81, 0x8D, 0x8F, 0×90, 0x9D

- V7 – Component length between 1 – 251 characters (assuming a default 3-letter extension and a maximum path length of 260 characters)

- V8 – Literal string CLOCK$ (NT 4.0 code base)

- V9 – a valid string with a reserved character 0×22 as the first and last character in the string

Invalid Class Subsets

- I1 – control codes (Ctrl + @, Ctrl + B, Ctrl + C, Ctrl +], Ctrl + N, etc.)

- I2 – escape sequence literal string NUL
- I3 – Tab character
- I4 – reserved words (LPT1 – LPT4, COM1 – COM4, CON, PRN, AUX, etc.)
- I5 – reserved words (LPT5 – LPT9, COM5 – COM9)
- I6 – reserved characters (/ : < > |)

  (0x2F, 0x3A, 0x3C, 0x3E, 0x7C) by themselves or as part of a string of characters
- I7 – reserved character 0x22 as the only character or > 2 characters in the string
- I8 – a string composed of > 1 reserved character 0x5C
- I9 – a string containing only 2 reserved characters 0x22
- I10 – period character (0x2E) as only character in a string
- I11 – two period characters (0x2E) as only characters in a string
- I12 – > 2 period characters (0x2E) as only characters in a string
- I13 – reserved character 0x5C as the only character in the string
- I14 – space character (0x20) as only character in a string
- I15 – space character (0x20) as first character in a string
- I16 – space character (0x20) as last character in a string
- I17 – reserved characters (* ?) (0x2A, 0x3F)
- I18 – a string of valid characters that contains at least one reserved character (* ?) (0x2A, 0x3F)
- I19 – a string of valid characters that contains at least one reserved character 0x5C but not in the first position
- I20 – string > 251 characters
- I21 – character case sensitivity
- I22 – empty

Discussion of valid equivalence class subsets

- Valid subset V1 is composed of the literal strings for control characters (or escape sequences) between 0x01 and 0x1F, and including 0x7F. The literal strings for control characters may cause problems under various configurations or unique situations. The book *How to Break Software: A Practical Guide to Testing* (Whittaker, 2003) goes into great detail explaining various fault models for these various character values. The literal strings in this subset should be tested as the base filename component and possibly in a separate test as an extension component. However, on the Windows platform the probability of one particular string in this subset behaving or being handled differently than any of the others is very low negating the need to test every string in this subset; although the overhead to test all would be minimal and once complete would not likely require repeated testing of all literal strings in this subset during a project cycle.

- Valid subset V2 provides guidance on the use of the space character in valid filenames. On the Windows operating system a space character (0x20) is allowed in a base filename, but is not permitted as the only character as a file name. Typical behavior on the Windows platform also truncates the space character if it is used as the first character of a base filename or the last character of a base filename. However, if the extension is appended to the base filename in the Filename edit control on the Save or Save As... dialog a space character can be the last character in the base filename. Also note that a space character by itself or as the first character in a filename is acceptable on a UNIX based operating system. Also, although we can force the Windows platform to save a file name with only a space character by typing " .txt" (including the quotes) in the Filename edit control on the Save/Save As... dialog this practice is not typical of reasonable Windows users' expectations.

◦ Valid subset V3 is the period character (0x2E) which is allowed in a base filename, but it is not a valid filename if it is the only character in the base filename (see Invalid subset for the period character).

◦ Valid subset V4 is composed of 'printable' ASCII characters that are valid ASCII characters in a Windows filename. The subset includes punctuation characters, numeric characters, and alpha characters. We could also decompose this subset further into additional subsets including valid punctuation characters, numbers, upper case, and lower case characters if we wanted to ensure that we test at least one element from the superset at least once.

◦ Valid subset V5 is the set of character code points between 0x80 and 0xFF.

◦ Valid subset V6 is a superset of subset V5 and are separated only because they are code points that do not have character glyphs assigned to those code point values. These would be interesting especially if we needed to test filenames for backwards compatibility on Windows 9x platforms.

◦ Valid subset V7 is the minimum and maximum component length assuming the filename is saved in the root directory (C:\).

◦ Valid subset V8 is probably a red-herring. On the NT 4 platform the string CLOCK$ was a reserved word. On an older application first created for the Windows NT 4 platform that does not use the system Save/Save As dialog we might want to test this string just to make sure the developer did not hard code the string in an error handling routine.

◦ Valid subset V9 is an interesting case because this invalid reserved character (0x22) is handled differently when used in first and last character positions of a base filename. When used in the first and last positions of a base filename the characters are truncated and if the remaining string is valid the filename is saved. If only one 0x22 character is used or if two or more 0x22 characters are used in a string other than the first and last character positions the result will be an error message.

Discussion of invalid equivalence class subsets

◦ Invalid subset I1 consists of the control code inputs for escape sequences in the range of 0x01 through 0x1F, and also includes 0x7F. Pressing the control key (CTRL) and any of the control codes keys will cause a system beep.

◦ Invalid subset I2 is the literal string "nul". Nul is a reserved word but could be processed differently than other reserved words on the Windows platform because it is also used in many coding languages as a character for string termination.

◦ Invalid subset I3 is the tab character which can be copied and pasted into the Filename textbox control. Pasting a tab into the [Filename textbox] and pressing the save button will generate an error message.

◦ The invalid subset I4 includes literal strings for reserved device names on the PC/AT machine and the Windows platform. Using any string in this subset results in an error message indicating the filename is a reserved device name.

◦ Invalid subset I5 also includes reserved device names for LPT5 – LPT9 and COM5 – COM9. However these must be separated into a unique subset because using these specific device names as the base filename on the Windows XP operating system result in an error message indicating the filename is invalid.

- Invalid subsets I6, I7, and I8, include reserved characters on a Windows platform. When characters in this subset are used by themselves or in any position in a string of characters the result is an error message indicating the above file name is invalid.

- Invalid subsets I9, I10, and I13, also include reserved characters and the space and period characters. When these subsets are tested as defined, no error message is displayed and focus is restored to the File name control on the Save/Save As... dialog.

- Invalid subsets I11 and I12, also include the reserved character (0x2E) as 2 characters in the string and greater than 2 characters in a string. The state machine changes are different.

- Invalid subsets I15 and I16 define the space character when used in the first or last character position of a string. These are placed in the invalid class because Windows' normal behavior is to truncate a leading or trailing space character in a file name. If the leading or trailing space character was not truncated and saved as part of the file name on a Windows platform, that would constitute a defect.

- Invalid subsets I17 and I18 contain two additional reserved characters: the asterisk and the question mark (0x2A and 0x3F respectively). If these characters are used by themselves or as a character in a string of other valid characters, a file will not be saved and no error message will occur. However, the state of the Save/Save As... dialog does change. If the default file type is .txt and there are text files displayed in the Folder View control on the Save As... dialog, the files with the .txt extension will be removed after the Save button is depressed. If the default file type is All files then all files will be removed from the Folder View control on the Save As... dialog after the Save button is depressed.

- Invalid subset I19 is a string of valid characters which contains at least backslash character except as the lead character in the string. (Of course, this assumes the string is random and the position of the backslash character in the string is not in a position which would resolve to a valid path.) The backslash character is a reserved character for use as a path delimiter in the file system. An error message will appear indicating the path is invalid.

- Invalid subset I20 tests for extremely long base file name length of greater than 252 characters. Note that an interesting anomaly occurs with string lengths. A base file name string length which tests the boundaries of 252 or 253 valid characters will cause an error message to display indicating the file name is invalid. However, a base file name string length of 254 or 255 characters will actually get saved as file name but not associated with any file type. Any base file name string longer than 255 characters again instantiates an error message.

- Invalid subset I21 describes the tests for case sensitivity. The Windows platform does not consider character case of characters that have an upper case and a lower case representation. For example, a file name with a lower case Latin character 'a' is considered the same as a file name with the upper case Latin character 'A'.

- Invalid subset I22 is, of course, an empty string

Of course, this is a partial list of the complete data set since the filename on a Windows XP operating system can be any valid Unicode value of which there are several thousand character code points, including surrogate pair characters.

The first and by far the most complex step in the application of the functional technique of equivalence class partitioning is data decomposition. This requires an incredible amount of knowledge about the system. Data decomposition is an exercise in modeling data. The less one understands the data set or the system under test the greater the probability of missing something. Next week we will analyze the equivalence class subsets to define are baseline set of tests to evaluate the base filename component.

Equivalence Class Partitioning – Part 3 – The Tests

Bj Rollison, November 29, 2007

http://www.testingmentor.com/imtesty/2009/11/13/equivalence-class-partitioning-part-3-the-tests/

In the last post we decomposed the set of characters in the ANSI character set into valid and invalid class subsets for use in a base filename component on the Windows XP operating system. The second part of the testing technique of equivalence class partitioning is to then use this information in tests that will adequately evaluate the functional capabilities of the base filename parameter used by COMDLG32.DLL in Windows XP.

(Note: It is appropriate here to differentiate between a test case and a test. A **test case** is the hypothesis or assertion that I am either trying to prove or disprove. A **test** is the process or procedure I am using to prove or disprove my hypothesis. In other words, a test case in this example might be "Validate a base filename can be saved using valid characters in the ANSI 1252 character set." In order to prove or disprove this hypothesis, I will execute multiple tests using the various subsets outlined in the previous post, and as described below. If any test fails, the test case fails.)

There are basically 2 procedures for defining the tests that use the data from an equivalence class table. Paul Jorgensen describes a procedure for robust equivalence class testing in which each valid class subset is tested individually. Glenford Myers suggests a procedure in which valid class subsets are combined in a test until all valid class subsets have been covered. (Jorgensen refers to this as weak equivalence class testing.) Both authors agree that subsets in the invalid subsets must be tested in a way that only one parameter is invalid and any other parameters use valid variables. Using Myers' approach (or what Jorgensen describes as weak equivalence class testing) the tests for the base filename parameter are illustrated in the table below.

[Edited 11/30 to clarify some assumptions.]

○ Any time a key is pressed there is essentially a state change. The primary state change we are concerned with for this particular functional test is whether or not a file is saved to the file system. However, in cases of invalid input, other state changes may be interesting. In most well designed Windows applications an erroneous input in an input control will be highlighted (usually after an error message is displayed). This is indeed an expected state change. The only time no noticeable state change occurs (there is still a state change because the machine is processing WM_Key messages) is with Test #5. But, another noticeable state change (the one primarily identified in the table below) is the state change to the list view control.

○ There are 3 ways to effectively affect the Save button. One way is to press Enter, another is to press the Alt + s key mnemonic, and thirdly to left mouse click the button control (including simulating any of those actions via automation). In some cases the visible state changes may vary; however, the purpose of these tests is to verify the existence of a file name in the file system for valid cases, and the non-existence and no abhorrent side effects in the case of members of the invalid class subsets. So, regardless of the visible state changes, the tester can use any of these procedures to affect the Save button.

○ Application of techniques (systematic procedures) at a granular level is very different than simply trying things to see what happens, exploratory testing, guessing or wild speculation. I made the assumption that readers are familiar with designing and executing atomic functional tests at a granular level in which certain variables are controlled. For example, once we enter an invalid string in the file name text box and press the save button, the Save As... dialog is now dirty; meaning that the next input could produce an error but I will not know if the error is a result of an error with the base filename parameter or with the Save As... dialog state. Equivalence class partitioning is a low level functional test of a single parameter, so in order to test the base filename parameter the tester (or automated test) should minimally close and instantiate the Save As... dialog on each test.

Tests	Data Subset	Example	Expected Result
1	V1	`ETX`	File saved to disk
2	V2, V3, V4, V5, V6, V7	`yæB1% 9!.ÅęxK`	File saved to disk
3	V8	`CLOCK$`	File saved to disk
4	V9, V2, V3, V4, V5 U V6, V7	`"myFileName"`	File saved to disk, but no file association
5	I1	`CTRL + B`	No error message, no listview state change, no File name textbox state change
6	I2	`NUL or nul`	Error message, reserved device name
7	I3	`[tab]`	Error message, file name invalid
8	I4	`lpt3`	Error message, reserved device name
9	I5	`com7`	Error message, file name invalid
10	I6	`: OR ht/7g|`	Error message, file name invalid
11	I7	`" OR \"""`	Error message, file name invalid
12	I8	`\\\\\`	Error message, file name invalid
13	I9	`\"`	No error message, state change
14	I10	`.`	No error message, no listview state change
15	I11	`. .`	No error message, listview state change
16	I12	`......`	No error message, listview state change
17	I13	`\`	No error message, listview state change
18	I14	`[space]`	No error message, listview state change
19	I15	`[space]myfile`	File saved to disk, leading space truncated
20	I16	`myfile[space]`	File saved to disk, trailing space truncated
21	I17	`*`	No error message, listview state change
22	I18	`my*file`	No error message, listview state change
23	I19	`myf\ile`	Error message, invalid path (assumes dir not exist)
24	I20	`strlen > 251`	Error message, file name invalid
25	I21	`myfile and MyFile`	Error message, file already exists
26	I22	`[empty]`	No error message, listview state change

Reducing tests while increasing breadth of coverage

The total number of possible tests of valid string combinations for just the base file-name parameter using only characters within the ANSI 1252 character set is $214^{251} + 214^{250} + 214^{249} + \ldots 214^{2} + 214^{1}$. This number of tests, of course, is a virtual impossibility, so by employing the equivalence class partitioning testing technique we are able to systematically produce a minimum baseline set of tests that has a high probability of proving or disproving our hypothesis or test purpose, as well as providing great variability in the test data to increase breadth of data coverage. The minimum possible number of valid tests determined by combining at least one element from each valid class subset is only four tests. But, let's look at each valid test a little more closely.

Test #3 is probably a red-herring! This is only an invalid filename on Windows NT 4.0 and below. So, if your application is ported from that time frame, and you are using a custom function for your file save functionality rather than Windows APIs then you might consider running this test once. If it passes, you can probably forget running this again ever again on that product. Test #1 evaluates the literal strings in valid subset V1. They can be listed in an array or enumeration and one element can be selected at random throughout the development lifecycle or each literal string can be tested once: the probability of failure in a later build is most likely less than .001%. Test #4 is also a test that probably doesn't require a great deal of retesting of various combinations of elements from subsets V2, V3, V4, V5 , & V7. Elements from the valid class subsets described in Test #2 are most interesting and this is the test that we will probably want to automate and run repeatedly throughout the development lifecycle because it provides great breadth of coverage.

Remember this is the minimum number of valid tests. What isn't covered in this set are common or 'real-world' data sets which we would certainly want to include. Additionally, Test #2 relies on at least one element from each indicated subset. We might want to consider additional tests that focus on subsets V4 and V5 only. Also, we might consider testing valid class subset V6 as a special case if we suspected a private function excluded code point values that were not assigned character glyphs. However, if these 4 valid tests pass, the probability of failure of any combination of these data sets used in this parameter is minimal. Random selection of elements for Test #2 (and possibly Test #4) may slightly increase the probability of exposing a defect in the base filename parsing routine. Tests #5 through #26 are tests for invalid filenames or in the case of Test #19 and #20 where the expected result is to truncate the leading or trailing space character.

This of course only analyzes (or tests) the base filename parameter and assumes a nominal valid 3-letter extension, valid filenames do not preexist on the file system, and within the specific context described in the first post. If the context changes, (e.g. this example does not apply to Unix platforms or Windows Vista or other parameters) then this set of tests (assuming we would run at least Tests #2, and #5 through #26 as part of our regression suite on each new build) would provide a high level of confidence in the functional capability of this specific parameter.

Next, we would decompose the data for the file extension parameter (which is different than the base filename parameter) because in the File name textbox we can enter either the base filename or the base filename and an extension. Once we verify the functionality of the base filename component, we can then proceed to the next step in analyzing the functionality of the arguments passed to the File name textbox parameter which we shall examine at a later date.

It is important to note that this and any other techniques are simply systematic procedures designed to help us wrap our minds around complex problems. They are not the only approach to testing (only a fool would advocate a single approach to testing), but when used in conjunction with various other techniques, methods, and approaches EQ can help to establish a strong foundation of confidence in low level operations. Of course, as has been previously stated, the limiting factor of this and other functional techniques is the knowledge of the professional tester to think critically and rationally analyze the "overall system" within the appropriate context.

We suggest one more group of tests for this superb list. Sometimes, you can save a file (or rename a file or import a file) with a name that Windows does not like. Perhaps being able to rename it this way is a bug, but once the file is in the file system, you probably want to be able to open it. What are the different ways that you could designate that file as the one you want to open? Will any of them work (let you open the file)?

GROUPING FILE NAMES BY TYPE

The extension carries fallible information about how data are stored in the file. Why do we say it is fallible? Consider...

- A file with extension pdf is probably a Portable Document Format file. However:
  - It might not be pdf at all.
  - It might be a version of pdf that only recent readers can read.
  - It might be a corrupt pdf file.

Thus, the set of files with extension pdf form a broad class that can be partitioned into equivalence classes that correspond to different versions of Portable Document Format and different non-pdf types.

The same breadth (many variations of format under the same name) apply to many other file types. Take a look, for example, at the Wikipedia articles:

- https://en.wikipedia.org/wiki/Tagged_image_file_format
- https://en.wikipedia.org/wiki/JPEG

J. LAY OUT THE ANALYSIS IN A CLASSICAL BOUNDARY/EQUIVALENCE TABLE. IDENTIFY BEST REPRESENTATIVES

See Rollison's list of test ideas and table of tests above.

K. CREATE TESTS FOR THE CONSEQUENCES OF THE DATA ENTERED, NOT JUST THE INPUT FILTER

Here are some examples of possible tests:

- Open files, check their contents are what you expect.
- Check the display of file names (in dialogs that list files, like the picture at the start of this example) to see whether it matches the names you entered.
- Open files, then save them. Do any files have unmanageable names or paths for saving?

L. IDENTIFY SECONDARY DIMENSIONS. ANALYZE THEM IN THE CLASSICAL WAY

Relative to the file name, these are all secondary:

- The contents of the file.
- The format of the file (the way the contents are organized). This *should be* consistent with the file extension. For example a file whose extension is pdf should be a Portable Document Format file. However, it might not be.
- The size of the file.
- The location of the file (specified by folder, path, URL, etc.).
- When the file was created.
- When it was last modified.
- Where the previous version of the file is and what the differences are between that one and this one.
- Who created the file.
- Who modified the file.
- Who owns the file.
- Whether the file can be opened without a password (and if not, what password).
- Whether the file can be copied or printed or edited.

Also:

- Can you select or name several files at once? How many?
- If the dialog displays a list that is actually larger than the display window can show, what if you name a file that is not visible?
- Can you concatenate files (name two files with a syntax that has the operating system open one and append the other to it?)
- Name a just-deleted file (still in the recycle bin or showing on the not-yet-repainted list of files)

M. SUMMARIZE YOUR ANALYSIS WITH A RISK/EQUIVALENCE TABLE

What we wanted to feature in this example was Rollison's list of test ideas and table of tests. A risk/equivalence table would be huge and the one we have in mind wouldn't add much information beyond Rollison's work. So we're going to skip this Task.

N. ANALYZE INDEPENDENT VARIABLES THAT SHOULD BE TESTED TOGETHER

None are mentioned in the problem description.

O. ANALYZE VARIABLES THAT HOLD RESULTS

We've done enough analysis in this Example, but if you want to consider it further, here are some result variables:

- If you use wild cards in the file name variable, the file list is a result variable.
- The file which is loaded by the open action is a result variable.
- The file name itself is a result variable if you click on an item in the file list.

P. TASKS P, Q & R ARE BEYOND WHAT WE'RE TRYING TO TEACH WITH THIS EXAMPLE.

SECTION 3. PART 2: ADVANCED EXAMPLES

In this Part, we look at more complex cases.

Each of these examples presents many variables. You have already seen examples of the standard analysis for the main data types. We aren't going to pick variables from these examples and show you the same analysis. Instead, we consider whether (and how and why) a domain analysis would be helpful *as part of* the design of the testing for this example.

In each example, the starting point is to look for variables.

- *Domain analysis is relevant when you focus on a variable that has so many possible values that it would be useful to test only a subset of the values.*

- *Domain analysis rests on a sampling approach: Divide the set of possible values of the variable into equivalence classes and then sample best representatives from each class.*

- *When you divide the values into equivalence classes, you're grouping them according to some type of similarity:*

  - *Traditionally, domain analysis focuses on similarity of size. For example, values might be grouped together as too small, too big or just right.*

  - *Instead of grouping by size, it might be possible to group values categorically.*

We described heuristics for grouping variables for domain analysis at *Examples of Variables that Can be Ordered* on page 85. Here is an overview / reminder of that description. For more details, including more-specific examples, see the main description:

- Examples of grouping by size:

  - Character-based encoding

  - How many

  - How big

  - Timing

  - Speed

- Examples of grouping by non-quantitative category:

  - Configuration

  - Variation between things that should be equivalent

  - Membership in the same group

  - Lead to the same consequence

  - Create exposure to the same risk

EXAMPLE 25: MOODLE ASSIGN USER ROLES

Moodle is a program that manages online courses. Here is one of its dialogs. The user can assign participants in a class to one or more roles in the course, such as student or teacher.

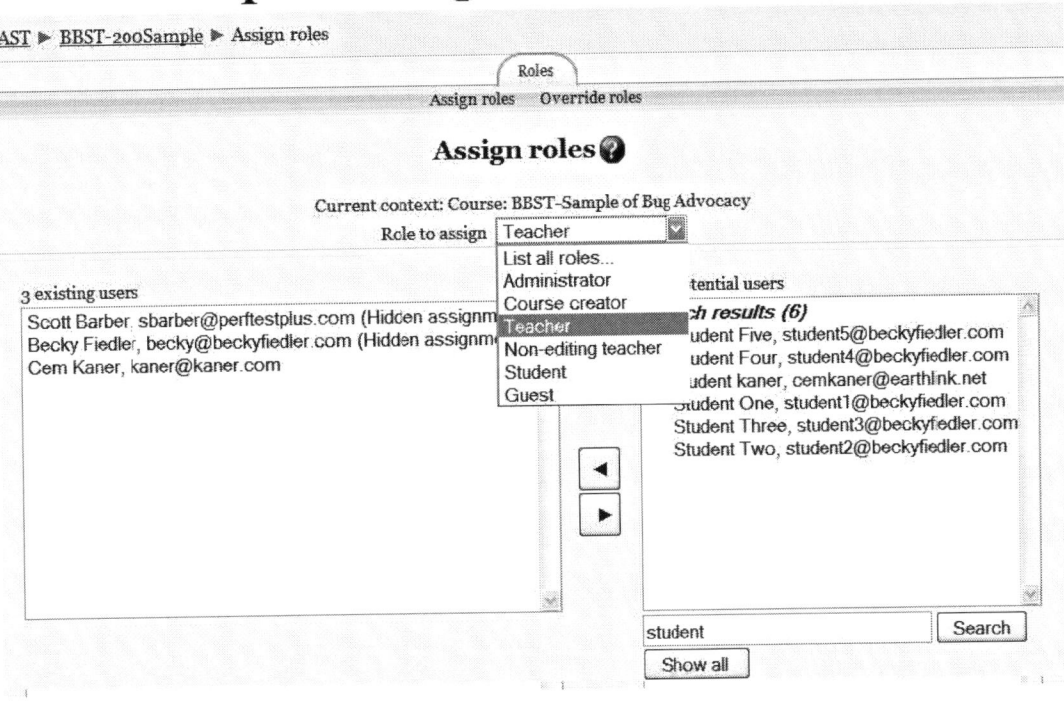

OVERVIEW

Moodle is a popular course management system. You can create and host courses on Moodle. Students can register in a course and then access course content (such as videos, documents, links to externally-stored content), engage in activities (such as discussions, games, quizzes, essay-style exams) and administer their profile and their view of the site. Moodle is open-source, available for use for free and is one of the most popular management systems for online courses.

A company can set up a Moodle site that can host many courses. This Example shows a screen that a course Administrator or Teacher would see while working in a course. It enables the course teacher to assign people to various roles in the course.

The pull-down list shows several roles. The set of privileges available for each role can be customized by the Site Administrator (the administrator of the entire site). The list on the screen shows these roles.

Typically, these roles have these privileges:

- The *Administrator* has all privileges available to someone working with courses. (It is possible to create an Administrator of courses who has fewer privileges than the Administrator of the entire Moodle site.)

- The *Course Creator* can create and modify courses. For example, the Course Creator might create the course, "Statistics 101". This is a "Master" course. She can then create a specific class, "Statistics 101 — Fall 2014" and another class, "Statistics 101 — Spring 2015". These are both copies (except for dates) from the Master course.

- The *Teacher* teaches a specific class, like "Statistics 101 — Fall 2014." In sites that distinguish between Course Creators and Teachers, the teacher might have less power than the Administrator or Course Creator to register students in the course or to create or modify elements of the course (such as quizzes or videos).

- The *Non-Editing Teacher* has only some of the privileges of the Teacher. For example, he can see student assignments and grade them. For example, he can post messages to the class or send messages to individual students through the course messaging system. However, he can't change any of the elements of the course (such as adding videos or discussion forums or changing how quizzes are graded.) If you have taken a university course that had a graduate student who served as Teaching Assistant, that person would probably be the Non-Editing Teacher in the Moodle course.

- The *Student* can see the content posted in the course (for example, watch videos) and can engage in the activities (take quizzes and post messages to discussion forums). However, much of what the Student submits will be private. For example, the Teacher will probably be able to see every Student's quiz answers but Students will probably see only their own answers.

- The *Guest* can see the content but can't engage in the activities.

An Administrator can change these privileges or delete or rename these roles or create new ones.

The left-hand pane on this screen shows a list of *Existing Users*.

- There is a different list for each role. It includes everyone who has been assigned this role.

- The list on the screen shows the three people (users) who have been assigned the role of Teacher.

The right-hand pane on this screen shows a list of *Potential Users*.

- This list includes everyone who has registered on the site and is potentially allowed to sign up for a course. Registration on the site is typically done once, when the person first visits the site. It is probably done before the person signs up for any particular course.

- There is a different list for each role. It shows everyone who has registered on this Moodle site who has not yet been assigned this role in this course. This can be a huge list.

- The list on the screen shows the six people (users) who have not been assigned the role of Teacher.

To assign a person to a role:

- Click on the name of the role (such as Teacher) in the pull-down list.
- Click on a name in the right-hand pane (Potential Users).
- Press the arrow pointing to the left-hand pane.

To remove a person from a role:

- Click on the name of the role (such as Teacher) in the pull-down list.
- Click on a name in the left-hand pane (Existing Users).
- Press the arrow pointing to the right-hand pane.

Note the Search box at the bottom of the right-hand pane. If you type a string (such as a letter or a name) in this box and click Search, Moodle will filter the list of Potential Users to show only users whose name-and-email-address include the search string.

At the top of the list of Potential Users in the screen shot, you can see *Search Results (6)*, which shows the number of elements in the filtered (the displayed) list.

WHERE CAN YOU APPLY DOMAIN ANALYSIS?

- The screen shows 6 roles.
  - How many are allowed?
  - How many can you assign to one person?
  - How many times can you assign a role to the same person?
- There are three visible lists of strings. There are actually more than that because there is one list for each role.
  - Are any strings permissible in one list but not the others?
  - Are any strings too long or too short for elements of one list but not the others?
  - How many elements can appear in each list?
  - Is there a maximum number of characters for the list that could sometimes reduce the number of possible elements for a particular list? (For example, imagine a list of people who all have very long names. Can you list as many people?)
  - Are any characters invalid?
  - Are any entries (such as email address) invalid because of format (for example a string that could not possibly be an email address because it contains no "@" symbol) or because of content (for example a valid-looking address that points to a nonexistent domain)?
  - Are duplicates allowed within a list? What about partial duplication (same name, different email or same email, different name)?
  - There are two visible user lists. Can a name appear in both lists?
  - Are any of the lists sorted or sortable? If so, is the sort-order correct across all possible contents of that list?
  - When you select a list type, how long does it take to present that list? For example, when the program presents a sorted list, does it have to take time to sort the list before presenting it? If so, do any problems arise out of the long sorting-time required for a long list?
  - How or where is the list stored? Can the list be made too long for the storage device?
  - What happens if you assign someone to every role?
  - What happens if you have a long list of students and you assign all of them to every role? Is there a memory limit somewhere?

- What values are permissible in the search box?
  - Consider the usual possibilities for testing strings (see *Test Idea Catalog for Strings* on page 278). Because these are names, pay special attention to accented characters and other characters that aren't common in your language.
  - Are search-control characters (such as wildcards) allowed?
  - What about search strings that lead to empty results?
  - What about search strings that yield the entire list?
    - Can you make the list long enough to overflow the Search Results (N) variable?
  - Are any strings equivalent (e.g., case-insensitivity)?
  - Does the search box correctly remember or clear the last value it contained when you navigate away and come back?
- What are the results of the search?
  - How many matches does it find?
  - Does it find matches with the first and last element in the list?
  - How well do the matches show in the display area? (Does the scroll bar appear when they overflow the display area?)
  - What if a match exceeds the width of the display area?
- What are the consequences of membership in a list?
  - Assigning a role to someone grants them certain permissions.
  - What happens if you rename a role (for example from Teacher to Instructor)? Do the permissions follow? Do all Instructors have the same privileges of Teachers?
  - What if you rename a role to a role with other privileges? For example, rename Guest to Visitor and then rename Teacher to Guest. What privileges will Guest have?
  - What happens when you assign two roles to the same person?
    - Cumulative privileges? (All privileges available to either role?) (That's our expectation.)
    - Only those privileges that are common to both roles?
    - Is it possible for selection of one role to reduce the privileges, in any way, that would be otherwise available to someone who had also been selected for a second role?
  - Can a person with lower privileges assign a role that has higher privileges? For example, can a Teacher make someone an Administrator?
  - What if you assign someone to a role (like, teacher) that gives them special privileges, they do things in that role and then you remove that role? For example, in Moodle, there is a course announcements forum that teachers can use to send messages to every student. Teachers can see and edit their posts to any forum. Students can't post messages to this forum. Suppose you make Joe a teacher, he posts messages to the forum and then you demote his privilege level from teacher to student. With this privilege level, can he access and edit one of his old posts?
  - What if you assign someone to a role and the Site Administrator eliminates that role? Do all the people in this situation get the next-highest set of privileges? No privileges? Something else?
  - If you remove someone from a role, does Moodle add their name back to the Potential users list for that role?

- Are there possible timing issues or race conditions?
  - Suppose someone signs up on the site while you're looking at the list of potential users. When do they show up in your list?
  - Suppose you attempt to assign someone to a role and while you're selecting and assigning them, the Site Administrator is booting them off the site. When do they lose privileges in your course?
  - Suppose that a Teacher (who is not also an Administrator or Course Creator) removes themself from the list of Teachers. This person no longer has the privilege to assign roles (or see student work, etc.). When does the system stop allowing them to exercise Teacher privileges?
- Are the roles hierarchical?
  - Can you create a role that has some privileges that another role has (but not all of them) and has other privileges the other role does not have?
  - If the roles aren't strictly hierarchical, how are they ordered in the Roles To Assign pulldown list?
  - If the roles are hierarchical, what happens if you reorder them?

EXAMPLE 26: INSTALL PRINTER SOFTWARE

The Microsoft Install Printer Software dialog installs the driver for the printer you select. There are a few thousand Windows-compatible printers. In this dialog, selecting the manufacturer brings up a list of printers made by that manufacturer.

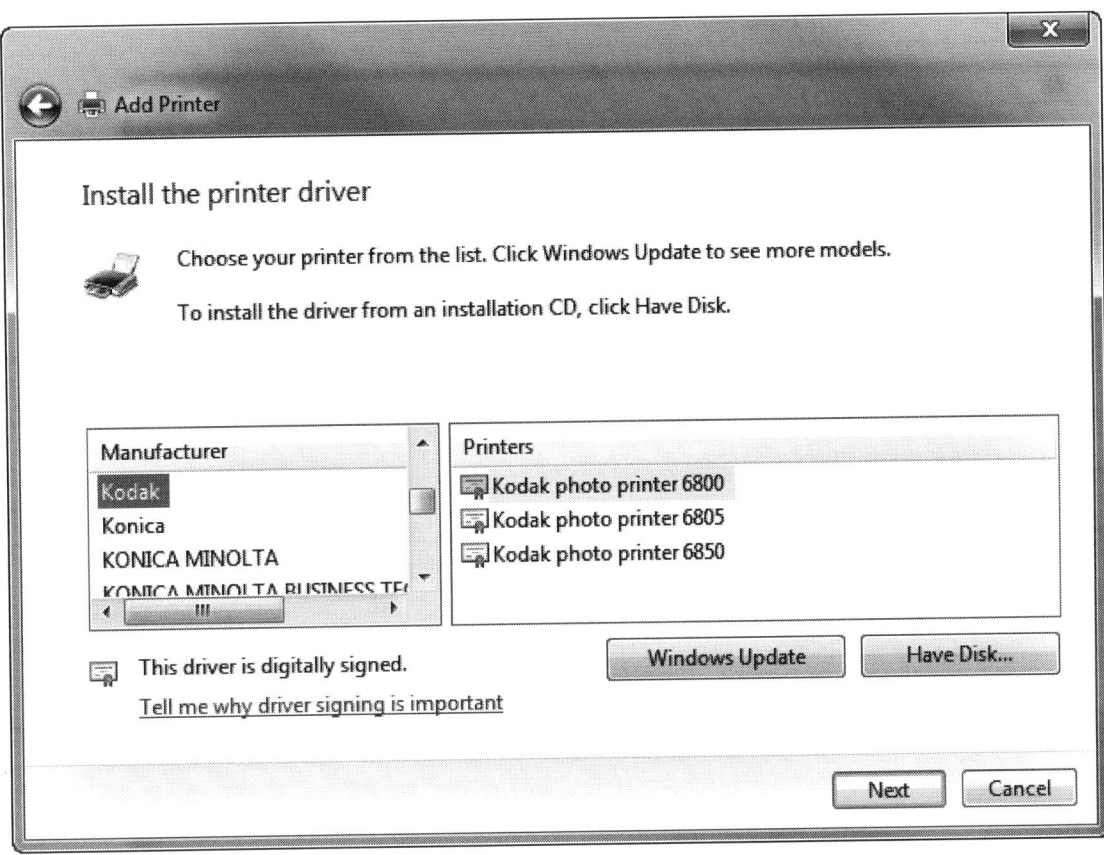

OVERVIEW

This shows a straightforward dialog. It shows two lists two lists, Manufacturers and Printers.

- Select a Manufacturer to determine which printers (made by that manufacturer) show in the Printers list.
- Select a Printer to install it.
- Click Windows Update to update both lists.

Once you've installed a printer, you can print a test page to check its basic functionality.

Most Windows 7-compatible programs are compatible with any printer that is compatible with Windows 7. It's not necessary to test a well-behaved Windows 7-compatible program with a large collection of printers to check compatibility. However, some programs rely more heavily on the details of the implementation of the individual printer or printer driver and might not be compatible with a specific printer. For example, see the printer compatibility documentation at PaperCut (2012, 2013).

WHERE CAN YOU APPLY DOMAIN ANALYSIS?

Suppose you're testing a program for its compatibility with Windows 7-compatible printers. Because there are so many potential printers to test, it is appropriate to sample from the set rather than to attempt to test a program's compatibility with each one.

There is no natural ordering for these printers (or their drivers). Perhaps the name of the HP LaserJet 2410 printer comes before Kodak 1392 in the alphabet and probably the file size of one of the drivers is bigger than the other. However, neither the name nor the file size has any relevance to whether the printer will actually work when an application sends it data to print.

An obvious grouping of the printers is by Manufacturer. However, this is not always the most useful high-level grouping and even if you group this way, within the list of Manufacturers, you still have to decide which printer(s) to test.

Kaner, Falk & Nguyen (1993) discussed this type of analysis in 25 pages of detail, laying out a strategy for organizing compatibility testing with printers, video cards, mice, network cards, scanners and any other type of peripheral.

In summary, working with printers as their primary example, they recommended testing in this order:

- *Test for device-independent, functionality errors first.* To achieve this, you can test the program with almost any printer.

- *Test for device-class-specific errors.* Divide the set of all printers into a relatively small group of classes that each contain many printers. Then test for errors that could appear in any member of this class.

  For example, consider all of the printers that can print using Printer Command Language 6 (PCL 6) (*See* https://en.wikipedia.org/wiki/Printer_Command_Language.) Many printers can use several different command languages, so testing for compatibility with PCL 6 printers involves selecting one or a few printers that *can* work with PCL 6, setting them *to* print using PCL 6 and then running your tests.

  Note that a printer will often belong to several classes. For example, a printer might be compatible with several different command languages and thus belong to several device classes.

- *Test for driver-class specific errors.* Some drivers are designed to work with several printers. Sample one or a few printers to check compatibility with the driver.

  Note that a printer will be compatible with several drivers. At a minimum, a printer will be compatible with the original version of a driver and its updates. In addition, a printer might be designed to emulate several other types of printers and to be compatible with the drivers created for those printers.

- *Test for errors that arise only with a specific (e.g., printer) model.*

- *Test for errors that arise when this device is used in conjunction with another one* (such as high-resolution print preview to a high-resolution display).

Note that each Printer Type has a rich set of secondary characteristics. For example, a printer might be multi-functional (scanner, fax, etc.). It might print in color. It might be a laser or inkjet printer. It has a memory capacity, type of hardware interface, printing speed (that might be adjustable, for example slowing as the printer heats up), it supports different paper sizes, has a number of paper trays, etc. These secondary dimensions may be useful for classification of similar devices or for categorization into separate subdomains.

It should be obvious that this is a messy categorization system. We spent years developing it as our way of coping with testing an enormous number of printers. In 1983, it was common for us to test WordStar with 600 printers per version and sometimes with several modes and several drivers per version. This was extremely expensive and time-consuming. By 1991, there were over 1000 printer models that were in common enough use that we wanted to test them. There were perhaps 2000 by 1994. Kaner, Falk and Nguyen developed an approach for rationally sampling 25-40 printers from this enormous set in the late 1980's as they managed software testing groups at Electronic Arts and at Power Up Software. (Test groups at other companies developed their own sampling systems. There is nothing special about Kaner *et al.*'s, compared to some others, beyond the fact it is described in some detail in print.) Kaner *et al.* applied the same approach to testing software compatibility with video cards and modems. Other testers followed the same approach, applying it to audio interfaces, mice, keyboards, disk drive controllers and a variety of other devices. This was imperfect but it was commercially viable, in the sense that we were able to reduce the number of printers (and driver versions and other settings) to a manageable level while keeping to an affordable level the number of customer-support calls that were caused by incompatibility of our software with specific printers.

We believe the same type of approach applies to smartphones and tablets (differing, for example, in which type of operating system and which version they run), to digital video recorders (which are subject to enormous compatibility issues with cable and satellite networks) and many other types of devices.[46]

Reviewers have asked us why we are still writing about printer compatibility. We agree that printer compatibility has gradually become a less serious problem. Printers are more standardized and many of the old compatibility issues are now resolved at the operating system level.

It is clear there is massive diversity in the mobile device space (*see* Velazco, 2012, for example). We have heard from software testers with experience in the field that this has been a significant challenge and that it requires some form of stratified sampling. Yet, we also hear from developers that this is not really a problem at all. Look, for example, at the long series of comments on Velazco's article. Many of them, purportedly from developers with experience in the field, dismiss the issue out of hand as the rantings of bloggers who know nothing of development or as motivated attacks from iOS zealots. Our intuition is there is knowledge and ignorance on all sides of this debate. We saw similar debates years ago over the impact of diversity of peripherals (like printers). Our impression is that, even though many valid claims and facts came out, those debates damaged the credibility of many people without contributing much to an understanding of the problem. We have no wish to wade into that swamp in this book.

---

46 The challenge is not just with device compatibility. Michael Hackett describes the same type of complexity:

"I have worked on 2 safety-critical hospital systems where this is an issue. Dividing medication into classes, class A, class B, class C (the ones people steal), divide by delivery: pill, IV oral, topical, nasal, etc. Age of patient: (a lot of reporting, dosage, approval and functionality built around medication/pharmacy for for neo-natal, infant, children, adult, senior, elderly). There are so many dimensions with life/safety-critical, legal, administrative role (researchers, "chief" Dr, intern, resident, PA, RN, LPN, etc.) all have different rules for prescribing), ingredients/combinations and interaction… the attempts to divide the MASSIVE databases of FDA approved medications into various domains would be helped by the analysis in this book. In every case, test coverage winds up being tiny."

The approach we describe for printers probably doesn't apply directly to Hackett's scenarios. What it does do is illustrate the idea of bringing order to a complex, multidimensional space by studying its variables in depth, looking for ways to group by similarity, probably by hierarchies of similarity.

We present printing in this book because we did enough research and testing with printers to know what we were talking about. We knew enough other people doing significant amounts of compatibility testing that we could check our work against theirs. We were able to document our work in some detail (Kaner, Falk & Nguyen, 1993). And a solid base of experience applying the ideas gave us confidence that it was useful. We can use this to present a general approach, that has worked for several types of devices, without getting bogged down in a swamp.

A key lesson we learned is that the more you know about a multidimensional variable that is hard to order (in this case, printers and their drivers), the better you'll be at recognizing similarities within the set of possible values and thus the better you'll be at partitioning into groups of similar values and at picking individual values that best represent each group.

EXAMPLE 27: OPENOFFICE IMPRESS GRID OPTIONS

Here is a dialog from the OpenOffice Impress product:

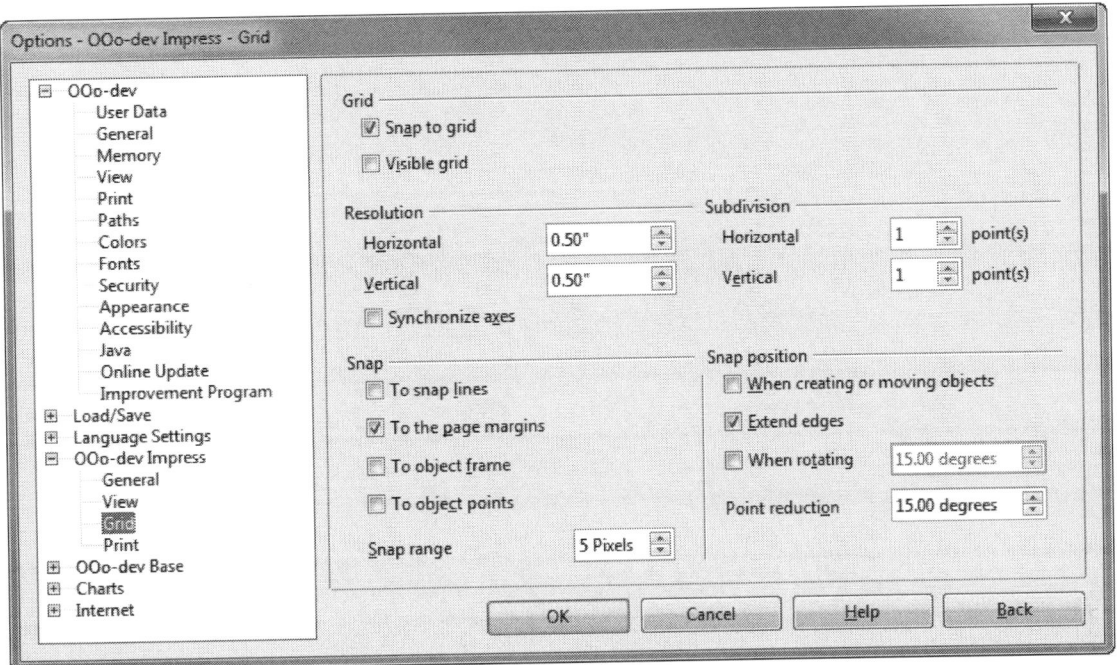

Note: OpenOffice is abbreviated as OOo.

OVERVIEW

OpenOffice Impress is a program that you can use to create presentations. Its main competitors are Microsoft Office PowerPoint and Apple iWork Keynote. Impress creates slides (just as word processors create pages).

Anything you can put on an Impress slide is an object.

- A line is an object.
- Any object other than a line has a contour (typically a bounding box) around it. The edges of the contour are marked by little squares, called *handles*.

You can create a grid in Impress. This grid is a set of evenly spaced lines (vertical and horizontal). If you display the grid, it shows on the screen as a set of dotted lines.

When you move the object, you can either:

- Move it to any point on the slide or you can
- Set Impress to position the contour on the grid lines. This is the *Snap To Grid* option.

The following screen shot shows a slide with a *Visible Grid* and a graphic (a thought balloon) with its handles.

The *Resolution* section of the dialog provides the following options:

- *Horizontal Resolution* specifies the distance between each grid point and the one to the left or right of it.
- *Vertical Resolution* specifies the distance between each grid point and the one above or below it.
- The *Horizontal* and *Vertical Subdivisions* specify the intermediate spacing between grid points. These allow you to create a finer grid than the one displayed on the screen.
- Check *Synchronize Axes* to keep the spacing between grids the same horizontally and vertically.

The next section of the menu specifies where Impress snaps an object to. The following is quoted from the OOo help (Apache OpenOffice 4.0.0):

SNAP

To snap lines

Snaps the edge of a dragged object to the nearest snap line when you release the mouse.

You can also define this setting by using the Snap to Guides icon, which is available in the Options bar in a presentation or drawing document.

To the page margins

Specifies whether to align the contour of the graphic object to the nearest page margin.

The cursor or a contour line of the graphics object must be in the snap range.

In a presentation or drawing document, this function can also be accessed with the Snap to Page Margins icon in the Options bar.

To object frame

Specifies whether to align the contour of the graphic object to the border of the nearest graphic object.

The cursor or a contour line of the graphics object must be in the snap range.

In a presentation or drawing document, this function can also be accessed with the Snap to Object Border icon in the Options bar.

To object points

Specifies whether to align the contour of the graphic object to the points of the nearest graphic object.

This only applies if the cursor or a contour line of the graphics object is in the snap range.

In a presentation or drawing document, this function can also be accessed with the Snap to Object Points icon in the Options bar.

Snap range

Defines the snap distance between the mouse pointer and the object contour. OOo-dev Impress snaps to a snap point if the mouse pointer is nearer than the distance selected in the Snap range control.

SNAP POSITION

When creating or moving objects

Specifies that graphic objects are restricted vertically, horizontally or diagonally (45°) when creating or moving them. You can temporarily deactivate this setting by pressing the Shift key.

Extend edges

Specifies that a square is created based on the longer side of a rectangle when the Shift key is pressed before you release the mouse button. This also applies to an ellipse (a circle will be created based on the longest diameter of the ellipse). When the Extend edges box is not marked, a square or a circle will be created based on the shorter side or diameter.

When rotating

Specifies that graphic objects can only be rotated within the rotation angle that you selected in the When rotating control. If you want to rotate an object outside the defined angle, press the Shift key when rotating. Release the key when the desired rotation angle is reached.

Point reduction

Defines the angle for point reduction. When working with polygons, you might find it useful to reduce their editing points.

WHERE CAN YOU APPLY DOMAIN ANALYSIS?

Five of the variables accept size/distance entries (units such as inches, centimeters or pixels). These are:

- `HorizontalResolution`
- `VerticalResolution`
- `HorizontalSubdivision`
- `VerticalSubdivision`
- `SnapRange`

Two others specify angles (in degrees):

- `SnapPositionWhenRotating`
- `PointReduction`

We would initially test these individually with the usual boundaries:

- Barely too small
- Smallest valid
- Largest valid
- Barely too large

After that, we would look for interactions among the variables. For example:

- Set `HorizontalSubdivision` to be larger than `HorizontalResolution`?
- Set `HorizontalResolution` to be wider than the slide?

Our primary interest is with the consequences of these settings. You are snapping *something* to the grid (or the margin or another object). ***Where does this something land on the slide and is that where it is supposed to land?***

The domain-testing part of studying that involves questions whose answers might vary depending on the value of one of the question's variables. For example:

- Does the `SnapRange` (the range of possible values of this variable) interact with the type of thing (grid, lines, etc.) that you snap to?
- Is there any difference in the accuracy of placement of the objects when you work with slides at a higher zoom level?

EXAMPLE 28: OPENOFFICE PRINTING OPTIONS

Here is a printing-options dialog from a development build of OpenOffice 4.

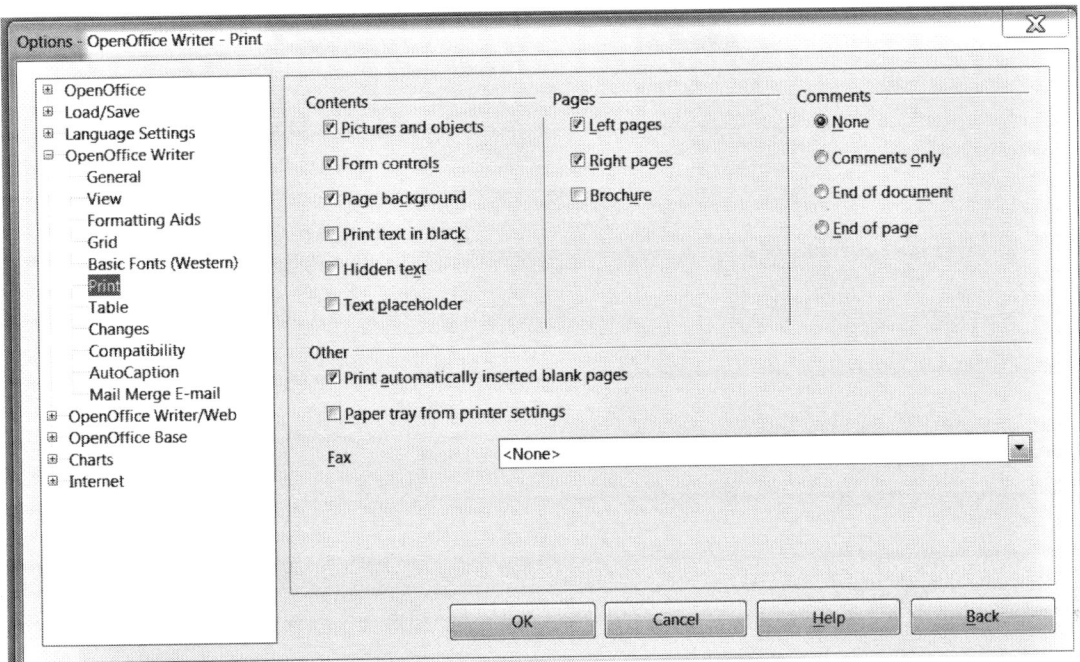

OVERVIEW

Apart from the Fax field, which we're going to ignore in this example:

- Most of these variables (11 of them) are Boolean. The values are either checked or unchecked, on or off.
- The Comments variable has four possible values (None, Comments only, End of document and End of page).

There is no reasonable partitioning for any of these. Each partition will have one and only one value.

WHERE CAN YOU APPLY DOMAIN ANALYSIS?

With 11 Boolean variables and one 4-value variable, there are 8192 ($2^{11} \times 4$) possible combinations of options on this page. This leads to more than 8192 possible tests because you should test the same combination of options with several pages that have different types of content.

Clearly, you'll want to sample from this huge set of possible tests, rather than running them all.

We would approach the sampling problem initially with combinatorial testing (a mechanical sampling strategy). Using the *Advanced Combinatorial Testing System* tool (National Institute of Science & Technology, 2013b). According to the tool's analysis:

- Achieving all-pairs coverage requires 10 tests.
- Achieving all-triples coverage requires 35 tests.
- Achieving all-quadruples coverage requires 81 tests.

This is a sampling strategy, but it is not domain testing:

- **There is a theory of equivalence**. Any test that covers a pair of values is treated as equally good as any other test that covers that pair.
- However, **there is no theory of risk to drive selection of best representatives**.

Domain testing *will* (or at least, can and probably should) come into play in setting up these tests, but it won't come into play directly with these variables. Instead, you'll probably use it to design appropriate test pages to print. For example:

- How large should the graphics be?
- Where should you place the text, the tables, etc.?
- Does density of the page (how packed it is with how many characters, images, etc.) matter?

EXAMPLE 29: SELECT AND FLIP PICTURE

In OpenOffice Impress (3.0), you can select a picture on a slide and then flip it vertically or horizontally.

This photo by Marc St. Gil is part of the Environmental Protection Agency's DOCUMERICA series. The National Archives identifier is 207/27/012387.

OVERVIEW

When you flip a picture, you rotate it 180°. If you flip it vertically, OpenOffice turns it upside down. If you flip it horizontally, OpenOffice reverses it, right to left. The result is the same size and fits in the same space as the original.

WHERE CAN YOU APPLY DOMAIN ANALYSIS?

Flipping the picture is an action, not a variable.

You could create a variable with 4 values: {Normal, Flipped Horizontally, Flipped Vertically, Flipped Horizontally and Vertically}. However, you would test this as an enumerated list, testing all the cases. There's no benefit from partitioning.

We prefer to think of the ability to flip the picture and the result of flipping the picture are *consequences* of the values of some variables, such as (perhaps):

- The format (such as a drawn shape, a text box, clip art placed on the slide (TIFF, JPEG, etc.), and several types of OLE objects).

- The size of the object.

- Its location on the slide.

The format (the type of object) is not a variable you can order. If you think that format might interact with your ability to flip the graphic, you'll do stratified sampling along the same lines as printers. See *Example 26: Install Printer Software* on page 401.

Picture size and location are quantities: numeric variables. You can determine and test their boundary values. These are suitable for a traditional domain analysis. Note that your tests will focus on the actual size and the actual location of the picture. This isn't about testing invalid inputs. It's about testing when you have a picture that has already been placed, that already has its size and location. What values of size or location might impact the ability to flip?

EXAMPLE 30: CONFIGURATION TESTING

We want to test our software with some or all of the following software and equipment:

- Operating system: Linux, Windows XP, Windows Vista, Windows 7
- RAM: 1 gByte, 2 gByte, 3 gByte, 4 gByte, 8 gByte
- Printer: Brother multifunction, Canon Laser, HP InkJet, Xerox Color Laser
- Video card: Nvidia GeForce, ATI Radeon, Diamond Stealth

- Disks: 1 hard drive, 2 hard drives, 3 hard drives

OVERVIEW

These variables are enumerated. The problem lists 4 operating systems, 5 levels of memory, 4 types of printers, 3 types of video cards, and 3 numbers of hard drives. None of these is equivalent to the others.

Testing all combinations, requires 720 ($4 \times 5 \times 4 \times 3 \times 3$) tests. Testing with all-pairs coverage reduces the set to 20 tests. Here's a table that satisfies the all-pairs requirement.

	RAM	O/S	Printer	Video	Drives
1	1 gB	Linux	Brother	Nvidia	1 drive
2	1 gB	Windows XP	Canon	ATI	2 drives
3	1 gB	Windows Vista	HP	Diamond	3 drives
4	1 gB	Windows 7	Xerox	Nvidia	1 drive
5	2 gB	Linux	Xerox	ATI	3 drives
6	2 gB	Windows XP	Brother	Diamond	2 drives
7	2 gB	Windows Vista	Canon	Nvidia	1 drives
8	2 gB	Windows 7	HP	ATI	2 drives
9	3 gB	Linux	HP	Diamond	2 drives
10	3 gB	Windows XP	Xerox	Nvidia	1 drives
11	3 gB	Windows Vista	Brother	ATI	3 drives
12	3 gB	Windows 7	Canon	Diamond	3 drives
13	4 gB	Linux	Canon	Nvidia	3 drives
14	4 gB	Windows XP	HP	ATI	1 drives
15	4 gB	Windows Vista	Xerox	Diamond	2 drives
16	4 gB	Windows 7	Brother	Nvidia	2 drives
17	8 gB	Linux	Brother	ATI	1 drive
18	8 gB	Windows XP	Canon	Diamond	3 drives
19	8 gB	Windows Vista	HP	Nvidia	2 drives
20	8 gB	Windows 7	Xerox	Diamond	1 drive

This list of configurations is not a list of tests.

When we have explicitly done configuration testing, we've used a carefully-designed set of tests. This type of testing is looking for failures that show up on one configuration but not on the others. Practices for creating configuration test suites vary across companies. One approach to creating the suite starts from a list of compatibility risks, often developed from support history with previous versions of this program or programs that are similar to it in some ways. Add to that tests based on known differences in how the operating systems manage memory, handle communication, etc. Other approaches have focused more on the functionality of the program, verifying that it does basic operations correctly on the different configurations. Whatever your approach, there are several tests and they each take time.

WHERE CAN YOU APPLY DOMAIN ANALYSIS?

Notice the implied equivalence analysis in the enumeration. Consider: *Which version of Linux* are you testing with? You can easily expand this set of operating systems to accept different versions of each operating system, but the total number of tests will get huge quickly. Instead, the configurations described here include one representative of each class (one Linux, one version of XP, one version of Windows 7, one type of Brother printer, etc.).

In practice, you will probably have to decide which values of each variable to test. For example, rather than being told which specific 4 printers to test, you'll probably have to decide how many printers to test and which specific printers are needed.

In this Example, you are picking best representatives of a variable that can't be ordered. We worked through this type of problem in detail in Chapter 8 of *Testing Computer Software* (Kaner, Falk & Nguyen, 1993, pp. 143-168). We summarize their approach at *Example 26: Install Printer Software* on page 401.

A SCHEMA FOR DOMAIN TESTING

1. CHARACTERIZE THE VARIABLE

A. Identify the potentially interesting variables.

B. Identify the variable(s) you can analyze now. This is the variable(s) of interest.

C. Determine the primary dimension of the variable of interest.

D. Determine the type and scale of the variable's primary dimension and what values it can take.

E. Determine whether you can order the variable's values (from smallest to largest).

F. Determine whether this is an input variable or a result.

G. Determine how the program uses this variable.

H. Determine whether other variables are related to this one.

2. ANALYZE THE VARIABLE AND CREATE TESTS

I. Partition the variable (its primary dimension).

- If the dimension is ordered, determine its sub-ranges and transition points.
- If the dimension is not ordered, base partitioning on similarity.

J. Lay out the analysis in a classical boundary/equivalence table. Identify best representatives.

K. Create tests for the consequences of the data entered, not just the input filter.

L. Identify secondary dimensions. Analyze them in the classical way.

M. Summarize your analysis with a risk/equivalence table.

3. GENERALIZE TO MULTIDIMENSIONAL VARIABLES

N. Analyze independent variables that should be tested together.

O. Analyze variables that hold results.

P. Analyze non-independent variables. Deal with relationships and constraints.

4. PREPARE FOR ADDITIONAL TESTING

Q. Identify and list unanalyzed variables. Gather information for later analysis.

R. Imagine and document risks that don't necessarily map to an obvious dimension.

AFTERWORD: DOMAIN TESTING AS PART OF A TESTING STRATEGY

Now that you have some experience with this technique, let's reflect on when to use it, what it's good for, and how to coordinate it with other techniques.

Here is a summary overview of our thinking:

1. *Use domain testing when you're just learning the program*: Working through the program with the goal of finding every variable and testing it with basic domain tests is a good way to find bugs while discovering what the program does.

2. *Simple domain testing has limits and will run out of steam*: Input-focused domain testing will check for many bugs that might never exist in software at your company. As to the ones domain testing does find, the programmers will fix them and your tests will no longer find them. Eventually, doing more simple system-level domain testing will become a waste of time and money.

3. *As you learn more about the program, use domain testing in a deeper way*: Use domain tests to hunt for problems in the ways the program uses a variable and in relationships among the variables.

4. *Use other test techniques too*: Domain testing is just one technique. There are many others. Each has strengths and weaknesses compared to the others. An effective testing strategy will use several test techniques that complement each other.

5. *Combine domain testing with other techniques to increase their efficiency and power*: Most tests set the values of one or more variables. The test technique might determine the values of some of those variables. Use domain testing to pick the values of the others.

USING DOMAIN TESTING WHEN YOU ARE JUST LEARNING THE PROGRAM

When you start testing a program, you might have very little information about it.[47] You don't need a lot of information to start designing and running domain tests. When you see a variable that appears to accept lots of different values, domain testing helps you check whether:

- The program does a reasonable job of collecting inputs for that variable.
- The program can use or store those values.

You saw this in many of the book's exercises and examples. These provided almost no context, almost no information about the surrounding program, but you could still design a lot of tests for the variable you were focusing on.

Used this way, you can achieve a high level of coverage of the program, quickly.[48] Just find as many variables as you can—and test them all. Domain testing gives you a simple structure for hunting bugs everywhere in the program, and while you're doing this in some new part of the program, you'll probably find other bugs just because you're there.

---

47 Even if you have a lot of program documentation, you probably haven't read and understood it yet. Domain testing operates as an active learning strategy—applying it throughout the program gives you a systematic way to learn about the program.

48 When you use domain testing this way, you're using it as a coverage-focused test technique.

*Used this way, domain testing is like an enthusiastic pet dog. If you **can** go somewhere, it wants to go there with you. And when you get there, it wants to sniff everything.*

This way of using domain testing looks a lot like Myers (1979) and like the opening example of Chapter 1.

In terms of the Schema, this testing involves Tasks A-F, I, J, and L.

This is certainly not the only way to guide early exploration of the program. (See Bolton, 2009 and Kelly, 2005, for example.) But we have found it a very useful one.

SIMPLE DOMAIN TESTING HAS LIMITS AND WILL RUN OUT OF STEAM

Simple domain testing is good for catching:

- Errors in input filters.
- Weak error-handling.
- Incorrectly specified boundary values.
- Incorrectly implemented boundaries.

We have presented several lists of test ideas that check the input filters in many different ways. Don't overuse these lists.

Historically, there have been lots of problems with input filters and the associated error-handling. These kinds of bugs have been around for a long time.

- These days, using standard library functions in most modern compiled programming languages will prevent most of these problems.
- Some of the bugs, such as buffer overflows, seem to still not be well-controlled.
- Other bugs seem to be mostly gone, but you might still see colonies of them in:
  - Programs written in custom-designed languages.
  - Some code written in some of the scripted languages.
  - Code that has been heavily speed-optimized and space-optimized to control specialized devices.[49]
  - Code written by programmers who still craft their own basic I/O instead of using the library functions. When they reinvent the wheel, they recreate the old bumps and wobbles with it.

Depending on how your programmers write and test their code, many of the bugs in the test idea catalogs might never appear at your company or might never make it to system-level testing.

---

49 Sewing machines provide a superb example of highly-specialized, complex embedded software created for consumers. These machines offer hundreds of built-in stitches, built-in alphabets and other embroidery designs, and support for user-created stitches and designs. The user interacts with them through a special-purpose user-interface that can include pedals, buttons, switches, and a touchscreen. The machine controls movement of the needle, the fabric and the thread at the same time. Control is complicated by the variety of threads and fabrics that the user works with. Even small timing errors can ruin the output.

You must determine which test ideas are relevant to the software you're testing and skip the rest. For any secondary dimension that looks interesting to you, check it on a few variables (preferably code written by different programmers). If you don't find a bug, with those tests, stop testing for that kind of bug. Too many other bugs have a higher probability of being in the code. Look for *them*.

You probably will find *some* bugs involving the filters, the boundaries and the basic input-error handling. Basic domain testing is a popular technique because generations of testers have found lots of bugs with it.

However, as you find these kinds of bugs, they'll get fixed. Over time, in the software under test, this class of bugs will go away.

Basic domain testing is especially useful when you first test some part of the program or retest a program that has gone through a lot of change. Its value declines as the program gets more stable.

- *We would include **lots** of tests like these in a unit-test regression suite that is regularly run by the programmer.* This type of suite is a safety net for the programmer. See Feathers ("Legacy code is code without tests", 2004, p. xvi) and Fowler (1999) on the value of unit test suites when you're revising code.

- *We would include **very few** tests like these in a library of system-level regression tests.* If you're doing manual regression testing, run more complex tests and check boundaries or secondary dimensions as a minor part of the larger tests. If you're automating regression testing, we think simple domain tests are often too expensive to code and maintain, compared to the value of what you will learn from them.[50]

AS YOU LEARN MORE ABOUT THE PROGRAM, USE DOMAIN TESTING IN A DEEPER WAY

When you test a feature, consider the variables that it uses:

- Where do they get their values?

  - If the values are directly from user input, what values might break this feature? (You are now doing Tasks G and K, probably supported by I or M).

  - If the values are calculated from other input, they're result variables. What values of the original inputs could drive the values of these variables (the one the feature is using) in ways that break the feature? (Tasks F, O, G, K, and I or M).

---

50 We see three obvious exceptions to this generalization.

  1. Many testers create suites of build-verification tests. (BVT) These are intended as simple tests that check whether the latest build of the software is stable enough to be worth testing. Simple domain tests often appear in BVT suites.

  2. If you can create a high-volume test automation script that can generate up-to-date versions of these tests whenever you want and then run them automatically, then your costs might be much cheaper than your benefits.

  3. If you're working with programmers who are unusually sloppy or junior or whose idea of maintenance is to replace one buggy routine that they copied from the web with some other buggy routine that they copy from the web or who won't use source control software, then any bug is possible at any time and therefore every test is potentially relevant. Good luck.

- What results do you get from this feature? Can it produce any invalid values or values that will cause trouble to other features? (Task O, K, etc.)

- Most features will work with more than one variable. Finding efficient ways to test those variables together (finding the multidimensional boundary cases) is the stuff of Tasks N and P.

You won't learn all this information about the product at the same time. And so you won't be able to do all the advanced tasks of the Schema (such as K, N, O, and P) at the same time. In our testing, we expect to add new domain tests to our collection of tests of the program throughout our testing of the program.

WHAT MAKES THESE TESTS DOMAIN TESTS?

The "more advanced" domain tests will often look like feature tests. What makes them domain tests?

In domain testing, you ask, "What values of this variable might cause the program to fail?"

Other techniques start from other places. For example:

- Function testing starts from the function/feature and asks, "What *can we do* to make this feature fail?" That's a different question, a more general question than, "*What values of this variable* could cause this feature to fail?"

- Scenario testing often starts from a benefit, from something valuable that the user expects to achieve with the program or get from the program. The scenario test tries to show that the user can't get it or that getting it is too hard, too expensive, too error-prone, too dangerous or too confusing. The values of variables play a role in these tests, but that role is rarely central.

If you design a test that hunts for a failure in a way that doesn't depend on the specific value of the variable, you are not doing domain testing. You are not testing the impact of the value of that variable on the program. You might be designing a good test, but it is not a good domain test.

USE OTHER TEST TECHNIQUES TOO

There are lots of other test techniques. Kaner & Fiedler (2011) describe over a hundred techniques and a few ways of categorizing them. They suggest ways to compare the strengths and weaknesses of the techniques.

For example, *scenario tests* are created as stories about things that might actually happen in the use of the software. They're typically complex, involving a complete task (many features, many variables). They're designed to be credible and motivating. Scenario tests aren't necessarily very powerful. They don't push the program to its limits without a credible story about a real user who would do this. Their strength is that a stakeholder who sees a failure of a well-designed scenario test will want to see that bug fixed.

In contrast, domain tests push every limit you can find. Give the program the nastiest combination of data you can cook up, even if no one would ever do that.[51] Power is central to domain tests. Credibility is for scenarios.

Domain tests won't tell you much about the overall value of the software. If you want to understand why someone would want to use the program and what would disappoint them, that insight won't come from putting its variables under a microscope. It will come from a well-designed collection of scenarios.

Every technique "won't tell you much about" some aspects of the program and "will tell you a lot about" other aspects of the program. To get a comprehensive view of the quality of the program, use several techniques that look at the program in significantly different ways.

COMBINE DOMAIN TESTING WITH OTHER TECHNIQUES TO INCREASE THEIR EFFICIENCY AND POWER

Hans Buwalda, (2000, 2004) describes *Soap Opera*s. These are scenarios, but with particularly vivid stories. Here's an example from Buwalda (2000):

> "William starts as a metal worker for Industrial Entropy Incorporated in 1955. During his career he becomes ill, works part time, marries, divorces, marries again, gets 3 children, one of which dies, then his wife dies and he marries again and gets 2 more children…."

From the perspective of the software that calculates how much pension should go to William (or his dependents or heirs), this might be a complex example. But it seems quite plausible.

A scenario test like this weaves many variables and many features into a realistic story about an important benefit that the software should deliver:

- From the point of view of the scenario, it might not matter exactly when he started working, how often he became ill, unemployed, married, divorced, etc..

- From the perspective of domain testing, those are all variables and their values are what makes tests interesting.

Maybe you could combine these techniques:

- Building a persuasive story line with whatever qualitative-analysis methods we use to create scenarios.

- Then stuffing its variables with boundary cases or other mischief-makers.

Buwalda calls these *Killer Soaps*. He recommends creating them after you have tested the program with scenarios that use more credible (and less stressful) values and fixed any bugs the gentler scenarios exposed. These more extreme cases will probably find more bugs, but perhaps bugs that would appear less often in real use.

A tester more focused on power might start with Killer Soaps. Whenever one of these tests exposed a bug, the tester might tone down the values to see if the failure comes up with those too. The resulting bug report could comment on the generality of the problem as well as the severity of the failure.

---

51 No one but a particularly creative hacker, a particularly annoyed cat or a user who should have gone to sleep an hour ago. Or someone trying to do something perfectly reasonable with the software that you never realized anyone would ever try to do.

Killer Soaps illustrate a general idea. When you use a test technique to design a test, that test will involve several variables.

- The technique will probably guide or determine the values of some of those variables. It probably won't determine the values of all of them, leaving you to set the values to "something reasonable."

- Instead of being "reasonable," consider combining the technique with domain testing. Do equivalence class and boundary value analysis on these other variables, to create powerful variants of that other technique's test.

Domain testing is a way of thinking about how to test well:

- Pay attention to variables.

- Divide the possible values of each variable into subsets of equivalent values.

- Pick one or two values from each equivalence set that maximize the likelihood of exposing a bug.

You can apply this way of thinking on its own or you can use it to inform your selection of variables' values in every test that you design, no matter what technique drives the overall character of the test.

APPENDIX: NOTES FOR INSTRUCTORS

This book provides useful material for a variety of course formats.

COMMERCIAL COURSES ON SOFTWARE TESTING

Commercial courses, also called *professional-development* courses or *industrial training* courses, are designed for people who have a job in the field (or are trying to qualify for one). They're typically short courses (1 to 5 days of face-to-face contact) or online courses that might last a week or a month.

Many of these courses are taught as part of a curriculum that leads to a certificate or certification in the professional field.

- In a standalone commercial course with an exclusive focus on Domain Testing, instructors can design in-class activities around the examples in the book. If the course lasts a long enough time, and the students have computers in-class, we suggest having students download and test a popular program (e.g., OpenOffice or Firefox). You can leverage the explanations in the book if you draw examples from those programs that are comparable to examples in this book.

- In a longer commercial software testing course (three to five days), this book can help you add depth and skill-based learning to a course that has to cover a broad spectrum of ideas in only a few days. As the focusing reference in the segment on domain testing, the book gives examples that are immediately available for use as in-class activities, with solutions and task descriptions that can clear up student confusions. From our experience as trainers, we believe that students value receiving source material that they can take home and extend the course experience with.

UNIVERSITY COURSES ON SOFTWARE TESTING

This book would be a supplement, not a main text.

- We have used early versions of this book in several university classes on software testing. The book explains the technique, the relationships between this technique and others, and gives students credible examples. It provides strong preparation for challenging assignments and exam questions. For a course that presents strong theory (such as a course based on Ammann & Offutt, 2008 or Tian 2005), this book can round out the course from an alternative viewpoint.

- We have used sections of some very early versions of this book in a course on programmer-testing. In our experience, books on TDD are often long on the use of tests in development and on the technology that supports those uses, but short on the design of the tests. We find it useful to emphasize different measures of coverage and ask students to write code and tests for the code that achieve near-complete coverage according to some of these measures. This book complements the RIGHT-BICEP approach taught in Hunt & Thomas (2004), offering students ideas for selecting test data and for considering several different types of boundaries to test.

DESIGNING A COURSE

Wiggins & McTighe (2005) write about the "twin sins" of traditional design for instruction:

- Activity-focused design

• Coverage-focused design

ACTIVITY-FOCUSED DESIGN

Wiggins & McTighe characterize activity-focused design as "hands-on without being minds-on" (p. 16). Such a course is packed with activities but it doesn't ask students to consider the meaning of each activity. The course lacks focus on important ideas. It collects little data to determine what students have come to understand about course content.

Courses like this can be fun to design and fun to take. You can toss in any activity that students will find interesting as long as you can make it appear somewhat relevant to the broad topic of the course. Magic tricks, games, puzzles, standup comics, demonstrations, simulated experiments, presentations, bull sessions, field trips, group projects—anything you want.

Students might learn nothing from a course like this, they might learn isolated facts or concepts or they might learn quite a bit (though not necessarily what you intended to teach them). If you don't assess (collect data about) their knowledge, you won't know what they have or have not learned, and neither will they.

COVERAGE-FOCUSED DESIGN

In a course that suffers from coverage-focused design, the instructor tries to cover a lot of material in a fixed period of time. Students push through the lectures and readings with little opportunity to practice with the material, question it, argue about it, compare or contrast the ideas with what they have learned elsewhere or generally, engage meaningfully beyond memorization and (if required in the course) basic application.

Multiple-choice exams and other simplistic "objective" tests are the natural assessment tools of this type of course. Students can demonstrate that they have noticed that a topic was mentioned and they remember a little bit about it, that they know some of its definitions or basic facts, and that they read the highlighted section in Chapter 3.

Many university faculty use a coverage-focused design and a huge textbook but give students harder exams that demand thoughtful essays or applications. These are hard courses. Many students flunk them, not because they're lazy or stupid, but because they never figured out how to teach themselves the material at a deeper level. Often the successful students succeed by creating their own activities, perhaps with friends in study groups.

Before condemning faculty who work this way, please understand that they're often driven to pack too much content into too short a course by external standards bodies. For example, look at the curriculum recommendations at ACM (2013), especially at the Software Engineering curriculum at ACM/IEEE Joint Task Force on Computing Curricula (2004).

Because this is a book on software testing, we encourage you to take a moment to marvel at the wondrous breadth of the one-semester course on Software Quality Assurance and Testing. According to this standard (ACM/IEEE Joint Task Force, 2004, p. 110-111):

"Upon completion of this course, students will have the ability to:
- Conduct effective and efficient inspections
- Design and implement comprehensive test plans
- Apply a wide variety of testing techniques in an effective and efficient manner
- Compute test coverage and yield, according to a variety of criteria
- Use statistical techniques to evaluate the defect density and the likelihood of faults

- Assess a software process to evaluate how effective it is at promoting quality."

This is supposed to be a three-month course taught in 3 hours of classroom activity (plus homework) per week.

We believe that any course that attempts to do all that in 3 months will have a coverage-focused design. We also doubt that a course twice as long could actually provide students enough meaningful interaction with the material to achieve half of these objectives.

Courses like this can look impressive. The course description is awe-inspiring. The rate at which students can (appear to) learn is limited only by how quickly the lecturer can talk.

Remarkably, many students in a commercial course think a course is high quality if it races through hundreds of slides that cover a broad set of topics. Without assessment (exams, tests, assignments, etc.) to tell them how much they haven't learned, many have no idea there is a problem.

BACKWARD DESIGN

Rather than march through a set of course topics, Wiggins & McTighe (2005) propose instructors design courses by beginning with the end in mind in what is often referred to as "backward design." They propose a three-stage approach to course design.

In the first stage, course designers reflect on the "big ideas and enduring understandings" they want students to carry with them beyond the course. What should students know? What should they be able to do? Are there overarching principles, concepts or ideas that can frame the learning objectives?

Once the big ideas are identified, course designers reflect on how they'll know whether students have achieved the intended learning outcomes. What performance tasks will students complete to demonstrate their understanding? What criteria will be used to judge student performance? What other evidence will instructors gather to provide insight about student understanding (e.g., quizzes, tests, assignments, etc.)? How will students reflect on their learning? What self-assessment activities will students engage in with respect to their learning?

The third stage is to plan for the learning instruction and experiences that will enable students to achieve and demonstrate the intended understanding. Wiggins & McTighe (2005, p. 22) offer the WHERETO acronym to remind course designers of the characteristic elements of effective and engaging course designs.

W =	Where is the unit going? What is expected? Where are the students coming from?
H =	Hook the students and hold their interest
E =	Equip students. Experience the key ideas. Explore the issues.
R =	Provide opportunities for students to Rethink and Revise their understanding and work.
E =	Allow students to Evaluate their work and its implications.
T =	Tailor instruction to student needs, interests, and abilities.
O =	Be Organized (within a course or the broader curriculum) to maximize initial and sustained engagement as well as effective learning.

Wiggins & McTighe (2005, p. 22)

Wiggins & McTighe's (2005) three-stage model sounds deceptively linear. In practice, course design is a messy, iterative process. Once complete, the outcome of the process should be a coherent design that falls into the described stages. However, getting to that outcome will almost certainly be a circuitous, meandering path for the course designer.

WE RECOMMEND ASSESSMENT-FOCUSED DESIGN

It is essential to understand what content you want students to learn. But you won't know whether they learned what you wanted them to learn or how well they learned it, unless you assess their knowledge.

Activities are very important instructional tools. However, they're only valuable in your course if they help students learn what you want those students to learn. And you won't know whether the activities are working unless you assess their knowledge.

Giving students questionnaires about how well they liked the course does not assess their knowledge. It tells you whether they feel good. But not what they know.

Assessments are activities that students engage in that allow you to determine what they do or don't know. Assessments include examinations, essays, projects, classroom presentations, anything a student can do, that you can use to figure out what they know.

Assessments aren't just good for finding out what people know. People learn while you assess them. People learn what they do. We'll come back to this in the next section, but here we'll note that this is true even when what the student is doing is as simple as taking a test. Students' knowledge of material improves while they're being tested on it (Butler, 2010 ; Larsen, Butler & Roediger, 2013; Roediger, Agarwal, McDaniel & McDermott, 2011; Roediger, McDaniel & McDermott, 2006).

The core idea underlying assessment-focused design is that if you want students to learn something, plan to assess it. Design the course as if you believed that anything you don't assess, they won't learn.

If you are teaching someone to do something with skill, assess them with tasks that are challenging. Make them show how well they can do something that actually requires the skill. Skills are not all-or-nothing. Use tasks that more-skilled people will do much better than less-skilled people.

Assessment takes time, so you can't assess everything. You have to prioritize what you assess and that means you prioritize what you teach.

Angelo & Cross (1993) provides a superb resource for prioritizing as part of your course design—the *Teaching Goals Inventory*. They also present a large collection of assessment techniques.

Backward Design is an example of what we're calling Assessment-Focused Design.

LEVELS OF KNOWLEDGE

In planning a course, it is useful to think about what *kind* of depth you're trying to add to it and how you will determine whether you're succeeding. This kind of planning is often guided by work on levels of knowledge (sometimes described as learning taxonomies).

- *People learn at different cognitive levels.* Being able to describe something is not the same as being able to apply it or evaluate it.

- *Evaluation of knowledge at one cognitive level tells you little about knowledge at another level.* Suppose a student does well on a test that focuses on definitions, descriptions and simple applications.
  - ◦ Does that tell us the student can actually apply this knowledge to a situation of real-life complexity? No. In fact, some students can apply the knowledge even though they can't articulate it (they can use it, but they can't explain it).
  - ◦ If we also test whether they can apply the knowledge, does that tell us about their judgment? No. For example, we won't know from this whether a student knows why to use a technique and when (and why) some other technique might be a better choice.

Knowledge Dimension	Cognitive Process Dimension					
	Remember	Understand	Apply	Analyze	Evaluate	Create
Facts						
Concepts						
Procedures						
Cognitive Strategies						
Models						
Skills						
Attitudes						
Metacognition						

Bloom's taxonomy of educational objectives, updated (Anderson et al., 2001; Bloom, 1956) and slightly modified for software testing (Kaner, 2006a, 2006b).

The table shows:

- Different types of knowledge (facts, procedures, cognitive strategies, etc.) that you can learn, and
- Different levels (remembering, applying, etc.) that you can learn at.

For example, you can memorize concepts, you can apply concepts, you can evaluate concepts by comparing and contrasting and combining them with other concepts.

This table evolved out of the ***Bloom's Taxonomy***, a famous summary of the Bloom Commission's study of levels of knowledge and the ways educators can assess student learning at different levels of cognitive depth (Bloom, 1956). This table is a minor variation of Anderson et al.'s (2001) update to Bloom's table—James Bach and I added a few concepts useful for testing (Kaner 2006a, 2006b). When we refer to *Bloom's Taxonomy* in this book, we're referring to this table.

APPROPRIATE EVALUATION

The most important lesson from the work of the Bloom commission (Bloom, 1956) is that teachers can't evaluate higher-level knowledge with lower-level tests.

- You can't determine whether someone knows how to apply a concept by testing how well they remember the concept's definition. For example, if you want to know if someone can apply a test technique to real programs, give them some real programs and watch them use the technique (and have them explain what they're doing and why).

- If you want to know whether someone can rationally decide which test technique is most useful for a given situation (this is an evaluation task), simulate the situations and have them pick the techniques they would use and explain their reasoning.

One of the major outgrowths of the Bloom taxonomy has been widespread discussion of ways to design questions or tasks to assess a student's knowledge at the level you want her or him working at. Bloom published examples of these types of questions and hundreds of websites have discussed or expanded this original work. For a few of *many* examples, *see* Clark (1999), Forehand (2005) or Long (2008) (or just ask Bing about Bloom's taxonomy).

APPROPRIATE INSTRUCTION

Traditional lectures are good for conveying the basic ideas and facts of a field. (Bligh, 2000). A skilled lecturer can convey the lecturer's enthusiasm, which improves student satisfaction (Williams & Ware, 1977) and provide memorable examples to help students learn complex concepts, tasks or cultural norms (Forsyth, 2003; Hamer, 1999; Kaufman & Bristol, 2001).

Lectures are less effective for teaching behavioral skills, promoting higher-level thinking or changing attitudes or values (Bligh, 2000). In terms of Bloom's taxonomy (Anderson et al., 2001; Bloom, 1956), lectures are most appropriate for conveying factual and conceptual knowledge at the remembering and understanding levels. Students of testing might get away with learning the material at the lower levels, but testing *work* requires more, much more.

For this, we have to engage students much more actively in their learning (Benjamin & Lowman, 1981; Benjamin et al., 1999; Bransford, Brown & Cocking, 2000; Butler, 2010; Dunlosky, Rawson, Marsh, Nathan & Willingham, 2013; Felder, 1996; Felder & Brent, 1996; Forsyth, 2003; Haskell, 2001; Knowles, 2005; Larsen, Butler & Roediger, 2013; Lave & Wenger, 1991; Lesh & Doerr, 2003; National Panel Report, 2003; Project Kaleidoscope, 2002; Santa, Havens & Valdes, 2004; Savery & Duffy, 2001; van Merrienboer, 1997). They will learn more from what they do than from what you say. Much of the design of an effective course involves deciding what tasks the students will do and how you as the instructor will prepare them to do it and give feedback on how well they did it.

Adding depth to a course is challenging. In our experience:

1. It is easy to *expose* people to new ideas, to teach them definitions and descriptions, and to use stories that connect emotionally, to shape their attitudes.

2. It is harder to teach people how to *apply* the new ideas—people learn at this level by doing. It takes a lot of time, a lot of practice with variations on the theme, for people to *develop skills*.

3. Along with skill, we have the challenge of *fostering judgment*. Which technique should the tester use in each specific case? What inquiry or investigation should the tester make to decide which course is optimal and why? Or how to extend a technique's core idea to a slightly new situation?

For many people, practice with many different examples helps build the foundation for deeper insight. There is evidence that development of expertise in an area requires experience with many different examples and problems over several years. (*See*, for example, Ericsson & Chase, 1982; Gobet & Charness, 2006; Hallam, 2010.) This (the idea of giving students extensive practice) was a starting point for our thinking about how to write this Workbook.

TRANSFER OF LEARNING AND THE EVOLUTION OF OUR SCHEMA

Our lab started work on creating a collection of worked examples of the main test techniques back in 2001. Back then, Sabrina Fay, Rebecca Fiedler, Ajay Jha, Pat McGee, Sowmya Padmanabhan, and Giri Vijayaraghavan worked on this project.

In 2003, Sowmya Padmanabhan started the specific project that yielded her M.Sc. thesis (Padmanabhan 2004) and inspired this book. We studied the application of an example-and-exercise focused approach to teaching domain testing (Kaner, 2004; Kaner & Padmanabhan, 2007; Padmanabhan, 2004).

Padmanabhan designed a 1-week class that included carefully designed exercises with extensive practice and feedback. She helped students learn:

- How to do a traditional domain analysis
- How to identify some common risks
- How to find domain-test-like test cases to address them, and
- How to express their analysis in the typical domain-test table and in a more modern (risk-oriented) version of the table.

We tested this in a final exam that included:

- Many questions that were similar to the problems that students solved in class. *Almost every student handled these very well.*

- One problem that required students to combine skills and knowledge in a way that we mentioned in lecture but did not force the students to specifically practice. We didn't think this task was much of a stretch from what the students had practiced, but we were mistaken. *Every student failed this part of the exam.*

Let me repeat that result:

- When we gave them problems that followed the same structure as we had taught, our students had no problem with them.

- When we gave them a problem that was a bit different and a bit more complex, they couldn't do it.

This wasn't the result we had wanted or expected, but it was the one we got.

- We had thought that we were going to solve ***the critical problem*** of teaching domain testing, ***the problem of skill***.

- What we learned from that experiment was that there were ***two critical problems***:

  ○ ***the problem of skill***, AND
  ○ ***the problem of transfer of learning***.

A student demonstrates ***transfer of learning*** when they use what they learned in one situation (such as one course) to another or when they use what they learned about doing one type of task (such as solving one type of problem) to do another type (Bransford, Brown & Cocking,

2000, Chapter 5; Halperin & Hakel, 2003; Haskell, 2001). In our experiment, the students were able to achieve transfer in most questions, but not with the one question that was a little bit more different and a little bit more complex than what they had practiced.

In general, learning theorists distinguish between **near transfer** and **far transfer**. We consider a task as a near transfer task if it is almost the same as something the student has already learned. The task becomes less near (more toward far transfer) as it becomes less similar—the underlying principle(s) might be the same, but the problem applies to a different subject area or is described using unfamiliar terms or is more complex.

In our experiment, our students demonstrated near transfer–they could solve problems that were similar to those they practice in class. But, they did not demonstrate far transfer – they could not solve problems that were slightly different in structure or slightly more complex.

This is consistent with a common finding in mathematics instruction. Stellar performance on examinations doesn't mean that students can transfer the knowledge beyond the classroom (Barnett & Ceci, 2002; Bransford, Brown & Cocking, 2000; Rebello, Cui, Bennett, Zollman & Ozimek, 2007).

Brookes, Ross & Mestre (2011) described a transfer-related problem in physics classes. Their students were biased by the examples they studied. Students would change how they described/drew the results they obtained in a second experiment to preserve consistency with what they had learned in a first experiment. Sowmya's and my students showed this kind of behavior as well, oversimplifying the problem in a way that allowed them to treat it as if it were the same as the examples they had studied.

The transfer problem is often considered the hardest problem in science education. Students often learn something well enough to pass an exam in that course, but not well enough to apply it beyond the course. Most courses in science and mathematics aren't effective in terms of providing students with transferable knowledge or skills.

In 2003, we had expected that writing a practice book for domain testing would go quickly. After all (we thought) domain testing is a straightforward technique (we thought) with a simple theme. *How hard could this be?*

What we realized from Sowmya's research and and ongoing classroom experiences teaching domain testing was that domain testing wasn't nearly as straightforward as we initially thought. Even simple cases require judgment—a lot of judgment. As we analyzed our own work on domain testing problems, we realized that we were analyzing the problems in several ways at the same time to address many different types of risks.

Our initial goal was to break our analyses into subtasks to create a test design *process*, something that someone could follow task by task. The initial goal was a process that, applied to a reasonable example, would yield a set of tests that would be essentially the same as the tests we would create when using our experience-based intuition to design domain tests for that example. The first generation of this process guided students in Sowmya's thesis research. The students followed her process somewhat rigidly. They failed when they encountered a task that went beyond their experience with the process.

We gradually realized that we had to teach students a way of *thinking about* the problem, not a set of steps or a few golden examples. Our subtasks could serve as aids or guides, but not as a rigid process. To achieve that, we had to pay closer attention to what we actually did, *and why we did it,* when we designed domain tests. What risks were we considering? What design heuristics were we applying, when were we applying them in our process, and why?

We called this set of tasks a Schema ... explored the idea for a decade ... and eventually wrote this book.

FOR MORE INFORMATION

Angelo & Cross' (1993) **Teaching Goals Inventory** is an excellent tool for helping you confront the limitations of what you can achieve in a single course. Most junior instructors need to understand these limitations. The ones who skip this harsh and sometimes-very-difficult prioritization inflict coverage-focused courses on their students.

Wiggins & McTighe's (2005) **Understand by Design** provides a variety of design templates, tools, and examples to help readers design instructional units or courses. Many of their samples are drawn from classrooms where young children are taught although the instructional design principles they espouse are appropriate for adults and children alike. Their work offers a clear explanation of their ideas. If you find the examples off-putting, consider L. Dee Fink's (2003) **Creating Significant Learning Experiences**, which explains similar design considerations and offers illustrations drawn from a university setting.

REFERENCES

Abramowitz, M. & Stegun, I.A. (Eds.) (1965). *Handbook of Mathematical Functions*. New York: Dover Publications.

Ainapure, B.S. (2007). *Software Testing and Quality Assurance*. Pune: Technical Publications Pune.

Ammann, P. & Offutt, J. (2008). *Introduction to Software Testing*. New York: Cambridge University Press.

Anderson, L. W., Krathwohl, D. R., Airasian, P. W., Cruikshank, K. A., Mayer, R. A., Pintrich, P. R., et al. (2001). *A Taxonomy for Learning, Teaching & Assessing: A Revision of Bloom's Taxonomy of Educational Objectives* (Complete ed.). New York: Longman.

Angelo, T.A. & Cross, K.P. (1993, 2nd Ed.) *Classroom Assessment Techniques: A Handbook for College Teachers*. Josey-Bass.

Arcuri, A., Iqbal, M.Z. & Briand, L. (2012). Random testing: Theoretical results and practical implications. *IEEE Transactions on Software Engineering, 38*(2), 258-277. doi: 10.1109/TSE.2011.121

Arsham, H. (2010) *Solving system of linear equations with application to matrix inversion*. Retrieved from http://home.ubalt.edu/ntsbarsh/business-stat/otherapplets/SysEq.htm

Association of Computing Machinery. (2013) *Curricula Recommendations*. Retrieved from http://www.acm.org/education/curricula-recommendations.

Association of Computing Machinery/Institute of Electrical and Electronics Engineers. Joint Task Force on Computing Curricula. (2004). *Software engineering 2004: Curriculum guidelines for undergraduate degree programs in software engineering (A volume of the Computing Curricula Series)* Retrieved from http://sites.computer.org/ccse/SE2004Volume.pdf

Bach, J. & Schroeder, P.J. (2004). *Pairwise testing: A best practice that isn't*. Presented at the 22nd Annual Pacific Northwest Software Quality Conference, Portland. Retrieved from http://www.testingeducation.org/wtst5/PairwisePNSQC2004.pdf

Bajaj, A. (2000). A study of senior information systems managers decision models in adopting new computing architectures. *Journal of the Association for Information Systems*: Vol. 1: Iss. 1, Article 4. Available at http://aisel.aisnet.org/jais/vol1/iss1/4

Baker, M.J. (2012a). *3-D Theory - Collision Detection*. Retrieved from http://www.euclideanspace.com/threed/animation/collisiondetect/index.htm

Baker, M.J. (2012b). *3-D Theory - Example - Car Racing Game - Collisions*. Retrieved from http://www.euclideanspace.com/threed/games/examples/cars/collisions/index.htm

Barnett, S. M. & Ceci, S. J. (2002). When and where do we apply what we learn? A taxonomy for far transfer. *Psychological Bulletin, 128*(4), 612-637.

Beizer, B. (1995). *Black-Box Testing: Techniques for Functional Testing of Software and Systems*. John Wiley & Sons, Inc.

Beizer, B. (1990, 2nd Ed.). *Software Testing Techniques*. New York: Van Nostrand Reinhold.

Benjamin, L. T. & Lowman, K., D. (Eds.). (1981). *Activities Handbook for the Teaching of Psychology* (Vol. 1). Washington, DC: American Psychological Association.

Benjamin, L. T., Nodine, B. F., Ernst, R. M. & Broeker, C. B. (Eds.). (1999). *Activities Handbook for the Teaching of Psychology* (Vol. 4). Washington, DC: American Psychological Association.

Binder, R. (2000). *Testing Object-oriented Systems: Models, Patterns & Tools.* Addison-Wesley Professional.

Binkley, D. & Gallagher, K.B. (1996). Program slicing. in M. Selkowitz (Ed.), *Advances in Computers* (Vol 43), pp. 1-50. doi: 10.1016/S0065-2458(08)60641-5

Binkley, D. & Harman, M. (2004). A survey of empirical results on program slicing. In M. Zelkowitz (Ed.) *Advances in Computers* (Vol 62), pp. 105-178. doi: 10.1016/S0065-2458(03)62003-6

Black, R. (2002). *Managing the Testing Process,* (2nd ed.). New York: John Wiley & Sons.

Black, R. (2007). *Pragmatic Software Testing.* Indianapolis: Wiley.

Bligh, D. A. (2000). *What's the Use of Lectures?* (American Edition). San Francisco: Jossey-Bass.

Bloom, B. S. (Ed.). (1956). *Taxonomy of Educational Objectives: Book 1 Cognitive Domain.* New York: Longman.

Bolton, M. (2009, April). Of testing tours and dashboards [Web log post]. Retrieved from http://www.developsense.com/blog/2009/04/of-testing-tours-and-dashboards/

Boisvert, R.F., Pozo, R., Remington, K., Barrett, R.F. & Dongarra, J.J. (1997) Matrix market: A web resource for test matrix collections. In Boisvert, R.F. (Ed.), *Quality of Numerical Software: Assessment and Enhancement.* London: Chapman & Hall.

Boyer, R. S., Elspas, B. & Levitt, K.N. (1975, April). *SELECT—A formal system for testing and debugging computer programs by symbolic execution.* Paper presented at the International Conference on Reliable Software, Los Angeles, CA.

Bransford, J. D., Brown, A. L. & Cocking, R.R. (Eds.). (2000). *How People Learn: Brain, Mind, Experience and School* (Expanded Edition). Washington, D.C.: National Academy Press. Retrieved from http://www.nap.edu

Burnstein, I. (2003). *Practical Software Testing.* New York: Springer.

Butler, A.C. (2010). Repeated testing produces superior transfer of learning relative to repeated studying. *Journal of Experimental Psychology: Learning, Memory, and Cognition. 36*(5), 1118-1133.

Buwalda, H. (2000). *Soap opera testing.* Presented at International Software Quality Week Europe. Retrieved from http://www.qualityweek.com/QWE2K/Papers/K22.html

Buwalda, H. (2004, February). Soap opera testing. *Better Software*, February, 30-37. Retrieved from http://www.logigear.com/component/downloadfile/f-soap_opera_testing.pdf.html

Carroll, J.M. (1999). Five reasons for scenario-based design. *Proceedings of the 32nd Hawaii International Conference on System Sciences.* Retrieved from http://www.massey.ac.nz/~hryu/157.757/Scenario.pdf

Chen, T. & Yu, Y. (1994). On the relationship between partition and random testing. *IEEE Transactions on Software Engineering, 20*(12), 997-980. doi: 10.1109/32.368132

Chen, T. & Yu, Y. (1996). On the expected number of failures detected by subdomain testing and random testing. *IEEE Transactions on Software Engineering, 22*(2), 109-119. doi: 10.1109/32.485221

Clark, D. R. (1999, 2007). *Bloom's Taxonomy of Learning Domains.* Retrieved from http://www.nwlink.com/~Donclark/hrd/bloom.html

Clarke, L. A. (1976). A system to generate test data and symbolically execute programs. *IEEE Transactions on Software Engineering*, SE-2(3), 215-222. doi: 10.1109/TSE.1976.233817

Clarke, L. A., Hassel, J. & Richardson, D. J. (1982). A close look at domain testing. *IEEE Transactions on Software Engineering*, SE-8(4), 380-390. doi: 10.1109/TSE.1982.235572

Cohen, D.M., Dalal, S.R., Parelius, J. & Patton, G.C. (1996, September). The combinatorial design approach to automatic test generation. *IEEE Software*, 13(5), 83-87. Retrieved from http://www.argreenhouse. com/papers/gcp/AETGissre96.shtml. doi: 10.1109/52.536462

Collard, R. (2003). *Developing Software Test Cases*. Unpublished manuscript in preparation, Draft dated 2/16/2003.

Copeland, L. (2004). *A Practitioner's Guide to Software Test Design*. Norwood, MA: Artech House.

Cork Constraint Computation Centre (2005). *Welcome to 4C's Outreach Programme: CSP Tutorial*. Retrieved from http://4c.ucc.ie/web/outreach/index.html

Craig, R. D. & Jaskiel, S. P. (2002). *Systematic Software Testing*. Norwood, MA: Artech House.

Crawford, I. M. (1997). *Marketing Research and Information Systems: Food and Agriculture Organization of the United Nations*. Retrieved from http://www.fao.org/docrep/W3241E/w3241e00.HTM

Cristopoulos, D. (2012). *Collision Detection*. NeHe Productions. Retrieved from http://nehe.gamedev.net/ tutorial/collision_detection/17005/

Czerwonka, J. (2008). *Pairwise testing in the real world. Practical extensions to test-case scenarios*. Retrieved from http://msdn.microsoft.com/en-us/library/cc150619.aspx

Czerwonka, J. (2011). *Pairwise testing: Combinatorial test case generation*. Retrieved from http://www. pairwise.org/

Dawson, B. (2012). *Comparing floating point numbers*, (2012 Ed.). Retrieved from http://randomascii. wordpress.com/2012/02/25/comparing-floating-point-numbers-2012-edition/

DeMillo, R. A., McCracken, W. M., Martin, R. J. & Passafiume, J. F. (1987). *Software Testing & Evaluation*. Menlo Park, CA: Benjamin/Cummings.

Desikan, S. & Ramesh, G. (2006). *Software Testing: Principles & Practices*. Patparganj, Delhi: Dorling Kindersley (India) Pvt. Ltd., licensees of Pearson Education in South Asia.

Doran, C. (2013). *A survey of the state of testing in the open source community*. Presented at the Workshop on Teaching Software Testing, Melbourne, FL. Retrieved from http://my.fit.edu/~cdoran2011/ OpenSource

Dunlosky, J., Rawson, K.A., Marsh, E.J., Nathan, M.J. & Willingham, D.T. (2013). Improving students' learning with effective learning techniques. Promising directions from cognitive and educational psychology. *Psychological Science in the Public Interest*, 14(1), 4-58. doi: 10.1177/1529100612453266

Duran, J. & Ntafos, S. (1984). An evaluation of random testing. *IEEE Transactions on Software Engineering*, 10(4), 438-444. doi: 10.1109/TSE.1984.5010257

Edgren, R. (2011). *The Little Black Book on Test Design*. Retrieved from http://www.thetesteye.com/papers/ TheLittleBlackBookOnTestDesign.pdf

Edgren, R., Jansson, M., Emilsson, H. (2012). *37 Sources for Test Ideas 1.0*. Retrieved from http://thetesteye. com/posters/TheTestEye_SourcesForTestIdeas.pdf

Eldh, S. (2011). *On Test Design*. (Doctoral dissertation, Mälardalen University). Retrieved from http://mdh. diva-portal.org/smash/get/diva2:442409/FULLTEXT01

Elmendorf, W.R. (1967). *Evaluation of the Functional Testing of Control Programs.* Poughkeepsie, NY: IBM Systems Development Division. Retrieved from http://www.benderrbt.com/Evaluation%20of%20 the%20Functional%20Testing%20of%20Control%20Programs%20-%201967.pdf

Elmendorf, W. R. (1973), *Cause-Effect graphs in functional testing,* (Technical Report TR-00.2487). Poughkeepsie, NY: IBM Systems Development Division. Retrieved from http://www.worldcat.org/title/ cause-effect-graphs-in-functional-testing/oclc/223828960

Ericsson, K.A. & Chase, W.G. (1982). Exceptional memory. *American Scientist, 6,* 607–612.

Feathers, M. (2004). *Working Effectively with Legacy Code.* Upper Saddle River, NJ: Pearson Education.

Feder, D. (2008, November 21). A perspective on the Jewish vote. Jewish Republicans of Colorado: A Blog of Townhall.com, [Web log post]. Retrieved from http://j-gop.blogtownhall.com/2008/11/21/a_ perspective_on_the_jewish_vote.thtml

Felder, R. M. (1996). Active, inductive, cooperative learning: An instructional model for chemistry? *Journal of Chemical Education, 73*(9), 832-836. doi: 10.1021/ed073p832

Felder, R. M. & Brent, R. (1996). Navigating the bumpy road to student-centered instruction. *College Teaching, 44*(2), 43-47. Available at http://www.jstor.org/stable/27558762

Fetzer, J. H. (1988). Program verification: The very idea. *Communications of the ACM, 31(9),* 1048. http:// dl.acm.org/citation.cfm?doid=48529.48530

Fink, L.D. (2003). *Creating Significant Learning Experiences: An Integrated Approach to Designing College Courses.* San Francisco, CA: Josey-Bass.

FMEA Info Center (undated). *FMEA Info Center: Everything You Want to Know About Failure Mode and Effect Analysis.* Retrieved from http://www.fmeainfocentre.com/index.htm

Forehand, M. (2005). Bloom's Taxonomy. In M. Orey (Ed.), *Emerging Perspectives on Learning, Teaching & Technology: Association for Educational Communications & Technology.* Retrieved from http://projects. coe.uga.edu/epltt/index.php?title=Bloom%27s_Taxonomy.

Forsyth, D., R. (2003). *The Professor's Guide to Teaching: Psychological Principles and Practices.* Washington, D.C.: American Psychological Association.

Foster, K. A. (1980). Error sensitive test cases analysis. *IEEE Transactions on Software Engineering, 6*(3), 258–264. doi: 10.1109/TSE.1980.234487

Foster, K. A. (1984). Sensitive test data for logic expressions. *ACM Software Engineering Notes, 9*(2), 120–125. doi: 10.1145/1010925.1010935

Fowler, M. (1999). *Refactoring: Improving the Design of Existing Code.* Westford, MA: Addison-Wesley Longman.

Gallagher, K. & Lyle J.R. (1991). Using program slicing in software maintenance. *IEEE Transactions on Software Engineering, 17*(8), 751-61. doi: 10.1109/32.83912

Gerrard, P. (2009). *The Tester's Pocketbook.* The Tester's Press. Retrieved from http://testers-pocketbook.com

Gerrard, P. & Thompson, N. (2002). *Risk-Based E-Business Testing.* Norwood, MA: Artech House.

Gobet, F. & Charness, N. (2006). Expertise in chess. In K.A. Ericsson, N. Charness, P.J. Feltovich & R.R. Hoffan (Eds.), *The Cambridge handbook of expertise and expert performance* (pp.523–538). Cambridge: Cambridge University Press.

Goldberg, D. (1991). What every computer scientist should know about floating point arithmetic. *ACM Computing Surveys, 23*(1), 5-48. doi: 10.1145/103162.103163. Retrieved from http://www.validlab.com/goldberg/paper.pdf

Gosling, J., Joy, B., Steele, G., Bracha, G. & Buckley, A. (2013). *The Java Language Specification* (Java SE 7 Edition.) Upper Saddle River, NJ: Addison-Wesley Professional. Retrieved from http://docs.oracle.com/javase/specs/jls/se7/html/index.html

Graham, D. & Fewster, M. (2012). *Experiences of Test Automation: Case Studies of Software Test Automation.* Upper Saddle River, NJ: Addison-Wesley Professional.

Gregory, R.T. & Karney, D.L. (1969). *A Collection of Matrices for Testing Computational Algorithms.* New York: Wiley.

Gutjahr, W.J. (1999). Partition testing vs. random testing: The influence of uncertainty. *IEEE Transactions on Software Engineering, 25*(5), 661-674. doi: 10.1109/32.815325

Hallam, S. (2010). Transitions and the development of expertise. *Psychology Teaching Review, 16*(2), 3-32.

Halperin, D. F. & Hakel, M. D. (2003, July/August). Applying the science of learning to the university and beyond: Teaching for long-term retention and transfer. *Change,* 36-41.

Hamer, L. (1999). A folkloristic approach to understanding teachers as storytellers. *International Journal of Qualitative Studies in Education, 12*(4), 363-380. Retrieved from http://ejournals.ebsco.com/direct.asp?ArticleID=NLAW20N8B16TQKHDEECM doi: 10.1080/095183999236033

Hamlet, D. (2006). When only random testing will do. *Proceedings of the First International Workshop on Random Testing.* 1-9. Retrieved from https://dl.acm.org/citation.cfm?id=1145737

Hamlet, D. (2010). Subdomain (partition) testing. *Encyclopedia of Software Engineering, 2,* 1188-1199. Auerbach Publications. Retrieved from http://www.tandfonline.com/doi/abs/10.1081/E-ESE-120044507

Hamlet, D. & Taylor, R. (1990). Partition testing does not inspire confidence. *IEEE Transactions on Software Engineering, 16*(12), 1402-1411. doi: 10.1109/32.62448

Harold, E.R. (2009). *Java's new math, Part 2: Floating-point numbers.* IBM developerWorks, Retrieved from http://www.ibm.com/developerworks/java/library/j-math2/index.html

Haskell, R. E. (2001). *Transfer of Learning: Cognition, Instruction, and Reasoning.* San Diego: Academic Press.

Hendrickson, E. (2006). *Test Heuristics Cheat Sheet.* Retrieved 4/23/2010 from http://testobsessed.com/wordpress/wp-content/uploads/2007/02/testheuristicscheatsheetv1.pdf

Hoffman, D., Strooper, P. & White, L. (1999). Boundary values and automated component testing. *Journal of Software Testing, Verification and Reliability.* (9), 3-26. doi: 10.1002/(SICI)1099-1689(199903)9:1

Hoffman, D. (2009). Why tests do not pass (or fail). Presented at the Pacific Northwest Software Quality Conference. Retrieved from http://www.softwarequalitymethods.com/Papers/WhyTestsDontPassPNSQC-B2.pdf

Holistic Numerical Methods Institute (2010) *Transforming Numerical Methods Education for the STEM Undergraduate.* Retrieved from http://numericalmethods.eng.usf.edu

Horowitz, S. & Reps, T. (2013). *Wisconsin Program-Slicing Project.* Retrieved from http://research.cs.wisc.edu/wpis/html/

Howden, W. E. (1980a). Functional testing and design abstractions. *Journal of Systems & Software, 1,* 307-313. doi: 10.1016/0164-1212(79)90032-3

Howden, W. E. (1980b). Functional program testing. *IEEE Transactions on Software Engineering, 6*(3), 162–169. doi: 10.1109/TSE.1980.230467

Howden, W. E. (1987). *Functional Program Testing & Analysis*. New York: McGraw-Hill.

Hunt, A. & Thomas, D. (2004). *Pragmatic Unit Testing in C# with NUnit*. Pragmatic Bookshelf, Raleigh, NC.

Hunter, M. (2010). *You Are Not Done Yet*. Retrieved from http://thebraidytester.com/downloads/ YouAreNotDoneYet.pdf

Hyde, R. (2006). *Write Great Code, Volume 2: Thinking Low-Level, Writing High-Level*. San Francisco: No Starch Press.

Institute for Electrical and Electronics Engineers (2008). *IEEE Standard for Floating-Point Arithmetic (IEEE 754)*. Retrieved from https://en.wikipedia.org/wiki/IEEE_754-2008

Jaegers, K. (2012) *XNA 4 3D Game Development by Example: Beginner's Guide*. Birmingham, UK: Packt Publishing.

Jeng, B. & Weyuker, E.J. (1989). Some observations on partition testing. Proceedings of the ACM SIGSOFT '89 Third Symposium on Software Testing, Analysis, and Verification. *Software Engineering Notes, 14*(8), 38-47. doi: 10.1145/75309.75314

Jeng, B. & Weyuker, E.J. (1994). A simplified domain testing strategy. *ACM Transactions on Software Engineering and Methodology, 3*(3), 254-270. doi: 10.1145/196092.193171

Johnson, K.N. (2007, January 29). Chars, strings, and injections. [Web log post] Retrieved from http:// testingreflections.com/node/4909

Joint Task Force on Computing Curricula (2004). *Software Engineering 2004: Curriculum Guidelines for Undergraduate Degree Programs in Software Engineering*. Retrieved from http://sites.computer.org/ccse/ SE2004Volume.pdf

Jonassen, D. H., Tessmer, M. & Hannum, W. H. (1999). *Task Analysis Methods for Instructional Design*: Mahway, NJ: Lawrence Erlbaum.

Jorgensen, P. C. (2008). *Software Testing: A Craftsman's Approach* (3rd ed.). New York: Taylor & Francis.

Jorgensen, A. (2003). Testing with hostile data streams, *ACM SIGSOFT Software Engineering Notes, 28*(2). Retrieved from http://cs.fit.edu/media/TechnicalReports/cs-2003-03.pdf doi: 10.1145/638750.638781

Kaner, C. (1988). *Testing Computer Software* (1st ed.). New York: McGraw Hill.

Kaner, C. (1996). *Software negligence and testing coverage*. Presented at Software Testing Analysis & Review Conference (STAR). Retrieved from http://www.kaner.com/pdfs/negligence_and_testing_ coverage.pdf

Kaner, C. (1997). The impossibility of complete testing. *Software QA, 4*(4), Retrieved from http://kaner.com/ pdfs/imposs.pdf

Kaner, C. (2001). *ITR/SY+PE: Improving the education of software testers*. Research proposal to the National Science Foundation. Submitted January 24, 2001. Project approved and started September 1, 2001.

Kaner, C. (2003a). *An introduction to scenario testing*. Retrieved from from http://www.kaner.com/pdfs/ ScenarioIntroVer4.pdf

Kaner, C. (2003b). *What is a good test case?*, Software Testing Analysis & Review Conference (STAR) East Orlando, FL. Retrieved from http://www.kaner.com/pdfs/GoodTest.pdf

Kaner, C. (2004). *Teaching domain testing: A status report.* Paper presented at the Conference on Software Engineering Education & Training. Retrieved from http://www.kaner.com/pdfs/teaching_sw_testing.pdf

Kaner, C. (2006a, December 6). *Assessment Objectives. Part 2: Anderson & Krathwohl's (2001) update to Bloom's taxonomy.* [Web log post] Retrieved from http://kaner.com/?p=32

Kaner, C. (2006b, December 9). Assessment objectives. Part 3: Adapting the Anderson & Krathwohl taxonomy for software testing. [Web log post] Retrieved from http://kaner.com/?p=33

Kaner, C. (2013). *An overview of high-volume automated testing.* Retrieved from http://kaner.com/?p=278

Kaner, C., Bach, J. & Pettichord, B. (2002). *Lessons Learned in Software Testing,* New York: Wiley.

Kaner, C., Falk, J. & Nguyen, H. Q. (1993). *Testing Computer Software* (2nd ed.): International Thomson Computer Press; Reprinted, 1999, by John Wiley & Sons.

Kaner, C. & Fiedler, R.L. (2007). *Adaptation & implementation of an activity-based online or hybrid course in software testing. Research proposal to the National Science Foundation.* Submitted January 10, 2007. Project approved and started October 1, 2007. Retrieved from http://www.kaner.com/pdfs/CirculatingCCLI2007.pdf

Kaner, C. & Fiedler, R.L. (2011). *Black Box Software Testing: Introduction to Test Design.* Retrieved from http://testingeducation.org/BBST/testdesign/

Kaner, C. Oliver, C. & Fioravanti, M. (2013) *How to actually DO high volume automated testing.* Presented at Software Testing, Analysis and Review (STAR) East Conference. Retrieved from http://kaner.com/pdfs/StarHiVAT2013KanerOliverFioravantiFinal.pdf

Kaner, C. & Padmanabhan, S. (2007). *Practice and transfer of learning in the teaching of software testing.* Paper presented at the Conference on Software Engineering Education & Training.

Kaufman, J. C. & Bristol, A. S. (2001). When Allport met Freud: Using anecdotes in the teaching of Psychology. *Teaching of Psychology, 28*(1), 44-46.

Kaw, A.K. (2008), Chapter 9, Adequacy of Solutions in *Introduction to Matrix Algebra*, Retrieved from http://numericalmethods.eng.usf.edu/mws/gen/04sle/mws_gen_sle_spe_adequacy.pdf

Kelly, M.D. (2005, September 20) *Touring Heuristic.* [Web log post] Retrieved from http://www.michaeldkelly.com/archives/50

Kit, E. (1995). *Software Testing in the Real World.* Wokingham, England: Addison-Wesley.

Knowles, M. S., Holton, E., F. & Swanson, R. A. (2005). *The Adult Learner: The Definitive Tradition in Adult Education and Human Resource Development* (6th ed.). Burlington, MA: Elsevier (Butterworth-Heinemann).

Koen, B.V. (1985). *Definition of the Engineering Method.* Washington: American Society for Engineering Education.

Koskela, L. (2008). *Test Driven: Practical TDD and Acceptance TDD for Java Developers.* Greenwich, CT: Manning.

Krieger, H. L. (2008, November 5). Exit polls: 78% of Jews voted for Obama. Jerusalem Post. [Web log post] Retrieved from http://www.jpost.com/servlet/Satellite?cid=1225715346628&pagename=JPost%2FJPArticle%2FShowFull

Kuhn, D.R., Kacker, R. & Lei, Y. (2009). Random vs. combinatorial methods for discrete event simulation of a grid computer network. *Proceedings of Mod Sim World 2009*, Virginia Beach. Retrieved from http://csrc.nist.gov/groups/SNS/acts/documents/kuhn-kacker-lei-09modsim.pdf

Larsen, D.P., Butler, A.C. & Roediger, H.L. (2013). Comparative effects of test-enhanced learning and self-explanation on long-term retention. *Medical Education, 47*(7), 674-682. doi: 10.1111/medu.12141

Lave, J. & Wenger, E. (1991). *Situated Learning: Legitimate Peripheral Participation*. Cambridge, England: Cambridge University Press.

Lesh, R. A. & Doerr, H. M. (2003). *Beyond constructivism: Models and modeling perspectives on mathematics, problem solving, learning and teaching*. Mahwah, NJ: Lawrence Erlbaum.

Lesh, R. A. & Lamon, S. J. (Eds.). (1992). *Assessment of authentic performance in school mathematics*. Washington, DC: AAAS Press.

Leveson, N.G. (1995). *Safeware: System Safety and Computers*. Reading, PA: Addison-Wesley.

Leveson, N.G. & Turner, C.S. (1993) An investigation of the Therac-25 accidents. *IEEE Computer 26*(7), 18–41. doi: 10.1109/MC.1993.274940

Long, K. (2008). *Bloom's Revised Taxonomy* Retrieved from http://www.kurwongbss.eq.edu.au/thinking/Bloom/blooms.htm

Marick, B. (1997) *How to misuse code coverage*. Retrieved from http://www.exampler.com/testing-com/writings/coverage.pdf

Marick, B. (2000). Faults of omission. *Software Testing & Quality Engineering. 2*(1). http://www.exampler.com/testing-com/writings/omissions.html

Marick, B. (2005) *The Craft of Software Testing*. Englewood Cliffs, NJ: Prentice Hall.

Mendelson, E. & Ayres, F. (1999). *Schaum's Outline of Calculus*. New York: McGraw-Hill.

Microsoft, Pairwise Independent Combination Testing tool [Computer software]. Retrieved from http://download.microsoft.com/download/f/5/5/f55484df-8494-48fa-8dbd-8c6f76cc014b/pict33.msi

Moody, J. (2001). Peer influence groups: Identifying dense clusters in large networks. *Social Networks, 23*, 261-283.

Myers, G. J. (1979). *The Art of Software Testing*. New York: Wiley.

Myers, G. J., Sandler, C., Badgett, T. & Thomas, T. (2004). *The Art of Software Testing* (2nd ed.). Hoboken, NJ: John Wiley & Sons.

National Aeronautics and Space Administration (NASA) Headquarters, (2013). *Research Opportunities in Aeronautics. NASA Research Announcement (NRA): NNH13ZEA001N. Soliciting Basic and Applied Research Proposals*. Retrieved from http://nspires.nasaprs.com/external/viewrepositorydocument/cmdocumentid=378330/solicitationId=%7B0A8625E4-D356-4A03-C358-EFD0D8A5562C%7D/viewSolicitationDocument=1/ROA%202013%20Amendment%203%2011July13.pdf

National Institute of Science & Technology (2007). *Matrix Market: A visual repository of test data for use in comparative studies of algorithms for numerical linear algebra*. Retrieved from http://math.nist.gov/MatrixMarket/index.html

National Institute of Science & Technology (2013a). *Combinatorial Methods in Software Testing*. Retrieved from http://csrc.nist.gov/groups/SNS/acts/index.html

National Institute of Science & Technology (2013b). *Advanced Combinatorial Testing System*. Retrieved from http://csrc.nist.gov/groups/SNS/acts/documents/comparison-report.html#acts

National Panel Report (2002). *Greater Expectations: A New Vision for Learning as a Nation Goes to College*. Washington, D.C.: Association of American Colleges and Universities. Retrieved from http://www.greaterexpectations.org

Nguyen, H. Q., Johnson, B. & Hackett, M. (2003). *Testing Applications on the Web* (2nd ed.). Indianapolis, IN: Wiley Publishing.

Ntafos, S.C. (2001). On comparisons of random, partition, and proportional partition testing. *IEEE Transactions on Software Engineering, 27*(10), 949-960. doi: 10.1109/32.962563

Ostrand, T. J. & Balcer, M. J. (1988). The Category-Partition Method for Specifying and Generating Functional Tests. *Communications of the ACM, 31*(6), 676-686. doi: 10.1145/62959.62964

Padmanabhan, S. (2004). *Domain Testing: Divide & Conquer*. (M.Sc. Thesis., Florida Institute of Technology, Melbourne, FL). Retrieved from http://www.testingeducation.org/a/DTD&C.pdf

Page, A., Johnston, K. & Rollison, B. (2009). *How We Test Software at Microsoft*. Redmond, WA: Microsoft Press.

PaperCut, Inc. (2012). *Testing a printer's compatibility without the physical printer*. Retrieved from http://www.papercut.com/kb/Main/PrePurchaseTesting

PaperCut, Inc. (2013). *Supported printers*. Retrieved from http://www.papercut.com/kb/Main/SupportedPrinters

Paradkar, A., Tai, K.C. & Vouk, M.A. (1997). Specification-based testing using cause-effect graphs. *Annals of Software Engineering, 4(1)*, 133-157. doi: 10.1023/A:1018979130614

Perry, W. E. (2006). *Effective Methods for Software Testing* (3rd ed.). Indianapolis, IN: Wiley Publishing.

Perry, W. E. & Rice, R. W. (1997). *Surviving the Top Ten Challenges of Software Testing: A People-Oriented Approach*. New York: Dorset House.

Petzold, C. (2000). *Code: The Hidden Language of Computer Hardware and Software*. Redmond: Microsoft Press.

Podgurski, A., Masri, W., McCleese, Y. & Wolff, F.G. (1999). Estimation of software reliability by stratified sampling. *ACM Transactions on Software Engineering and Methodology, 8*(3) (July) 263–283. doi: 10.1145/310663.310667

Podgurski, A. & Yang, C. (1993). Partition testing, stratified sampling, and cluster analysis. *SIGSOFT Software Engineering Notes 18*(5) (December), 169–181.

Price, D.J. de Solla (July 30, 1965). Networks of scientific papers: The pattern of bibliographic references indicates the nature of the scientific research front. *Science, 149(3683)*, 510-515.

Project Kaleidoscope, (2002) *Report on Reports: Recommendations for Action in support of Undergraduate Science, Technology, Engineering, and Mathematics: Investing in Human Potential: Science and Engineering at the Crossroads*. Washington, D.C. Retrieved from: http://www.aacu.org/pkal/publications/documents/ReportonReports2002.pdf

Python Software Foundation (2009). *The Python Tutorial*. Retrieved from http://docs.python.org/tutorial/index.html

Rainsberger, J. B. (2004). *JUnit Recipes: Practical Methods for Programmer Testing*. Greenwich, CT: Manning Publications Co.

Rebello, N. S., Cui, L., Bennett, A. G., Zollman, D. A. & Ozimek, D. J. (2007). Transfer of learning in problem solving in the context of mathematics & physics. In D. H. Jonassen (Ed.), *Learning to Solve Complex Scientific Problems*. Mahwah, NJ: Lawrence Erlbaum.

Reid, S.C. (1997a). An empirical analysis of equivalence partitioning, boundary value analysis and random testing. *Proceedings of the Fourth International Software Metrics Symposium*, pp 64-73. Retrieved from http://www.cis.famu.edu/~ejones/papers/2008-09/bva-bbt.pdf

Reid, S.C. (1997b). Module testing techniques—which are the most effective? *Proceedings of EuroSTAR97: The Fifth European Conference on Software Testing*.

Richardson, D.J. & Clarke, L.A. (1985). Partition analysis: a method combining testing and verification. *IEEE Transactions on Software Engineering, 11*(12), 1477-1490. doi: 10.1109/TSE.1985.231892

Roediger, H.L., III, McDaniel, M. & McDermott, K. (2006) Test enhanced learning. *Observer, 19*(3). Retrieved from http://www.psychologicalscience.org/index.php/publications/observer/2006/march-06/test-enhanced-learning-2.html

Roediger, H.L, III, Agarwal, P.K, McDaniel, M.A. & McDermott, K.B. (2011). Test-enhanced learning in the classroom: Long-term improvements from quizzing. *Journal of Experimental Psychology: Applied, 17*(4), 382-395. doi: 10.1037/a0026252

Rollison, B.J. (2007a, October 31). Equivalence class partitioning—Part 1. [Web log post] Retrieved from http://www.testingmentor.com/imtesty/2009/11/13/equivalence-class-partitioning-part-1/

Rollison, B.J. (2007b, November 15). Equivalence class partitioning—Part 2: Character/String Data Decomposition. [Web log post] Retrieved from http://www.testingmentor.com/imtesty/2009/11/13/equivalence-class-partitioning-part-2-characterstring-data-decomposition/

Rollison, B.J. (2007c, November 29). Equivalence class partitioning—Part 3: The Tests. [Web log post] Retrieved from http://www.testingmentor.com/imtesty/2009/11/13/equivalence-class-partitioning-part-3-the-tests/

Santa, C., Havens, L. & Valdes, B. (2004). *Project CRISS: Creating independence through student owned strategies*. Dubuque, IA: Kendall/Hunt Publishing Company.

Savery, J. R. & Duffy, T. M. (2001). *Problem Based Learning: An Instructional Model and Its Constructivist Framework* (No. CRLT Technical Report No. 16-01). Bloomington, IN: Indiana University Retrieved from http://java.cs.vt.edu/public/classes/communities/readings/Savery-Duffy-ConstructivePBL.pdf

Schaefer, H. (2002). Risk based testing. In van Veenendaal (Ed.) *The Testing Practitioner*, Den Bosch: UTN Publishers, pp. 57-75.

Sedgewick, R. and Wayne, K (2007). *Introduction to Programming in Java*. Boston: Addison-Wesley. Their material on Floating Point is available and under revision at press time at http://introcs.cs.princeton.edu/java/91float/

Small, H.G. (1978). Cited documents as symbols. *Social Studies of Social Science, 8(3)*, 327-340. http://www.jstor.org/stable/284908

Small, H.G. (2003). Paradigms, citations, and maps of science: A personal history. *Journal of the American Society for Information Science and Technology, 54(5)*, 394-399.

SoftRel (undated) Software FMEA service. Retrieved from http://www.softrel.com/fmea.htm

Spillner, A., Linz, T. & Schaefer, H. (2007). *Software Testing Foundations* (2nd Edition). Santa Barbara, CA: Rocky Nook.

Stevens, S.S. (1946). On the theory of scales of measurement. *Science, 103*(2684), 677-680. Retrieved from http://www.jstor.org/stable/1671815. doi: 10.1126/science.103.2684.677

Stevens, S.S. (1951). Mathematics, measurement and psychophysics. In S.S. Stevens (Ed.), *Handbook of Experimental Psychology* (pp. 1–49). New York: Wiley.

Sun Microsystems (2000). *Numeric Computation Guide*. Retrieved from http://docs.sun.com/source/806-3568/ncgTOC.html

Sveshnikov, A. A. (1968). *Problems in Probability Theory, Mathematical Statistics and Theory of Random Functions*. Philadelphia: Saunders.

Tian, J. (2005). *Software Quality Engineering : Testing, Quality Assurance, and Quantifiable Improvement*, Hoboken, NJ: Wiley-IEEE Computer Society Press.

Tip, F. (1995). A survey of program slicing techniques. *Journal of Programming Languages*. 3(3), 121-189.

Trochim, W. M. K. (2006). Levels of measurement in *Research Methods Knowledge Base*. Retrieved from http://www.socialresearchmethods.net/kb/measlevl.htm

Upham, S.P., Rosenkopf, L. & Ungar, L.H. (2010). Positioning knowledge: schools of thought and new knowledge creation. *Scientometrics, 83*, 555-581.

Van Merrienboer, J. J. G. (1997). *Training complex cognitive skills: A four-component instructional design model for technical training*. Englewood Cliffs, NJ: Educational Technology Publications.

van Veenendaal, E. & Seubers, J. (2002). Black box techniques. In van Veenendaal (Ed.) (2002) *The Testing Practitioner*, Den Bosch: UTN Publishers, pp. 227-260.

Velazco, C. (2012, May 15). *3997 Models: Android fragmentation as seen by the developers of OpenSignalMaps*. [Web log post]. Retrieved from http://techcrunch.com/2012/05/15/3997-models-android-fragmentation-as-seen-by-the-developers-of-opensignalmaps/

Venners, B. (1996, October 1). Floating point arithmetic: A look at the floating-point support of the Java virtual machine. *JavaWorld*. Retrieved from http://www.javaworld.com/javaworld/jw-10-1996/jw-10-hood.html

Vijayaraghavan, G. & Kaner, C. (2003). Bug taxonomies: Use them to generate better tests. Presented at *Software Testing, Analysis & Review Conference* (Star East). Orlando, FL. Retrieved from http://www.testingeducation.org/a/bugtax.pdf

Weinberg, G. M. (2008). *Perfect Software and Other Illusions About Testing*. New York: Dorset House.

Weiser, M. (1984). Program slicing. *IEEE Transactions on Software Engineering, 10*(4), 352-357.

Weyuker, E. J. & Jeng, B. (1991). Analyzing partition testing strategies. *IEEE Transactions on Software Engineering, 17*(7), 703-711. doi: 10.1109/32.83906

Weyuker, E.J. & Ostrand, T.J. (1980). Theories of program testing and the application of revealing subdomains. *IEEE Transactions on Software Engineering, SE-6*(3), 236-245. doi: 10.1109/TSE.1980.234485

White, L. J., Cohen, E.I. & Zeil, S.J. (1981). A domain strategy for computer program testing. In B. C. S. Radicchi (Ed.), *Computer Program Testing* (pp. 103-112). Amsterdam: North Holland Publishing.

Whittaker, J. & Jorgensen, A. (1999). Why Software Fails. *ACM Software Engineering Notes. 24*(4). Retrieved from http://www.stickyminds.com/sitewide.asp?Function=edetail&ObjectType=ART&Obje ctId=2091

Whittaker, J. (2003). *How to Break Software: A Practical Guide to Software Testing.* Boston: Pearson Addison-Wesley.

Whittaker, J., and Jorgensen, A. (2000). *How to Break Software.* Keynote presentation, EUROSTAR 2000, Copenhagen, Denmark, December 6, 2000, Keynote presentation, ASIASTAR 2001, Sydney, Australia, July 9, 2001.

Wiggins, G. & McTighe, J. (2005). *Understanding by Design*, Expanded 2nd Edition. Pearson.

Williams, R. G. & Ware, J. E. (1977). An extended visit with Dr. Fox: Validity of student satisfaction with instruction ratings after repeated exposures to a lecturer. *American Educational Research Journal, 14*(4), 449-457. Stable link at http://www.jstor.org/stable/1162342

INDEX

DOMAIN TESTING TABLES

Tables help you organize your thoughts, work through an analysis a piece at a time and explain your reasoning. People often use tables (tables that make your reasoning and test choices clear) instead of much more cumbersome test scripts.

THE CLASSICAL BOUNDARY/EQUIVALENCE TABLE

Here is the usual form of this table.

Variable	Valid case equivalence class	Invalid case equivalence class	Boundaries and special cases	Notes
Variable 1				
Variable 2				
Variable 3				

Some people prefer another column that traces the variable to the key places in the specification that describes it.

Variable	Specification section	Valid case equivalence class	Invalid case equivalence class	Boundaries and special cases	Notes
Variable 1					
Variable 2					
Variable 3					

Each variable has its own section. There is a new row within the section for every test.

Variable	Valid case equivalence class	Invalid case equivalence class	Boundaries and special cases	None
Variable 1	1-100		1	
			100	
		<1	0	
		>100	101	

The classical table excels at making the boundary tests obvious so that, with a minimum of training, people can create the table or read and understand it.

This table focuses on equivalence classes of the variable's primary dimension. The program can mishandle the variable in other ways. For exaample, how does it handle letters? Or null inputs or too many digits or negative numbers or Floating Points (if this is supposed to be an Integer), etc. When you think of one of these, you can create one or more equivalence classes and then pick best representatives.

THE RISK / EQUIVALENCE TABLE

Here is the usual form of this table. As with the classical table, you can also add a column that traces back to a specification or other document.

Variable	Risk (potential failure)	Classes that should not trigger failure	Classes that might trigger failure	Test cases (best representatives)	Notes
Variable 1					
Variable 2					
Variable 3					

As with the classical table, each variable gets its own section. This one starts with a risk and then analyzes equivalence in terms of that risk. For example, consider again the Integer variable that is supposed to run from 1-100:

Variable	Risk (potential failure)	Classes that should not trigger failure	Classes that might trigger failure	Test cases (best representatives)	Notes
Variable 1	mishanldes values that are too small	>0	<1	0	
				-1	
				-99999999 etc	buffer overflow
	mishandles values that are too large	<101	>100	101	
				999999999 etc	
	misclassifies valid values	<1, >100	1-100	1	
				100	
	fails on non-digits	digits	non-digits	/	ASCII 47
				:	ASCII 58
				A	

We often prefer the classical table for simple, academic examples because the risk-oriented table is more complex to work with when you're dealing with simple variables. The weakness of simple examples is that they're divorced from real-life software. You analyze a variable, but you don't know why a program needs it, what the program will do with it, what other variables will be used in conjunction with it. Once you know the real-life information, many risks (should) become apparent, risks you can study by testing different values of this variable. The risk-oriented table helps organize that testing. Any time you're thinking beyond the basic "too big/ too small" tests, this style of table might be more helpful than the classical one.

You will probably modify the table when working with variables in combination. *Risk/Equivalence Table Showing Multiple Related Variables* on page 304 for two examples.

Printed in Great Britain
by Amazon